Microsoft®
Visual
FoxPro 6.0
Programmer's
Guide

Microsoft Press

PUBLISHED BY
Microsoft Press
A Division of Microsoft Corporation
One Microsoft Way
Redmond, Washington 98052-6399

Library of Congress Cataloging-in-Publication Data
Microsoft Visual FoxPro 6.0 Programmer's Guide / Microsoft
    Corporation.
         p.   cm.
    Includes index.
    ISBN 1-57231-868-6
    1. Visual FoxPro for Windows.   2. Database management.   3. Object
-oriented programming (Computer science)   I. Microsoft Corporation.
QA76.9.D3M5745   1998
005.75'65--dc21   98-15689
                                                               CIP

Printed and bound in the United States of America.

1 2 3 4 5 6 7 8 9   WCWC   3 2 1 0 9 8

Distributed in Canada by ITP Nelson, a division of Thomson Canada Limited.

A CIP catalogue record for this book is available from the British Library.

Microsoft Press books are available through booksellers and distributors worldwide. For further information about international editions, contact your local Microsoft Corporation office or contact Microsoft Press International directly at fax (425) 936-7329. Visit our Web site at mspress.microsoft.com.

Acquisitions Editor: Eric Stroo
Project Editor: Anne Taussig

Contents

Introduction

Welcome to Microsoft Visual FoxPro, the relational database system that simplifies data management and streamlines.

Visual FoxPro makes it easy for you to organize data, define database rules, and build applications. You can quickly create forms, queries, and reports with the visual design tools and wizards. Visual FoxPro also makes it possible for you to rapidly create full-featured applications by providing an integrated development environment with powerful object-oriented programming tools, client/server capabilities, and ActiveX support.

About This Book

This book introduces you to application development with Visual FoxPro. Read this book to learn how to create an application using the Visual FoxPro design tools and object-oriented programming techniques.

This book consists of the following parts:

Part 1   Programming in Visual FoxPro   Provides an overview of procedural and object-oriented programming techniques, discusses the Visual FoxPro language elements and event model, and gives an overview of the application development process.

Part 2   Working with Data   Discusses how to set up tables, indexes, and databases for effective application development.

Part 3   Creating the Interface   Discusses how to create the forms, menus, and toolbars that make up the interface of a Visual FoxPro application.

Part 4   Putting It All Together   Covers compiling, debugging, and optimizing Visual FoxPro applications, as well as incorporating queries and reports into your applications.

Part 5   Extending Applications   Explains how to enhance your applications by enabling their use by multiple users, taking advantage of OLE and ActiveX, and preparing applications for use in international markets.

Part 6   Creating Client/Server Solutions   Discusses how to prototype, create, implement, and optimize an effective client/server application.

Part 7   Creating Help Files   Describes how to create a customized online Help system for your applications. Includes information about Winhelp 4.0, HTML Help, and .DBF-style (character-based) Help.

Part 8 Distributing Applications Shows how to turn your application into a distributable executable (.EXE) file.

Part 9 Accessing APIs Discusses how you can create C or C++ function libraries that access the Visual FoxPro Application Programming Interface (API).

Part 10 Creating Enterprise Solutions Describes team development and other solutions you can create to help you in enterprise-wide computing.

Part 11 What's New in Visual FoxPro Describes the latest enhancements to Visual FoxPro.

Getting Help

The Visual FoxPro Help system gives you quick access to information about using the Visual FoxPro design tools and language elements.

Need Help? Press F1

If you are working with a command or keyword you need more information about, highlight the command or keyword in the Command window and press F1 to display a context-sensitive Help topic on that item. Note that to get Help you have to choose the MSDN Library option during setup.

Sample Files

A variety of sample applications, databases, and files are included with Visual FoxPro and the MSDN Library to demonstrate programming techniques. To find more information, see the "Welcome to Visual FoxPro" screen when you start Visual FoxPro.

Using Code Examples

Many language topics in Help contain code examples that you can run in a program window. You must install the sample files provided in Setup before you can run the program examples.

To run a code example

1. At the top of the Help topic, click the "Example" link.

2. Select the code entirely and copy it to the Clipboard (Ctrl+C).

3. Click the Command window in Visual FoxPro and type MODIFY COMMAND to open a program window, or choose New from the File menu in Visual FoxPro, click the Program window.

   – or –

   Choose New from the File menu in Visual FoxPro, click the Program option button in the New dialog box, then click the New File button.

4. Paste the code into the program window (Ctrl+V).

5. Click the "!" button to run the program.

6. Name and save the program when prompted. When saved, the program runs.

Document Conventions

The following typographic conventions are used in Visual FoxPro documentation:

Example	Convention
setup	Bold font indicates words, other than language commands, that you must type.
In the Query Designer toolbar, choose Add Table.	Bold font is also used in procedures to highlight interface elements such as the name of a window, menu, dialog box, toolbar, button, or option.
SET HELP TO	Capital letters denote commands and keywords, acronyms, constants, and device names.
Press the TAB key. Press SHIFT+F1.	Capital letters denote the names of keys on the keyboard. A plus sign (+) indicates a combination of keys.
Buttons.vcx	Initial capital letters indicate file names.
C:\My Computer\Working Files\Document	Initial capital letters identify folders and directories. In a path, folders, directories, and file names are separated by backslashes.
http://www.microsoft.com/	Lowercase letters indicate are used for URLs. Server, share, and file names are separated by forward slashes.
FontSize	Initial capital letters indicate the names of objects, properties, events, and methods. If the name consists of more than one word, the initial-capital words are concatenated.
event-driven	Italic letters denote defined terms the first time they occur in text. Defined terms are part of the product Glossary. Click on the italicized word to see the definition.
IF StatusText() = "Test" = MESSAGEBOX("OK") ENDIF	Monospace font indicates command lines you type, code examples, and references in text to the code examples.
USE customer	Lowercase letters indicate table and field names.
nTotal, cName	Lowercase letters prefix variable names and placeholders. The prefix indicates the data type of the variable: "c" for Character, "n" for Numeric, "l" for Logical, "d" for Date, "t" for DateTime, "y" for Currency, "o" for Object, and "e" for any expression.

In syntax, the following conventions are used:

Example	Convention
DELETE VIEW ViewName	In syntax, words in italics are placeholders for information you supply.
[STYLE cStyleName]	In syntax, brackets enclose optional items.
SET BELL ON | OFF	In syntax, a vertical bar separates two mutually exclusive choices.
[, WindowName2 ...]	In syntax, an ellipsis indicates that an item can be repeated in a list any number of times. A comma separates the list items.

PART 1

Programming in Visual FoxPro

Visual FoxPro is a powerful, interactive data-management tool, but you can also access the full power of Visual FoxPro by creating applications. Understanding object-oriented programming techniques and the event-driven model can maximize your programming productivity.

Chapter 1   Introduction to Programming

If you're new to programming, learn about the programming process and the mechanics of programming in Visual FoxPro.

Chapter 2   Developing an Application

As you develop an application, organize its pieces with the Project Manager, an integrated way to build and test your application as you go.

Chapter 3   Object-Oriented Programming

With object-oriented programming, you can create self-contained application components that respond to user actions and to the system, and which can be easily maintained and reused.

Chapter 4   Understanding the Event Model

The event model defines when and how user and system interactions occur.

CHAPTER 1

Introduction to Programming

In Visual FoxPro, procedural and object-oriented programming work together so you can create powerful, flexible applications. Conceptually, you can think of programming as writing a sequence of instructions for accomplishing specific tasks. At a structural level, programming in Visual FoxPro involves manipulating stored data.

If you are new to programming, this chapter helps you get started. If you are familiar with other programming languages and want to see how Visual FoxPro compares, see "Visual FoxPro and Other Programming Languages" in Help. For an explanation of object-oriented programming, see Chapter 3, "Object-Oriented Programming."

This chapter covers:

- Advantages of Programming
- The Mechanics of Programming in Visual FoxPro
- Basic Programming Concepts
- The Process of Programming
- Using Procedures and User-Defined Functions
- Moving Forward

Advantages of Programming

Generally, anything that you can do in a program can also be done manually if you have enough time. For example, if you wanted to look at information about a single customer in a table of customers, say the Ernst Handel company, you could do it manually by following a specific sequence of instructions.

To manually find a single order in a table

1. From the **File** menu, choose **Open**.

2. From the **Files of type** box, choose **Table**.

3. Double-click **Customer.dbf** in the list of files.

4. From the **View** menu, choose **Browse**.

5. Scroll through the table, checking the Company field of the records for "Ernst Handel."

Programmatically, you could achieve the same results by typing the following Visual FoxPro commands in the Command window:

```
USE Customer
LOCATE FOR Company = "Ernst Handel"
BROWSE
```

After you locate the order for this company, you might want to increase the maximum order amount by 3 percent.

To manually increase the maximum order amount

1. Tab to the `max_ord_amt` field.

2. Multiply the value in `max_ord_amt` by 1.03 and type the new value in the field.

To achieve the same result programmatically, type the following Visual FoxPro command in the Command window:

```
REPLACE max_ord_amt WITH max_ord_amt * 1.03
```

It is relatively simple to change the maximum order amount for a single customer, either manually or by typing the instructions in the Command window. Suppose, however, that you wanted to increase the maximum order amount of every customer by 3 percent. To do this manually would be laborious and prone to mistakes. If you give the right instructions in a program file, Visual FoxPro can accomplish this task quickly and easily, without error.

Sample Program to Increase Maximum Order Amounts for All Customers

Code	Comments
`USE customer`	Open the CUSTOMER table.
`SCAN`	Go through every record in the table and perform all the instructions between SCAN and ENDSCAN for every record.
`REPLACE max_ord_amt WITH ;` `    max_ord_amt * 1.03`	Increase the maximum order amount by 3%. (The semicolon (;) indicates that the command is continued on the next line.)
`ENDSCAN`	End of the code that is executed for every record in the table.

Running a program has some advantages over entering individual commands in the Command window:

- Programs can be modified and run again.

- You can run programs from your menus, forms, and toolbars.

- Programs can run other programs.

The following sections detail the mechanics, concepts, and processes behind this and other Visual FoxPro programs.

The Mechanics of Programming in Visual FoxPro

You can program Visual FoxPro by writing code: instructions in the form of commands, functions, or operations that Visual FoxPro can understand. You can include these instructions in:

- The Command window.
- Program files.
- Event or method code windows in the Form Designer or Class Designer.
- Procedure code windows in the Menu Designer.
- Procedure code windows in the Report Designer.

Using the Command Window

You can execute a Visual FoxPro command by typing it into the Command window and pressing ENTER. To re-execute the command, move the cursor to the line containing the command and press ENTER again.

You can even run multiple lines of code from the Command window as though they were a self-contained program.

To run multiple lines of code in the Command window

1. Select the lines of code.

2. Press ENTER or choose **Execute Selection** from the shortcut menu.

Since the Command window is an editing window, you can edit commands using the editing tools available in Visual FoxPro. You can edit, insert, delete, cut, copy, or paste text in the Command window.

The advantage of entering code in the Command window is that the instructions are carried out immediately. There is no need to save a file and run it as a program.

In addition, choices you make from menus and dialog boxes are echoed in the Command window as commands. You can copy and paste these commands into a Visual FoxPro program, then run the program repeatedly, making it easy to execute thousands of commands again and again.

Creating Programs

A Visual FoxPro program is a text file containing a series of commands. You can create a program in Visual FoxPro in one of these ways:

To create a program

1. In the Project Manager, select **Programs** under the **Code** tab.

2. Choose **New**.

    – or –

    From the **File** menu, choose **New**.

3. In the **New** dialog box, select **Program**.

4. Choose **New File**.

– or –

In the Command window, type:

```
MODIFY COMMAND
```

Visual FoxPro opens a new window named Program1. You can now type your program into this window.

Saving Programs

After you create a program, be sure to save it.

To save a program

- From the **File** menu, choose **Save**.

If you try to close an unsaved program, a dialog box opens, prompting you to either save or discard the changes you made to it.

If you save a program that was created from the Project Manager, the program is added to the project.

If you save a program that hasn't been named yet, the Save As dialog box opens so you can specify a name for the program. After you save your program, you can run or modify it.

Modifying Programs

After you save your program, you can modify it. First, open the program in one of these ways:

To open a program

- If the program is contained in a project, select it in the Project Manager and choose **Modify**.

– or –

- From the **File** menu, choose **Open**. A dialog box with a list of available files appears. From the **Files of type** list, choose **Program**. From the list of files, select the program you want to modify, then choose **Open**.

– or –

- In the Command window, type the name of the program to modify:

```
MODIFY COMMAND myprogrm
```

– or –

In the Command window, type:

```
MODIFY COMMAND ?
```

From the list of files, select the program you want to modify, then choose **Open**.

After you open the program, you can make changes. When you finish making your changes, be sure to save the program.

Running Programs

After you create a program, you can run it.

To run a program

- If the program is contained in a project, select it in the Project Manager and choose **Run**.

  – or –

  From the **Program** menu, choose **Do**. From the list of programs, select the program to run, then choose **Do**.

  – or –

  In the Command window, type DO and the name of the program to run:

  ```
  DO myprogram
  ```

Writing Code in the Visual FoxPro Design Tools

The Form Designer, Class Designer, and Menu Designer allow you to easily integrate program code with the user interface so that the appropriate code executes in response to user actions. The Report Designer allows you to create complex and customizable reports by integrating code into the report file.

To take advantage of the full power of Visual FoxPro, you need to use these design tools. For more information about the Report Designer, see Chapter 7, "Designing Reports and Labels," in the *User's Guide*. For more information about the Class Designer, see Chapter 3, "Object-Oriented Programming," in this book. For more information about the Form Designer, see Chapter 9, "Creating Forms," and for more information about the Menu Designer, see Chapter 11, "Designing Menus and Toolbars."

Basic Programming Concepts

When you program, you store data and manipulate it with a series of instructions. The data and data storage containers are the raw materials of programming. The tools you use to manipulate this raw material are commands, functions, and operators.

Storing Data

The data you work with probably includes amounts of time, money, and countable items, as well as dates, names, descriptions, and so on. Each piece of data is a certain type: it belongs to a category of data that you manipulate in similar ways. You could work directly with this data without storing it, but you would lose most of the flexibility and power of Visual FoxPro. Visual FoxPro provides numerous storage containers to extend your ability to easily manipulate data.

Data types determine how data is stored and how it can be used. You can multiply two numbers together, but you can't multiply characters. You can print characters in uppercase, but you can't print numbers in uppercase. Some of the primary data types in Visual FoxPro are listed in the following table:

Data Types

Type	Examples
Numeric	123 3.1415 –7
Character	"Test String" "123" "01/01/98"
Logical	.T. .F.
Date	{^1998-01-01}
DateTime	{^1998-01-01 12:30:00 p}

Data Containers

Data containers allow you to perform the same operations on multiple pieces of data. For example, you add the hours an employee has worked, multiply them by the hourly wage, and then deduct the taxes to determine the amount of pay the employee has earned. You'll have to perform these operations for every employee and every pay period. If you store this information in containers, and perform the operations on the containers, you can just replace the old data with new data and run the same program again. This table lists some of the main containers for data in Visual FoxPro:

Type	Description
Variables	Single elements of data stored in your computer's RAM (Random Access Memory).
Table Records	Multiple rows of predetermined fields, each of which can contain a predefined piece of data. Tables are saved to disk.
Arrays	Multiple elements of data stored in RAM.

Manipulating Data

Containers and data types give you the building blocks you need to manipulate data. The final pieces are operators, functions, and commands.

Using Operators

Operators tie data together. Here are the most common operators in Visual FoxPro.

Operator	Valid Data Types	Example	Result
=	All	? n = 7	Prints .T. if the value stored in the variable n is 7, .F. otherwise
+	Numeric, Character, Date, DateTime	? "Fox" + "Pro"	Prints "FoxPro"
! or NOT	Logical	? !.T.	Prints .F.
*, /	Numeric	? 5 * 5 ? 25 / 5	Prints 25 Prints 5

Note   A question mark ("?") in front of an expression causes a new line character and the results of the expression to be printed in the active output window, which is usually the main Visual FoxPro window.

Remember that you must use the same type of data with any one operator. The following statements store two numeric pieces of data to two variables. The variables have been given names that start with n so we can tell at a glance that they contain numeric data, but you could name them with any combination of alphanumeric characters and underscores.

```
nFirst = 123
nSecond = 45
```

The following statements store two pieces of character data to two variables. The variables have been given names that start with c to indicate that they contain character data.

```
cFirst = "123"
cSecond = "45"
```

The following two operations, addition and concatenation, yield different results because the type of data in the variables is different.

```
? nFirst + nSecond
? cFirst + cSecond
```

Output

```
168
12345
```

Because cFirst is character data and nSecond is numeric data, you get a data type mismatch error if you try the following command:

```
? cFirst + nSecond
```

You can avoid this problem by using conversion functions. For example, STR( ) returns the character equivalent of a numeric value and VAL( ) returns the numeric equivalent of a character string of numbers. These functions and LTRIM( ), which removes leading spaces, enable you to perform the following operations:

```
? cFirst + LTRIM(STR(nSecond))
? VAL(cFirst) + nSecond
```

Output

```
12345
168
```

Using Functions

Functions return a specific type of data. For example, the functions STR( ) and VAL( ), used in the previous section, return character and numeric values, respectively. As with all functions, these return types are documented along with the functions.

There are five ways to call a Visual FoxPro function:

- Assign the return value of the function to a variable. The following line of code stores the current system date to a variable named dToday:

  ```
  dToday = DATE( )
  ```

- Include the function call in a Visual FoxPro command. The following command sets the default directory to the value returned from the GETDIR( ) function:

  ```
  CD GETDIR( )
  ```

- Print the return value in the active output window. The following line of code prints the current system time in the active output window:

  ```
  ? TIME( )
  ```

- Call the function without storing the return value anywhere. The following function call turns the cursor off:

```
SYS(2002)
```

- Embed the function in another function. The following line of code prints the day of the week:

```
? DOW(DATE( ))
```

Some other examples of functions used in this chapter are:

Function	Description
ISDIGIT( )	Returns true (.T.) if the leftmost character in a string is a number; otherwise, returns false (.F.).
FIELD( )	Returns the name of a field.
LEN( )	Returns the number of characters in a character expression.
RECCOUNT( )	Returns the number of records in the currently active table.
SUBSTR( )	Returns the specified number of characters from a character string, starting at a specified location in the string.

For a complete descriptions of these functions, see Help.

Using Commands

A command causes a certain action to be performed. Each command has a specific syntax which indicates what must be included in order for the command to work. There are also optional clauses associated with commands that allow you to specify in more detail what you want.

For example, the USE command allows you to open and close tables:

USE Syntax	Description
USE	Closes the table in the current work area.
USE customer	Opens the CUSTOMER table in the current work area, closing any table that was already open in the work area.
USE customer IN 0	Opens the CUSTOMER table in the next available work area.
USE customer IN 0 ; ALIAS mycust	Opens the CUSTOMER table in the next available work area and assigns the work area an alias of mycust.

Some examples of commands used in this chapter are:

Command	Description
DELETE	Marks specified records in a table for deletion.
REPLACE	Replaces the value stored in record field with a new value.
Go	Positions the record pointer to a specific location in the table.

For a complete description of these commands, see Help.

Controlling Program Flow

Visual FoxPro includes a special category of commands that "wrap around" other commands and functions, determining when and how often the other commands and functions are executed. These commands allow conditional branching and looping, two very powerful programming tools. The following program illustrates conditional branches and loops. These concepts are described in more detail after the example.

Suppose that you had 10,000 employees and wanted to give everybody making $30,000 or more a 3 percent raise, and everybody making under $30,000 a 6 percent raise. The following sample program accomplishes this task.

This program assumes that a table with a numeric field named salary is open in the current work area. For information about work areas, see "Using Multiple Tables" in Chapter 7, "Working with Tables."

Sample Program to Increase Employee Salaries

Code	Comments
SCAN	The code between SCAN and ENDSCAN is executed as many times as there are records in the table. Each time the code is executed, the record pointer moves to the next record in the table.
IF salary >= 30000.00 REPLACE salary WITH ; salary * 1.03	For each record, if the salary is greater than or equal to 30,000, replace this value with a new salary that is 3% higher.
	The semicolon (;) after WITH indicates that the command is continued on the next line.
ELSE REPLACE salary WITH ; salary * 1.06	For each record, if the salary is not greater than or equal to 30,000, replace this value with a new salary that is 6% higher.
ENDIF	End of the conditional IF statement.
ENDSCAN	End of the code that is executed for each record in the table.

This example uses both conditional branching and looping commands to control the flow of the program.

Conditional Branching

Conditional branching allows you to test conditions and then, depending on the results of that test, perform different operations. There are two commands in Visual FoxPro that allow conditional branching:

- IF ... ELSE ... ENDIF

- DO CASE ... ENDCASE

The code between the initial statement and the ENDIF or ENDCASE statement is executed only if a logical condition evaluates to true (.T.). In the example program, the IF command is used to distinguish between two states: either the salary is $30,000 or more, or it isn't. Different actions are taken depending on the state.

In the following example, if the value stored in the variable nWaterTemp is less than 100, no action is taken:

```
* set a logical variable to true if a condition is met.
IF nWaterTemp >= 100
   lBoiling = .T.
ENDIF
```

> **Note**   An asterisk at the beginning of a line in a program indicates that the line is a comment. Comments help the programmer remember what each segment of code is designed to do, but are ignored by Visual FoxPro.

If there are several possible conditions to check for, a DO CASE ... ENDCASE block can be more efficient and easier to keep track of than multiple IF statements.

Looping

Looping allows you to execute one or more lines of code as many times as you need to. There are three commands in Visual FoxPro that allow looping:

- SCAN ... ENDSCAN

- FOR ... ENDFOR

- DO WHILE ... ENDDO

Use SCAN when you are performing a series of actions for each record in a table, as in the example program just described. The SCAN loop enables you to write the code once and have it executed for each record as the record pointer moves through the table.

Use FOR when you know how many times the section of code needs to be executed. For example, you know there are a specific number of fields in a table. Because the Visual FoxPro function FCOUNT( ) returns this number, you can use a FOR loop to print the names of all the fields in the table:

```
FOR nCnt = 1 TO FCOUNT( )
   ? FIELD(nCnt)
ENDFOR
```

Use DO WHILE when you want to execute a section of code as long as a certain condition is met. You might not know how many times the code will have to execute, but you know when it should stop executing. For example, let's assume you have a table with people's names and initials, and you want to use the initials to look people up. You would have a problem the first time you tried to add a person who had the same initials as someone else already in your table.

To solve the problem, you could add a number to the initials. For example, Michael Suyama's identification code could be MS. The next person with the same initials, Margaret Sun, would be MS1. If you then added Michelle Smith to the table, her identification code would be MS2. A DO WHILE loop enables you to find the right number to append to the initials.

Sample Program with DO WHILE to Generate a Unique ID

Code	Comments
`nHere = RECNO()`	Save the location of the record.

`cInitials = LEFT(firstname,1) + ;`
`    LEFT(lastname,1)`
`nSuffix = 0`
	Get the person's initials from the first letters of the `firstname` and `lastname` fields.
	Establish a variable to hold the number to be added to the end of a person's initials if necessary.

`LOCATE FOR person_id = cInitials`	See if there is another person in the table with the same initials.
`DO WHILE FOUND( )`	If another record in the table has a person_id value that is the same as `cInitials`, the FOUND( ) function returns true (.T.) and the code in the DO WHILE loop executes. If no match is found, the next line of code to be executed is the line following ENDDO.

`    nSuffix = nSuffix + 1`
`    cInitials = ;`
`        LEFT(cInitials,2);`
`        + ALLTRIM(STR(nSuffix))`
	Prepare a fresh suffix and append it to the end of the initials.

`    CONTINUE`	CONTINUE causes the last LOCATE command to be evaluated again. The program checks to see if the new value in `cInitials` already exists in the person_id field of another record. If so, FOUND( ) will still return .T. and the code in the DO WHILE loop will execute again. If the new value in `cInitials` is indeed unique, FOUND( ) will return .F. and program execution continues with the line of code following ENDDO.
`ENDDO`	End of the DO WHILE loop.
`GOTO nHere` `REPLACE person_id WITH cInitials`	Return to the record and store the unique identification code in the `person_id` field.

Because you can't know beforehand how many times you'll find matching identification codes already in use, you use the DO WHILE loop.

The Process of Programming

When you understand the basic concepts, programming is an iterative process. You go through the steps many times, refining your code as you go. When you are starting out, you test frequently, using a lot of trial and error. The more familiar you become with the language, the more quickly you can program and the more preliminary testing you can do in your head.

The basic programming steps include:

- Stating the problem.
- Breaking the problem down into discrete elements.
- Constructing the pieces.
- Testing and fixing the pieces.
- Assembling the pieces.
- Testing the whole program.

Here are some things to remember when you are getting started:

- Clearly delineate the problem before trying to solve it. If you don't, you'll end up having to make a lot of changes, throw away code, start over, or be satisfied with something that is less than what you really want.

- Break the problem down into manageable steps instead of trying to solve the whole problem at once.

- Test and debug sections of code as you develop. Test to see if the code does what you want it to do. Debugging is the process of finding and fixing the problems that prevent the code from doing what you want it to do.

- Refine your data and data storage to make it easier to manipulate the data through program code. This often means structuring your tables properly.

The rest of this section traces the steps in constructing a small Visual FoxPro program.

Stating the Problem

Before you can solve a problem, you need to formulate it clearly. Sometimes if you adjust the way you formulate the problem, you'll be able to see more or better options for solving it.

Suppose you get a lot of data from various sources. Though most of the data is strictly numeric, some data values contain dashes and spaces in addition to numbers. You should remove all the spaces and dashes from those fields and save the numeric data.

Instead of trying to remove spaces and dashes from the original data, you could formulate the goal of the program as:

Goal   Replace the existing values in a field with other values that contain everything from the original values except the spaces and dashes.

This formulation avoids the difficulty of manipulating a string of characters whose length keeps changing as you work with it.

Breaking the Problem Down

Because you have to provide specific instructions to Visual FoxPro in terms of operations, commands, and functions, you need to break the problem down into discrete steps. The most discrete task for the example problem is to look at each character in the string. Until you can look at a character individually, you can't determine whether you want to save it.

After you look at a character, you need to check to see if it is a dash or a space. At this point, you might want to refine the statement of the problem. What if you get data later that contains open and closed parentheses? What if you want to get rid of currency symbols, commas, and periods? The more generic you can make the code, the more work you can save yourself later; the whole point is to save work. Here is a formulation of the problem that works with a much greater variety of data:

Refined Goal   Replace the existing values in a field with other values that contain only the numeric characters from the original values.

With this formulation, you can now restate the problem at the character level: if the character is numeric, save the character; if the character is not numeric, move on to the next character. When you have constructed a string that contains only the numeric elements of the initial string, you can replace the first string and move on to the next record until you have gone through all the data.

To summarize, the problem breaks down into these pieces:

1. Look at each character.

2. Decide if the character is numeric or not.

3. If it is numeric, copy it to the second string.

4. When you have gone through every character in the original string, replace the original string with the numeric-only string.

5. Repeat these steps for all the records in the table.

Constructing the Pieces

When you know what you need to do, you can start to formulate the pieces in terms of Visual FoxPro commands, functions, and operators. If you know exactly what command or function you need, you can check Help to see the correct syntax. If you know what you want to do, but don't know the appropriate commands or functions, search for "Language Categories" in Help.

Since the commands and functions will be used to manipulate data, you need some test data to work with. You want the test data to resemble the actual data as closely as possible.

For this example, you can store a test string to a variable by entering the following command in the Command window:

```
cTest = "123-456-7 89 0"
```

Look at Each Character

First, you want to look at a single character in the string. For a list of functions that can be used to manipulate strings, see "Character Functions" in Help.

First, you want to look at a single character in the string. For a list of functions that can be used to manipulate strings, see "Character Functions."

You will find three functions that return specific sections of a string: LEFT( ), RIGHT( ), and SUBSTR( ). Of the three, SUBSTR( ) returns characters from any part of the string.

SUBSTR( ) takes three arguments or parameters: the string, the initial location in the string, and the number of characters to return from the string, starting from the initial location. To test if SUBSTR( ) is going to do what you want, type the following commands in the Command window:

```
? SUBSTR(cTest, 1, 1)
? SUBSTR(cTest, 3, 1)
? SUBSTR(cTest, 8, 1)
```

Output

```
1
3
-
```

You can see that the first, third, and eighth characters of the test string have been displayed in the main Visual FoxPro window.

To do the same thing a number of times, use a loop. Since the test string has a specific number of characters (14), you can use a FOR loop. The counter in the FOR loop is incremented each time the code in the loop is executed, so you can use the counter in the SUBSTR( ) function. You could test the looping constructs in the Command window, but at some point you'll want to save your work to build on it later. Now would be a good time to create a new program.

To create a new program

1. Type the following command in the **Command** window:

    ```
    MODIFY COMMAND numonly
    ```

2. In the window that opens, type the following lines of code:

    ```
    FOR nCnt = 1 TO 14
        ? SUBSTR(cTest, nCnt, 1)
    ENDFOR
    ```

Now that you've created a program, you can run it.

To run a program

1. In the open program window, press CTRL+E.

2. If a **Save** dialog box appears, choose **OK**.

When you run this program, the individual characters in the test string are printed on separate lines in the main Visual FoxPro window.

Testing Part of the Program

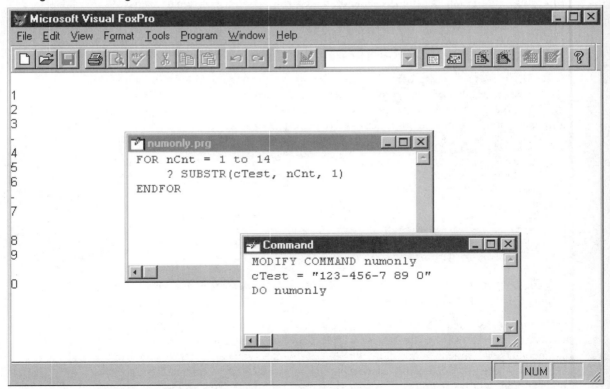

The first task has been accomplished. You can now look at each character in the string.

Decide If the Character is Numeric

After you have fetched a single character from the string, you need to know if it is a number. You can find this out using ISDIGIT( ).

Type the following commands in the Command window:

```
? ISDIGIT('2')
? ISDIGIT('-')
? ISDIGIT(SUBSTR(cTest, 3, 1))
```

Output

```
.T.
.F.
.T.
```

From this output, you can see that '2' is a number, '−' is not a number, and the third character in cTest, 3, is a number.

If the Character Is Numeric, Copy It to the Second String

Now that you can look at the characters and determine whether they are numeric, you need a variable to hold the numeric values: cNumOnly.

To create the variable, assign it an initial value, a zero-length string:

```
cNumOnly = ""
```

As the FOR loop moves through the string, it's a good idea to create another variable to temporarily hold each character from the string as it is being manipulated:

```
cCharacter = SUBSTR(cTest, nCnt, 1)
```

> **Tip**   It's often better to store the result of a calculation, evaluation, or function to a variable. You can then manipulate the variable without having to repeat the calculation or evaluation.

The following line of code can be used each time a number is encountered to add the number to the second string:

```
cNumOnly = cNumOnly + cCharacter
```

The program so far is:

```
cNumOnly = ""
FOR nCnt = 1 TO 14
   cCharacter = SUBSTR(cTest, nCnt, 1)
   IF ISDIGIT(cCharacter)
      cNumOnly = cNumOnly + cCharacter
   ENDIF
ENDFOR
```

Testing the Pieces

If you add a couple of commands to the end to display the strings, and then run the program, you can see that the program works with the test string:

```
cNumOnly = ""
FOR nCnt = 1 TO 14
    cCharacter = SUBSTR(cTest, nCnt, 1)
    IF ISDIGIT(cCharacter)
        cNumOnly = cNumOnly + cCharacter
    ENDIF
ENDFOR
? cTest
? cNumOnly
```

Output

```
123-456-7 89 0
1234567890
```

The output looks correct. But if you change the test string as you are testing the pieces, you can run into problems. Type the following command in the Command window and run the program again:

```
cTest = "456-789 22"
```

The program generates an error message. The FOR loop tried to execute 14 times, but there were only 10 characters in the string. You need a way to adjust for varying string lengths. Use LEN( ) to return the number of characters in a string. If you substitute this command in the FOR loop, you'll find that the program works correctly with both test strings:

```
cNumOnly = ""
FOR nCnt = 1 TO LEN(cTest)
    cCharacter = SUBSTR(cTest, nCnt, 1)
    IF ISDIGIT(cCharacter)
        cNumOnly = cNumOnly + cCharacter
    ENDIF
ENDFOR
? cTest
? cNumOnly
```

Putting the Pieces Together

To complete the programming solution for this problem, you might want to switch to reading your data from a table. When you have selected a table to use, scan the records in it and apply your program code to a field in the table rather than to a variable.

First, you could create a temporary table containing a variety of sample strings. Such a table could contain a single character field called TestField and four or five records:

TestField Contents

123-456-7 89 0	-9221 9220 94321 99-
456-789 22	000001 98-99-234

When you substitute the name of the field for the name of the test string, the program looks like this:

```
FOR nCnt = 1 TO LEN(TestField)
   cCharacter = SUBSTR(TestField, nCnt, 1)
   IF ISDIGIT(cCharacter)
      cNumOnly = cNumOnly + cCharacter
   ENDIF
ENDFOR
? TestField
? cNumOnly
```

You can manually adjust the record pointer by browsing the table and scrolling through it. When the record pointer is on each of the records, the program works the way you want it to. Or, you can now wrap table navigation code around the rest of your program:

```
SCAN
   cNumOnly = ""
   FOR nCnt = 1 TO LEN(TestField)
      cCharacter = SUBSTR(TestField, nCnt, 1)
      IF ISDIGIT(cCharacter)
         cNumOnly = cNumOnly + cCharacter
      ENDIF
   ENDFOR
? TestField
? cNumOnly
?
ENDSCAN
```

Output

```
123-456-7 89 0
1234567890

456-789 22
45678922

-9221 9220 94321 99-
922192209432199

000001 98-99-234
0000019899234
```

Testing the Whole Program

Instead of printing the string at the end of the program, you want to save it in your table. Use the following line of code to do this:

```
REPLACE TestField WITH cNumOnly
```

The complete program becomes:

```
SCAN
   cNumOnly = ""
   FOR nCnt = 1 TO LEN(TestField)
      cCharacter = SUBSTR(TestField, nCnt, 1)
      IF ISDIGIT(cCharacter)
         cNumOnly = cNumOnly + cCharacter
      ENDIF
   ENDFOR
   REPLACE TestField WITH cNumOnly
ENDSCAN
```

When you have finished the complete program, you need to test it on the sample data before trying it on your real data.

Making the Program More Robust

A robust program does what you want it to, but it also anticipates and deals with possible things that could go wrong. The example program does what you want it to do, but it makes some assumptions that must be true if the program is to work:

- A table is open in the current work area.

- The table has a character field named TestField.

If the table isn't open in the current work area or if the table doesn't have a character field with the expected name, the program will generate an error message and fail to accomplish the task.

Program to Remove the Non-Numeric Characters from a Field for All Records

Code	Comments
| ```
lFieldOK = .F.
``` | This variable determines if the necessary conditions exist for the program to work. Initially, set the variable to false (.F.) to assume that the necessary conditions do not exist. |
| ```
FOR nCnt = 1 TO FCOUNT( )
   IF FIELD(nCnt) = ;
      UPPER("TestField")
      IF TYPE("TestField") = "C"
         lFieldOK = .T.
      ENDIF
      EXIT
   ENDIF
ENDFOR
``` | This section of code goes through every field in the current table until it finds a character field named TestField. As soon as the correct field is found, lFieldOK is set to true (.T.) and EXIT ends the loop (there is no reason to keep checking after the correct field is identified). If no field matches the criteria, lFieldOK remains false (.F.). |
| ```
IF lFieldOK
``` | The conversion section of the program is executed only if a character field named TestField is present in the currently active table. |
| ```
SCAN
   cNumOnly = ""
   FOR nCnt = 1 TO LEN(TestField)
      cCharacter = ;
   SUBSTR(TestField, nCnt, 1)
      IF ISDIGIT(cCharacter)
      cNumOnly = cNumOnly + ;
      cCharacter
      ENDIF
   ENDFOR
   REPLACE TestField WITH ;
   cNumOnly
ENDSCAN
``` | The conversion code. |
| ```
ENDIF
``` | End of the IF lFieldOK condition. |

The most limiting feature of this program is that you can use it for only one field. If you want to remove the non-numeric characters from a field other than TestField, you have to go through the program and change every occurrence of TestField to the name of the other field.

Converting the program to a function, as explained in the following sections, allows you to make the code you have written more generic and more reusable, saving you work later.

Using Procedures and User-Defined Functions

Procedures and functions allow you to keep commonly used code in a single place and call it throughout your application whenever you need it. This makes your code easier to read and easier to maintain because a change can be made once in the procedure rather than multiple times in your programs.
```

In Visual FoxPro, procedures look like this:

```
PROCEDURE myproc
   * This is a comment, but it could be executable code
ENDPROC
```

Traditionally, procedures contain code that you write to perform an operation, and functions do some operations and return a value. In Visual FoxPro, functions are similar to procedures:

```
FUNCTION myfunc
   * This is a comment, but it could be executable code
ENDFUNC
```

You can include procedures and functions in a separate program file or at the end of a program file that contains normal program code. You cannot have normal executable program code included in a program file following procedures and functions.

If you include your procedures and functions in a separate program file, you can make these procedures and functions accessible in your program by using the SET PROCEDURE TO command. For example, for a file called FUNPROC.PRG, use this command in the Command window:

```
SET PROCEDURE TO funproc.prg
```

Calling a Procedure or Function

There are two ways to call a procedure or function in your programs:

- Use the DO command. For example:

  ```
  DO myproc
  ```

  – or –

  Include a set of parentheses after the function name. For example:

  ```
  myfunc( )
  ```

Each of these methods can be expanded by sending or receiving values from the procedure or function.

Sending Values to a Procedure or Function

To send values to procedures or functions, you include parameters. The following procedure, for example, accepts a single parameter:

```
PROCEDURE myproc( cString )
   * The following line displays a message
   MESSAGEBOX ("myproc" + cString)
ENDPROC
```

Note Including the parameters inside parentheses in a procedure or function definition line, for example, `PROCEDURE myproc(cString)`, indicates that the parameter is scoped locally to the procedure or function. You can also allow a function or procedure to accept locally scoped parameters with LPARAMETERS.

Parameters work identically in a function. To send a value as a parameter to this procedure or to a function, you can use a string or a variable that contains a string, as shown in the following table.

Passing Parameters

Code	Comments
`DO myproc WITH cTestString` `DO myproc WITH "test string"`	Calls a procedure and passes a literal string or character variable.
`myfunc("test string")` `myfunc( cTestString )`	Calls a function and passes a copy of a character variable or literal string.

Note If you call a procedure or function without using the DO command, the UDFPARMS setting controls how parameters are passed. By default, UDFPARMS is set to VALUE, so copies of the parameters are passed. When you use DO, the actual parameter is used (the parameter is passed by reference), and any changes within the procedure or function are reflected in the original data, regardless of the setting of UDFPARMS.

You can send multiple values to a procedure or function by separating them with commas. For example, the following procedure expects three parameters: a date, a character string, and a number.

```
PROCEDURE myproc( dDate, cString, nTimesToPrint )
   FOR nCnt = 1 to nTimesToPrint
      ? DTOC(dDate) + " " + cString + " " + STR(nCnt)
   ENDFOR
ENDPROC
```

You could call this procedure with this line of code:

```
DO myproc WITH DATE(), "Hello World", 10
```

Receiving Values from a Function

The default return value is true (.T.), but you can use the RETURN command to return any value. For example, the following function returns a date that is two weeks later than date passed to it as a parameter.

```
FUNCTION plus2weeks
PARAMETERS dDate
   RETURN dDate + 14
ENDFUNC
```

The following line of code stores the value returned from this function to a variable:

```
dDeadLine = plus2weeks(DATE())
```

The following table lists the ways you can store or display values returned from a function:

Manipulating Return Values

Code	Comments
var = myfunc( )	Stores the value returned by the function to a variable.
? myfunc( )	Prints the value returned by the function in the active output window.

Verifying Parameters in a Procedure or Function

It's a good idea to verify that the parameters sent to your procedure or function are what you expect to receive. You can use the TYPE( ) and PARAMETERS( ) functions to verify the type and number of parameters sent to your procedure or function.

The example in the previous section, for instance, needs to receive a Date type parameter. You can use the TYPE( ) function to make sure the value your function receives is the right type.

```
FUNCTION plus2weeks( dDate )
   IF TYPE("dDate") = "D"
      RETURN dDate + 14
   ELSE
      MESSAGEBOX( "You must pass a date!" )
      RETURN { - - }        && Return an empty date
   ENDIF
ENDFUNC
```

If a procedure expects fewer parameters than it receives, Visual FoxPro generates an error message. For example, if you listed two parameters, but you call the procedure with three parameters, you'll get an error message. But if a procedure expects more parameters than it receives, the additional parameters are simply initialized to false (.F.). Because there is no way to tell whether the last parameter was set to false (.F.) or omitted, the following procedure checks to make sure the appropriate number of parameters was sent:

```
PROCEDURE SaveValue( cStoreTo, cNewVal, lIsInTable )
   IF PARAMETERS( ) < 3
      MESSAGEBOX( "Too few parameters passed." )
      RETURN .F.
   ENDIF
   IF lIsInTable
      REPLACE (cStoreTo) WITH (cNewVal)
   ELSE
      &cStoreTo = cNewVal
   ENDIF
   RETURN .T.
ENDPROC
```

Converting the NUMONLY Program to a Function

NUMONLY.PRG, the example program discussed earlier in The Process of Programming
section, can be made more robust and useful by creating a function for the part of the
program that removes the non-numeric characters from a string.

Sample Procedure to Return Numeric Characters from a String

Code	Comments
`FUNCTION NumbersOnly( cMixedVal )`	Start of the function, which accepts a character string.

`  cNumOnly = ""`
`  FOR nCnt = 1 TO LEN(cMixedVal)`
`   cCharacter = ;`
`  SUBSTR(cMixedVal, nCnt, 1)`
`     IF ISDIGIT(cCharacter)`
`        cNumOnly = ;`
`   cNumOnly + cCharacter`
`     ENDIF`
`  ENDFOR`
	Create a string that has only the numeric characters from the original string.

`RETURN cNumOnly`	Return the string that has only numeric characters.
`ENDFUNC`	End of the function.

In addition to allowing you to use this code in multiple situations, this function makes the
program easier to read:

```
SCAN
   REPLACE FieldName WITH NumbersOnly(FieldName)
ENDSCAN
```

Or, even more simply:

```
REPLACE ALL FieldName WITH NumbersOnly(FieldName)
```

Moving Forward

Procedural programming, together with object-oriented programming and the
Visual FoxPro design tools, can help you develop a versatile Visual FoxPro application.
The rest of this book addresses topics you'll encounter as you develop Visual FoxPro
applications.

For more information on programming with an object-oriented approach, see Chapter 3,
"Object-Oriented Programming." To learn about designing forms with the Form Designer,
see Chapter 9, "Creating Forms."

Developing an Application

A Visual FoxPro application typically includes one or more databases, a main program that sets up the application's system environment, and a user interface comprised of forms, toolbars, and menus. Queries and reports allow users to retrieve information from their data.

This chapter discusses:

- Planning the Application
- Creating Databases
- Creating Classes
- Providing Access to Functionality
- Providing Access to Information
- Testing and Debugging

For information on developing applications using the Application Builder and the enhanced Application Framework, see "Developing Applications Using the Applications Framework" in Help.

Planning the Application

Careful planning saves time, effort, money, and sanity. The more you involve your end users in the planning process, the better. No matter how carefully you plan, though, you'll probably end up refining the specifications as you progress through the project and your end users provide feedback.

Some of the design decisions you make will impact how you create elements of the application. Who will be using the application? What is the center of user activity? How large a data set will you conceivably be working with? Will back-end data servers be used or will the data be exclusively local to a single user or multiple users over a network? Consider these factors before getting too far into the project.

Common User Activities

Even if your end users are working with customers, orders, and parts, how they are working with this information will determine how your application should deal with the data. An order entry form, like the one in Tastraded.app (in the Visual Studio …\Samples\Vfp98\Tastrade directory), might be necessary for some applications, but wouldn't be a good tool for managing inventory or tracking sales, for example.

Database Size

You'll want to think more about performance if you are dealing with large sets of data. Chapter 15, "Optimizing Applications," explains methods of optimizing performance. You may also want to adjust the way you allow users to move through the data. If you have twenty or thirty records in a table, it's okay to let users move the record pointer in a table one record at a time. If you have twenty or thirty thousand records, you'll have to provide other ways of getting to the desired data: adding search lists or dialogs, filters, custom queries, and so on. Chapter 10, "Using Controls," explains how to use a list to select specific table records. Chapter 8, "Creating Views," discusses creating parameterized queries.

Single User vs. Multiple Users

It's a good idea to create your application with the assumption that multiple users will be accessing the database at the same time. Visual FoxPro makes it easy to program for shared access. Chapter 17, "Programming for Shared Access," describes techniques for allowing multiple users to simultaneously access your database.

International Considerations

If you know your application will be used only in a single-language environment, you don't have to worry about internationalization. If, on the other hand, you want to expand your market, or if your users could be dealing with international data or environment settings, you'll want to take these factors into account as you create the application. Chapter 18, "Developing International Applications," discusses the issues you'll need to deal with as you develop applications for international use.

Local vs. Remote Data

If your application deals with remote data, you'll manage it differently than you would manage native Visual FoxPro data. Chapter 8, "Creating Views," explains how to create views to local or remote data. Part 6 of the *Microsoft Visual FoxPro 6.0 Programmer's Guide*, "Creating Client/Server Solutions," discusses how to design applications that work seamlessly with remote data.

Overview of the Process

The process of creating an application is largely iterative. Since no two applications are exactly the same, you'll probably develop prototypes and refine some components several times before achieving a finished product. End-user expectations or commitments can also change, requiring you to redefine aspects of the application. And nobody writes bug-free code all the time, so testing and debugging usually lead to some redesigning or rewriting.

The process of creating an application

In addition to taking the big picture into account in your planning stage, you'll need to decide what functionality is required, what data is involved, and how the database should be structured. You'll need to design an interface to give users access to the functionality in the application. You can create reports and queries so that users can extract useful information from their data.

Starting Development

After you have planned which components you need in your application, you might want to set up a directory framework and project to organize the component files you want to create for your application. You can make the framework yourself in the Windows Explorer and the project in the Project Manager, or use the Application Wizard to set up both at one time. This new Application Wizard opens the Application Builder so you can further customize a project and components you start in the wizard. For backward compatibility, you can still choose the earlier Application Wizard (5.0).

For more information, search for "Application Wizard" in Help.

Using the Project Manager

The Project Manager allows you to compile your completed application, but in the development phase of the application, the Project Manager makes it easy to design, modify, and run the individual components of your application.

The Project Manager

When you use the Project Manager, you can:

- Modify and run pieces of your application (forms, menus, programs) with just a few clicks.

- Drag classes, tables, and fields from the Project Manager to the Form Designer or Class Designer.

- Drag classes between class libraries.

- View and modify your tables and databases easily.

- Add descriptions for the components in your application.

- Drag-and-drop elements between projects.

For detailed information about how to use the Project Manager, see Chapter 1, "Getting Started," in the *User's Guide*. For information about compiling applications, see Chapter 13, "Compiling an Application," in this book.

Creating Databases

Because a database application is so dependent on the underlying data, the best way to begin designing your application is to start with the data. You can set up your database and determine what the relationships are between tables, what business rules you want to enforce, and so on, before you design any interface or data manipulation components. A sound database foundation makes development work much easier.

Chapter 5, "Designing Databases," Chapter 6, "Creating Databases," and Chapter 7, "Working with Tables," discuss design issues and explain how to use Visual FoxPro to design effective and efficient tables and databases.

Creating Classes

You can create a robust, object-oriented, event-driven application using only the Visual FoxPro base classes. You might not ever have to create a class, but you'll want to. In addition to making code more manageable and easier to maintain, a solid class library allows you to rapidly create prototypes and quickly plug functionality into an application. You can create classes in a program file, in the Form Designer (using the Save As Class command on the File menu), or in the Class Designer.

Chapter 3, "Object-Oriented Programming," discusses some of the benefits of creating classes and details how to create them either with the Class Designer or programmatically.

Providing Access to Functionality

User satisfaction will be strongly influenced by the interface you provide for the functionality of your application. You can have a very clean class model, elegant code, and clever solutions to difficult problems in your application, but these are almost always hidden from your customers. What they see is the interface you provide. Fortunately, the Visual FoxPro design tools make it easy to create attractive, feature-rich interfaces.

The user interface consists primarily of forms, toolbars, and menus. You can associate all the functionality in your application with controls or menu commands in the interface. Chapter 9, "Creating Forms," describes how to create forms and form sets. Utilizing Visual FoxPro controls in your forms is discussed in Chapter 10, "Using Controls." See Chapter 11, "Designing Menus and Toolbars," to put the finishing touches on your application.

Providing Access to Information

You'll probably display some information for your users in forms, but you'll also want to give your users the ability to specify exactly what information they want to see and the option to print it out in reports or labels. Queries, especially queries that accept user-defined parameters, allow users to have greater control over their data. Reports allow users to print full, partial, or summary pictures of their data. ActiveX controls and automation allow your application to share information and functionality with other applications.

The Query Designer and the Report Designer are discussed in chapters 4 through 7 of the *User's Guide*. Chapter 12 of this book, "Adding Queries and Reports," discusses integrating queries and reports into an application. Chapter 16, "Adding OLE," describes integrating OLE in an application.

Testing and Debugging

Testing and debugging is something most developers do at each step in the development process. It's a good idea to test and debug as you go. If you create a form, you'll want to make sure it does what you want it to do before moving on to other elements of your application.

Chapter 14, "Testing and Debugging Applications," explains how to use the Visual FoxPro debugging tools to debug your applications and provides tips on how to make the debugging process easier.

Object-Oriented Programming

While Visual FoxPro still supports standard procedural programming, new extensions to the language give you the power and flexibility of object-oriented programming.

Object-oriented design and object-oriented programming represent a change in focus from standard procedural programming. Instead of thinking about program flow from the first line of code to the last line of code, you need to think about creating objects: self-contained components of an application that have private functionality as well as functionality that you can expose to the user.

This chapter discusses:

- Understanding Objects in Visual FoxPro
- Understanding Classes in Visual FoxPro
- Matching the Class to the Task
- Creating Classes
- Adding Classes to Forms
- Defining Classes Programmatically

Understanding Objects in Visual FoxPro

In Visual FoxPro, forms and controls are objects that you include in your applications. You manipulate these objects through their properties, events, and methods.

The object-oriented Visual FoxPro language extensions provide you with a great deal of control over the objects in your applications. These extensions also make it easier to create and maintain libraries of reusable code, giving you:

- More compact code.
- Easier incorporation of code into applications without elaborate naming schemes.
- Less complexity when integrating code from different files into an application.

Object-oriented programming is largely a way of packaging code so that it can be reused and maintained more easily. The primary package is called a class.

Classes and Objects: The Building Blocks of Applications

Classes and objects are closely related, but they are not the same. A class contains information about how an object should look and behave. A class is the blueprint or schematic of an object. The electrical schematic and design layout of a telephone, for example, would approximate a class. The object, or an instance of the class, would be a telephone.

The class determines the characteristics of the object.

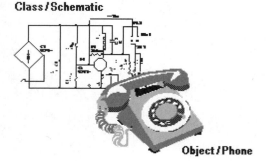

Objects Have Properties

An object has certain properties, or attributes. For example, a phone is a certain color and size. When you put a phone in your office, it has a certain position on your desk. The receiver can be on or off the hook.

Objects you create in Visual FoxPro also have properties that are determined by the class the object is based on. These properties can be set at design time or at run time.

For example, some of the properties that a check box can have are listed in the following table:

Property	Description
Caption	The descriptive text beside the check box.
Enabled	Specifies whether the check box can be chosen by a user.
ForeColor	The color of the caption text.
Left	The position of the left side of the check box.
MousePointer	How the mouse pointer looks when over the check box.
Top	The position of the top of the check box.
Visible	Specifies whether the check box is visible.

Objects Have Associated Events and Methods

Each object recognizes and can respond to certain actions called events. An event is a specific and predetermined activity, initiated by either a user or the system. Events, in most cases, are generated by user interaction. For example, with a phone, an event is triggered when a user takes the receiver off the hook. Events are also triggered when the user presses the buttons to make a call.

In Visual FoxPro, user actions that trigger events include clicks, mouse moves, and key presses. Initializing an object and encountering a line of code that causes an error are system-initiated events.

Methods are procedures that are associated with an object. Methods are different from normal Visual FoxPro procedures: methods are inextricably bound with an object and are called differently than normal Visual FoxPro procedures are called.

Events can have methods associated with them. For example, if you write method code for the Click event, that code is executed when the Click event occurs. Methods can also exist independently of any events. These methods must be explicitly called in code.

The event set, while extensive, is fixed. You can't create new events. The method set, however, is infinitely extendible.

The following table lists some of the events associated with a check box:

Event	Description
Click	User clicks the check box.
GotFocus	User selects the check box by clicking it or tabbing to it.
LostFocus	User selects another control.

The following table lists some of the methods associated with a check box:

Method	Description
Refresh	The value of the check box is updated to reflect any changes that may have occurred to the underlying data source.
SetFocus	The focus is set to the check box just as though the user had pressed the TAB key until the check box was selected.

See Chapter 4, "Understanding the Event Model," for a discussion of the order in which events occur. For a description of each property, event, and method, see Help.

Understanding Classes in Visual FoxPro

All of the properties, events, and methods for an object are specified in the class definition. In addition, classes have the following characteristics that make them especially useful for creating reusable, easily maintained code:

- Encapsulation
- Subclasses
- Inheritance

Hiding Unnecessary Complexity

When you include a phone in your office, you probably don't care how the phone internally receives a call, initiates or terminates connections to electronic switchboards, or translates key presses into electronic signals. All you need to know is that you can lift the receiver, dial the appropriate numbers, and talk to the person you want to talk to. The complexity of making that connection is hidden. The benefit of being able to ignore the inner details of an object so you can focus on the aspects of the object you need to use is called abstraction.

Internal complexity can be hidden.

Encapsulation, which involves packaging method and property code together in an object, contributes to abstraction. For example, the properties that determine the items in a list box and the code that executes when you choose an item in the list can be encapsulated in a single control that you add to a form.

Leveraging the Power of Existing Classes

A subclass can have all the functionality of an existing class, plus any additional controls or functionality you want to give it. If your class is a basic telephone, you can have subclasses that have all the functionality of the original telephone and any specialized features you want to give them.

Subclassing allows you to reuse code.

Subclassing is one way to decrease the amount of code you have to write. Start with the definition of an object that is close to what you want, and customize it.

Streamlining Code Maintenance

With inheritance, if you make a change to a class, that change is reflected in all subclasses based on the class. This automatic update saves you time and effort. For example, if a phone manufacturer wanted to change from dial to push-button style phones, it would save a lot of work to be able to make the change to the master schematic and have all previously manufactured phones based on that master schematic automatically inherit this new feature, rather than having to add the new feature to all the existing phones individually.

Inheritance makes maintaining your code easy.

Change dial to buttons in the base class.

Subclasses with dials...   ...automatically inherit buttons.

Inheritance doesn't work with hardware, but you do have this capability in software. If you discover a bug in your class, instead of having to go to each subclass and change the code, you fix it once in the class and the change propagates throughout all subclasses of the class.

The Visual FoxPro Class Hierarchy

When you are creating user-defined classes, it helps to understand the Visual FoxPro class hierarchy.

The Visual FoxPro class hierarchy

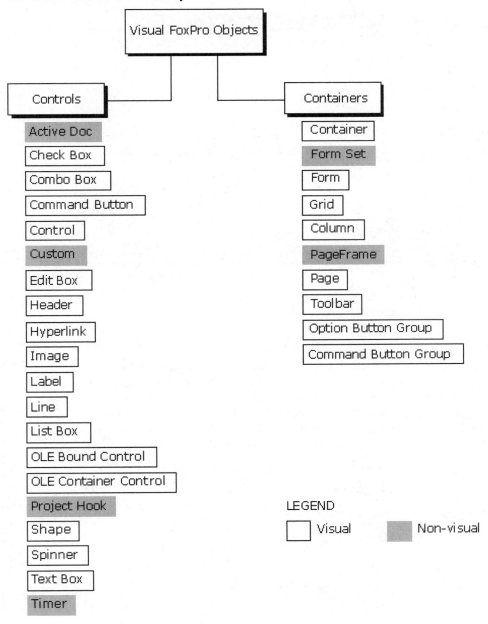

Containers and Non-Containers

The two primary types of Visual FoxPro classes, and by extension Visual FoxPro objects, are container classes and control classes.

Container and Control Classes

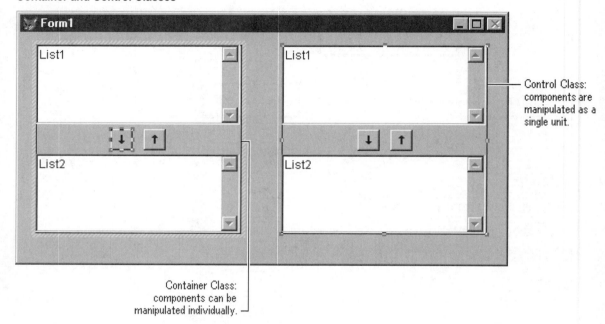

Control Class: components are manipulated as a single unit.

Container Class: components can be manipulated individually.

Container Classes

Containers can contain other objects and allow access to the objects contained within them. For example, if you create a container class that consists of two list boxes and two command buttons, and then add an object based on this class to a form, each individual object can be manipulated at run time and design time. You can easily change the positions of the list boxes or the captions of the command buttons. You can also add objects to the control at design time; for example, you can add labels to identify the list boxes.

The following table lists what each container class can contain:

Container	Can contain
Command button groups	Command buttons
Container	Any controls
Control	Any controls
Custom	Any controls, page frame, container, custom

(continued)

Container	Can contain
Form sets	Forms, toolbars
Forms	Page frames, any controls, containers, custom
Grid columns	Headers and any objects except form sets, forms, toolbars, timers, and other columns
Grids	Grid columns
Option button groups	Option buttons
Page frames	Pages
Pages	Any controls, containers, custom
Project	Files, servers
Toolbars	Any controls, page frame, container

Control Classes

Control classes are more completely encapsulated than container classes are, but can be less flexible for that reason. Control classes do not have an AddObject method.

Matching the Class to the Task

You want to be able to use classes in many different contexts. Smart planning will enable you to most effectively decide what classes to design and what functionality to include in the class.

Deciding When to Create Classes

You could create a class for every control and every form you might ever use, but this isn't the most effective way to design your applications. You'll likely end up with multiple classes that do much the same thing but must be maintained separately.

Encapsulate Generic Functionality

You can create a control class for generic functionality. For example, command buttons that allow a user to move the record pointer in a table, a button to close a form, and a help button, can all be saved as classes and added to forms any time you want the forms to have this functionality.

You can expose properties and methods on a class so that the user can integrate them into the particular data environment of a form or form set.

Provide a Consistent Application Look and Feel

You can create form set, form, and control classes with a distinctive appearance so that all the components of your application have the same look. For example, you could add graphics and specific color patterns to a form class and use that as a template for all forms you create. You could create a text box class with a distinctive appearance, such as a shadowed effect, and use this class throughout your application any time you want to add a text box.

Deciding What Type of Class to Create

Visual FoxPro allows you to create several different kinds of classes, each with its own characteristics. You specify the type of class you want to create in the New Class dialog box or in the AS clause in the CREATE CLASS command.

The Visual FoxPro Base Classes

You can create subclasses of most of the Visual FoxPro base classes in the Class Designer.

Visual FoxPro Base Classes

ActiveDoc	Custom	Label	PageFrame
CheckBox	EditBox	Line	ProjectHook
Column*	Form	ListBox	Separator
CommandButton	FormSet	OLEBoundControl	Shape
CommandGroup	Grid	OLEContainerControl	Spinner
ComboBox	Header*	OptionButton*	TextBox
Container	Hyperlink Object	OptionGroup	Timer
Control	Image	Page*	ToolBar

* These classes are an integral part of a parent container and cannot be subclassed in the Class Designer.

For more information on Visual FoxPro base classes, see Help.

All Visual FoxPro base classes recognize the following minimum set of events:

Event	Description
Init	Occurs when the object is created.
Destroy	Occurs when the object is released from memory.
Error	Occurs whenever an error occurs in event or method procedures of the class.

All Visual FoxPro base classes have the following minimum set of properties:

Property	Description
Class	What type of class it is.
BaseClass	The base class it was derived from, such as Form, Commandbutton, Custom, and so on.
ClassLibrary	The class library the class is stored in.
ParentClass	The class that the current class was derived from. If the class was derived directly from a Visual FoxPro base class, the ParentClass property is the same as the BaseClass property.

For more information on these properties and events, see Help.

Extending the Visual FoxPro Base Classes

You can subclass these classes to set your own default control properties. For example, if you want the default names of controls you add to forms in your applications to automatically reflect your naming conventions, you can create classes based on the Visual FoxPro base classes to do this. You can create form classes with a customized look or behavior to serve as templates for all the forms you create.

You could also subclass the Visual FoxPro base classes to create controls with encapsulated functionality. If you want a button to release forms when the button is clicked, you can create a class based on the Visual FoxPro command button class, set the caption property to "Quit" and include the following command in the Click event:

```
THISFORM.Release
```

You can add this new button to any form in your application.

Customized command button added to a form

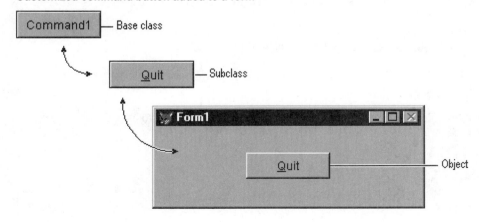

Creating Controls with Multiple Components

Your subclasses aren't limited to single base classes. You can add multiple controls into a single container class definition. Many of the classes in the Visual FoxPro sample class library fall into this category. For example, the VCR class in Buttons.vcx, located in the Visual Studio …\Samples\Vfp98\Classes directory, contains four command buttons for navigating the records in a table.

Creating Non-Visual Classes

A class based on the Visual FoxPro custom class doesn't have a run-time visual element. You can create methods and properties for your custom class using the Class Designer environment. For example, you could create a custom class named StrMethods and include a number of methods to manipulate character strings. You could add this class to a form with an edit box and call the methods as needed. If you had a method called WordCount, you could call it when needed:

```
THISFORM.txtCount.Value = ;
    THISFORM.StrMethods.WordCount(THISFORM.edtText.Value)
```

Non-visual classes (like the custom control and the timer control) have a visual representation only at design time in the Form Designer. Set the picture property of the custom class to the .bmp file you want displayed in the Form Designer when the custom class is added to a form.

Creating Classes

You can create new classes in the Class Designer and you can see how each object will appear to the user as you design it.

To create a new class

- In the Project Manager, select the **Classes** tab and choose **New**.

  – or –

  From the **File** menu, choose **New**, select **Class**, and choose **New File**.

  – or –

  Use the CREATE CLASS command.

The New Class dialog box lets you specify what to call the new class, the class to base the new class on, and the library to store it in.

Creating a new class

```
New Class                                          ✕

  Class Name:  myclass                        ┌─────────┐
                                              │   OK    │
  Based On:   Control          ▼   ...        └─────────┘
  From:                                       ┌─────────┐
                                              │ Cancel  │
  Store In:    mylib.vcx           ...         └─────────┘
```

Choose the parent class from
this drop-down list. ─┘

Modifying a Class Definition

Once you have created a class, you can modify it. Changes made to a class affect all the subclasses and all the objects based on this class. You can add an enhancement to a class or fix a bug in the class, and all the subclasses and objects based on the class will inherit the change.

To modify a class in the Project Manager

1. Select the class you want to modify.

2. Choose **Modify**.

    The **Class Designer** opens.

You can also modify a visual class definition with the MODIFY CLASS command. For more information, search for MODIFY CLASS in Help.

> **Important**   Don't change the Name property of a class if the class is already being used in any other application components. Otherwise, Visual FoxPro will not be able to locate the class when needed.

Subclassing a Class Definition

You can create a subclass of a user-defined class in one of two ways.

To create a subclass of a user-defined class

1. In the **New Class** dialog box, click the dialog button to the right of the **Based On** box.

2. In the **Open** dialog box, choose the class you want to base the new class on.

    – or –

    Use the CREATE CLASS command.

For example, to base a new class, x, on `parentclass` in Mylibrary.vcx, use this code:

```
CREATE CLASS x OF y AS parentclass ;
    FROM mylibrary
```

Using the Class Designer

When you specify what class your new class is based on and the library to store the class in, the Class Designer opens.

Class Designer

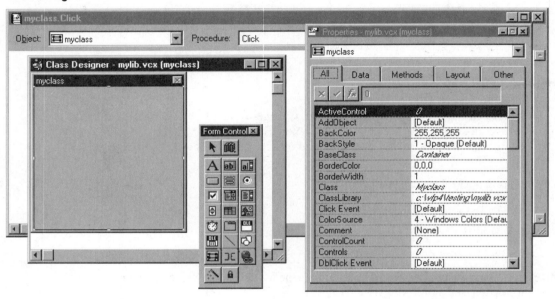

The Class Designer provides the same interface that the Form Designer does, allowing you to see and edit the properties of your class in the Properties window. Code editing windows allow you to write code to be executed when events occur or methods are called.

Adding Objects to a Control or Container Class

If you base the new class on the control or container class, you can add controls to it the same way you add controls in the Form Designer: choose the control button on the Form Controls toolbar and drag to size in the Class Designer.

No matter what type of class you base the new class on, you can set properties and write method code. You can also create new properties and methods for the class.

Adding Properties and Methods to a Class

You can add as many new properties and methods to the new class as you want. Properties hold values; methods hold procedural code to be run when you call the method.

Creating New Properties and Methods

When you create new properties and methods for classes, the properties and methods are scoped to the class, not to individual components in the class.

To add a new property to a class

1. From the **Class** menu, choose **New Property**.

2. In the **New Property** dialog box, type the name of the property.

3. Specify the visibility: **Public**, **Protected**, or **Hidden**.

   A Public property can be accessed anywhere in your application. Protected and Hidden properties and methods are discussed in "Protecting and Hiding Class Members" later in this chapter.

   #### New Property dialog box

4. Choose **Add**.

   You can also include a description of the property that will be displayed at the bottom of the Properties window in the **Class Designer** and in the **Form Designer** when the control is added to a form.

   Troubleshooting   When you add a property to a class that can be set by a user of the class, the user could enter an invalid setting for your property that could cause run-time errors. You need to explicitly document the valid settings for the property. If your property can be set to 0, 1, or 2, for example, say so in the Description box of the New Property dialog box. You might also want to verify the value of the property in code that references it.

To create an array property

- In the **Name** box of the **New Property** dialog box, specify the name, size, and dimensions of the array.

  For example, to create an array property named myarray with ten rows and two columns, type the following in the Name box:

  ```
  myarray[10,2]
  ```

The array property is read-only at design time and is displayed in the Properties window in italics. The array property can be managed and redimensioned at run time. For an example of using an array property, see "Managing Multiple Instances of a Form" in Chapter 9, "Creating Forms."

To add a new method to a class

1. From the **Class** menu, choose **New Method**.

2. In the **New Method** dialog box, type the name of the method.

3. Specify the visibility: **Public**, **Protected**, or **Hidden**.

4. Select the **Access** check box to create an Access method, select the Assign check box to create an Assign method, or select both check boxes to create Access and Assign methods.

Access and Assign methods let you execute code when the value of a property is queried or when you attempt to change the property's value.

The code in an Access method is executed when the value of a property is queried, typically by using the property in an object reference, storing the value of the property to a variable, or displaying the value of property with a question mark (?).

The code in an Assign method is executed when you attempt to change the value of a property, typically by using the STORE or = command to assign a new value to the property.

For more information about Access and Assign methods, see "Access and Assign Methods," in Chapter 33, "Programming Improvements."

You can also include a description of the method.

Protecting and Hiding Class Members

Properties and methods in a class definition are **Public** by default: code in other classes or procedures can set the properties or call the methods. Properties and methods that you designate as **Protected** can be accessed only by other methods in the class definition or in subclasses of the class. Properties and methods designated as **Hidden** can be accessed only by other members in the class definition. Subclasses of the class cannot "see" or reference hidden members.

To ensure correct functioning in some classes, you need to prevent users from programmatically changing the properties or calling the method from outside the class.

The following example illustrates using protected properties and methods in a class.

The stopwatch class included in Samples.vcx, in the Visual Studio ...\Samples \Vfp98\Classes directory, includes a timer and five labels to display the elapsed time:

The stopwatch class in Samples.vcx

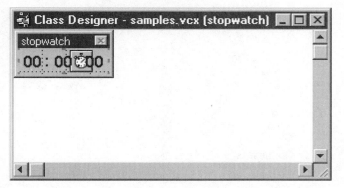

The Stopwatch class contains labels and a timer.

Property Settings for the Stopwatch Class

Control	Property	Setting
lblSeconds	Caption	00
lblColon1	Caption	:
lblMinutes	Caption	00
lblColon2	Caption	:
lblHours	Caption	00
tmrSWatch	Interval	1000

This class also has three protected properties, nSec, nMin, and nHour, and one protected method, UpdateDisplay. The other three custom methods in the class, Start, Stop, and Reset, are not protected.

> **Tip** Choose Class Info on the Class menu to see the visibility of all properties and methods of a class.

The protected properties are used in internal calculations in the UpdateDisplay method and the Timer event. The UpdateDisplay method sets the captions of the labels to reflect the elapsed time.

The UpdateDisplay Method

Code	Comments
```cSecDisplay = ALLTRIM(STR(THIS.nSec))\ncMinDisplay = ALLTRIM(STR(THIS.nMin))\ncHourDisplay = ALLTRIM(STR(THIS.nHour))```	Convert the numeric properties to Character type for display in the label captions.
```THIS.lblSeconds.Caption = ;\n IIF(THIS.nSec < 10, ;\n "0" ,"") + cSecDisplay\nTHIS.lblMinutes.Caption = ;\n IIF(THIS.nMin < 10, ;\n "0", "") + cMinDisplay\nTHIS.lblHours.Caption = ;\n IIF(THIS.nHour < 10, ;\n "0", "") + cHourDisplay```	Set the label captions, retaining the leading 0 if the value of the numeric property is less than 10.

The following table lists the code in the tmrSWatch.Timer event:

The Timer Event

Code	Comments
```THIS.Parent.nSec = THIS.Parent.nSec + 1```	Increment the nSec property every time the timer event fires: every second.
```IF THIS.Parent.nSec = 60\n THIS.Parent.nSec = 0\n THIS.Parent.nMin = ;\n THIS.Parent.nMin + 1\nENDIF```	If nSec has reached 60, reset it to 0 and increment the nMin property.
```IF THIS.Parent.nMin = 60\n THIS.Parent.nMin = 0\n THIS.Parent.nHour = ;\n THIS.Parent.nHour + 1\nENDIF\nTHIS.Parent.UpdateDisplay```	If nMin has reached 60, reset it to 0 and increment the nHour property. Call the UpdateDisplay method when the new property values are set.

The stopwatch class has three methods that are not protected: Start, Stop, and Reset. A user can call these methods directly to control the stopwatch.

The Start method contains the following line of code:

```
THIS.tmrSWatch.Enabled = .T.
```

The Stop method contains the following line of code:

```
THIS.tmrSWatch.Enabled = .F.
```

The Reset method sets the protected properties to zero and calls the protected method:

```
THIS.nSec = 0
THIS.nMin = 0
THIS.nHour = 0
THIS.UpdateDisplay
```

The user cannot directly set these properties or call this method, but code in the Reset method can.

Specifying the Default Value for a Property

When you create a new property, the default setting is false (.F.). To specify a different default setting for a property, use the Properties window. In the Other tab, click on your property and set it to the desired value. This will be the initial property setting when the class is added to a form or form set.

You can also set any of the base class properties in the Class Designer. When an object based on the class is added to the form, the object reflects your property settings rather than the Visual FoxPro base class property settings.

> **Tip**   If you want to make the default setting of a property an empty string, select the setting in the Property Editing box and press the BACKSPACE key.

Specifying Design Time Appearance

You can specify the toolbar icon and the container icon for your class in the Class Info dialog box.

To set a toolbar icon for a class

1. In the Class Designer, choose **Class Info** from the **Class** menu.

2. In the **Class Info** dialog box, type the name and path of the .BMP file in the **Toolbar icon** box.

> **Tip**   The bitmap (.bmp file) for the toolbar icon is 15 by 16 pixels. If the picture is larger or smaller, it is sized to 15 by 16 pixels and might not look the way you want it to.

The toolbar icon you specify is displayed in the Form Controls toolbar when you populate the toolbar with the classes in your class library.

You can also specify the icon to be displayed for the class in the Project Manager and Class Browser by setting the container icon.

To set a container icon for a class

1. In the Class Designer, choose **Class Info** from the **Class** menu.

2. In the **Container icon** box, type the name and path of the .bmp file to be displayed on the button in the Form Controls toolbar.

Using Class Library Files

Every visually designed class is stored in a class library with a .vcx file extension.

Creating a Class Library

You can create a class library in one of three ways.

To create a class library

- When you create a class, specify a new class library file in the **Store In** box of the **New Class** dialog box.

  – or –

  Use the CREATE CLASS command, specifying the name of the new class library.

  For example, the following statement creates a new class named `myclass` and a new class library named `new_lib`:

  ```
  CREATE CLASS myclass OF new_lib AS CUSTOM
  ```

  – or –

  Use the CREATE CLASSLIB command.

  For example, type the following command in the Command window to create a class library named `new_lib`:

  ```
  CREATE CLASSLIB new_lib
  ```

Copying and Removing Class Library Classes

Once you add a class library to a project, you can easily copy classes from one library to another or simply remove classes from libraries.

To copy a class from one library to another

1. Make sure both libraries are in a project (not necessarily the same project).

2. In the Project Manager, select the **Classes** tab.

3. Click the plus sign (+) to the left of the class library that the class is now in.

4. Drag the class from the original library and drop it in the new library.

   Tip   For convenience and speed, you might want to keep a class and all the subclasses based on it in one class library. If you have a class that contains elements from many different class libraries, these libraries must all be open, so it will take a little longer to initially load your class at run time and at design time.

To remove a class from a library

- Select the class in the Project Manager and choose **Remove**.

  – or –

  Use the REMOVE CLASS command.

To change the name of a class in a class library, use the RENAME CLASS command. Remember, however, that when you change the name of a class, forms that contain the class and subclasses in other .vcx files continue to reference the old name and will no longer function correctly. For more information, search for REMOVE CLASS and RENAME CLASS in Help.

Visual FoxPro includes a Class Browser to facilitate using and managing classes and class libraries. For more information, search for "Class Browser window" in Help.

Adding Classes to Forms

You can drag a class from the Project Manager to the Form Designer or to the Class Designer. You can also register your classes so that they can be displayed directly on the Form Controls toolbar in the Class Designer or Form Designer and added to containers the same way the standard controls are added.

To register a class library

1. From the **Tools** menu, choose **Options**.

2. In the **Options** dialog box, choose the **Controls** tab.

3. Select **Visual Class Libraries** and choose **Add**.

4. In the **Open** dialog box, choose a class library to add to the registry and choose **Open**.

5. Choose **Set as Default** if you want the class library to be available in the **Form Controls** toolbar in future sessions of Visual FoxPro.

You can also add your class library to the Form Controls toolbar by choosing Add in the submenu of the View Classes button. To make these classes available in the Form Controls toolbar in future sessions of Visual FoxPro, you still need to set the default in the Options dialog box.

Overriding Default Property Settings

When you add objects based on a user-defined class to a form, you can change the settings of all the properties of the class that are not protected, overriding the default settings. If you change the class properties in the Class Designer later, the settings in the object on the form are not affected. If you have not changed a property setting in the form and you change the property setting in the class, the change will take effect in the object as well.

For example, a user could add an object based on your class to a form and change the BackColor property from white to red. If you change the BackColor property of the class to green, the object on the user's form will still have a background color of red. If, on the other hand, the user did not change the BackColor property of the object and you changed the background color of the class to green, the BackColor property of the object on the form would inherit the change and also be green.

Calling Parent Class Method Code

An object or class based on another class automatically inherits the functionality of the original. However, you can easily override the inherited method code. For example, you can write new code for the Click event of a class after you subclass it or after you add an object based on the class to a container. In both cases, the new code is executed at run time; the original code is not executed.

More frequently, however, you want to add functionality to the new class or object while keeping the original functionality. In fact, one of the key decisions you have to make in object-oriented programming is what functionality to include at the class level, at the subclass level, and at the object level. You can optimize your class design by using the DODEFAULT( ) function or scope resolution operator (::) to add code at different levels in the class or container hierarchy.

Adding Functionality to Subclasses

You can call the parent class code from a subclass by using the DODEFAULT( ) function.

For example, cmdOK is a command button class stored in Buttons.vcx, located in the Visual Studio …\Samples\Vfp98\Classes directory. The code associated with the Click event of cmdOk releases the form the button is on. CmdCancel is a subclass of cmdOk in the same class library. To add functionality to cmdCancel to discard changes, for example, you could add the following code to the Click event:

```
IF USED( ) AND CURSORGETPROP("Buffering") != 1
   TABLEREVERT(.T.)
ENDIF
DODEFAULT( )
```

Because changes are written to a buffered table by default when the table is closed, you don't need to add TABLEUPDATE( ) code to cmdOk. The additional code in cmdCancel reverts changes to the table before calling the code in cmdOk, the ParentClass, to release the form.

Class and Container Hierarchies

The class hierarchy and the container are two separate entities. Visual FoxPro looks for event code up through the class hierarchy, whereas objects are referenced in the container hierarchy. The following section, "Referencing Objects in the Container Hierarchy," discusses container hierarchies. Later in this chapter, class hierarchies are explained in the section "Calling Event Code up the Class Hierarchy."

Referencing Objects in the Container Hierarchy

To manipulate an object, you need to identify it in relation to the container hierarchy. For example, to manipulate a control on a form in a form set, you need to reference the form set, the form, and then the control.

You can compare the referencing of an object within its container hierarchy to giving Visual FoxPro an address to your object. When you describe the location of a house to someone outside your immediate frame of reference, you need to indicate the country, the state or region, the city, the street, or just the street number of the house, depending on how far they are from you. Otherwise, there could be some confusion.

The following illustration shows a possible container nesting situation.

Nested containers

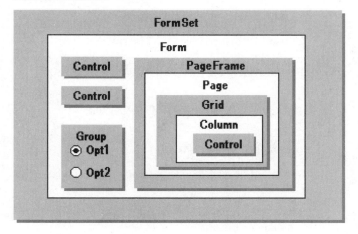

To disable the control in the grid column, you need to provide the following address:

```
Formset.Form.PageFrame.Page.;
   Grid.Column.Control.Enabled = .F.
```

The ActiveForm property of the application object (_VFP) allows you to manipulate the active form even if you don't know the name of the form. For example, the following line of code changes the background color of the active form, no matter what form set it belongs to:

```
_VFP.ActiveForm.BackColor = RGB(255,255,255)
```

Similarly, the ActiveControl property allows you to manipulate the active control on the active form. For example, the following expression entered in the Watch window displays the name of the active control on a form as you interactively choose the various controls:

```
_VFP.ActiveForm.ActiveControl.Name
```

Relative Referencing

When you are referencing objects from within the container hierarchy (for example, in the Click event of a command button on a form in a form set), you can use some shortcuts to identify the object you want to manipulate. The following table lists properties or keywords that make it easier to reference an object from within the object hierarchy:

Property or keyword	Reference
Parent	The immediate container of the object.
THIS	The object. *(continued)*

(continued)

Property or keyword	Reference
THISFORM	The form that contains the object.
THISFORMSET	The form set that contains the object.

Note You can use THIS, THISFORM, and THISFORMSET only in method or event code.

The following table provides examples of using THISFORMSET, THISFORM, THIS, and Parent to set object properties:

Command	Where to include the command
`THISFORMSET.frm1.cmd1.Caption = "OK"`	In the event or method code of any controls on any form in the form set.
`THISFORM.cmd1.Caption = "OK"`	In the event or method code of any control on the same form that `cmd1` is on.
`THIS.Caption = "OK"`	In the event or method code of the control whose caption you want to change.
`THIS.Parent.BackColor = RGB(192,0,0)`	In the event or method code of a control on a form. The command changes the background color of the form to dark red.

Setting Properties

You can set the properties of an object at run time or design time.

To set a property

- Use this syntax:

  Container.Object.Property = Value

  For example, the following statements set various properties of a text box named `txtDate` on a form named `frmPhoneLog`:

  ```
  frmPhoneLog.txtDate.Value = DATE( ) && Display the current date
  frmPhoneLog.txtDate.Enabled = .T. && The control is enabled
  frmPhoneLog.txtDate.ForeColor = RGB(0,0,0)     && black text
  frmPhoneLog.txtDate.BackColor = RGB(192,192,192)  && gray background
  ```

For the property settings in the preceding examples, `frmPhoneLog` is the highest level container object. If `frmPhoneLog` were contained in a form set, you would also need to include the form set in the parent path:

```
frsContacts.frmPhoneLog.txtDate.Value = DATE( )
```

Setting Multiple Properties

The WITH ... ENDWITH structure simplifies setting multiple properties. For example, to set multiple properties of a column in a grid in a form in a form set, you could use the following syntax:

```
WITH THISFORMSET.frmForm1.grdGrid1.grcColumn1
    .Width = 5
    .Resizable = .F.
    .ForeColor = RGB(0,0,0)
    .BackColor = RGB(255,255,255)
    .SelectOnEntry = .T.
ENDWITH
```

Calling Methods

Once an object has been created, you can call the methods of that object from anywhere in your application.

To call a method

- Use this syntax:

  Parent.Object.Method

The following statements call methods to display a form and set the focus to a text box:

```
frsFormSet.frmForm1.Show
frsFormSet.frmForm1.txtGetText1.SetFocus
```

Methods that return values and are used in expressions must end in open and closed parentheses. For example, the following statement sets the caption of a form to the value returned from the user-defined method `GetNewCaption`:

```
Form1.Caption = Form1.GetNewCaption( )
```

> **Note**   Parameters passed to methods must be included in parentheses after the method name; for example, `Form1.Show(nStyle)`. passes `nStyle` to Form1's Show method code.

Responding to Events

The code you include in an event procedure is executed when the event takes place. For example, the code you include in the Click event procedure of a command button is executed when the user clicks the command button.

You can programmatically cause Click, DblClick, MouseMove, and DragDrop events with the MOUSE command, or use the ERROR command to generate Error events and the KEYBOARD command to generate KeyPress events. You cannot programmatically cause any other events to occur, but you can call the procedure associated with the event. For example, the following statement causes the code in the Activate event of `frmPhoneLog` to be executed, but it doesn't activate the form:

```
frmPhoneLog.Activate
```

If you do want to activate the form, use the Show method of the form. Calling the Show method causes the form to be displayed and activated, at which point the code in the Activate event is also executed:

```
frmPhoneLog.Show
```

Defining Classes Programmatically

You can define classes visually in the Class Designer and the Form Designer or programmatically in .PRG files. This section describes how to write class definitions. For information about the specific commands, functions, and operators, see Help. For more information about forms, see Chapter 9, "Creating Forms."

In a program file, you can have program code prior to the class definitions, but not after the class definitions, in the same way that program code cannot come after procedures in a program. The basic shell for class creation has this syntax:

DEFINE CLASS *ClassName1* AS *ParentClass* [OLEPUBLIC]
    [[PROTECTED | HIDDEN *PropertyName1*, *PropertyName2* ...]
        [Object.]*PropertyName* = *eExpression* ...]
    [ADD OBJECT [PROTECTED] *ObjectName* AS *ClassName2* [NOINIT]
        [WITH *cPropertylist*]]...
    [[PROTECTED | HIDDEN] FUNCTION | PROCEDURE *Name*[_ACCESS | _ASSIGN]
        [NODEFAULT]
        cStatements
    [ENDFUNC | ENDPROC]]...
ENDDEFINE

Protecting and Hiding Class Members

You can protect or hide properties and methods in a class definition with the PROTECTED and HIDDEN keywords of the DEFINE CLASS command.

For example, if you create a class to hold employee information, and you don't want users to be able to change the hire date, you can protect the HireDate property. If users need to find out when an employee was hired, you can include a method to return the hire date.

```
DEFINE CLASS employee AS CUSTOM
PROTECTED HireDate
    First_Name = ""
    Last_Name = ""
    Address = ""
    HireDate = { - - }
```

```
PROCEDURE GetHireDate
   RETURN This.HireDate
ENDPROC
ENDDEFINE
```

Creating Objects from Classes

When you have saved a visual class, you can create an object based on it with the CREATEOBJECT( ) function. The following example demonstrates running a form saved as a class definition in the class library file Forms.vcx:

Creating and Showing a Form Object Whose Class Was Designed in the Form Designer

Code	Comments
`SET CLASSLIB TO Forms ADDITIVE`	Set the class library to the .vcx file that the form definition was saved in. The ADDITIVE keyword prevents this command from closing any other class libraries that happened to be open.
`frmTest = CREATEOBJECT("TestForm")`	This code assumes that the name of the form class saved in the class library is TestForm.
`frmTest.Show`	Display the form.

For more information, search for SET CLASSLIB or CREATEOBJECT( ) in Help.

Adding Objects to a Container Class

You can use the ADD OBJECT clause in the DEFINE CLASS command or the AddObject method to add objects to a container.

For example, the following class definition is based on a form. The ADD OBJECT command adds two command buttons to the form:

```
DEFINE CLASS myform AS FORM
   ADD OBJECT cmdOK AS COMMANDBUTTON
   ADD OBJECT PROTECTED cmdCancel AS COMMANDBUTTON
ENDDEFINE
```

Use the AddObject method to add objects to a container after the container object has been created. For example, the following lines of code create a form object and add two command buttons to it:

```
frmMessage = CREATEOBJECT("FORM")
frmMessage.AddObject("txt1", "TEXTBOX")
frmMessage.AddObject("txt2", "TEXTBOX")
```

You can also use the AddObject method in the method code of a class. For example, the following class definition uses AddObject in the code associated with the Init event to add a control to a grid column.

```
DEFINE CLASS mygrid AS GRID
ColumnCount = 3
PROCEDURE Init
   THIS.Column2.AddObject("cboClient", "COMBOBOX")
   THIS.Column2.CurrentControl = "cboClient"
ENDPROC
ENDDEFINE
```

Adding and Creating Classes in Method Code

You can programmatically add objects to a container with the AddObject method. You can also create objects with the CREATEOBJECT( ) function in the Load, Init, or any other method of the class.

When you add an object with the AddObject method, the object becomes a member of the container. The Parent property of the added object refers to the container. When an object based on the container or control class is released from memory, the added object is also released.

When you create an object with the CREATEOBJECT( ) function, the object is scoped to a property of the class or a variable in the method that calls this function. The parent property of the object is undefined.

Assigning Method and Event Code

In addition to writing code for the methods and events of an object, you can extend the set of methods in subclasses of Visual FoxPro base classes. Here are the rules for writing event code and methods:

- The event set for the Visual FoxPro base classes is fixed and cannot be extended.

- Every class recognizes a set of fixed default events, the minimum set of which includes Init, Destroy, and Error events.

- When you create a method in a class definition with the same name as an event that the class can recognize, the code in the method is executed when the event occurs.

- You can add methods to your classes by creating a procedure or function within the class definition.

- You can create Access and Assign methods for your classes by creating a procedure or function with the same name as a class property and _ACCESS or _ASSIGN appended to the procedure or function name.

Calling Event Code up the Class Hierarchy

When you create a class, the class automatically inherits all the properties, methods, and events of the parent class. If code is written for an event in the parent class, that code is executed when the event occurs with respect to an object based on the subclass. You can, however, overwrite the parent class code by writing code for the event in the subclass.

To explicitly call the event code in a parent class when the subclass has code written for the same event, use the DODEFAULT( ) function.

For example, you could have a class named cmdBottom based on the command button base class that has the following code in the Click event:

```
GO BOTTOM
THISFORM.Refresh
```

When you add an object based on this class to a form, named, for example, cmdBottom1, you might decide that you also want to display a message for the user so that he or she knows that the record pointer is at the bottom of the table. You could add the following code to the Click event of the object to display the message:

```
WAIT WINDOW "At the Bottom of the Table" TIMEOUT 1
```

When you run the form, however, the message is displayed, but the record pointer doesn't move because the code in the Click event of the parent class is never executed. To make sure the code in the Click event of the parent class is also executed, include the following lines of code in the Click event procedure of the object:

```
DODEFAULT( )
WAIT WINDOW "At the Bottom of the Table" TIMEOUT 1
```

Note   You can use the ACLASS( ) function to determine all the classes in an object's class hierarchy.

Preventing Base Class Code from Executing

Sometimes you'll want to prevent the base class default behavior from taking place in an event or method. You can do this by including the NODEFAULT keyword in the method code you write. For example, the following program uses the NODEFAULT keyword in the KeyPress event of a text box to prevent the typed characters from being displayed in the text box:

```
frmKeyExample = CREATEOBJECT("test")
frmKeyExample.Show
READ EVENTS
DEFINE CLASS test AS FORM
    ADD OBJECT text1 AS TEXTBOX
    PROCEDURE text1.KeyPress
        PARAMETERS nKeyCode, nShiftAltCtrl
```

```
            NODEFAULT
            IF BETWEEN(nKeyCode, 65, 122) && between 'A' and 'z'
               This.Value = ALLTRIM(This.Value) + "*"
               ACTIVATE SCREEN        && send output to main Visual FoxPro window
               ?? CHR(nKeyCode)
            ENDIF
         ENDPROC
         PROCEDURE Destroy
            CLEAR EVENTS
         ENDPROC
      ENDDEFINE
```

Creating a Set of Table Navigation Buttons

A common feature of many applications is a series of navigation buttons that allow users to move through a table. These typically include buttons to move the record pointer to the next or prior record in the table, as well as to the top or bottom record in the table.

Table navigation buttons

Designing the Navigation Buttons

Each of the buttons will have some characteristics and functionality in common, so it is a good idea to create a navigation button class. Then the individual buttons can easily derive this common appearance and functionality. This parent class is the Navbutton class defined later in this section.

Once the parent class is defined, the following subclasses define the functionality and appearance specific to each of the four navigation buttons: navTop, navPrior, navNext, navBottom.

Finally, a container class, vcr, is created and each of the navigation buttons is added to the container class. The container can be added to a form or a toolbar to provide table navigation functionality.

NAVBUTTON Class Definition

To create Navbutton, save the following six class definitions (Navbutton, navTop, navBottom, navPrior, navNext, and vcr) to a program file such as Navclass.prg.

Definition of the Generic Navigation Commandbutton Class

Code	Comments
DEFINE CLASS Navbutton AS COMMANDBUTTON	Define the parent class of the navigation buttons.
Height = 25	Give the class some dimensions.
Width = 25	
TableAlias = ""	Include a custom property, TableAlias, to hold the name of the alias to navigate through.

(continued)

Code	Comments
| ```
PROCEDURE Click
   IF NOT EMPTY(This.TableAlias)
      SELECT (This.TableAlias)
   ENDIF
ENDPROC
``` | If `TableAlias` has been set, this parent class procedure selects the alias before the actual navigation code in the subclasses is executed. Otherwise, assume that the user wants to navigate through the table in the currently selected work area. |
| ```
PROCEDURE RefreshForm
   _SCREEN.ActiveForm.Refresh
ENDPROC
``` | Using _SCREEN.ActiveForm.Refresh instead of THISFORM.Refresh allows you to add the class to a form or a toolbar and have it function equally well. |
| ```
ENDDEFINE
``` | End the class definition. |

The specific navigation buttons are all based on the `Navbutton` class. The following code defines the Top button for the set of navigation buttons. The remaining three navigation buttons are defined in the following table. The four class definitions are similar, so only the first one has extensive comments.

Definition of the Top Navigation Button Class

Code	Comments
| ```
DEFINE CLASS navTop AS Navbutton
   Caption = "|<"
``` | Define the Top navigation button class and set the Caption property. |
| ```
PROCEDURE Click
``` | Create method code to be executed when the Click event for the control occurs. |
| ```
   DODEFAULT( )
``` | Call the Click event code in the parent class, `Navbutton`, so that the appropriate alias can be selected if the TableAlias property has been set. |
| ```
   GO TOP
``` | Include the code to set the record pointer to the first record in the table: GO TOP. |
| ```
   THIS.RefreshForm
``` | Call the RefreshForm method in the parent class. It is not necessary to use the scope resolution operator (::) in this case because there is no method in the subclass with the same name as the method in the parent class. On the other hand, both the parent and the subclass have method code for the Click event. |
| ```
ENDPROC
``` | End the Click procedure. |
| ```
ENDDEFINE
``` | End the class definition. |

The other navigation buttons have similar class definitions.

Definition of the Other Navigation Button Classes

Code	Comments
```DEFINE CLASS navNext AS Navbutton``` ``` Caption = ">"```	Define the Next navigation button class and set the Caption property.

```PROCEDURE Click```
 ```   DODEFAULT( )```
 ```   SKIP 1```
 ```   IF EOF( )```
 ```   GO BOTTOM```
 ```   ENDIF```
 ```   THIS.RefreshForm```
 ```ENDPROC```
	Include the code to set the record pointer to the next record in the table.

```ENDDEFINE```	End the class definition.
```DEFINE CLASS navPrior AS Navbutton``` ``` Caption = "<"```	Define the Prior navigation button class and set the Caption property.

```PROCEDURE Click```
 ```   DODEFAULT( )```
 ```   SKIP -1```
 ```   IF BOF( )```
 ```   GO TOP```
 ```   ENDIF```
 ```   THIS.RefreshForm```
 ```ENDPROC```
	Include the code to set the record pointer to the previous record in the table.

```ENDDEFINE```	End the class definition.
```DEFINE CLASS navBottom AS Navbutton``` ``` Caption = ">|"```	Define the Bottom navigation button class and set the Caption property.

```PROCEDURE Click```
 ```   DODEFAULT( )```
 ```   GO BOTTOM```
 ```   THIS.RefreshForm```
 ```ENDPROC```
	Include the code to set the record pointer to the bottom record in the table.

```ENDDEFINE```	End the class definition.

The following class definition contains all four navigation buttons so that they can be added as a unit to a form. The class also includes a method to set the TableAlias property of the buttons.

Definition of a Table Navigation Control Class

Code	Comments
```DEFINE CLASS vcr AS CONTAINER```	Begin the class definition. The Height property is set to the same height as the command buttons it will contain.

```
DEFINE CLASS vcr AS CONTAINER
   Height = 25
   Width = 100
   Left = 3
   Top = 3
   ADD OBJECT cmdTop AS navTop ;
      WITH Left = 0
   ADD OBJECT cmdPrior AS navPrior ;
      WITH Left = 25
   ADD OBJECT cmdNext AS navNext ;
      WITH Left = 50
   ADD OBJECT cmdBot AS navBottom ;
      WITH Left = 75
PROCEDURE SetTable(cTableAlias)
   IF TYPE("cTableAlias") = 'C'
      THIS.cmdTop.TableAlias = ;
         cTableAlias
         THIS.cmdPrior.TableAlias = ;
         cTableAlias
      THIS.cmdNext.TableAlias = ;
         cTableAlias
      THIS.cmdBot.TableAlias = ;
         cTableAlias
   ENDIF
ENDPROC

ENDDEFINE
```

Begin the class definition. The Height property is set to the same height as the command buttons it will contain.

Add the navigation buttons.

This method is used to set the TableAlias property of the buttons. TableAlias is defined in the parent class `Navbutton`.

You could also use the SetAll method to set this property:
```
IF TYPE ("cTableAlias") = 'C'
    This.SetAll("TableAlias", "cTableAlias")
ENDIF
```
However, this would cause an error if an object were ever added to the class that did not have a TableAlias property.

End class definition.

Once you have defined the class, you can subclass it or add it to a form.

Creating a Subclass Based on the New Class

You can also create subclasses based on vcr that have additional buttons such as Search, Edit, Save, and Quit. For example, vcr2 includes a Quit button:

Table navigation buttons with a button to close the form

Definition of a Table Navigation Control Subclass

Code	Comments
| ```
DEFINE CLASS vcr2 AS vcr
ADD OBJECT cmdQuit AS
COMMANDBUTTON WITH ;
   Caption = "Quit",.;
   Height = 25, ;
   Width = 50
Width = THIS.Width + THIS.cmdQuit.Width
cmdQuit.Left = THIS.Width - ;
   THIS.cmdQuit.Width
``` | Define a class based on vcr and add a command button to it. |
| ```
PROCEDURE cmdQuit.CLICK
   RELEASE THISFORM
ENDPROC
``` | When the user clicks cmdQuit, this code releases the form. |
| ```
ENDDEFINE
``` | End class definition. |

Vcr2 has everything that vcr does, plus the new command button, and you don't have to rewrite any of the existing code.

Changes to VCR Reflected in the Subclass

Because of inheritance, changes to the parent class are reflected in all subclasses based on the parent. For example, you could let the user know that the bottom of the table has been reached by changing the IF EOF( ) statement in navNext.Click to the following:

```
IF EOF( )
   GO BOTTOM
   SET MESSAGE TO "Bottom of the table"
ELSE
   SET MESSAGE TO
ENDIF
```

You could let the user know that the top of the table has been reached by changing the IF BOF( ) statement in navPrior.Click to the following:

```
IF BOF()
   GO TOP
   SET MESSAGE TO "Top of the table"
ELSE
   SET MESSAGE TO
ENDIF
```

If these changes are made to the navNext and navPrior classes, they will also apply automatically to the appropriate buttons in vcr and vcr2.
```

Adding VCR to a Form Class

Once vcr is defined as a control, the control can be added in the definition of a container. For example, the following code added to Navclass.prg defines a form with added navigation buttons:

```
DEFINE CLASS NavForm AS Form
    ADD OBJECT oVCR AS vcr
ENDDEFINE
```

Running the Form Containing VCR

Once the form subclass is defined, you can display it easily with the appropriate commands.

To display the form

1. Load the class definition:

   ```
   SET PROCEDURE TO navclass ADDITIVE
   ```

2. Create an object based on the navform class:

   ```
   frmTest = CREATEOBJECT("navform")
   ```

3. Invoke the Show method of the form:

   ```
   frmTest.Show
   ```

If you don't call the SetTable method of oVCR (the VCR object in NavForm) when the user clicks the navigation buttons, the record pointer moves in the table in the currently selected work area. You can call the SetTable method to specify what table to move through.

```
frmTest.oVCR.SetTable("customer")
```

> **Note**   When the user closes the form, frmTest is set to a null value (.NULL.). To release the object variable from memory, use the RELEASE command. Object variables created in program files are released from memory when the program is completed.

Defining a Grid Control

A grid contains columns, which in turn can contain headers and any other control. The default control contained in a column is a text box, so that the default functionality of the grid approximates a Browse window. However, the underlying architecture of the grid opens it up to endless extensibility.

The following example creates a form that contains a Grid object with two columns. The second column contains a check box to display the values in a logical field in a table.

Grid control with a check box in one column

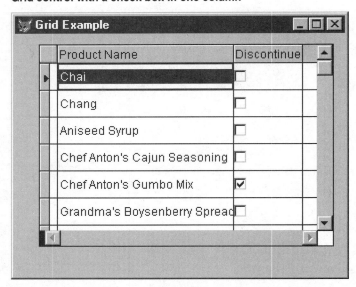

Definition of a Grid Class with a Check Box in a Grid Column

Code	Comments

```DEFINE CLASS grdProducts AS Grid```
``` ·Left = 24```
``` Top = 10```
``` Width = 295```
``` Height = 210```
``` Visible = .T.```
``` RowHeight = 28```
``` ColumnCount = 2```
	Start the class definition and set properties that determine the grid appearance.
	
	When you set the ColumnCount property to 2, you add two columns to the grid. Each column contains a header with the name Header1. In addition, each column has an independent group of properties that determines its appearance and behavior.

```Column1.ControlSource ="prod_name"``` ```Column2.ControlSource ="discontinu"```	When you set the ControlSource of a column, the column displays that field's values for all the records in the table. ```Discontinu``` is a logical field.
```Column2.Sparse = .F.```	Column2 will contain the check box. Set the column's Sparse property to .F. so that the check box will be visible in all rows, not just in the selected cell.

```Procedure Init```
``` THIS.Column1.Width = 175```
``` THIS.Column2.Width = 68```
``` THIS.Column1.Header1.Caption = ;```
```   "Product Name"```
``` THIS.Column2.Header1.Caption = ;```
```   "Discontinued"```
	Set column widths and header captions.

Definition of a Grid Class with a Check Box in a Grid Column   *(continued)*

Code	Comments

```THIS.Column2.AddObject("chk1", ;```
 ```   "checkbox")```
 ```THIS.Column2.CurrentControl = ;```
 ```   "chk1"```
 ```THIS.Column2.chk1.Visible = .T.```
 ```THIS.Column2.chk1.Caption = ""```
 ```ENDPROC```
	The AddObject method allows you to add an object to a container — in this case, a check box named `chk1`. Set the CurrentControl of the column to the check box so that the check box will be displayed. Make sure that the check box is visible. Set the caption to an empty string so that the default caption "chk1" won't be displayed.

```ENDDEFINE```	End of the class definition.

The following class definition is the form that contains the grid. Both class definitions can be included in the same program file.

Definition of a Form Class that Contains the Grid Class

Code	Comments

```DEFINE CLASS GridForm AS FORM```
 ```   Width = 330```
 ```   Height = 250```
 ```   Caption = "Grid Example"```
 ```   ADD OBJECT grid1 AS grdProducts```
	Create a form class and add an object, based on the grid class, to it.

```PROCEDURE Destroy```
 ```   CLEAR EVENTS```
 ```ENDPROC```
 	
 ```ENDDEFINE```
	The program that creates an object based on this class will use READ EVENTS. Including CLEAR EVENTS in the Destroy event of the form allows the program to finish running when the user closes the form. End of the class definition.

The following program opens the table with the fields to be displayed in the grid columns, creates an object based on the GridForm class, and issues the READ EVENTS command:

```
CLOSE DATABASE
OPEN DATABASE (HOME(2) + "data\testdata.dbc")
USE products
frmTest= CREATEOBJECT("GridForm")
frmTest.Show
READ EVENTS
```

This program can be included in the same file with the class definitions if it comes at the beginning of the file. You could also use the SET PROCEDURE TO command to specify the program with the class definitions and include this code in a separate program.

Creating Object References

Instead of making a copy of an object, you can create a reference to the object. A reference takes less memory than an additional object, can easily be passed between procedures, and can aid in writing generic code.

Returning a Reference to an Object

Sometimes, you might want to manipulate an object by means of one or more references to the object. For example, the following program defines a class, creates an object based on the class, and returns a reference to the object:

```
*--NEWINV.PRG
*--Returns a reference to a new invoice form.
frmInv = CREATEOBJECT("InvoiceForm")
RETURN frmInv

DEFINE CLASS InvoiceForm AS FORM
   ADD OBJECT txtCompany AS TEXTBOX
   * code to set properties, add other objects, and so on
ENDDEFINE
```

The following program establishes a reference to the object created in Newinv.prg. The reference variable can be manipulated in exactly the same way as the object variable can:

```
frmInvoice = NewInv() && store the object reference to a variable
frmInvoice.SHOW
```

You can also create a reference to an object on a form, as in the following example:

```
txtCustName = frmInvoice.txtCompany
txtCustName.Value = "Fox User"
```

Tip   Once you've created an object, you can use the DISPLAY OBJECTS command to display the object's class hierarchy, property settings, contained objects, and available methods and events. You can fill an array with the properties (not the property settings), events, methods, and contained objects of an object with the AMEMBERS( ) function. For more information, see DISPLAY OBJECTS and AMEMBERS( ) in Help.

Releasing Objects and References from Memory

If a reference to an object exists, releasing the object does not clear the object from memory. For example, the following command releases frmInvoice:, the original object:

```
RELEASE frmInvoice
```

However, because a reference to an object belonging to frmInvoice still exists, the object is not released from memory until txtCustName is released with the following command:

```
RELEASE txtCustName
```

Checking to See if an Object Exists

You can use the TYPE( ), ISNULL( ), and VARTYPE( ) functions to determine if an object exists. For example, the following lines of code check to see whether an object named oConnection exists:

```
IF TYPE("oConnection") = "O" AND NOT ISNULL(oConnection)
   * Object exists
ELSE
   * Object does not exist
ENDIF
```

Note ISNULL( ) is necessary because .NULL. is stored to the form object variable when a user closes a form, but the type of the variable remains "O".

Creating Arrays of Members

You can define members of classes as arrays. In the following example, choices is an array of controls:

```
DEFINE CLASS MoverListBox AS CONTAINER
DIMENSION choices[3]
ADD OBJECT lstFromListBox AS LISTBOX
ADD OBJECT lstToListBox AS LISTBOX
ADD OBJECT choices[1] AS COMMANDBUTTON
ADD OBJECT choices[2] AS COMMANDBUTTON
ADD OBJECT choices[3] AS CHECKBOX
PROCEDURE choices.CLICK
   PARAMETER nIndex
   DO CASE
      CASE nIndex = 1
         * code
      CASE nIndex = 2
         * code
      CASE nIndex = 3
         * code
   ENDCASE
ENDPROC
ENDDEFINE
```

When the user clicks a control in an array of controls, Visual FoxPro passes the index number of the control to the Click event procedure. In this procedure, you can use a CASE statement to execute different code depending on which button was clicked.

Creating Arrays of Objects

You can also create arrays of objects. For example, `MyArray` holds five command buttons:

```
DIMENSION MyArray[5]
FOR x = 1 TO 5
   MyArray[x] = CREATEOBJECT("COMMANDBUTTON")
ENDFOR
```

There are some considerations to keep in mind with arrays of objects:

- You can't assign an object to an entire array with one command. You need to assign the object to each member of the array individually.

- You can't assign a value to a property of an entire array. The following command would result in an error:

```
MyArray.Enabled = .F.
```

- When you redimension an object array so that it is larger than the original array, the new elements are initialized to false (.F.), as is the case with all arrays in Visual FoxPro. When you redimension an object array so that it is smaller than the original array, the objects with a subscript greater than the largest new subscript are released.

Using Objects to Store Data

In object-oriented languages, a class offers a useful and convenient vehicle for storing data and procedures related to an entity. For example, you could define a customer class to hold information about a customer as well as a method to calculate the customer's age:

```
DEFINE CLASS customer AS CUSTOM
   LastName = ""
   FirstName = ""
   Birthday = { - - }
   PROCEDURE Age
      IF !EMPTY(THIS.Birthday)
         RETURN YEAR(DATE()) - YEAR(THIS.Birthday)
      ELSE
         RETURN 0
      ENDIF
   ENDPROC
ENDDEFINE
```

However, data stored in objects based on the customer class are stored only in memory. If this data were in a table, the table would be stored on disk. If you had more than one customer to keep track of, the table would give you access to all of the Visual FoxPro database management commands and functions. As a result, you could quickly locate information, sort it, group it, perform calculations on it, create reports and queries based on it, and so on.

Storing and manipulating data in databases and tables is what Visual FoxPro does best. There are times, however, when you'll want to store data in objects. Usually, the data will be significant only while your application is running and it will pertain to a single entity.

For example, in an application that includes a security system, you would typically have a table of users who have access to the application. The table would include user identification, password, and access level. Once a user has logged on, you won't need all the information in the table. All you need is information about the current user, and this information can be easily stored and manipulated in an object. The following class definition, for example, initiates a logon when an object based on the class is created:

```
DEFINE CLASS NewUser AS CUSTOM
    PROTECTED LogonTime, AccessLevel
    UserId = ""
    PassWord = ""
    LogonTime = { - - : : }
    AccessLevel = 0
    PROCEDURE Init
        DO FORM LOGON WITH ; && assuming you have created this form
            This.UserId, ;
            This.PassWord, ;
            This.AccessLevel
        This.LogonTime = DATETIME( )
    ENDPROC
* Create methods to return protected property values.
    PROCEDURE GetLogonTime
        RETURN This.LogonTime
    ENDPROC
    PROCEDURE GetAccessLevel
        RETURN This.AccessLevel
    ENDPROC

ENDDEFINE
```

In the main program of your application, you could create an object based on the NewUserclass:

```
oUser = CREATEOBJECT('NewUser')
oUser.Logon
```

Throughout your application, when you need information about the current user, you can get it from the oUser object. For example:

```
IF oUser.GetAccessLevel( ) >= 4
    DO ADMIN.MPR
ENDIF
```

Integrating Objects and Data

In most applications, you can best utilize the power of Visual FoxPro by integrating objects and data. Most Visual FoxPro classes have properties and methods that allow you to integrate the power of a relational database manager and a full object-oriented system.

Properties for Integrating Visual FoxPro Classes and Database Data

Class	Data properties
Grid	RecordSource, ChildOrder, LinkMaster
All other controls	ControlSource
List box and combo box	ControlSource, RowSource
Form and form set	DataSession

Because these data properties can be changed at design or run time, you can create generic controls with encapsulated functionality that operates on diverse data.

For more information about integrating data and objects, see Chapter 9, "Creating Forms," and Chapter 10, "Using Controls."

CHAPTER 4

Understanding the Event Model

Visual FoxPro provides true modeless operation so that you can easily coordinate multiple forms automatically and run multiple instances of a form simultaneously. Visual FoxPro also manages event processing for you so you can give your users a much richer interactive environment.

This chapter describes:

- Events in Visual FoxPro
- Tracking Event Sequences
- Assigning Code to Events

Events in Visual FoxPro

Event code is triggered automatically by the system in response to some user action. For example, code written for the Click event is automatically processed by the system when the user clicks on a control. Event code can also be triggered by system events, as in the case of the Timer event in a timer control.

The Core Events

The following table contains a list of the core set of Visual FoxPro events, which apply to most controls.

Core Event Set

Event	When the event is triggered
Init	An object is created.
Destroy	An object is released from memory.
Click	The user clicks the object using the primary mouse button.
DblClick	The user double-clicks the object using the primary mouse button.
RightClick	The user clicks the object using the secondary mouse button.
GotFocus	The object receives the focus, either by user action such as tabbing or clicking, or by changing the focus in code using the SetFocus method.

(continued)

Core Event Set   *(continued)*

Event	When the event is triggered
LostFocus	The object loses the focus, either by user action such as tabbing to or clicking another object, or by changing the focus in code using the SetFocus method.
KeyPress	The user presses and releases a key.
MouseDown	The user presses the mouse button while the mouse pointer is over the object.
MouseMove	The user moves the mouse over the object.
MouseUp	The user releases the mouse button while the mouse pointer is over the object.

Containers and Object Events

There are two basic rules to keep in mind when you are writing event code for controls:

- Containers do not process events associated with the controls they contain.

- If no event code is associated with a control, Visual FoxPro checks to see if there is code associated with the event higher up the class hierarchy for the control.

When a user interacts with an object in any way — by tabbing to it, clicking it, moving the mouse pointer over it, and so on — object events take place. Each object receives its events independently. For example, even though a command button is on a form, the form's Click event is not triggered when a user clicks the command button; only the command button's Click event is triggered.

Container event code is separate from control event code

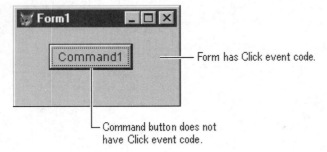

Form has Click event code.

Command button does not have Click event code.

If there is no Click event code associated with the command button, nothing happens when the user clicks the button, even though there is Click event code associated with the form.

This rule is also true of grid controls. The grid contains columns which in turn contain headers and controls. When events occur, only the innermost object involved in the event recognizes the event. The higher-level containers do not recognize the event. The following illustration shows which objects process the MouseMove events that are generated when a user moves the mouse pointer across the grid.

MouseMove events for a grid

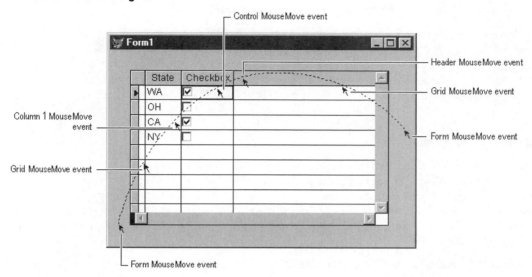

There is an exception to this rule, however. If you have written event code for an option button group or a command button group but there is no code for the event in a particular button in the group, the group event code *is* executed when the button event occurs.

For example, you can have an option button group with associated Click event code. Only one of the two option buttons in the group has associated Click event code:

Event code for button groups can be used as the default

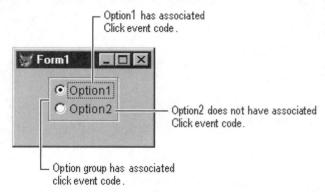

If a user clicks Option1, the Click event code associated with Option1 is executed. The Click event code associated with the option button group is not executed.

Because there is no Click event code associated with Option2, if the user clicks Option2, the option group Click event code is executed.

Note   When a sequence of events, such as MouseDown then MouseUp, is initiated for a control, the whole sequence of events belongs to the control.

For example, if you click the left mouse button on a command button and drag the mouse pointer away from the command button, the command button's MouseMove events continue to occur, even though the mouse pointer is moving over the form. If you release the left mouse button over the form instead of over the command button, the MouseUp event that occurs is associated with the command button rather than the form.

Classes and Control Events

If a control on a form is based on a user-defined class (which, in turn, could be based on another user-defined class), Visual FoxPro checks in the immediate control for event code when an event occurs. If there is code in that event procedure, Visual FoxPro executes it. If no code exists in the event procedure, Visual FoxPro checks the next level up in the class hierarchy. If at any point in the class hierarchy Visual FoxPro finds code for the event, that code is executed. Any code further up the hierarchy is not executed.

If no event code is associated with an object, Visual FoxPro checks the parent class.

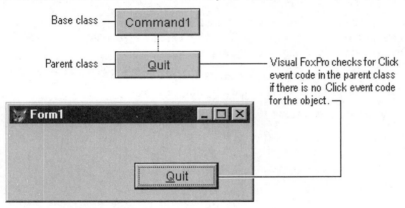

You can, however, include code in an event procedure and explicitly call the code in classes that the control is based on by using the DODEFAULT( ) function.

Tracking Event Sequences

The Visual FoxPro event model is extensive, allowing you a great deal of control over the components of your application in response to a wide variety of user actions. Some of the event sequences are fixed, as for example, when a form is created or destroyed. Some events occur independently, but most occur in conjunction with several other events based on user interaction.

Setting Event Tracking On

The best way to see the Visual FoxPro event sequences is to set event tracking on in the debugger. Event tracking allows you to see when each event associated with your own forms and controls occurs in relation to other events, so that you can determine the most efficient place to include your code.

To set event tracking on

1. From the **Tools** menu in the Debugger window, choose **Event Tracking**.

2. In the **Event Tracking** dialog box, select **Turn event tracking on**.

The events in the Events to track list are written to the Debugger Output window or a file as they occur.

The Event Tracking dialog box

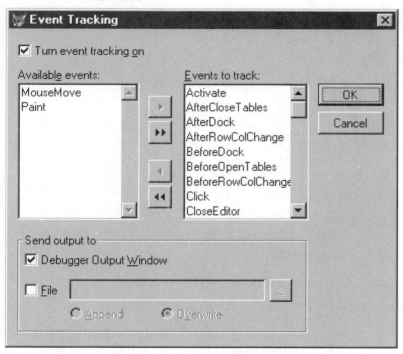

Note   this example, the MouseMove and Paint events have been removed from the Events to track list because these events occur so frequently that they make it more difficult to see the sequences of the other events.

Watching Events Occur

Sometimes a single event is triggered by a user action, such as the user moving the mouse pointer over a control. Often, however, a user action triggers multiple events.

This section describes the order in which events occur in response to user interaction, using the following form as an example.

A sample form to illustrate event sequences

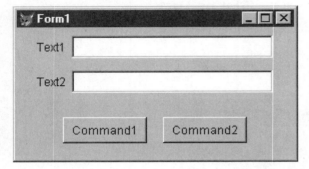

In this example scenario, the user performs the following actions on the form:

1. Runs the form.

2. Types text in Text1.

3. Selects the field, and copies it to the clipboard.

4. Moves to Text2.

5. Pastes the text into Text2.

6. Closes the form by clicking Command2.

These actions trigger one or more system events for each object. The following tables detail the events triggered in response to each user action.

Action 1

The user runs the form by typing the following command in the Command window:

```
DO FORM form1 NAME frmObject
```

Visual FoxPro loads the form, initializes each object, then initializes the form; the form is activated and then the first field receives input focus.

Object	Event
DataEnvironment	BeforeOpenTables
Form1	Load
DataEnvironment	Init

(continued)

Object	Event
Text1	Init
Text2	Init
Command1	Init
Command2	Init
Form1	Init
Form1	Activate
Form1	GotFocus
Text1	When
Text1	GotFocus

Action 2

The user types **Test** in Text1. Each keystroke generates two events. The KeyPress event receives 2 parameters: the pressed key and the state of the SHIFT, ALT, and CTRL keys.

Object	Event
Text1	KeyPress(84, 1) "T"
Text1	InteractiveChange
Text1	KeyPress(101, 0) "e"
Text1	InteractiveChange
Text1	KeyPress(115,0) "s"
Text1	InteractiveChange
Text1	KeyPress(116,0) "t"
Text1	InteractiveChange

Action 3

The user double-clicks Text1 to select the text, then presses CTRL+C to copy the text to the Clipboard. Mouse events and a Click event accompany the DblClick event. The MouseMove and MouseDown events receive four parameters: a number indicating which button was pressed, the Shift state, and X and Y locations. The X and Y locations are relative to the form and reflect the scale mode (for example, pixels) of the form. Only one MouseMove event is listed for each control. In actuality, this event would probably fire half a dozen times or more.

Object	Event
Form1	MouseMove(0, 0, 100, 35)
Text1	MouseMove(0,0,44,22)
Text1	MouseDown(1, 0, 44, 22)
Text1	MouseUp(1, 0, 44, 22)
Text1	Click
Text1	MouseDown(1, 0, 44, 22)
Text1	MouseUp(1, 0, 44, 22)
Text1	DblClick

Action 4

The user presses TAB to move to Text2.

Object	Event
Text1	KeyPress(9, 0)
Text1	Valid
Text1	LostFocus
Text2	When
Text2	GotFocus

Action 5

The user pastes the copied text into Text2 by pressing CTRL+V.

Object	Event
Text2	InteractiveChange

Action 6

The user clicks Command2, which closes the form.

Object	Event
Form1	MouseMove
Command2	MouseMove
Text2	Valid
Command2	When
Text2	LostFocus

(continued)

Object	Event
Command2	GotFocus
Command2	MouseDown(1, 0, 143, 128)
Command2	MouseUp(1, 0, 143, 128)
Command2	Click
Command2	Valid
Command2	When

As the form closes and the object is released, these additional events take place, in opposite order to the events in Action 1.

Object	Event
Form1	Destroy
Command2	Destroy
Command1	Destroy
Text2	Destroy
Text1	Destroy
Form1	Unload
DataEnvironment	AfterCloseTables
DataEnvironment	Destroy

The Visual FoxPro Event Sequence

The following table shows the general firing sequence of Visual FoxPro events. The data environment's AutoOpenTables property is assumed to be set to true (.T.). Other events can occur based on user interaction and system response.

Object	Events
Data environment	BeforeOpenTables
Form set	Load
Form	Load
Data environment cursor(s)	Init
Data environment	Init

(continued)

(continued)

Object	Events
Objects [1]	Init
Form	Init
Form set	Init
Form set	Activate
Form	Activate
Object1 [2]	When
Form	GotFocus
Object1	GotFocus
Object1	Message
Object1	Valid [3]
Object1	LostFocus
Object2 [3]	When
Object2	GotFocus
Object2	Message
Object2	Valid [4]
Object2	LostFocus
Form	QueryUnload
Form	Destroy
Object [5]	Destroy
Form	Unload
Form set	Unload
Data environment	AfterCloseTables
Data environment	Destroy
Data environment cursor(s)	Destroy

1. For each object, from innermost object to outermostcontainer

2. First object in the tab order

3. Next object to get focus

4. As the object loses focus

5. For each object, from outermost container to innermost object

Assigning Code to Events

Unless you associate code with an event, nothing happens when that event occurs. You'll almost never write code for all of the events associated with any Visual FoxPro object, but you'll want to incorporate functionality in response to certain key events in your applications. To add code to be executed when an event occurs, use the Properties window in the Form Designer.

The sequence of events affects where you should put code. Keep in mind the following tips:

- The Init events of all the controls on a form execute before the Init event of the form, so you can include code in the Init event of the form to manipulate any of the controls on the form before the form is displayed.

- If you want some code to be processed whenever the value of a list box, combo box, or check box changes, associate it with the InteractiveChange event. The Click event might not occur or might be called even if the value hasn't changed.

- When you are dragging a control, the other mouse events are suspended. For example, the MouseUp and MouseMove events do not occur during a drag-and-drop operation.

- The Valid and When events return a value. True (.T.) is the default. If you return false (.F.) or 0 from the When event, the control cannot get the focus. If you return false (.F.) or 0 from the Valid event, the focus cannot leave the control.

For more information about using the Form Designer, see Chapter 9, "Creating Forms." For information on coding classes and adding event code, see Chapter 3, "Object-Oriented Programming."

Working with Data

To create effective applications, you need to analyze your data requirements, then design your databases, tables, and indexes to meet these needs.

Chapter 5   Designing Databases

Take advantage of relational database technology in Visual FoxPro with well-planned databases.

Chapter 6   Creating Databases

Use databases in Visual FoxPro to establish relationships between tables, enforce referential integrity, and manage local and remote data.

Chapter 7   Working with Tables

Make sure your tables have the structure that your application requires. Data type and index choices are essential to the success of your application.

Chapter 8   Creating Views

Use views to access and update records from multiple tables. With views, you can update local and remote data.

Designing Databases

In Visual FoxPro, you use databases to organize and relate tables and views. Databases provide the architecture for storing your data and have additional benefits as well. When you use a database, you can create table-level extensions such as field- and record-level rules, default field values, and triggers. You can also create stored procedures and persistent table relationships. You can use your database to access connections to remote data sources and to create views of local and remote tables.

This chapter provides guidelines for planning the tables that go into a Visual FoxPro database. It walks you through the database design of the Tasmanian Traders sample database and provides you with additional sample database designs. The Tasmanian Traders sample database, Tastrade.dbc, is located in the Visual Studio …\Samples\Vfp98\Tastrade\Data directory.

For information on creating Visual FoxPro databases after you design them, see Chapter 6, "Creating Databases." For information on creating Visual FoxPro tables, see Chapter 7, "Working with Tables."

This chapter discusses:

- Using a Database Design Process
- Analyzing Data Requirements
- Grouping Requirements into Tables
- Determining the Fields You Need
- Identifying Relationships
- Refining the Design
- Sample Database Diagrams

Using a Database Design Process

If you use an established database design process, you can quickly and effectively create a well-designed database that provides you with convenient access to the information you want. With a solid design, you'll spend less time constructing the database and you'll end up with faster, more accurate results.

Note   The terms "database" and "table" are not synonymous in Visual FoxPro. The term database (.dbc file) refers to a relational database that is a container of information about one or more tables (.dbf files) or views.

The key to effective database design lies in understanding exactly what information you want to store and the way a relational database management system, such as Visual FoxPro, stores data. To efficiently and accurately provide you with information, Visual FoxPro needs to have the facts about different subjects organized into separate tables. For example, you might have one table that stores facts only about employees and another that stores facts only about sales.

When you organize your data appropriately, you design flexibility into your database and gain the capability to combine and present facts in many different ways. For example, you can print reports that combine facts about employees and facts about sales.

Separating facts into tables adds flexibility to your database.

Store all facts about employees...

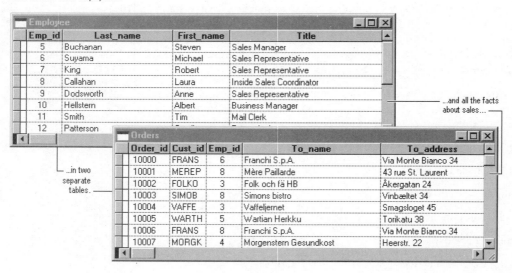

...and all the facts about sales...

...in two separate tables.

When you design a database, you first break down the information you want to keep as separate subjects, and then you tell Visual FoxPro how the subjects are related to each other so that Visual FoxPro can bring the right information together when you need it. By maintaining information in separate tables, you make it easier to organize and maintain your data, as well as to build a high-performance application.

Here are the steps in the database design process. Each step is discussed in greater detail in the remaining sections of this chapter.

1. **Determine the purpose of your database**   Knowing the purpose will help you decide which facts you want Visual FoxPro to store.

2. **Determine the tables you need**   When you have a clear purpose for your database, you can divide your information into separate subjects, such as "Employees" or "Orders." Each subject will be a table in your database.

3. **Determine the fields you need**   Decide what information you want to keep in each table. Each category of information in a table is called a field and is displayed as a column when you browse the table. For example, one field in an Employee table could be Last_name; another could be Hire_date.

4. **Determine the relationships**   Look at each table and decide how the data in one table is related to the data in other tables. Add fields to tables or create new tables to clarify the relationships, as necessary.

5. **Refine your design**   Analyze your design for errors. Create the tables and add a few records of sample data. See if you can get the results you want from your tables. Make adjustments to the design as needed.

Don't worry if you make mistakes or leave things out of your initial design. Think of it as a rough draft that you can refine later. Experiment with sample data and prototypes of your forms and reports. With Visual FoxPro, it's easy to change the design of your database as you're creating it. However, it becomes much more difficult to make changes to tables after they're filled with data and after you've built forms and reports. For this reason, make sure that you have a solid design before you proceed too far into building your application.

Analyzing Data Requirements

Your first step in designing a Visual FoxPro database is to analyze your data requirements by determining the purpose of the database and how it is to be used. This tells you what information you want from the database. From that, you can determine what subjects you need to store facts about (the tables) and what facts you need to store about each subject (the fields in the tables).

Talk to the people who will use the database. Brainstorm about the questions you'd like the database to answer. Sketch out the reports you'd like it to produce. Gather the forms you currently use to record your data. You'll use all this information in the remaining steps of the design process.

Example: Tracking Sales and Inventory

Suppose that Tasmanian Traders, an import/export company that sells specialty foods from around the world, wants a database that can track information about the company's sales and inventory.

Start by writing down a list of questions the database should be able to answer. How many sales of our featured product did we make last month? Where do our best customers live? Who's the supplier for our best-selling product?

Next, gather all the forms and reports that contain information the database should be able to produce. The company currently uses a printed report to keep track of products being ordered and an order form to take new orders. The following illustration shows these two documents.

Forms and reports show some data requirements for your database.

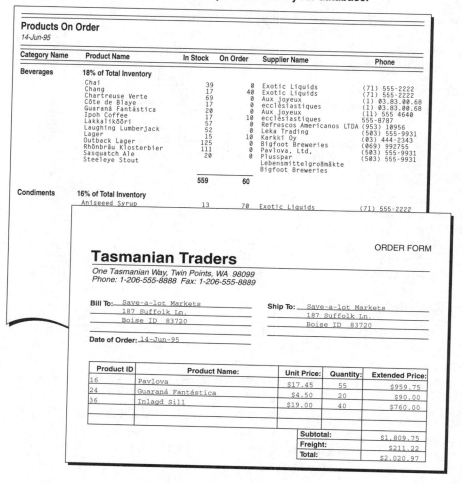

Tasmanian Traders also needs to print mailing labels for customers, employees, and suppliers.

After gathering this information, you're ready for the next step.

Grouping Requirements into Tables

Determining the tables in your database can be the trickiest step in the database design process. That's because the results you want from your database — the reports you want to print, the forms you want to use, and the questions you want answered — don't necessarily provide clues about the structure of the tables that produce them. They tell you what you want to know but not how to categorize the information into tables.

See the preceding order form as an example. It includes facts about the customer — the customer's address and phone number — along with facts about the order. This form provides you with a number of facts that you know you want to store in your database. Although the facts are all on the same form, you can easily prevent common data integrity problems by storing them in separate tables.

Storing information once reduces chance of error

For example, if you only use one table to store the information for an order form, suppose that one customer places three different orders. You could add the customer's address and phone number to your database three times, once for each order. But this multiplies the chance of data entry errors.

The Customer table stores address information once.

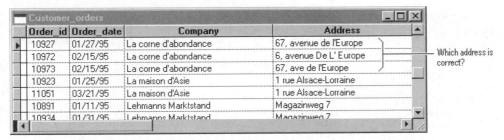

Which address is correct?

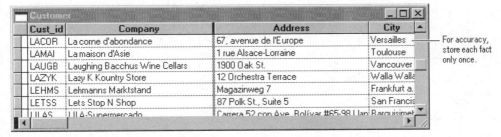

For accuracy, store each fact only once.

Also, if the customer moves, you'd have to either accept contradictory information or find and change each of that customer's sales records in the table. It's much better to create a Customer table that stores the customer's address in your database once. Then, if you need to change the data, you change it only once.

Preventing deletion of valuable information

Suppose a new customer places an order and then cancels. When you delete the order from the table containing information on both customers and their orders, you would delete the customer's name and address as well. But you want to keep this new customer in your database so you can send the customer your next catalog. Again, it's better to put the information about the customer in a separate Customer table. That way you can delete the order without deleting customer information.

Look at the information you want to get out of your database and divide it into fundamental subjects you want to track, such as customers, employees, products you sell, services you provide, and so on. Each of these subjects is a candidate for a separate table.

> **Tip** One strategy for dividing information into tables is to look at individual facts and determine what each fact is actually about. For example, on the Tasmanian Traders order form, the customer address isn't about the sale; it's about the customer. This suggests that you need a separate table for customers. In the Products On Order report, the supplier's phone number isn't about the product in stock; it's about the supplier. This suggests that you need a separate table for suppliers.

Example: Designing Tables in the Tasmanian Traders Database

The Tasmanian Traders Order Form and Products On Order report include information about these subjects:

- Employees

- Customers

- Suppliers

- Products

- Orders

From this list, you can come up with a rough draft of the tables in the database and some of the fields for each table.

Rough draft of tables and fields required for Tasmanian Traders database

Although the finished Tasmanian Traders database contains other tables, this list is a good start. Later in this chapter, you'll see how to add other tables to refine your design.

Determining the Fields You Need

To determine the fields in a table, decide what you need to know about the people, things, or events recorded in the table. You can think of fields as attributes of the table. Each record (or row) in the table contains the same set of fields or attributes. For example, an address field in a customer table contains customers' addresses. Each record in the table contains data about one customer, and the address field contains the address for that customer.

Identifying Fields

Here are a few tips for determining your fields:

Relate each field directly to the subject of the table

A field that describes the subject of a different table belongs in that other table. Later, when you define relationships between your tables, you'll see how you can combine the data from fields in multiple tables. For now, make sure that each field in a table directly describes the subject of the table. If you find yourself repeating the same information in several tables, it's a clue that you have unnecessary fields in some of the tables.

Don't include derived or calculated data

In most cases, you don't want to store the result of calculations in tables. Instead, you can have Visual FoxPro perform the calculations when you want to see the result. For example, the order form shown earlier in this chapter displays the extended price for each line of the order in the Tasmanian Traders database. However, there's no Extended Price subtotal field in any Tasmanian Traders table. Instead, the Order_Line_Items table includes a quantity field that stores the units on order for each individual product, as well as the unit price for each item ordered. Using that data, Visual FoxPro calculates the subtotal each time you print an order form. The subtotal itself doesn't need to be stored in a table.

Include all the information you need

It's easy to overlook important information. Return to the information you gathered in the first step of the design process. Look at your paper forms and reports to make sure all the information you have required in the past is included in your Visual FoxPro tables or can be derived from them. Think of the questions you will ask Visual FoxPro. Can Visual FoxPro find all the answers using the information in your tables? Have you identified fields that will store unique data, such as the customer ID? Which tables include information that you'll combine into one report or form? For more information on identifying key fields and relating tables, see the sections "Using Primary Key Fields" and "Identifying Relationships" later in this chapter.

Store information in its smallest logical parts

You might be tempted to have a single field for full names, or for product names, along with product descriptions. If you combine more than one kind of information in a field, it's difficult to retrieve individual facts later. Try to break down information into logical parts; for example, create separate fields for first and last name, or for product name, category, and description.

Example: Adding Fields to the Products Table

Tasmanian Traders sells imported specialty foods from around the world. The employees use a Products On Order report to keep track of products being ordered.

Report for tracking the inventory of products

Products On Order
14-Jun-95

Category Name	Product Name	In Stock	On Order	Supplier Name	Phone
Beverages	**18% of Total Inventory**				
	Chai	39	0	Exotic Liquids	(71) 555-2222
	Chang	17	40	Exotic Liquids	(71) 555-2222
	Chartreuse Verte	69	0	Aux joyeux ecclésiastiques	(1) 03.83.00.68
	Côte de Blaye	17	0	Aux joyeux ecclésiastiques	(1) 03.83.00.68
	Guaraná Fantástica	20	0	Refrescos Americanos LTDA	(11) 555 4640
	Ipoh Coffee	17	10	Leka Trading	555-8787
	Lakkalikööri	57	0	Karkki Oy	(953) 10956
	Laughing Lumberjack	52	0	Bigfoot Breweries	(503) 555-9931
	Lager	15	10	Pavlova, Ltd.	(03) 444-2343
	Outback Lager	125	0	Plusspar	(069) 992755
	Rhönbräu Klosterbier	111	0	Lebensmittelgroßmäkte	(503) 555-9931
	Sasquatch Ale	20	0	Bigfoot Breweries	(503) 555-9931
	Steeleye Stout			Bigfoot Breweries	
Condiments	**16% of Total Inventory**				
	Aniseed Syrup	13	70	Exotic Liquids	(71) 555-2222
	Chef Anton's Cajun Seasoning	53	0	New Orleans Cajun Delights	(100) 555-4822
	Chef Anton's Gumbo Mix	0	0	New Orleans Cajun Delights	(100) 555-4822
	Genen Shouyu	39	0	Mayumi's	(06) 431-7877

The report indicates that the Products table, which contains facts about products sold, needs to include fields for the product name, units in stock, and units on order, among others. But what about fields for the supplier name and phone number? To produce the report, Visual FoxPro needs to know which supplier goes with each product.

Draft of the Supplier table containing fields for supplier name and phone number

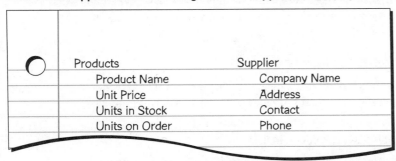

Products	Supplier
Product Name	Company Name
Unit Price	Address
Units in Stock	Contact
Units on Order	Phone

You can solve this without storing redundant data in your tables by creating a Supplier table with separate fields for the supplier's name and phone number. In the next step, you'll add a field to the Products table that identifies the supplier information you need.

Using Primary Key Fields

The power in a relational database management system such as Visual FoxPro comes from its ability to quickly find and bring together information stored in separate tables. In order for Visual FoxPro to work most efficiently, each table in your database should include a field or set of fields that uniquely identifies each individual record stored in the table. This is often a unique identification number, such as an employee ID number or a serial number. In database terminology, this information is called the primary key of the table. Visual FoxPro uses primary key fields to quickly associate data from multiple tables and bring the data together for you.

If you already have a unique identifier for a table, such as a set of product numbers you've developed to identify the items in your stock, you can use that identifier as the table's primary key. But make sure the values in this field will always be different for each record — Visual FoxPro doesn't allow duplicate values in a primary key field. For example, don't use someone's name as a primary key, because names aren't unique. You could easily have two people with the same name in the same table.

When choosing primary key fields, keep these points in mind:

- Visual FoxPro doesn't allow duplicate or null values in a primary key field. For this reason, you shouldn't choose a primary key that could contain such values.

- You can use the value in the primary key field to look up records, so it shouldn't be too long to remember or type. You might want it to have a certain number of letters or digits, or be within a certain range of values.

- The size of the primary key affects the speed of operations in your database. When you create primary key fields, use the smallest size that will accommodate the values you need to store in the field.

Example: Setting the Primary Key for the Products Table

The primary key of the Tasmanian Traders Products table contains product ID numbers. Because each product number identifies a different product, you don't want two products with the same number.

The Primary key for the Products table is the Product_id field.

Primary key

Product_id	Product_name	English_name	Unit_cost
1	Chai	Dharamsala Tea	12.6000
2	Chang	Tibetan Barley Beer	13.3000
3	Aniseed Syrup	Licorice Syrup	12.6000
4	Chef Anton's Cajun Seasoning	Chef Anton's Cajun Seasoning	15.4000
5	Chef Anton's Gumbo Mix	Chef Anton's Gumbo Mix	14.9450

No two product numbers are the same...   ...but other fields may contain duplicate values.

In some cases, you might want to use two or more fields that together provide the primary key of a table. For example, the Order_Line_Items table in the Tasmanian Traders database uses two fields as its primary key: Order_id and Product_id. In the next step, you'll see why.

Identifying Relationships

Now that you've divided your information into tables, you need a way to tell Visual FoxPro how to bring it back together again in meaningful ways. For example, the following form includes information from several tables.

The Order Entry form uses information from several tables.

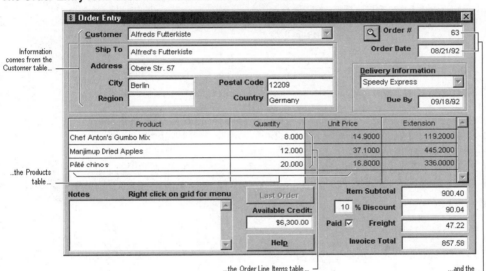

Visual FoxPro is a relational database management system. That means you store related data in separate tables. Then you define relationships between the tables and Visual FoxPro uses the relationships to find associated information stored in your database.

For example, suppose that you want to phone an employee with questions about a sale the employee made. Employee phone numbers are recorded in the Employee table; sales are recorded in the Orders table. When you tell Visual FoxPro which sale you're interested in, Visual FoxPro can look up the phone number based on the relationship between the two tables. It works because Employee_id, the primary key for the Employee table, is also a field in the Orders table. In database terminology, the Employee_id field in the Orders table is called a foreign key, because it refers to a primary key from a different, or foreign, table.

Employee_id field as primary key for Employee table and foreign key for Orders table

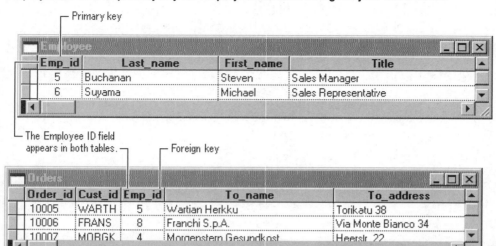

So, to set up a relationship between two tables — Table A and Table B — you add one table's primary key to the other table, so that it appears in both tables. But how do you decide which table's primary key to use? To set up the relationship correctly, you must first determine the nature of the relationship. There are three types of relationships between tables:

- One-to-many relationships
- Many-to-many relationships
- One-to-one relationships

The rest of this section presents an example of each type of relationship and explains how to design your tables so that Visual FoxPro can associate the data correctly. The purpose of each example is to explain how you determine the relationships between your tables and how you decide which fields belong in the tables to support those relationships — it doesn't describe how to use the Visual FoxPro interface to relate tables.

Example: Creating a One-to-Many Relationship

A one-to-many relationship is the most common type of relationship in a relational database. In a one-to-many relationship, a record in Table A can have more than one matching record in Table B, but a record in Table B has, at most, one matching record in Table A.

For example, the Category and Products tables in the Tasmanian Traders database have a one-to-many relationship.

The Category and Products tables represent a one-to-many relationship.

Category_id	Name:	Description	Picture_file	Picture
1	Beverages	Memo	Memo	Gen
2	Condiments	Memo	Memo	Gen
3	Confections	Memo	Memo	Gen
4	Dairy Products	Memo	Memo	Gen

One category can relate to many products.

Product_id	Supplier_id	Category_id	Product_name
43	20	1	Ipoh Coffee
67	16	1	Laughing Lumberjack Lager
70	7	1	Outback Lager
75	12	1	Rhönbräu Klosterbier
76	23	1	Lakkalikööri
3	7	2	Aniseed Syrup

To set up the relationship, you add the field or fields that make up the primary key on the "one" side of the relationship to the table on the "many" side of the relationship. You use a primary or candidate index key for the "one" side of the relationship, and a regular index key for the "many" side. In this case, you would add the Category_id field from the Category table to the Products table, because one category includes many products. Visual FoxPro uses the category ID number to locate the correct category for each product.

For information about creating index keys, see Chapter 7, "Working with Tables."

Example: Creating a Many-to-Many Relationship

In a many-to-many relationship, a record in Table A can have more than one matching record in Table B, and a record in Table B can have more than one matching record in Table A. This type of relationship requires changes in your database design before you can correctly specify the relationship to Visual FoxPro.

To detect many-to-many relationships between your tables, it's important that you look at both directions of the relationship. For example, consider the relationship between orders and products in the Tasmanian Traders business. One order can include more than one product. So for each record in the Orders table, there can be many records in the Products table. But that's not the whole story. Each product can appear on many orders. So for each record in the Products table, there can be many records in the Orders table.

The Orders and Products tables represent a many-to-many relationship.

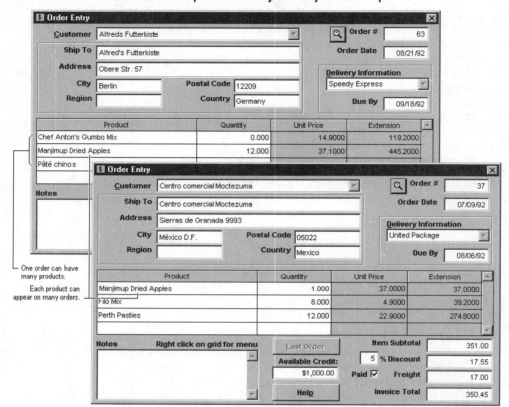

One order can have many products.

Each product can appear on many orders.

The subjects of the two tables — orders and products — have a many-to-many relationship. This presents a challenge in database design. To understand the problem, imagine what would happen if you tried to set up the relationship between the two tables by adding the Product_id field to the Orders table. To have more than one product per order, you need more than one record in the Orders table per order. You'd be repeating order information over and over for each record that relates to a single order — an inefficient design that could lead to inaccurate data. You run into the same problem if you put the Order_id field in the Products table — you'd have more than one record in the Products table for each product. How do you solve this problem?

The answer is to create a third table that breaks down the many-to-many relationship into two one-to-many relationships. This third table is called a junction table, because it acts as the junction between two tables. You put the primary key from each of the two tables into the junction table.

The Order_Line_Items table creates a one-to-many link between Orders and Products.

Primary key from the
Orders table

Primary key from the
Products table

Line_no	Order_id	Product_id	Unit_price	Quantity
1	10000	17	27.0000	4.000
1	10001	25	9.8000	42.000
2	10001	40	12.8000	36.000
3	10001	59	38.5000	24.000
4	10001	64	23.0000	12.000
1	10002	31	8.0000	15.000
2	10002	39	12.6000	19.000
3	10002	71	15.0000	15.000
1	10003	18	43.7000	12.000

Information that relates to both
the order and the product.

A junction table might hold only the two primary keys from the tables it links together or, as in the Order_Line_Items table, the junction table might hold additional information.

Each record in the Order_Line_Items table represents one line item on an order. The Order_Line_Items table's primary key consists of two fields — the foreign keys from the Orders and Products tables. The Order_id field alone doesn't work as the primary key for this table, because one order can have many line items. The order ID is repeated for each line item on an order, so the field doesn't contain unique values. The Product_id field alone doesn't work either, because one product can appear on many different orders. But together the two fields in the junction table always produce a unique value for each record. The junction table does not require its own primary key.

In the Tasmanian Traders database, the Orders table and the Products table aren't related to each other directly. Instead, they are related indirectly through the Order_Line_Items table. The many-to-many relationship between orders and products is represented in the database using two one-to-many relationships:

- The Orders and Order_Line_Items tables have a one-to-many relationship. Each order can have more than one line item, but each line item is connected to only one order.

- The Products and Order_Line_Items tables have a one-to-many relationship. Each product can have many line items associated with it, but each line item refers to only one product.

Example: Creating a One-to-One Relationship

In a one-to-one relationship, a record in Table A can have no more than one matching record in Table B, and a record in Table B can have no more than one matching record in Table A. This type of relationship is unusual and might call for some changes in your database design.

One-to-one relationships between tables are unusual because in many cases, the
information in the two tables can simply be combined into one table. For example,
suppose you created a table, called Ping-Pong Players, to track information about a
Tasmanian Traders Ping-Pong fundraising event. Because the ping-pong players are
all employees of Tasmanian Traders, this table has a one-to-one relationship with the
Employee table in the Tasmanian Traders database.

The Employee and Ping_Pong_Players represent a one-to-one relationship.

Emp_id	Player_nickname	Preferred_date	Skill_level	Pledge
6	Ace	07/07/96	1	2.0000
7	King John	07/09/96	2	2.0000
8	Calmeister	07/07/96	1	2.0000
9	Slammin' Nan	07/07/96	1	2.0000

— Each ping-pong player has one matching record in the Employee table.

Emp_id	Last_name	First_name	Title
6	Suyama	Michael	Sales Representative
7	King	Robert	Sales Representative
8	Callahan	Laura	Inside Sales Coordinator
9	Dodsworth	Anne	Sales Representative

— This set of values is a subset of the
Employee_id field in the Employee table.

You could add all the fields from the Ping-Pong Players table to the Employee table. But
the Ping-Pong Players table tracks a one-time event, and you won't need the information
after the event is over. Additionally, not all employees play Ping-Pong, so if these fields
were in the Employee table, they would be empty for many records. For these reasons, it
makes sense to create a separate table.

When you detect the need for a one-to-one relationship in your database, consider whether
you can put the information together in one table. For example, in the Employee table, one
employee can have one manager, who is also an employee. You can add a field for the
manager's id number. To pull the information together later, you can use a self join in your
query or view. You don't need a separate table to resolve the one-to-one relationship. If
you don't want to do that for some reason, here's how to set up the one-to-one relationship
between two tables:

- If the two tables have the same subject, you can probably set up the relationship by using the same primary key field in both tables.

- If the two tables have different subjects with different primary keys, choose one of the tables (either one) and put its primary key field in the other table as a foreign key.

Refining the Design

When you have the tables, fields, and relationships you need, it's time to study the design and detect any flaws that might remain.

You might encounter several pitfalls while you are designing your database. These common problems can cause your data to be harder to use and maintain:

- Do you have one table with a large number of fields that don't all relate to the same subject? For example, one table might contain fields pertaining to your customers as well as fields that contain sales information. Try to make sure each table contains data about only one subject.

- Do you have fields that are intentionally left blank in many records because they aren't applicable to those records? This usually means that the fields belong in another table.

- Do you have a large number of tables, many of which contain the same fields? For example, you have separate tables for January sales and February sales, or for local customers and remote customers, in which you store the same type of information. Try consolidating all the information pertaining to a single subject in one table. You might also need to add an extra field, for example, to identify the sales date.

Create your tables, specify relationships between the tables, and enter a few records of data in each table. See if you can use the database to get the answers you want. Create rough drafts of your forms and reports and see if they show the data you expect. Look for unnecessary duplications of data and eliminate them.

As you try out your initial database, you will probably discover room for improvement. Here are a few things to check for:

- Did you forget any fields? Is there information that you need that isn't included? If so, does it belong in the existing tables? If it's information about something else, you might need to create another table.

- Did you choose a good primary key for each table? If you use it to search for specific records, is it easy to remember and type? Make sure that you won't need to enter a value in a primary key field that duplicates another value in the field.

- Are you repeatedly entering duplicate information in one of your tables? If so, you probably need to divide the table into two tables with a one-to-many relationship.

- Do you have tables with many fields, a limited number of records, and many empty fields in individual records? If so, think about redesigning the table so it has fewer fields and more records.

As you identify the changes you want to make, you can alter your tables and fields to reflect the improved design. For information about modifying tables, see Chapter 7, "Working with Tables."

Example: Refining the Products Table

Each product in the Tasmanian Traders stock falls under a general category, such as Beverages, Condiments, or Seafood. The Products table could include a field that shows the category of each product.

Products table with a Category_name field

Product_id	Product_name	Units_in_stock	Category_name
1	Chai	39.000	Produce
2	Chang	17.000	Beverages
3	Aniseed Syrup	13.000	Condiments
4	Chef Anton's Cajun Seasoning	53.000	Beverages
5	Chef Anton's Gumbo Mix	0.000	Condiments
6	Grandma's Boysenberry Spread	120.000	Condiments
7	Uncle Bob's Organic Dried Pears	15.000	Produce
8	Northwoods Cranberry Sauce	6.000	Condiments

Each product has a category.

Suppose that in examining and refining the database, Tasmanian Traders decides to store a description of the category along with its name. If you add a Category Description field to the Products table, you have to repeat each category description for each product that falls under the category — not a good solution.

A better solution is to make Category a new subject for the database to track, with its own table and its own primary key. Then you can add the primary key from the Category table to the Products table as a foreign key.

The Category table provides a place to store category information efficiently.

Category_id	Name:	Description	Picture_file	Picture
1	Beverages	Memo	Memo	Gen
2	Condiments	Memo	Memo	Gen
3	Confections	Memo	Memo	Gen
4	Dairy Products	Memo	Memo	Gen
5	Grains/Cereals	Memo	Memo	Gen
6	Meat/Poultry	Memo	Memo	Gen
7				
8				

Primary key

Product_id	Product_name	English_name	Category_id
1	Chai	Dharamsala Tea	7
2	Chang	Tibetan Barley Beer	1
3	Aniseed Syrup	Licorice Syrup	2
4	Chef Anton's Cajun Seasoning	Chef Anton's Cajun Seasoning	1
5	Chef Anton's Gumbo Mix	Chef Anton's Gumbo Mix	2
6	Grandma's Boysenberry Spread	Grandma's Boysenberry Spread	2
7	Uncle Bob's Organic Dried Pears	Uncle Bob's Organic Dried Pears	7
8	Northwoods Cranberry Sauce	Northwoods Cranberry Sauce	2
9	Mishi Kobe Niku	Mishi Kobe Beef	6

Foreign key

The Category and Products tables have a one-to-many relationship: one category can have more than one product in it, but any individual product can belong to only one category.

Sample Database Diagrams

The database diagrams in this section might give you ideas for designing your own database. These databases aren't included with Visual FoxPro; they're included here as examples of the types of databases and tables you can create.

Appointments Database

This database structure stores appointments for a professional office, and could easily be modified for use in an office of doctors, dentists, lawyers, or accountants. The Appointments table has a multiple-field primary key to uniquely identify each appointment. This primary key, the "client_sta" index, is created by indexing on an expression that combines the client_id and date_start time fields.

Example of an appointments database

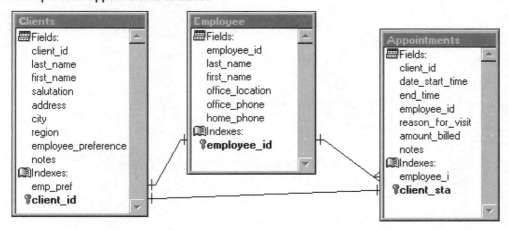

Personnel Database

This database structure stores human resources information. The Job History table stores information on each hire or promotion, so it can contain many records for each employee.

Example of a personnel database

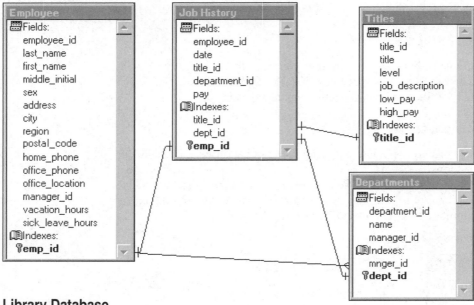

Library Database

This database stores information about library books and loans to patrons. Notice the many-to-many relationships between the Books and Authors tables and between the Books and Subjects tables.

Example of a library database

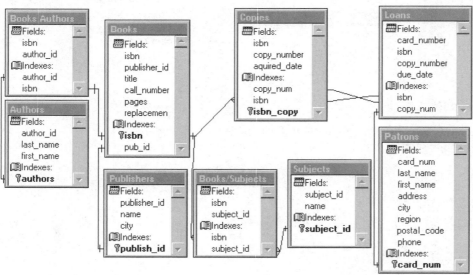

CHAPTER 6

Creating Databases

After you've designed your database, you can build the database through the interface or with the language. You might want to add existing tables to your database, and then modify them to take advantage of the data dictionary features in Visual FoxPro. If you are working within a project in the Project Manager, you can add the tables as you create them.

For more information about creating a database for a multiple-user environment, see Chapter 17, "Programming for Shared Access."

This chapter discusses:

- Creating a Database
- Viewing and Modifying Database Architecture
- Managing a Database
- Referencing Multiple Databases
- Handling Database Errors

Creating a Database

When you create a database, you gather tables together into one collection and gain the benefit of data dictionary features.

A data dictionary gives you greater flexibility in designing and modifying the database, and frees you from having to write code to create field-level and row-level validation or to ensure the uniqueness of values within primary key fields. The Visual FoxPro data dictionary enables you to create or specify:

- Primary and candidate keys.
- Persistent relationships between database tables.
- Long names for tables and fields.
- Captions on fields that display in Browse windows and Grid columns as headers.
- Default values on fields.
- The default control class used in forms.
- Input masks and display formats for fields.

- Field-level rules and record-level rules.

- Triggers.

- Stored procedures.

- Connections to remote data sources.

- Local and remote views.

- Comments for each field, table, and database.

Some data dictionary features, such as long field names, primary and candidate keys, default values, field-level and record-level rules, and triggers, are stored in the .dbc file but are created as part of the process of building a table or view. For information about these features, see Chapter 7, "Working with Tables," and Chapter 8, "Creating Views."

Collecting Tables into a Database

To collect tables into a database, you need to create a database container to hold all of the objects such as views, connections, and stored procedures associated with the tables that make up your database.

To create a new database

- In the Project Manager, select the **Data** tab, then select **Databases** from the list and choose **New**.

    – or –

    Use the CREATE DATABASE command.

For example, the following code creates and exclusively opens a new database called `Sample`:

```
CREATE DATABASE Sample
```

When you create a new database, it is empty, containing no associated tables or other objects. Adding a table creates links between the table file and the database container. The link information stored in the database about a table is a forward link. The link information stored in the table about the database container is the backlink.

Links specify the associations between a database container and tables.

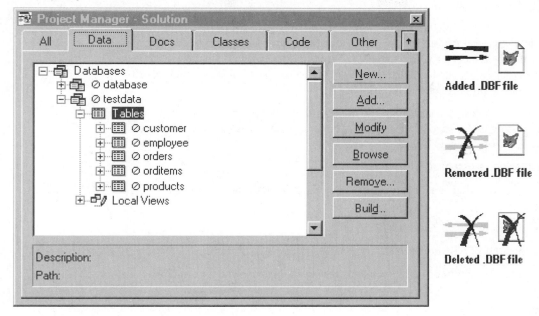

Backlink ◄━━━━━   ━━━━━► Forward link

You can use the following commands and functions to work with a database and its objects programmatically.

Commands and Functions That Manipulate Databases and Database Objects

ADATABASES( )	CREATE VIEW	MODIFY CONNECTION
ADBOBJECTS( )	DBC( )	MODIFY DATABASE
ADD TABLE	DBGETPROP( )	MODIFY PROCEDURE
ALTER TABLE	DBSETPROP( )	MODIFY STRUCTURE
APPEND PROCEDURES	DELETE CONNECTION	MODIFY VIEW
CLOSE DATABASE	DELETE DATABASE	OPEN DATABASE
COPY PROCEDURES	DELETE VIEW	PACK DATABASE
CREATE CONNECTION	DISPLAY DATABASE	RENAME TABLE
CREATE DATABASE	DROP TABLE	REMOVE TABLE
CREATE SQL VIEW	INDBC( )	SET DATABASE
CREATE TABLE	LIST DATABASE	VALIDATE DATABASE

For more information about a specific command or function, see Help.

Adding Tables to a Database

Each Visual FoxPro table can exist in one of two states: either as a free table, which is a .dbf file that is not associated with any database, or as a database table, which is a .dbf file that is associated with a database. Tables associated with a database can have properties that tables outside a database do not have, such as field-level and record-level rules, triggers, and persistent relationships.

You associate tables with a database by creating them within an open database, or by adding existing tables to a database. For information about creating new tables, see Chapter 7, "Working with Tables."

To add a free table to a database

- In the Project Manager, select **Tables** from the **All** tab or the **Data** tab, then choose **Add**.

  – or –

  Use the ADD TABLE command.

For example, the following code opens the `testdata` database and adds the `orditems` table:

```
OPEN DATABASE testdata
ADD TABLE orditems
```

You must explicitly add an existing free table to a database to make it a part of a database. Modifying the structure of a free table does not cause Visual FoxPro to add the free table to a database, even if a database is open when you issue the MODIFY STRUCTURE command.

Using Free Tables

You can associate a given table with only one database. However, you can use the data in an existing .dbf file without incorporating it into your database.

To access a table in another database

- Create a view in your database that references the table.

  – or –

  Access the table with the USE command and the "!" symbol.

Use the "!" symbol to refer to a table in a database other than the current database. For example, if you want to browse the `orditems` table in the `testdata` database, you can type:

```
USE testdata!orditems
BROWSE
```

In the previous example, the testdata database is opened automatically for you when you issue the USE command, but Visual FoxPro does not set testdata as the current database. A database opened automatically, as in the previous example, is automatically closed when the table is closed, unless you open the database explicitly before closing the table.

For information about using a view to access information outside your database, see Chapter 8, "Creating Views."

Removing a Table from a Database

When you add a table to a database, Visual FoxPro modifies the table file's header record to document the path and file name for the database that now owns the table. This path and file name information is called a backlink, because it links the table back to the owning database. The process of removing a table from a database not only removes the table and associated data dictionary information from the database file, but also updates the backlink information to reflect the table's new status as a free table.

You can remove a table from a database through the interface or with the REMOVE TABLE command. As you remove the table from the database, you can also choose to physically delete the table file from the disk.

To remove a table from a database

- In the Project Manager, select the table name, then choose **Remove**.

  – or –

  From the Database Designer, select the table and choose Remove from the Database menu.

  – or –

  Use the REMOVE TABLE command.

For example, the following code opens the testdata database and removes the orditems table:

```
OPEN DATABASE testdata
REMOVE TABLE orditems
```

Removing a table from a database does not automatically delete the table file. If you want to both remove the table from the database and delete the table's .dbf file from the disk, use the DELETE clause of the REMOVE TABLE command or the DROP TABLE command. For example, the following code opens the testdata database and deletes the orditems table from disk:

```
OPEN DATABASE testdata
REMOVE TABLE orditems DELETE
```

The following code also opens the testdata database, then deletes the orditems table without moving a copy to the Windows Recycle bin:

```
OPEN DATABASE testdata
DROP TABLE orditems NORECYCLE
```

Updating Table and Database Links

If you move database files (.dbc, .dct, and .dcx), or a table associated with a database, the relative paths change and might break the backlinks and forward links that Visual FoxPro uses to associate database and table files:

- The backlink links the table back to the table's owning database. It consists of the relative path and file name for the .dbc file associated with the table, and is stored in the header of the Visual FoxPro table file (.dbf).

- The forward link tells the database which tables belong to it. Forward links are stored in the database file (.dbc), and consist of the relative path and file name for each associated table file.

You can reestablish links and update the relative path information to reflect the new file location.

To update links after moving a table or a database

- Use the RECOVER clause of the VALIDATE DATABASE command.

For example, the following code opens the `testdata` database and displays dialog boxes that allow you to locate tables that are not in the locations contained in the database:

```
OPEN DATABASE testdata
VALIDATE DATABASE RECOVER
```

> **Tip**   If you want to use a table without taking time to reestablish the links for all tables in the database, you can open the table with the USE command. Visual FoxPro displays the Open dialog box to allow you to locate the owning database or delete the links.

For information on removing the backlink from a table whose owning database has been deleted accidentally from disk, see FREE TABLE in Help.

Creating Persistent Relationships

You can create persistent relationships between tables in a database. Persistent relationships are relationships between database tables that are stored in the database file and are:

- Automatically used as default join conditions in the Query and View Designers.

- Displayed in the Database Designer as lines relating table indexes.

- Displayed in the Data Environment Designer as default relationships for forms and reports.

- Used to store referential integrity information.

Unlike temporary relationships created with the SET RELATION command, persistent relationships do not need to be re-created each time you use tables. However, because persistent relationships do not control the relationship between record pointers in tables, you will use both temporary SET RELATION relationships and persistent relationships when developing Visual FoxPro applications.

In Visual FoxPro, you use indexes to establish persistent relationships between tables in a database. You create a persistent relationship between indexes rather than between fields, which enables you to relate tables based on a simple or a complex index expression.

To create a persistent relationship between tables

- In the Database Designer, choose the index name you want to relate, then drag it to the index name of the related table.

  – or –

  Use the FOREIGN KEY clause with the CREATE TABLE or ALTER TABLE commands.

For example, the following command adds a one-to-many persistent relationship between the customer and orders table, based on the primary cust_id key in the customer table, and a new foreign key, cust_id, in the orders table:

```
ALTER TABLE orders;
   ADD FOREIGN KEY cust_id TAG ;
      cust_id REFERENCES customer
```

If you were to then examine the database schema in the Database Designer, you would see a line joining orders and customer, representing the new persistent relationship.

Indexes provide the basis for persistent relationships

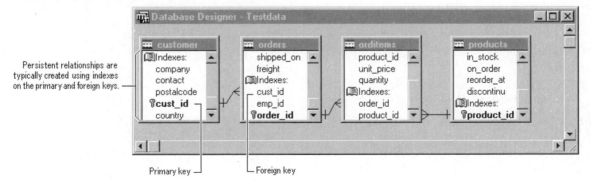

Persistent relationships are typically created using indexes on the primary and foreign keys.

Primary key ⌐ Foreign key

The type of index tag or key determines the type of persistent relationship you can create. You must use a primary or candidate index tag or key for the "one" side of a one-to-many relationship; for the "many" side, you must use a regular index tag or key. For more information on index types and creating indexes, see Chapter 7, "Working with Tables."

To delete a persistent relationship between tables

1. In the Database Designer, click the relationship line between the two tables.

   The width of the relationship line increases to indicate that you have selected the relationship.

2. Press the DELETE key

   – or –

   Use the DROP FOREIGN KEY clause with the ALTER TABLE command.

For example, the following command deletes a persistent relationship between the `customer` and `orders` table, based on the primary `cust_id` key in the `customer` table, and a foreign key, `cust_id`, in the `orders` table:

```
ALTER TABLE orders DROP FOREIGN KEY TAG cust_id SAVE
```

Building Referential Integrity

Establishing referential integrity involves building a set of rules to preserve the defined relationships between tables when you enter or delete records.

If you enforce referential integrity, Visual FoxPro prevents you from:

- Adding records to a related table when there is no associated record in the primary table.

- Changing values in a primary table that would result in orphan records in a related table.

- Deleting records from a primary table when there are matching related records.

You can choose to write your own triggers and stored procedure code to enforce referential integrity. However, the Visual FoxPro Referential Integrity (RI) Builder enables you to determine the types of rules you want to enforce, the tables on which you want the rules enforced, and the system events that will cause Visual FoxPro to check referential integrity rules.

The RI Builder handles multiple levels of cascading for cascade deletes and updates and is recommended as a tool for building referential integrity.

To open the RI Builder

1. Open the Database Designer.

2. From the **Database** menu, choose **Referential Integrity**.

When you use the RI Builder to build rules for your database, Visual FoxPro generates code to enforce relational integrity rules, then saves it as triggers that reference stored procedures. You can view this code by opening the stored procedure text editor for your database. For more information on using the RI Builder, search for "Referential Integrity Builder" in Help. For information about creating triggers programmatically, see "Using Triggers" in Chapter 7, "Working with Tables."

Caution   When you make changes to the design of a database, such as modifying database tables or altering indexes used in a persistent relationship, you should rerun the RI Builder before you use the database. Rerunning the RI Builder revises the stored procedure code and table triggers used to enforce referential integrity so that they reflect the new design. If you don't rerun the RI Builder, you might have unexpected results, because the stored procedures and triggers are not rewritten to reflect your changes.

Creating Stored Procedures

You can create stored procedures for the tables in your database. A stored procedure is Visual FoxPro code that is stored in the .dbc file. Stored procedures are code procedures that operate specifically on the data in the database. Stored procedures can improve performance because they are loaded into memory when a database is opened.

To create, modify, or remove a stored procedure

- In the Project Manager, select a database and select **Stored Procedures**, then choose **New**, **Modify**, or **Remove**.

  – or –

  In the Database Designer, choose **Edit Stored Procedures** from the **Database** menu.

  – or –

  In the Command window, use the MODIFY PROCEDURE command.

Each of these options opens the Visual FoxPro text editor, allowing you to create, modify, or remove stored procedures in the current database.

You can use stored procedures for creating user-defined functions that you reference in field- and record-level validation rules. When you save a user-defined function as a stored procedure in your database, the code for the function is saved in the .dbc file and automatically moves with the database if you relocate the database. Using stored procedures also makes your application more portable because you don't have to manage user-defined function files separately from your database file.

Viewing and Setting Database Properties

Each Visual FoxPro database has Version and Comment properties. You can view and set these properties with the DBGETPROP( ) and DBSETPROP( ) functions.

For example, the following code displays the version number of the testdata database:

```
? DBGETPROP('testdata', 'database', 'version')
```

The value returned represents the Visual FoxPro .dbc version number, and is read-only. Using the same function, you can view the comment, if one exists for the database:

```
? DBGETPROP('testdata', 'database', 'comment')
```

Unlike the Version property, the Comment property can be set. Use the DBSETPROP( ) function to enter a description or other text that you want to store with the database.

To set the comment property on the current database

- In the Database Designer, choose **Properties** from the **Database** menu and type a comment in the **Comment** box.

  – or –

  Use the comment option of the DBSETPROP( ) function.

For example, the following code changes the comment for the testdata database:

```
? DBSETPROP('testdata', 'database', 'comment', ;
   'TestData is included with Visual FoxPro')
```

You can also use the DBGETPROP( ) and DBSETPROP( ) functions to view and set properties on other database objects such as connections and views. For more information on these functions, see Help.

Viewing and Modifying Database Architecture

When you create a database, Visual FoxPro creates and exclusively opens a .dbc (DataBase Container) file. The .dbc file stores all the information about the database, including the names of files and objects associated with it. The .dbc file does not physically contain any top-level objects such as tables or fields. Rather, Visual FoxPro stores file path pointers to the tables in the .dbc file.

To examine the architecture of your database, you can browse the database file, view the schema, browse the database objects, validate the database, and even extend the .dbc file.

Viewing the Database Schema

The database schema is a visual representation of the table structures and persistent relationships established in your database. The Database Designer window displays the schema of the open database.

To view the database schema

- Use the MODIFY DATABASE command.

For example, the following code opens the testdata database and displays the schema in the Database Designer:

```
MODIFY DATABASE testdata
```

A database schema is a representation of the objects in a database.

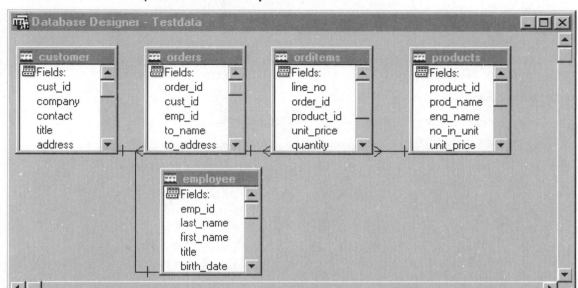

From the Database Designer, you can use the Database toolbar to create a new table, add an existing table to the database, remove a table from the database, or modify the structure of a table. You can also create connections and edit stored procedures.

Browsing the Database File

The database file contains a record for each table, view, index, index tag, persistent relationship, and connection associated with the database, as well as for each table field or view field having extended properties. It also includes a single record that contains all the stored procedures for the database.

For information about the structure of the .dbc file, see "Table File Structure" in Help.

While the Database Designer provides a conceptual representation of the database schema, sometimes you might need to browse the contents of the database file itself. You can browse a closed database by issuing the USE command on the .dbc file. The following example opens a Browse window displaying the contents of the sales database in table form.

```
CLOSE DATABASE sales
USE sales.dbc EXCLUSIVE
BROWSE
```

> **Caution**   Don't use the BROWSE command to alter the database file unless you are knowledgeable about the structure of the .dbc file. If you make an error while attempting to change the .dbc file you can invalidate the database and potentially lose data.

Extending Database Files

Each .dbc file contains a Memo field named User that you can use to store your own information about each record in the database. You can also extend a .dbc file to add fields to accommodate your own needs as a developer. Fields must be added to the end of the structure. You must have exclusive access to a .dbc file to modify its structure.

To add a field to a .dbc file

1. Open the .dbc file for exclusive use with the USE command.

2. Use the MODIFY STRUCTURE command.

For example, the following code opens the Table Designer so you can add a field to the structure of Testdata.dbc:

```
USE TESTDATA.DBC EXCLUSIVE
MODIFY STRUCTURE
```

When you add a new field to a database file, begin the field name with "U" to designate it as a user-defined field. This designation prevents your field from conflicting with any future extensions to the .dbc file.

> **Caution**   Don't change any existing Visual FoxPro-defined fields in a .dbc file. Any changes you make to a .dbc file could affect the integrity of your database.

Validating a Database

Validating a database ensures that the rows of the database are storing accurate representations of the meta-data in the database. You can check the integrity of the current database with the VALIDATE DATABASE command.

To validate a database

*   Use the VALIDATE DATABASE command.

For example, the following code uses and validates the .dbc file for the testdata database:

```
OPEN DATABASE testdata EXCLUSIVE
VALIDATE DATABASE
```

For more information on the validation processes performed by the VALIDATE DATABASE command, see Help.

Managing a Database

After creating a database, you might want to add it to a project if it isn't already part of one. If your database is already part of a project, you can remove it from a project. Also, if you no longer need the database, you can delete it from the disk.

A database in the Project Manager

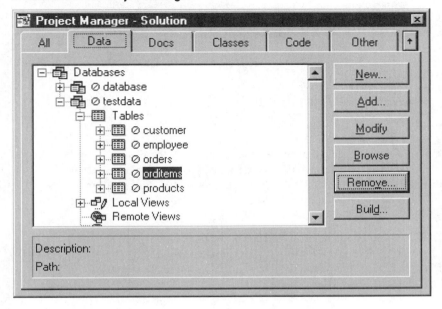

Adding a Database to a Project

When you create a database with the CREATE DATABASE command, the database is not automatically a part of a project, even if the Project Manager is open. You can add the database to a project to make it easier to organize, view and manipulate database objects through the interface, as well as to simplify the process of building an application. You can add a database to a project only through the Project Manager.

To add a database to a project

* In the Project Manager, select **Databases** and choose **Add**.

Removing a Database from a Project

You can remove a database from a project only through the Project Manager.

To remove a database from a project

* In the Project Manager, select the database and choose **Remove**, and then choose **Remove** again.

Deleting a Database

You can delete a database from disk using the Project Manager or the DELETE DATABASE command.

To delete a database

- In the Project Manager, select the database and choose **Remove**, and then choose **Delete**.

  – or –

  Use the DELETE DATABASE command.

For example, the following code deletes the `sample` database:

```
DELETE DATABASE sample
```

Always use one of the methods above to delete a database from disk. Using the Project Manager or the DELETE DATABASE command enables Visual FoxPro to remove backlinks to the database from the tables in a database. If you use another file manipulation utility to delete a database file, such as the Windows Explorer, these backlinks are not removed. For more information on the DELETE DATABASE command, see Help.

Note   The DELETE DATABASE command does not delete the tables associated with a database from the disk; rather, the tables that were associated with the database become free tables. If you want to delete both a database and all its associated tables from disk, use the DELETETABLES clause with the DELETE DATABASE command.

Referencing Multiple Databases

You can have many Visual FoxPro databases on your system to meet organizational needs in a multi-user environment. Multiple databases offer the following advantages:

- Controlling user access to a subset of tables in the overall system.

- Organizing the data to efficiently meet the information needs of various groups using the system.

- Allowing exclusive use of a subset of tables for creating local and remote views at run time.

For example, you might have a sales database that maintains sales information used primarily by the sales force working with customers and another database that maintains inventory information used primarily by the buyers working with suppliers. At times the information needs of these groups will overlap. These databases can be opened at the same time and accessed at will but they contain completely different types of information.

Multiple databases can add flexibility to your system.

You can use multiple databases either by opening more than one database simultaneously or by referencing tables in a closed database. Once multiple databases are open, you can set the current database and select tables in it.

Opening More Than One Database

When a database is open, the tables and relationships between tables are controlled by the information stored in the open database. You can have more than one database open at a time. For example, you might use multiple open databases when you run multiple applications, each based on a different database. You might also want to open multiple databases to use information, such as custom controls, stored in a database that is separate from your application's database.

To open more than one database

- In the Project Manager, select a database and choose **Modify** or **Open**.

    – or –

    Use the OPEN DATABASE command.

Opening a new database does not close any databases you've opened previously. Other open databases remain open, and the newly opened database becomes the current database.

Setting the Current Database

When you open multiple databases, Visual FoxPro sets the most recently opened database as the current database. Any tables or other objects you create or add to the database become a part of the current database by default. Commands and functions that manipulate open databases, such as ADD TABLE and DBC( ), operate on the current database.

You can choose a different database as the current database through the interface or with the SET DATABASE command.

To set the current database

- On the standard toolbar, select a database from the **Databases** box.

  – or –

  Use the SET DATABASE command.

For example, the following code opens three databases, sets the first database as the current database, then uses the DBC( ) function to display the name of the current database:

```
OPEN DATABASE testdata
OPEN DATABASE tastrade
OPEN DATABASE sample
SET DATABASE TO testdata
? DBC( )
```

> **Tip** Visual FoxPro might open one or more databases automatically when you execute a query or a form that requires the databases to be open. To be sure you are operating on the correct database, set the current database explicitly before issuing any commands that operate on the current database.

Selecting Tables in the Current Database

You can choose from a list of tables in the current database with the USE command.

To choose a table from the current database

- Issue the USE command with a "?" symbol.

  The **Use** dialog box displays so that you can select a table to open.

For example, the following code opens the sales database and prompts you to select a table from the list of tables in the database.

```
OPEN DATABASE SALES
USE ?
```

If you want to select a table that is not associated with the open database, you can choose Other in the Use dialog box.

Closing a Database

You can close an open database from the Project Manager or with the CLOSE DATABASE command.

To close a database

- From the Project Manager, select the database and choose **Close**.

  – or –

  Use the CLOSE DATABASE command.

For example, the following code closes the testdata database:

```
SET DATABASE TO testdata
CLOSE DATABASE
```

Both options close the database automatically. You can also close databases and all other open objects with the ALL clause of the CLOSE command.

Issuing the CLOSE DATABASE command from the Command window does not close a database if the database was opened by:

- The Project Manager when you expanded the outline to view the contents of a database.

- A form that is running in its own data session.

In these circumstances, the database remains open until the Project Manager closes the database, or until the form using the database is closed. For more information on the CLOSE command, see Help.

Scope Resolution

Visual FoxPro uses the current database as the primary scope for named objects, such as tables. When a database is open, Visual FoxPro first searches within the open database for any objects you request, such as tables, views, connections, and so on. If the object is not in the database, Visual FoxPro looks in the default search path.

For example, if the customer table is associated with the sales database, Visual FoxPro would always find the customer table in the database when you issue the following commands:

```
OPEN DATABASE SALES
ADD TABLE F:\SOURCE\CUSTOMER.DBF
USE CUSTOMER
```

If you issue the following command, Visual FoxPro will first look in the current database for the products table.

```
USE PRODUCTS
```

If products is not in the current database, Visual FoxPro will look outside the database, using the default search path.

> **Note** You can specify the full path for a table if you want to be able to access it inside or outside a database — for example, if you anticipate a change in the location of a table. However, you increase performance when you reference only the table name, because Visual FoxPro accesses database table names more quickly than names specified with a full path.

Handling Database Errors

Database errors, also called "engine errors," occur when run-time errors occur in record-level event code. For example, a database error occurs when a user attempts to store a null value to a field that doesn't allow null values.

When a database error occurs, the underlying database engine that detects the error typically posts an error message. However, the exact nature of the error message depends on what database is being accessed — for example, the error messages produced by a remote database server (such as Microsoft SQL Server) will probably be different from those produced if a database error occurs in a local Visual FoxPro table.

In addition, engine-level errors are sometimes very generic, because the database engine has no information about the context in which a record is being updated. As a consequence, error messages produced by a database engine are often less useful to the end user of a Visual FoxPro application.

To handle database errors in a more application-specific way, you can create triggers using the CREATE TRIGGER command. The trigger is called when a record update is attempted (delete, insert, or update). Your custom trigger code can then look for application-specific error conditions and report these.

If you handle database errors using triggers, you should turn buffering on. That way, when a record is updated your trigger is called, but the record is not immediately sent to the underlying database. You therefore avoid the possibility of producing two error messages: one from your trigger, and another from the underlying database engine.

To create custom error messages using triggers

1. Inside a user-defined function or stored procedure, write your own message text.

2. Enable buffering with the CURSORSETPROP( ) function to display your custom text. If buffering is off, the user will see both your custom text and the engine error message.

CHAPTER 7

Working with Tables

Building your database includes creating tables. When you designed your database, you specified the table fields and relationships needed for your application. Now, as you create those tables, you make more detailed choices about the data types, captions, and potential default values for each field, the triggers for each table, as well as the table indexes you build to establish relationships between tables. This chapter describes the process of creating, refining, and relating tables and indexes as you develop an application. It focuses primarily on using the language to work with tables and records, but also explains using the interface to handle common tasks.

This chapter discusses:

- Creating Tables
- Working with Records
- Indexing Tables
- Using Multiple Tables

Creating Tables

You can create a table in a database, or just create a free table not associated with a database. If you put the table in a database, you can create long table and field names for database tables. You can also take advantage of data dictionary capabilities for database tables, long field names, default field values, field- and record-level rules, as well as triggers.

Designing Database vs. Free Tables

A Visual FoxPro table, or .dbf file, can exist in one of two states: either as a database table (a table associated with a database) or as a free table that is not associated with any database. Tables associated with a database have several benefits over free tables. When a table is a part of a database you can create:

- Long names for the table and for each field in the table.
- Captions and comments for each table field.
- Default values, input masks, and format for table fields.
- Default control class for table fields.

- Field-level and record-level rules.

- Primary key indexes and table relationships to support referential integrity rules.

- One trigger for each INSERT, UPDATE, or DELETE event.

Some features apply only to database tables. For information about associating tables with a database, see Chapter 6, "Creating Databases."

Database tables have properties that free tables don't.

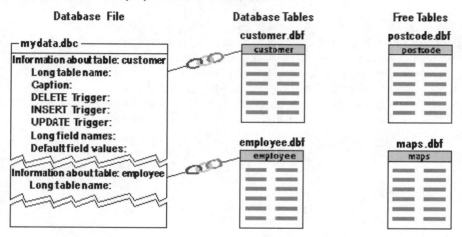

You can design and create a table interactively with the Table Designer, accessible through the Project Manager or the File menu, or you can create a table programmatically with the language. This section primarily describes building a table programmatically. For information on using the Table Designer to build tables interactively, see Chapter 2, "Creating Tables and Indexes," in the *User's Guide*.

You use the following commands to create and edit a table programmatically:

Commands for Creating and Editing Tables

ALTER TABLE	CLOSE TABLES
CREATE TABLE	DELETE FILE
REMOVE TABLE	RENAME TABLE
DROP TABLE	

For detailed information about these commands, see Help.

Creating a Database Table

You can create a new table in a database through the menu system, the Project Manager, or through the language. As you create the table, you can create long table and field names, default field values, field- and record-level rules, as well as triggers.

To create a new database table

- In the Project Manager, select a database, then **Tables**, and then **New** to open the Table Designer.

  – or –

  Use the CREATE TABLE command with a database open.

For example, the following code creates the table smalltbl with one column, called name:

```
OPEN DATABASE Sales
CREATE TABLE smalltbl (name c(50))
```

The new table is automatically associated with the database that is open at the time you create it. This association is defined by a backlink stored in the table's header record.

Creating a Free Table

A free table is a table that is not associated with a database. You might want to create a free table, for example, to store lookup information that many databases share.

To create a new free table

- In the Project Manager, select **Free Tables**, and then **New** to open the Table Designer.

  – or –

  Use the FREE keyword with the CREATE TABLE command.

For example, the following code creates the free table smalltbl with one column, called name:

```
CLOSE DATABASES
CREATE TABLE smalltbl FREE (name c(50))
```

If no database is open at the time you create the table, you do not need to use the keyword FREE.

Naming a Table

When you issue the CREATE TABLE command, you specify the file name for the .dbf file Visual FoxPro creates to store your new table. The file name is the default table name for both database and free tables. Table names can consist of letters, digits, or underscores and must begin with a letter or underscore.

If your table is in a database, you can also specify a long table name. Long table names can contain up to 128 characters and can be used in place of short file names to identify the table in the database. Visual FoxPro displays long table names, if you've defined them, whenever the table appears in the interface, such as in the Project Manager, the Database Designer, the Query Designer, and the View Designer, as well as in the title bar of a Browse window.

To give a database table a long name

- In the Table Designer, enter a long name in the **Table Name** box.

  – or –

  Use the NAME clause of the CREATE TABLE command.

For example, the following code creates the table vendintl and gives the table a more understandable long name of vendors_international:

```
CREATE TABLE vendintl NAME vendors_international (company C(40))
```

You can also use the Table Designer to rename tables or add long names to tables that were created without long names. For example, when you add a free table to a database, you can use the Table Designer to add a long table name. Long names can contain letters, digits, or underscores, and must begin with a letter or underscore. You can't use spaces in long table names.

Renaming a Table

You can rename database tables through the interface because you are changing the long name. If you remove the table from the database, the file name for the table retains the original name. Free tables do not have a long name and can only be renamed using the language.

To rename a table in a database

1. In the Database Designer, select the table to rename.

2. From the **Database** menu, choose **Modify**.

3. In the **Table Designer,** type a new name for the table in the **Table Name** box on the **Table** tab.

To rename a free table

- Use the RENAME command.

  Caution   If you use the RENAME command on tables associated with a database, the command does not update the backlink to the database and can cause table access errors.

Deleting a Database Table

If a table is associated with a database, you can delete the table as a by-product of removing the table from its database. Deleting a table is different from removing a table from a database, however. If you just want to remove a table from a database but do not want to physically delete the table from disk, see "Removing a Table from a Database" in Chapter 6, "Creating Databases."

To delete a database table from disk

- In the Project Manager, select the table name, choose **Remove**, and then choose **Delete**.

  – or –

  From the Database Designer, select the table, choose **Remove** from the **Database** menu, and then choose **Delete**.

  – or –

  To delete the table plus all primary indexes, default values, and validation rules associated with the table, use the DROP TABLE command.

  – or –

  To delete just the table file (.dbf), use the ERASE command.

  > **Caution**   If you use the ERASE command on tables associated with a database, the command does not update the backlink to the database and can cause table access errors.

The following code opens the database testdata and deletes the table orditems and its indexes, default values, and validation rules:

```
OPEN DATABASE testdata
DROP TABLE orditems
```

If you delete a table using the DELETE clause of the REMOVE TABLE command, you also remove the associated .fpt memo file and .cdx structural index file.

Deleting a Free Table

If a table is not associated with a database, you can delete the table file through the Project Manager or with the DELETE FILE command.

To delete a free table

- In the Project Manager, select the free table, choose **Remove**, and then choose **Delete**.

  – or –

  Use the DELETE FILE command.

For example, if `sample` is the current table, the following code closes the table and deletes the file from disk:

```
USE
DELETE FILE sample.dbf
```

The file you want to delete cannot be open when DELETE FILE is issued. If you delete a table that has other associated files, such as a memo file (.fpt) or index files (.cdx or .idx), be sure to delete those files as well. For example, if the file `sample.dbf` also has an associated memo file, you could delete both files with the following commands:

```
USE
DELETE FILE sample.dbf
DELETE FILE sample.fpt
```

For more information on the DELETE FILE command, see Help.

Duplicating a Table

You can make a copy of a tables structure, its stored procedures, trigger expressions, and default field values by using the language. There is no menu option to perform the same function. This procedure does not copy the contents of the table.

To duplicate a table

1. Open the original table.
2. Use the COPY STRUCTURE command to make a copy of the original table.
3. Open the empty table created with the COPY STRUCTURE command.
4. Use the APPEND FROM command to copy the data from the original table.

Copying and Editing Table Structure

To modify the structure of an existing table, you can use the Table Designer or ALTER TABLE. Alternatively, you can create a new table based on the structure of an existing table, then modify the structure of the new table.

To copy and edit a table structure

1. Open the original table.
2. Use the COPY STRUCTURE EXTENDED command to produce a new table containing the structural information of the old table.
3. Edit the new table containing the structural information to alter the structure of any new table created from that information.
4. Create a new table using the CREATE FROM command.

   The new table is empty.
5. Use APPEND FROM or one of the data copying commands to fill the table if necessary.

Saving a Table as HTML

You can use the **Save As HTML** option on the **File** menu when you are browsing a table to save the contents of a table as an HTML (Hypertext Markup Language) file.

To save a table as HTML

1. Open the table.

2. Browse the table by issuing the BROWSE command in the Command window or by choosing **Browse** from the **View** menu.

3. Choose **Save As HTML** on the **File** menu.

4. Enter the name of the HTML file to create and choose **Save**.

Creating Fields

When you create table fields, you determine how data is identified and stored in the table by specifying a field name, a data type, and a field width. You also can control what data is allowed into the field by specifying whether the field allows null values, has a default value, or must meet validation rules. Setting the display properties, you can specify the type of form control created when the field is added onto a form, the format for the contents of the fields, or the caption that labels the content of field.

> **Note**   Tables in Visual FoxPro can contain up to 255 fields. If one or more fields can contain null values, the maximum number of fields the table can contain is reduced by one, from 255 to 254.

Naming Fields

You specify field names as you build a new table. These field names can be 10 characters long for free tables or 128 characters long for database tables. If you remove a table from a database, the table's long field names are truncated to 10 characters.

To name a table field

- In the Table Designer, enter a field name in the **Name** box.

  – or –

  Use the CREATE TABLE command or ALTER TABLE command.

For example, to create and open the table `customer` with three fields, `cust_id`, `company`, and `contact`, you could issue the following command:

```
CREATE TABLE customer (cust_id C(6), company C(40), contact C(30))
```

In the previous example, the `C(6)` signifies a field with Character data and a field width of 6. Choosing data types for your table fields is discussed later in this section.

Using the ALTER TABLE command, you add fields, company, and contact to an existing table customer:

```
ALTER TABLE customer ;
   ADD COLUMN (company C(40), contact C(30))
```

Using Short Field Names

When you create a table in a database, Visual FoxPro stores the long name for the table's fields in a record of the .dbc file. The first 10 characters of the long name are also stored in the .dbf file as the field name.

If the first 10 characters of the long field name are not unique to the table, Visual FoxPro generates a name that is the first n characters of the long name with the sequential number value appended to the end so that the field name is 10 characters. For example, these long field names are converted to the following 10-character names:

Long Name	Short Name
customer_contact_name	customer_c
customer_contact_address	customer_2
customer_contact_city	customer_3
...	...
customer_contact_fax	customer11

While a table is associated with a database, you must use the long field names to refer to table fields. It is not possible to use the 10-character field names to refer to fields of a table in a database. If you remove a table from its database, the long names for the fields are lost and you must use the 10-character field names (stored in the .dbf) as the field names.

You can use long field names composed of characters, not numbers, in your index files. However, if you create an index using long field names and then remove the referenced table from the database, your index will not work. In this case, you can either shorten the names in the index and then rebuild the index; or delete the index and re-create it, using short field names. For information on deleting an index, see "Deleting an Index" later in this chapter.

The rules for creating long field names are the same as those for creating any Visual FoxPro identifier, except that the names can contain up to 128 characters.

For more information about naming Visual FoxPro identifiers, see "Creating Visual FoxPro Names" in Help.

Choosing Data Types

As you create each table field you also choose a data type for the data the field is to store. When you choose a field's data type, you're deciding:

- What kind of values to allow in the field. For example, you can't store text in a Numeric field.

- How much storage space Visual FoxPro is to set aside for the values stored in that field. For example, any value with the Currency data type uses 8 bytes of storage.

- What types of operations can be performed on the values in that field. For example, Visual FoxPro can find the sum of Numeric or Currency values but not of Character or General values.

- Whether Visual FoxPro can index or sort values in the field. You can't sort or create an index for Memo or General fields.

  Tip   For phone numbers, part numbers, and other numbers you don't intend to use for mathematical calculations, you should select the Character data type, not the Numeric data type.

To choose a data type for a field

- In the Table Designer, choose a data type from the **Type** list.

  – or –

- Use the CREATE TABLE command.

For example, to create and open the table products with three fields, prod_id, prod_name, and unit_price, you could issue the following command:

```
CREATE TABLE products (prod_id C(6), prod_name C(40), unit_price Y)
```

In the previous example, the "Y" after the unit_price field name specifies a Currency data type.

For more information about specific data types, see "Data and Field Types" in Help.

Adding a Regular Index Quickly

As you add a field, you can quickly define a regular index on the field by specifying ascending or descending in the Index column of the Table Designer. The index you create is automatically added to the Index tab and uses the field as the expression. To modify the index, you can switch to the Index tab to change the index name, type, or to add a filter.

Using Null Values

As you build a new table, you can specify whether one or more table fields will accept null values. When you use a null value, you are documenting the fact that information that would normally be stored in a field or record is not currently available. For example,

an employee's health benefits or tax status may be undetermined at the time a record
is populated. Rather than storing a zero or a blank, which could be interpreted to have
meaning, you could store a null value in the field until the information becomes available.

To control entering null values per field

- In the Table Designer, select or clear the **Null** column for the field.

  When the **Null** column is selected, you can enter null values in the field.

  – or –

  Use the NULL and NOT NULL clauses of the CREATE TABLE command.

For example, the following command creates and opens a table that does not permit null
values for the cust_id and company fields but does permit null values in the contact field:

```
CREATE TABLE customer (cust_id C(6) NOT NULL, ;
    company C(40) NOT NULL, contact C(30) NULL)
```

You can also control whether null values are permitted in table fields by using the
SET NULL ON command.

To permit null values in all table fields

- In the Table Designer, select the **Null** column for each table field.

  – or –

  Use the SET NULL ON command before using the CREATE TABLE command.

When you issue the SET NULL ON command, Visual FoxPro automatically checks the
NULL column for each table field as you add fields in the Table Designer. If you issue
the SET NULL command before issuing CREATE TABLE, you don't have to specify the
NULL or NOT NULL clauses. For example, the following code creates a table that allows
nulls in every table field:

```
SET NULL ON
CREATE TABLE test (field1 C(6), field2 C(40), field3 Y)
```

The presence of null values affects the behavior of tables and indexes. For example, if
you use APPEND FROM or INSERT INTO to copy records from a table containing null
values to a table that does not permit null values, then appended fields that contained
null values would be treated as blank, empty, or zero in the current table.

For more information about how null values interact with Visual FoxPro commands,
see "Handling Null Values" in Help.

Adding Comments to Fields

After you create a table in an open database, you can add a description of each table field
to make your tables easier to understand and update. Visual FoxPro displays a field's
comment text in the Project Manager when you select the field in the list of fields for
the table.

To add a comment to a field in a database table

- In the Table Designer, enter the text for your comment in the **Field Comment** box.

  – or –

  Use the DBSETPROP( ) function.

For example, you might want to clarify what is stored in the unit_price field in your orditems table by entering "Current retail price per unit" as comment text for the field:

```
?DBSETPROP('orditems.price', 'field', 'comment', ;
        'Current retail price per unit')
```

For more information on using DBSETPROP( ) to set properties on database table fields, see DBSETPROP( ) in Help, or see Chapter 6, "Creating Databases."

Creating Default Field Values

If you want Visual FoxPro to fill the contents of a field automatically as you add a new record, you can create a default value for the field. A default value is a quantity or string that you designate as the "default" content for a field when a new record is added to a database table.The default value is applied whether you enter data through a form, in a Browse window, a view, or programmatically, and remains in the field until you enter a new value.

You create default values either through the Table Designer or through the language. You can specify default values for any data type except General.

To assign a default value to a database table field

- In the Table Designer, enter the value in the **Default value** box in the **Field validation** area.

  – or –

  Use the DEFAULT clause of the CREATE TABLE command.

For example, you might want your application to limit the amount of merchandise a new customer can order until you've had time to complete a credit check and determine the amount of credit you're willing to extend to that customer. The following example creates a maxordamt field with a default value of 1000:

```
CREATE TABLE customer (cust_id C(6), company C(40), contact C(30), ;
        maxordamt Y(4) DEFAULT 1000)
```

If your customer table already included the maxordamt column, you could add a default value for the column with this command:

```
ALTER TABLE customer ALTER COLUMN maxordamt SET DEFAULT 1000
```

For information on the ALTER TABLE command, see Help.

Using Default Values to Speed Data Entry

You can use default values to speed data entry for your application's users, enabling them to skip a field unless they want to enter a different value. For example, if your business primarily deals with domestic customers, you may want the country field in the customer table in a database to be filled with the name of your country automatically. If you're entering a customer record for an international customer, you can then overwrite the name of your country with their country name.

> **Tip**   If one of your application's business rules requires that a field contain an entry, providing a default value helps to ensure that a particular field-level or record-level rule will not be violated.

If you remove or delete a table from a database, all default values bound to that table are deleted from the database. Stored procedures referenced by the removed or deleted default value remain even after the default value has been removed.

When you don't specify a default value, a blank value (as defined for each data type) is inserted unless SET NULL is on. This preserves backward compatibility with any existing FoxPro code you might have.

You can use .NULL. as a default value if you want the field to use null values. Whether SET NULL is on or off, if you use .NULL. as a default value, Visual FoxPro inserts .NULL. for all commands except APPEND BLANK.

Allowable Default Values

You can specify default values that are either scalar values (such as "a number") or expressions that evaluate to a scalar quantity. You can also specify any valid Xbase expression that returns a value consistent with the data type for the field.

Visual FoxPro evaluates expressions for data type when the table structure is closed. If the data type doesn't match the associated field type, Visual FoxPro generates an error. If the expression is a user-defined function (UDF) or contains a UDF, it is not evaluated.

When you create the default value through the language, the CREATE TABLE or ALTER TABLE commands will generate an error if the data types do not match. If the expression is a UDF or contains a UDF, it is not evaluated at CREATE time and no error is returned.

When Default Values are Applied

Default values are evaluated (if necessary) and placed in the appropriate fields when the APPEND, APPEND BLANK, or INSERT commands are issued.

When you assign values with the APPEND FROM or INSERT – SQL commands, Visual FoxPro assigns default values to any fields not explicitly assigned. The APPEND FROM and INSERT – SQL commands also respect default values. However, when either of these commands is issued, defaults will not overwrite existing values in fields. If appended or inserted fields contain values, the existing value is retained as the record is appended or inserted and the default value is not applied.

Using Default Values to Auto-Populate NOT NULL Fields

Default values are particularly useful to automatically populate fields that do not allow null values. When you add a new record, default values are applied first, then each field is checked in definition order for missing information. This ensures fields designated as NOT NULL have the opportunity to be populated with default values before the NOT NULL constraint is applied.

Specifying an Input Mask

By specifying an input mask, you define the punctuation, spacing, and other format attributes of values as they are entered into the field. The values are then stored in a uniform manner which can reduce data entry errors and make processing more efficient. For example, adding a mask to a numeric field storing telephone numbers helps the user to quickly fill out the field because the punctuation and spaces are already provided by the mask.

To provide an input mask

- In the Table Designer, enter the mask in the **Input mask** box in the **Display** area.

  – or –

  Use the DBSETPROP( ) function to set the InputMask property.

  For example, the following code specifies an input mask for a date:

  ```
  DBSetProp("orders.postalcode","field","InputMask", "99999-9999")
  ```

Controlling Display of a Field

Additional properties for fields allow you to control how a field and its values appear on forms, Browse windows, and reports. You can specify a display format, a default field caption, and a default class and class library.

Defining a Format

A format provides an output mask that determines the manner in which the value of a field is displayed in a form, Browse window, or report. For example:

To provide a format

- In the Table Designer, enter the mask in the **Format** box in the **Display** area.

  – or –

  Use the DBSETPROP( ) function to set the Format property.

For example, the following code specifies a display format for a postal code:

```
DBSetProp("orders.postalcode","field","Format","@R 99999-9999")
```

Creating Captions for Fields

You can create a caption for each field in a database table. Visual FoxPro displays a field's caption text as the column header in a Browse window and as the default header name in a form grid.

To add a caption to a field in a database table

- In the Table Designer, enter the text for your caption in the **Caption** box in the **Display** area.

  – or –

  Use the DBSETPROP( ) function.

For example, you might want to create a caption for the `fax` field in your `supplier` table by entering "Supplier_Fax" as the caption for the field:

```
?DBSETPROP('supplier.fax', 'field', 'caption', 'Supplier_Fax')
```

For more information on using DBSETPROP( ) to set properties on database table fields, see DBSETPROP( ) in Help, or see Chapter 6, "Creating Databases."

Setting a Default Class

To save time later when you're creating forms, you can set a default class for a field. Once set, each time you add the field to a form, the control on the form uses the class you specify as the default. For example, character fields automatically appear as text box controls when you add them to a form. If you want to automatically create a combo box control instead when you use the field in a form, you can set that class as the default for this field. You can also use class libraries that you've created.

To set a default class

- In the Table Designer, choose a class and library in the **Default Class** box and the **Default Library** box.

If you find you're often changing the library and class for your fields, you can map the fields data types to a library and class in the Options dialog box. For more information about mapping your field data types to classes, see Chapter 3, "Configuring Visual FoxPro," in the *Installation Guide*. For more information about creating classes, see Chapter 3, "Object-Oriented Programming," in this book.

Enforcing Business Rules

You can enforce business rules for data entry by creating field-level and record-level rules, called validation rules, to control the data entered into database table fields and records. Field- and record-level rules compare the values entered against the rule expressions that you define. If the entered value does not meet the requirements of the rule, the value is rejected. Validation rules exist only in database tables.

Field- and record-level rules enable you to control the types of information entered into a table, whether the data is accessed through a Browse window, a form, or programmatically through the language. They allow you to consistently enforce the rule for a field with less coding than if you wrote the rule expression as code in a VALID clause on a form, or in a portion of program code. In addition, the rules you establish in a database are enforced for all users of the table, regardless of the requirements of the application.

You can also create candidate or primary indexes that prevent duplicate entries in a field, and triggers to enforce referential integrity or perform other actions when the data in your database is changed.

Knowing When Constraints Are Enforced

You choose database constraints based on the level at which you want to enforce a business or referential integrity rule, as well as the action that causes the constraint to be activated. The following table lists the data validation constraints in the order in which they are enforced by the Visual FoxPro engine, the level at which they are applied, and when the engine activates the validation.

Enforcement Mechanism	Level	Activated
NULL validation	Field or column	When you move out of the field/column in a browse, or when the field value changes during an INSERT or REPLACE.
Field-level rules	Field or column	When you move out of the field/column in a browse, or when the field value changes during an INSERT or REPLACE.
Record-level rules	Record	When the record update occurs.
Candidate/primary index	Record	When the record update occurs.
VALID clause	Form	When you move off the record.
Triggers	Table	When table values change during an INSERT, UPDATE, or DELETE event.

Constraints are activated in the order in which they appear in the table. The first violation of any validation test stops the command.

Candidate and primary indexes are explained later in this chapter in the section "Controlling Duplicate Values."

Limiting Values in a Field

When you want to control the type of information a user can enter into a field, and you can validate the data in a field independently of any other entry in the record, you use a field-level validation rule. For example, you might use a field-level validation rule to ensure that the user doesn't enter a negative number in a field that should contain only positive values. You can also use a field-level rule to compare the values entered in a field against the values in another table.

You should not create field- or record-level rules that are application-specific. Use field- and record-level validation rules to enforce data integrity and business rules that always apply to the data in your database, regardless of who may access the data. For example, you might create a rule that compares the entry in the postal_code field of a table against a lookup table that contains the postal abbreviation codes for your country, and rejects any value that is not already present as a valid postal code abbreviation.

To create a field-level rule

- In the Table Designer, enter the rule expression in the **Rule** box in the **Field validation** area.

  – or –

  Use the CHECK clause of the CREATE TABLE command.

  – or –

  Use the SET CHECK clause of the ALTER TABLE command.

For example, the following code adds a field-level validation rule to the orditems table requiring that numbers entered into the quantity field be 1 or greater:

```
ALTER TABLE orditems
   ALTER COLUMN quantity SET CHECK quantity >= 1
```

When the user attempts to enter a value less than 1, Visual FoxPro displays an error and the value is rejected.

You can customize the message displayed when the rule is violated by adding validation text to the field. The text you enter is displayed instead of the default error message.

To add a custom error message to a field-level rule

- In the Table Designer, enter the error message you want in the **Message** box in the **Field validation** area.

  – or –

  Use the optional ERROR clause with the CHECK clause of the CREATE TABLE or ALTER TABLE commands.

For example, the following code adds both a field-level validation rule for the orditems table requiring that numbers entered into the quantity column must be 1 or greater, as well as a custom error message:

```
ALTER TABLE orditems ;
   ALTER COLUMN quantity SET CHECK quantity >= 1 ;
   ERROR "Quantities must be greater than or equal to 1"
```

When the user attempts to enter a value less than 1, Visual FoxPro displays an error with the custom error message you defined, and rejects the failed value. You can also use the SET CHECK clause of the ALTER TABLE command with the optional ERROR clause to create a custom error message.

Knowing When Field-Level Rules are Checked

Field-level rules are checked when the field's value changes. Unlike triggers, field-level rules fire even if data is buffered. When you work with data in a Browse window, form, or other window, Visual FoxPro checks field-level rules as you move away from the field. If a field value has not been changed, the rule is not checked. This means that you are free to tab through fields without the system validating any of the data.

Field-level Rule Checking

Data entry method	Window or command	Field-level rule checked
User interface	Browse window Form Other window	As you move away from the field, if the field value has changed. (If the field value has not been changed, the rule is not checked.)
Commands that do not specify fields	APPEND APPEND GENERAL APPEND MEMO BROWSE CHANGE DELETE EDIT GATHER	As field value changes, in field definition order.
	APPEND BLANK INSERT INSERT – SQL	As the record is appended or inserted.
Commands that specify fields	UPDATE UPDATE – SQL REPLACE	In the order in which fields are specified in the command.

Validating Record-Level Values

You use record-level validation rules to control the type of information a user can enter into a record. Record-level validation rules typically compare the values of two or more fields in the same record to make sure they follow the business rules established for the database. For example, you can use a record-level validation rule to ensure that one field's value is always greater than that of another in the same record.

To create a record-level validation rule and custom error message

- In the **Table** tab of the Table Designer, enter the rule and error message you want in the **Rule** and **Message** boxes.

  – or –

  Use the CHECK clause of the CREATE TABLE or ALTER TABLE commands.

For example, you might want to ensure employees are 18 years or older when hired. The following code adds a record-level validation rule and error text for the `employee` table requiring that the date of hire entered into the `hire_date` column is greater than or equal to their birth date plus 18 years:

```
ALTER TABLE employee SET CHECK ;
   hire_date >= birth_date + (18 * 365.25) ;
   ERROR "Employees must be 18 years or older by date of hire"
```

If the user enters an employee record with an invalid date, Visual FoxPro displays an error with the custom error message you defined, and does not update the record.

You can also use the SET CHECK clause of the ALTER TABLE command to create a record-level validation rule. You should ensure that any rules specified for fields do not conflict semantically with the rules you define for the table. Visual FoxPro makes no attempt to compare the field-level and record-level expressions for consistency.

Knowing When Record-Level Rules are Checked

Record-level rules, like field-level rules, activate when the record value changes. No matter how you work with data, whether in a Browse window, form, or other user interface window, or through commands that alter data, Visual FoxPro checks record-level rules as you move the record pointer off the record. If no values within the record have changed, the record-level rule is not checked when you move the record pointer. You are free to move through records without the system validating any of the data.

If you modify a record, but don't move the record pointer, and then close the Browse window, the rule is still checked. You're warned of any errors that occur, and the Browse window is closed.

> **Caution**   Do not include any commands or functions in your validation rules that attempt to move the record pointer in the current work area (that is, in the work area whose rules are being checked). Including commands or functions such as SEEK, LOCATE, SKIP, APPEND, APPEND BLANK, INSERT, or AVERAGE, COUNT, BROWSE, and REPLACE FOR in validation rules may cause them to trigger recursively, creating an error condition.

Unlike triggers, record-level rules fire even if data is buffered. When a record-level rule fires during a running application, you need to include error handling code. Typically, this will mean not allowing the application to leave the form (or change the active environment, to be more generic) until the user either corrects the reported error or cancels the update.

Removing a Table with Associated Rules from a Database

If you remove or delete a table from a database, all field-level and record-level rules bound to that table are deleted from the database. This is because the rules are stored in the .dbc file, and removing a table from the database breaks the link between the .dbf file and its .dbc file. However, stored procedures referenced by the removed or deleted rule are not deleted. They are not automatically removed, because they may be used by rules in other tables that remain in the database.

Using Triggers

A trigger is an expression that is bound to a table and is invoked when any of the table's records are modified by one of the specified data-modification commands. Triggers can be used to perform any side-effect operations that a database application requires when data is modified. For example, you can use triggers to:

- Log database modifications.

- Enforce referential integrity.

- Create an automatic reorder for a product that is low on stock.

Triggers are created and stored as properties on a specific table. If you remove a table from a database, the triggers associated with that table are deleted. Triggers fire after all other checks, such as validation rules, primary key enforcement, and null value enforcement, are performed. And unlike field- and record-level validation rules, triggers don't fire on buffered data.

Creating Triggers

You create triggers using the Table Designer or the CREATE TRIGGER command. For each table, you can create one trigger for each of the three events: INSERT, UPDATE, and DELETE. A table can have a maximum of three triggers at any one time. A trigger must return a true (.T.) or false (.F.) value.

To create a trigger

- In the **Table** tab of the Table Designer, enter the trigger expression or the name of a stored procedure containing the trigger expression in the **Insert trigger**, **Update trigger**, or **Delete trigger** box.

  – or –

  Use the CREATE TRIGGER command.

For example, perhaps each time Tasmanian Traders sells an item, they want to compare the remaining `Units_in_stock` against the `Reorder_level` and be notified if they need to reorder that item. You can create an Update trigger on the `products` table to accomplish this. Every time a product is sold, the Update trigger will fire and the `Units_in_stock` field will be updated to reflect the remaining items in stock.

To create the trigger, you can specify `updProductsTrigger( )` as your Update trigger for the `products` table. You can add a field to `products`, named `reorder_amount`, which stores the amount you want to order each time you reorder the item, and create a `reorder` table with the fields: `product_id` and `reorder_amount`. You can then add this code to your stored procedure:

```
PROCEDURE updProductsTrigger
    IF (units_in_stock+units_on_order) <= reorder_level
    INSERT INTO Reorder VALUES(Products.product_id, ;
    Products.reorder_amount)
    ENDIF
ENDPROC
```

You can create similar triggers for an insert or delete event by using the FOR INSERT or FOR DELETE clause, respectively, instead of the FOR UPDATE clause. If you attempt to create a trigger that already exists for a particular event and table while SET SAFETY is on, Visual FoxPro asks you if you want to overwrite the existing trigger.

Removing or Deleting Triggers

You can remove a trigger from a database table through the interface or with the DELETE TRIGGER command.

To delete a trigger

- In the **Table** tab of the Table Designer, select the trigger expression in the **Insert trigger**, **Update trigger**, or **Delete trigger** box and delete it.

    – or –

    Use the DELETE TRIGGER command.

The following example removes the update trigger for the `customer` table:

```
DELETE TRIGGER ON customer FOR UPDATE
```

If you remove or delete a table from a database, all triggers bound to that table are deleted from the database. However, stored procedures referenced by the removed or deleted trigger are not deleted.

Modifying Triggers

You can modify triggers through the Table Designer or through the language.

To modify a trigger

- In the **Table** tab of the Table Designer, enter the new trigger expression in the **Insert trigger**, **Update trigger**, or **Delete trigger** box.

    – or –

    Issue the SET SAFETY OFF command, and then use the CREATE TRIGGER command.

When you modify a trigger by first issuing the SET SAFETY OFF command and then re-creating the trigger, the old trigger expression is automatically deleted and replaced by the re-created trigger expression.

Using Triggers to Build Referential Integrity

Visual FoxPro provides a Referential Integrity Builder to generate triggers and stored procedures that will enforce Referential Integrity (RI) for your database. For more information on using the RI Builder, search for "Referential Integrity Builder" in Help or see Chapter 6, "Creating Databases."

Modifying the Table Structure

After you've built a table you can always modify the table structure and properties. You may want to add, change or delete field names, widths, data types, change default values or rules, or add comments or captions.

You can open the Table Designer to modify your table's structure, or you can make changes programmatically using the ALTER TABLE command. Make sure you have exclusive access to the table before modifying its structure.

To modify the structure of a table with the Table Designer

- In the Project Manager, select the table name and then choose **Modify**.

  – or –

  In the Database Designer, select the table in the schema and choose **Modify** from the **Database** menu.

  – or –

  Use the MODIFY STRUCTURE command.

For example, you can modify the structure of the database table employee with the following commands:

```
OPEN DATABASE testdata
USE employee EXCLUSIVE
MODIFY STRUCTURE
```

Each of the previous options opens the Table Designer.

To modify the structure of a table programmatically

- Use the ALTER TABLE command.

The ALTER TABLE command offers extensive clauses that enable you to add or drop table fields, create or drop primary or unique keys or foreign key tags, and rename existing fields. Some clauses apply only to tables associated with a database. A few specific examples are included in this section. For more information on ALTER TABLE and its clauses, see Help.

Adding Fields

You can add a new field to a table with the Table Designer or with the language.

To add a field to a table

- In the Table Designer, choose **Insert**.

  – or –

  Use the ADD COLUMN clause of the ALTER TABLE command.

For example, the following command adds a field called `fax` to the `customer` table and allows the field to have null values:

```
ALTER TABLE customer ADD COLUMN fax c(20) NULL
```

Deleting Fields

You can delete an existing field from a table with the Table Designer or with the language.

To delete a field from a table

- In the Table Designer, select the field and choose **Delete**.

  – or –

  Use the DROP COLUMN clause of the ALTER TABLE command.

For example, the following command drops the field called `fax` from the `customer` table:

```
ALTER TABLE customer DROP COLUMN fax
```

Removing a field from a table also removes the field's default value setting, rule definitions, and caption. If index key or trigger expressions reference the field, the expressions become invalid when the field is removed. The invalid index key or trigger expression will not generate an error until run time.

Renaming Fields

You can rename existing table fields in two ways.

To rename a table field

- In the Table Designer, enter a new field name in the **Name** box for the existing field.

  – or –

  Use the RENAME COLUMN clause of the ALTER TABLE command.

For example, to rename the column `company` in the `customer` table, you could issue the following command:

```
ALTER TABLE customer RENAME COLUMN company TO company_long_new_name
```

In the previous example, the new field name takes advantage of the ability to create long field names in database tables.

Setting or Changing Field-Level or Table Rules

You can set new field-level or table rule expressions and rule text, as well as alter rules and text you established with CREATE TABLE or ALTER TABLE commands.

To change an existing rule

- In the Table Designer, select the **Table** tab and enter the new rule expression or rule text in the **Rule** and **Message** boxes in the **Record validation** section.

  – or –

  Use the ALTER TABLE command.

To view the current rule expression and associated text, you can use the DBGETPROP( ) function; these values are read-only for tables and can only be changed using the ALTER TABLE command.

Setting or Changing Default Values

You can set or change default values for table fields after you've built your table.

To change an existing default value

- In the Table Designer, enter the new value in the **Default value** box of the **Fields** tab.

  – or –

  Use the ALTER TABLE command.

To view the current default value for a field, use the DBGETPROP( ) function; these values are read-only for tables and can only be changed using the ALTER TABLE command.

Working with Records

Once you've designed and created the structure for a table, you can store data in the table by adding new records. Later, you'll change and delete existing records. Each of these tasks can be accomplished either through the interface or by using commands. This section focuses primarily on working with records programmatically. For more information about working with records through the interface, see Chapter 2, "Creating Tables and Indexes," in the *User's Guide*.

Adding Records

When you first create a Visual FoxPro table, it is open but empty. If you try to store data to a table without first creating a record in the table, nothing happens. The first step in adding records to a new table is to add rows to store the new data.

To add records to a table

- Use the INSERT – SQL command.

The INSERT – SQL command can be used to insert values specified with the command or to insert values from an array or variable. For example, to insert a new record into the TasTrade database `customer` table, you could issue the following command:

```
INSERT INTO customer (cust_id, company, contact) ;
    VALUES ("SMI007", "Smith's Delicatessen", "Sarah Smith")
```

The INSERT – SQL command is useful with remote data, as it uses ANSI-compliant SQL syntax. For more information on INSERT – SQL, see Help.

You can also use the APPEND BLANK command followed by the REPLACE command to add a blank record to a table and then store data in a field. The APPEND BLANK appends a new, blank record to a table. The REPLACE command replaces the current value of a field, even an empty field, with a new value.

The REPLACE command requires:

- An open table.

- An existing record.

- The name of the field in which to store the value.

- A value for each field that is valid for the field's data type.

The following example uses the APPEND BLANK command to create one record in which you can store data using the REPLACE command:

```
APPEND BLANK                    && record now available
REPLACE lastname WITH "SMITH"   && store character value to the field
```

You can use the UPDATE – SQL command instead of the REPLACE command to update records in a table. For information about UPDATE – SQL, see Help.

Appending Records from Another Table

Another way to store data in records is to copy them from other tables or files. For example, you can append records from another table or file.

To append records from another file

- Use the APPEND FROM command.

    – or –

    Use the IMPORT command.

Records can accept data directly, as in the previous example, where the INSERT command specified the text to be inserted into specific fields in the `customer` table, as well as from constants, variables, arrays, objects, and other data sources. For more information about other ways to import data, see Chapter 9, "Importing and Exporting Data," in the *User's Guide*.

Adding Records in Browse Mode

If you want to add a new record while viewing a table in browse mode, you can choose Append Record from the Table menu. Conversely, if you want to prevent users from being able to append a new record while in browse mode, you can use the NOAPPEND clause of the BROWSE command. For more information about the BROWSE command, see Help.

Entering Data in a Table

You can enter data in a table interactively, through a Browse window, or programmatically, with the REPLACE or UPDATE – SQL commands. When you use the REPLACE or UPDATE – SQL in a multi-user application, you can turn on record or table buffering, which enables you to edit data without locking the record until you want to commit changes. For more information on record and table buffering, see Chapter 17, "Programming for Shared Access."

Editing Records in a Table

You can display and edit existing records in a table through the interface or programmatically.

To display records for editing

- Use the EDIT command.

  – or –

  Use the CHANGE command.

For example, the following code displays the `customer` table in a Browse window in edit mode:

```
USE customer
EDIT
```

If you want to use a form to edit a record, create a text box in your form and set its DataSource property to the name of the table you want to edit. For more information about forms, see Chapter 9, "Creating Forms."

You can also use the CHANGE and EDIT commands to make changes to specific fields in a table. For information about CHANGE and EDIT, see Help.

Adding Graphics to a Table

You can store graphics in a Visual FoxPro table by creating a General field and importing or pasting OLE objects, such as bitmaps or charts, into the field. The APPEND GENERAL command places an OLE object into a General field. The following example stores a Microsoft Excel chart file from the default Visual FoxPro directory into a General field named Chart:

```
APPEND GENERAL Chart FROM "CHART1.CLX" CLASS EXCELCHART
```

For more information about working with OLE objects in Visual FoxPro tables, see Chapter 16, "Adding OLE."

Entering Null Values in Fields

You can enter a null value in a field through the language with the NULL token, or through the interface with a key combination if the field accepts null values.

To store a null value in a field

- In a Browse window or form control, press CTRL+0 (zero).

    – or –

    Use the NULL token.

For example, the following code replaces the existing value in the field `automobile` with a null value:

```
REPLACE automobile WITH NULL
```

> **Note**   Use the SET NULLDISPLAY command to specify the text displayed for null values.

Deleting Records

You delete records by marking them for deletion, then removing the deleted records. Until you remove the records that are flagged for deletion, they are still on disk and can be unmarked and restored. This section describes how to mark, unmark, and remove records from your table.

Marking Records for Deletion

You can mark records for deletion through the interface or with the DELETE – SQL command.

To mark a record for deletion

- In a Browse window, click the deletion marker to flag the record.

    – or –

    From the **Table** menu, choose **Delete Records**.

    – or –

    Use the DELETE – SQL command.

You can use the DELETE – SQL command to specify a range of records, as well as a condition based on a logical expression that records must meet to be marked for deletion. For example, the following code marks for deletion all product records with "T" in the `Discontinu` field:

```
USE products
DELETE FROM products WHERE discontinu = .T.
BROWSE
```

Records you mark for deletion are not physically removed from the table until you issue a PACK command. When you view the table in the Browse window, you'll see that the deletion marker is flagged for each deleted record, but the record is still visible in the table, if SET DELETED is set to off. If SET DELETED is set to on, the records marked for deletion are excluded from the Browse window.

The setting of the SET DELETED command also affects whether records marked for deletion are accessible by commands that operate on records. For more information on SET DELETED, see Help.

Retrieving Records Marked for Deletion

You can unmark records that were marked for deletion with the RECALL command. The RECALL command can recover records only if you have not issued a PACK or ZAP command, which physically deletes the records from the table.

To unmark a record marked for deletion

- In a Browse window, click the deletion marker to unmark the record.

    – or –

    From the **Table** menu, choose **Recall Records**.

    – or –

    Use the RECALL command.

You can use the RECALL command to specify a range of records, as well as a condition based on a logical expression that records must meet to be unmarked for deletion. For example, the following code unmarks for deletion all product records with "T" in the discontinu field:

```
USE products
RECALL FOR discontinu = .T.
BROWSE
```

When you view the table in the Browse window, you'll see that the deletion marker is not flagged for the records.

Removing Records Marked for Deletion

After you've marked records for deletion, you can permanently remove them from disk through the interface or the language.

To remove records marked for deletion from disk

- In a Browse window, choose **Remove Deleted Records** from the **Table** menu.

    – or –

    Use the PACK command.

The PACK command has two clauses: MEMO and DBF. When you issue PACK without the MEMO or DBF clauses, records in both the table file and the associated memo file are removed. Make sure you have exclusive access to the table. For example, the following code removes records marked for deletion:

```
USE customer EXCLUSIVE
PACK
```

To delete records in the table file only and leave the memo file untouched, use PACK DBF. For more information about PACK, see Help.

Conserving Space

Information in table memo fields is stored in an associated memo file with the same name as the table and an .fpt extension. If you want to remove unused space from the memo file without removing records that are marked for deletion, issue the PACK command with the MEMO clause. Make sure you have exclusive access to the table.

Removing All Records from a Table

If you want to remove all records from a table, and leave just the table structure, you can use the ZAP command. Issuing ZAP is equivalent to issuing DELETE ALL followed by PACK, but ZAP is much faster. Make sure you have exclusive access to the table.

Caution Records zapped from the current table cannot be recalled.

For information on the ZAP command, see Help.

Indexing Tables

When you want to navigate, view, or manipulate table records in a particular order, you use an index. Visual FoxPro uses indexes as ordering mechanisms to provide you with flexibility and power as you develop your application. You have the flexibility to create and use many different index keys for the same table, enabling you to work with records in different orders, according to your application's requirements. You have the power to create custom relationships between tables based on their indexes, enabling you to access exactly the records you want.

A Visual FoxPro index is a file that contains pointers that are logically ordered by the values of an index key. The index file is separate from the table's .dbf file, and does not change the physical order of the records in the table. Rather, when you create an index, you create a file that maintains pointers to the records in the .dbf file. When you want to work with table records in a particular order, you choose an index to control the order and increase the speed in which the table is viewed and accessed.

Creating One Index

When you first create a table, Visual FoxPro creates the table's .dbf file and, if your table includes Memo or General fields, the associated .fpt file. You can choose to quickly add an index to a field as you define the field; otherwise, no index files are generated at that time. Records you enter into the new table are stored in the order you entered them; when you browse the new table, they appear in the order they were entered.

Typically, you'll want to be able to view and access the records in your new table in a specific order. For example, you may want to view the records in your customer table alphabetically by company name. When you want to control the order in which records are displayed and accessed, you create an index file for your table by creating the first ordering scenario, or index key, for your table. You can then set the order of the table to the new index key, and access the table's records in the new order.

To create an index key for a table

- In the Table Designer, choose the **Index** tab and enter the information for one index key. Choose **Regular** as the index type.

  – or –

  Use the INDEX command.

For example, the following code uses the table `customer` and creates an index key on the `city` field. The keyword TAG and the word "city" afterward specifies a name, or tag, for the new index key on the city field.

```
USE customer
INDEX ON city TAG city
```

In the previous example, the tag for the index key uses the same name as the field you're indexing. The names don't have to match — you could also choose to give the index key a different name.

When you first create an index using the INDEX command, Visual FoxPro automatically uses the new index to set the order of the records in the table. For example, if you entered some data into the sample table created in the previous example, and then browsed the table, the records would appear in order by city.

Creating an Index File

As you created the first index key for your table in the previous example, Visual FoxPro automatically created a new file, Customer.cdx, to store the new index key. The .cdx index file, called a structural compound index, is the most common and important type of index file you'll create in Visual FoxPro. The structural .cdx file:

- Opens automatically when you open a table.
- Can contain multiple ordering scenarios, or index keys, in the same index file.
- Is automatically maintained as you add, change, or delete table records.

If a Visual FoxPro table has any index file associated with it at all, it is typically a structural .cdx file. The term "structural" refers to the fact that Visual FoxPro treats the file as an intrinsic part of the table and opens it automatically when you use a table. Whether you use the Table Designer or the simplest form of the INDEX command, as shown in the previous example, Visual FoxPro creates the .cdx file with the same base name as the current table, and stores the index information for the new key, or tag, inside. You use the structural .cdx file for frequently used index keys, such as those used for ordering records for daily viewing, data entry, SET RELATION linkages, Rushmore optimization on viewing records, or frequently printed reports.

Visual FoxPro offers you two additional types of index files: the non-structural .cdx file and the single-key .idx file. Because the .cdx (or structural compound compact index) is the most important index type, most of the examples in this section will discuss using index keys in the .cdx file to order table records. The other two index file types are less frequently used and are discussed at the end of this section.

Viewing Index Information

You can see how many records are indexed during the indexing process by setting TALK to ON. The record interval displayed during indexing can be specified with SET ODOMETER. For more information about open index files, use the DISPLAY STATUS command. This command lists the names of all open index files, their types (structural, .cdx, .idx), their index expressions, and the name of the master index file or master tag.

The number of index files (.idx or .cdx) you can open is limited only by memory and system resources.

Controlling Duplicate Values

Visual FoxPro supports four types of indexes: primary, candidate, unique, and regular. These index types control whether duplicate values are permitted or prohibited in table fields and records.

Preventing Duplicate Values

A primary index is an index that never permits duplicate values on the specified fields or expression. Primary indexes are principally used within the primary or "referenced" table for establishing referential integrity in a persistent relationship. You can create only one primary index for a table. Visual FoxPro returns an error if you specify a primary index on any field that already contains duplicate data.

A candidate index is an index that never permits duplicate values on the specified fields or expression. The name "Candidate" refers to the status of the index; since candidate indexes prohibit duplicate values, they qualify as "candidates" to be selected as the primary index on a table.

You can create multiple candidate indexes for a table. You use candidate indexes as either the referenced or referencing index in a persistent relationship for establishing referential integrity.

Visual FoxPro returns an error if you specify a candidate index on any field that already contains duplicate data.

Setting a Primary or Candidate Index

You create primary and candidate indexes with the CREATE TABLE or ALTER TABLE commands. You can use both candidate and primary indexes in defining the "one" side of a one-to-many or a one-to-one persistent relationship.

To create a primary or candidate index

- In the Table Designer, select the **Index** tab and create an index, selecting **Primary** or **Candidate** as the index type.

  – or –

  Use the ALTER TABLE command.

For example, either of the following commands make `cust_id` the primary key of the `customer` table:

```
ALTER TABLE customer ADD PRIMARY KEY cust_id TAG cust_id
ALTER TABLE customer ALTER COLUMN cust_id c(5) PRIMARY KEY
```

Primary and candidate indexes are stored in the structural .cdx file for a given table. The database stores the names of the indexes in the .cdx file and whether or not the indexes are Primary or Candidate. It is not possible to store these types of indexes in other .cdx files, nor is it possible to use .idx files for these types of indexes. The principal reason is that the index file that contains these indexes should always be open whenever their associated table is opened.

Primary keys are part of a table within a database. If you free a table from a database, the primary key is removed.

If you use a user-defined function in an index expression associated with a database, Visual FoxPro handles the expression in the same way it handles rule and trigger expressions that contain UDFs.

Permitting Duplicate Values

In Visual FoxPro, a unique index does not prevent duplicate values from being created; rather, a unique index stores only the first occurrence of the value in the index file. In this sense, the word "unique" refers to the entries in the index file, which contains only unique values, because it doesn't store a particular key more than once, and ignores the second or later occurrence of a non-unique value. The table indexed by a unique index could contain duplicate values. Unique index types are provided primarily for backward compatibility.

A regular index is simply an index that is not unique, primary, or candidate. You use a regular index for ordering and seeking records, but not to enforce the uniqueness of the data in those records. You also use a regular index as the many side of a one-to-many persistent relationship.

To create a regular index

- In the Table Designer, select the **Index** tab and create an index, by selecting **Regular** as the index type.

  – or –

  Use the INDEX command.

For example, the following commands make `city` a regular key for the `customer` table:

```
USE customer
INDEX ON city TAG city
```

Creating Multiple Indexes

As you work with the records in your table, you'll discover the need for accessing table records in several different sequences. For example, you might want to order the `customer` table by contact to quickly find a name you're looking for, or by postal code to generate mailing labels that are presorted for more efficient mailing.

You can create and store many different ordering scenarios for your table by creating multiple index keys for the same table. This enables you to order table records at different times according to different purposes.

To create additional index keys for a table

- In the Table Designer choose the Index tab and enter the information for additional index keys.

  – or –

  Use the INDEX command.

For example, the following code creates two new index keys on the `employee` table: one on the `last_name` field and another on the `country` field:

```
USE employee
INDEX ON last_name TAG last_name
INDEX ON country TAG country
```

When you create an index tag without specifying the name of an index file, the tag is added automatically to the table's structural .cdx index file. The following diagram shows a .cdx index file with three index tags.

.cdx index contains multiple tags representing multiple record-ordering scenarios.

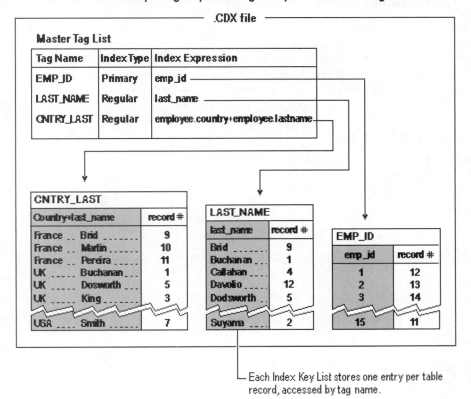

Each Index Key List stores one entry per table record, accessed by tag name.

Two of the tags in the diagram, `emp_id` and `last_name`, represent indexes based on single fields. The `cntry_last` index orders records using a simple two-field index expression. For more information on building an index based on multiple fields, see "Indexing on Expressions" later in this chapter.

Controlling the Order in which Records Are Accessed

After you create index keys for the `customer` table on the `company`, `city`, and `country` fields, you can access and display the table in different orders, simply by choosing the index key you prefer. You use the SET ORDER command to choose a specific index key as the ordering key for the table.

For example, the following code opens a Browse window displaying the records in the `customer` table in order by country:

```
SET ORDER TO country
BROWSE
```

Setting Record Order at Run Time

Using the SET ORDER command, you can designate the controlling index file or tag. A table can have many index files open simultaneously. However, you determine the order in which the records in a table are displayed or accessed by setting one single-index (.idx) file (the controlling index file) or tag from a compound index (.cdx) file (the controlling tag) as the controlling index. Certain commands, such as SEEK, use the controlling index tag to search for records. You do not need to SET ORDER for running queries.

Setting Record Order Interactively in a Form

You can use SET ORDER at run time to change the order of records in a form. For example, you might want to enable your application's users to reorder the records in a grid by clicking on the header of the column they want to order by.

To sort the records in a grid by columns

1. Create a form with a Grid control.

2. Set the ColumnCount property of the grid to the number of fields you want displayed in the grid.

3. In the Click event for the header of each column in the grid, insert code that:

   - Sets the record order to an index key based on the column.

   - Refreshes the form.

For example, if you created a form based on the Customer table in the Testdata database with a grid containing four columns — company, contact, postal code, and phone — the grid would first appear sorted alphabetically because the records in that table were entered alphabetically.

Customer table in grid, ordered alphabetically by company name

y

You could then enable the user to view the grid in contact or postal_code order by inserting the following code in the Click event of each column header:

Sample event code to order records in a Grid by clicking on the column header

Code	Comment

`SET ORDER TO company`
`GO TOP`
`THISFORM.Refresh`
	In the Company header Click event code, reorder the grid by the company index key and refresh the form to display records in order by company.

`SET ORDER TO contact`
`GO TOP`
`THISFORM.Refresh`
	In the Contact header Click event code, reorder the grid by the contact index key and refresh the form to display records in order by contact name.

(continued)

Code	Comment

`SET ORDER TO`
`postalcode`
`GO TOP`
`THISFORM.Refresh`
	In the `Postal_Code` header Click event code, reorder the grid by the `postalcode` index key and refresh the form to display records in order by postal code.
	
	Because sorting by phone number is not relevant to this application, leave the `Phone` header Click event code blank.

In this example, when the form is first displayed, the grid appears in alphabetical order by company. When the user clicks the header of the Contact column, Visual FoxPro displays the records in the grid in alphabetical order by contact name.

Customer table in grid, reordered alphabetically by contact name

If the user clicks on the `Postal_code` column header, the grid is resorted and displayed in order by postal code.

Customer table in grid, reordered by postal code

Since there isn't a pressing need in our example application to sort contacts by phone numbers, no SET ORDER code is inserted into the Click event for the `phone` column header. When the user clicks the Phone column header, the grid display does not change.

Using Other Index Types

In addition to the most common index — the compact compound structural .cdx index — Visual FoxPro supports two other types of index files: the non-structural .cdx, and the stand-alone .idx index. Non-structural .cdx indexes are used for less frequently used multiple-key tags. Stand-alone, or .idx indexes are used for temporary or infrequently used single-key indexes, and are available primarily for backward compatibility.

The following table is a summary of the three index types, how they are named, the number of keys they can contain, and the character limitations for each.

Visual FoxPro Index Types

Index type	Description	Number of keys	Limits
Structural .cdx	Uses same base name as the table file name; opens with table automatically	Multiple-key expressions, called tags	240-character limit on evaluated expression
Non-structural .cdx	Must be opened explicitly; uses a different name from the base table name	Multiple-key expressions, called tags	240-character limit on evaluated expression

(continued)

Index type	Description	Number of keys	Limits
Stand-alone .idx	Must be opened explicitly; base name of .idx file is user-defined	Single key expression	100-character limit on evaluated expression

Using Non-Structural .cdx Indexes

A non-structural .cdx index is useful when you want to create multiple index tags for a special purpose, but don't want to burden your application with maintaining these indexes on an ongoing basis. For example, your application may have a special set of reports that analyzes data based on fields not normally indexed. Your application program can create a non-structural .cdx index with the necessary index tags, run the special reports, then delete the non-structural .cdx file.

To create a non-structural .cdx index tag

- Use the TAG and OF clauses with the INDEX command.

You use the OF clause with the INDEX command to direct Visual FoxPro to store the tag in a file other than the structural .cdx index file for the table. For example, the following command creates tags called `title` and `hire_date` on the `employee` table and stores them in a non-structural .cdx file named `QRTLYRPT.CDX`:

```
USE employee
INDEX ON title TO TAG title OF QRTLYRPT
INDEX ON hire_date TO TAG hiredate OF QRTLYRPT
```

Using Stand-Alone Indexes

The stand-alone index file, based on a single key expression, is stored as an .idx file. In contrast to .cdx indexes, which can store multiple key expressions, the .idx index stores only a single key expression.

You typically use stand-alone indexes as temporary indexes, creating or re-indexing them right before you need them. For example, you may have an index that you use only for a quarterly or annual summary report. Rather than include this infrequently used index in the structural .cdx, where it would be maintained every time you use the table, you can create a stand-alone .idx index. You can create as many .idx files as you want for a particular table.

To create a stand-alone .idx index

- Use the COMPACT clause of the INDEX command.

  – or –

  Use the COPY TAG command.

Using the INDEX command with the COMPACT clause creates a new stand-alone index in a small, quickly accessed index file. You can omit the COMPACT clause if you want to create a non-compact stand-alone .idx file for compatibility with the older FoxBASE+ and FoxPro version 1.0 index formats.

The following code creates a stand-alone .idx file on `order_date` in the `orders` table, sets the order to the new index, then opens a Browse window showing the orders in `order_date` sequence:

```
USE ORDERS
INDEX ON order_date TO orddate COMPACT
SET ORDER TO orddate
BROWSE
```

You can use the COPY TAG command to generate a stand-alone index file from an index tag in an existing .cdx file. For example, you may find that one of the indexes you currently maintain in the structural .cdx is used only for quarterly or annual reports. The following code creates a stand-alone index from a tag `birth_date` in the `employee` table:

```
COPY TAG birth_date to birthdt COMPACT
```

After you've created a stand-alone index from a tag in a .cdx file, you'll typically delete this now unneeded tag from the .cdx file. The next section describes deleting an index.

Deleting an Index

You can delete indexes you're no longer using by deleting the tag within the .cdx file, or by deleting the .idx file itself for stand-alone indexes. Deleting unused index tags improves performance by removing the need for Visual FoxPro to update unused tags to reflect changes in a table's data.

Deleting a Tag from the Structural .cdx File

You can remove a tag from the structural .cdx file using the Table Designer or the language.

To delete an index tag in the structural .cdx

- In the Table Designer, use the **Index** tab to select and delete the index.

  – or –

  Use the DELETE TAG command.

  – or –

  Use the DROP PRIMARY KEY or DROP UNIQUE TAG clauses of the ALTER TABLE command.

For example, if your employee table contained a tag called title, you could delete it using the following code:

```
USE employee
DELETE TAG title
```

If the tag you wanted to delete was the primary key for the employee table, you could use the ALTER TABLE command:

```
USE employee
ALTER TABLE DROP PRIMARY KEY
```

For more information on ALTER TABLE, see Help.

Deleting a Tag from a Non-Structural .cdx File

A non-structural .cdx index and its tags are not visible in the Table Designer. You use the language to delete a tag from a non-structural .cdx file.

To delete an index in a non-structural .cdx file

- Use the OF clause of the DELETE TAG command.

You use the OF clause with the DELETE TAG command to direct Visual FoxPro to delete a tag from a .cdx other than the structural .cdx file. For example, if you have a non-structural .cdx file named QRTLYRPT.CDX with a tag called title, you could delete the title tag with the following command:

```
DELETE TAG title OF qtrlyrpt
```

You delete all the tags in a structural or non-structural .cdx file with the ALL clause of the DELETE TAG command. For more information on DELETE TAG, see Help.

Deleting a Stand-Alone .idx Index File

Because a stand-alone index file contains only a single index key expression, you delete the expression by deleting the .idx file from disk.

To delete a stand-alone .idx file

- Use the DELETE FILE command.

For example, the following code deletes the stand-alone .idx index file Orddate.idx:

```
DELETE FILE orddate.idx
```

You could also use a utility, such as Windows Explorer, to delete an unneeded stand-alone .idx file. For more information on DELETE FILE, see Help.

Indexing on Expressions

You can increase the power of your applications by creating indexes based on expressions. These expressions can be simple or complex, depending upon what you want to accomplish.

Indexing on Simple Expressions

Simple index expressions are indexes based on single fields, or on the concatenation of two or more character fields to form a multifield key. For example, you might want to create an index for the Customer table in the TasTrade database based on the expression:

```
country + region + cust_id
```

When you browse the Customer table sorted by this index tag, you see the customers ordered by country, then region, then customer ID.

Preventing Duplicates in a Combination of Fields

If you want to prevent duplicating values across multiple fields, you can create a primary or candidate index based on an expression combining multiple fields.

For example, you may have a table that stores the area code and phone number in two columns:

Area Code	Phone Number
206	444-nnnn
206	555-nnnn
313	444-nnnn

Both the area code field and the phone number field contain values that duplicate the values in other rows. However, no phone numbers are duplicated, because it is the combination of the two fields that makes up the value. Yet, if the primary or candidate index specified both columns in the index expression, the rows in the example would not be considered duplicates. If you attempted to enter a value that was exactly the same area code and phone number as one of the existing rows, Visual FoxPro would reject the entry as a duplicate.

Using Null Values in Index Expressions

You can create indexes on fields that contain null values. Index expressions that evaluate to .NULL. are inserted into the .cdx or .idx file before non-null entries. All null values are placed at the beginning of the index.

The following example demonstrates one effect of indexing null values. This is the state of the table before the index is applied:

Null values appear in the SocSec **field for two records.**

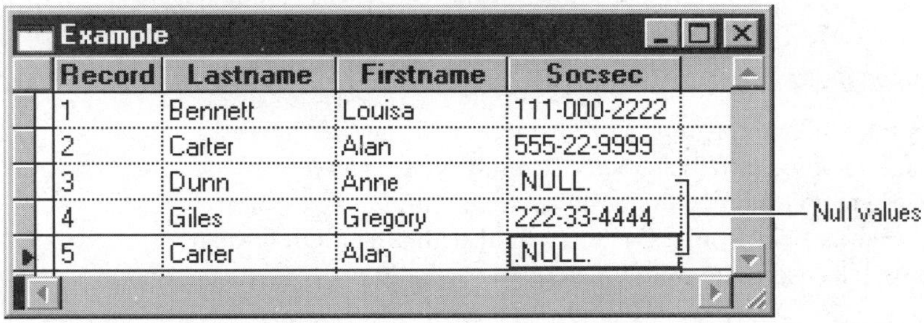

— Null values

The value .NULL. in two records represents the fact that Social Security numbers for Anne Dunn and Alan Carter are either unknown or unavailable. You then create an index with the Social Security number using the following example:

```
INDEX ON SocSec + LastName + FirstName TAG MyIndex
```

When you view the table sorted by this index, you see the sort order as shown in the following figure.

After indexing on SocSec, **records containing null** SocSec **values appear first.**

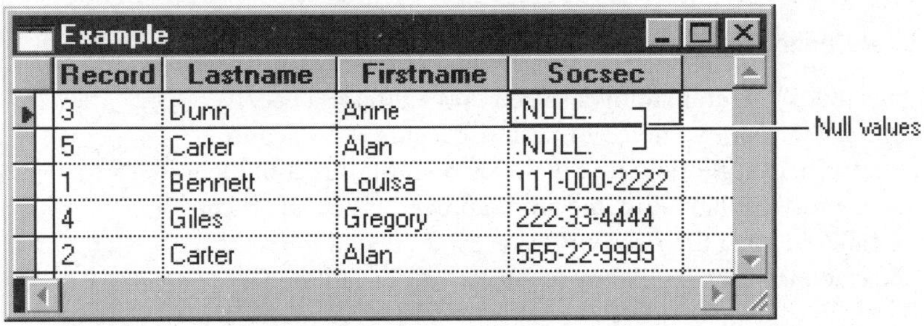

— Null values

When the index expression contains null values, the records whose SocSec values are .NULL. are sorted first (by LastName), followed by the records whose SocSec values are non-null. Notice that there are two entries for Alan Carter. Because record 5 contains a null value, record 5 is indexed before record 2.

Indexing on Complex Expressions

You can also create indexes based on more complex expressions. Visual FoxPro index key expressions can include Visual FoxPro functions, constants, or user-defined functions.

The expression you create must evaluate to no more than 100 characters for a stand-alone (.idx) index or 240 characters for a .cdx index tag. You can use fields of different data types together in a single tag by converting the individual components of the expression to character data.

To take advantage of Rushmore optimization, the index expression must exactly match the criteria.

Using Visual FoxPro Functions in an Index Tag

You can use Visual FoxPro functions in an index tag. For example, you can use the STR( ) function to convert a numeric value into a character string. If you wanted to create an index tag for the `customer` table that combined the `cust_id` field with the `maxordamt` field, you could convert the `maxordamt` field from a Currency field with a width of 8 to an 8-character field with 2 decimal places using the following code:

```
INDEX ON cust_id + STR(maxordamt, 8, 2) TAG custmaxord
```

If you want to reduce the size of indexes for fields with integer values, you can convert the integer values to a binary character representation using the BINTOC( ) function. You can also convert the binary values to integer values using the CTOBIN( ) function.

If you want to create an index to sort a table in chronological order, you can use the DTOS( ) function to convert a date field to a character string. To access the `employee` table by `hire_date` and `emp_id`, you can create this index key expression:

```
INDEX ON DTOS(hire_date) + emp_id TAG id_hired
```

Including Stored Procedures or User-Defined Functions

You can increase the power of your index by referencing a stored procedure or a user-defined function in your index expression. For example, you can use a stored procedure or a UDF to extract the street name from a single field that includes both the street number and street name. If the street number is always numeric, the stored procedure or UDF can return the character portion of the field and pad the field with spaces as needed to create a constant-length index key. You can then use this index key to access records in the table in street-name order.

You may prefer to use a stored procedure rather than a UDF in your index tag, if your table is associated with a database. Because a UDF is stored in a file that is separate from the database, it is possible to move or delete the UDF file, which then causes the index tag referencing the UDF to become invalid. In contrast, stored procedure code is stored in the .dbc file and can always be located by Visual FoxPro.

Another benefit to using a stored procedure in an index tag is that referencing a stored procedure guarantees that the index is based on the exact code you specify. If you use a UDF in your index expression, any UDF that is in scope at the time of indexing and has the same name as the UDF referenced in your index will be used.

Note   Exercise care when referencing a stored procedure or UDF in an index expression, as it increases the time required to create or update the index.

Using Data in a Field in Another Table

You can create an index tag that refers to a table open in another work area. It's wise to use a stand-alone index (.idx) for any tag that refers to more than one table. This is because if you were to include a tag referring to another table in a structural .cdx file, Visual FoxPro wouldn't allow you to open the table until you opened the table referenced in the index tag.

Accessing Records in Descending Order

You can view records in descending order by creating a descending index, or by reading an existing index in descending order.

To create a descending index

- In the **Index** tab of the Table Designer, choose the arrow button to the left of the **Name** box so that the arrow points down.

    – or –

    Use the DESCENDING clause with the INDEX ON command to create a descending index.

To create a compound structural index file, you can use either method. To create other types of index files, you can use the second method. For example, you could create a new descending index ordering your product table from highest to lowest unit_price and browse the table in the new order with the following code:

```
USE products
INDEX ON unit_price TAG unit_price DESCENDING
BROWSE
```

To read an existing index in descending order

- Use the DESCENDING clause of the SET ORDER command to read an existing index in descending order.

Reading an existing index in descending order enables you to leverage an existing index rather than create a new one. For example, you may have already created an index ordering your product table by unit_price with the following code:

```
USE products
INDEX ON unit_price TAG unit_price
```

By default, the order is ascending. You could browse the table in descending order with the following code:

```
USE products
SET ORDER TO unit_price DESCENDING
BROWSE
```

The previous examples focus on accessing information in descending order. Both the SET ORDER and INDEX commands also offer an ASCENDING clause. You can combine these two commands to gain tremendous flexibility in your application. For example, if you use the ASCENDING or DESCENDING clause to create an index in the most frequently used order, you can then use the opposite clause with the SET ORDER command to view or access the information in the opposite order, when that order is more convenient.

Filtering Data

You can limit the records you access to only the data you want by using a filtered index. When you create a filtered index, only records that match the filter expression are available for display and access.

To filter data using a filtered index

- In the Table Designer, select the **Index** tab and enter a filter expression in the **Filter** box for the index you want to filter.

  – or –

  Use the optional FOR clause with the INDEX command.

If you include the optional FOR clause with the INDEX command, the index file acts as a filter on the table. Index keys are created in the index file for just those records that match the filter expression. For example, if you were preparing a mailing to go to the sales representatives in your company, and you wanted to sort the mailing by country, you could create an index that filtered the employee table so that only the records for sales representatives appeared, ordered by their country and their last name. The following code creates a filtered index and displays the filtered data in a Browse window:

```
USE employee
INDEX ON country+last_name FOR title = "Sales Representative" ;
TAG reps_cntry
BROWSE
```

When you view the Browse window, only the sales representatives are shown; the records for other employees do not appear at all in the Browse window.

A filtered index builds an index only for records that match the filter expression.

INDEX ON country+last_name FOR title = "Sales Representative" TAG reps_cntry

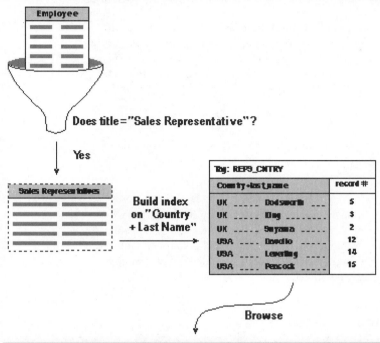

Tag: REPS_CNTRY

Country+last_name	record #
UK ..... Dodsworth ...	5
UK ..... King	3
UK ..... Suyama	2
USA .... Davolio	12
USA .... Leverling	14
USA .... Peacock	15

Browse

Employee

Last_name	First_name	Title	Address
Dodsworth	Anne	Sales Representative	7 Houndstooth Rd.
King	Robert	Sales Representative	Edgeham Hollow, Winchester Way
Suyama	Michael	Sales Representative	Coventry House, Miner Rd.
Davolio	Nancy	Sales Representative	507 - 20th Ave. E., Apt. 2A
Leverling	Janet	Sales Representative	722 Moss Bay Blvd.
Peacock	Margaret	Sales Representative	4110 Old Redmond Rd.

Filtering Data Temporarily

You can use the SET FILTER command to filter data temporarily, without building a special filtered index. This command is particularly useful when you want to specify a temporary condition that records in a table must meet in order to be accessible. To turn off the filter for the current table, you can issue SET FILTER TO without an expression. For example, you could issue the following command to filter the customer table to show only the customers in Germany:

```
USE customer
SET FILTER TO country = "Germany"
BROWSE
```

The SET FILTER command accepts any valid Visual FoxPro logical expression as the filter condition. Once you issue the SET FILTER command, only the records that satisfy the filter condition are available in the table. All commands that access the table respect the SET FILTER condition. You can set a separate filter for every open table. For more information on SET FILTER, see Help.

Using Indexes Efficiently

You can improve the performance of indexed tables by keeping indexes current and using optimizable expressions in your indexes.

Rebuilding an Active Index File

Index files become outdated when you open a table without opening its corresponding index files and make changes to the key fields in the table. Index files can also become invalid as a result of a system crash, or potentially by accessing and updating a table from a program other than Visual FoxPro. When index files become outdated, you can update them by re-indexing with the REINDEX command.

To rebuild an active index file

- From the **Table** menu, choose **Rebuild Indexes**.

  – or –

  Use the REINDEX command.

For example, the following code updates the index file for the Customer table:

```
USE customer
REINDEX
```

REINDEX updates all index files open in the selected work area. Visual FoxPro recognizes each index file type (compound index .cdx files, structural .cdx files, and single index .idx files) and re-indexes accordingly. It updates all tags in .cdx files, and updates structural .cdx files, which open automatically with the table.

You can also update outdated index files with the REINDEX command. For more information on REINDEX, see Help.

Re-Indexing at Run Time

Re-indexing takes time, particularly when you're re-indexing large tables. You should re-index only when necessary. You can enhance performance by re-indexing during the initialization or termination portion of your program, rather than performing indexing maintenance during the main portion of an application.

Using Indexes to Optimize Queries

You can use indexes to speed queries and other operations. For information on creating Rushmore-optimizable index expressions, see Chapter 15, "Optimizing Applications."

Using Multiple Tables

To use multiple tables, you use data sessions to control the tables that are available to forms, and work areas to set which tables are open. A work area is a numbered region that identifies an open table. You can open and manipulate Visual FoxPro tables in 32,767 work areas. Work areas are normally identified in your application by using the table alias of the table open in the work area. A table alias is a name that refers to a table open in a work area.

Using Data Sessions

In addition to the work areas visible in the Data Session window, Visual FoxPro automatically provides a separate environment for each instance of a form or form set through data sessions. A data session is a representation of the current dynamic work environment used by a form, form set, or report. Each data session contains its own set of work areas. These work areas contain the tables open in the work areas, their indexes, and relationships. For information on using data sessions, see Chapter 17, "Programming for Shared Access."

Viewing Work Areas

You can see the list of tables open in a Visual FoxPro session by opening the Data Session window.

To open the Data Session window

- From the **Window** menu, choose **Data Session**.

  – or –

  Use the SET command.

When you enter SET in the Command window, Visual FoxPro opens the Data Session window and displays the work area aliases for the tables open in the current data session.

Data Session window with the Employees table open

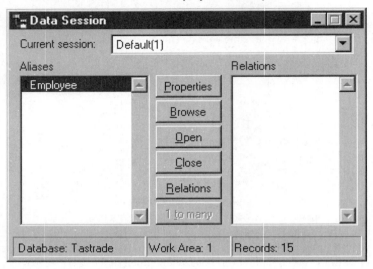

Opening a Table in a Work Area

You can open a table in a work area with the Data Session window or with the USE command.

To open a table in a work area

- In the Data Session window, choose **Open**.

  – or –

  Type USE in the **Command** window.

To open a table in the lowest available work area, use the IN clause of the USE command with work area 0. For example, if tables are open in work areas 1 through 10, the following command opens the customer table in work area 11.

```
USE customer IN 0
```

You can also choose Open from the File menu to open a table in a work area.

Closing a Table in a Work Area

You can close a table in a work area through the Data Session window or by using the language.

To close a table in a work area

- From the Data Session window, select the alias of the table, and then choose **Close**.

  – or –

  Type USE without a table name.

  – or –

  Use the IN clause of the USE command to reference the work area of the table you want to close.

When you issue the USE command without a table name and a table file is open in the currently selected work area, the table is closed. For example, the following code opens the `customer` table, displays a Browse window, and then closes the table:

```
USE customer
BROWSE
USE
```

You also close a table automatically when you open another table in the same work area, or issue the USE command with the IN clause and reference the current work area. The following code opens, displays, and then closes the `customer` table by issuing USE IN and the table alias `customer`:

```
USE customer
BROWSE
USE IN customer
```

You can't have more than one table open in a work area at one time.

Referencing a Work Area

You can reference the next available work area before you open a table by using the work area number as shown below:

```
SELECT 0
```

Using Table Aliases

A table alias is the name that Visual FoxPro uses to refer to a table open in a work area. Visual FoxPro automatically uses the file name for the default alias when you open a table. For example, if you open the file Customer.dbf in work area 0 with the following commands, the default alias `customer` is automatically assigned to the table:

```
SELECT 0
USE customer
```

You can then use the alias `customer` to identify the table in a command or function. You can also create your own alias.

Creating a User-Defined Alias

You can assign your own user-defined alias to a table when you open it.

To open a table with a user-defined alias

- Type USE with a table alias name.

For example, to open the file Customer.dbf in work area 0 and assign it an alias of `people`, use the following command:

```
SELECT 0
USE customer ALIAS people
```

You must then use the alias `people` to refer to the open table. An alias can consist of up to 254 letters, digits, or underscores and it must begin with a letter or an underscore. Visual FoxPro automatically creates an alias if the alias you provide contains an unsupported alias character. For more information on assigning table aliases, see USE in Help.

Using a Visual FoxPro-Assigned Alias

Visual FoxPro automatically assigns an alias to a table in certain instances:

- If you open a single table simultaneously in multiple work areas by including the AGAIN clause with the USE command and you don't specify an alias when opening the table in each work area.

- If a conflict occurs with aliases.

The default aliases assigned in the first 10 work areas are the work area letters "A" through "J"; the aliases assigned in work areas 11 through 32767 are W11 through W32767. You can use these Visual FoxPro-assigned aliases just as you would any default or user-defined alias to refer to a table open in a work area.

Selecting a Work Area Using an Alias

You can move to a work area from another work area with the SELECT command. For example, if Customer.dbf is open in a work area and the default alias of CUSTOMER is assigned, you can move to this work area with the following SELECT command:

```
SELECT customer
```

Referring to Tables Open in Other Work Areas

You can also refer to fields in other work areas by prefacing the field name with the alias name and a period, or the –> operator. For example, if you're in a work area and you want to access the field `contact` from the Customer table open in a different work area, you could use the following to reference the field:

```
customer.contact
```

If the table you want to reference is opened with an alias, you can use the alias name. For example, if the Customer table is opened with the alias `people`, you can reference the `lastname` field with the following to refer to the field:

`people.lastname`

Using the table name or table alias specifically identifies the desired table independently from the work area in which the table is open.

Setting Temporary Relationships Between Tables

When you establish a temporary relationship between tables, you cause the record pointer of one table (the child table) to automatically follow the movements of the record pointer in the other, or parent, table. This allows you to select a record on the "one," or parent side, of a relationship and automatically access the related records on the "many," or child side, of the table relationship.

For example, you may want to relate the `customer` and `orders` tables so that when you move the record pointer in the `customer` table to a particular customer, the record pointer in the `orders` table moves to the record with the same customer number.

You can use table work areas and table aliases to establish relationships between two open tables with the SET RELATION command. If you're using a form to work with tables, you can store these relationships as part of the data environment for the form.

Temporarily Relating Tables

You can use the Data Session window or the language to create temporary relationships between tables.

To temporarily relate tables

- In the Data Session window, select tables and use the **Relations** button to create relationships.

  – or –

  Use the SET RELATION command.

You use the SET RELATION command to establish a relationship between a table open in the currently selected work area, and another table open in another work area. You typically relate tables that have a common field, and the expression you use to establish the relationship is usually the index expression of the controlling index of the child table.

For example, a customer may have many orders. If you create a relationship between the field that is common to both customer and order tables, you can easily see all the orders for any customer. The following program uses a field, cust_id, that is common to both tables and creates a relationship between the two tables based on the field cust_id in the `customer` table and the cust_id index tag in the `orders` table.

Using SET RELATION to Establish Relationship Between Two Tables

Code	Comments
`USE customer IN 1`	Open the `customer` table (parent table) in work area 1.
`USE orders IN 2`	Open the `orders` table (child table) in work area 2.
`SELECT orders`	Select the child work area.
`SET ORDER TO TAG cust_id`	Specify the table order for the child table using the index tag `cust_id`.
`SELECT customer`	Select the parent work area.
`SET RELATION TO cust_id` `INTO orders`	Create the relationship between the parent table and the controlling index in the child table.

`SELECT orders`
`BROWSE NOWAIT`
`SELECT customer`
`BROWSE NOWAIT`
	Open two Browse windows; notice that moving the record pointer in the parent table changes the set of data viewed in the child table.

The Data Session window displays the two open tables, Orders and Customer, and the relationship established by the SET RELATION command.

The Data Session window displays open table aliases and temporary relationships.

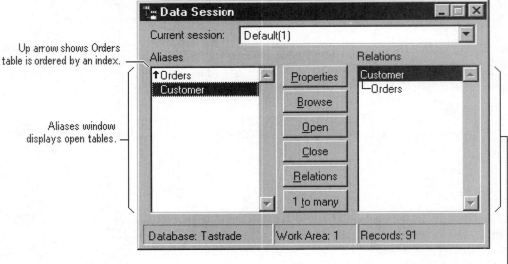

Up arrow shows Orders table is ordered by an index.

Aliases window displays open tables.

Relations window shows temporary relationship between Customer and Orders table.

You created an index on the child table, orders, to organize records in the orders table into groups, according to the customer who placed the order. When you create a relationship between the parent table and the index of the child table, Visual FoxPro selects only those child table records whose index key matches the index key of the parent record you've selected.

The previous example established a single relationship between two tables. You can also use the SET RELATION command to establish multiple relationships between a single parent table and various child tables. For more information on setting relationships programmatically, see SET RELATION in Help.

Saving Table Relationships in a Data Environment

If you are creating a form that uses more than one table, you can use the data environment to create table relationships and store them with the form. Relationships you establish in the data environment are opened automatically when you run the form. For information on creating a data environment, see Chapter 9, "Creating Forms."

Relating Records in a Single Table

You can also create a relationship between records in a single table. This relationship, known as a self-referential relation, can be useful in situations where you have all the information you need stored in a single table. For example, you may want to move through the managers in the Employees table and have the employees who report to each manager automatically change as you move the record pointer from manager to manager.

To temporarily relate records in a single table

- In the Data Session window, select tables and use the **Relations** button to create relationships.

  – or –

  Use the SET RELATION command.

To create a self-referential relation, open the same table twice: once in one work area and then a second time, with the USE AGAIN command, in another work area. Then use an index to relate the records. For example, the following code establishes and browses a self-referential relationship by creating an index tag named mgr_id that orders the Employee table by the reports_to field:

```
SELECT 0
USE employee ALIAS managers
SELECT 0
USE employee AGAIN ALIAS employees
INDEX ON reports_to TAG mgr_id
SET ORDER TO mgr_id
SELECT managers
SET RELATION TO emp_id INTO employees
BROWSE
SELECT employees
BROWSE
```

When you move the record pointer in the managers Browse window, the employees Browse window is refreshed to show only those employees who report to the selected manager.

Setting Persistent Relationships with Indexes

Indexes are used to establish persistent relationships between tables in a database. Persistent relationships are relationships between database tables that are stored in the database file and are automatically used as default join conditions in the Query and View Designers. Persistent relationships are also displayed in the Database Designer as lines joining table indexes, and as default relationships when you use the tables in the data environment.

Unlike temporary relationships set with the SET RELATION command, persistent relationships do not need to be re-created each time you use tables. However, because persistent relationships do not control the relationship between record pointers in tables, you will use both temporary SET RELATION relationships as well as persistent relationships in developing Visual FoxPro applications. For more information on setting persistent relationships, see Chapter 6, "Creating Databases."

CHAPTER 8

Creating Views

If you want a custom, updatable data set for your application, you can use views. Views combine the qualities of tables and queries: like a query, you can use a view to extract a set of data from one or more related tables; like a table, you can use a view to update the information in the view and permanently store the results to disk. You can also use views to take your data offline to collect or modify data away from your main system.

This chapter covers creating and updating views programmatically, as well as setting properties to optimize the performance of your views. For more information about databases, see Chapter 6, "Creating Databases." If you want more information about tables or indexes, see Chapter 7, "Working with Tables." For more information about the View Designer, see Chapter 5, "Updating Data with Views," in the *User's Guide*.

This chapter includes:

- Creating a View
- Using Views
- Updating Data in a View
- Combining Views
- Working with Offline Data
- Optimizing View Performance

Creating a View

Because views and queries have much in common, your steps in creating a view are like the steps you take in creating a query. You choose the tables and fields you want to include in the view, specify the join conditions used to relate the tables, and specify filters to select specific records. Unlike in queries, in views you can also select how the changes you make to the data in a view are sent to the original, or base tables, from which the view is built.

When you create a view, Visual FoxPro stores a view definition in the current database. The definition contains the names of the tables used in the view, and selected fields and the settings for their properties. When you use the view, the view definition is used to build a SQL statement that defines the view's data set.

For information about view properties, see "Setting View and Connection Properties" later in this chapter, and see DBGETPROP( ) or CURSORGETPROP( ) in Help.

You can create two types of views: local and remote. Remote views use remote SQL syntax to select information from tables on a remote ODBC data source. Local views use Visual FoxPro SQL syntax to select information from tables or views. You can add one or more remote views into a local view, allowing you to access information from Visual FoxPro and remote ODBC data sources in the same view. For information on accessing local and remote data in a single view, see "Combining Local and Remote Data in a View" later in this chapter.

Creating a Local View

You can create a local view with the View Designer or the CREATE SQL VIEW command.

To create a local view

- In the Project Manager, select a database, and then choose **Local Views**, and then choose **New** to open the View Designer.

  – or –

  Use the CREATE SQL VIEW command when a database is open to display the View Designer.

  – or –

  Use the CREATE SQL VIEW command with the AS clause.

For example, the following code creates a view containing all the fields in the products table :

```
CREATE SQL VIEW product_view AS SELECT * ;
   FROM testdata!products
```

The new view name appears in the Project Manager. If you open the Database Designer, the view is displayed in the same manner as a table in the schema, with the view name in place of a table name.

In the previous example, the table name is preceded, or qualified, by the name of the table's database and the "!" symbol. If you qualify the table name when you create a view, Visual FoxPro searches for the table both in the open database list, including the current and any non-current databases, and in the default search path for the table.

If you don't qualify a table with a database name in a view definition, the database must be open before you can use the view.

> **Tip**   When you create or use a view in the Project Manager, the Project Manager opens the database automatically for you. If you subsequently use a view outside the project, you must open the database or ensure the database is in scope before you can use the view.

Creating Views with Stored SQL SELECT Statements

You can use macro substitution to store the SQL SELECT statement into a variable which you can call with the AS clause of the CREATE SQL VIEW command. For example, the following code stores a SQL SELECT statement into the variable `emp_cust_sql`, which is then used to create a new view:

```
emp_cust_sql = "SELECT employee.emp_id, ;
   customer.cust_id, customer.emp_id, ;
   customer.contact, customer.company ;
   FROM employee, customer ;
   WHERE employee.emp_id = customer.emp_id"
CREATE SQL VIEW emp_cust_view AS &emp_cust_sql
```

Modifying Views

You can modify existing views in the View Designer using the Project Manager or the language. If you want to modify the view's SQL string programmatically, you must create a new view. You can then save the new view definition and overwrite the existing view name. To modify a view's properties, see "Setting View and Connection Properties" later in this chapter.

Tip   In the View Designer, you can open an existing view, and then copy the read-only SQL string and paste it in your code as a shortcut in creating a view programmatically.

To modify a view in the View Designer

- In the Project Manager, select the name of the view, and then choose **Modify** to open the View Designer.

  – or –

  Open a database and use the MODIFY VIEW command with the name of the view.

In the View Designer, you can use the Query menu or the View Designer toolbar to add a new table to the view. The following code displays `product_view` in the View Designer:

```
OPEN DATABASE testdata
MODIFY VIEW product_view
```

Renaming a View

You can rename a view from the Project Manager or with the RENAME VIEW command.

To change the name of a view

- In the Project Manager, select a database, and then select the view name, and then choose **Rename File** from the **Project** menu.

  – or –

  Use the RENAME VIEW command.

For example, the following code renames `product_view` to `products_all_view`:

```
RENAME VIEW product_view TO products_all_view
```

The database containing the view must be open before you can rename the view.

Deleting a View

You can delete a view definition from a database using the Project Manager or the DELETE VIEW command. Before deleting the view, make sure the database containing the view is open and set as the current database.

To delete a view

- In the Project Manager, select a database, and then the view name, and then choose **Remove**.

  – or –

  Use the DELETE VIEW or DROP VIEW command.

For example, the following code deletes `product_view` and `customer_view` from the database:

```
DELETE VIEW product_view
DROP VIEW customer_view
```

> **Note**   These commands have the same effect; DROP VIEW is the ANSI SQL standard syntax for deleting a SQL view.

Creating a Multitable View

To access related information that is stored in separate tables, you can create a view and add two or more tables, or you can modify an existing view by adding tables. To add the tables, you can use the View Designer or the CREATE SQL VIEW command. After adding the tables, you can expand your control of the view results using the join condition you define between the tables.

To create a multitable view

- In the Project Manager, create a view and add the tables you want in the View Designer.

  – or –

  Open a database and use the CREATE SQL VIEW command, adding table names to the FROM clause and join conditions.

Just adding the tables to the CREATE SQL VIEW command produces a cross-product. You need to specify a join condition in either the FROM clause or the WHERE clause of the statement to match related records between the tables. If persistent relationships between the tables exist, they are automatically used as join conditions.

Defining and Modifying Join Conditions

Typically, to define a join condition, you use the relationships established on the primary and foreign key fields between the tables. For example, you might want to find information on the orders, including information on the customer who placed the order. You can create a view using the Customer and Orders tables. You specify a join condition to compare values in the fields they have in common and, usually, return those that are equal. In the example, Customer and Orders both have a Customer ID field.

To define join conditions in a view

- In the Project Manager, create or modify a view, and then add the tables you want in the View Designer.

  – or –

  Open a database and use the CREATE SQL VIEW command, adding table names to the FROM clause and join conditions to the FROM clause.

Inner joins specified in the View Designer and displayed in the SELECT – SQL statement

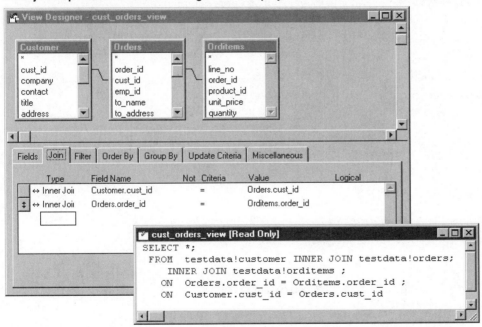

The following code creates the new view as described in the example above, using the FROM clause to specify the join conditions for the view:

```
OPEN DATABASE testdata
CREATE SQL VIEW cust_orders_view AS ;
   SELECT * FROM testdata!customer ;
      INNER JOIN testdata!orders ;
      ON customer.cust_id = orders.cust_id
```

The join condition has several aspects: the type of join, the fields to join on, and the operator for comparing the fields. In this case, which is an inner join, only rows from the customer table that match one or more records in the orders table are included in the result.

To change the results of the view to meet your specific needs, you can specify:

- Fields in the join

- Comparison operators between the fields

- A sequence of joins, if you have two tables in your view

- The type of join

Specifying joins on fields other than the primary and foreign keys can be useful in specific instances, but are not used in most views.

By changing the comparison operator, you can control which records are compared and returned in a manner similar to a filter. For example, if you are using a date field in the join, you can use the comparison operator to include only records before or after a certain date.

For more information about the sequence of joins, see "Defining Multiple Join Conditions" later in this chapter.

Choosing a different join type allows you to expand your query results to include both records that match the join condition and those that do not. If you have more than two tables in your view, you can change your results by changing the order of joins in the FROM clause.

You can modify the join types in your view using the View Designer or the language.

To modify a join type

- Select the **Join** tab.

  – or –

  Double-click the join line.

  – or –

  Open a database and use the CREATE SQL VIEW command, adding table names and join conditions to the FROM clause.

Including Non-Matching Records in Results

If you want to include non-matching rows in your results, you can use an outer join. For example, you might want a list of all customers and whether or not they have placed an order. In addition, for customers that have placed orders, you might want the order numbers included in the view. When you use an outer join, the empty fields of the non-matching rows return null values.

You can also use the language to create this view by using the following code:

```
OPEN DATABASE testdata
CREATE SQL VIEW cust_orders_view AS ;
   SELECT * FROM testdata!customer ;
      LEFT OUTER JOIN testdata!orders ;
      ON customer.cust_id = orders.cust_id
```

To control which non-matching records are included in your view, you can choose from the following join types.

To	Use
Return only records from both tables that match the comparison condition set between the two fields in the join condition.	Inner join
Return all records from the table to the left of the JOIN keyword and only matching records from the table to the right of the keyword.	Left outer join
Return all records from the table to the right of the JOIN keyword and only matching records from the table to the left of the keyword.	Right outer join
Return matching and non-matching records from both tables	Full outer join

Defining Multiple Join Conditions

If you create views or queries with more than two tables, you can change the results by the order your join conditions are specified. For example, you might want to find information on the orders, including information on the employee who made the sale and the customer who placed the order. You can create a view using the customer, orders, and employee tables and specify inner join conditions on the fields they have in common: customer and orders both have a customer ID field; orders and employee both have an employee ID field.

This view has the following underlying SQL statement:

```
OPEN DATABASE testdata
CREATE SQL VIEW cust_orders_emp_view AS ;
   SELECT * FROM testdata!customer ;
      INNER JOIN testdata!orders ;
      ON customer.cust_id = orders.cust_id ;
      INNER JOIN testdata!employee ;
      ON orders.emp_id = employee.emp_id
```

Using Joins in the WHERE Clause

You can specify your join conditions in the WHERE clause; however, you cannot specify a join type as you can in joins in the FROM clause. For remote views, the join clause always appears in the WHERE clause.

The following code creates the same view as the previous example, using the WHERE clause to specify the join conditions for the view:

```
OPEN DATABASE testdata
CREATE SQL VIEW cust_orders_emp_view AS ;
   SELECT * FROM testdata!customer, ;
      testdata!orders, testdata!employee ;
   WHERE customer.cust_id = orders.cust_id ;
   AND orders.emp_id = employee.emp_id
```

Accessing Remote Data

When you want to use data located on a remote server, you create a remote view. To create a remote view, you must first be able to connect to a data source.

Connecting to a Remote Data Source

A remote data source is typically a remote server for which you've installed an ODBC driver and set up an ODBC data source name. To have a valid data source, you must ensure that ODBC is installed. From within Visual FoxPro, you can define a data source and connections.

For more information about setting up an ODBC data source, see Chapter 1, "Installing Visual FoxPro," in the *Installation Guide*.

Defining a Connection

In Visual FoxPro, you can create and store a named connection definition in a database, which you can then refer to by name when you create a remote view. You can also set properties of the named connection to optimize the communication between Visual FoxPro and the remote data source. When you activate a remote view, the view's connection becomes the pipeline to the remote data source.

To create a named connection

- In the Project Manager, select **Connections**, and then choose **New** to open the Connection Designer.

  – or –

  Open a database and use the CREATE CONNECTION command to open the **Connection Designer**.

  – or –

  Use the CREATE CONNECTION command with a connection name.

For example, to create a connection in the testdata database that stores the information needed to connect to the ODBC data source sqlremote, you can enter the following code:

```
OPEN DATABASE testdata
CREATE CONNECTION remote_01 DATASOURCE sqlremote userid password
```

Visual FoxPro displays `remote_01` as the name of the connection in the Project Manager.

Creating a named connection in your database does not use any network or remote resources, because Visual FoxPro doesn't activate the connection until you use the view. Until you activate the connection, the named connection merely exists as a connection definition stored as a row in the database's .dbc file. When you use a remote view, Visual FoxPro uses the named connection referenced in the view to create a live connection to the remote data source, and then sends the request for data to the remote source using the active connection as the pipeline.

You can optionally create a view that specifies only the name of the data source, rather than a connection name. When you use the view, Visual FoxPro uses the ODBC information about the data source to create and activate a connection to the data source. When you close the view, the connection is closed.

Naming Precedence for Connections and Data Sources

When you use the CREATE SQL VIEW command with the CONNECTION clause, you specify a name that represents either a connection or a data source. Visual FoxPro first searches the current database for a connection with the name you specified. If no connection with the specified name exists in the database, then Visual FoxPro looks for an established ODBC data source with the specified name. If your current database contains a named connection with the same name as an ODBC data source on your system, Visual FoxPro will find and use the named connection.

Displaying ODBC Login Prompts

When you use a view whose connection login information is not fully specified, Visual FoxPro might display a data source-specific box that prompts you for the missing information.

You can control whether Visual FoxPro prompts you for information that was left unspecified at connection time.

To control the display of ODBC login prompts

- In the Project Manager, select the name of the connection, and then choose **Modify** to open the Connection Designer.

- In the **Display ODBC login prompts** area, choose an option.

  – or –

  Use the DispLogin property of the DBSETPROP( ) or SQLSETPROP( ) functions.

Using an Existing Connection

You can use an existing named connection to create a remote view. You can see a list of the connections available in a database by using the Project Manager or the DISPLAY CONNECTIONS command.

To determine existing connections

- In the Project Manager, select a database, and then select **Connections**.

  – or –

  Use the DISPLAY CONNECTIONS command.

For example, the following code displays the connections in the `testdata` database:

```
OPEN DATABASE testdata
DISPLAY CONNECTIONS
```

Creating a Remote View

Once you have a valid data source or named connection, you can create a remote view using the Project Manager or the language. A remote view is similar to a local view, but you add a connection or data source name when you define the view. The remote view's SQL statement uses the native server dialect.

To create a remote view

- In the Project Manager, select a database, select **Remote Views**, and then choose **New** to open the View Designer.

  – or –

  Use the CREATE SQL VIEW command with the REMOTE and/or the CONNECTION clause.

If you use the CONNECTION clause with the CREATE SQL VIEW command, you don't need to include the REMOTE keyword. Visual FoxPro identifies the view as a remote view by the presence of the CONNECTION keyword. For example, if you have the `products` table from the Testdata database on a remote server, the following code creates a remote view of the `products` table:

```
OPEN DATABASE testdata
CREATE SQL VIEW product_remote_view ;
   CONNECTION remote_01 ;
   AS SELECT * FROM products
```

You can use a data source name rather than a connection name when you create a remote view. You can also choose to omit a connection or data source name when you use the CREATE SQL VIEW command with the REMOTE clause. Visual FoxPro then displays the Selection Connection or Datasource dialog box, from which you can choose a valid connection or data source.

After you create a view, you can open the Database Designer and see that the view is in the schema displayed in the same manner as a table, with the view name and icon in place of a table name and icon.

If you join two or more tables in the Remote View Designer, the Designer uses inner joins (or equi-joins) and places the join condition in the WHERE clause. If you want to use an outer join, the Remote View Designer provides only left outer joins, the syntax supported by ODBC. If you need right or full outer joins or just want to use a native syntax for a left outer join, create the view programmatically.

Using Views

After you've created a view, you can use the view to display and update data. You can also modify the properties of a view to increase view performance. You treat a view like a table:

- Open the view with the USE command and include the name of the view.
- Close the view with the USE command.
- Display view records in a Browse window.
- Display open view aliases in the Data Session window.
- Use the view as a data source, such as in a text or Grid control, form, or report.

You can use a view through the Project Manager or the language.

To use a view

- In the Project Manager, select a database, choose the name of the view, and then choose **Browse** to display the view in a Browse window.

  – or –

  Access the view programmatically with the USE command.

The following code displays `product_view` in a Browse window:

```
OPEN DATABASE testdata
USE product_view
BROWSE
```

When you use a view, the view is opened as a cursor in its own work area. If the view is based on local tables, Visual FoxPro also opens the base tables in separate work areas. The base tables for a view are the tables accessed by the SELECT – SQL statement you include in the CREATE SQL VIEW command when you create a view. In the previous example, using `product_view` automatically opens the `products` table as well.

Data Session window displays the view and its base table

View is open in a work area.

View's base table is open in a separate work area.

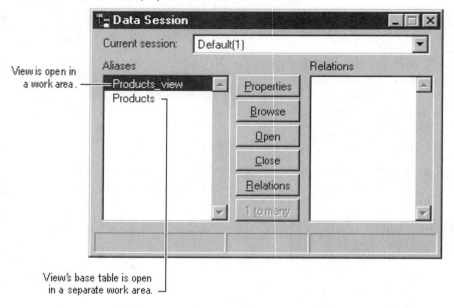

When a view is based on remote tables, the base tables are not opened in work areas. Only the name of the remote view appears in the Data Session window.

Limiting the Scope of a View

When you access a remote data source, you're accessing potentially massive amounts of data. You can limit the scope of data selected into your view to be just the records you need at a given moment. This reduces network traffic and increases the performance of your view. For example, if you want to view information about customers in a particular country and their orders, you gain performance by downloading only the records for that country, rather than all customers, into your view.

One method you can use to limit the scope of your view is to add a WHERE clause to your view's SQL statement. If you want to look at the records for the customers in Sweden, you would create this SQL WHERE clause for your view:

```
SELECT * FROM customer ;
   WHERE customer.country = 'Sweden'
```

This code would effectively limit the scope of your view by downloading records for just the Swedish customers, but it would also require that you create a separate view for each country, because the actual value for one country's `customer.country` is hard-coded into your view's SELECT statement.

Creating a Parameterized View

You can limit the scope of a view without creating a separate view for each subset of records by creating a parameterized view. A parameterized view creates a WHERE clause in the view's SQL SELECT statement that limits the records downloaded to only those records that meet the conditions of the WHERE clause built using the value supplied for the parameter. This value can be supplied at run time, or passed programmatically to the view.

In the case of the previous example, you can create one view that allows you to download records for any country, simply by entering the country's name as you use the view.

To create a parameterized view

- In the View Designer, choose **View Parameters** from the **Query** menu.

  – or –

  Use the CREATE SQL VIEW command with a "?" symbol and a parameter.

The parameter you supply is evaluated as a Visual FoxPro expression and the value is sent as part of the view's SQL statement. If the evaluation fails, Visual FoxPro prompts for the parameter value. For example, if you have the `customer` table from the Testdata database on a remote server, the following code creates a parameterized remote view that limits the view to those customers whose country matches the value supplied for the `?cCountry` parameter:

```
OPEN DATABASE testdata
CREATE SQL VIEW customer_remote_view ;
   CONNECTION remote_01 ;
   AS SELECT * FROM customer ;
   WHERE customer.country = ?cCountry
```

You can supply a value for `?cCountry` programmatically when you use the view. For example, you could type the following code:

```
cCountry = 'Sweden'
USE Testdata!customer_remote_view IN 0
BROWSE
```

Visual FoxPro displays the customer records for Swedish companies in the Browse window for `Customer_remote_view`.

View displaying records whose country matches the supplied parameter

Cust_id	Company	Address	City	Country	Contact
BERGS	Berglunds snabbköp	Berguvsvägen 8	Luleå	Sweden	Christina Berglund
FOLKO	Folk och fä HB	Åkergatan 24	Bräcke	Sweden	Maria Larsson

Tip   If your parameter is an expression, enclose the parameter expression in parentheses. This allows the entire expression to be evaluated as part of the parameter.

Prompting for User Input of a Parameter Value

If your parameter is not a variable or expression, you might want to prompt the user to supply the parameter value by using a quoted string as your view parameter. When you create a view parameter using a quoted string after the "?" symbol, Visual FoxPro does not interpret the string as an expression. Rather, you are prompted to enter the value for the parameter at run time. For example, the following code creates a parameterized remote view that prompts the user to supply a value for the ?'my customer id' parameter:

```
OPEN DATABASE testdata
CREATE SQL VIEW customer_remote_view ;
   CONNECTION remote_01 ;
   AS SELECT * FROM customer ;
   WHERE customer.cust_id = ?'my customer id'
USE customer_remote_view
```

When you use the view in the previous example, the View Parameter dialog box is displayed.

View Parameter dialog box prompts for the value in quoted string

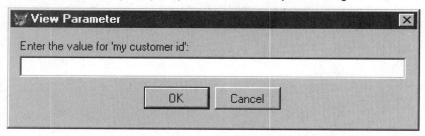

After you enter a valid customer ID, Visual FoxPro retrieves the record that matches that ID. If you enter the value "ALFKI" in the previous example and then browse Customer_remote_view, you see the customer record displayed in the Browse window.

Browse window displaying record for cust_id ALFKI

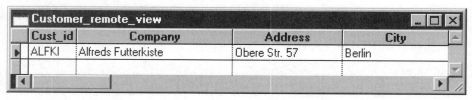

By using a quoted string as a view parameter, you ensure that Visual FoxPro will always prompt the user for the parameter value.

Opening Multiple Instances of a View

You can open multiple instances of a view in separate work areas, just as you can open a table in more than one work area. Unlike tables, views fetch a new data set by default each time you use the view.

To open a view in multiple work areas

- In the Project Manager, choose the name of the view, and then choose Browse to display the view in a Browse window. Repeat this process to open the view in additional work areas.

  – or –

  In the Data Session window, choose **Open**, and then the name of the view. Repeat this process to open the view in additional work areas.

  – or –

  Access the view programmatically with the USE command.

When you access the view programmatically with the USE command, you can choose to open another instance of a view without requerying the data source. This is particularly useful when you want to open a remote view in multiple work areas without waiting for data to be downloaded from a remote data source.

To use a view again without downloading data

- Use the NOREQUERY clause with the USE command.

  – or –

  Use the AGAIN clause with the USE command.

The following code uses the NOREQUERY clause to display the cursor fetched from the first instance of product_remote_view in two Browse windows without requerying the remote data source:

```
OPEN DATABASE testdata
CREATE SQL VIEW product_remote_view ;
   CONNECTION remote_01 ;
   AS SELECT * FROM products
USE product_remote_view
BROWSE
SELECT 0
USE product_remote_view NOREQUERY
BROWSE
```

You can specify a session number with the NOREQUERY clause. If you don't specify a session number, Visual FoxPro searches in all sessions. If an opened result set is found for the view, a cursor is opened again on the same result set. If no open result set is found, a new result set is fetched for the view. As is true for tables, if the view is not found, a new view cursor is opened for you.

If you want Visual FoxPro to search only the current session for an opened result set for your view, you can use the AGAIN clause. The following code displays `product_remote_view` in two Browse windows:

```
OPEN DATABASE testdata
USE product_remote_view
BROWSE
USE product_remote_view AGAIN in 0
BROWSE
```

When you use the AGAIN clause, Visual FoxPro looks for an existing view cursor in the current session, and opens an additional alias pointing to this view cursor. Opening another instance of a view with the AGAIN clause is the equivalent of issuing a USE with the NOREQUERY clause with the current session number.

Displaying the Structure of a View

You can open and display just the structure of a view with the NODATA clause of the USE command. This option is particularly useful when you want to look at the structure of a remote view without waiting to download data.

To open a view without data

- Access the view programmatically with the USE command and the NODATA clause.

The following code displays `customer_remote_view` without data in a Browse window:

```
OPEN DATABASE testdata
USE customer_remote_view NODATA in 0
BROWSE
```

Using a view with the NODATA clause always opens a new view cursor. The NODATA clause is the fastest way to get the view's structure because it creates the smallest cursor possible on the remote data source. When you use the NODATA clause, Visual FoxPro creates a WHERE clause for the view that always returns a false value. Because no records on the data source can meet the WHERE clause condition, no rows are selected into the remote data source's cursor. Your view is retrieved quickly because you're not waiting for the remote data source to build a potentially large cursor.

> **Tip**   Using the NODATA clause is more efficient than using a MaxRecords property setting of 0 on your view or cursor. When you use the MaxRecords property, you must wait while the remote data source builds a cursor for the view containing all data rows that meet the view's normal WHERE clause conditions. Rows from the full remote view cursor are then downloaded according to the setting of the MaxRecords property.

Creating an Index on a View

You can create local indexes on a view, just as on a table, using the INDEX ON command. Unlike indexes you build on a table, local indexes you create on a view are not stored persistently: they vanish when you close the view.

Tip   Consider the size of your view's result set when deciding whether to create a local index on a view. Indexing a large result set can take a long time, and slow down performance of your view.

For more information on creating indexes, see Chapter 7, "Working with Tables," or see INDEX in Help.

Creating Temporary Relationships on Views

You can create temporary relationships between view indexes or between view indexes and table indexes with the SET RELATION command.

For better performance, when you use the SET RELATION command to relate a view and a table, make the view the parent and the table the child in the relationship. Making the table the child is more efficient because the structural index of the table is constantly maintained, quickly accessed, and can be used by the data environment to order the records. The index on the view must be rebuilt each time the view is activated and takes more time than the index on the table. An index on a view is not part of the view definition; so, if you use a data environment, the view cannot be the child because the index on the child has to exist as part of the definition, which views don't support.

Setting View and Connection Properties

When you create a view, the view inherits property settings, such as UpdateType and UseMemoSize, from the environment cursor, or cursor 0 of the current session. You can change these default property settings by using the CURSORSETPROP( ) function with 0 as the cursor number. After the view has been created and is stored in a database, you can change view properties with the DBSETPROP( ) function. The changes you make to view properties in a database are stored persistently in the database.

When you use a view, the property settings stored for the view in the database are inherited by the active view cursor. You can change these properties on the active cursor using the CURSORSETPROP( ) function for the view cursor. Changes you make with the CURSORSETPROP( ) function are temporary. The temporary settings for the active view disappear when you close the view; the temporary settings for cursor 0 go away when you close the Visual FoxPro session.

Connections inherit properties in a similar fashion. Default properties for connection 0 are inherited when you create and store a named connection in a database. You can change these default property settings for connection 0 with the SQLSETPROP( ) function. After the connection has been created and is stored in a database, you can change connection properties with the DBSETPROP( ) function. When you use a connection, the property settings stored for the connection in the database are inherited by the active connection. You can change these properties on the active connection using the SQLSETPROP( ) function for the connection handle.

Both views and connections can use a named ODBC data source. If you use an ODBC data source in a view, the connection inherits properties from the session defaults. For more information on CURSORSETPROP( ), DBSETPROP( ), and SQLSETPROP( ), see Help.

The following diagram illustrates property inheritance for views and connections. The gray lines represent the flow of property inheritance; the black lines represent Visual FoxPro commands.

View and Connection properties and their inheritance

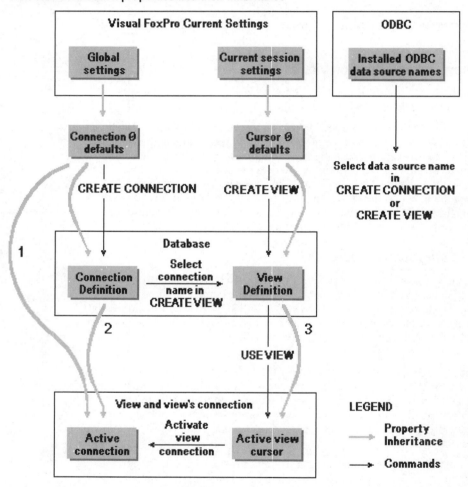

[1] If view is based on an ODBC data source, active connection properties are inherited from connection Ø.

[2] If view is based on a database connection, active connection properties are inherited from the connection definition in the database.

[3] Active view cursor's properties are inherited from the view definition in the database.

Changing Default Data Types When Downloading Remote Views

When you create a view, the DataType property for all fields in the view is set to a default value. The value is the data type letter (D, G, I, L, M, P, T, Y) for fixed-length data types and the letter followed by precision and scale parameters in parentheses (B(*d*), C(*n*), N(*n,d*)) for variable length types. This property is read-only for local views. For a list of default data types, see "Downloading and Uploading Remote View Data" in Chapter 21, "Implementing a Client/Server Application."

You can modify the setting of the DataType property for the remote view field with the DBSETPROP( ) function as shown in this table.

ODBC data type of remote field	Possible data types in Visual FoxPro cursor
SQL_CHAR SQL_VARCHAR SQL_LONGVARCHAR	Character or Memo[1] (default); also General or Picture
SQL_BINARY SQL_VARBINARY SQL_LONGVARBINARY	Memo (default); also Character, General, or Picture
SQL_DECIMAL SQL_NUMERIC	Numeric or Currency[2] (default); also Character, Integer, or Double
SQL_BIT	Logical (default); also Character
SQL_TINYINT SQL_SMALLINT SQL_INTEGER	Integer (default); also Character, Numeric, Double, or Currency
SQL_BIGINT	Character (default); also Integer, Numeric, Double, or Currency
SQL_REAL SQL_FLOAT SQL_DOUBLE	Double (default); the number of decimal places is the value of SET DECIMALS in Visual FoxPro; also Character, Integer, Numeric, or Currency
SQL_DATE	Date (default); also Character or DateTime
SQL_TIME	DateTime[3] (default); also Character
SQL_TIMESTAMP	DateTime[4] (default); also Character or Date

1. If the ODBC field width is less than the value of the cursor property UseMemoSize, it becomes a Character field in the Visual FoxPro cursor; otherwise, it becomes a Memo field.

2. If the server field is a money data type, it becomes a Currency data type in Visual FoxPro.

3. The day defaults to 1/1/1900.

4. If the value in the SQL_TIMESTAMP field contains fractions of seconds, the fractions are truncated when the value is converted to a Visual FoxPro DateTime data type.

Using the DataType Property

You can use the DataType property to choose a different data type than the default. For example, you might want to download a server timestamp field to Visual FoxPro, but the default data type mapping into a Visual FoxPro DateTime field would truncate any fractions of seconds stored in the server timestamp. You might use the DataType property to map the remote timestamp field into a Visual FoxPro character field to preserve the fractions of seconds.

Closing a View's Base Tables

The local base tables opened automatically when you use a view are not automatically closed when you close a view; you must explicitly close them. This is consistent with the SELECT – SQL command.

Updating Data in a View

You update data in a view just as you would update data in a table. With a view you can also update the view's base tables. Views are, by default, buffered with optimistic row buffering. You can change this to table buffering; for more information on buffering, see Chapter 17, "Programming for Shared Access."

You can update data in a view through the interface or the language. The first step in updating view data is to make the view updatable. In most cases, the default property settings automatically prepare the view to be updatable, but updates are not sent to the data source until you instruct Visual FoxPro to do so by setting the SendUpdates property to On.

A view uses five properties to control updates. These properties are listed here with their default settings:

View Update Properties and Default Settings

View Property	Default Setting
Tables	Includes all tables that have updatable fields and have at least one primary key field.
KeyField	Database key fields and remote primary keys on the table.
UpdateName	Table_name.column_name for all fields.
Updatable	All fields except the primary key fields.
SendUpdates	Defaults to the session default, which is originally set to false (.F.); if you change it to true (.T.), that becomes the default for all views created in the session.
CompareMemo	Defaults to true (.T.), means that memo fields are included in the WHERE clause and used for detecting update conflicts.

While all five properties are required to update data, the SendUpdates property serves as a "master switch" controlling whether or not updates are sent. As you develop your application, you might set the SendUpdates property off and then configure the other properties to enable updates to the fields you want updated. When you're ready to test your application, you can set the SendUpdates property on to start updates flowing.

In some more complex situations, the default update settings may not provide updates for a view you create through the language. To enable updates, look at the default settings for each of the update properties and adjust them as needed. You can also specify additional properties, such as UpdateType, WhereType, and so on, according to your preferences. For a complete list of view properties, see DBGETPROP( ) in Help.

To make a view updatable from the View Designer

- In the View Designer, select the **Update Criteria** tab and verify the default settings.

The default settings for views you create through the View Designer usually prepare the view to be updatable; you only need to select the Send SQL Updates check box to turn updates on. You can further modify the tables, fields, SQL WHERE clause, and Update options as you desire.

To make a view updatable by setting view update properties

- Examine the current default settings with the DISPLAY DATABASE command, and then modify properties for the view definition as you desire with the DBSETPROP( ) function.

The following example lists the steps you would follow to specify the five view update properties programmatically:

> **Note**   The default View properties may supply all the information needed to update your view.

1. Set the Tables property with at least one table name.

   For example, if you have a view based on the `customer` table called `cust_view`, you could set the table name with the following function:

   ```
   DBSETPROP('cust_view','View','Tables','customer')
   ```

   > **Tip**   If a table appears as a qualifier in the UpdateName property but is not included in the default list for the Tables property, the table might not have a primary key field specified. Make the table updatable by adding the field you consider to be a key field to the KeyField property list, and then add the table to the Tables property list.

2. Set the KeyField property with one or more local Visual FoxPro field names that together define a unique key for the update table.

   Using the same example, you could make `cust_id` the key field using the following code:

   ```
   DBSETPROP('cust_view.cust_id','Field','KeyField',.T.)
   ```

Caution   Be sure the key field(s) you specify define a unique key both in the base table you want to update and in the view.

3. Map the view fields to their base table fields with the UpdateName property. This property is particularly useful when your view is based on a join of two tables with a common field name, or when the fields are aliased in the view. To update the desired base table, you map the Visual FoxPro view field name to the base table field and table name.

```
DBSETPROP('cust_view.cust_id','Field','UpdateName',;
        'customer.cust_id')
```

Tip   To avoid creating synonym fields in your view, you can qualify field names in the SQL statement you use to build your view. Then use the Visual FoxPro UpdateName property of the view to map each qualified field to the correct base table and field name.

4. Specify the scope of fields you want to update with the Updatable property. You should specify only those fields also specified with the UpdateName property.

```
DBSETPROP('cust_view.cust_id','Field','Updatable',;
        .T.)
```

5. Set the SendUpdates property to true (.T.). This is the master switch that instructs Visual FoxPro to create and send updates to any of the tables and fields you've specified as updatable.

```
DBSETPROP('cust_view','View','SendUpdates',.T.)
```

When you use DBSETPROP( ) to set properties on a view before you use the view, the settings are stored in the database and are used automatically whenever you activate the view. Once the view is active, you can use CURSORSETPROP( ) to change property settings on the active view. Property settings you set on an active view with CURSORSETPROP( ) are not saved when you close the view.

Updating Multiple Tables in a View

You can update multiple base tables from a view. When your view combines two or more tables, you set properties to ensure that only the many side of the view query is updatable.

Views are updated on a table-by-table basis. You must ensure that for each table accessed in a view, the key field set is a unique key for both the view result set and the base table.

To make a multitable view updatable

*   In the View Designer, choose the **Update Criteria** tab, and then select the tables and field names you want to update.

    – or –

    Use the DBSETPROP( ) function.

In most cases, the default values provided by Visual FoxPro prepare a multitable view to be updatable, even when you create the view programmatically. The following code example creates and explicitly sets properties to update a two-table view. You can use this example as a guide for customizing update property settings on a view.

Updating Multiple Tables in a View

Code	Comments
``CREATE SQL VIEW emp_cust_view AS ;
SELECT employee.emp_id, ;
employee.phone, customer.cust_id, ;
customer.emp_id, customer.contact, ;
customer.company ;
FROM employee, customer ;
WHERE employee.emp_id = customer.emp_id```	Create a view that accesses fields from two tables.
``DBSETPROP('emp_cust_view', 'View', 'Tables',
'employee, customer')```	Set the tables to be updated.
``DBSETPROP('emp_cust_view.emp_id', 'Field', ;
'UpdateName', 'employee.emp_id')
DBSETPROP('emp_cust_view.phone', 'Field', ;
'UpdateName', 'employee.phone')
DBSETPROP('emp_cust_view.cust_id', 'Field', ;
'UpdateName', 'customer.cust_id')
DBSETPROP('emp_cust_view.emp_id1', 'Field', ;
'UpdateName', 'customer.emp_id')
DBSETPROP('emp_cust_view.contact', 'Field', ;
'UpdateName', 'customer.contact')
DBSETPROP('emp_cust_view.company', 'Field', ;
'UpdateName', 'customer.company')```	Set update names.
``DBSETPROP('emp_cust_view.emp_id', 'Field', ;
'KeyField', .T.)```	Set a single-field unique key for the Employee table.
``DBSETPROP('emp_cust_view.cust_id', 'Field', ;
'KeyField', .T.)
DBSETPROP('emp_cust_view.emp_id1', 'Field', ;
'KeyField', .T.)```	Set a two-field unique key for the Customer table.
``DBSETPROP('emp_cust_view.phone', 'Field', ;
'UpdatableField', .T.)
DBSETPROP('emp_cust_view.contact', 'Field', ;
'UpdatableField', .T.)
DBSETPROP('emp_cust_view.company', 'Field', ;
'UpdatableField', .T.)```	Set the updatable fields. Typically, key fields are not updatable.
``DBSETPROP('emp_cust_view', 'View', ;
'SendUpdates', .T.)```	Activate the update functionality.

(continued)

(continued)

Code	Comments

`GO TOP`
`REPLACE employee.phone WITH "(206)111-2222"`
`REPLACE customer.contact WITH "John Doe"`
	Modify data in the view.

`TABLEUPDATE()`	Commit the changes by updating both the Employee and Customer base tables.

Customizing Views with the Data Dictionary

Because views are stored in a database, you can create:

- Captions

- Comments for the view and view fields

- Default values for view fields

- Field- and row-level rules and rule error messages

The data dictionary features for views are similar in function to their counterparts for database tables. However, you use the language rather than the Table Designer to create captions, comments, default values and rules for views.

Creating Default Values for View Fields

Like default values for table fields, view field default values are stored in the database and are available each time you use the view. Visual FoxPro doesn't compare the default values you create locally with any default values established on the remote data source. You must create default values that are acceptable for the data source.

To assign a default value to a view field

- In the **Fields** tab in the **View Designer**, select a field, and then choose **Properties** and enter the default value for the field.

    – or –

    Use the DefaultValue property of the DBSETPROP( ) function.

For example, you may want your application to limit the amount of merchandise a new customer can order until you've had time to complete a credit check and determine the amount of credit you're willing to extend to that customer. The following example creates a `maxordamt` field with a default value of 1000:

```
OPEN DATABASE testdata
USE VIEW customer_view
?DBSETPROP ('Customer_view.maxordamt', 'Field', 'DefaultValue', 1000)
```

You might also use default values to populate some rows automatically for the user. For example, you might add a Grid control to an order entry form that is based on a remote view of an order line items table. The order_id field is the key field that maps each row of the Grid to its counterpart in the remote order line items table. Because the order ID for each row in the grid will be the same for one order, you can use a default value to save keystrokes by populating the order_id field automatically.

Tip   If one of your application's business rules requires that a field contain an entry, providing a default value helps to ensure that a particular field-level or record-level rule will not be violated.

Creating Rules on View Fields and Rows

You can create local versions of remote data source rules to:

- Reduce response time.
- Reduce impact on network resources.
- Test data before sending it to the remote data source.
- Prevent sending faulty data to the remote data source.

Visual FoxPro doesn't compare the rules you create locally with remote rules. You must create rules that are acceptable for the data source. If remote rules change, you must change your local rules to match.

To create a rule on a view field or row

- In the **Fields** tab in the **View Designer**, select a field, and then choose **Properties** and enter the rule expression and message text for the field.

  – or –

  Use the RuleExpression and RuleText properties of the DBSETPROP( ) function.

For example, the following code creates a field-level rule on orditems_view that prevents entering a quantity of less than 1:

```
OPEN DATABASE testdata
USE VIEW orditems_view
DBSETPROP('Orditems_view.quantity','Field', ;
        'RuleExpression', 'quantity >= 1')
DBSETPROP('Orditems_view.quantity','Field', ;
        'RuleText', ;
'"Quantities must be greater than or equal to 1"')
```

You can also use the DBSETPROP( ) function to create row-level rules. For more information on DBSETPROP( ), see Help.

Combining Views

You can build a view that is based on other views. You might want to do this if you need a subset of the information available in multiple other views, or if you want to combine local and remote data in a single view. A view based on other views, or on a combination of local tables and local or remote views, is called a multitiered view. The view that combines other views is the top-level view. You can have multiple levels of views in between the top-level view and the local or remote base tables. When you use a multitiered view, the views on which the top-level view is based and any Visual FoxPro base tables used in the top-level or intermediate-level views appear in the Data Session window. Remote tables do not appear in the Data Session window.

Combining Local and Remote Data in a View

You can combine local and remote data in a view by creating a new local view based on a local view and a remote view.

To create a view that combines local and remote data

- In the Project Manager, select a database, choose **Local Views**, and choose **New** to open the View Designer. Add any combination of tables, local views, and remote views into your view.

  – or –

  Use the CREATE SQL VIEW command.

For example, to create a local view that combines information from the local Employee table and the remote Orders table, you can use the following code:

```
OPEN DATABASE testdata
CREATE SQL VIEW remote_orders_view ;
   CONNECTION remote_01 ;
   AS SELECT * FROM orders
CREATE SQL VIEW local_employee_remote_orders_view ;
   AS SELECT * FROM testdata!local_employee_view, ;
   testdata!remote_orders_view ;
   WHERE local_employee_view.emp_id = ;
      remote_orders_view.emp_id
```

Updating Local and Remote Data in a View

When you update data in a multitiered view, the updates go down one level, to the view on which the top-level view is based. If you want to update the base tables on which a multitiered view is built, you must issue a TABLEUPDATE command for each view in the structure.

Working with Offline Data

There are times when you might want to display, collect, or modify data independent of the host database. By using the offline view features in Visual FoxPro, you can use views to connect to a host database and create a subset of data for use offline. Then, working offline, you can use the view directly or through an application you create. When you are done, you can upload the changes stored in the view back to the host database.

Some scenarios where offline views are useful include:

- A data warehousing situation, where large databases are maintained centrally on MIS servers. If you are only interested in data pertaining to, for example, the Marketing department, you can construct a view including only the data that is relevant to you. You can then take the data offline, allow multiple users in the Marketing department to update the data, then commit the changed data to the source database.

- A geographically remote location which requires that you take a subset of data with you on a laptop, modify the data independently of the host database, then update the host database with the changed data at a later time.

- Time-sensitive data. For example, you might want to update data reflecting employee pay raises before the new pay rates actually take effect.

Working with offline views

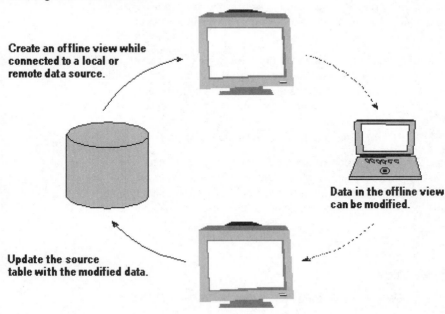

Create an offline view while connected to a local or remote data source.

Data in the offline view can be modified.

Update the source table with the modified data.

To create and use view data offline, you can use the following language features:

- The CREATEOFFLINE( ) function
- The USE *SQLViewName* command with the ADMIN and ONLINE clauses
- The TABLEUPDATE function
- The DROPOFFLINE( ) function

If you plan to use the offline view on a machine other than the one on which you created the offline view, you must prepare the offline destination by creating a copy of the host database file (.dbc); making sure the ODBC data source used by the view exists on the destination machine; and analyzing your data requirements to determine the contents of the view you need.

Note Use the ODBC Administrator program to install data sources on a machine. You can access the ODBC Administrator program from either the Visual FoxPro program group or from Control Panel.

Creating Offline Views

As with online data, analyze your requirements before creating offline views to determine the design of the views you will need in the offline database. Once you know the subset of data you want to use offline, you can start with an existing view or create a new view. If a view already exists that returns the records you want to use offline, you can use it, or you can create one programmatically. The view you take offline is stored in a .dbf file in the offline database container.

Note If you plan to modify data in an offline view, be sure to make the view updatable before you take it offline. Once a view is offline, you can only set its update properties programmatically; you cannot modify an offline view in the View Designer.

To use an existing view offline

- Use the CREATEOFFLINE( ) function and the name of the view.

For example, if you want to go to client sites to update accounts, add customers, and record new sales, you need the customer information as well as current orders and the online product descriptions. You might have a view called `customerinfo` that combines information from the Customers table, Orders table, and OrderItems table. To create the view, use this code:

```
CREATEOFFLINE("customerinfo")
```

To programmatically create a view offline

- Use the CREATE SQL VIEW command, followed by the CREATEOFFLINE( ) command.

For example, the following code creates a view that displays data from the `Products` table and the `Inventory` table from the online database. Since no update criteria are specified, this view is read-only:

```
CREATE SQL VIEW showproducts ;
   CONNECTION dsource ;
   AS SELECT * FROM Products INNER JOIN Inventory ;
   ON Products.ProductID = Inventory.ProductID ;
CREATEOFFLINE("showproducts")
```

Displaying and Modifying Offline Data

After you create the view for your offline data, you can use it as you would any view in your application: you can add, change, and delete records. Multiple users can access the offline view concurrently using the same database in shared mode. If you decide you do not want to keep any of the changes, you can revert the information to reflect the original information.

Using Data Offline

Using the offline view, you can display and update data much as you do online with the same forms, reports, or applications. For example, the following code opens the view `Showproducts`:

```
USE Showproducts
```

> **Tip** If you are not getting the subset of data that you expected, check the optimization settings for the remote view. If you set the MaxRecords property using the DBSETPROP( ) function, only that many records appear in your views offline. However, if you include a Memo field in the field list of your view, it is automatically included in the result set even if FetchMemo is set to false (.F.).

Administering Data Offline

In some cases — especially in a multiple-user environment where data is modified by numerous people — you might want to examine changes made to the offline view before committing the changes to the source database. With the USE command and the ADMIN clause, you can see all changes that have been committed to a view since it was taken offline. You can then selectively revert changes that have been made without being connected to the data source. For example, the following code opens the view `Showproducts` in administrator mode:

```
USE Showproducts ADMIN
```

Updating to Online Data

After you're finished offline, you can update the data on the sever using the same table update transactions you usually use with online data. When working with remote data, keep in mind the following tips:

- For single record updates, use automatic transactions.

- For batch updates, use manual transactions.

- As necessary, include code to detect update conflicts, create a log of conflicts, and resolve conflicts.

Before you can process your updates, you need to use the USE command and the ONLINE keyword to reconnect to the host database. After you issue the command, Visual FoxPro attempts to locate the host database using the data source information stored in the view. After the connection is established, you can use TABLEUPDATE( ) to process the updates stored in the offline data.

To make sure the connection information is correct regardless of the location of either the host or view tables, you need to use connection string syntax rather than a named connection.

Updating Batches of Records in Local Tables

To process a batch of changes against local tables, you can use manual transactions that allow you to process the entire batch of changes within a single transaction rather a series of separate transactions.

Updating local tables with offline views

Code	Comments
`USE myofflineview ONLINE EXCLUSIVE`	Reconnect to the host and open the view

`BEGIN TRANSACTION`
`IF TABLEUPDATE (2, .F., "myofflineview")`
`   END TRANSACTION`
`ELSE`
`   MESSAGEBOX("Error Occurred: Update unsuccessful.")`
`   ROLLBACK`
`ENDIF`
	Check for update conflicts and update as appropriate.

Updating Batches of Records in Remote Tables

To process a batch of changes against remote tables, use manual transactions: begin with TABLEUPDATE( ) and finish processing with either SQLCOMMIT( ) or SQLROLLBACK( ).

To set the connection to manage your transactions manually, you need to use CURSORGETPROP( ) on the view cursor to get the connection handle, then set the Transactions property to manual mode.

In the following code, the current connection identification for the view, myview, is stored into hConn1. hConn1 is used to set the Transactions property to "2" for manual transactions.

```
hConn1 = CURSORGETPROP("CONNECTHANDLE","myview") ;
SQLSETPROP(hConn1,"TRANSACTIONS",2)
```

After you set the connection to handle the updates, you can use TABLEUPDATE( ) to handle your transactions.

If the host tables reside on a remote server, such as SQL Server, you might use the following code as a guideline.

Updating remote tables with offline views

Code	Comment
`USE myofflineview ONLINE EXCLUSIVE`	Reconnect to the host and open the view.

`SQLSetProp(liviewhandle,"transactions",2)`
`SQLSetProp(custviewhandle,"transactions",2)`
`SQLSetProp(ordviewhandle,"transactions",2)`
	Setting the connections on the views to handle transaction manually.

`IF NOT TABLEUPDATE(.T.,.F.,"lineitemsview")`	Handling updates and update conflicts.

```
IF NOT TABLEUPDATE(.T.,.F.,"lineitemsview")
   =SQLROLLBACK(ordviewhandle)
   =MESSAGEBOX("Can't update line items table")
   IF NOT TableUpdate(.T.,.F.,"ordersview")
      =SQLROLLBACK(liviewhandle)
      =MESSAGEBOX("unable to update the orders table")
      IF NOT TABLEUPDATE(.T.,.F.,"customerview")
         =SQLROLLBACK(custviewhandle)
         =MESSAGEBOX("Can't update customer table")
      Else *# check out failure scenarios
         IF NOT SQLCOMMIT(liviewhandle)
            =SQLROLLBACK(liviewhandle)
            IF NOT SQLCOMMIT(ordviewhandle)
               =SQLROLLBACK(ordviewhandle)
               IF NOT SQLCOMMIT(custviewhandle)
                  =SQLROLLBACK(custviewhandle)
               ENDIF
            ENDIF
         ENDIF
      ENDIF
   ENDIF
ENDIF
```

Updating One Record

If you are updating a single row, you can use automatic transactions. Because each statement to process an update, delete, or insert is handled as a separate transaction, rollbacks against prior transaction statements are not possible.

```
USE customerview ONLINE EXCLUSIVE
GO TO 3
   IF TABLEUPDATE (0, .F. workarea)
   * conflict handling code
   ENDIF
```

Tip   To update a single record in a local table, use the GETNEXTMODIFIED( ) function.

Canceling Offline Updates

If you decide you want to delete the offline data and convert the view back to an online view, you can use the DROPOFFLINE( ) function.

To cancel offline updates

- Use DROPOFFLINE( ) with the name of the view.

Be sure to check the return values. True (.T.) indicates success and false (.F.) indicates that the view was not closed before the command was issued.

The following code drops all of the changes made to the subset of data in myview. The view remains part of the database, but its current set of data is dropped.

```
DROPOFFLINE("myview")
```

You can delete offline records, but you can't use the PACK, ZAP, or INSERT commands with an offline view.

Optimizing View Performance

You can optimize the performance of your views by setting view properties.

Controlling Progressive Fetching Fetch Size

You can control the number of rows Visual FoxPro progressively fetches at one time from the host database with the FetchSize property of the view and active view cursor. You use DBSETPROP( ) and CURSORSETPROP( ) to set these properties.

Controlling Memo Fetching

You can use the delayed memo fetching feature to speed retrieval of view data. When you choose delayed memo fetching, Visual FoxPro does not retrieve the contents of a Memo field until you choose to open and display the field. Because Visual FoxPro needs the key field and table name to locate a row on the remote data source, you must set the UpdateName or UpdatableFieldList property, the KeyField or KeyFieldList property, and the Tables property for delayed Memo fetching to work. However, you don't have to set the SendUpdates or Updatable properties to on in order to make delayed memo fetching work.

Setting the Maximum Number of Records Downloaded

You can control the amount of data downloaded when you open a view by setting the MaxRecords property. When Visual FoxPro sends a SQL statement to the data source to create a view, the data source builds and stores a result set. The MaxRecords property specifies the maximum number of rows fetched from the remote result set into your view. The default setting is –1, which downloads all rows in the result set.

To control the number of rows downloaded into a view

- From the **Tools** menu, choose **Options** and select the **Remote Data** tab; then in the **Remote view defaults** area, next to the **Maximum records to fetch** box, clear **All**, enter a value in the text box, and then choose **OK**.

  – or –

  Use the MaxRecords property of the DBSETPROP( ) or CURSORSETPROP( ) function.

For example, the following code alters the view definition to limit the number of rows downloaded into the view to 50, regardless of the size of the result set built on the remote data source:

```
OPEN DATABASE testdata
USE VIEW remote_customer_view
?DBSETPROP ('Remote_customer_view', ;    'View','MaxRecords', 50)
```

You can use the CURSORSETPROP( ) function to set the MaxRecords limit for an active view.

> **Tip**   You can't use the MaxRecords property to stop a runaway query, because the MaxRecords property doesn't control the building of the result set. Use the QueryTimeOut property to control the execution time on the remote data source.

Optimizing Filters and Joins

To make optimization decisions for a view or query, you might need to know the execution plan: the order that joins and filter clauses will be evaluated. Using the SYS(3054) function, you can display one of three Rushmore optimization levels. The three levels indicate the degree to which the filter conditions or join conditions were able to use Rushmore optimization. The levels are completely (Full), partially (Partial) or not at all (None).

To display the execution plan for filters

1. In the Command window, type **SYS(3054,1)** to enable SQL ShowPlan.

2. Type your SQL SELECT statement.

   For example, you might type:

```
SELECT * FROM customer, orders ;
AND Upper(country) = "MEXICO"
```

3. On the screen, read the execution plan.

For this example, the screen might display:

```
Using Index Tag Country to optimize table customer
Rushmore Optimization Level for table customer: Full
Rushmore Optimization level for table orders: none
```

4. In the Command window, type **SYS(3054,0)** to turn off SQL ShowPlan.

You can then pass 11 to the SYS function to evaluate joins in the FROM or WHERE clauses.

To display the execution plan for joins

1. In the Command window, type **SYS(3054,11)** to enable SQL ShowPlan.

2. Enter your SQL SELECT statement.

For example, you might type:

```
SELECT * ;
FROM customer INNER JOIN orders ;
    ON customer.cust_id = orders.cust_id ;
WHERE Upper(country) = "MEXICO"
```

3. On the screen, read the execution plan.

For this example, the screen might display:

```
Using Index Tag Country to optimize table customer
Rushmore Optimization Level for table customer: Full
Rushmore Optimization level for table orders: none
Joining table customer and table orders using Cust_id
```

4. In the Command window, type **SYS(3054,0)** to turn off SQL ShowPlan.

Controlling Join Evaluation

If the execution plan for your joins does not match your specific needs, you can force your join order to execute exactly as written without optimization from the processor. To force the evaluation order of the join, you need to add the FORCE keyword and place your join conditions in the FROM clause. Join conditions placed within the WHERE clause are not included in a forced join evaluation.

Note   You can't use the FORCE keyword in SQL pass-through statements or remote views because this keyword is a Visual FoxPro extension of the ANSI standard and is not supported in other SQL dictionaries.

The FORCE clause is global and therefore applies to all tables in the JOIN clause. Be sure that the order in which the join tables appear is exactly the order in which they should be joined. You can also use parentheses to control the evaluation order of joins.

In this example, the first join specified is also the first join evaluated. The Customer table is joined with the Orders table first. The result of that join is then joined with the OrdItems table:

```
SELECT * ;
   FROM FORCE Customers ;
   INNER JOIN Orders ;
      ON Orders.Company_ID = Customers.Company_ID ;
   INNER JOIN OrItems;
      ON OrdItems.Order_NO = Orders.Order_NO
```

In this example, the join within the parentheses for the table Orders and OrdItems is evaluated first. The result of that join is then used in the evaluation of the join with Customers:

```
SELECT * ;
FROM FORCE Customers ;
   INNER JOIN (orders INNER JOIN OrdItems ;
      ON OrdItems.Order_No = Orders.Order_No) ;
      ON Orders.Company_ID = Customers.Company_ID
```

Sharing Connections for Multiple Remote Views

You can use one active connection as the information pipeline for multiple remote views by sharing a connection. When you share an active connection, you:

- Reduce the number of connections on a remote server.

- Reduce costs for connections to servers that charge on a per-connection basis.

You share connections by setting the view definition to use a shared connection upon activation. When the view is used, Visual FoxPro connects to the remote data source using the existing shared connection (if any). If a shared connection isn't in use, Visual FoxPro creates a unique connection when the view is opened, which can then be shared with other views.

Only one active instance of a named connection definition is shared during a Visual FoxPro session. If multiple instances of the same connection definition are active, the first instance to be used as a shared connection becomes the designated shared connection. All views that use that connection definition and employ connection sharing will access the remote server through the designated shared connection.

Connections other than the designated shared connection are not shared. Connection sharing is not scoped to sessions.

To share a connection

- From the **Tools** menu, choose **Options** and select the **Remote Data** tab; then select **Share connection** in the **Remote view defaults** area and choose **OK**.

  – or –

  Use the View Designer.

  – or –

  Use the CREATE SQL VIEW command with the SHARE clause.

The following code creates a view that, when activated with the USE command, shares a connection:

```
CREATE SQL VIEW product_view_remote ;
   CONNECTION remote_01 SHARE AS ;
   SELECT * FROM products
USE product_view_remote
```

Testing a Connection for Busyness

When a connection is busy, such as when Visual FoxPro is progressively fetching data into a cursor, you don't want to start another fetch or send updates on the same connection. You can determine whether a connection is busy with the ConnectBusy property, which returns a value of true (.T.) if the connection is busy. You can use this property in your application to test a connection before sending a request over a shared connection to a remote data source.

To determine whether a connection is busy

- Use the ConnectBusy property of SQLGETPROP( ).

You need the connection handle to use the SQLGETPROP( ) function. You can identify the connection handle for an active view with the ConnectHandle property of the CURSORGETPROP( ) function. The following code identifies a connection handle and then uses the connection handle to test whether the connection is busy:

```
nConnectionHandle=CURSORGETPROP('ConnectHandle')
SQLGETPROP(nConnectionHandle, "ConnectBusy")
```

Creating the Interface

A well-designed interface can guide users through your application. Forms, classes, controls, menus, and toolbars provide a rich set of tools for designing a great user interface.

Chapter 9   Creating Forms

Your application needs forms to allow users to view and enter data. But you can also customize standard forms visually and programmatically to create a specialized environment for your users.

Chapter 10   Using Controls

Controls manage the interactions between users and your application. Visual FoxPro offers a variety of controls to enhance your application interface.

Chapter 11   Designing Menus and Toolbars

A good menu system tells your users a lot about the design and structure of your application. Planning menus and toolbars carefully can improve the usability of your application, provide immediate access to common tasks, and add a Windows look and feel to your application.

Creating Forms

You can use forms to give your users a familiar interface for viewing and entering data into a database, but forms provide far more than just an interface. Forms provide a rich set of objects that can respond to user (or system) events so that you can enable your users to accomplish their information management tasks as easily and as intuitively as possible.

This chapter covers:

- Designing Forms
- Creating a New Form
- Adding Objects to Forms
- Manipulating Objects
- Managing Forms

Designing Forms

Visual FoxPro provides you with a powerful Form Designer to make form design fast and easy. You can have:

- Various types of objects on the forms.
- Data bound to objects on the form.
- Top-level or child forms.
- Multiple forms that can be manipulated together.
- Forms based on your own custom templates.

Forms and form sets are objects with their own properties, events, and methods that you can set in the Form Designer. A form set consists of one or more forms that can be manipulated as a unit. If you have four forms in your form set, for example, you can display or hide them as a unit with a single command at run time.

Creating a New Form

You can create new forms in the Form Designer, and you can see how each object will appear to the user as you design it.

To create a new form

- In the Project Manager, select **Forms** and choose **New**.

  – or –

  From the **File** menu, choose **New**, select **Form**, and choose **New File**.

  – or –

  Use the CREATE FORM command.

The Form Designer with toolbars: Form Designer, Controls, Layout, and Palette

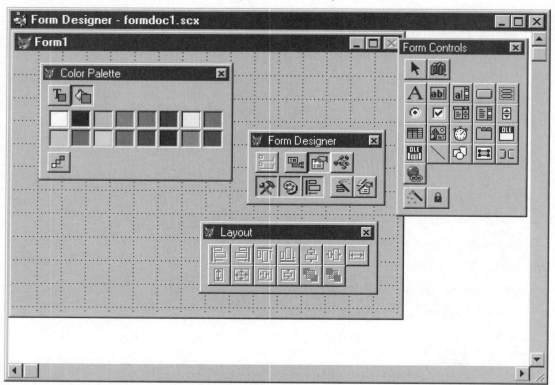

For a more detailed description of the Form Designer, see Chapter 8, "Managing Data Through Forms," in the *User's Guide*. For more information on the toolbars, search for "toolbars" in Help and select the toolbar you need information on.

Setting the Data Environment

Each form or set of forms includes a data environment. The data environment is an object that includes the tables or views the form interacts with and the relationships between tables that the form expects. You can visually design the data environment in the Data Environment Designer and save it with the form.

The data environment can automate opening and closing tables and views when the form is run. In addition, the data environment helps you set the ControlSource property for controls by populating the ControlSource property setting box in the Properties window with all the fields in your data environment.

To open the Data Environment Designer

1. From the **View** menu, choose **Data Environment**.

2. From the **Shortcut** menu, choose **Add**.

3. In the **Open** dialog box, choose a table or view to add to the data environment.

The Data Environment Designer

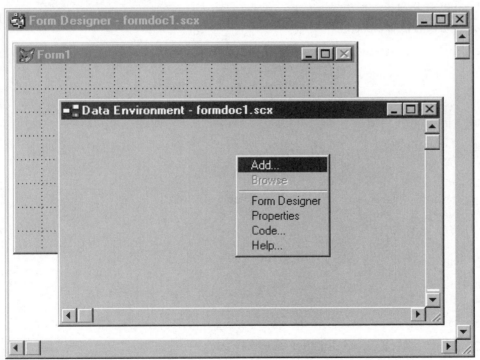

Common Data Environment Properties

The following data environment properties are commonly set in the Properties window:

Property	Description	Default Setting
AutoCloseTables	Controls whether tables and views are closed when the form is released.	True (.T.)
AutoOpenTables	Controls whether tables and views in the data environment are opened when the form is run.	True (.T.)
InitialSelectedAlias	Specifies the table or view that is selected when the form is run.	"" at design time. If not specified, at run time the first cursor added to the DataEnvironment is initially selected.

Adding a Table or View to the Data Environment Designer

When you add tables or views to the Data Environment Designer, you can see the fields and indexes that belong to the table or view.

To add a table or view to the Data Environment

1. From the Data Environment Designer, choose **Add** from the **DataEnvironment** menu.

2. In the **Add Table** or **View** dialog box, choose a table or view from the list.

   – or –

   If no database or project is open, choose **Other** to select a table.

You can also drag a table or view from an open project or the Database Designer into the Data Environment Designer.

When the Data Environment Designer is active, the Properties window displays objects and properties associated with the data environment. Each table or view in the data environment, each relationship between tables, and the data environment itself is a separate object in the Object box of the Properties window.

Removing a Table from the Data Environment Designer

When you remove a table from the data environment, any relationships that the table is involved in are also removed.

To remove a table or view from the Data Environment Designer

1. In the Data Environment Designer, select the table or view.

2. From the **DataEnvironment** menu, choose **Remove**.

Setting Relationships in the Data Environment Designer

If you add tables to the Data Environment Designer that have persistent relationships set in a database, the relationships are automatically added in the data environment. If the tables don't have persistent relationships, you can still relate them in the Data Environment Designer.

To set relationships in the Data Environment Designer

- Drag a field from the primary table onto the matching index tag in the related table.

The Data Environment Designer with relationships set between tables

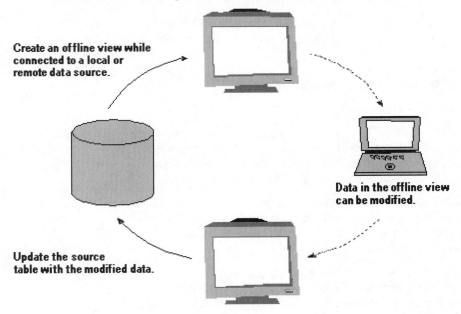

Create an offline view while connected to a local or remote data source.

Data in the offline view can be modified.

Update the source table with the modified data.

You can also drag a field from the primary table to a field in the related table. If there is no index tag in the related table corresponding to the field in the primary table, you're prompted to create the index tag.

Editing Relationships in the Data Environment Designer

When you set a relation in the Data Environment Designer, a line between the tables indicates the relationship.

To edit the properties of the relation

- In the Properties window, select the relation from the **Object** box.

The properties of the relation correspond to clauses and keywords in the SET RELATION and SET SKIP commands. For more information, see the Help topics for these commands.

The RelationalExpr property is set by default to the name of the primary key field in the primary table. If the related table is indexed on an expression, you need to set the RelationalExpr property to this expression. For example, if the related table is indexed on UPPER(cust_id), you need to set RelationalExpr to UPPER(cust_id).

If the relation is not a one-to-many relationship, set the OneToMany property to false (.F.). This corresponds to using the SET RELATION command without issuing SET SKIP.

Setting the OneToMany property of a relation to true (.T.) corresponds to issuing the SET SKIP command. When you skip through the parent table, the record pointer remains on the same parent record until the record pointer moves through all related records in the child table.

Note   If you want a one-to-many relationship in the form, set the OneToMany property to true (.T.), even if a persistent one-to-many relationship has been established in a database.

Creating Single- and Multiple-Document Interfaces

Visual FoxPro allows to you to create two types of applications:

- Multiple-document interface(MDI) applications consist of a single main window, and the application's windows are contained within or float on top of the main window. Visual FoxPro is primarily an MDI application, with the command window, edit windows, and designer windows contained within the main Visual FoxPro window.

- Single-document interface(SDI) applications consist of one or more independent windows, each of which appears separately on the Windows desktop. Microsoft Exchange is an example of an SDI application, in which each message you open appears in its own independent window.

An application consisting of single window is usually an SDI application, but some applications mix SDI and MDI elements. For example, Visual FoxPro displays its debugger as an SDI application, which in turn contains MDI windows of its own.

To support both types of interfaces, Visual FoxPro allows you to create several types of forms:

- *Child form.* A form contained within another window, used in creating MDI applications. Child forms cannot be moved outside the bounds of their parent form (the main form), and when minimized appear at the bottom of their parent form. If their parent form is minimized, they are minimized along with it.

- *Floating form.* A form that belongs to a parent (main) form, but is not contained within it. Instead, floating forms can be moved anywhere on the screen. They cannot be moved behind their parent window. If minimized, a floating form appears at the bottom of the desktop. If their parent form is minimized, floating forms are minimized along with it. Floating forms are also used in creating MDI applications.

- *Top-level form.* An independent form without parent form, used to create an SDI application, or to serve as the parent for other child forms in an MDI application. Top-level forms work at the same level as other Windows applications, and can appear in front of or behind them. They appear on the Windows taskbar.

Child, floating, and top-level forms

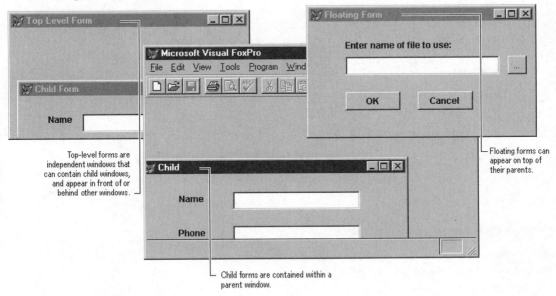

Top-level forms are independent windows that can contain child windows, and appear in front of or behind other windows.

Floating forms can appear on top of their parents.

Child forms are contained within a parent window.

Specifying a Form Type

You create all types of forms in much the same way, but you set specific properties to indicate how the form should behave.

If you're creating a child form, you specify not only that it should appear inside another form, but also whether it is an MDI-compliant child form, which indicates how the form behaves when maximized. If the child form is MDI-compliant, it combines with the parent form, sharing the parent form's title bar and caption, menus, and toolbars. A child form that is not MDI-compliant maximizes into the full client area of the parent, but retains its own caption and title bar.

To specify a child form

1. Create or edit the form using the Form Designer.

2. Set the form's ShowWindow property to one of the following values:

   - **0 – In Screen**. The child form's parent will be the main Visual FoxPro window.

   - **1 – In Top-Level Form**. The child form's parent will be the top-level form that is active when the child window is displayed. Use this setting if you want the child window to appear inside any top-level window other than the main Visual FoxPro window.

3. Set the form's MDIForm property to .T. (true) if you want the child form to be combined with the parent when maximized, or to .F. (false) if the child window should be retained as a separate window when maximized.

A floating form is a variation of a child form.

To specify a floating form

1. Create or edit the form using the Form Designer.

2. Set the form's ShowWindow property to one of the following values:

   - **0 – In Screen**. The floating form's parent will be the main Visual FoxPro window.

   - **1 – In Top-Level Form**. The floating form's parent will be the top-level form that is active when the floating window is displayed.

3. Set the form's Desktop property to .T. (true).

To specify a top-level form

1. Create or edit the form using the Form Designer.

2. Set the form's ShowWindow property to **2 – As Top-Level Form**.

Displaying a Child Form Inside a Top-Level Form

If you've created a child form in which the ShowWindow property is set to **1 – In Top-Level Form**, you don't directly specify the top-level form that acts as the child form's parent. Instead, Visual FoxPro assigns the child form to a parent at the time the child window is displayed.

To display a child form inside a top-level form

1. Create a top-level form.

2. In the event code of the top-level form, include the DO FORM command, specifying the name of the child form to display.

   For example, create a button in the top-level form, and then in the Click event code for the button, include a command such as this one:

   ```
   DO FORM MyChild
   ```

   Note   The top-level form must be visible and active when the child form is displayed. Therefore, you cannot use the Init event of the top-level form to display a child form, because the top-level form will not yet be active.

3. Activate the top-level form, and then if necessary, trigger the event that displays the child form.

Hiding the Main Visual FoxPro Window

If you're running a top-level form, you might not want the main Visual FoxPro window to be visible. You can use the Visible property of the Application object to hide and show the main Visual FoxPro window as needed.

To hide the main Visual FoxPro window

1. In the Init event of the form, include the following line of code:

```
Application.Visible = .F.
```

2. In the Destroy event of the form, include the following line of code:

```
Application.Visible = .T.
```

Make sure that you also provide a way to close the form by using THISFORM.Release in some method or event.

> **Note**   You can also include the following line in a configuration file to hide the main Visual FoxPro window:
>
> ```
> SCREEN = OFF
> ```
>
> For more information about configuring Visual FoxPro, see Chapter 3, "Configuring Visual FoxPro," in the *Installation Guide*.

Adding a Menu to a Top-Level Form

To add a menu to a top-level form

1. Create a top-level form menu. For more information about creating menus for top-level forms, see Chapter 11, "Designing Menus and Toolbars."

2. Set the form's ShowWindow property to **2 – As Top-Level Form**.

3. In the Init event of the form, run the menu program and pass it two parameters:

   DO *menuname.mpr* WITH *oForm, lAutoRename*

   oForm is an object reference to the form. In the Init event of the form, pass THIS as the first parameter.

   lAutoRename specifies whether or not a new unique name is generated for the menu. If you plan to run multiple instances of the form, pass .T. for *lAutoRename*.

   For example, you can call a menu called mySDImenu with this code:

   ```
   DO mySDImenu.mpr WITH THIS, .T.
   ```

Extending Forms with Form Sets

You can manipulate multiple forms as a group by including them in a form set. A form set has these benefits:

- You can show or hide all the forms in a form set at one time.

- You can visually arrange multiple forms at once to control their relative positions.

- Because all the forms in a form set are defined in a single .scx file with a single data environment, you can automatically synchronize record pointers in multiple forms. If you change the record pointer in a parent table in one form, the child records in another form are updated and displayed.

   Note   All the forms and all the objects on the forms are loaded when you run the form set. Loading many forms with a lot of controls might take several seconds.

Creating a New Form Set

A form set is a parent container for one or more forms. When you are in the Form Designer, you can create a form set.

To create a form set

- From the **Form** menu, choose **Create Formset**.

If you don't want to work with multiple forms as a group of forms, you don't need to create a form set. Once you've created a form set, you can add forms to it.

Adding and Removing Forms

Once you've created a form set, you can add new forms and remove forms.

To add additional forms to a form set

- From the **Form** menu, choose **Add New Form**.

To remove a form from a form set

1. In the **Form** box at the bottom of the Form Designer, select the form.

2. From the **Form** menu, choose **Remove Form**.

If you have a single form in a form set, you can remove the form set so that you have only the form.

To remove a form set

- From the **Form** menu, choose **Remove Formset**.

Forms are saved in table format to a file with an .scx extension. When you create a form, the .scx table contains a record for the form, a record for the data environment, and two records for internal use. A record is added for each object you add to the form or to the data environment. If you create a form set, an additional record is added for the form set and for each new form. The parent container of each form is the form set. The parent container of each control is the form that it is placed on.

Tip   When you run a form set, you may not want all forms in the form set initially visible. Set the Visible property to false (.F.) for forms you don't want displayed when the form set runs. Set the Visible property to true (.T.) when you want the forms displayed.

Adding Objects to Forms

To design the functionality you want in a form, you add the appropriate controls, set form and control properties, and write event code.

You can add the following types of objects to a form:

- Controls
- Containers
- User-defined classes
- OLE objects

Understanding Container and Control Objects

Objects in Visual FoxPro belong in one of two categories, depending on the nature of the class they are based on:

- Containers can hold other containers or controls. They can act as the parent object for other objects. For example, a form, as a container, is the parent object of a check box on that form.
- Controls can be placed in containers, but cannot be the parent for other objects. For example, a check box cannot contain any other object.

The Form Designer allows you to design both containers and controls.

Container	Can contain
Column	Headers, and any objects except form sets, forms, toolbars, timers, and other columns
Command button group	Command buttons
Form set	Forms, toolbars
Form	Page frames, grids, any controls
Grid	Columns
Option button group	Option buttons
Page frame	Pages
Page	Grids, any controls

Adding Visual FoxPro Containers

In addition to form sets and forms, Visual FoxPro provides four base container classes.

Visual FoxPro Container Classes

Command button group	Option button group
Grid	Page frame

To add container objects to a form

- In the Form Controls toolbar, select the desired container object (button group, grid, or page frame) button and drag it to size in the form.

When you add a command button group or an option button group to a form in the Form Designer, the group contains two buttons by default. When you add a page frame to a form, the page frame contains two pages by default. You can add more buttons or pages by setting the ButtonCount property or the PageCount property to the number you want.

When you add a grid to a form, the ColumnCount property is set to –1 by default, which indicates AutoFill. At run time, the grid will display as many columns as there are fields in the RowSource table. If you don't want AutoFill, you can specify the number of columns by setting the grid's ColumnCount property.

For more information about these container objects, see Chapter 10, "Using Controls."

Collection and Count Properties

All container objects in Visual FoxPro have a count property and a collection property associated with them. The collection property is an array referencing each contained object. The count property is a numeric property indicating the number of contained objects.

The collection and count properties for each container are named according to the type of object that can be contained in the container. The following table lists the containers and the corresponding collection and count properties.

Container	Collection Property	Count Property
Application	Objects	Count
	Forms	FormCount
FormSet	Forms	FormCount
Form	Objects	Count
	Controls	ControlCount
PageFrame	Pages	PageCount
Page	Controls	ControlCount

(continued)

Container	Collection Property	Count Property
Grid	Columns	ColumnCount
CommandGroup	Buttons	ButtonCount
OptionGroup	Buttons	ButtonCount
Column	Controls	ControlCount
ToolBar	Controls	ControlCount
Container	Controls	ControlCount
Control	Controls	ControlCount

These properties allow you to use a loop to programmatically manipulate all or specific contained objects. For example, the following lines of code set the BackColor property of columns in a grid to alternating green and red:

```
o = THISFORM.grd1
FOR i = 1 to o.ColumnCount
   IF i % 2 = 0 && Even-numbered column
      o.Columns(i).BackColor = RGB(0,255,0) && Green
   ELSE
      o.Columns(i).BackColor = RGB(255,0,0) && Red
   ENDIF
ENDFOR
```

Adding Visual FoxPro Controls to a Form

You can easily add any of the standard Visual FoxPro controls to your form by using the Controls toolbar.

Standard Visual FoxPro Controls

Check box	Hyperlink	List box	Spinner
Combo box	Image	OLE Bound Control	Text box
Command button	Label	OLE Container Control	Timer
Edit box	Line	Shape	

To add controls to a form

- In the Form Controls toolbar, select the desired control button and click or drag it to size in the form.

For more information about which control to choose, see Chapter 10, "Using Controls."

Adding Data-Bound Controls to a Form

You can bind controls to data in a table, view, table field, or view field by setting the ControlSource property of a control to a field or the RecordSource property of a grid to a table or view. But you can also create data-bound controls by dragging fields or tables to the form directly from:

- The Project Manager
- The Database Designer
- The Data Environment Designer

The class of control created this way depends on the Field Mappings settings in the Properties tab of the Table Designer or the Field Mapping tab of the Options dialog box.

For more information about setting default control classes, search for "Table Designer" or "Field Mapping Tab" in Help.

Adding User-Defined Objects to a Form

One of the most powerful features of Visual FoxPro is the ability to create classes that can easily be used and reused in various pieces of your applications. Once you've created classes, you can add them to your forms.

To add an object based on a custom class

- In the Project Manager, drag the class onto the container.

You can also add your classes directly from the Form Controls toolbar when you add them to your toolbar.

Adding Class Libraries to the Controls Toolbar

You need to register your class libraries before they can be displayed in the Form Controls toolbar.

To register a class library

1. From the **Tools** menu, choose **Options**.
2. In the **Options** dialog box, choose the **Controls** tab.
3. Choose **Add**.
4. In the **Open** dialog box, choose a class library to add to the **Selected** list and choose **Open**.
5. Repeat steps 3 and 4 until you've added all the libraries you want to register.

Classes in the class libraries in the Selected list can be used in the Form Designer as easily as Visual FoxPro base classes can be used.

Controls tab of the Options dialog box

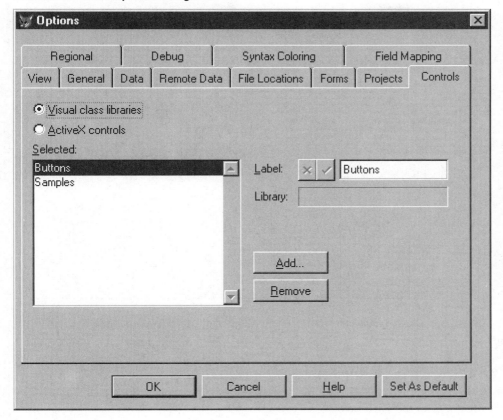

Tip   If you want the class libraries to be available from the Form Controls toolbar every time you run Visual FoxPro, choose Set as Default in the Options dialog box.

You can also register libraries directly in the Form Designer.

To register a class library in the Form Designer

1. In the Form Controls toolbar, choose the **View Classes** button.

2. From the submenu, choose **Add**.

Submenu of the View Classes button

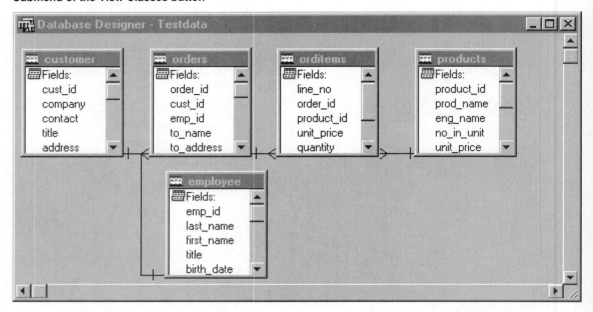

3. In the **Open** dialog box, choose a class library to add to the Form Controls toolbar and choose **Open**.

Adding Objects to a Form from a Class Library

Once you've added class libraries in the Classes tab of the Options dialog box or from the View Classes submenu, you can access them in the Form Designer.

To add a custom object from the Controls toolbar

1. In the Form Controls toolbar, choose the **View Classes** button.

2. From the list of registered class libraries, select the library that contains the control you want to add to the form.

    The toolbar is populated with the controls in the library you selected.

User-defined class library added to the View Classes submenu

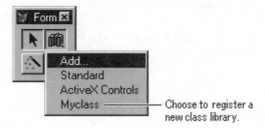

Choose to register a
new class library.

3. Click the control you want and drag it to size in the form.

    Note   You can remove a visual class library from the View Classes toolbar menu by
    selecting the library in the Selected list in the Controls tab of the Options dialog box,
    and choosing Remove.

When you add objects to a form based on anything other than the Visual FoxPro base
classes, a relative path to the class library (.vcx file) is stored in the form's .scx file. If you
move either the form or the class library to a different location, Visual FoxPro displays a
dialog box when you try to run the form so that you can manually locate the class library.

Determining What Controls Are on a Form

To determine how many controls are on the form, you can use the ControlCount property.
The Controls[n] property of the form allows you to reference each control on the form.
The following program prints the Name property of all the controls on the currently
active form.

```
ACTIVATE SCREEN  && to print to the main Visual FoxPro window
FOR nCnt = 1 TO Application.ActiveForm.ControlCount
    ? Application.ActiveForm.Controls[nCnt].Name
ENDFOR
```

Adding Properties and Methods to a Form

You can add as many new properties and methods as you want to a form set or to a form
that isn't part of a form set. Properties hold a value; methods hold procedural code to be
run when you call the method. The new properties and methods are scoped to the form and
you reference them the same way you reference other properties or methods of the form.

Creating New Properties

If you have a form set, properties and methods that you add in the Form Designer are
scoped to the form set. If you don't have a form set, the properties and methods are scoped
to the form.

To add a new property to a form

1. From the **Form** menu, choose **New Property**.

2. In the **New Property** dialog box, type the name of the property. You can also include a description of the property that can be displayed at the bottom of the Properties window.

Adding a property to a form

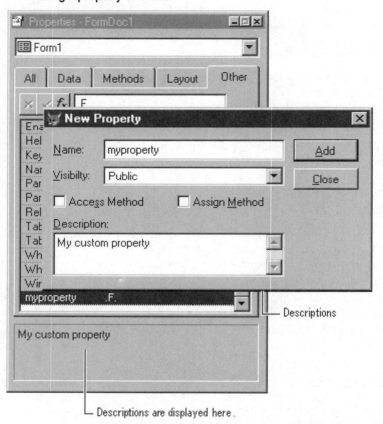

Descriptions

Descriptions are displayed here.

Creating an Array Property

An array property is scoped to the form like any other property, but can be manipulated with the Visual FoxPro array commands and functions.

To create an array property

1. Add a new property to the form.

2. In the **Name** box of the **New Property** dialog box, type the name of the array property and include the size and dimensions of the array.

    For example, to create a two-dimensional array with 10 rows, you could type **arrayprop[10,2]** in the **Name** box of the **New Property** dialog box.

Array properties are read-only in design mode, but you can manage, redimension, and assign values to the elements of the array property at run time. For an example of using an array property, see "Managing Multiple Instances of a Form" later in this chapter.

Creating New Methods

You can add methods to the form that can be called the same way the form class methods can be called.

To create a new method for a form

1. From the **Form** menu, choose **New Method**.

2. In the **New Method** dialog box, type the name of the method. You can optionally include a description of the method.

You call a user-defined method the same way you call base class methods, using the following syntax:

ObjectName.MethodName

Your method can also accept parameters and return values. In this case, you call the method in an assignment statement:

cVariable = ObjectName.MethodName(cParameter, nParameter)

Including Predefined Constants

To use predefined constants in your methods, you can include a header file in a form or a form set using #INCLUDE. A header file typically contains compile-time constants defined with the #DEFINE preprocessor directive.

For more information, see #INCLUDE and #DEFINE in Help.

To include a file in a form

1. From the **Form** menu, choose **Include File**.

2. In the **Include File** dialog box, specify the file in the **Include File** text box.

    – or –

    Choose the dialog button to open the **Include** dialog box and choose the file.

3. Choose **OK**.

Manipulating Objects

There are several ways you can manipulate objects at design time:

- Set the size and position of objects by dragging them in the Form Designer window.

- Align controls by choosing alignment tools on the Layout toolbar or options on the Format menu.

- Set colors by choosing foreground and background colors in the Palette toolbar.

- Set properties in the Properties window. The primary point of control for all objects in your form is the Properties window.

For information on using the toolbars and menu options and for information on the components of the Properties window, search for the toolbar name or "Properties Window" in Help.

Setting Properties at Design Time

The Properties window opens with the properties or events of the selected object displayed. If more than one object is selected, the properties that the objects have in common are displayed in the Properties window. To edit the properties or events of a different object, choose the appropriate object from the Object box or select a different control in the form.

The Properties window

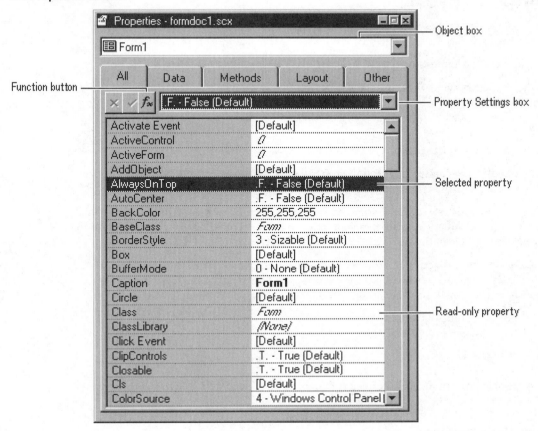

Object box

Function button

Property Settings box

Selected property

Read-only property

To set a property

1. In the Properties window, select a property in the **Property and Events** list.

2. In the **Property Settings** box, type or choose the desired setting for the selected property.

   Note   Properties that are read-only at design time, such as the Class property of an object, are displayed in the Properties and Events list in the Properties window in italics.

If the property requires a character value, you don't have to include the value in quotation marks. If you want the caption of a form to be CUSTOMER, type **CUSTOMER** in the Property Settings box. If you want the caption of a form to be "CUSTOMER," with the quotation marks displayed in the window title, type **"CUSTOMER"** in the Property Settings box.

Setting Properties with Expressions

You can also set properties to the results of expressions or functions through the Properties window.

To set a property with an expression

- In the Properties window, choose the **Function** button to open the **Expression Builder**.

  – or –

  In the **Property Settings** box, type = followed by an expression.

  For example, you can set the Caption property of a form to indicate the currently active table when the form is run by typing **=ALIAS( )** in the Property Settings box.

A property expression is evaluated when the you set it in the Properties window and when the object is initialized at run time or design time. Once the object is created, the property setting doesn't change until you or a user explicitly changes it.

  Troubleshooting   If you set a property to the result of a user-defined function, the function is evaluated when you set the property or modify or run the form. If there is an error in the user-defined function, you might not be able to open your form.

  You can also set the property to the user-defined function in the Init event of the object, as in the following example:

```
THIS.Caption = myfunction( )
```

  If there is an error in the user-defined function, you still won't be able to run the form this way, but you'll be able to modify it.

Defining Form Behavior

When you are designing a form in the Form Designer, the form is live: except for setting the Visible property to false (.F.), visual and behavioral changes you make are immediately reflected in the form. If you set the WindowState property to 1 – Minimized or 2 – Maximized, the form in the Form Designer immediately reflects this setting. If you set the Movable property to false (.F.), a user will not be able to move the form at run time and you won't be able to move the form at design time either. You might want to design the functionality of your form and add all the appropriate controls before you set some of the properties that determine form behavior.

The following form properties are commonly set at design time to define the appearance and behavior of the form.

Property	Description	Default
AlwaysOnTop	Controls whether a form is always on top of other open windows.	False (.F.)
AutoCenter	Controls whether the form is automatically centered in the main Visual FoxPro window or on the desktop when the form is initialized.	False (.F.)
BackColor	Determines the color of the form window.	255,255,255
BorderStyle	Controls whether the form has no border, a single-line border, a double-wide border, or a system border. If the BorderStyle is 3 – System, the user will be able to resize the form.	3
Caption	Determines the text displayed in the title bar of the form.	Form1
Closable	Controls whether the user can close the form by double-clicking the close box.	True (.T.)
DataSession	Controls whether the tables in the form are opened in work areas that are globally accessible or private to the form.	1
MaxButton	Controls whether or not the form has a maximize button.	True (.T.)
MinButton	Controls whether or not the form has a minimize button.	True (.T.)
Movable	Controls whether or not the form can be moved to a new location on the screen.	True (.T.)
ScaleMode	Controls whether the unit of measurement in object size and position properties is foxels or pixels.	Determined by settings in the Options dialog box.
Scrollbars	Controls the type of scroll bars a form has.	0 – None
TitleBar	Controls whether a title bar appears at the top of the form.	1 – On
ShowWindow	Controls whether the window is a child (in screen), floating, or top-level window.	0 – In Screen
WindowState	Controls whether the form is minimized (in Windows only), maximized, or normal.	0 – Normal
WindowType	Controls whether the form is modeless (the default) or modal. If the form is modal, the user must close the form before accessing any other elements of your application's user interface.	0 – Modeless

You can use the LockScreen property to make run-time adjustment of control layout properties appear cleaner.

Assigning Icons to Forms

In Visual FoxPro for Windows, you can assign an icon to the form; the icon is displayed when the window is minimized in Windows NT and in the title bar in Windows 95. To assign an icon to a form, set the form's Icon property to the name of an .ico file.

To assign an icon to a form

1. Open the form.

2. Open the Properties window.

3. Set the Icon property to the .ico file that you want to display.

Editing Event and Method Code

Events are user actions, such as clicks and mouse movements, or system actions, such as the progression of the system clock. Methods are procedures that are associated with the object and that are specifically invoked programmatically. For a discussion of events and methods, see Chapter 3, "Object-Oriented Programming." You can specify the code to be processed when an event is triggered or a method is invoked.

To edit event or method code

1. From the **View** menu, choose **Code**.

2. Select the event or method in the Procedure box.

3. In the **Edit** window, write the code you want to be processed when the event is triggered or the method is invoked.

    For example, you could have a command button on a form with the caption "Quit." In the Click event for the button, include the line:

    ```
    THISFORM.Release
    ```

    Tip   To move between procedures in the Code Editing window, press PAGE DOWN or PAGE UP.

When the user clicks the command button, the form is removed from the screen and from memory. If you don't want to release the form from memory, you could instead include the following line in the click event:

```
THISFORM.Hide
```

Note   If code associated with the Init event of a form set, a form, or any object on any form in a form set returns false (.F.), the form will not be created.

Saving Forms

You need to save your form before you can run it. If you try to close the Form Designer when the form has not been saved, Visual FoxPro prompts you to save or discard the changes you've made.

To save a form

- In the Form Designer, choose **Save** from the **File** menu.

Saving Forms and Controls as Classes

You can also save a form, or a subset of the controls on a form, as a class definition. If you intend to create subclasses based on the form or reuse the controls in other forms, save the form as a class definition.

To save a form or selected controls as a class definition

1. From the **File** menu, choose **Save As Class**.

2. In the **Save As Class** dialog box, choose **Current form** or **Selected controls**.

   The Save As Class dialog box

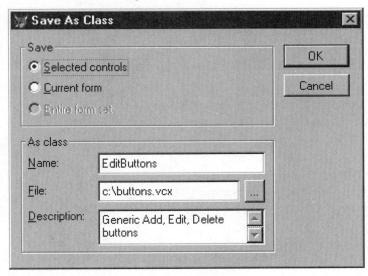

3. In the **Name** box, enter a name for the class.

4. In the **File** box, enter a filename for the class to be stored to.

5. Choose **OK**.

If you don't give the filename an extension, the default extension of .vcx is added when the file is saved. Once a form has been saved as a class definition, you can modify it with the MODIFY CLASS command. For more information about creating classes, see Chapter 3, "Object-Oriented Programming."

Running a Form

You can run a form directly from the interface or in program code.

Running a Form Interactively

There are several ways to run the form you've designed.

> **Note**   If you're working in the Form Designer, you can test the form by clicking the
> Run button on the Form Designer toolbar. To reopen the form in the Form Designer,
> close the form or choose the Modify Form button on the toolbar.

You can also run a form from a project or programmatically.

To run a form interactively

- In the Project Manager, select the form and choose **Run**.

   – or –

   Type DO FORM in the Command window.

You can also run the form by choosing Do from the Program menu, choosing Form in the
List Files of Type box, selecting the form, and choosing Do.

Running a Form from a Program

To programmatically run a form, include the DO FORM command in the code associated
with an event, in method code, or in a program or procedure.

Naming the Form Object

By default, when you use the DO FORM command, the name of the form object is the
same as the name of the .scx file. For example, the following line of code runs
Customer.scx. Visual FoxPro automatically creates an object variable for the form named
`customer`:

```
DO FORM Customer
```

To name a form object

- Use the NAME clause of the DO FORM command.

For example, the following commands run a form, creating two form object variable
names:

```
DO FORM Customer NAME frmCust1
DO FORM Customer NAME frmCust2
```

Manipulating the Form Object

If you issue the DO FORM command from the Command window, the form object is associated with a public variable. You can access the form object through the variable name. For example, the following commands, issued in the Command window, open a form named `Customer` and change its caption.

```
DO FORM Customer
Customer.Caption = "Hello"
```

If you then issue the following command in the Command window, 0 is displayed in the active output window, indicating that `Customer` is an object:

```
? TYPE("Customer")
```

If you issue the DO FORM command in a program, the form object is scoped to the program. If the program or procedure completes, the object is gone, but the form remains visible. For example, you could run the following program:

```
*formtest.prg
DO FORM Customer
```

After you run the program, the form remains visible and all of the controls on the form are active, but `TYPE("Customer")` returns `U` indicating that `Customer` is an undefined variable. The following command, issued in the Command window, would generate an error:

```
Customer.Caption = "Hello"
```

You can, however, access the form by using the ActiveForm, Forms, and FormCount properties of the application object.

Scoping the Form to the Form Object Variable

The LINKED keyword of the DO FORM command allows you to link the form to the form object. If you include the LINKED keyword, when the variable associated with the form object goes out of scope, the form is released.

For example, the following command creates a form linked to the object variable `frmCust2`:

```
DO FORM Customer NAME frmCust2 LINKED
```

When `frmCust2` is released, the form is closed.

Closing an Active Form

To allow users to close the active form by clicking the close button or by choosing Close from the form's Control menu, set the Closable property of the form.

To allow a user to close the active form

- In the Properties window, set the Closable property to true (.T.).

   – or –

   Use the RELEASE command.

For example, you can close and release the `frmCustomer` form by issuing the following command in a program or in the Command window:

```
RELEASE frmCustomer
```

You can also allow a user to close and release a form by including the following command in the Click event code for a control, such as a command button with a caption of "Quit":

```
THISFORM.Release
```

You can also use the RELEASE command in the code associated with an object on the form, but any code you've included in the Release method will not be executed.

> **Troubleshooting**   When you release a form, you release from memory the object variable created for the form. There is a single variable for a form set, so you can't release forms in a form set without releasing the form set. If you want to release the form set, you can use `RELEASE THISFORMSET`. If you want to remove a form from the screen so that a user can no longer see it or interact with it, you can use `THISFORM.Hide`.

Setting Properties at Run Time

The object model in Visual FoxPro gives you a great deal of control over properties at run time.

Referencing Objects in the Object Hierarchy

To manipulate an object, you need to identify it in relation to the container hierarchy. At the highest level of the container hierarchy (the form set or form) you need to reference the object variable. Unless you use the NAME clause of the DO FORM command, the object variable has the same name as the .scx file.

Properties are manipulated by referencing the object variable, the control, and the property, separated by dots (.):

objectvariable.[form.]control.property = Setting

The following table lists properties or keywords that make it easier to reference an object in the object hierarchy:

Property or keyword	Reference
ActiveControl	The control on the currently active form that has the focus
ActiveForm	The currently active form
ActivePage	The active page on the currently active form
Parent	The immediate container of the object
THIS	The object or a procedure or event of the object
THISFORM	The form that contains the object
THISFORMSET	The form set that contains the object

For example, to change the caption of a command button on the form `frmCust` in a form set stored in Custview.scx, use the following command in a program or in the Command window:

```
CustView.frmCust.cmdButton1.Caption = "Edit"
```

Use the THIS, THISFORM, and THISFORMSET keywords to reference objects from within a form. For example, to change the Caption of a command button when the command button is clicked, include the following command in the Click event code for the command button:

```
THIS.Caption = "Edit"
```

The following table gives examples of using THISFORMSET, THISFORM, THIS, and Parent to set object properties:

Command	Where to include the command
`THISFORMSET.frm1.cmd1.Caption = 'OK'`	In the event or method code of any control on any form in the form set except for `frm1`.
`THISFORM.cmd1.Caption = 'OK'`	In the event or method code of any control except for `cmd1` on the same form that `cmd1` is on.
`THIS.Caption = 'OK'`	In the event or method code of the control whose caption you want to change.
`THIS.Parent.BackColor = RGB(192,0,0)`	In the event or method code of a control on a form. The command changes the background color of the form to dark red.

Setting Properties at Run Time with Expressions

You can also set properties at run time using expressions or functions.

To set properties to expressions at run time

- Assign an expression to the property.

  – or –

  Assign the result of a user-defined function to the property.

  For example, you could set the caption of a button to be Edit or Save, depending on the value of a variable. Declare the variable in the calling program for your form:

```
PUBLIC glEditing
glEditing = .F.
```

Then use an IIF expression in the Caption setting:

```
frsSet1.frmForm1.cmdButton1.Caption = ;
    IIF(glEditing = .F., "Edit", "Save")
```

You could determine the size of a button and set the caption using expressions with fields in a table:

```
* set button width to length of 'Call ' + first and last names
frmForm1.cmdButton1.Width = 5 + ;
   LEN(ALLTRIM(employee.first_name    + " " + employee.last_name))
* set button caption to 'Call ' + first and last names
frmForm1.cmdButton1.Caption = "Call " + ;
   ALLTRIM(employee.first_name + " " + employee.last_name)
```

You could also set the caption using a user-defined function:

```
frsSet1.frmForm1.cmdButton1.Caption = setcaption()
```

Setting Multiple Properties

You can set multiple properties at once.

To set multiple properties

- Use the WITH ... ENDWITH structure.

  For example, to set multiple properties of a column in a grid in a form, you could include the following statement in any event or method code in the form:

```
WITH THISFORM.grdGrid1.grcColumn1
    .Width = 5
    .Resizable = .F.
    .ForeColor = RGB(0,0,0)
    .BackColor = RGB(255,255,255)
    .SelectOnEntry = .T.
ENDWITH
```

Calling Methods at Run Time

The syntax for calling methods of an object is:

Parent.Object.Method

Once an object has been created, you can call the methods of that object from anywhere in your application. The following commands call methods to display a form and set the focus to a command button:

```
* form set saved in MYF_SET.SCX
myf_set.frmForm1.Show
myf_set.frmForm1.cmdButton1.SetFocus
```

To hide the form, issue this command:

```
myf_set.frmForm1.Hide
```

Responding to Events

The code you include in an event procedure is executed when the event takes place. For example, the code you include in the Click event procedure of a command button runs when the user clicks the command button.

Calling the procedural code associated with an event does not cause the event to occur. For example, the following statement causes the code in the Activate event of `frmPhoneLog` to be executed, but it doesn't activate the form:

```
frmPhoneLog.Activate
```

Calling the Show method of a form causes the form to be displayed and activated, at which point the code in the Activate event is executed:

```
frmPhoneLog.Show
```

Example of Manipulating Objects

The following example sets properties and calls event code from various objects within a form set. The example includes two forms, frmLeft and frmRight, in a formset.

Sample form set in the Form Designer

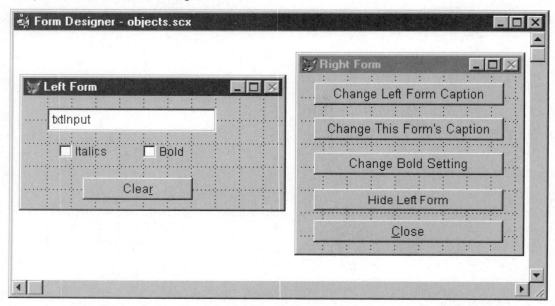

The two check boxes and the command button on frmLeft have event code associated with them. The name of the text box on frmLeft is txtInput.

Event Code for Objects in LeftForm

Object	Event	Code
ChkItalic	Click	`THISFORM.txtInput.FontItalic = ;` `    THIS.Value`
ChkBold	Click	`THIS.txtInput.FontBold = THIS.Value`

CmdClear	Click	`THISFORM.txtInput.Value = ""`
		`THISFORM.txtInput.FontBold = .F.`
		`THISFORM.txtInput.FontItalic = .F.`
		`THISFORM.chkItalic.Value = .F.`
		`THISFORM.chkBold.Value = .F.`

Setting a Property of Another Control on the Same Form

You can set the properties of one control from within the event code of another by using the THISFORM keyword or the Parent property. The following two commands are executed when a user initially clicks on the Italic and the Bold check boxes, setting the appropriate text box properties:

```
THISFORM.txtInput.FontItalic = .T.
THIS.Parent.txtInput.FontBold = .T.
```

In this case, THISFORM and THIS.Parent can be used interchangeably.

Sample form set at run time

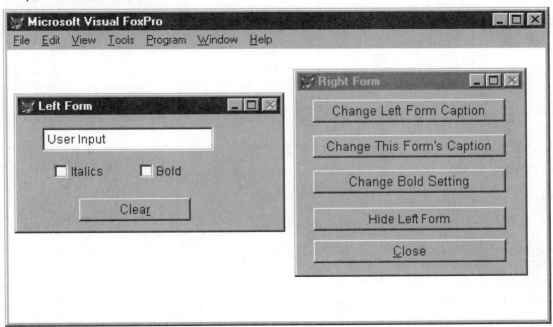

The code in the click event for `cmdClear` uses THISFORM to reset the values of the other controls on the form.

Setting Another Form's Properties

You can also set properties of one form from another. Form2 contains five command buttons. The first button on the form has this code in its Click event:

```
THISFORMSET.frmLeft.Caption = ;
   ALLTRIM(ThisFormSet.frmLeft.txtInput.Value)
```

Notice that the form set and the form need to be referenced when setting properties from within a different form.

User clicks "Change Left Form Caption" command button on Right Form

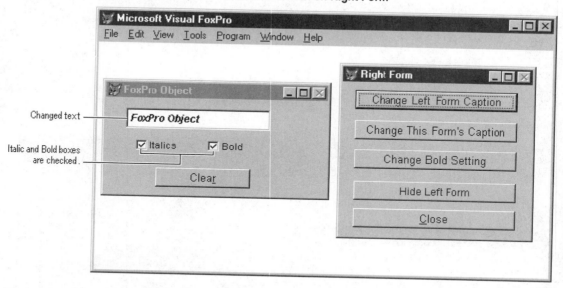

The click event code of the second command button on frmRight demonstrates setting a property of a form from within an object on the form:

```
THISFORM.Caption = ;
   ALLTRIM(ThisFormSet.frmLeft.txtInput.Value)
```

If the user chooses this button, the caption of frmRight changes to the value in the text box on frmLeft.

Accessing Objects on Different Forms

The following code in the Click event of the Change Bold Setting command button changes the value of the Bold check box on frmLeft and calls the event code associated with this control.

```
THISFORMSET.frmLeft.chkBold.Value = ;
   NOT THISFORMSET.frmLeft.chkBold.Value
THISFORMSET.frmLeft.chkBold.InteractiveChange
```

The last line of the example calls the InteractiveChange event of chkBold. You could also call this procedure with the following command:

```
THISFORMSET.frmForm1.chkBold.InteractiveChange( )
```

If this procedure call is omitted, the value of the check box changes, but the FontBold property of the text box is never changed.

User clicks "Change Bold Setting" command button on Right Form

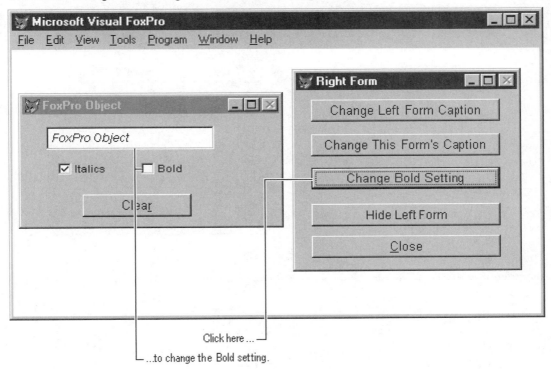

Click here ...
...to change the Bold setting.

Checking Properties and Calling Method Code of Another Form

The following code in the Click event of the Hide Left Form command button hides or shows frmLeft, depending on the value of the Visible property, and changes the button caption as appropriate:

```
IF ThisFormSet.frmLeft.Visible
   ThisFormSet.frmLeft.Hide
   THIS.Caption = "Show Left Form"
ELSE
   ThisFormSet.frmLeft.Show
   THIS.Caption = "Hide Left Form"
ENDIF
```

Notice that the THIS keyword is used within event code of a control to reference properties of the control.

User clicks "Hide Left Form" command button on Right Form

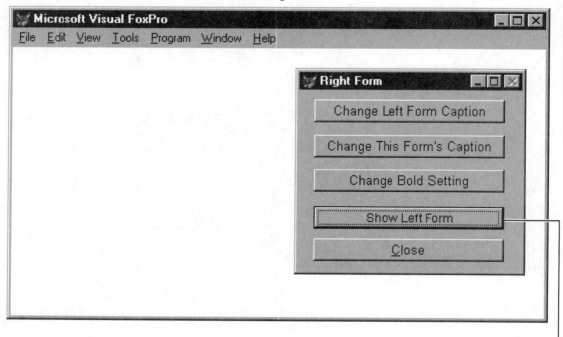

Note caption change.

The following command in the Click event of the Quit command button releases the form set, causing both forms to close:

```
RELEASE ThisFormSet
```

Managing Forms

The following procedures describe common tasks associated with managing forms in an application.

Hiding a Form

You can hide a form so that it is not visible to a user. When the form is hidden, the user cannot interact with the form, but you still have full programmatic control of them.

To hide a form

- Use the Hide method.

  For example, in the code associated with the Click event of a command button, you could include the following line of code:

  ```
  THISFORM.Hide
  ```

When the user clicks the command button, the form remains in memory, but is not visible.

Releasing a Form

You can allow a user to release a form when he or she is finished interacting with it. When you release a form, you can no longer access properties and methods of the form.

To release a form

- Call the Release method.

For example, in the code associated with the Click event of a command button, you could include the following line of code:

```
THISFORM.Release
```

When the user clicks the command button, the form closes.

Passing Parameters to a Form

Sometimes you want to pass parameters to forms when you run them to set property values or specify operational defaults.

To pass a parameter to a form created in the Form Designer

1. Create properties on the form to hold the parameters, such as ItemName and ItemQuantity.

2. In the Init event code for the form, include a PARAMETERS statement such as:

```
PARAMETERS cString, nNumber
```

3. In the Init event code for the form, assign the parameters to the properties, as in this example:

```
THIS.ItemName = cString
THIS.ItemQuantity = nNumber
```

4. When running the form, include a WITH clause in the DO FORM command:

```
DO FORM myform WITH "Bagel", 24
```

Returning a Value From a Form

You can use forms throughout your application to allow users to specify a value.

To return a value from a form

1. Set the WindowType property of the form to 1 to make the form modal.

2. In the code associated with the Unload event of the form, include a RETURN command with the return value.

3. In the program or method that runs the form, include the TO keyword in the DO FORM command.

    For example, if `FindCustID` is a modal form that returns a character value, the following line of code stores the return value to a variable named `cCustID`:

    ```
    DO FORM FindCustID TO cCustID
    ```

For more information, see the Help topics for RETURN and DO FORM.

> **Troubleshooting**   If you get an error, make sure the WindowType is set to 1 (Modal).

Saving a Form as HTML

You can use the **Save As HTML** option on the **File** menu when you're creating a form to save the contents of a form as an HTML (Hypertext Markup Language) file.

To save a form as HTML

1. Open the form.

2. Choose **Save As HTML** on the **File** menu. (You will be asked to save the form if it has been modified.)

3. Enter the name of the HTML file to create and choose **Save**.

Managing Multiple Instances of a Form

You can have multiple instances of a class definition active at a time. For example, you can design one order form but have several open orders in your application. Each uses the same form definition but is displayed and manipulated individually.

When you have multiple instances of a form, the key points to remember are:

*   Create an array property in the launching form to hold the object variables associated with each instance of the multiple instance form. The easiest way to keep track of instance variables when you don't know ahead of time how many there will be is to use an array.

*   For the form that is to have multiple instances, set the DataSession property to 2 – Private Data Session. A private data session provides a separate set of work areas for each instance of the form so that selected tables and record pointer positions are all independent.

The following example provides code that demonstrates creating multiple instances of a form. For the sake of brevity, this code is not optimized; it is intended only to present the concepts.

The following form launches multiple instances:

Launcher Form

Property Setting for Launch.scx

Object	Property	Setting
FrmLaunch	aForms[1]	" "

Event Code for Launch.scx

Object	Event	Code
CmdQuit	Click	RELEASE THISFORM
CmdLaunch	Click	nInstance = ALEN(THISFORM.aForms) DO FORM Multi ; NAME THISFORM.aForms[nInstance] ; LINKED DIMENSION ; THISFORM.aForms[nInstance + 1]

In refining the code in this example, you could manage the array of form objects so that empty array elements reused as forms are closed and new forms are opened, rather than always redimensioning the array and increasing the number of elements by one.

The form that can have multiple instances is Multi.scx. The data environment for this form contains the Employee table.

Multiple instances of Multi.scx

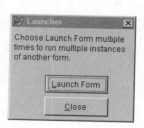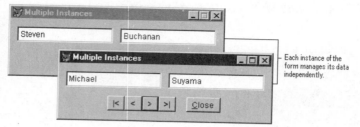

Each instance of the form manages its data independently.

Property Setting for Multi.scx

Object	Property	Setting
TxtFirstname	ControlSource	Employee.first_name
TxtLastName	ControlSource	Employee.last_name
FrmMulti	DataSession	2 – Private Data Session

When you choose Launch Form in the Launcher form, an instance of the Multi form is created. When you close the Launcher form, the property array aForms is released and all instances of Multi are destroyed.

Visual FoxPro provides some functions and properties to help you manage multiple instances of objects. For more information, see AINSTANCE( ), AUSED( ), and DataSessionID in the *Microsoft Visual FoxPro 6.0 Language Reference*.

Setting the Design Area for a Form

You can set the maximum design area for the Form Designer in the Options dialog box.

Forms tab of the Options dialog box

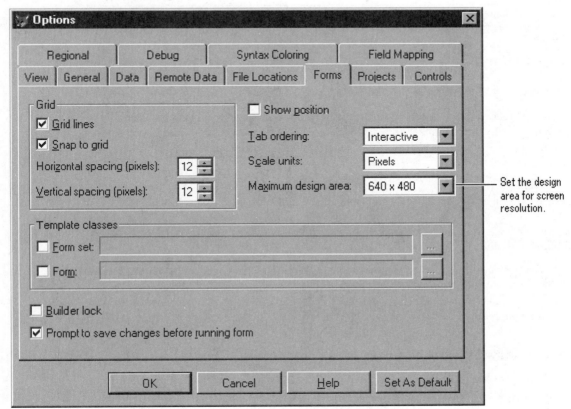

Set the design area for screen resolution.

To set the maximum design area for a form

1. From the **Tools** menu, choose **Options**.

2. In the **Options** dialog box, choose the **Forms** tab.

3. In the **Maximum design area** box, choose the pixel coordinates for the maximum design area.

When you set the maximum design area, the background of the Form Designer is white within the design area boundaries and gray in areas beyond the maximum design area. If you develop applications on a monitor with a resolution of 1024 x 768, for example, you can set your design resolution to 640 x 480 and know that the forms you design will always fit on 640 x 480 screens.

Within the design area, be sure to account for standard window attributes such as toolbars. For example, in a 640 x 480 screen, a form with a status bar and one toolbar docked at the top or the bottom of the screen can have a maximum height of 390 pixels.

Main Visual FoxPro window attribute	Required pixels
Title and menu	38
Status bar	23
Docked toolbar	29

Using Local and Remote Data in a Form

You can create forms that can be easily switched between using local data and data that is stored remotely (for example, on a database server). This allows you to create a prototype application using local or test data, then switch to remote or live data without substantial changes to your forms.

For example, if your Visual FoxPro application is a front end for a large customer table stored on a database server, you can create a local .dbf file that contains a small but representative sampling of the data. You can then create, test, and debug your forms based on this small set of data. When you're ready to distribute your application, you can link your form to the large data set.

The key to being able to switch between local and remote data is to make sure that you use views instead of directly linking your form (and its controls) to a table. To access remote data, you must use a view in any event. Therefore, to facilitate switching between local and remote data, create a view for the local data as well. When you create the form, you can add both views to its data environment, then switch between them as needed.

To create a form that can switch between local and remote data

1. Create two views of the data, one that points to the remote data, and another that points to the local data.

2. Create a new form.

3. Open the Data Environment Designer for the form, and then add both views.

4. Right-click the **Data Environment Designer**, and then choose **Properties**.

5. In the Properties window, set the Alias property for both cursors to the same name.

6. Set the data environment's OpenViews property to either **1 – Local Only** or **2 – Remote Only**, depending on which view you wanted to use when running the form.

   Note   Because you are using the same alias for both views, do not choose **0 – Local and Remote** (the default).

7. On the form, add the controls you need and set their ControlSource properties to the appropriate fields in the view. Because both views have the same alias, the controls will respond automatically to whichever view is active when the form is run.

After the form is created, you can switch the views alias by changing the data environment's OpenViews property. You can do this in the Data Environment while using the Form Designer. Alternatively, you can write code and attach it to an event, which is useful if you want to switch views at run time. For example, you could put this code in the form's Activate event:

```
THISFORM.DataEnvironment.OpenViews = 2 && Use remote view
```

If you create a form that can be switched between local and remote data, you must also design your navigation code to accommodate both views, particularly if you are designing forms with one-to-many relationships. For example, if your form only accesses a local table or view, you might use code such as the following in a Next command button to move to the next record in a cursor:

```
SKIP 1
THISFORM.Refresh()
```

However, this code is inefficient when you're navigating in a remote view, because it assumes that the cursor contains all the data required by the form. As a rule, you want to minimize the amount of data that you download from the remote data source.

The solution is to use a parameterized view. For example, the definition for a view used to edit customer information could be:

```
SELECT * FROM CUSTOMERS WHERE ;
CUSTOMERS.COMPANY_NAME = ?pCompanyName
```

When the form runs, it can prompt the user for a customer name using a dialog box or by allowing the user to enter a name in a text box. The code for a Display button would then be similar to the following:

```
pCompanyName = THISFORM.txtCompanyName.Value
REQUERY("customer")
THISFORM.Refresh()
```

For more information about parameterized views, see "Creating a Parameterized View" in Chapter 8, "Creating Views."

Setting Form Templates

You can create your own form class to use a template for all your new forms, or you can use one of the sample classes that ship with Visual FoxPro.

When you create a new form, it is based on the template form that is set in the Options dialog box. If no template is specified, the new form is based on the Visual FoxPro Form base class. For more information about Visual FoxPro classes, see Chapter 3, "Object-Oriented Programming."

Advantages of Using Form Templates

Form templates allow you to set default properties for your forms so that you can easily give all the forms in your application a consistent look and feel. You could include a company logo, for instance, and use a consistent color scheme in all your forms by designing a template form class with these attributes. If the company logo changes, you could change the picture in the template form class and all the forms you created based on the template would automatically inherit the new logo.

You can add custom properties and methods to the Visual FoxPro form class so that these properties and methods are available to each form in your application. If you are used to creating variables and user-defined procedures that are scoped to a form, using custom properties and methods provides this functionality, and also allows you to have a cleaner encapsulation model.

Specifying the Default Form Template

You can specify a form class from a registered class library for your form template.

To specify a default form template

1. From the **Tools** menu, choose **Options**.

2. In the **Options** dialog box, choose the **Forms** tab.

3. In the **Template classes** area, select the **Form** check box.

   If no form template has been selected, the **Open** dialog box opens so that you can choose a form class. If a form template has been selected, you can change it by choosing the dialog button and selecting another class.

4. Choose **Set as Default** if you want the template to be used in subsequent sessions of Visual FoxPro.

5. Choose **OK**.

Forms tab of the Options dialog box

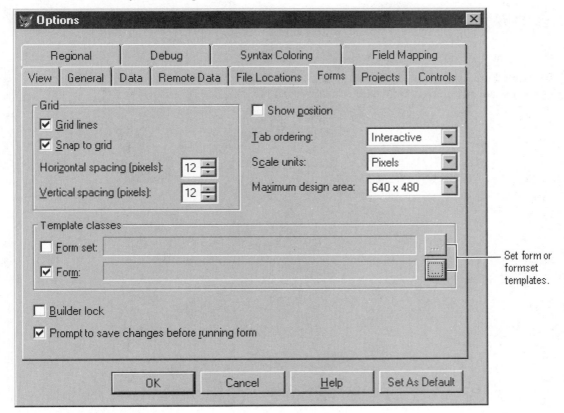

Set form or formset templates.

Using Form Templates

You can specify form set templates the same way you set form templates. The following combinations are possible:

- Both form set and form templates are specified.

    Choosing Form in the New dialog box (and all the other ways to create a new form) will automatically create a form set based on the template form set class. When you choose Add New Form from the Form menu in the Form Designer, a form based on your form template is added to the form set.

- Only the form set template is specified.

    Choosing Form in the New dialog box (and all the other ways to create a new form) will automatically create a form set based on the template FormSet class. When you choose Add New Form from the Form menu in the Form Designer, a form based on the Visual FoxPro Form base class is added to the form set.

- Only the form template is specified.

  Choosing Form in the New dialog box (and all the other ways to create a new form) will automatically create a form based on the template Form class.

- No templates are specified.

  Choosing Form in the New dialog box (and all the other ways to create a new form) will automatically create a form based on the Visual FoxPro Form base class.

Using Controls

Controls are the primary medium of user interaction. By typing and clicking, and by moving through controls on the forms in your application, users can manipulate their data and accomplish the tasks they want to do.

This chapter discusses:

- Understanding Controls and Data
- Choosing the Right Control for the Task
- Making Controls Easier to Use
- Extending Forms

For additional information, see "Controls and Objects" in the *Microsoft Visual FoxPro 6.0 Language Reference*.

Understanding Controls and Data

You can have two types of controls on your forms: controls that are bound to data and controls that are not. When users interact with bound controls, the values that they enter or choose are stored in the data source, which can be a table field, a cursor field, or a variable. You bind a control to data by setting its ControlSource property, or, in the case of grids, its RecordSource property.

If you don't set the ControlSource property of a control, the value that the user enters or chooses in the control is only stored as a property setting. The value is not written to disk or stored in memory beyond the lifetime of the control.

Effect of a ControlSource Property Setting on Controls

Control	Effect
Check box	If the ControlSource is a field in a table, then NULL values, logical values true (.T.) or false (.F.), or numeric values 0, 1, or 2 in the ControlSource field cause the check box to be selected, cleared, or grayed as the record pointer moves through the table.
Column	If the ControlSource is a table field, the user is directly editing the field when editing values in the column. To bind an entire grid to data, set the RecordSource property of the grid.

(continued)

Effect of a ControlSource Property Setting on Controls   *(continued)*

Control	Effect
List box or combo box	If the ControlSource is a variable, the value the user chooses in the list is stored in the variable. If the ControlSource is a field in a table, the value is stored in the field at the record pointer. If an item in the list matches the value of the field in the table, the item is selected in the list when the record pointer moves through the table.
Option button	If the ControlSource is a numeric field, 0 or 1 is written to the field, depending on whether or not the button is chosen.
	If the ControlSource is logical, .T. or .F. is written to the field, depending on whether the button is chosen. If the record pointer moves in the table, the value of the option button is updated to reflect the new value in the field.
	If the ControlSource of the option button's OptionGroup control (not the option button itself) is a character field, the caption of the option button is stored to the field if the option button is chosen. Note that the control source for an option button (as distinct from an OptionGroup control) cannot be a character field, or Visual FoxPro will report a data type mismatch when the form is run.
Spinner	The spinner reflects and writes numeric values to the underlying field or variable.
Text box or edit box	The value in the table field is displayed in the text box. Changes the user makes to this value are written back to the table. Moving the record pointer affects the Value property of the text box.

Some of the tasks you want to accomplish with controls require having data bound to the control. Other tasks will not.

Choosing the Right Control for the Task

Visual FoxPro controls are flexible and versatile. Though there are multiple controls you could use to accomplish any particular task, you need to have a consistent approach to the controls you use so that users can tell what to expect when they see the interface you provide. For example, a label has a Click event in the same way that a command button does, but users familiar with graphical interfaces expect to click on command buttons to perform actions.

Most of the functionality you'll want to build into your forms will fall under one of the following categories:

- Providing users with a set of predetermined choices
- Accepting user input that can't be predetermined

- Accepting user input in a given range

- Allowing users to perform specific actions

- Performing specific actions at given intervals

- Displaying information

Providing a Set of Predetermined Choices

One of the most straightforward ways to ensure the validity of the data in a database is to give users a predetermined set of options. By controlling user choices, you can make sure that no invalid data is stored in the database. The following controls allow you to provide users with a set of predetermined choices:

- Option button groups

- List boxes and drop-down lists

- Check boxes

Using Option Button Groups

Option button groups are containers that contain option buttons. Typically, option buttons allow users to specify one of a number of operational options in a dialog box rather than data entry. For example, option buttons can be used to specify output to a file, a printer, or to print preview as described in Chapter 12, "Adding Queries and Reports."

Setting the Number of Option Buttons in an Option Button Group

When you create an option button group on a form, two option buttons are included by default. You can determine how many option buttons are in a group by changing the ButtonCount property.

To set the number of option buttons in a group

- Set the **ButtonCount** property to the desired number of option buttons.

  For example, to have a group of six option buttons, set the **ButtonCount** property of the option button group to 6.

The Value property of the group indicates which of the buttons has been chosen. For example, if a user chooses the fourth option button in a group of six option buttons, the value of the option button group is 4.

If the group's **ControlSource** property is a character field, or if the **Value** property is set to a character value before the form is run, the group's Value property is the caption of the selected option button.

Setting Option Button Properties

To manually adjust individual elements of an option button or command button group in the Form Designer, choose Edit from the group's shortcut menu.

You can set properties on individual buttons in the Properties window. You can also set these properties at run time by specifying the name of the option button and the desired property setting. For example, the following line of code, included in the method or event code of some object on the same form as the option button group, sets the caption of optCust in the option button group opgChoices:

```
THISFORM.opgChoices.optCust.Caption = "Sort by Customer"
```

You can also set these properties at run time by using the Buttons property and specifying the index number of the option button in the group. For example, if optCust is the third button in the group, the following line of code also sets the caption of optCust:

```
THISFORM.opgChoices.Buttons(3).Caption = "Sort by Customer"
```

To set properties on all buttons in a group

- Use the SetAll method of the group.

    For example, the following line of code disables all the buttons in an option button group named opgMyGroup on a form:

    ```
    THISFORM.opgMyGroup.SetAll("Enabled",.F., "OptionButton")
    ```

Enabling and Disabling Buttons in a Group

The previous example shows how to programmatically disable all option buttons in a group. When the buttons are disabled, they are displayed in the colors specified in the DisabledForeColor and DisabledBackColor properties of the option buttons. You could also set the Enabled property of the option button group to false (.F.) to disable the group; however, there would be no visual clue for the user.

Determining Which Option Button Is Currently Selected

You can use the Value property of the option button group to determine which option button in the group is selected. If the control source for the button is numeric, you have five option buttons in a group. If the third button is selected, the Value property of the option button group is 3; if no option buttons are selected, the Value property of the option button group is 0.

You can also determine the caption of the selected option button by using the Value and Buttons properties of the group. For example, the following line of code stores the Caption property of the selected option button to a variable cSelected.

```
oGroup = THISFORM.opg1
cSelected = oGroup.Buttons(oGroup.Value).Caption
```

Filtering Lists with Option Buttons

If you have a small set of predetermined table filters, you could use option buttons to allow users to switch between the filters.

The following example assumes a form with a list box (lstCustomers) and an option button group that contains three option buttons.

Property Settings for the List Box

Object	Property	Setting
lstCustomers	RowSourceType	2 – Alias
lstCustomers	RowSource	Customer

The filters are set in the Click event code of the option buttons.

Event Code for Filtering a List When a User Chooses an Option Button

Object	Event	Code

optAll	Click	`SET FILTER TO`
		`GO TOP`
		`THISFORM.lstCustomers.Requery`

optCanada	Click	`SET FILTER TO customer.country = "Canada"`
		`GO TOP`
		`THISFORM.lstCustomers.Requery`

optUK	Click	`SET FILTER TO customer.country = "UK"`
		`GO TOP`
		`THISFORM.lstCustomers.Requery`

When the user closes the form, don't forget to reset the filter by including SET FILTER TO in the Click event of the closing button or in the Destroy event.

> **Tip**   To refresh a list when the list source might have changed, use the Requery method.

Using Option Buttons to Store User Choices to a Table

While it is not as common, you can use option buttons to get information from a user to be stored in a table by saving the Caption property. If you have a standardized testing application, for example, you could use option buttons to allow a user to choose among multiple choice options A, B, C, or D. You could also use option buttons to indicate gender in an employee table.

To store the Caption property of an option button to a table

1. Set the Value property of the option button group to an empty string.

2. Set the ControlSource property of the option button group to a character field in a table.

For example, if the captions of the option buttons in a group are "A," "B," "C," and "D," and the ControlSource of the option button group is a character field, when a user chooses the button with the caption "B," "B" is stored in the field.

To see an example of a multiple-choice test using option buttons

1. Run Solution.app in the Visual Studio ...\Samples\Vfp98\Solution directory.

2. In the treeview, click **Controls**, then click **Options buttons**.

3. Click **Present a user with multiple choices**.

Using List Boxes and Drop-Down List Boxes

List boxes and drop-down list boxes (combo box controls with the Style property set to 2 – Dropdown List) provide a user with scrollable lists that contain a number of options or pieces of information. In a list box, multiple items can be visible at all times. In a drop-down list box, only one item is visible, but a user can click the down button to display a scrolling list of all the items in the drop-down list box.

Run Solution.app in the Visual Studio ...\Samples\Vfp98\Solution directory to see several examples that demonstrate using list boxes and drop-down list boxes, including the following:

• Add pictures to a list.

• Multiselect items in a list.

• Fill a list with values from different sources.

• Display multiple columns in a list.

• Sort list items.

• Move items between lists.

List box and a drop-down list box with the same RowSource property setting

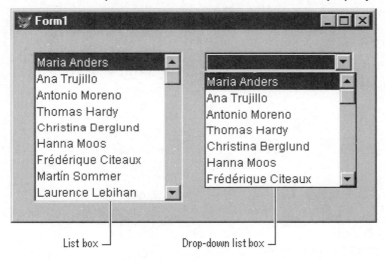

List box ┘   Drop-down list box ┘

Tip   If you have room on the form and if you want to emphasize the choices a user has, use a list. To conserve space and emphasize the currently selected item, use a drop-down list box.

Common List Properties and Methods

The following list box properties are commonly set at design time.

Property	Description
ColumnCount	The number of columns in the list box.
ControlSource	Where the value that a user chooses from the list is stored.
MoverBars	Whether mover bars are displayed to the left of list items so that a user can easily rearrange the order of items in the list.
Multiselect	Whether the user can select more than one item in the list at a time.
RowSource	Where the values displayed in the list come from.
RowSourceType	Whether the RowSource is a value, a table, a SQL statement, a query, an array, a list of files, or a list of fields.

Note   The Value property of a list can be numeric or character. The default is numeric. Set the Value property to an empty string if the RowSource is a character value and if you want the Value property to reflect the character string of the selected item in the list. You can press the SPACEBAR and then the BACKSPACE key to enter an empty string for a property in the Properties window.

The following list box methods are commonly used.

Method	Description
AddItem	Adds an item to a list with a RowSourceType of 0.
RemoveItem	Removes an item from a list with a RowSourceType of 0.
Requery	Updates the list if the values in the RowSource have changed.

Filling a List Box or a Combo Box

You can fill a list box with items from a variety of sources by setting the RowSourceType and RowSource properties.

Choosing the Type of Data for a List or Combo Box

The RowSourceType property determines what kind of source populates the list box or combo box — for example, an array or a table. Once you have set the RowSourceType, specify the source of the list items by setting the RowSource property.

RowSourceType	Source of the List Items
0	None. Programmatically add items to the list.
1	Value
2	Alias
3	SQL Statement
4	Query (.qpr)
5	Array
6	Fields
7	Files
8	Structure
9	Popup. Included for backward compatibility.

The following sections describe the various RowSourceType settings.

None   If you set the RowSourceType property to 0, the default, the list is not automatically populated. You can add items to the list by using the AddItem method:

```
frmForm1.lstMyList.RowSourceType = 0
frmForm1.lstMyList.AddItem("First Item")
frmForm1.lstMyList.AddItem("Second Item")
frmForm1.lstMyList.AddItem("Third Item")
```

The RemoveItem method allows you to remove items from the list. For example, the following line of code removes "Second Item" from the list:

```
frmForm1.lstMyList.RemoveItem(2)
```

Value   If you set the RowSourceType property to 1, you can specify multiple values in the RowSource property to be displayed in the list. If you set the RowSource property through the Properties window, include a comma-delimited list of items. If you set the RowSource programmatically, include the comma-delimited list in quotation marks:

```
Form1.lstMyList.RowSourceType = 1
Form1.lstMyList.RowSource = "one,two,three,four"
```

Alias   If you set the RowSourceType property to 2, you can include values from one or more fields in an open table.

If the ColumnCount property is 0 or 1, the list displays values in the first field of the table. If you set the ColumnCount property to 3, the list displays values in the first three fields of the table. To display fields in a different order than they are stored in the table, set the RowSourceType property to 3 – SQL Statement or 6 – Fields.

> **Note**   If the RowSourceType is 2 – Alias or 6 – Fields, when a user chooses a new value in the list, the table record pointer moves to the record with the value of that item.

SQL Statement   If you set the RowSourceType property to 3 – SQL Statement, include a SELECT – SQL statement in the RowSource property. For example, the following statement selects all fields and all records from the Customer table into a cursor:

```
SELECT * FROM Customer INTO CURSOR mylist
```

If you set the RowSource programmatically, remember to enclose the SELECT statement in quotation marks.

> **Note**   By default, Visual FoxPro SELECT statements without INTO clauses immediately display the resulting cursor in a Browse window. Since you rarely want this behavior in a RowSource SQL statement, include an INTO CURSOR clause in your SELECT statement.

Query   If you set the RowSourceType property to 4, you can populate your list box with the results of a query you designed in the Query Designer. When RowSourceType is set to 4, set RowSource to the .qpr file. For example, the following line of code sets the RowSource property of a list to a query.

```
THISFORM.List1.RowSource = "region.qpr"
```

If you don't specify a file extension, Visual FoxPro assumes an extension of .qpr.

Array   If you set the RowSourceType property to 5, the list is populated with the items in an array. You can create an array property of the form or form set for the RowSource or use an array created elsewhere in your application.

For information about creating array properties, see Chapter 9, "Creating Forms."

Troubleshooting   The RowSource setting of a list is evaluated by Visual FoxPro as needed in your application, not just in the method in which you set the RowSource. You need to keep this scope in mind. If you create a local array in a method, that array will be scoped to the method and will not be available in all cases when Visual FoxPro needs to evaluate the property setting. If you set the RowSource of a list to an array property of the form or form set, you need to reference the property relative to the list, not relative to the method in which you set the property. For example, if you have a form array property named `arrayprop`, the following lines of code in the Init of the form produce different results:

```
THIS.lstl.RowSource = "THIS.arrayprop"    && Error
THIS.lstl.RowSource = "THISFORM.arrayprop" && No error.
```

To populate a list with the elements in a multi-dimensional array

1. Set the **RowSourceType** property to 5.

2. Set the **RowSource** property to the multi-dimensional array.

3. Set the **ColumnCount** property to the number of columns to display.

4. Set the **ColumnWidths** property to the desired widths for each column.

Fields   If you set the RowSourceType property to 6, you can specify a field or comma-delimited list of fields to populate the list, such as:

```
contact,company,country
```

You can include the following types of information in the RowSource property of a list with a RowSourceType of 6 – Fields:

- field
- alias.field
- alias.field, field, field, ...

If you want to have fields from multiple tables in the list, set the RowSourceType property to 3 – SQL Statement.

Unlike a RowSourceType of 2 – Alias, a RowSourceType of 6 – Fields allows you to display fields independent of their actual positions in the table.

Files   If you set the RowSourceType property to 7, the list is populated with files in the current directory. Additionally, options in the list allow you to choose a different drive and directory for file names to be displayed in the list.

List populated with files in a directory

Set RowSource to the skeleton of the type of files you want to be displayed in the list. For example, to display Visual FoxPro tables in the list, set the RowSource property to ***.dbf**.

Structure   If you set the RowSourceType property to 8, the list is populated with the fields in the table that you specify when you set the RowSource property. This RowSourceType setting is useful if you want to present the user with a list of fields to search for values in or a list of fields to order a table by.

Popup   If you set the RowSourceType property to 9, you can fill the list from a previously defined popup. This option is included for backward compatibility.

Creating Multicolumn List Boxes

Although the default number of columns in a list box is one, a list box in Visual FoxPro can contain as many columns as you want. A multicolumn list box differs from a grid in that you select a row at a time in a multicolumn list box while you can select individual cells in a grid, and data in the list cannot be directly edited.

To display multiple columns in a list box

1. Set the **ColumnCount** property to the number of desired columns.

2. Set the **ColumnWidths** property. For example, if there are three columns in the list box, the following command would set the column widths to 10, 15, and 30, respectively:

   ```
   THISFORM.listbox.ColumnWidths = "10, 15, 30"
   ```

3. Set the **RowSourceType** property to **6 – Fields**.

4. Set the **RowSource property** to the fields to be displayed in the columns. For example, the following command sets the sources of three columns in a 3-column list box to the contact, city, and country fields of the customer table:

```
form.listbox.RowSource = "contact,city,country"
```

Note For the columns to align correctly, you need to either set the ColumnWidths property or change the FontName property to a monospaced font.

When the RowSourceType of the list is set to 0 – None, you can use the AddListItem method to add items to a multicolumn list box. For example, the following code adds text to specific columns in a list box:

```
THISFORM.lst1.ColumnCount = 3
THISFORM.lst1.Columnwidths = "100,100,100"
THISFORM.lst1.AddListItem("row1 col1", 1,1)
THISFORM.lst1.AddListItem("row1 col2", 1,2)
THISFORM.lst1.AddListItem("row1 col3", 1,3)
THISFORM.lst1.AddListItem("row2 col2", 2,2)
```

Allowing Users to Select Multiple Items in a List Box

The default behavior of a list allows one item at a time to be selected. You can, however, allow a user to select multiple items in a list.

To allow multiple selected items in a list

*   Set the MultiSelect property of the list to true (.T.).

To process the selected items — to copy them to an array or incorporate them elsewhere in your application — loop through the list items and process those for which the Selected property is true (.T.). The following code could be included in the InteractiveChange event of a list box to display the selected items in a combo box, cboSelected, and the number of selected items in a text box, txtNoSelected:

```
nNumberSelected = 0  && a variable to track the number
THISFORM.cboSelected.Clear && clear the combo box
FOR nCnt = 1 TO THIS.ListCount
   IF THIS.Selected(nCnt)
      nNumberSelected = nNumberSelected + 1
      THISFORM.cboSelected.Additem (THIS.List(nCnt))
   ENDIF
ENDFOR
THISFORM.txtNoSelected.Value = nNumberSelected
```

Allowing Users to Add Items to a List Box

In addition to allowing users to select items from a list box, you can allow users to interactively add items to a list.

To add items to a list interactively

- Use the **AddItem** method.

In the following example, when the user presses ENTER, the code in the KeyPress event of a text box adds the text in the text box to the list box and clears the text in the text box:

```
LPARAMETERS nKeyCode, nShiftAltCtrl
IF nKeyCode = 13    && Enter Key
   THISFORM.lstAdd.AddItem(This.Value)
   THIS.Value = ""
ENDIF
```

Allowing Users to Enter Data into a Table from a List

If the ControlSource property is set to a field, whatever the user selects in the list is written to the table. This is an easy way to help ensure the integrity of the data in your table. While the user can still enter the wrong data, an illegal value cannot be entered.

For example, if you have a list of states or counties for a user to choose from, the user cannot enter an invalid state or county abbreviation.

Allowing Users to Go to a Record by Picking a Value in a List

Often, you want to let users select the record they want to view or edit. For example, you could provide users with a list of customer names. When the user selects a customer from the list, you select that customer's record in the table and display customer information in text boxes on the form. You can do this several ways, depending on the source of data in your form.

RowSourceType	Selecting the appropriate record
2 – Alias 6 – Fields	When the user chooses a value in the list, the record pointer is automatically set to the desired record. Issue THISFORM.Refresh in the InteractiveChange event of the list to show the new values in other controls on the form.

0 – None
1 – Value
3 – SQL Statement
4 – QPR
5 – Array
	In the InteractiveChange event, select the table that has the record with the desired values, then search for the desired value. For example, if the RowSource holds customer identification numbers from the customer table, use this code:
	
	`SELECT customer`
	`LOCATE FOR THIS.Value = cust_id`
	`THISFORM.Refresh`

Refreshing a One-To-Many Display Based on a List Value

When the user chooses to go to a record by picking a value in a list, you might have a one-to-many relationship that needs to reflect the changed record pointer in the parent table. You can implement this functionality with both local tables and local or remote views.

Local Tables

If the RowSourceType of the list is 2 – Alias or 6 – Fields and the RowSource is a local table with a relationship set in the form's data environment, issue THISFORM.Refresh in the InteractiveChange event when the user chooses a new value. The many side of the one-to-many relationship automatically displays only the records that match the expression of the parent table involved in the relation.

Views

Refreshing a one-to-many display is a little different if the RowSource of the list box is a local or remote view. The following example describes creating a form with a list box and a grid. The list box displays the values from the cust_id field in the TESTDATA!Customer table. The grid displays the orders associated with the cust_id field selected in the list box.

First, in the View Designer create a parameterized view for the orders. When you create the view in the View Designer, set the selection criterion for the foreign key to a variable. In the following example, the variable is called m.cCust_id.

Parameterized view using a variable

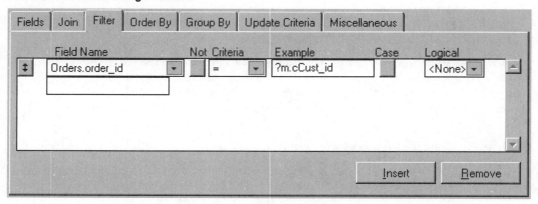

Then, when you design the form, follow the steps in the following procedure. Note that the view requires a value for the parameter that isn't available when the form is loaded. By setting the NoDataOnLoad property of the view cursor object to true (.T.), you prevent the view from being run until the REQUERY( ) function is called, at which time the user would have selected a value for the variable used in the parameterized view.

To design a one-to-many list based on local or remote views

1. Add the table and the parameterized view to the data environment.

2. In the Properties window for the view cursor object in the **Data Environment**, set the NoDataOnLoad property to true (.T.).

3. Set the RowSourceType property of the list box to **6 – Fields**, and set its RowSource property to the field referenced as the foreign key in the view's parameter.

    In the example, you would set the **RowSource** property to customer.cust_id.

4. Set the **RecordSource** property of the grid to the name of the view you created earlier.

5. In the **InteractiveChange** event code of the list box, store the value of the list box to the variable, then requery the view, as in this example:

```
m.cCust_id = THIS.Value
*assuming the name of the view is orders_view
=REQUERY("orders_view")
```

For more information about local and remote views, see Chapter 8, "Creating Views."

Displaying Child Records in a List

You can display records from a one-to-many relationship in a list so that the list displays the child records in the relationship as the record pointer moves through the parent table.

To display child records in a list

1. Add a list to the form.

2. Set the **ColumnCount** property of the list to the number of columns you want to display.

   For example, if you want to display the Order_id, Order_net, and Shipped_on fields in the list, set the **ColumnCount** property to 3.

3. Set the **ColumnWidths** property to the appropriate widths for displaying your selected fields.

4. Set the **RowSourceType** of the list to **3 – SQL Statement**.

5. Set the **RowSource** to the SELECT statement. For example, the following statement selects three fields from the orders table for the current record in the customer table:

```
SELECT order_id, order_net, shipped_on from orders ;
   WHERE order.cust_id = customer.cust_id ;
   INTO CURSOR temp
```

6. In the **Init** event of the form and in the code that moves the record pointer through the table, requery the list:

```
THISFORM.lstChild.Requery
```

Adding Pictures to Items in a List

You can set the Picture property of the list to the .bmp file you want displayed next to the items in the list.

For example, you could have a list box populated with files. You might want to have a different bitmap next to the file if it is a table, a program, or some other file type.

List box with pictures

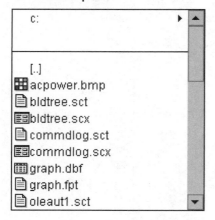

The following code is associated with the Click event of the list box:

```
FOR iItem = 5 TO THIS.ListCount       && files start at the 5th item
    cExtension = UPPER(RIGHT(THIS.List(iItem),3))
    DO CASE
       CASE cExtension = "DBF"
          THIS.Picture(iItem) = "tables.bmp"
       CASE cExtension = "BMP"
          THIS.Picture(iItem) = "other.bmp"
       CASE cExtension = "PRG"
          THIS.Picture(iItem) = "programs.bmp"
       CASE cExtension = "SCX"
          THIS.Picture(iItem) = "form.bmp"
       OTHERWISE
           THIS.Picture(iItem) = IIF("]" $ cExtension, ; "", "textfile.bmp")
    ENDCASE
ENDFOR
```

Using Check Boxes

You can use check boxes to allow a user to specify a Boolean state: True or False, On or Off, Open or Closed. However, there are times when it isn't accurate to evaluate something as True or False, such as unanswered questions on a True/False questionnaire.

To see examples of using check boxes

1. Run Solution.app in the Visual Studio ...\Samples\Vfp98\Solution directory.

2. In the treeview, click **Controls,** then click **Check boxes.**

There are four possible states for a check box, as determined by the Value property.

Display	Value property
☐ Check1	0 or .F.
☑ Check2	1 or .T.
☑ Check3	2
☐ Check4	.NULL.

The Value property of the check box reflects the data type of the last assignment. If you set the property to true (.T.) or false (.F.), the type is Logical until you set the property to a numeric value.

Tip   A user can display a null value in a check box by pressing CTRL+0.

Storing or Displaying Logical Fields

If you set the ControlSource property of the check box to a logical field in a table, the check box is displayed as checked when the value in the current record is true (.T.), as not checked when the value in the current record is false (.F.), and as grayed when a null value (.NULL.) is in the current record.

Accepting Input That Can't Be Predetermined

It is not always possible to anticipate all the possible values that a user might need to enter into a control. The following controls allow you to accept user input that can't be predetermined:

- Text boxes
- Edit boxes
- Combo boxes

Using Text Boxes

The text box is the basic control that allows users to add or edit data stored in a non-memo field in a table.

To see examples of using text boxes

1. Run Solution.app in the Visual Studio …\Samples\Vfp98\Solution directory.

2. In the treeview, click **Controls**, then click **Text boxes.**

To programmatically reference or change the text displayed in the text box

- Set or reference the **Value** property.

If you set a ControlSource for the text box, the value displayed in the text box is stored in the Value property of the text box and in the variable or field specified in the ControlSource property.

Validating the Data in a Text Box

To check or verify the value in the text box, include code in the method associated with the Valid event. If the value is invalid, return false (.F.) or 0. If the Valid returns false (.F.) an "Invalid input" message is displayed. If you want to display your own message, include the WAIT WINDOW command or the MESSAGEBOX( ) function in the Valid code and return 0.

For example, if you have a text box that allows a user to type an appointment date, you could check to make sure that the date is not already past by including the following code in the Valid event of the text box:

```
IF CTOD(THIS.Value) < DATE( )
   = MESSAGEBOX("You need to enter a future date",1)
   RETURN 0
ENDIF
```

Selecting Text When the Text Box Gets the Focus

To select all text when the user enters the text box with the keyboard, set the SelectOnEntry property to true (.T.).

Formatting the Text in a Text Box

You can use the InputMask property to determine the values that can be typed in the text box and the Format property to determine the way values are displayed in the text box.

Using the InputMask Property

The InputMask property determines the characteristics of each character typed into the text box. For example, you could set the InputMask property to 999,999.99 to limit user input to numeric values less than 1,000,000 with two decimal places. The comma and the period would be displayed in the text box before the user entered any values. If the user pressed a character key, the character would not be displayed in the text box.

If you have a logical field and want a user to be able to type "Y" or "N" but not "T" or "F," set the InputMask property to "Y."

Accepting User Passwords in a Text Box

Often in an application, you want to obtain secure information from a user, such as a password. You can use a text box to get this information without making the information visible on the screen.

To accept user input without displaying the actual value

- Set the PasswordChar property of the text box to * or some other generic character.

If you set the PasswordChar property to anything other than an empty string, the Value and Text properties of the text box contain the actual value that the user typed in the text box, but the text box displays a generic character for every key the user pressed.

Entering Dates in a Text Box

Text boxes have several properties that you can set to make it easy for your users to enter date values.

Property	Description
Century	Whether the first two digits of the year are displayed or not.
DateFormat	Format the date in the text box to one of fifteen predetermined formats, such as American, German, Japanese.
StrictDateEntry	Setting StrictDateEntry to 0 – Loose allows a user to enter dates in more flexible formats than the default 99/99/99.

For more information on these properties, see Help.

Common Text Box Properties

The following text box properties are commonly set at design time.

Property	Description
Alignment	Whether the contents of the text box are left justified, right justified, centered, or automatic. Automatic alignment depends on the data type. Numbers, for example, are right justified and characters are left justified.
ControlSource	The table field or variable whose value is displayed in the text box.
InputMask	Specifies the data entry rule each character entered must follow. For specific information about InputMask, see Help.
SelectOnEntry	Whether the contents of the text box are automatically selected when the text box receives the focus.
TabStop	Whether the user can tab to the control. If TabStop is set to .F., a user can still select the text box by clicking it.

Using Edit Boxes

You can allow users to edit text from long character fields or memo fields in edit boxes. Edit boxes allow automatic word-wrapping and the ability to move through the text using the arrow keys, page up and page down keys, and scrollbars.

To see examples of using edit boxes

1. Run Solution.app in the Visual Studio ...\Samples\Vfp98\Solution directory.

2. In the treeview, click **Controls**, then click **Edit boxes.**

Allowing Users to Edit a Memo Field in an Edit Box

All you have to do to allow a user to edit a memo field in an edit box is set the ControlSource property of the edit box to the memo field. For example, if you have a memo field named `comments` in a table named `log`, you can set the ControlSource property of an edit box to `log.comments` to enable a user to edit the memo field in the edit box.

Allowing Users to Edit a Text File in an Edit Box

You can also allow a user to edit a text file in an edit box. The following form demonstrates this.

Example form for editing a text file in an edit box

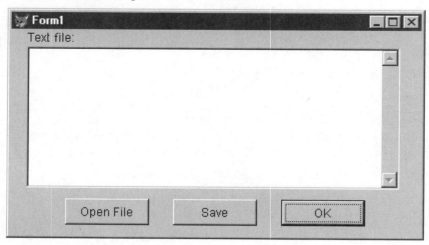

An OK button on the form closes the form with the following command in the Click event code:

```
RELEASE THISFORM
```

The other two buttons in this example, cmdOpenFile and cmdSave, allow a user to open a text file and save the file after edits.

Code Associated with the Click Event of cmdOpenFile

Code	Comments
```CREATE CURSOR textfile ;``` ``` (filename c(35), mem m)```	Create a cursor with a character field to hold the name of the text file and a memo field to hold the contents of the text file.
```APPEND BLANK```	Add a blank record to the cursor.
```REPLACE textfile.FileName WITH ;``` ``` GETFILE("TXT")```	Use the GETFILE( ) function to return the name of the file to open. Store the name in the FileName field of the cursor.

```IF EMPTY(textfile.FileName)```
 ```   RETURN```
 ```ENDIF```
	If the user chooses Cancel in the Get File dialog box, the FileName field will be empty and there will be no file to open.

```APPEND MEMO mem FROM ;``` ``` (textfile.FileName) OVERWRITE```	Fill the memo field with the text in the file.

```THISFORM.edtText.ControlSource = ;```
 ```   "textfile.mem"```
 ```THISFORM.Refresh```
	Set the ControlSource of the edit box on the form.

```THISFORM.cmdSave.Enabled = .T.```	Enable the Save button.

Once the file has been opened and edited, the Save button allows a user to write changes back out to the file.

Code Associated with the Click Event of cmdSave

Code	Comments
```COPY MEMO textfile.mem TO ;``` ``` (textfile.filename)```	Overwrites the old value in the file with the text in the memo field.

Manipulating Selected Text in an Edit Box

Edit boxes and text boxes hav4e three properties that allow you to work with selected text: SelLength, SelStart, and SelText.

You can select text programmatically using the SelStart and SelLength properties. For example, the following lines of code select the first word in an edit box.

```
Form1.edtText.SelStart = 0
Form1.edtText.SelLength = AT(" ", Form1.edtText.Text) - 1
```

Tip   When you change the SelStart property, the edit box scrolls to display the new SelStart. If you change the SelStart in a loop, for example when searching for text, your code will execute faster if you include `THISFORM.LockScreen = .T.` before processing and `THISFORM.LockScreen = .F.` after processing.

You can access selected text in an edit box or text box with the SelText property. For example, the following line of code makes the selected text all uppercase:

```
Form1.edtText.SelText = UPPER(Form1.edtText.SelText)
```

Common Edit Box Properties

The following edit box properties are commonly set at design time.

Property	Description
AllowTabs	Whether the user can insert tabs in the edit box instead of moving to the next control. If you allow tabs, be sure to indicate that users can move to the next control by pressing CTRL+TAB.
HideSelection	Whether selected text in the edit box is visibly selected when the edit box doesn't have the focus.
ReadOnly	Whether the user can change the text in the edit box.
ScrollBars	Whether there are vertical scrollbars.

Using Combo Boxes

The combo box control has the functionality of a list box and a text box. There are two styles for a combo box: Drop-down combo and Drop-down list. Specify which one you want by changing the Style property of the control. Drop-down lists are discussed in "Using List Boxes and Drop-Down List Boxes" earlier in this chapter.

Drop-Down Combo

A user can click the button on a drop-down combo box to see a list of choices or enter a new item directly in the box beside the button. The default Style property of a combo box is 0 — Dropdown Combo.

Adding User Items to Drop-Down Combo Lists

To add the new user value to the drop-down combo box, you can use the following line of code in the method associated with the Valid event of the combo box:

```
THIS.AddItem(THIS.Text)
```

Before adding an item, however, it would be a good idea to check to make sure that the value isn't already in the combo box drop-down:

```
lItemExists = .F. && assume the value isn't in the list.
FOR i = 1 to THIS.ListCount
   IF THIS.List(i) = THIS.Text
      lItemExists = .T.
      EXIT
   ENDIF
ENDFOR

IF !lItemExists
   THIS.AddItem(THIS.Text)
ENDIF
```

Common Combo Box Properties

The following combo box properties are commonly set at design time.

Property	Description
ControlSource	Specifies the table field where the value that the user chooses or enters is stored.
DisplayCount	Specifies the maximum number of items displayed in the list.
InputMask	For drop-down combo boxes, specifies the type of values that can be typed in.
IncrementalSearch	Specifies whether the control tries to match an item in the list as the user types each letter.
RowSource	Specifies the source of the items in the combo box.
RowSourceType	Specifies the type of the source for the combo box. The RowSourceType values for a combo box are the same as for a List. For an explanation of each, see Help or the discussion on list boxes earlier in this chapter.
Style	Specifies whether the combo box is a drop-down combo or a drop-down list.

Accepting Numeric Input in a Given Range

Although you can set the InputMask property and include code in the Valid event to make sure that numeric values entered into text boxes fall within a given range, the easiest way to check the range of values is to use a spinner.

Using Spinners

You can use spinners to allow users to make choices by "spinning" through values or directly typing the values in the spinner box.

Setting the Range of Values That Users Can Choose

Set the KeyboardHighValue and the SpinnerHighValue properties to the highest number you want users to be able to enter in the spinner.

Set the KeyboardLowValue and the SpinnerLowValue properties to the lowest number you want users to be able to enter in the spinner.

Decrementing a Spinner When the User Clicks the Up Button

Sometimes, if your spinner reflects a value like "priority," you want the user to be able to increase the priority from 2 to 1 by clicking the Up button. To cause the spinner number to decrement when the user clicks the Up button, set the Increment property to –1.

Spinning Through Non-Numeric Values

While the value of a spinner is numeric, you can use the Spinner control and a text box to allow users to spin through multiple types of data. For instance, if you want a user to be able to spin through a range of dates, you could size the spinner so that only the buttons are visible and position a text box beside the spinner buttons. Set the Value property of the text box to a date and in the UpClick and DownClick events of the spinner, increment or decrement the date.

Tip   You can use the Windows API function GetSystemMetrics to set the width of your spinner so that only the buttons are visible and the buttons are the best width for the up and down arrow bitmap display.

1. Set the spinner's **BorderStyle** property to 0.

2. Include the following code in the Init of the spinner:

```
DECLARE INTEGER GetSystemMetrics IN Win32api INTEGER
THIS.Width = GetSystemMetrics(2) && SM_CXVSCROLL
```

Common Spinner Properties

The following spinner properties are commonly set at design time.

Property	Description
Interval	How much to increment or decrement the value each time the user clicks the Up or Down buttons.
KeyboardHighValue	The highest value that can be entered into the spinner text box.
KeyboardLowValue	The lowest value that can be entered into the spinner text box.
SpinnerHighValue	The highest value that the spinner will display when the user clicks the Up button.
SpinnerLowValue	The lowest value that the spinner will display when the user clicks the Down button.

Allowing Specific Actions

Frequently, you want to enable users to take specific actions that have nothing to do with manipulating values. For example, you can allow a user to close a form, open another form, move through a table, save or cancel edits, run a report or query, jump to an address of a destination on the Internet or an intranet, or any number of other actions.

Using Command Buttons and Command Button Groups

One of the most common places to put the code for specific actions is the Click event of a command button.

Making a Command Button the Default Choice

Set the Default property to true (.T.) to make the command button the default choice. The default choice has a thicker border than other command buttons. If a command button is the default choice, when the user presses ENTER, the Click event of the command button executes.

> **Note**   If the selected object on a form is an edit box or a grid, the code associated with the Click event of the default choice is not executed when the user presses ENTER. Pressing ENTER in an edit box adds a carriage return and line feed to the value in the edit box. Pressing ENTER in a grid selects an adjacent field. To execute the Click event of the default button, press CTRL+ENTER.

Common Command Button Properties

The following command button properties are commonly set at design time.

Property	Description
Cancel	Specifies that the code associated with the Click event of the command button executes when a user presses ESC.
Caption	Text displayed on the button.
DisabledPicture	The .bmp file displayed when the button is disabled.
DownPicture	The .bmp file displayed when the button is pressed.
Enabled	Whether the button can be chosen.
Picture	The .bmp file displayed on the button.

You can also include command buttons in a group so that you can manipulate them individually or as a group.

Managing Command Button Choices at the Group Level

If you want to work with a single method procedure for all the code for the Click events of command buttons in a group, you can attach the code to the Click event of the command button group. The Value property of the command button group indicates which of the buttons was clicked, as demonstrated in the following code example:

```
DO CASE
   CASE THIS.Value = 1
      WAIT WINDOW "You clicked " + THIS.cmdCommand1.Caption NOWAIT
      * do some action
   CASE THIS.Value = 2
      WAIT WINDOW "You clicked " + THIS.cmdCommand2.Caption NOWAIT
      * do some other action
   CASE THIS.Value = 3
      WAIT WINDOW "You clicked " + THIS.cmdCommand3.Caption NOWAIT
      * do a third action
ENDCASE
```

Note If the user clicks in the command button group but not on a particular button, the Value property still reflects the last command button that was selected.

If you have written code for the Click event of a particular button in the group, that code is executed rather than the group Click event code when the user chooses that button.

Common Command Button Group Properties

The following command button group properties are commonly set at design time.

Property	Description
ButtonCount	Number of command buttons in the group.
BackStyle	Whether the command button group has a transparent or opaque background. A transparent background appears to be the same color that the underlying object, usually the form or a page, is.

Using the Hyperlink Object

You can use the Hyperlink object to jump to an address of a destination on the Internet or an intranet. The Hyperlink object can be used to start a hyperlink aware application, typically an Internet browser such as the Microsoft Internet Explorer, and open the page specified in the address. The Hyperlink NavigateTo( ) method allows you to specify the address of the destination that you jump to.

For example, to navigate to the Microsoft Internet site on the World Wide Web from a form, first add the Hyperlink control to the form. Add a command button to the form, and then add the following code to the Click event for the command button:

```
THISFORM.Hyperlink1.NavigateTo('www.microsoft.com')
```

When the form is run, you can click the command button to jump to the Microsoft Web site.

Performing Specific Actions at Given Intervals

The Timer control allows you to perform actions or check values at specific intervals.

Using the Timer Control

Timer controls respond to the passage of time independent of user interaction, so you can program them to take actions at regular intervals. A typical use is checking the system clock to see if it is time to do a particular task. Timers are also useful for other kinds of background processing.

To see examples of using timers

1. Run Solution.app in the Visual Studio …\Samples\Vfp98\Solution directory.

2. In the treeview, click **Controls**, then click **Timer.**

Each timer has an Interval property, which specifies the number of milliseconds that pass between one timer event and the next. Unless disabled, a timer continues to receive an event (appropriately named the Timer event) at roughly equal intervals of time. The Interval property has a few limitations to consider when you're programming a timer:

*   The interval can be between 0 and 2,147,483,647, inclusive, which means that the longest interval is about 596.5 hours (over 24 days).

*   The interval is not guaranteed to elapse exactly on time. To ensure accuracy, the timer should check the system clock when it needs to, rather than try to keep track of accumulated time internally.

*   The system generates 18 clock ticks per second, so even though the Interval property is measured in milliseconds, the true precision of an interval is no more than one-eighteenth of a second.

*   If your application or another application is making heavy demands on the system — such as long loops, intensive calculations, or disk, network, or port access — your application may not get timer events as often as the Interval property specifies.

Placing a Timer Control on a Form

Placing a Timer control on a form is like drawing any other control: you choose the timer tool on the Controls toolbar and click and drag on the form.

A Timer control

The timer appears on the form at design time so you can select it, view its properties, and write an event procedure for it. At run time, a timer is invisible and its position and size are irrelevant.

Initializing a Timer Control

A Timer control has two key properties.

Property	Setting
Enabled	If you want the timer to start working as soon as the form loads, set to true (.T.). Otherwise, leave this property set to false (.F.). You may choose to have an outside event (such as a click of a command button) start operation of the timer.
Interval	Number of milliseconds between timer events.

Note that the Enabled property for the timer is different than for other objects. With most objects, the Enabled property determines whether the object can respond to an event caused by the user. With the Timer control, setting Enabled to false (.F.) suspends timer operation.

Remember that the Timer event is periodic. The Interval property doesn't determine "how long" as much as it determines "how often." The length of the interval should depend on how much precision you want. Because there is some built-in potential for error, make the interval one-half the desired amount of precision.

> **Note** The more often a timer event is generated, the more processor time is consumed in responding to the event. This can slow down overall performance. Don't set a particularly small interval unless you need it.

Responding to the Timer Event

When a Timer control's interval elapses, Visual FoxPro generates the Timer event. Typically, you respond to this event by checking some general condition, such as the system clock.

A digital clock is a very simple but highly useful application involving a Timer control. Once you understand how the application works, you can enhance it to work as an alarm clock, stopwatch, or other timing device.

The digital clock application includes a timer and a label with a border. At design time, the application looks like this:

The digital clock application

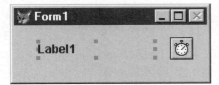

At run time, the timer is invisible.

Control	Property	Setting
lblTime	Caption	
Timer1	Interval	500 (half a second)
Timer1	Enabled	True

The sole procedure in the application is the Timer event procedure:

```
IF THISFORM.lblTime.Caption != Time()
    THISFORM.lblTime.Caption = Time()
ENDIF
```

The Interval property for the timer is set to 500, following the rule of setting the Interval to half of the shortest period you want to distinguish (one second in this case). This may cause the timer code to update the label with the same time twice in one second. This could cause some visible flicker, so the code tests to see if the time is different from what is displayed in the label before it changes the caption.

Displaying Information

One of the principles of good design is to make relevant information visible. You can use the following controls to display information to your users:

- Images
- Labels
- Text Boxes
- Edit Boxes
- Shapes

Using Images

The Image control allows you to add pictures (.bmp files) to your form. An Image control has the full range of properties, events, and methods that other controls have, so an Image control can be changed dynamically at run time, Users can interact with images by clicking, double-clicking, and so on.

The following table lists some of the key properties of an Image control.

Property	Description
Picture	The picture (.bmp file) to display.
BorderStyle	Whether there is a visible border for the image.
Stretch	If Stretch is set to 0 – Clip, portions of the picture that extend beyond the dimensions of the Image control are not displayed. If Stretch is set to 1 – Isometric, the Image control preserves the original dimensions of the picture and displays as much of the picture as the dimensions of the Image control will allow. If Stretch is set to 2 – Stretch, the picture is adjusted to exactly match the height and width of the Image control.

Using Labels

Labels differ from text boxes in that they:

- Cannot have a data source.
- Cannot be directly edited.
- Cannot be tabbed to.

You can programmatically change the Caption and Visible properties of labels to tailor the label display to the situation at hand.

Common Label Properties

The following label properties are commonly set at design time.

Property	Description
Caption	The text displayed by the label.
AutoSize	Whether the size of the label is adjusted to the length of the Caption.
BackStyle	Whether the label is Opaque or Transparent.
WordWrap	Whether the text displayed on the label can wrap to additional lines.

Using Text and Edit Boxes to Display Information

Set the ReadOnly property of text and edit boxes to display information that the user can view but not edit. If you only disable an edit box, the user won't be able to scroll through the text.

Using Shapes and Lines

Shapes and lines help you visually group elements of your form together. Research has shown that associating related items helps users to learn and understand an interface, which makes it easier for them to use your application.

The following Shape properties are commonly set at design time.

Property	Description
Curvature	A value between 0 (90 degree angles) and 99 (circle or oval).
FillStyle	Whether the shape is transparent or has a specified background fill pattern.
SpecialEffect	Whether the shape is plain or 3D. This only has an effect when the Curvature property is set to 0.

The following Line properties are commonly set at design time.

Property	Description
BorderWidth	How many pixels wide the line is.
LineSlant	When the line is not horizontal or vertical, the direction of the slant. Valid values for this property are a slash (/) and a backslash (\ ).

Using Form Graphics to Display Information

You can graphically display information on a form by using the following form methods.

Method	Description
Circle	Draws a circular figure or arc on a form.
Cls	Clears graphics and text from a form.
Line	Draws a line on a form.
Pset	Sets a point on a form to a specific color.
Print	Prints a character string on a form.

To see examples that demonstrate form graphics

1. Run Solution.app in the Visual Studio ...\Samples\Vfp98\Solution directory.

2. In the treeview, click **Forms**, then click **Form graphics**.

Enhancing Control Display

Command buttons, check boxes, and option buttons can display pictures in addition to captions. These controls all have properties that allow you to specify pictures to be displayed on the controls.

Property	Description
DisabledPicture	Picture displayed on the button when the button is disabled.
DownPicture	Picture displayed on the button when the button is pressed.
Picture	Picture displayed on the button when the button is enabled and not pressed.

If you don't specify a DisabledPicture value, Visual FoxPro displays the Picture grayed when the control is disabled. If you don't specify a DownPicture value, Visual FoxPro displays the Picture with the background colors changed so that the button appears pressed when the button is pressed.

If you don't want a caption displayed in addition to the picture, set the Caption property to an empty string by deleting the default caption in the Property Editing box of the Properties window.

Using Picture Masks

Often, a .bmp picture contains white space you don't want to appear on your controls. A white border around an irregularly shaped image could make your control look bad. To avoid this problem, Visual FoxPro creates a temporary default mask for your picture. White areas are given a transparent attribute so that the underlying color of the button or background shows through. To keep certain white areas of your .bmp white, create a mask for it that will override the default.

To create a mask for a .bmp

1. Open the .bmp file in Paint or another bitmap utility.

2. Blacken all areas of the picture that you want to be displayed exactly as they are in the .bmp file. Leave the areas you want to be transparent as white.

3. Save the file in the same directory and with the same name as the .bmp file but with an .msk extension.

When Visual FoxPro loads a .bmp file specified by the Picture property for a command button, option button, or check box, it looks in the same directory for a matching .msk file. If an .msk file with the same name as the .bmp is in the directory, Visual FoxPro uses it as a mask for the picture. All white areas in the .msk picture are made transparent in the .bmp. All black areas in the .msk picture are displayed exactly as they are in the .bmp.

Note   The .bmp picture and the .msk picture must have the same dimensions for the mask to be able to represent the area of the .bmp.

Manipulating Multiple Rows of Data

Visual FoxPro provides a very powerful tool — the grid object — for displaying and manipulating multiple rows of data.

Using Grids

The grid is a container object. Just as a form set can contain forms, a grid can contain columns. In addition, the columns contain headers and controls, each with their own sets of properties, events, and methods, giving you a great deal of control over the elements of the grid.

Container	Can contain
Grid	Columns
Column	Headers, controls

The Grid object allows you to present and manipulate rows and columns of data in a form or page. A particularly useful application of the Grid control is creating one-to-many forms, such as an invoice form.

To see examples of using grids

1. Run Solution.app in the Visual Studio …\Samples\Vfp98\Solution directory.

2. In the treeview, click **Controls**, then click **Grid**.

A form with a populated grid

To add a Grid control to a form

*   In the Form Controls toolbar, choose the **Grid** button and drag to size in the **Form** window.

If you do not specify a RecordSource value for the grid and there is a table open in the current work area, the grid will display all the fields in that table.

Setting the Number of Columns in a Grid

One of the first properties you might want to set for the Grid control is the number of columns.

To set the number of columns in a grid

1. Select the **ColumnCount** property in the **Property and Methods** list.

2. In the **Property** box, type the number of columns you want.

If the ColumnCount property is set to –1 (the default), the grid will contain, at run time, as many columns as there are fields in the table associated with the grid.

Manually Adjusting Grid Display at Design Time

Once you have added columns to the grid, you can change the width of the columns and the height of the rows. You can manually set the height and width properties of the column and row objects in the Properties window or visually set these properties in grid design mode.

To switch to grid design mode

- Choose **Edit** from the grid's shortcut menu.

  – or –

  In the **Object** box of the Properties window, select a column of the grid.

When you are in grid design mode, a thick border is displayed around the grid. To switch out of grid design mode, select the form or another control.

To adjust the width of the columns in a grid

1. In grid design mode, position the mouse pointer between grid column headers so that the pointer changes to a bar with arrows pointing left and right.

2. Select the column and drag until the column is the desired width

   – or –

   Set the column's Width property in the Properties window.

To adjust the height of the rows in a grid

1. In grid design mode, position the mouse pointer between the first and second buttons on the left side of the **Grid** control so that the pointer changes to a bar with arrows pointing up and down.

2. Select the row and drag until the row is the desired height.

   – or –

   Set the column's Height property in the Properties window.

   Tip   You can prevent a user from changing the height of the grid rows at run time by setting AllowRowSizing to false (.F.).

Setting the Source of the Data Displayed in the Grid

You can set the data source for the grid and for each column individually.

To set the data source for a grid

1. Select the grid, then click the **RecordSourceType** property in the Properties window.

2. Set the **RecordSourceType** property to **0 – Table**, if you want Visual FoxPro to open the table for you, or **1 – Alias** if you want the grid to be populated with the fields in a table that is already open.

3. Click the **RecordSource** property in the Properties window.

4. Type the name of the alias or table to serve as the data source for the grid.

If you want to specify particular fields to be displayed in particular columns, you can also set the data source for a column.

To set the data source for a column

1. Select the column, then click the **ControlSource** property in the Properties window.

2. Type the name of the alias or table and the field to serve as the source for the values displayed in the column. For example, you can type:

```
Orders.order_id
```

Adding Records to a Grid

You can allow users to add new records to a table displayed in a grid by setting the AllowAddNew property of the grid to true (.T.). When the AllowAddNew property is set to true, new records are added to the table when the last record is selected and the user presses the DOWN ARROW key.

If you want more control over when a user adds new records to a table, you can set the AllowAddNew property to false (.F.), the default, and use the APPEND BLANK or INSERT commands to add new records.

Setting Up a One-To-Many Form Using the Grid Control

One of the most common uses for a grid is to display the child records for a table while text boxes display the data for the parent records. When the user moves through the records in the parent table, the grid displays the appropriate child records.

If you have a data environment for your form that includes a one-to-many relationship between two tables, displaying the one-to-many relationship in the form is very easy.

To set up a one-to-many form with a data environment

1. Drag desired fields from the parent table in the Data Environment Designer to your form.

2. Drag the related table from the **Data Environment Designer** to the form.

In almost all cases, you'll want to create a data environment for your form or form set. However, it's not much more complicated to create a one-to-many form without using the Data Environment Designer.

To set up a one-to-many form without creating a data environment

1. Add text boxes to your form to display the desired fields from the primary table.

2. Set the **ControlSource** property of the text boxes to the primary table.

3. Add a grid to the form.

4. Set the **RecordSource** property of the grid to the name of the related table.

5. Set the **LinkMaster** property of the grid to the name of the primary table.

6. Set the **ChildOrder** property of the grid to the name of the index tag in the related table that corresponds to the relational expression of the primary table.

7. Set the **RelationalExpr** property of the grid to the expression that joins the related table to the primary table. For example, if the ChildOrder tag is indexed on "lastname + firstname", set **RelationalExpr** to the same expression.

Either way you set up the one-to-many form, you can add navigation controls to move through the parent table and refresh the form objects. For example, the following code could be included in the Click event of a command button:

```
SELECT orders && if orders is the parent table
SKIP
IF EOF( )
   GO BOTTOM
ENDIF
THISFORM.Refresh
```

Displaying Controls in Grid Columns

In addition to displaying field data in a grid, you can have controls in the columns of a grid so that you can present a user with embedded text boxes, check boxes, drop-down list boxes, spinners, and other controls. For example, if you have a logical field in a table, when you run the form, a user can tell which record values are true (.T.) and which record values are false (.F.) by seeing whether the check box is set. Changing the value is as easy as setting or clearing the check box.

You can add controls to grid columns interactively in the Form Designer or write code to add the controls to the columns at run time.

To interactively add controls to a grid column

1. Add a grid to a form.

2. In the Properties window, set the ColumnCount property of the grid to the number of desired columns.

   For example, type **2** for a two-column grid.

3. In the **Properties** window, select the parent column for the control from the Object box.

   For example, select Column1 to add a control to Column1. The border of the grid changes to indicate that you are editing a contained object when you select the column.

4. Select the desired control on the Form Controls toolbar and click in the parent column.

   The new control will not be displayed in the grid column in the **Form Designer**, but it will be visible at run time.

5. In the **Properties** window, make sure the control is displayed indented under the parent column in the **Object** box.

A check box added to a grid column

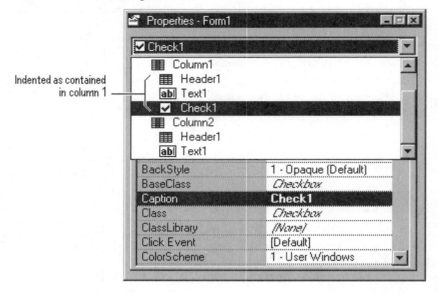

Indented as contained in column 1

If the new control is a check box, set the Caption property of the check box to " " and the Sparse property of the column to false (.F.).

6. Set the **ControlSource** property of the parent column to the desired table field.

   For example, the ControlSource of the column in the following illustration is `products.discontinu` from Testdata.dbc in the Visual Studio ...\Samples\Vfp98\Data directory.

7. Set the **CurrentControl** property of the parent column to the new control.

When you run the form, the control is displayed in the grid column.

The check box is displayed in the column at run time.

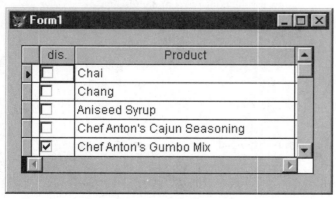

Tip   If you want to be able to center a check box in a grid column, create a container class, add a check box to the container class, and adjust the position of the check box in the container class. Add the container class to the grid column and set the ControlSource of the check box to the desired field.

To remove controls from grid columns in the Form Designer

1. In the **Object** box of the Properties window, select the control.

2. Activate the Form Designer.

   If the Properties window is visible, the control name is displayed in the **Object** box.

3. Press the DELETE key.

You can also add controls to a grid column using the AddObject method in code.

To programmatically add controls to a grid column

- In the **Init** event of the grid, use the **AddObject** method to add the control to the grid column and set the **CurrentControl** property of the column.

For example, the following lines of code in the Init event of a grid add two controls to a grid column and specify one of them as the current control:

```
THIS.grcColumn1.AddObject("spnQuantity", "SPINNER")
THIS.grcColumn1.AddObject("cboQuantity", "COMBOBOX")
THIS.grcColumn1.CurrentControl = "spnQuantity"
* The following lines of code make sure the control is visible
* and is diplayed in every row in the grid
THIS.grcColumn1.spnQuantity.Visible = .T.
THIS.grcColumn1.Sparse = .F.
```

In this example, Column1 has three possible current control values:

- spnQuantity

- cboQuantity

- Text1 (the default control)

   Note   Properties set on the Grid level are not passed on to the columns or headers. In the same way, you must set properties of the headers and contained controls directly; they do not inherit their properties from settings at the Column level.

   Tip   For the best display of combo boxes in grid columns, set the following combo box properties:

```
BackStyle = 0      && Transparent
Margin = 0
SpecialEffect = 1 && Plain
BorderStyle = 0    && None
```

Using Conditional Formatting in Grids

Special formatting in a grid can make it easier for a user to scan through the records in the grid and locate certain information. To provide conditional formatting, use the dynamic font and color properties of a column.

For example, you can add a grid to a form and set the ColumnCount property to 2. Set the ControlSource property of the first column to orders.to_name and the ControlSource property of the second column to orders.order_net. To display order totals less than 500.00 with a forecolor of black and order totals greater than or equal to 500.00 with a foreground color of red, include the following line in the grid's Init event code:

```
THIS.Column2.DynamicForeColor = ;
    "IIF(orders.order_net >= 500, RGB(255,0,0), RGB(0,0,0))"
```

Common Grid Properties

The following grid properties are commonly set at design time.

Property	Description
ChildOrder	The foreign key of the child table that is joined with the primary key of the parent table.
ColumnCount	Number of columns. If ColumnCount is set to –1, the grid has as many columns as there are fields in the grid's RecordSource.
LinkMaster	The parent table for child records displayed in the grid.
RecordSource	The data to be displayed in the grid.
RecordSourceType	Where the data displayed in the grid comes from: a table, an alias, a query, or a table selected by the user in response to a prompt.

Common Column Properties

The following column properties are commonly set at design time.

Property	Description
ControlSource	The data to be displayed in the column. This is often a field in a table.
Sparse	If Sparse is set to true (.T.), controls in a grid are displayed as controls only when the cell in the column is selected. Other cells in the column display the underlying data value in a text box. Setting Sparse to true (.T.) allows faster repainting if a user is scrolling through a grid with a lot of displayed rows.
CurrentControl	Which control in the grid is active. The default is Text1, but if you add a control to the column, you can specify it as the CurrentControl.

Note   The ReadOnly property of a control inside the column is overridden by the ReadOnly property of the Column. If you set the ReadOnly property of the control in a column in the code associated with the AfterRowColChange event, the new setting will be valid while you are in that cell.

Making Controls Easier to Use

You want to make it as easy as possible for users to understand and use your controls. Access keys, tab order, ToolTip text, and selective disabling all contribute to a more usable design.

Setting Access Keys

An access key allows a user to choose a control from anywhere in the form by pressing ALT and the key.

To specify an access key for a control

- Precede the desired letter in the **Caption** property for the control with a backslash and a less-than sign (\<).

For example, the following property setting for the Caption of a command button makes O the access key.

```
\<Open
```

A user can choose the command button from anywhere in the form by pressing ALT+O.

To specify an access key for a text box or edit box

1. Create a label with a backslash and less than sign (\<) in front of the desired letter, such as C\<ustomer.

2. Make sure the label is the control in the tab order immediately preceding the text box or edit box you want to receive the focus.

Setting the Tab Order of Controls

The default tab order of controls on your form is the order in which you added the controls to the form.

> **Tip**   Set the tab order of controls so that the user can easily move through your controls in a logical order.

To change the tab order of controls

1. In the Form Designer toolbar, choose **Set Tab Order**.

2. Double-click the box next to the control you want to have the initial focus when the form opens.

3. Click the box next to the other controls in the order you want them to be tabbed to.

4. Click anywhere outside the tab order boxes to finish.

You can also set the tab order for the objects on your form by list, depending on the setting in the Form Design tab of the Options dialog box.

You can set the selection order for the option and command buttons within a control group. To move to a control group with the keyboard, a user tabs to the first button in the control group and then uses the arrow keys to select other buttons in the group.

To change the selection order of buttons within a control group

1. In the Properties window, select the group in the **Object** list. A thick border indicates that the group is in edit mode.

2. Select the Form Designer window.

3. From the **View** menu, choose **Tab Order**.

4. Set the selection order as you would the tab order for controls.

Setting ToolTip Text

Each control has a ToolTipText property that allows you to specify the text displayed when the user pauses the mouse pointer over the control. Tips are especially useful for buttons with icons instead of text.

To specify ToolTip text

• In the Properties window, select the **ToolTipText** property and type the desired text.

The form's ShowTips property determines whether ToolTip text is displayed.

Change the Mouse Pointer Display

You can change the mouse pointer display to provide visual clues to your users about different states your application might be in.

For example, in the tsBaseForm class of the Tasmanian Traders sample application, a WaitMode method changes the mouse pointer to the default wait state cursor. Before running any code that might take a while to process, the Tasmanian Traders application passes a value of true (.T.) to the WaitMode method to change the pointer and let the user know that processing is going on. After the processing is completed, a call to WaitMode with false (.F.) restores the default mouse pointer.

```
* WaitMode Method of tsBaseForm class
LPARAMETERS tlWaitMode

lnMousePointer = IIF(tlWaitMode, MOUSE_HOURGLASS, MOUSE_DEFAULT)
THISFORM.MousePointer = lnMousePointer
THISFORM.SetAll('MousePointer', lnMousePointer)
```

If you want to change the mouse pointer to something other than one of the default pointers, set the MousePointer property to 99 – Custom and set the MouseIcon property to your own cursor (.cur) or icon (.ico) file.

Enabling and Disabling Controls

Set a control's Enabled property to false (.F.) if the functionality of the control is not available in a given situation.

Enabling and Disabling Buttons in a Group

You can enable or disable individual option buttons or command buttons in a group by setting the Enabled property of each button to either true (.T.) or false (.F.). You can also disable or enable all the buttons in a group by setting the Enabled property of the group, as in the following line of code:

```
frmForm1.cmgCommandGroup1.Enabled = .T.
```

When you set the Enabled property of an option button group or a command button group to false (.F.), all the buttons in the group are disabled, but won't be displayed with the disabled ForeColor and BackColor. Setting the Enabled property of the group does not change the Enabled property of the individual buttons in the group. This allows you to disable a group of buttons with some of the buttons already disabled. When you enable the group, buttons that were originally disabled remain disabled.

If you want to disable all the buttons in a group so that they appear disabled, and if you don't want to preserve information about which buttons were originally disabled or enabled, you can use the SetAll method of the group, like this:

```
frmForm1.opgOptionGroup1.SetAll("Enabled", .F.)
```

Allowing Users to Drag-and-Drop

When you design Visual FoxPro applications, you can drag text, files, and objects from the Component Gallery, Project Manager, the Database Designer, and the Data Environment Designer to desired locations on forms and reports. The drag-and-drop features in Visual FoxPro allow you to extend this ability to the user at run time.

This drag-and-drop capability extends to multiple-form operations. The user can drag text, files, and controls anywhere on the screen, including other forms.

Two types of drag-and-drop are now supported in Visual FoxPro: OLE drag-and-drop and control drag-and-drop. OLE drag-and-drop allows you to move data between other applications that support OLE drag-and-drop (such as Visual FoxPro, Visual Basic, the Windows Explorer, Microsoft Word and Excel, and so on). In a distributed Visual FoxPro application, you can move data between controls in the application, or between controls and other Window applications that support OLE drag-and-drop.

Control drag-and-drop allows you to drag-and-drop Visual FoxPro controls within your Visual FoxPro applications. Control drag-and-drop is also supported in earlier versions of Visual FoxPro. As the user drags a control, Visual FoxPro provides a gray outline that is the same size as the object and moves with the mouse pointer. You can override this default behavior by specifying a cursor file (.cur) for the DragIcon property of a control.

This section describes control drag-and-drop. For more information about OLE drag-and-drop, see "OLE Drag-and-Drop" in Chapter 31, "Interoperability and the Internet."

To see examples of control drag-and-drop

1. Run Solution.app in the Visual Studio …\Samples\Vfp98\Solution directory.

2. In the treeview, click **Controls**, then click **General**.

Dragging an Image control at run time

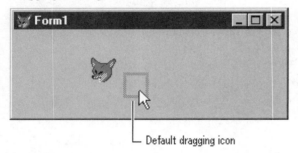

Note   Run-time dragging of a control doesn't automatically change its location. You can do this, but you must program the relocation yourself, as described in the section "Causing Control Movement in a Drag-and Drop Operation," later in this chapter. Often, dragging is used only to indicate that some action should be performed; the control retains its original position after the user releases the mouse button.

Using the following drag-and-drop properties, events, and method, you can specify both the meaning of a drag operation and how dragging can be initiated (if at all) for any given control.

To	Use this feature
Enable automatic or manual dragging of a control.	DragMode property
Specify what icon is displayed when the control is dragged.	DragIcon property
Recognize when a control is dropped onto the object.	DragDrop event
Recognize when a control is dragged over the object.	DragOver event
Start or stop manual dragging.	Drag method

All visual controls can be dragged at run time and all controls share the properties listed in the preceding table. Forms recognize the DragDrop and DragOver events, but they don't have DragMode and DragIcon properties.

Enabling Automatic Drag Mode

To allow the user to drag a control whenever the user clicks the control, set its DragMode property to 1. This enables automatic dragging of the control. When you set dragging to Automatic, dragging is always on.

Note   While an automatic drag operation is taking place, the control being dragged doesn't recognize other mouse events.

Responding When the User Drops the Object

When the user releases the mouse button after dragging a control, Visual FoxPro generates a DragDrop event. You can respond to this event in many ways. You can relocate the control at the new location (indicated by the last position of the gray outline). Remember that the control doesn't automatically move to the new location.

Two terms are important when discussing drag-and-drop operations — *source* and *target*.

Term	Meaning
Source	The control being dragged.
Target	The object onto which the user drops the control. This object, which can be a form or control, recognizes the DragDrop event.

A control becomes the target if the mouse position is within its borders when the button is released. A form is the target if the pointer is in a blank portion of the form.

The DragDrop event receives three parameters: *oSource*, *nXCoord*, and *nYCoord*. The parameter *oSource* is a reference to the control that was dropped onto the target. The parameters *nXCoord* and *nYCoord* contain the horizontal and vertical coordinates, respectively, of the mouse pointer within the target.

Because *oSource* is an object, you use it just as you would a control — you can refer to its properties or call one of its methods. For example, the following statements in the code associated with the DragDrop event checks to see whether the user has dropped a control on itself:

```
LPARAMETERS oSource, nXCoord, nYCoord
IF oSource.Name != THIS.Name
   * Take some action.
ELSE
   * Control was dropped on itself.
   * Take some other action.
ENDIF
```

All possible control types for *oSource* have a Visible property. Therefore, you can make a control invisible when it's dropped on a certain part of a form or on another control. The following line in the code associated with the DragDrop event of an Image control causes a dragged control to disappear when it's dropped on the image:

```
LPARAMETERS oSource, nXCoord, nYCoord
oSource.Visible = .F.
```

Indicating Valid Drop Zones

When you enable drag-and-drop, you can help your users by including visual clues about where a user can and cannot drop a control. The best way to do this is to change the DragIcon of the source in the code associated with the DragOver event.

The following code in the DragOver event of a control indicates to a user that the control is not a valid drop target. In this example, cOldIcon is a user-defined property of the form.

```
LPARAMETERS oSource, nXCoord, nYCoord, nState
DO CASE
   CASE nState = 0 && Enter
      THISFORM.cOldIcon = oSource.DragIcon
      oSource.DragIcon = "NODROP01.CUR"
   CASE nState = 1 && Leave
      oSource.DragIcon = THISFORM.cOldIcon
ENDCASE
```

Controlling When Dragging Starts or Stops

Visual FoxPro has a setting of Manual for the DragMode property that gives you more control than the Automatic setting. The Manual setting allows you to specify when a control can and cannot be dragged. (When DragMode is set to Automatic, the control can always be dragged as long as the setting isn't changed.)

For instance, you may want to enable dragging in response to MouseDown and MouseUp events, or in response to a keyboard or menu command. The Manual setting also allows you to recognize a MouseDown event before dragging starts, so that you can record the mouse position.

To enable dragging from code, leave DragMode in its default setting (0 – Manual). Then use the Drag method whenever you want to begin or stop dragging an object:

container.control.Drag(*nAction*)

If *nAction* is 1, the Drag method initiates dragging of the control. If *nAction* is 2, the control is dropped, causing a DragDrop event. The value 0 for *nAction* cancels the drag. The effect is similar to giving the value 2, except that no DragDrop event occurs.

Note   To enable a drag-and-drop operation from a list box, the best place to call the Drag method is in the code associated with the MouseMove event of the source list box, after determining that the mouse button is down. For an example, see Lmover.scx in the Visual Studio …\Samples\Vfp98\Solution\Controls\Lists directory.

Causing Control Movement in a Drag-and-Drop Operation

You may want the source control to change position after the user releases the mouse button. To make a control move to the new mouse location, use the Move method. For example, the following code in the DragDrop event of a form moves the control that is dragged to the location of the drop:

```
LPARAMETERS oSource, nXCoord, nYCoord
oSource.Move(nXCoord, nYCoord)
```

This code may not produce precisely the effects you want, because the upper-left corner of the control is positioned at the mouse location. The following code positions the center of the control at the mouse location:

```
LPARAMETERS oSource, nXCoord, nYCoord
oSource.Move ((nXCoord - oSource.Width / 2), ; (nYCoord - oSource.Height / 2))
```

The code works best when the DragIcon property is set to a value other than the default (the gray rectangle). When the gray rectangle is being used, the user normally wants the control to move precisely into the final position of the gray rectangle. To do this, record the initial mouse position within the source control. Then use this position as an offset when the control is moved. For an example, see Ddrop.scx in the Visual Studio …\Samples\Vfp98\Solution\Forms directory.

To record the initial mouse position

1. Specify manual dragging of the control.

2. Declare two form-level variables, nDragX and nDragY.

3. Turn on dragging when a **MouseDown** event occurs. Also, store the value of *nXCoord* and *nYCoord* in the form-level variables in this event.

4. Turn dragging off when the **MouseUp** event occurs.

Extending Forms

Page frames allow you to extend the surface area of your forms, and ActiveX controls allow you to extend the functionality of your forms.

Using Page Frames

A page frame is a container object that contains pages. Pages in turn contain controls. Properties can be set at the page frame, page, or control level.

To see examples of using page frames

1. Run Solution.app in the Visual Studio …\Samples\Vfp98\Solution directory.

2. In the treeview, click **Controls**, then click **Page frame**.

You can think of the page frame as a three-dimensional container that presents layered pages. Only controls on the top page (or on top of the page frame) can be visible and active.

Multiple pages in a page frame on a form

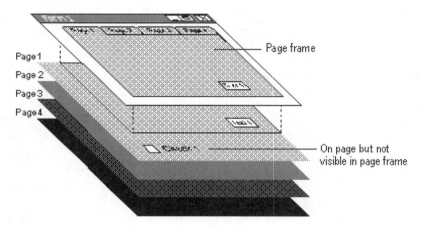

The page frame defines the location of the pages and the amount of the page that is visible. The upper-left corner of a page is anchored to the upper-left corner of the page frame. Controls can be placed on pages which are beyond the dimensions of the page frame. These controls are active, but are not visible unless you programmatically change the Height and Width properties of the page frame to make the controls visible.

Using Pages in an Application

With page frames and pages, you can create tabbed forms or dialog boxes with the same kind of interface capabilities that you see in the Project Manager.

In addition, page frames allow you to define a region of the form where you can easily swap controls in and out. For example, in Wizards, most of the form remains constant, but an area of the form changes with each step. Instead of creating five forms for the wizard steps, you could create one form with a page frame and five pages.

Solution.app, in the Visual Studio …\Samples\Vfp98\Solution directory, contains two page frame examples that demonstrate using frames with and without tabs.

Adding Page Frames to a Form

You can include one or more page frames on any form.

To add a page frame to a form

1. In the Form Controls toolbar, choose the **Page Frame** button and drag to size in the **Form** window.

2. Set the PageCount property to indicate the number of pages to include in the frame.

Page frame with four pages

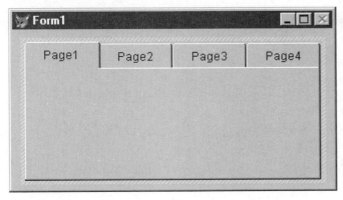

3. From the frame's shortcut menu, choose **Edit** to activate the frame as a container. The page frame border widens to indicate that it is active.

4. Add controls the same way you would add them to a form.

   Note   Like other container controls, you must select the page frame and choose **Edit** from the right mouse menu, or select the container in the Object drop-down list in the Properties window, so that the container is selected (has a wider border) before you add controls to the page you are designing. If you do not activate the page as a container before adding controls, the controls will be added to the form instead of the page, even though they may appear to be on the page.

To select a different page in the page frame

1. Activate the page frame as a container by right-clicking it and choosing **Edit**.

2. Select the tab of the page you want to use.

   – or –

   Select the page in the **Object** box in the Properties window.

   – or –

   Select the page in the **Page** box at the bottom of the Form Designer.

Adding Controls to a Page

When you add controls to a page, they are visible and active only when their page is active.

To add controls to a page

1. In the **Object** box of the Properties window, select the page. A border appears around the page frame indicating that you can manipulate contained objects.

2. In the Form Controls toolbar, choose the control button you want and drag to size in the page.

Managing Long Captions on Page Tabs

If the captions on your tabs are longer than can be displayed on the tab given the width of the page frame and the number of pages, you have two options:

- Set the TabStretch property to **1 – Single Row** to show only the characters of the captions that will fit on the tabs. Single Row is the default.

- Set the TabStretch property to **0 – Multiple Rows** to stack the tabs so that the entire caption on all the tabs is visible.

Changing Pages Programmatically

Whether a page frame is displayed with tabs or not, you can programmatically make a page active by using the ActivePage property. For example, the following code in the Click event procedure of a command button on a form changes the active page of a frame page on the form to the third page:

```
THISFORM.pgfOptions.ActivePage = 3
```

Common Page Frame Properties

The following page frame properties are commonly set at design time.

Property	Description
Tabs	Whether tabs are visible for the pages.
TabStyle	Whether or not the tabs are all the same size and together the same width as the page frame.
PageCount	The number of pages in the page frame.

OLE Container Control

You add an OLE object to a form by clicking this tool and dragging it to size in the Form window. This tool can represent a server object such as Microsoft Excel or Word, or it can represent an ActiveX control if your Windows SYSTEM directory contains ActiveX controls (files with an .ocx extension). For general information about ActiveX controls, see Chapter 16, "Adding OLE."

OLE Bound Control

You can create a bound OLE object on a form by clicking this tool and dragging it to size in the Form window. After creating the object, you connect it to a General field in a table. Then, you use the object to display the contents of the field. For example, if you store Word documents in a General field, you can display the contents of these documents by using a bound OLE object on a form.

To create a bound OLE object

1. Create or open a form.

2. In the Form Controls toolbar, choose the **OLE Bound Control** button and drag it to size on the form.

3. Bind the OLE object to a General field by setting the object's **ControlSource** property.

For an example of using the OLE Bound control, see Chapter 16, "Adding OLE."

Designing Menus and Toolbars

Menus and toolbars provide a structured and accessible route for users to leverage the commands and tools contained in your applications. Proper planning and design of menus and toolbars will ensure that the key functionality of your applications is exposed, and that users will not become frustrated as they try to use your applications.

For information about customizing Visual FoxPro toolbars, see Chapter 3, "Configuring Visual FoxPro," in the *Installation Guide*.

This chapter discusses:

- Using Menus in Your Applications
- Creating Custom Toolbars
- Testing and Debugging a Menu System
- Customizing a Menu System

Using Menus in Your Applications

Users often browse menus before looking elsewhere for information about your application. If your menus are well designed, users can organize their understanding of the application by developing a mental model based on the menu organization and content alone. With the Visual FoxPro Menu Designer, you can create menus that enhance the quality of your applications.

Each part of a Visual FoxPro application can have its own menu system, or set of menus. The following sections describe how to create a menu system, but don't explain how to incorporate the menu system into your application. For details about adding menus to an application, see Chapter 13, "Compiling an Application."

The following sections describe:

- Creating a Menu System
- Planning a Menu System
- Creating Menus, Shortcut Menus, Menu Items, and Submenus
- Assigning Tasks to a Menu System

Creating a Menu System

Much of the work involved in creating a menu system is done in the Menu Designer, where you create the actual menus, submenus, and menu options.

Menu Designer

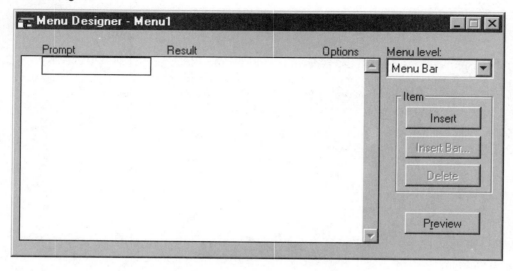

Creating a menu system involves several steps. Regardless of the size of your application and the complexities of the menus you plan to use, you should:

- Plan and design the system.

  Decide what menus you need, where they appear in the interface, which ones need submenus, and so on. For more information about planning menu systems, see "Planning a Menu System" later in this chapter.

- Create the menus and submenus.

  Define the menu titles, menu items, and submenus using the Menu Designer.

- Assign tasks to the system so that it does what you want.

  Specify tasks for the menus to perform, such as displaying forms and dialog boxes. Additionally, include setup code and cleanup code if appropriate. Setup code executes before the menu system is defined and can include code for opening files, declaring variables, or placing the menu system on a stack so that it can be retrieved later. Cleanup code contains code to be executed after the menu definition code, and makes menus and menu items available or unavailable for selection.

- Generate the menu program.

- Run the program to test the system.

Planning a Menu System

The usefulness of an application can depend on the quality of its menu systems. If you invest planning time in your menus, users will accept them readily and learn them quickly.

While designing your menu system, consider the following guidelines:

- Organize the system according to the tasks users will perform, not according to the hierarchy of programs in the application.

  Users can form a mental model of how the application is organized by looking at the menus and menu items. To design these menus and menu items effectively, you should know how your users will think about and accomplish their work.

- Give each menu a meaningful title.

- Organize menu items according to their expected frequency of use, their logical sequence, or their alphabetical order.

  If you can't predict the frequency and can't determine a logical order, then organize menu items alphabetically. Alphabetical ordering is particularly effective when a menu contains more than eight items. With so many items, the user spends time scanning them; alphabetical ordering facilitates scanning.

- Put separator lines between logical groups of menu items.

- Limit the number of items on a menu to one screen.

- If the number exceeds the length of a screen, create submenus for appropriate menu items.

- Choose access keys and keyboard shortcuts for menus and menu items.

  For example, ALT+F could be an access key for a File menu.

- Use words that clearly describe the menu items.

  Use common words rather than computer jargon, and use simple, active verbs to indicate what actions will result from choosing each menu item. Don't use nouns as verbs. Additionally, describe the menu items using parallel construction. For example, if you use single words for all the items, then use the same part of speech for all of them.

- Use mixed upper and lowercase letters in menu items.

  Tip   To see an example of a menu system, run the Tasmanian Traders application, Tastrade.app, located in the Visual Studio …\Samples\Vfp98\Tastrade directory.

Creating Menus, Shortcut Menus, Menu Items, and Submenus

After planning your menu system, you can create it with the Menu Designer. You can create menus, shortcut menus, menu items, submenus of menu items, lines that separate groups of related menu items, and so on. The following sections provide the details.

Creating Menus

You can create menus by customizing the existing Visual FoxPro menu system or by developing your own menu system. To start with the existing Visual FoxPro menu system, use the Quick Menu feature.

To create a menu system with Quick Menu

1. From the Project Manager, select the **Other** tab, select **Menus**, and then select **New**.

2. Select **Menu**.

   The **Menu Designer** appears.

3. From the **Menu** menu, choose **Quick Menu**.

   The **Menu Designer** now contains information about the main Visual FoxPro menus.

   A menu system created with the Quick Menu feature

   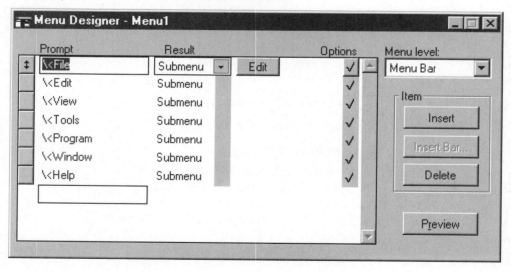

4. Customize the menu system by adding or changing menu items.

   For example, insert a Customer menu before the Help menu by choosing the mover button associated with the Help menu, choosing the **Insert** button, and then typing **Customer** in the **Prompt** column. The result looks like this:

A customized menu system

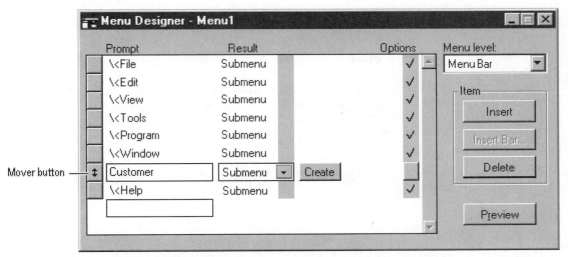

Mover button

Tip   Drag mover buttons to change the location of menus on the menu bar.

If you need a Help menu, make it the last menu on the menu bar so that users can find it quickly.

Before you can use your menu in an application, you must generate it.

To generate a menu

- From the Menu menu, choose **Generate**.

Visual FoxPro prompts you to save the menu system in a file with an .mnx extension. This file is a table that will store all the information about the menu system. After you save the menu system, Visual FoxPro prompts for an output file with an .mpr extension. This file will contain the generated menu program.

Creating Shortcut Menus

Shortcut menus appear when you click the right mouse button on a control or object, and provide a quick way to expose all of the functions that apply to just that object. You can use Visual FoxPro to create shortcut menus, then attach these menus to controls. For example, you can create a shortcut menu containing the commands Cut, Copy, and Paste that will appear when a user right-clicks on data contained in a Grid control.

To create a shortcut menu

1. From the Project Manager, select the **Other** tab, select **Menus**, and then choose **New**.

2. Choose **Shortcut**.

   The **Shortcut Designer** appears.

Once you are in the Shortcut Menu designer, the process for adding menu items is the same as it is for creating menus.

For an example of shortcut menus, run Solution.app in the Visual Studio ...\Samples\Solution\Vfp98\Solution directory.

Creating SDI Menus

SDI menus are menus that appear in single-document interface (SDI) windows. To create an SDI menu you must indicate that the menu will be used on an SDI form while you're designing the menu. Other than that, the process of creating an SDI menu is the same as that for creating a normal menu.

To create an SDI menu

- While the Menu Designer is open, choose **General Options** from the **View** menu, and select **Top-Level Form**.

Creating Menu Items

After creating menus, you can place menu items on the menus. Menu items can represent Visual FoxPro commands or procedures that you want the user to execute, or menu items can contain submenus that offer additional menu items.

To add menu items to a menu

1. In the **Prompt** column, select the menu title to which you want to add menu items.

   For example, select the Customer menu title created previously.

2. In the **Result** box, select **Submenu**.

   A **Create** button appears to the right of the list.

3. Choose the **Create** button.

   An empty design window appears. In this window, you enter the menu items.

4. In the **Prompt** column, type the names of the new menu items.

   For example, distinguish between cash and credit customers by typing **Cash** for one menu item and **Credit** for another.

Creating Submenus

For each menu item, you can create a submenu containing additional menu items.

To create a submenu

1. In the **Prompt** column, select the menu item to which you want to add a submenu.

   For example, select the Credit menu item created earlier.

2. In the **Result** box, select **Submenu**.

   A **Create** button appears to the right of the list. If a submenu already exists, an **Edit** button appears instead.

3. Select **Create** or **Edit**.

4. In the **Prompt** column, type the names of the new menu items.

    For example, add two items to the Credit submenu: type **Visa** for Visa cardholders and **MasterCard** for MasterCard holders.

Adding Menus Programmatically

Though you typically create menus and menu items using the Menu Designer, you can also create them using Visual FoxPro commands. For example, you can create a menu using DEFINE PAD, a submenu using DEFINE POPUP, and items on the submenu using a series of DEFINE BAR commands. For details, see these topics in Help.

Grouping Menu Items

For readability, separate groups of similar menu items with dividing lines. For example, in Visual FoxPro, the Edit menu has a line separating the Undo and Redo commands from the Cut, Copy, Paste, Paste Special, and Clear commands.

Grouped menu items

To group menu items

1. In the **Prompt** column, type **\-**. This creates a dividing line.

2. Drag the button to the left of the **\-** prompt to move the dividing line until it appears where you want it.

Saving a Menu as HTML

You can use the **Save As HTML** option on the **File** menu when you're creating a menu to save the contents of a menu as an HTML (Hypertext Markup Language) file.

To save a form as HTML

1. Open the menu.

2. Choose **Save As HTML** on the **File** menu. (You will be asked to save the menu if it has been modified.)

3. Enter the name of the HTML file to create and choose **Save**.

Including Menus in an Application

Once you create a menu system, you can include it in your application.

To include a menu system in your application

- Add the .mnx file to your project, then build the application from the project. For more information about building your application, see Chapter 13, "Compiling an Application."

Attaching Shortcut Menus to Controls

Once you create and generate a shortcut menu, you can attach it to a control. Shortcut menus typically appear when a user right-clicks on a control. You can attach a shortcut menu to a particular control by entering a small amount of code in the right-click event of the control.

1. Select the control to which you want to attach the shortcut menu.

2. In the Properties window, choose the **Methods** tab and select **Right Click Event**.

3. In the code window, type **DO** *menu***.MPR**, where *menu* is the name of the shortcut menu.

   Note   Be sure to use the .mpr extension when referencing shortcut menus.

Attaching SDI Menus to Forms

Once you create an SDI menu, you can attach it to an SDI form. In addition, you must:

- Set the form's **ShowWindow** property.

- Add a DO statement to the form's **Init** event.

To attach an SDI menu to a form

1. In the Form Designer, set the form's ShowWindow property to **2 – As Top Level Form**.

2. In the **Init** event of the form, call the menu.

   For example, if your menu is called SDIMENU.MPR, add this code:

   ```
   DO SDIMENU.MPR WITH THIS,.T.
   ```

Assigning Tasks to a Menu System

As you create a menu system, you should consider ease of access to the system, and you must assign tasks to the system. You must give menus and menu items tasks to perform, such as displaying forms, toolbars, and other menu systems. You should define access keys to permit entry to the menu system. You can also add keyboard shortcuts and enable or disable menu items for more control.

Assigning Access Keys

Well-designed menus have access keys for quick keyboard access to the menu functionality. The access key is represented by the underlined letter in the menu title or menu item. For instance, the Visual FoxPro File menu uses "F" as its access key.

If you don't assign an access key to a menu title or menu item, Visual FoxPro automatically assigns the first letter as the access key. For example, the Customer menu created previously didn't have a defined access key. Accordingly, Visual FoxPro assigned the first letter (C) as the access key.

Menus with access keys

To specify the access key for a menu or menu item

- Type \< to the left of the letter you want as the access key.

   For example, to set the access key to "u" in the Customer menu title, replace **Customer** with **C\<ustomer** in the Prompt column.

   Troubleshooting   If an access key for your menu system doesn't work, look for duplicate access keys.

Assigning Keyboard Shortcuts

In addition to assigning access keys, you can specify keyboard shortcuts for menus or menu items. As with access keys, keyboard shortcuts let you choose a menu or menu item by holding down one key while pressing another. The difference between access keys and keyboard shortcuts is that you can use a keyboard shortcut to choose a menu item without first displaying its menu.

Keyboard shortcuts for Visual FoxPro menu items are combinations of the CTRL or ALT key and another key. For instance, you can create a new file in Visual FoxPro by pressing CTRL+N.

To specify a keyboard shortcut for a menu or menu item

1. In the **Prompt** column, select the appropriate menu title or menu item.

2. Choose the button in the **Options** column to display the **Prompt Options** dialog box.

3. In the **Key Label** box, press a key combination to create a keyboard shortcut.

   If a menu item doesn't have a keyboard shortcut, Visual FoxPro displays "(press the key)" in the **Key Label** box.

4. In the **Key Text** box, add the text you want to appear beside the menu item.

    By default, Visual FoxPro repeats the keyboard shortcut from the **Key Label** box in the **Key Text** box. However, you can change the text in the **Key Text** box if you want your application to display different text. For example, if both the **Key Label** and **Key Text** were CTRL+R, you could change the **Key Text** value to ^R.

    Note   CTRL+J is an invalid keyboard shortcut because it is used to close certain dialog boxes in Visual FoxPro.

Enabling and Disabling Menu Items

You can enable or disable a menu or menu item based on a logical condition.

To enable or disable a menu or menu item

1. In the **Prompt** column, select the appropriate menu title or menu item.
2. Choose the button in the **Options** column to display the **Prompt Options** dialog box.
3. Select **Skip For**.

    The **Expression Builder** appears.

Expression Builder Dialog Box

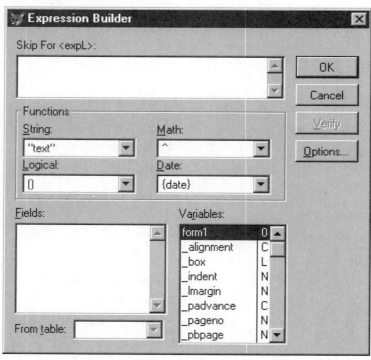

4. In the **Skip For** box, type the expression that determines whether the menu or menu item is enabled or disabled.

    If the expression evaluates to false (.F.), the menu or menu item is enabled. If the expression evaluates to true (.T.), the menu or menu item is disabled and cannot be selected or chosen. For details, see DEFINE BAR and DEFINE PAD in Help.

    Note   After the menu system has been displayed, you can enable and disable menus and menu items by using the SET SKIP OF command. For details, see Help.

Marking the State of a Menu Item

On a menu, a check mark next to a menu item indicates that it is in effect. For example, if you put a check mark next to the Credit item on the Customer menu created earlier, Credit is in effect.

At run time, you can place a check mark next to a menu item by using the SET MARK OF command. For details, see Help.

For an example of disabling and marking the state of menu items, run Solution.app in the Visual Studio …\Samples\Vfp98\Solution directory.

Assigning Tasks to Menus or Menu Items

When a menu or menu item is selected, it performs a task, such as displaying a form, a toolbar, or another menu system. To perform a task, a menu or menu item must execute a Visual FoxPro command. The command can be contained in one line, or it can be a procedure call.

Tip   If you expect to use a set of commands in several places, write a procedure. The procedure should be explicitly named and written in the menu cleanup code, or somewhere where it can be referenced by any menu or object.

Performing Tasks with Commands

To perform a task, you can assign a command to a menu or menu item. A command can be any valid Visual FoxPro command, including a call to a program that exists on your path or a procedure defined in the Cleanup option of the General Options dialog box. For more information, see "Creating a Default Procedure for a Menu System" later in this chapter.

To assign a command to a menu or menu item

1. In the **Prompt** column, select the appropriate menu title or menu item.

2. In the **Result** box, select **Command**.

3. In the box to the right of the **Result** box, type the appropriate command:

Assigning a command to a menu

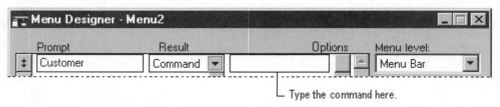

— Type the command here.

If the command calls a procedure in the menu's cleanup code, use the DO command with the following syntax:

DO *procname* IN *menuname*

In this syntax, *menuname* specifies the location of the procedure. This is the name of the menu file and must have the .mpr extension. If you don't specify the location in *menuname*, you must specify it with SET PROCEDURE TO *menuname*.mpr, if the procedure is in the menu cleanup code. For more information about these commands, see Help.

Displaying Forms and Dialog Boxes

From a menu or menu item, you can display a compiled form or dialog box by calling it with a command or procedure. For example, to display a form named "Orders," use the following command:

```
DO FORM Orders
```

Tip   When you create a menu or menu item that displays a form or dialog box, put three dots at the end of the prompt to indicate that more user input is required.

Dots after a menu item show that user input is required.

Displaying Toolbars

If you create a custom toolbar for an application, you can display it by calling it from a menu or menu item. For details, see "Creating Custom Toolbars" later in this chapter.

Performing Tasks with Procedures

You can assign a procedure to a menu or menu item. The way you assign a procedure depends on whether the menu or menu item has submenus.

To assign a procedure to a menu or menu item without submenus

1. In the **Prompt** column, select the appropriate menu title or menu item.

2. In the **Result** box, select **Procedure**.

   A **Create** button appears to the right of the list. If a procedure has been defined previously, an **Edit** button appears instead.

3. Select **Create** or **Edit**.

   Assigning a procedure to a menu with submenus

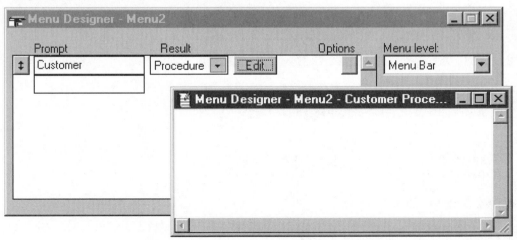

4. Type the appropriate code in the window.

   Note   You don't need to type the PROCEDURE command in the procedure editing window because Visual FoxPro generates this statement for you. The only place you need the PROCEDURE statement is in the cleanup code.

To assign a procedure to a menu or menu item with submenus

1. In the **Menu level** box, select the level that includes the appropriate menu or menu item. For example, suppose your menu system includes the Customer menu created earlier. To assign a procedure to the Customer menu, select the "Menu Bar" level in the Menu Level box. Similarly, to assign a procedure to an item on the Customer menu, select the "Customer" level in the list.

2. From the **View** menu, choose **Menu Options**.

   Visual FoxPro displays the **Menu Options** dialog box.

   ### Assigning a procedure to a menu with submenus

   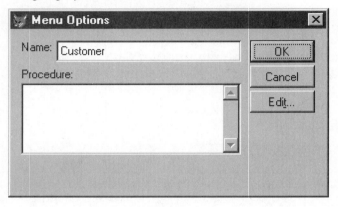

3. Assign the procedure by doing one of the following:

   - Write or call a procedure in the **Procedure** box.

     – or –

     Choose **Edit** and then **OK** to open a separate editing window and write or call a procedure.

Adding Setup Code to a Menu System

You can customize a menu system by adding setup code to it. Setup code can include code for creating the environment, defining variables, opening necessary files, and saving or restoring menu systems with the PUSH MENU and POP MENU commands. For details, see the PUSH MENU and POP MENU command topics in Help.

To add setup code to a menu system

1. From the **View** menu, choose **General Options**.

2. In the **Menu Code** area, select **Setup** and then choose **OK**.

3. In the setup code window, type the appropriate setup code.

   Your changes are saved when you close the Menu Designer.

Adding Cleanup Code to a Menu System

You can tailor your menu system by adding cleanup code to it. Cleanup code typically contains code that initially enables or disables menus and menu items. When you generate and run the menu program, setup code and menu definition code is processed before cleanup code.

To add cleanup code to a menu system

1. From the **View** menu, choose **General Options**.

2. In the **Menu Code** area, select **Cleanup** and then choose **OK**.

3. In the code window, type the appropriate cleanup code.

   Your changes are saved when you close the **Menu Designer**.

   Tip   If your menu is the main program in an application, include a READ EVENTS command in the cleanup code and assign a CLEAR EVENTS command to the menu command used to exit the menu system. This prevents your run-time applications from terminating prematurely.

Controlling Menus at Run Time

Each Visual FoxPro menu has two names, and each menu item has a name and a number. Visual FoxPro uses one name in the user interface and the other name or number in the generated menu program (.mpr). You can use these names or numbers to reference and control menus and menu items at run time. If you don't provide a name or number when creating menus and menu items, Visual FoxPro creates one when you generate the menu program.

For an example of adding and removing menu items at run time, see Solution.app in the Visual Studio …\Samples\Vfp98\Solution directory.

   Caution   Avoid using Visual FoxPro-generated names and numbers in code, because they change each time you generate the menu program. If you refer to a generated name or number, your code might fail.

In the Menu Designer, the Prompt column shows what appears in the user interface, and the column to the right of the Result box shows what appears in the generated program.

Using Pad Name to reference a menu pad in the generated menu program

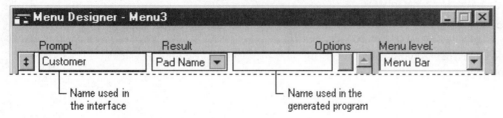

Using Bar # to reference a menu item in the generated menu program

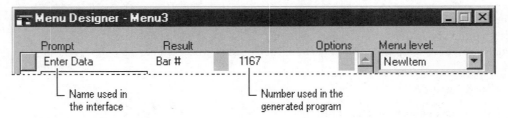

To specify a name for a menu pad

1. In the **Prompt** column, select the appropriate menu title.

   Note   The **Result** column must show **Command**, **Submenu**, or **Procedure** — not **Pad Name**.

2. Choose the button in the **Options** column to display the **Prompt Options** dialog box.

3. In the **Pad Name** box, type the name of your choice.

4. Choose **OK** to return to the **Menu Designer**.

To specify a number for a menu item

1. In the **Prompt** column, select the appropriate menu item.

   Note   The **Result** column must show **Command**, **Submenu**, or **Procedure** — not **Bar #**.

2. Choose the button in the **Options** column to display the **Prompt Options** dialog box.

3. In the **Bar #** box, type the number of your choice.

4. Choose **OK** to return to the **Menu Designer**.

   Tip   If you use the Quick Menu feature, don't change the names or numbers that Visual FoxPro provides for system menus or menu items; otherwise, you might get unpredictable results when you run the generated menu program.

For a list of the commands and functions you can use to control menus at run time, search for "menu and menu bars" in Help.

Creating Custom Toolbars

If your application includes repetitive tasks that users perform frequently, you can add custom toolbars to simplify or speed up the tasks. For example, if users typically print a report by choosing a menu command, you can simplify the task by providing a toolbar with a print button.

The following sections describe how to create custom toolbars for your applications. For details about customizing the toolbars that come with Visual FoxPro, search for "Customize Toolbar Dialog Box" in Help.

The following sections discuss:

- Defining a Toolbar Class
- Adding Objects to a Custom Toolbar Class
- Adding Custom Toolbars to Form Sets

Defining a Toolbar Class

If you want to create a toolbar that contains buttons not already found on existing toolbars, you can do so by defining a custom toolbar class. Visual FoxPro provides a Toolbar base class from which you can create the class you need.

After defining a toolbar class, you can add objects to the toolbar class, then define the properties, events, and methods for the custom toolbar. Finally, you can add the toolbar to a form set.

To define a custom toolbar class

1. From the Project Manager, select **Classes** and then choose **New**.

2. In the **Class Name** box, type the name of your class.

3. From the **Based On** box, select **Toolbar** to use the Toolbar base class.

    – or –

    Choose the dialog button to choose another toolbar class.

4. In the **Store In** box, type the name of the library in which you want to save the new class.

    – or –

    Choose the dialog button to select an existing library.

5. Add objects to the new toolbar class.

For example, you could store a printing class based on the Toolbar base class in an inventory library.

Creating a new class in the New Class dialog box

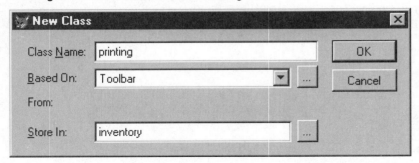

When you complete the New Class dialog box, the Class Designer appears.

A new custom toolbar in the Class Designer

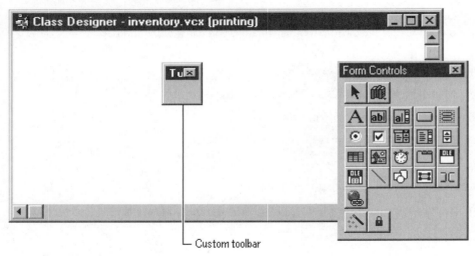

— Custom toolbar

You can also define a toolbar class by doing one of the following:

- Choosing New from the File menu and then choosing Class.

- Using the CREATE CLASS or MODIFY CLASS command.

- Defining the class programmatically with the DEFINE CLASS command.

For details, search for CREATE CLASS, DEFINE CLASS, and MODIFY CLASS in Help.

Adding Objects to a Custom Toolbar Class

After creating a custom toolbar class, you can add objects to it, including any objects supported by Visual FoxPro. For example, you can add objects from the Controls toolbar.

To add objects to your custom toolbar class

1. Open the class library containing the custom toolbar class, and then open the class.

2. On the Form Controls toolbar, choose an object you want to add.

3. Place the object on the custom toolbar by selecting the custom toolbar.

4. Repeat steps 2 and 3 until the custom toolbar is complete.

5. Reorganize the objects on the custom toolbar, if appropriate.

    For example, you can size objects, move them by dragging them, delete them by pressing the DELETE key, or add extra space between them by inserting Separator objects from the Form Controls toolbar.

    Note   You can move only one object at a time.

6. Set properties of the toolbar in the Properties window.

7. Save the custom toolbar class.

    Tip   You can add a bitmap or icon to a toolbar button by setting its Picture property.

Adding Custom Toolbars to Form Sets

After defining a toolbar class, you can create a toolbar from it. You can coordinate toolbars and forms by using the Form Designer or writing code.

Coordinating Toolbars and Forms in the Form Designer

You can add a toolbar to a form set so that the toolbar opens along with the forms in the form set. You cannot add the toolbar directly to the form.

To add a toolbar to a form set using the Form Designer

1. Register and select the library containing the toolbar class.

2. Open the form set with which you want to use the toolbar class, click the **View Classes** button on the **Form Controls** toolbar, and then select the toolbar class from the list displayed.

3. From the **Form Controls** toolbar, choose the toolbar class.

4. Click in the **Form Designer** to add the toolbar, and then drag the toolbar to its appropriate location.

    Visual FoxPro adds the toolbar to the form set. If a form set isn't open, Visual FoxPro prompts you for one.

5. Define the actions of the toolbar and its buttons (see "Defining Toolbar Actions" later in this chapter).

    Tip   To determine an object's class, look at its ToolTip in the Form Controls toolbar.

For more information on how to register and select the library containing the toolbar class, see "Adding Classes to Forms," in Chapter 3, "Object-Oriented Programming."

Coordinating Toolbars and Forms Using Code

In addition to using the Form Designer, you can add toolbars to form sets by using code.

To add a toolbar to a form set using code

- In the form set's Init event, use the SET CLASSLIB command to specify the library containing the toolbar class, and then create a toolbar from that class in the form set.

For example, to add and display the toolbar tbrPrint, which is based on the printing class in the inventory class library, add the following code to the form set's Init event:

```
SET CLASSLIB TO inventory
THIS.AddObject("tbrPrint","printing")
THIS.tbrPrint.Show
```

> **Note** If the toolbar class does not define the actions of the toolbar and its buttons, you must define the actions in the event procedures associated with the toolbar and its buttons. For more information, see "Defining Toolbar Actions" later in this chapter.

Example: Creating a Custom Toolbar

You can define all aspects of a toolbar in code. For example, if you add the following code to a form set's Init event, when the form set is loaded Visual FoxPro creates and displays the toolbar defined in the code. This toolbar contains two buttons.

Toolbar with two buttons

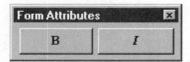

When chosen, these buttons change the font attributes of the form frmForm1 in the form set.

Form Set Init Event Code

Code	Comments
`THIS.AddObject("tbrTool1","mytoolbar")` `THIS.tbrTool1.Show`	Adds a toolbar of the class mytoolbar to the current form set and makes the toolbar visible. This code is in the form set's Init event.

Class definition code

Code	Comments

```
DEFINE CLASS myToolBar AS TOOLBAR
```
Start of the class definition: one toolbar with a command button, a separator, and another command button.

```
ADD OBJECT cmdBold AS COMMANDBUTTON
ADD OBJECT sep1    AS SEPARATOR
ADD OBJECT cmdItalic AS COMMANDBUTTON
Left = 1
Top  = 1
Width = 25
Caption = "Form Attributes"
```
Sets properties of the toolbar object.

```
cmdBold.Caption = "B"
cmdBold.Height = 1.7
cmdBold.Width = 10

cmdItalic.Caption = "I"
cmdItalic.Height = 1.7
cmdItalic.Width = 10
cmdItalic.FontBold = .F.
```
Sets properties of the controls. Notice that there are no Top or Left property settings for controls on a toolbar. Controls on a toolbar are automatically positioned in the order they are added.

The FontBold property of cmdItalic is set to false (.F.) because FontBold is true (.T.) by default.

```
PROCEDURE Activate
   THIS.cmdBold.FontBold = ;
      THISFORMSET.frmForm1.FontBold
   THIS.cmdItalic.FontItalic = ;
      THISFORMSET.frmForm1.FontItalic
ENDPROC
```
When the toolbar is activated, the font attributes of the two command buttons are set to reflect the Bold and Italic font settings of frmForm1.

```
PROCEDURE cmdBold.CLICK
   THISFORMSET.frmForm1.FontBold = ;
      !THISFORMSET.frmForm1.FontBold
   THIS.FontBold = ;
      THISFORMSET.frmForm1.FontBold
ENDPROC
```
When the user clicks cmdBold, the FontBold setting of frmForm1 is reversed, and the FontBold setting of cmdBold is set to match it.

```
PROCEDURE cmdItalic.CLICK
   THISFORMSET.frmForm1.FontItalic = ;
      !THISFORMSET.frmForm1.FontItalic
   THIS.FontItalic = ;
      THISFORMSET.frmForm1.FontItalic
ENDPROC
ENDDEFINE
```
When the user clicks cmdItalic, the FontItalic setting of frmForm1 is reversed, and the FontItalic setting of cmdItalic is set to match it.

End of the class definition.

Setting Properties of Custom Toolbars

While designing a custom toolbar, you can set its properties. For example, you can set the Movable property to allow the user to move the toolbar.

Additionally, you can use methods and events to control custom toolbars. For example, you can use the Dock method to dock or float a toolbar, and you can use the BeforeDock event and AfterDock event to control what happens before and after a toolbar is docked. For details about these properties, events, and methods, see Help.

Defining Toolbar Actions

After creating a toolbar, you must define the actions associated with the toolbar and its objects. For example, you must define what happens when the user clicks the toolbar or one of its buttons.

To define a toolbar action

1. Select the object for which you want to define an action: the toolbar or one of its buttons.

2. In the Properties window, choose the **Methods** tab.

3. Edit the appropriate event.

4. Add the code that specifies the action.

Additionally, you can set properties and methods of the toolbar and its objects. For details, see Help.

Coordinating Menus and Custom Toolbars

If you create a toolbar, you should synchronize menu commands with their corresponding toolbar buttons. For example, if you enable a toolbar button, you should enable its corresponding menu command.

You should design and create your application to:

- Perform the same actions when the user chooses associated toolbar buttons and menu items.

- Coordinate the enabling and disabling of associated toolbar buttons and menu items.

Follow these general steps when coordinating menu items and toolbar buttons:

1. Create a toolbar by defining a toolbar class, add command buttons, and include the operational code in the methods associated with the Click events of the command buttons.

2. Create the coordinated menu.

3. Add the coordinated toolbar and menu to a form set.

Creating the Coordinated Menu

When you coordinate a menu with a toolbar, the menu items accomplish the same tasks as the associated toolbar buttons, and the menu items are automatically disabled when the associated toolbar button is disabled.

To create a menu that is coordinated with a toolbar

1. In the Menu Designer, create a submenu with a descriptive prompt for every button on the toolbar.

2. In the result column for each submenu item, choose **Command**.

3. For each submenu item, call the code associated with the Click event of the appropriate toolbar command button.

    For example, if the name of the button on the toolbar is cmdA, add the following line of code in the edit box for the submenu item command:

    ```
    Formset.toolbar.cmdA.Click
    ```

4. Choose the button in the **Options** column to open the **Prompt Options** dialog box and choose **Skip For**.

5. In the Expression Builder, enter an expression that indicates that the menu option should be skipped when the toolbar command button is not enabled.

    For example, if the name of the button on the toolbar is cmdA, enter the following expression in the **Skip For** box:

    ```
    NOT formset.toolbar.cmdA.Enabled
    ```

6. Generate the menu.

7. Add the menu to the form set with the toolbar and run the form set.

When the user opens the menu, Visual FoxPro evaluates the Skip For condition, disabling the menu item if the associated toolbar command button is disabled. When the user chooses an item on the menu, the code in the Click event of the associated toolbar command button is executed.

Adding a Coordinated Toolbar and Menu to a Form Set

Once you have created a toolbar class and a menu that are designed to work together, it is easy to incorporate them in a form set.

To incorporate a coordinated toolbar and menu in a form set

1. Add the toolbar to the form set in one of three ways:

   - Drag the toolbar class from the Project Manager into the Form Designer.

   - Register the toolbar class library and add the toolbar to the form set from the Controls toolbar.

   - In the Init event of the form set, include code with the AddObject method to add the toolbar.

2. In the Load event of the form set, save the existing menu and run your menu program.

   For example, if your menu name is mymenu, include the following lines of code using the PUSH MENU and DO commands:

   ```
   PUSH MENU _MSYSMENU
   DO mymenu.mpr
   ```

3. In the Unload event of the form set, restore the original menu with the POP MENU command:

   ```
   POP MENU _MSYSMENU
   ```

If some menu commands are used more than others, you can create custom toolbars containing buttons for those commands. Then, users can simply press the buttons whenever they need the commands. However, if you create a toolbar, you should synchronize the menu commands with their corresponding buttons. For example, if you enable a button, you should enable its corresponding menu command.

Testing and Debugging a Menu System

You can preview a menu system as you design it or you can test and debug it after generating the menu program.

To preview a menu system as you design it

- In the Menu Designer, choose **Preview**.

When you choose Preview, the menu system you've defined appears at the top of the screen. Additionally, the Preview dialog box displays the file name (or a temporary file name) of the menu system.

Previewing a menu system

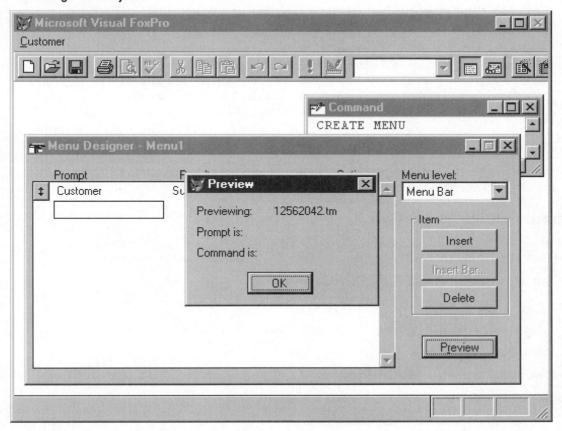

If you select a menu title or menu item, it also appears in the Preview dialog box, along with the command assigned to it, if there is one.

To test a menu system

1. From the **Menu** menu, choose **Generate**.

   If you've changed the menu, Visual FoxPro prompts you to save the changes.

2. In the **Generate Menu** dialog box, enter a name for the generated menu program by typing the name in the **Output File** box or by choosing the dialog button.

3. Choose **Generate** to produce a menu program file with an .mpr extension.

4. From the **Program** menu, choose **Do** to run the program.

   Caution   If you modify the generated menu program (the .mpr file), you'll lose the changes when you modify the menu using the Menu Designer and then regenerate the menu program.

If the menu program doesn't work as intended, use the diagnostic tools provided with Visual FoxPro. For more information, see Chapter 14, "Testing and Debugging Applications."

> **Troubleshooting**   If you run an application (.exe file) in which the main program is a menu and the application terminates as soon as the menu is displayed, include the READ EVENTS command in the cleanup code. You must also assign a CLEAR EVENTS command to the menu command that allows the user to exit the menu system. For details about READ EVENTS and CLEAR EVENTS, see Help.

Customizing a Menu System

After creating a basic menu system, you can customize it. For example, you can create status bar messages, define menu locations, or define default procedures.

Displaying Status Bar Messages

When a menu or menu item is selected, you can display a status bar message describing the choice. Such a message helps the user by adding information about the menu choice.

To display a message when a menu or menu item is selected

1. In the **Prompt** column, select the appropriate menu title or menu item.

2. Choose the button in the **Options** column to display the **Prompt Options** dialog box.

3. Select **Message**.

   The **Expression Builder** dialog box appears.

4. In the **Message** box, type the appropriate message.

   > **Tip**   Enclose character strings in quotation marks.

Defining the Location of Menu Titles

You can customize the location of user-defined menu titles in your applications. You can customize the location relative to the active menu system by choosing options in the General Options dialog box. Additionally, you can specify the location of menu titles when the user edits an object visually.

To specify a relative location for user-defined menu titles

1. From the **View** menu, choose **General Options**.

2. Choose the appropriate **Location** option: **Replace**, **Append**, **Before**, or **After**.

Visual FoxPro relocates all of the menu titles you've defined. If you want to relocate some but not all of them, drag the mover buttons next to the appropriate menu titles in the Menu Designer.

Additionally, you can specify the location of menu titles when the user edits an object in your application. If you include an object and the user activates it, your menu titles will not appear on the resulting menu bar unless you indicate that you want them there.

To control menu title location during object visual editing

1. In the **Prompt** column, select the appropriate menu title.

2. Choose the button in the **Options** column to display the **Prompt Options** dialog box.

3. Set the **Negotiate** check box.

4. Choose one of the following option buttons:

   - **None** does not place the menu title on the menu bar. Choosing **None** is the same as not choosing any option.

   - **Left** places the menu title in the left group of menu titles on the menu bar.

   - **Middle** places the menu title in the middle group of menu titles on the menu bar.

   - **Right** places the menu title in the right group of menu titles on the menu bar.

If you don't choose Left, Middle, or Right, the menu title will not appear on the menu bar when the user edits an object. For more information about editing objects visually, see Chapter 16, "Adding OLE."

Saving and Restoring Menus

You can save and restore menus on the stack with the PUSH MENU and POP MENU commands. Pushing and popping is useful when you want to remove a menu temporarily, replace it with another, and then restore the original later on. For details, see the PUSH MENU and POP MENU topics in Help.

The number of menus you save in memory is limited only by the amount of available memory.

> **Tip**   Check the available memory with the SYS(1016) function. For example, to check how much memory your menu system uses, call SYS(1016), push the menu on the stack, then call SYS(1016) again.

Creating a Default Procedure for a Menu System

You can create a global procedure that applies to your entire menu system. Such a procedure runs whenever a menu without an assigned procedure is chosen.

For example, suppose you're developing an application for which some menus do not yet have submenus, procedures, and so on. For these menus, you can create a code stub that executes when the menus are chosen. For instance, you could create a general procedure that includes this function:

```
MESSAGEBOX("Feature not available")
```

To create a default procedure

1. Open the menu system you're designing.

2. From the **View** menu, choose **General Options**.

3. Assign the procedure by doing one of the following:

   - Write or call a procedure in the **Procedure** box.

     – or –

     Select **Edit** and then **OK** to open a separate editing window and write or call a procedure.

Setting the System Menu

You can manipulate menus that use the Visual FoxPro menu system by using the SET SYSMENU command. With SET SYSMENU, you can disable your menus, add and remove items from your menus, restore the default Visual FoxPro menus, and control access to your menus during program execution. For details, search for SET SYSMENU in Help.

Putting It All Together

Now you're ready to complete your application and to test its functionality. Add queries and reports to provide your users with the information they need, then run the application and look for areas to optimize.

Chapter 12   Adding Queries and Reports

After creating data and an interface for your application, you can add power and depth with queries and reports that provide important information for your users.

Chapter 13   Compiling an Application

Create your applications one piece at a time, verifying each component as you go. When all your components are in place, it's easy to compile them into an application.

Chapter 14   Testing and Debugging Applications

When you develop an application, you need to test for errors within and across components. Visual FoxPro provides debugging tools to help you find and correct any errors you discover in your applications.

Chapter 15   Optimizing Applications

Once you have a stable, running application, consider ways to optimize its performance by making your application smaller and faster.

Adding Queries and Reports

Once you create tables and forms for your application, you can add queries and reports to select and display data for your users. Your queries can be directed to a variety of destinations so that you can use them in the other components of your application. You can also run reports separately without using a query. This chapter highlights some of the ways you can use queries, add reports, and expose queries and reports to the user.

When you use a query or a view in your application, you are actually using a SELECT – SQL statement. This chapter describes how you can use a SELECT – SQL statement in your application whether you create it through a query defined in the Query Designer, a view defined in the View Designer, or code entered for an event or procedure. For detailed information about views, see Part 2, "Finding Information," in the *User's Guide*.

This chapter discusses:

- Adding Queries
- Adding Reports and Labels
- Integrating Queries and Reports

Adding Queries

When you add queries to your application, you can combine a variety of data sources, finely filter records, manipulate data, and sort the results — all with the SELECT – SQL statement. By using the SQL statement, you have complete control over the results your query produces and where the results are stored.

A query is a SELECT – SQL statement.

**SELECT-SQL
statement collects
and filters data...**

...then points results to a destination.

You can add SELECT – SQL statements to procedures or to event code. For more information about events, see Chapter 4, "Understanding the Event Model."

Creating SELECT – SQL Statements

To create a SELECT – SQL statement

- Use the Query Designer or the View Designer to build the statement, then copy the contents of the SQL window into a code window.

  – or –

  In a code window, type the SELECT – SQL statement.

For example, you can select all the records from the `Customer` table in the `TasTrade` database where the `country` field contains the value "Canada":

```
SELECT * ;
   FROM tastrade!customer ;
   WHERE customer.country = "Canada"
```

To execute the command immediately, you can enter the statement in the Command window. If you want each clause to appear on a separate line within the window, end each line except the last one with a semicolon so that Visual FoxPro processes the command only after the last line.

Selecting a Number or Percentage of Records

If you only need a certain number or percentage of records from the result set that your query would return, you can use the Top property on the Miscellaneous tab in the Query or View Designers or you can add a TOP clause to your SELECT – SQL statement. The number you provide in a TOP clause can range from 1 to 32,767. For a percentage, you can use from 0.001 to 99.99.

For example, if you want to select the top 10 customers with the highest order amounts, you can specify a GROUP BY on CUST_ID to show one aggregate record for each customer and sort by ORDER_AMT in the ORDER BY clause. To get a true TOP 10, you need to specify a descending sort on the ORDER_AMT so that the records with the highest order amounts appear first in the results. If you use an ascending sort, the result records are ordered from the least order amount to the most. The top records you select from the result set would actually have the lowest values.

```
SELECT TOP 10 *;
 FROM  testdata!customer INNER JOIN testdata!orders ;
 ON  Customer.cust_id = Orders.cust_id;
GROUP BY Customer.cust_id;
ORDER BY Orders.order_amt DESC
```

Specifying Destinations for Query Results

By using clauses of the SELECT – SQL statement, you can specify several destinations to store your query results.

To send results to this destination	Use this clause
Separate table	INTO TABLE mytable
Array	INTO ARRAY aMyArray
Temporary table	INTO CURSOR mycursor
Active window	TO SCREEN
Browse window	The default if no other destination is specified.

Once the results are stored, you can use commands to control how the stored results are integrated for display or printing. For more information about the syntax of the SELECT – SQL statement, see Help.

Storing Results in a Table, Array, or Cursor

You can store your query results in a table, array, or cursor for other uses such as populating forms and printing reports and labels. If you want to store the results only temporarily, send the results to an array or cursor. If you want to store the results permanently, send the results to a table.

To specify a table as the destination

- Use the INTO clause of the SELECT – SQL statement to specify a destination.

The following example shows an INTO clause for a table:

```
SELECT * ;
   FROM tastrade!customer ;
   WHERE customer.country = "Canada" ;
   INTO TABLE mytable
```

To specify an array as the destination

- Use the INTO clause of the SELECT – SQL statement to specify a destination.

The following example shows an INTO clause for an array:

```
SELECT * ;
   FROM tastrade!customer ;
   WHERE customer.country = "Canada" ;
   INTO ARRAY aMyArray
```

To specify a cursor as the destination

- Use the INTO clause of the SELECT – SQL statement to specify a destination.

The following example shows an INTO clause for a cursor named mycursor:

```
SELECT * ;
   FROM tastrade!customer ;
   WHERE customer.country = "Canada" ;
   INTO CURSOR mycursor
```

If you create a table or an array, you can use it like any other table or array in Visual FoxPro. If you create a cursor, you can browse through its contents. The cursor is opened in the lowest available work area. You can access it by using the name you gave it in the SELECT – SQL statement.

The following two procedures describe two common ways to include query results stored in tables and cursors into an application.

Populating a Form Control

If you want to display your query results in a form, you can use a table, array, or cursor to populate a grid, list box, or combo box.

To populate a list box or combo box control with a table or cursor

1. In the Form Designer, modify the form that has the control you want to populate.

2. Set the RowSourceType property to **3 – SQL Statement**.

3. In the control's RowSource property, enter a SELECT – SQL statement that includes an INTO TABLE or INTO CURSOR clause.

To populate a grid control with a table or cursor

1. In the Form Designer, modify the form that has the control you want to populate.

2. In the form's Load event, enter a SELECT – SQL statement that includes an INTO TABLE or INTO CURSOR clause.

3. Set the grid's RecordSource property to the name of the table or cursor you created in Step 2.

4. Set the grid's RecordSourceType property to **0 – Table** (for a table) or **1 – Alias** (for a cursor).

Printing Results in a Report or Label

If your report or label includes groups or you otherwise need to order the data, you can use the various clauses of the SELECT – SQL statement to get the exact results you need.

To send results to an existing report or label

- Use the SELECT – SQL statement with a REPORT or LABEL command.

  The following example uses the GROUP BY and ORDER BY clauses as well as the REPORT FORM command:

```
SELECT * ;
    FROM tastrade!customer ;
    WHERE customer.country = "Canada" ;
    GROUP BY customer.region ;
    ORDER BY customer.postal_code, customer.company_name ;
    INTO CURSOR MyCursor
REPORT FORM MYREPORT.FRX
```

  The following example uses a LABEL FORM command:

```
SELECT * ;
    FROM tastrade!customer ;
    WHERE customer.country = "Canada" ;
    GROUP BY customer.region ;
    ORDER BY customer.postal_code, customer.company_name ;
    INTO CURSOR mycursor
LABEL FORM MYLABEL.LBX
```

While the SELECT – SQL statement is the most flexible method for populating your report or label, it is not the only method. For more information about setting report data sources, see the section "Controlling Data Sources" later in this chapter. For more information about integrating the report destinations into your application, see "Integrating Queries and Reports" later in this chapter.

Displaying Results in a Window

If you want to display the results of your SELECT – SQL statement, you can send the results to a window. The Browse window is the default destination for query results and you don't need to include a destination clause. You can also send the results to the main Visual FoxPro window or another active window.

To display results in the main Visual FoxPro window

- Use the TO SCREEN clause of a SELECT – SQL statement.

To display results in another active window

- Define a window, show it to activate it, and then run a SQL query or other command that displays results in a window.

This code example shows the definition for a temporary window titled "Top Customers" that displays the names of companies with more than $5,000 in total orders for the year.

Displaying query results in a window

Code	Comment
| ```
frmMyForm=createobj("form")
frmMyForm.Left = 1
frmMyForm.Top = 1
frmMyForm.Width = 130
frmMyForm.Height = 25
frmMyForm.Caption = "Top Customers"
frmMyForm.Show
``` | Create and start a temporary window object. |
| ```
SELECT customer.company_name,
   SUM(orders.freight) ;
   FROM tastrade!customer,
   tastrade!orders ;
   WHERE customer.customer_id =
   orders.customer_id ;
   GROUP BY customer.company_name ;
   HAVING SUM(orders.freight) > 5000 ;
   ORDER BY 2 DESC
``` | Enter a SELECT – SQL statement. |

Adding Reports and Labels

After you collect and organize your data, you can add reports or labels to your application to print the data or display it on the screen. You can control the data in your report through the data sources you choose, and manipulate and combine raw data with report variables. *Report variables* store values that are calculated and used in a report.

Controlling Data Sources

To control the data sources for a report, you can define a data environment that is stored with the report or you can activate specific data sources in code each time you run a report. For more information about using the Data Environment Designer, see Chapter 9, "Creating Forms."

To	Add
Always use the same data sources.	Tables or views to the report's data environment.
	DO *query* or SELECT – SQL to the Init event of the report's data environment.
Use separate sets of data sources.	USE *table*, USE *view*, DO *query*, or SELECT – SQL to the Click event or other code that precedes a REPORT or LABEL command.

If you use a table as the data source, use aliases on the fields in the report only if you don't plan to use the report with any other data source than the table itself. If you use a view or query as the data source and aliases are included in the report controls, the report might display the same record repeatedly on the report page.

Controlling Record Order

You can use the data sources used by the report to control the order the records print in your report. The records are processed and printed in the order they appear in the table, view, or query. To order the records in a table, you can set an index in code or as part of the report's data environment. For a query, view, or SELECT – SQL code, you can use the ORDER BY clause. If you don't order the records using the data sources, the only way to use just the report to order the records is through the ORDER property on a cursor in the data environment.

Controlling Record Selection

In addition to the order records appear in the report, you can select which records are printed by using the data source, the report printing options, or a combination of both.

To use	Add
View or query	Conditions in the Filter tab
SELECT – SQL	WHERE or HAVING clause
Report Designer	Setting in the Print Options dialog box
REPORT command	Scope, FOR, or WHILE expressions
Table	Filtered index

Protecting a Report's Data Session

To prevent your report's data session from being affected by the global data session as a result of changes made in other designers, you can set the report's data session to Private.

To set a private data session

- From the **Report** menu, choose **Private Data Session**.

For more information about using the Data Environment Designer, see Chapter 9, "Creating Forms." For more information about data sessions, see Chapter 17, "Programming for Shared Access."

If you want to display your query results in a graph, you can use the Graph Wizard, the Query Designer, or a SELECT – SQL command. To use the Query Designer or a SELECT – SQL command, follow the steps below. You need to include at least one numeric field in your result set to create a graph. After completing the query, you can select one of six types of graphs, each with two variations.

To modify the graph

1. Browse the table containing the graph.

2. Double-click the general field to display the graph.

3. Double-click the graph to open Microsoft Graph and display the Microsoft Graph toolbar.

4. Modify the graph in Microsoft Graph.

Refining Page Layout

You can refine the layout of your report pages by defining multiple columns and changing the area of the page reserved for a band by changing the height of each band.

Defining Multiple Columns on a Page

To create phone directories, mailing labels, or other types of listings, you can define multiple columns per page.

To define a multi-column report

1. From the **File** menu, choose **Page Setup**.

   Page Setup dialog box with columns defined

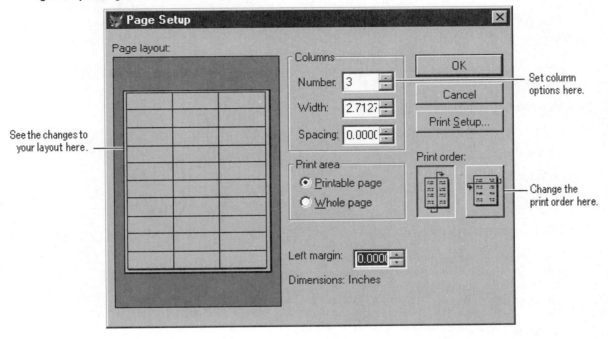

2. In the **Columns** area, enter the number of columns for the page. This is the same as the number of records you want to print across the page.

3. In the **Width** box, enter a value for column width.

4. In the **Spacing** box, enter a value for the space you want to appear between each column.

   Tip If you're printing groups set to start on a new page, don't use the Print Order option.

5. Choose **OK**.

   The **Report Designer** reflects your changes.

If your layout already contained report controls in the Detail band, you may need to move or resize them to fit within the boundaries of the new column.

Setting Report Band Height

While designing your report, you can change the height of a report band. The height of a report band determines the amount of space that each report band uses on the page within the page margins. For example, if the Title band is set at a half inch, the Title will appear in the first half inch of space after the top margin. The detail band shows the amount of space devoted to each printed record. The following information applies to all of the report bands. You can set additional parameters for Group Header and Footer bands. For more information about Group bands, see the section "Grouping Data on Your Layout" in Chapter 7, "Designing Reports and Labels," in the *User's Guide*.

To set a precise band height

1. Double-click the bar for the appropriate band.

   A dialog box for the band appears.

2. In the **Height** box, enter a value for the height.

3. Choose **OK**.

Using Expressions and Functions in Field Controls

You can include field controls in your report or label to display values from a variety of expressions, including fields from tables and views, variables, and calculations. The following sections describe some commonly used expressions and functions such as multiple fields, dates, and page numbers.

Adding Field Controls

You can add field controls in several ways.

To add table fields from the data environment

1. Open the report's data environment.

2. Select a table or view.

3. Drag fields onto the layout.

To add table fields from the toolbar

1. From the **Report Controls** toolbar, insert a **Field** control.

2. In the **Report Expression** dialog box, choose the dialog button after the **Expression** box.

3. In the **Fields** box, double-click the name of the field you want.

   The table name and field name appear in the **Expression for Field on Report** box.

Note   If the **Fields** box is empty, add a table or view to the data environment.

You don't have to keep the table name alias in the expression. You can delete it or you can clear the Expression Builder options. For more information, search for "Expression Builder" in Help.

4. Choose **OK**.

5. In the **Report Expression** dialog box, choose **OK**.

After entering the expression, you can change the format or set printing, position, or stretch options. For more information, see "Adding a Comment to a Control" in Chapter 7, "Designing Reports and Labels," in the *User's Guide,* and see "Setting a Control's Print Options" later in this chapter.

Inserting Concatenated Field Controls

After you add your table fields, you might notice that they don't print the way you would like on the page. For example, printing the field controls for City, Region, and Postal Code separately produces unwanted spaces between each value. You can trim or concatenate the table fields into one field expression. The space required by each value for this control will vary. You can set the control to adjust for each value.

To combine several table fields into an expression

1. From the **Report Controls** toolbar, insert a **Field** control.

   Tip   Size the field to the least amount of room the expression will require. If more space is needed, you can set the control to stretch for larger values, but you can't set it to shrink if less space is needed.

2. In the **Report Expression** dialog box, select the dialog button after the **Expression** box.

3. In the Expression Builder, select **ALLTRIM(expC)** from the **String** box.

   The string function appears in the **Expression** box with expC selected.

4. Double-click the first field name you want to appear in the control.

   The field name replaces the expC.

5. Type a plus sign after the field name or select + from the **String** functions box.

6. Type **,** or select **Text** from the String functions list and then enter a comma.

7. Repeat steps 3 and 4 for additional fields to complete the expression and then choose **OK**.

8. In the **Report Expression** dialog box, select **Stretch with Overflow**.

   When the control is populated, the space allocated to the control adjusts downward to accommodate the value of the expression. For more information about **Stretch with Overflow**, see "Printing Controls with Variable-Length Values" later in this chapter.

To combine several fields in an expression, place an ALLTRIM( ) function before each field name, place punctuation inside quotation marks, and place a plus sign between each of the elements in the expression. If the field value lengths don't vary, such as with postal codes or abbreviations, you can insert just the field name, as in this example:

```
ALLTRIM(city)+", "+region+"  "+postal_code
```

Notice the spaces in quotes, rather than a comma, to separate the region and the postal code.

For more examples, see the report Invoice.frx in the Visual Studio ...\Sample\Vfp98\Solution\Reports directory.

Trimming and Concatenating Character Expressions

To quickly trim and concatenate character expressions in the Expression Builder, you can place commas between character expressions. The value of the expression preceding the comma is trimmed. You can also use semicolons to place the expression on a new line, provided that the trimmed value has a length greater than zero. The following example shows character expressions for fields in a mailing address:

```
contact_name; address; city, region, postal_code
```

> **Note**   Use these when you don't want to include punctuation in the value.

If you use these methods, make sure the field is set to Stretch with Overflow. For more information, see "Printing Controls with Variable-Length Values" later in this chapter.

Inserting the Current Date

You can insert a field control that prints the current date.

To insert the current date

1. From the **Report Controls** toolbar, insert a **Field** control.
2. In the **Report Expression** dialog box, select the dialog button after the **Expression** box.
3. In the Expression Builder, select **DATE( )** from the **Date** list.
4. Choose **OK**.
5. In the **Report Expression** dialog box, choose **OK**.

Inserting a Page Number

The Page Header or Footer bands usually contain a page number. If you use a wizard or Quick Report, a page number is inserted for you into the Page Footer band.

To insert a page number

1. From the **Report Controls** toolbar, insert a **Field** control.

2. In the **Report Expression** dialog box, select the dialog button after the **Expression** box.

3. In the Expression Builder, select **_pageno** from the **Variables** list.

4. Choose **OK**.

5. In the **Report Expression** dialog box, choose **OK**.

   Tip   You can use this procedure to insert any of the system variables from the Variables list into your report.

Defining Report Variables

To manipulate data and display calculated results in a report, you can use report variables. Using report variables, you can calculate values and then use those values to calculate subsequent values.

To define a report variable

1. Open or create a report.

2. From the **Report** menu, choose **Variables**.

3. In the Report Variables dialog box, select the **Variables** box and type a name for the variable.

4. In the **Value to store** box, type a field name or any other expression.

5. If appropriate, select a calculation option.

6. If appropriate, in the **Initial value** box, type an expression that sets the initial value.

7. Choose **OK**.

   You can use the variable in any expression you enter in the report.

To count all the Canadian entries in the Company table, use this expression and select Count as the calculation option.

```
IIF(country="Canada",1,0)
```

The following example shows three variables for a simple time sheet:

To store this value	Create this variable	Using this expression
Time employee arrived	tArrive	hour_in + (min_in / 60)
Time employee left	tLeave	hour_out + (min_out / 60)
Total time employee was present	tDayTotal	tLeave - tArrive

You can use the tDayTotal variable in a variety of other calculations, such as the number of hours worked in a week, a month, or a year; the average number of hours worked each day; and so on.

For examples of report variables, see the reports Percent.frx and Invoice.frx in the Visual Studio ...\Samples\Vfp98\Solution\Reports directory.

Reordering Report Variables

Report variables are evaluated in the order that they appear in the list and can affect the value of expressions that use them. For example, if variable 1 is used to define the value of variable 2, variable 1 must appear before variable 2. In the previous time sheet example, tArrive and tLeave must precede tDayTotal.

To change the order of report variables

1. From the **Report** menu, choose **Variables**.

2. In the **Variable** box, drag the button to the left of the variable to rearrange the order.

3. Choose **OK**.

Setting a Variable's Initial Value

If you use a variable in calculations, be sure that you initialize the variable with a non-zero value to avoid a division-by-zero error. If you don't specify a value, Visual FoxPro assigns a default value of 0.

To set a variable's initial value

1. From the **Report** menu, choose **Variables**.

2. In the **Variable** box, select the variable you want to set.

3. In the **Initial value** box, enter the value.

4. Choose **OK**.

If you reorder the groups in your report, your report variables might not be resetting on the correct field. For example, if your report has two groups, the first grouping by country and the second grouping by date, and you switch the order of the groups, the variables still reset according to the original positions of the groups.

You can change the value of a calculation by specifying when the variable is reset.
By default, Visual FoxPro resets the report variables at the end of the report.

To reset a variable at the end of a report, a page, or a column

1. From the **Report** menu, choose **Variables**.

2. In the **Reset at** box, choose an option.

3. Choose **OK**.

To reset a variable on entry or exit of any band

1. In the Report Designer, open the report.

2. Double-click the bar for the report band.

3. In the **Run expression** area of the band's dialog box, choose the dialog button at the end of the **On entry** or **On exit** box.

4. Enter an expression to reset the variable each time the band is entered or exited.

Formatting Field Controls

After inserting a field control, you can change the control's data type and print format. Data types can be Character, Numeric, or Date. Each of these data types has its own format options, including the option to create your own format template. The format determines how the field is displayed when the report or label is printed.

You can enter format functions directly in the Expressions box of the Report Expression dialog box or you can select options from the Format dialog box.

Typically, you might convert all alphabetical output to uppercase, insert commas or decimal points in numeric output, display numeric output in currency format, or convert one date format to another.

Formatting Options for Report Controls

For field controls, you can set a variety of format options for each data type.

To format a field control

1. Choose the **Field** control.

2. In the **Report Expression** dialog box, choose the dialog button after the **Format** box.

3. In the **Format** dialog box, select the data type for the field: **Character**, **Numeric**, or **Date**.

   The **Editing options** area displays the formatting options available for that data type.

   > **Note**   This data type applies only to the report control. It reflects the data type of the expression and doesn't change the data type of the field in the table.

4. Select the justification and format options you want.

The Format dialog box displays different options depending on the data type you choose. You can also create a format template by entering characters in the Format box.

Justifying Text in a Field

You can justify field contents within the control in two ways. This setting does not change the position of the control on the report, only the contents within the space of the control.

To justify text in a field control

1. Select the controls you want to change.

2. From the **Format** menu, choose **Text Alignment**.

3. From the submenu, choose the appropriate command.

To justify text in a field

1. Choose the **Field** control.

2. In the **Report Expression** dialog box, choose the dialog button after the **Format** box.

    Format dialog box for a Numeric expression

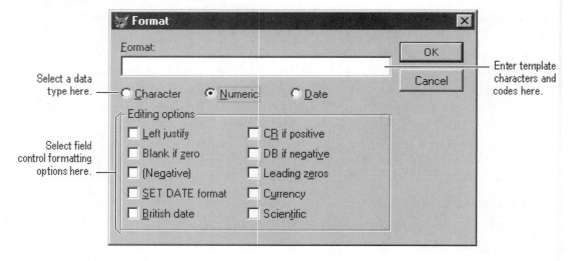

3. In the **Format** dialog box, select the data type for the field: **Character**, **Numeric**, or **Date**.

4. Select the justification and format options you want.

Defining Field Format Templates

A format template allows you to customize the format of the field. By entering a combination of characters and codes in the Format box of the Report Expression dialog box or the Format dialog box, you can create a wide variety of print formats. The characters you enter appear as literal text along with the field value. The codes you enter determine the appearance of the field output. For example, if you use the following format template for a 10-digit numeric field, the characters (parentheses, spaces, and dashes) are printed along with the numeric data.

Format Template	Printed Output
(999) 999-9999	(123) 456-7890

Changing Fonts

You can change the font and size of text for each field or label control or you can change the default font for the report.

To change fonts and size in a report

1. Select the control.

2. From the **Format** menu, select **Font**.

   The **Font** dialog box appears.

3. Select the appropriate font and point size and then choose **OK**.

To change the default font

1. From the **Report** menu, choose **Default Font**.

2. In the **Font** dialog box, select the appropriate font and point size you want as the default and then choose **OK**.

   Only the controls inserted after you changed the default font will reflect the new font settings. To change existing objects, select them all, and then change the font using the Font option on the Format menu.

Cropping a Picture or OLE Object

The picture or OLE object you inserted might not fit the frame you drew when you created the control. By default, the picture or object retains its original size. You can clip or scale it to fit into your frame.

If the picture or OLE object is bigger than the frame you created in the Report Designer, only a portion of the picture or object appears in the frame. The picture or object is anchored at the top and at the left of the frame. You cannot see the lower right portion that extends beyond the frame.

To fit a picture in the frame

1. In the Report Designer, create a Picture/OLE Bound Control.

2. In the **Report Picture** dialog box, select **Scale picture – Retain shape**.

The whole picture appears, filling as much of the frame as possible while retaining its relative proportions. This protects your picture from vertical or horizontal distortion.

To fill the frame with the picture

1. In the **Report Designer**, create a **Picture/OLE Bound Control**.

2. In the **Report Picture** dialog box, select **Scale picture – Fill the frame**.

The whole picture changes to fill the frame that you sized. If necessary, the picture is stretched vertically or horizontally to fit the frame.

To see an example of a report with pictures, see the report Wrapping.frx in the Visual Studio …\Sample\Vfp98\Solution directory.

Centering an OLE Object

The OLE objects included in a General field can vary in shape and size. If the object in a General field is smaller than the frame, it appears in the upper left corner of the frame. You can center it to ensure that all objects smaller than the frame are centered in the frame in the report or label. File pictures don't need to be centered because they don't vary.

To center General field OLE objects

1. In the Report Designer, create a Picture/OLE Bound Control.

2. In the **Report Picture** dialog box, select **Center picture**.

The printed OLE objects are centered within the area when the report is previewed or printed.

Changing Colors of Report Controls

You can change the color of a field, label, line, or rectangle.

To change colors

1. Select the controls to change.

2. In the **Color Palette** toolbar, choose **Foreground Color** or **Background Color**.

3. Select the color you want.

Saving a Report as HTML

You can use the **Save As HTML** option on the **File** menu when you're creating a report to save the contents of a form as an HTML (Hypertext Markup Language) file.

To save a report as HTML

1. Open the report.

2. Choose **Save As HTML** on the **File** menu. (You will be asked to save the report if it has been modified.)

3. Enter the name of the HTML file to create and choose **Save**.

Setting Print Options for Controls

The general layout and band position of your controls determine the time and place they are printed. You can also set specific print options for each control. Each control has a default size based either on its value (fields and labels) or the size you created (lines, rectangles, and pictures). The length of the control on the layout defines the display width of the control. Because the value of some controls will vary from record to record, you can set the height of the control to stretch downward to display the entire value. If you don't set it to stretch, the value will be truncated within the display width. You cannot resize Label controls, but you can resize all other controls.

Printing Controls with Variable-Length Values

If you want a control to use only the space needed by its value, you can set it to stretch. For example, the values in an expression can vary from record to record. Rather than allot a fixed amount of space on the report that accommodates the longest value, you can set the control to stretch downward to display the entire value. You can set controls below the stretching control to float down the page relative to the stretching control.

Examples of controls set to stretch and float

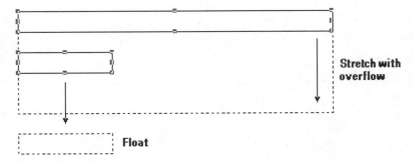

The stretch option is available for fields, vertical lines, rectangles, and rounded rectangles.

For an example of controls that stretch and float, see the report Wrapping.frx in the Visual Studio …\Sample\Vfp98\Solution\Reports directory.

To set a field to stretch with its value

1.   Double-click the field control to display its dialog box.

2.   Select **Stretch with overflow**.

Controls that are placed relative to controls that stretch must be set to float or they will
be overwritten.

To set a control to float

1.   Double-click the control to display its dialog box.

2.   In the control's dialog box, select **Float**.

> **Caution**   Some of your data could be overwritten during printing if: (1) you
> position a field relative to the bottom of the band and include *below* this field
> another field that is positioned relative to the top of the band and can stretch; or
> (2) you position a field relative to the top of the band and include *above* this field
> another field that is positioned relative to the top of the band and can stretch.

You can also set lines, rectangles, and rounded rectangles to stretch. They can stretch
relative to the band or, if part of a group of controls, they can stretch relative to the largest
control in the group.

To set a line or rectangle to stretch

1.   Double-click the control to display its dialog box.

2.   In the **Stretch downwards** area, select an option.

To print a border around a stretchable control

1.   Draw a rectangle around the stretchable controls.

2.   Double-click the rectangle to display the **Rectangle/Line** dialog box.

3.   In the **Stretch downwards** area, select **Stretch relative to the tallest object in group**.

4.   Choose **OK**.

5.   Drag a selection box around the rectangle.

6.   From the **Format** menu, choose **Group**.

> Selection handles appear at the corners of the rectangle. From now on you can treat
> all of the controls as one. The rectangle will stretch along with the stretchable field.
> Regardless of how far down the value in the field stretches, the rectangle will maintain
> its border around the field. You can place two of these groups side by side in the layout
> and one will not be affected by the stretching of the other.

To print one stretchable control below another

1.   Insert the two controls one below the other in the layout.

2.   Double-click the top control to display the control's dialog box.

3. In the **Field Position** area, select **Fix relative to top band**, and then choose **OK**.

4. Double-click the bottom control to display the control's dialog box.

5. In the **Field Position** area, select **Float**, and then choose **OK**.

The two record values will print in their entirety and will not overwrite each other.

Setting a Control's Print Options

You can control when and how often each report control is printed in your report. For more information about a control's print options, search for "Print When Dialog Box" in Help.

Suppressing Repeated Values

For field controls, you can suppress values repeated for consecutive records so that the value is printed once for the first record but doesn't appear for subsequent records until the value changes. For example, if you're printing an invoice, and one of the fields contains the date of the transaction, the date would only be printed once for transactions that took place on the same date.

To suppress repeated values

1. Double-click the control to display the control's dialog box.

2. Choose **Print When** to display the **Print When** dialog box.

   Print When dialog box

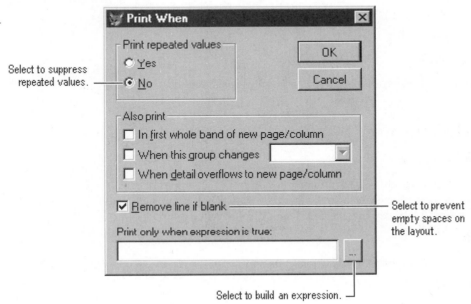

3. In the **Print Repeated Values** area, select **No**, and then choose **OK**.

To repeat only on a new page or column

1. Double-click the control.

2. Choose **Print When**.

3. In the **Print repeated values** area, select **No**.

4. In the **Also print** area, select **In first whole band of new page/column**, and then choose **OK**.

To repeat when the detail band overflows to a new page or column

1. Double-click the control.

2. Choose **Print When**.

3. In the **Also Print** area, select **When detail overflows to new page/column**, and then choose **OK**.

Building Print Expressions

You can add expressions to a control: they are evaluated before the field prints. If the expression evaluates to false (.F.), the field will not print. If you add an expression, all of the other options in the Print When dialog box are disabled except Remove Line If Blank.

For examples of Print When conditions, see the reports Colors.frx and Ledger.frx in the Visual Studio ...\Sample\Vfp98\Solution\Reports directory.

To add a print expression

1. Double-click the control.

2. Choose **Print When**.

3. In the **Print only when expression is true** box, enter an expression.

   – or –

   Click the dialog button to create an expression with the Expression Builder.

Suppressing Blank Lines

Your report may include records that don't contain values for every field control. By default, Visual FoxPro leaves the area for that field blank. You can remove these blank areas to create a more pleasing and continuous display of the information.

To suppress blank lines

1. Double-click the control that's likely to cause blank lines in the report.

2. Choose **Print When**.

3. Select **Remove line if blank**.

Visual FoxPro will remove the line from the report if it evaluates to blank. If the field doesn't print or if the table field is empty, Visual FoxPro checks for other controls in the line. If none are found, the line is removed. If you don't select this option and no other controls are on the same line, a blank line is printed.

Setting Print Options for Groups

You can control how groups are printed in your report. Sometimes you may want each group to start on a separate page or you may want to control when the group header prints.

Setting Group Page Breaks

In addition to selecting the field or expression to be grouped, the Data Grouping dialog box allows you to specify page break options for groups.

Choosing a Group Header Option

You might want your groups to appear in the next column for multi-column reports, on a new page for forms, or with a new page numbered at 1. The Data Grouping dialog box offers four options to accomplish these tasks. You can:

- Start a group on a new column.

- Start each group on a new page.

- Reset the page number to 1 for each group.

- Reprint the group header on each page.

After you enter an expression, you can select these options from the Group Properties area.

Preventing Orphaned Group Headers

Sometimes a group may print partially on one page and then finish on the next. To avoid a group header from printing near the bottom of the page with the majority of records on the next page, you can set the minimum distance from the bottom that a group header will print. If the header would be positioned closer to the bottom of the page than the number of inches or centimeters you enter, Visual FoxPro prints the header on a new page.

To prevent orphaned group headers

1. From the **Report** menu, choose **Data Grouping**.

2. In the **Data Grouping** dialog box, choose or enter a value in the **Start group on new page** box.

> **Tip**   To determine a good value for orphan control, add the Group Header height to one to three times the Detail height.

Printing Suppressed Values When the Group Changes

If repeated values are suppressed, you may want them to print when a particular group changes.

To print repeated values when the group changes

1. Double-click the control to display the control's dialog box.

2. Choose the **Print When** button to display the **Print When** dialog box.

3. Select **When this group changes**.

   The groups defined for the report appear in the box.

4. Select a group from the box, and then choose **OK**.

Repeating Group Headers

When a group continues onto the next page, you might want the group header to repeat at the top of the group of continued information. If you have multiple data groups on your report, the header on the subsequent pages will be from the last group in the group list. Place all of the controls you want to print for the group header in the header band of the last group on the list.

To repeat the group header on the next page

- In the Data Grouping dialog box, select the group you want to repeat and then choose **Reprint group header on each page**.

  If you don't want to repeat the group header, clear this check box.

Controlling Report and Label Output

You can control where report and label output is sent by using one of these keywords with the REPORT or LABEL command:

- PRINT
- PREVIEW
- FILE

If you don't use any keywords, the report is sent to the screen or active window.

Selecting Records to Print

When you print a report, you might want to limit the number of records that appear in the report by providing selection criteria. You can:

- Choose a scope of records by specifying a quantity or range.
- Build a FOR expression that selects records that match a condition.

- Build a WHILE expression that selects records until one record is found that doesn't match a condition.

You can use any combination of these options. The WHILE expression overrides the other criteria.

Printing a Quantity or Range of Records

One way you can limit the number of records is to specify a quantity or range of records. Using the Scope option, you can select a single record or a group of records positioned sequentially in the file.

Note   The active index and the current record pointer affect the results of the scope options Next and Rest. For example, the next record in a table indexed by last name is probably different than one in a table indexed by state. This doesn't affect the Record option because the number for a record doesn't change when the table is indexed.

To select a limited number of records

1. From the **File** menu, choose **Print**.

2. In the **Print** dialog box, choose **Options**.

3. In the **Print Options** dialog box, choose **Options**.

   Report and Label Print Options dialog box

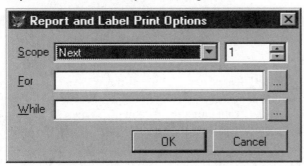

4. In the **Print and Label Print Options** dialog box, choose **Scope**.

5. Select the appropriate scope option.

To print	Choose this scope option
Every record from the source file	**ALL**
A range of records starting with 1	**NEXT**
A specific record by number	**RECORD**
The current record plus all of those after it to the end of the file	**REST**

Visual FoxPro prints the report using data from the records within the scope you selected.

Printing Records That Match a Condition

If the records you want to select are not sequential within the table, you can build a logical expression that specifies selection criteria a record must meet to be printed. For example, you can choose to print all records with a particular value in a field.

To enter criteria for selecting records

1. From the **File** menu, choose **Print**.

2. In the **Print** dialog box, choose **Options**.

3. In the **Print Options** dialog box, choose **Options**.

4. In the **Print and Label Print Options** dialog box, choose **Scope**.

5. In the **For** box, enter a FOR expression.

   – or –

   Make sure the records sources used by the report are open, and then choose the **For** button to use the Expression Builder.

   > **Note**   You don't need to include the FOR command in the expression. For example, type **country = "Canada"** to see only Canadian data.

   Visual FoxPro evaluates all of the records and prints the report using those records that match the condition in the expression.

Controlling Selection of Records to Print

When printing, you can specify a condition that must be met to continue evaluating and selecting records. You enter this condition as a WHILE expression. As long as the WHILE expression remains true, Visual FoxPro processes the data source. After finding a record that doesn't meet the condition, Visual FoxPro ends the evaluation process and prints the selected records. This option allows you to select records based on information outside the values contained in the fields.

> **Tip**   If you use a WHILE expression on a file that hasn't been indexed, the selection process may end before evaluating all of the appropriate records. Before printing the report, be sure the source table has the appropriate index active for the WHILE expression you want to use.

To enter criteria for ending record selection

1. From the **File** menu, choose **Print**.

2. In the **Print** dialog box, choose **Options**.

3. In the **Print Options** dialog box, choose **Options**.

4. In the **Print and Label Print Options** dialog box, choose **Scope**.

5. In the **While** box, enter a WHILE expression.

– or –

Choose the **While** button to use the Expression Builder.

> **Note**   You don't need to include the WHILE command in the statement.
> For example, type **sales > 1000** to see only sales above one-thousand dollars.

Visual FoxPro prints the report using the records it evaluates while the expression is true.

Printing Reports and Labels

If you want to send the report to the printer, you can send it directly to the printer or display the Print Setup dialog box.

To send a report to the printer

- Use the TO PRINTER clause of the REPORT or LABEL command.

For example, the following code sends the report `MyReport` to the default printer and stops the report from printing on the screen:

```
REPORT FORM MYREPORT.FRX TO PRINTER NOCONSOLE
```

To display the Print Setup dialog box before sending the report to the printer

- Use the TO PRINTER PROMPT clause of the REPORT or LABEL command.

For example, the following code displays the Print Setup dialog box, sends the report `MyReport` to the default printer, and stops the report from printing in the active window:

```
REPORT FORM MYREPORT.FRX TO PRINTER PROMPT NOCONSOLE
```

Previewing Reports and Labels

If you want to display a preview of the report, you can send it to the Preview window in the Report Designer.

To preview a report

- Use the PREVIEW clause of the REPORT command

For example, the following code displays the report in a modal window:

```
REPORT FORM MYREPORT.FRX PREVIEW
```

By default, the Preview window is modal but allows access to the Preview toolbar. If you want to make the preview modeless, you can add the keyword NOWAIT to the REPORT command.

For example, the following code displays the report in a modeless window:

```
REPORT FORM MYREPORT.FRX PREVIEW NOWAIT
```

If you want to preview the results in a specific window, you can include the WINDOW clause to specify a window created with DEFINE WINDOW.

```
REPORT FORM MYREPORT.FRX PREVIEW WINDOW MYWINDOW
```

Printing Reports to File

If you want to create an electronic version of the report, you can send it to a file formatted for your printer or to an ASCII file. Sending reports to a file allows you to print them in a batch on your printer at a later time.

If you want to create an ASCII file, you can create a file that includes only the text, dashes, and plus signs to represent lines and shapes. Font and color choices are not included. You can also specify the number of characters to place on each line and the number of lines to place on each page. For more information about the REPORT command, see Help.

To print a report to an ASCII file

- Use the FILE and ASCII keywords of the REPORT command.

The following example defines the variables for the ASCII page, then prints a report called Myreport.frx to an ASCII file name Myfile.txt.

Printing to an ASCII File

Code	Comment
`_asciirows = nLines`	Define the number of lines per page.
`_asciicols = nChars`	Define the number of characters per line.
`REPORT FORM MYREPORT.FRX` `    TO FILE MYFILE.TXT ASCII`	Run the report.

Saving a Report as HTML

You can use the **Save As HTML** option on the **File** menu when creating or modifying a report to save the contents of the report as an HTML (Hypertext Markup Language) file.

To save a report as HTML

1. Open the report.

2. Choose **Save As HTML** on the **File** menu. This option is only available when the report has been saved to disk.

3. Enter the name of the HTML file to create and choose **Save**.

Integrating Queries and Reports

After you've created the components of your application, you can integrate them. The following illustration shows some ways you can add queries and reports to your application.

Some ways to integrate queries and reports

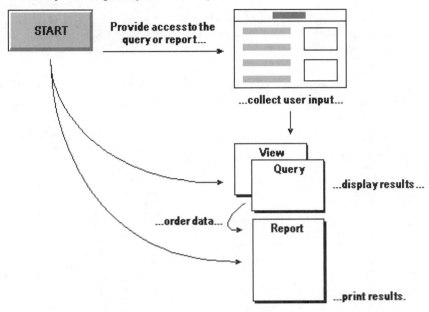

You can add code that executes a query or a report to the following objects in your application.

- A button on a form. For more information about forms and buttons, see Chapter 9, "Creating Forms."

- An item on a menu or a button on a toolbar. For more information, see Chapter 11, "Designing Menus and Toolbars."

To add a query, view, or program

- Add a DO or USE command to the code behind a command button on a form, a button on a toolbar, or a menu item.

  For example, add code similar to one of the following lines:

```
DO MYQUERY.QPR
DO MYPROGRAM.PRG
USE myview
```

You have several options for integrating reports into your application.

- If you want the user to simply start the report and collect the printout, you can have the user initiate a report by adding the REPORT command to a control on a form, a command on a menu, or a button on a toolbar.

- If you want to allow your user to enter some variables used in the report, you can gather values from the user just as you did for queries. For example, the user could enter a specified date range that the report will include. For more information, see "Collecting User Input with Queries" later in this chapter.

- If you want the user to create custom reports, you can offer the user the ability to create new reports or modify existing reports with the Report Designer.

To run reports and labels

- Use the REPORT or LABEL commands.

  For example, you could use code similar to one of the following lines:

```
REPORT FORM MYREPORT.FRX
LABEL FORM MYLABEL.LBX
```

To modify reports and labels

- Use the MODIFY REPORT or MODIFY LABEL commands.

  For example, add code similar to one of the following lines:

```
MODIFY REPORT MYREPORT.FRX
MODIFY LABEL MYLABEL.LBX
```

To create reports and labels

- Use the CREATE REPORT or CREATE LABEL commands.

  For example, you could use code similar to one of the following lines:

```
CREATE REPORT MYREPORT.FRX
CREATE LABEL MYLABEL.LBX
```

For more information about the MODIFY and CREATE commands, see Help.

Collecting User Input with Queries

If you want to collect values from a form, you can use variables in a SELECT – SQL statement and then use them immediately in the statement, or execute the statement later.

To collect values for immediate use, you can either explicitly name the form or use a shortcut reference for the form in your SELECT – SQL statement. In this example, shortcut reference is in the WHERE clause.

Collecting Values Using Shortcut References in a SELECT – SQL Statement

Code	Comment
| ```
SELECT * ;
   FROM tastrade!customer ;
   WHERE customer.country = ;
      THISFORM.ControlName1.Value ;
   AND customer.region =
THISFORM.ControlName2.Value ;
   GROUP BY customer.postal_code ;
   ORDER BY customer.postal_code,
customer.company_name
``` | Use THISFORM as a shortcut reference for the currently active form and substitute control names for ControlName1 and ControlName2. |

If you don't want to use references to the control, you can define variables in the code. Use code variables if you want to store the values from a form but don't necessarily expect to use them while the form is active.

Collecting Values for Later Use

Code	Comment
| ```
cValue = THISFORM.ControlName.Value
``` | Define the variable. |
| ```
SELECT * ;
   FROM tastrade!customer ;
   WHERE customer.country = cValue ;
   GROUP BY customer.postal_code ;
   ORDER BY customer.postal_code, ;
      customer.company_name
``` | Use the variable you defined in the SELECT – SQL statement. |

If you don't define the variable before you run the query, an error message appears stating that the variable couldn't be found. If the variable isn't defined in code, Visual FoxPro assumes that the variable is pre-initialized.
```

Compiling an Application

You can easily create event-driven, object-oriented applications one piece at a time. This modular approach allows you to verify the functionality of each component as you create it. After you've created all the functional components, you can compile them into an application, which assembles the executable components of your project — forms, reports, menus, programs, and so on — into a single file that you can distribute to your users along with your data.

To quickly create a complete project with Application Framework, you can use the Application Wizard. After the project is created, the new Application Builder opens so you can add a database, tables, reports, and forms.

This chapter describes how to build a typical Visual FoxPro application. For more information about the process of developing Visual FoxPro applications, see Chapter 2, "Developing an Application," and Chapter 14, "Testing and Debugging Applications." If you want to distribute your application, see Part 8, "Distributing Applications."

The application building process requires:

- Structuring an Application
- Adding Files to a Project
- Creating an Application from a Project

Structuring an Application

A typical database application consists of data structures, a user interface, query options, and reporting capabilities. To design the structure of your application, carefully consider the function each component provides and its relationship to other components.

An assembled Visual FoxPro application typically presents a user with a menu and one or more forms for entering or displaying data. You provide functionality and maintain data integrity and security by attaching code to certain events. Queries and reports allow your users to extract information from the database.

Structure of a typical Visual FoxPro application

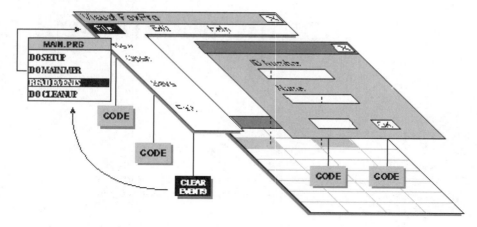

When structuring your application, you need to consider the following tasks:

- Setting the application's starting point.

- Initializing the environment.

- Displaying the interface.

- Controlling the event loop.

- Restoring the original environment when the application quits.

The following sections provide details about each of these tasks. Typically you would create an application object to complete these tasks; see the Tasmanian Traders sample application located in the Visual Studio …\Samples\Vfp98\Tastrade directory for an example of this technique. Also, if you use the Application Wizard to compile your application, it creates an application object. Or, if you want, you can use a program as the main file that handles these tasks. For more information, see "Structuring a Program as a Main File" later in this chapter.

Setting the Starting Point

You link each component together and set a starting point for your application with a main file. The main file serves as the execution starting point for your application, and can consist of a program or form. When users run your application, Visual FoxPro launches the main file for your application, which in turn runs all other components as needed. All applications must have a main file. Usually, the best choice is to create a main program in your application. However, you can combine the functionality of the main program and the initial user interface by using a form as the main program.

If you use the Application Wizard to create your application, you can allow the wizard to create a main file program for you. You don't need to specify a main file yourself unless you want to change the main file after the wizard is done.

To set the starting point for an application

1. In the Project Manager, select the file.

2. From the **Project** menu, choose **Set Main**.

> **Note**   The file that you set as the application's main file is automatically marked as included so that it is treated as read-only after you compile the application.

Only one file in the project can be set as the main file. The main file is displayed in bold type, as shown in the following illustration.

Setting a main file in the Project Manager

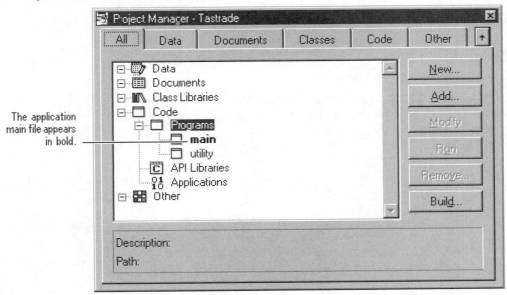

The application main file appears in bold.

Initializing the Environment

The first task that a main file or application object must accomplish is to set up your application's environment. The default Visual FoxPro development environment establishes certain values of SET commands and system variables when Visual FoxPro opens. However, these settings might not be the best environment for your application.

> **Tip**   To see the default values of the Visual FoxPro development environment, start Visual FoxPro without a configuration file by typing **VFP –C** and then issue the DISPLAY STATUS command.

It is always a good idea to save the initial environment settings and set up a specific environment for your application in your setup code.

To capture commands for the current environment

1. From the **Tools** menu, choose **Options**.

2. Press **Shift** and select **OK** to display the environment SET commands in the
   Command window.

3. From the Command window, copy and paste into your program.

In an environment specific to your application, you might want to include code to:

- Initialize variables.

- Establish a default path.

- Open any needed databases, free tables, and indexes. If your application requires
  access to remote data, the initialization routine can also prompt the user for the
  necessary login information.

- Reference external library and procedure files.

For example, if you wanted to test the default value of the SET TALK command, store
the value, and set TALK to OFF for your application, you could place the following
code in your setup procedure:

```
IF SET('TALK') = "ON"
    SET TALK OFF
    cTalkVal = "ON"
ELSE
    cTalkVal = "OFF"
ENDIF
```

It is usually a good idea to save default settings in public variables, in a custom class, or
as properties of an application object so that you can restore these values when quitting
the application.

```
SET TALK &cTalkVal
```

Displaying the Initial Interface

The initial user interface can be a menu, form, or any other user component. Often, an
application will display a sign-on screen or logon dialog box before displaying the opening
menu or form.

You can initiate the user interface in the main program by using a DO command to run a
menu or a DO FORM command to run a form. For more information on these commands,
see Help.

Controlling the Event Loop

Once the environment is set up and you've displayed the initial user interface, you're ready to establish an event loop to wait for user interaction.

To control the event loop

- Issue the READ EVENTS command, which causes Visual FoxPro to begin processing user events such as mouse clicks and keystrokes.

It is important to place the READ EVENTS command correctly in your main file, because all processing in the main file is suspended from the time the READ EVENTS command is executed until a subsequent CLEAR EVENTS command is issued. For example, you might issue a READ EVENTS command as the last command in an initialization procedure, executed after the environment has been initialized and the user interface displayed. If you don't include the READ EVENTS command, your application will return to the operating system after running.

After the event loop has been started, the application is under the control of the user interface element that was last displayed. For example, if the following two commands are issued in the main file, the application displays the form Startup.scx:

```
DO FORM STARTUP.SCX
READ EVENTS
```

If you don't include a READ EVENTS command or its equivalent in your main file, your application will run properly from the Command window within the development environment. However, when you run it from your menu or main screen, the application will appear briefly, then quit.

Your application must also provide a way to end the event loop.

To terminate the event loop

- Issue the CLEAR EVENTS command.

Typically, you issue the CLEAR EVENTS command from a menu or a button in a form. The CLEAR EVENTS command suspends the event processing for Visual FoxPro and returns control to the program that issued the READ EVENTS command that started the event loop.

For a simple program example, see "Structuring a Program as a Main File" later in this chapter.

> **Caution**   You need to establish a way to exit the event loop before you start it. Make sure your interface has a mechanism (such as an Exit button or menu command) to issue the CLEAR EVENTS command.

Restoring the Original Environment

To restore the original value of saved variables, you can macrosubstitute them into the original SET commands. For example, if you saved the SET TALK setting into the public variable cTalkVal, issue the following command:

```
SET TALK &cTalkval
```

> **Note**   Variable names used with macro substitution shouldn't contain the "m." prefix because the period assumes a variable concatenation and will produce a syntax error.

If you initialized the environment in a different program than the one in which you are restoring it — for example, if you initialize by calling one procedure, but restore the environment by calling another — be sure you can access the values you stored. For example, store the values to restore in public variables, custom classes, or as properties of an application object.

Structuring a Program as a Main File

If you use a program (.prg) file as the main file in your application, you must be sure that it includes commands to handle the tasks associated with major application tasks. The main file doesn't have to issue commands directly to accomplish all the tasks. For example, it is common to call procedures or functions to handle tasks such as initializing the environment and cleaning up.

> **Note**   If you used the Application Wizard and allowed it to create the program Main.prg, you can modify the program the wizard created instead of creating a new one. The wizards uses a special class to define an object for the application. The main program includes sections to instantiate and configure the object.

To build a simple main program

1. Initialize the environment by opening databases, declaring variables, and so on.
2. Establish the initial user interface by calling a menu or form.
3. Establish the event loop by issuing the READ EVENTS command.
4. Issue CLEAR EVENTS command from a menu (such as an Exit command) or a button (such as an Exit command button). The main program shouldn't issue this command.
5. Restore the environment when the user quits the application.

For example, your main program might look like this:

Code	Comments
DO SETUP.PRG	Call program to set up environment (store values in public variables)
DO MAINMENU.MPR	Display menu as initial interface
READ EVENTS	Establish event loop. A different program (such as Mainmenu.mpr must issue a CLEAR EVENTS command)
DO CLEANUP.PRG	Restore environment before quitting

Adding Files to a Project

A Visual FoxPro project consists of separate components that are stored as individual files. For example, a simple project might consist of forms (.scx files), reports (.frx files), and programs (.prg and .fxp files). In addition, a project usually has one or more databases (.dbc files), tables (stored in .dbf and .fpt files) and indexes (.cdx and .idx files). To be included in an application, a file has to be added to your project. That way, when you compile your application, Visual FoxPro can include the files for that component in the finished product.

You can easily add files to a project in a number of ways:

- To create a project and add existing files, use the Application Wizard.

- To automatically add new files to a project, open a project, then create the new files from within the Project Manager.

- To add existing files to a project, open a project and add them using the Project Manager.

If you've used the Application Wizard or Project Manager to create the files, you usually don't need to do anything else — the file is automatically included in the project. One exception, however, is if your application includes a file that will be modified by the user. Because included files are read-only, you must mark the file as excluded. For details, see "Referencing Modifiable Files" later in this chapter.

Tip   For a list of file types and extensions used in Visual FoxPro, search for "File Extensions and File Types" in Help.

If an existing file is not already part of your project, you can add it manually.

To add a file to a project manually

1. In the Project Manager, choose the type of component you want to add by selecting it in the hierarchy, and then click **Add**.

2. In the **Open** dialog box, select the file to add.

Visual FoxPro also adds files to your project if you reference them in a program or form. For example, if a program in your project includes the following line, Visual FoxPro adds the file Orders.scx to your project:

```
DO FORM ORDERS.SCX
```

If a file is referenced in this way, it is not immediately included in a project. Later, when you build the project, Visual FoxPro resolves references to all files and automatically includes implicit files in the project. Additionally, if any other file is referenced through user-defined code within the new file, building the project will also resolve that reference and include the file. The referenced files appear in the Project Manager the next time you view the project.

Important   Visual FoxPro might not be able to resolve references to picture (.bmp and
.msk) files, depending on how they are used in code. Therefore, add pictures to your
files manually. In addition, Visual FoxPro cannot automatically include files that are
referenced using macro substitution, because the name of the file is not known until the
application is running. If your application references files using macro substitution,
include the referenced files manually.

Referencing Modifiable Files

When you compile a project into an application, files included in the project are assembled
into a single application file. After the project is built, files in the project that are marked
"included" become read-only.

Often, files that are part of your project, such as tables, are intended to be modified by
users. In those cases, you should add the files to your project but mark them as excluded.
Excluded files are still part of your application, so Visual FoxPro still tracks them as part
of your project, but they are not compiled in the application file, so users can update them.

Note   Tables are marked as excluded by default, because Visual FoxPro assumes that
tables will be modifiable in an application.

As a general rule, files containing executable programs (forms, reports, queries, menus,
and programs) should be included in the application file, and data files should be excluded.
However, you should determine whether to include or exclude files based on your
application requirements. For example, a table that contains sensitive system information
or information used only for lookup can be included in the application file to protect it
from inadvertent change. Conversely, you might exclude a report (.frx) file if your
application allows users to change it dynamically.

If you exclude a file, you must make sure that Visual FoxPro can find the excluded file
when the application runs. For example, when a form references a visual class library, the
form stores a relative path to that library. If you include the library in the project, it is made
part of the application file, and the form will always be able to locate the library. However,
if you exclude the library, the form must search for the library using the relative path or the
Visual FoxPro search path (as set using the SET PATH command). If the library is not in
the expected locations — for example, if you have moved the library since creating the
form — Visual FoxPro displays a dialog box asking the user to locate the library. You
might not want users to see this dialog box. To be safe, include all files that don't need to
be updated by users.

Note   You cannot include application (.app) files, and you should choose to exclude
library files (.ocx, .fll, and .dll).

To exclude modifiable files

1. In the Project Manager, select the modifiable file.

2. From the **Project** menu, choose **Exclude**.

   If the file is already excluded, the **Exclude** command is not available; the **Include** command appears in its place.

Excluded files have the ∅ symbol to the left of their names.

> **Note**   Files marked as main files cannot be marked as excluded. For details about main files, see "Setting the Starting Point" earlier in this chapter.

Tables marked as excluded in a project

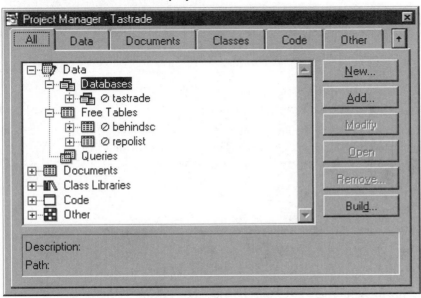

> **Tip**   To view all project files at once, choose **Project Info** from the **Project** menu and select the **Files** tab.

Creating an Application from a Project

The final step in compiling a project is to build it. The end result of this process is a single file that includes all the files referenced in your project into a single application file (except those marked as excluded). You can distribute the application file along with the data files (and any other files you've excluded from the project) to your users, who can then launch the file to run your application.

The steps involved in creating an application from your project are:

- Testing the project.

- Building an application file from the project.

Testing a Project

To verify references and check that all components are available, you can test the project. To do so, you rebuild the project, which forces Visual FoxPro to resolve file references and to recompile files that are out of date.

To test a project

1. In the Project Manager, choose **Build**.

2. In the **Build Options** dialog box, select **Rebuild Project**.

3. Select any other options you need and choose **OK**.

   – or –

   Use the BUILD PROJECT command.

For example, to build a project named Myproj.pjx, type:

```
BUILD PROJECT myproj
```

For more information on the BUILD PROJECT command, see Help.

If errors occur during the build process, they are collected into a file in your current directory with the name of your project and an .err extension. The compilation error count is displayed on the status bar. You can also see the error file immediately.

To display the error file immediately

- Select the **Display Errors** box.

After the project has been built successfully, you should try to run it before creating an application.

To run the application

- In the **Project Manager**, highlight the main program, and then choose **Run**.

  – or –

  In the Command window, issue a DO command with the name of the main program:

```
DO MAINPROG.PRG
```

If the program runs properly, you're ready to build an application file that will contain all the files included in the project.

You should repeat the steps of rebuilding and running your project as you add components to your project. Unless you choose Recompile All Files in the Build Options dialog box, only files that have been modified since the last build are recompiled.

Building an Application File from the Project

To create a finished file from your application, you build it into an application file. An application file has an extension of .app. To run the application, users first start Visual FoxPro, then load the .app file.

You can choose to build either an application (.app) or an executable (.exe) file from your project. Users can run an .app file if they already have a copy of Visual FoxPro. Alternatively, you can create an .exe file. The .exe file works in conjunction with two Visual FoxPro dynamic link libraries (Vfp6r.dll and Vfp6enu.dll) that you ship with your application to provide a complete run-time environment for Visual FoxPro. The second file is specific to the region of the world your application targets. For more information, see Part 8, "Distributing Applications."

To build an application

1. In the **Project Manager**, choose **Build**.

2. In the **Build Options** dialog box, choose **Build Application** to build an .app file, or **Build Executable** to build an .exe file.

3. Select any other options you need, then choose **OK**.

   – or –

   Use the BUILD APP or BUILD EXE command.

For example, to build an application called Myapp.app from a project named Myproj.pjx, you can type:

```
BUILD APP myapp FROM myproj
```

To create an application called Myapp.exe from a project named Myproj.pjx, you can type:

```
BUILD EXE myapp FROM myproj
```

For more information on the BUILD APP and BUILD EXE commands, see Help.

> **Note**   You can also use the Build dialog box to create an Automation server from your Visual FoxPro application. For more information, see "Creating Automation Servers" in Chapter 16, "Adding OLE."

After you've created a finished application file for your project, you and your users can run it.

To run an application as an .app file

- In Visual FoxPro, choose **Do** from the **Program** menu and select the application file.

  – or –

  In the Command window, type DO and the name of your application file.

  For example, to run an application called MYAPP, type:

  ```
  DO myapp.app
  ```

For more information on the DO command, see Help.

If you have created an .exe file from your application, users can run it in a variety of ways.

To run an application as an .exe file

- In Visual FoxPro, choose **Do** from the **Program** menu and select the application file, or in the Command window, type DO and the name of your application file.

  For example, to run an .exe file called Myapp.exe, type:

  ```
  DO myapp.exe
  ```

  – or –

  In Windows, double-click the icon for the .exe file.

     Note   You can use the Setup Wizard to create an installation routine that installs the appropriate files.

CHAPTER 14

Testing and Debugging Applications

Testing involves finding problems in your code; debugging consists of isolating and fixing the problems. Testing and debugging are necessary stages in the development cycle, and they are best incorporated early in the cycle. Thoroughly testing and debugging individual components makes testing and debugging integrated applications much easier.

For more information about creating an application, see Chapter 2, "Developing an Application," and Chapter 13, "Compiling an Application."

This chapter discusses:

- Planning to Test and Debug
- Debugging Before You Have Bugs
- Isolating Problems
- Displaying Output
- Logging Code Coverage
- Handling Run-Time Errors

Planning to Test and Debug

Typically, developers look for different levels of robustness as they are testing and debugging their applications:

1. Running without crashing or generating error messages.

2. Appropriate action in common scenarios.

3. Reasonable action or error messages in a range of scenarios.

4. Graceful recovery from unexpected user interactions.

Visual FoxPro provides a rich set of tools to help you isolate and identify the problems in your code so that you can fix them effectively. However, one of the best ways to create a robust application is to look for potential problems before they occur.

Debugging Before You Have Bugs

Studies have shown that good coding practices (using white space, including comments, adhering to naming conventions, and so on) automatically tend to reduce the number of bugs in your code. In addition, there are some steps you can take early in the development process to make testing and debugging easier later on, including:

- Creating a Test Environment
- Setting Asserts
- Seeing Event Sequences

Creating a Test Environment

The system environment that you expect an application to run in is as important as the data environment you have set up for the application itself. To ensure portability and to create an appropriate context for testing and debugging, you need to consider the following:

- Hardware and software
- System paths and file properties
- Directory structure and file locations

Hardware and Software

For maximum portability, you should develop applications on the lowest common platform you expect them to run on. To establish a baseline platform:

- Develop your applications using the lowest common video mode.
- Determine base requirements for RAM and media storage space, including any necessary drivers or concurrently running software.
- Consider special memory, file, and record-locking scenarios for network versus stand-alone versions of applications.

System Paths and File Properties

To ensure all necessary program files are readily accessible on each machine that will run your application, you might also require a baseline file configuration. To help you define a configuration baseline, answer the following questions:

- Does your application require common system paths?
- Have you set appropriate file access properties?
- Are network permissions set correctly for each user?

Directory Structure and File Locations

If your source code references absolute paths or file names, those exact paths and files must exist when your application is installed on any other computer. To avoid this scenario, you can:

- Use Visual FoxPro configuration files. For additional information on using configuration files, see Chapter 3, "Configuring Visual FoxPro," in the *Installation Guide.*

- Create a separate directory or directory structure to keep source files apart from the generated application files. This way, you can test the references of the completed application and know exactly which files to distribute.

- Use relative paths.

Setting Asserts

You can include asserts in your code to verify assumptions you have about the run-time environment for the code.

To set an assert

- Use the ASSERT command to identify assumptions in your program.

  When the condition stipulated in the ASSERT command evaluates to false (.F.), an assert message box is displayed and echoed to the Debug Output window.

For example, you could be writing a function that expects a non-zero parameter value. The following line of code in the function alerts you if the value of the parameter is 0:

```
ASSERT nParm != 0 MESSAGE "Received a parameter of 0"
```

You can specify whether assert messages are displayed with the SET ASSERTS command. By default, assert messages are not displayed.

Seeing Event Sequences

When you see events occur in relation to other events, you can determine the most efficient place to include your code.

To track events

- From the **Tools** menu in the Debugger window, choose **Event Tracking**.

  – or –

  Use the SET EVENTTRACKING command.

The **Event Tracking** Dialog Box allows you to select the events that you want to see.

Event Tracking Dialog Box

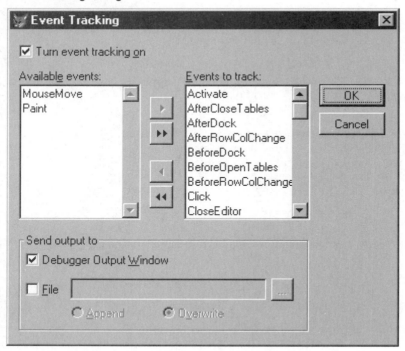

Note   In this example, the MouseMove and Paint events have been removed from the Events to track list because these events occur so frequently that they make it more difficult to see the sequences of the other events.

When event tracking is enabled, every time a system event in the Events to track list occurs, the name of the event is displayed in the Debug Output window or written to a file. If you choose to have the events displayed in the Debug Output window, you can still save them to a file as described in "Displaying Output" later in this chapter.

Note   If the Debug Output window is not open, events will not be listed, even if the Debugger Output Window box is set.

Isolating Problems

Once your testing has identified problems, you can use the Visual FoxPro debugging environment to isolate those problems by:

- Starting a debugging session
- Tracing through code
- Suspending program execution
- Seeing stored values
- Displaying output

Starting a Debugging Session

You start a debugging session by opening the debugging environment.

To open the debugger

- From the **Tools** menu, choose **Debugger**.

    Note If you're debugging in the Visual FoxPro environment, choose the debugging tool you want to open from the Tools menu.

You can also open the debugger with any of the following commands:

```
DEBUG
```

```
SET STEP ON
```

```
SET ECHO ON
```

The debugger opens automatically whenever a breakpoint condition is met.

Tracing Through Code

One of the most useful debugging strategies at your disposal is the ability to trace through code, see each line of code as it executes, and check the values of all variables, properties, and environment settings.

Code in the Trace window

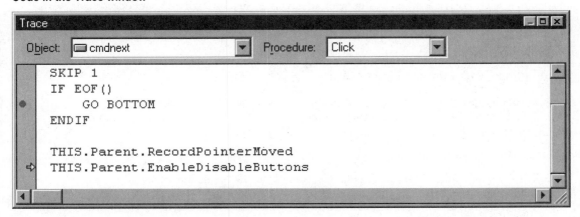

To trace through code

1. Start a debugging session.

2. If no program is open in the Trace window, choose **Do** from the **Debug** menu.

3. Choose **Step Into** from the **Debug** menu or click the **Step Into** toolbar button.

An arrow in the gray area to the left of the code indicates the next line to execute.

Tips   The following tips apply:

- Set breakpoints to narrow the range of code you need to step through.

- You can skip a line of code you know will generate an error by placing the cursor on the line of code after the problem line and choosing **Set Next Statement** from the **Debug** menu.

- If you have much code associated with Timer events, you can avoid tracing through this code by clearing **Display Timer Event** in the **Debugging** tab of the **Options** dialog box.

If you isolate a problem when you're debugging a program or object code, you can immediately fix it.

To fix problems encountered while tracing code

- From the **Debug** menu, choose **Fix**.

When you choose Fix from the Debug menu, program execution is canceled and the code editor is opened to the location of the cursor in the Trace window.

Suspending Program Execution

Breakpoints allow you to suspend program execution. Once program execution has been suspended, you can check the values of variables and properties, see environment settings, and examine sections of code line by line without having to step through all your code.

Tip   You can also suspend execution of a program running in the Trace window by pressing ESC.

Suspending Execution at a Line of Code

You can set breakpoints in your code to suspend program execution in several different ways. If you know where you want to suspend program execution, you can set a breakpoint directly on that line of code.

To set a breakpoint on a particular line of code

In the Trace window, locate the line of code you want to set the breakpoint on and do one of the following:

1. Position the cursor on the line of code.

2. Press F9 or click the **Toggle Breakpoints** button in the **Debugger** toolbar.

   – or –

   Double-click in the gray area to the left of the line of code.

A solid dot is displayed in the gray area to the left of the line of code to indicate that a breakpoint has been set on that line.

   Tip   If you are debugging objects, you can locate particular lines of code in the Trace window by choosing the object from the Object list and the method or event from the Procedure list.

You can also set breakpoints by specifying locations and files in the Breakpoints dialog box.

Breaking at a location

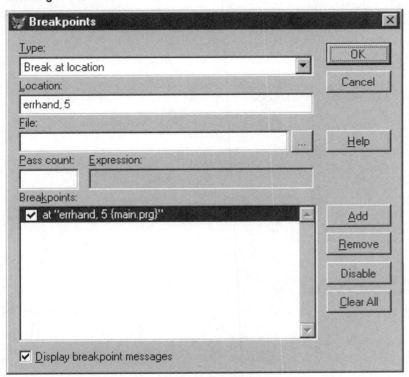

Examples of Locations and Files for Breakpoints

Location	File	Where execution suspends
ErrHandler	C:\Myapp\Main.prg	The first executable line in a procedure named ErrHandler in Main.prg.
Click	C:\Myapp\Form.scx	The first executable line of any procedure, function, method or event named Click in Form.scx.
Main,10	C:\Myapp\Main.prg	The tenth line in the program named Main.

(continued)

Examples of Locations and Files for Breakpoints *(continued)*

Location	File	Where execution suspends
cmdNext.Click	C:\Myapp\Form.scx	The first executable line associated with the Click event of cmdNext in Form.scx.
cmdNext::Click		The first executable line in the Click event of any control whose ParentClass is cmdNext in any file.

Suspending Execution When Values Change

If you want to know when the value of a variable or property changes, or when a run-time condition changes, you can set a breakpoint on an expression.

Breaking when an expression changes

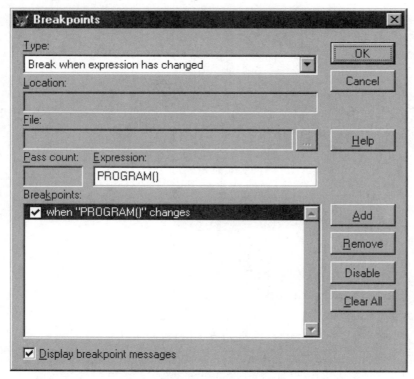

To suspend program execution when the value of an expression changes

1. From the **Tools** menu in the Debugger window, choose **Breakpoints** to open the **Breakpoints** dialog box.

2. From the **Type** list, choose **Break when expression has changed**.

3. Enter the expression in the **Expression** box.

Examples of breakpoint expressions

Expression	Use
RECNO( )	Suspend execution when the record pointer moves in the table.
PROGRAM( )	Suspend execution on the first line of any new program, procedure, method, or event.
myform.Text1.Value	Suspend execution any time the value of this property is changed interactively or programmatically.

Suspending Execution Conditionally

Often you'll want to suspend program execution, not at a particular line, but when a certain condition is true.

Breaking on an expression

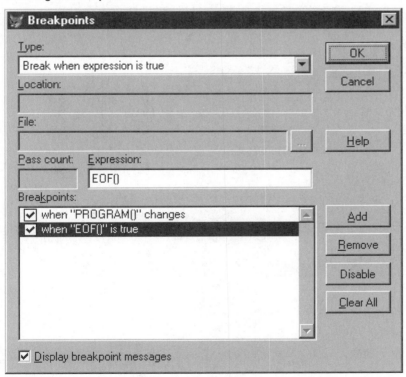

To suspend program execution when an expression evaluates to true

1. From the **Tools** menu in the Debugger window, choose **Breakpoints** to open the Breakpoints dialog box.

2. From the **Type** list, choose **Break when expression is true**.

3.   Enter the expression in the **Expression** box.

4.   Choose **Add** to add the breakpoint to the **Breakpoints** list.

Examples of breakpoint expressions

Expression	Use
EOF( )	Suspend execution when the record pointer has moved past the last record in a table.
'CLICK'$PROGRAM( )	Suspend execution on the first line of code associated with a Click or DblClick event.
nReturnValue = 6	If the return value of a message box is stored to nReturnValue, suspend execution when a user chooses **Yes** in the message box.

Suspending Execution Conditionally at a Line of Code

You can specify that program execution be suspended at a particular line only when a particular condition is true.

Breaking when an expression is true

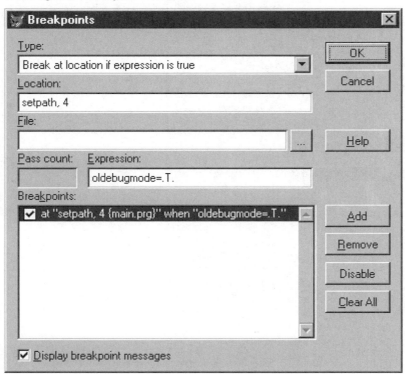

To suspend program execution at a particular line when an expression evaluates to true

1. From the **Tools** menu in the Debugger window, choose **Breakpoints** to open the Breakpoints dialog box.

2. From the **Type** list, choose **Break at location if expression is true**.

3. Enter the location in the **Location** box.

4. Enter the expression in the **Expression** box.

5. Choose **Add** to add the breakpoint to the **Breakpoints** list.

6. Choose **OK**.

> **Tip** It is sometimes easier to locate the line of code in the Trace window, set a breakpoint, and then edit that breakpoint in the Breakpoints dialog box. To do this, change the **Type** from **Break at location** to **Break at location if expression is true** and then add the expression.

Removing Breakpoints

You can disable breakpoints without removing them in the Breakpoints dialog box. You can delete "break at location" breakpoints in the Trace window.

To remove a breakpoint from a line of code

In the Trace window, locate the breakpoint and do one of the following:

- Position the cursor on the line of code, and then choose **Toggle Breakpoints** from the **Debugger** toolbar.

  – or –

  Double-click the gray area to the left of the line of code.

Seeing Stored Values

In the Debugger window, you can easily see the run-time values of variables, array elements, properties, and expressions in the following windows:

- Locals Window
- Watch Window
- Trace Window

Seeing Stored Values in the Locals Window

The Locals window displays all the variables, arrays, objects, and object members that are visible in any program, procedure, or method on the call stack. By default, values for the currently executing program are displayed in the Locals window. You can see these values for other programs or procedures on the call stack by choosing the programs or procedures from the Locals For list.

Locals window

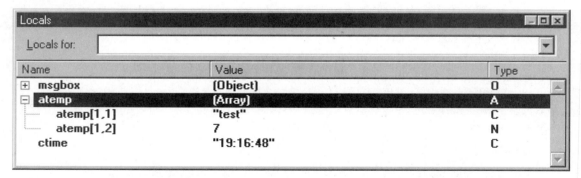

You can drill down into arrays or objects by clicking the plus (+) beside the array or object name in the Locals and Watch windows. When you drill down, you can see the values of all the elements in the arrays and all the property settings in objects.

You can even change the values in variables, array elements, and properties in the Locals and Watch windows by selecting the variable, array element, or property, clicking in the Value column, and typing a new value.

Seeing Stored Values in the Watch Window

In the Watch box of the Watch window, type any valid Visual FoxPro expression and press ENTER. The value and type of the expression appears in the Watch window list.

Watch window

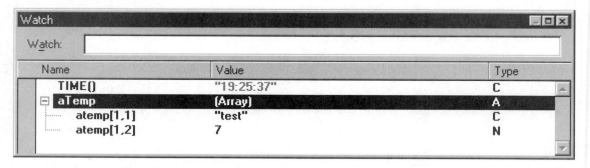

Note   You can't enter expressions in the Watch window that create objects.

You can also select variables or expressions in the Trace window or other Debugger windows and drag them into the Watch window.

Values that have changed are displayed in red in the Watch window.

To remove an item from the Watch window list

Select the item and choose one of the following:

- Press DEL.

  – or –

  From the shortcut menu, choose **Delete Watch**.

To edit a watch

- Double-click the watch in the Watch window and edit in place.

Seeing Stored Values in the Trace Window

Position the cursor over any variable, array element, or property in the Trace window to display its current value in a value tip.

A value tip in the Trace window

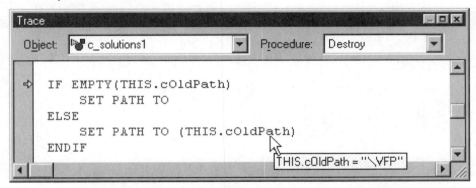

Displaying Output

The DEBUGOUT command allows you to write values in the Debug Output window to a text file log. Alternatively, you can use the SET DEBUGOUT TO command or the Debug tab of the Options dialog box.

If you aren't writing DEBUGOUT commands to a text file, the Debug Output window must be open in order for the DEBUGOUT values to be written. The following line of code prints in the Debug Output window at the time that the line of code executes:

```
DEBUGOUT DATETIME( )
```

In addition, you can enable event tracking, described earlier in this chapter, and choose to have the name and parameters of each event that occurs displayed in the Debug Output window.

Logging Code Coverage

Later in the development process, you might want to refine your code for performance and ensure that you've adequately tested the code by logging code coverage information.

Code coverage gives you information about which lines of code have been executed and how long it took to execute them. This information can help you identify areas of code that aren't being executed and therefore aren't being tested, as well as areas of the code that you may want to fine tune for performance.

You can toggle code coverage on and off by clicking the Code Coverage toolbar button in the Debugger window. If you toggle code coverage on, the Coverage dialog box opens so that you can specify a file to save the coverage information to.

Coverage Dialog Box

You can also toggle coverage logging on and off programmatically by using the SET COVERAGE TO command. You could, for example, include the following command in your application just before a piece of code you want to investigate:

```
SET COVERAGE TO mylog.log
```

After the section of code you want to log coverage for, you could include the following command to set code coverage off:

```
SET COVERAGE TO
```

When you've specified a file for the coverage information, switch to the main Visual FoxPro window and run your program, form, or application. For every line of code that is executed, the following information is written to the log file:

- How long in seconds the line took to execute.
- The class, if any, that the code belongs to.
- The method or procedure the line of code is in.
- The number of the line of code.
- The file that the code is in.

The easiest way to extract information from the log file is to convert it into a table so that you can set filters, run queries and reports, execute commands, and manipulate the table in other ways.

The Coverage Profiler application creates a cursor from the data generated in coverage logging and uses this cursor in a window for easy analysis.

The Coverage Profiler application creates a cursor from the data generated in coverage logging and uses this cursor in a window for easy analysis. For more information on the Coverage Profiler application, see Chapter 32, "Application Development and Developer Productivity."

The following program converts the text file created by the coverage log into a table:

```
cFileName = GETFILE('DBF')
IF EMPTY(cFileName)
    RETURN
ENDIF
CREATE TABLE (cFileName) ;
    (duration n(7,3), ;
    class c(30), ;
    procedure c(60), ;
    line i, ;
    file c(100))

APPEND FROM GETFILE('log') TYPE DELIMITED
```

Handling Run-Time Errors

Run-time errors occur after the application starts to execute. Actions that would generate run-time errors include: writing to a file that doesn't exist, attempting to open a table that is already open, trying to select a table that has been closed, encountering a data conflict, dividing a value by zero, and so on.

The following commands and functions are useful when anticipating and managing run-time errors.

To	Use
Fill an array with error information	AERROR( )
Open the Debugger or Trace window	DEBUG or SET STEP ON
Generate a specific error to test your error handling	ERROR
Return an error number	ERROR( )
Return an executing program line	LINENO( )

(continued)

(continued)

To	Use
Return an error message string	MESSAGE( )
Execute a command when an error occurs	ON ERROR
Return commands assigned to error handling commands	ON( )
Return the name of the currently executing program	PROGRAM( ) OR SYS(16)
Re-execute the previous command	RETRY
Return any current error message parameter	SYS(2018)

For full descriptions and examples of these commands and functions, see Help.

Anticipating Errors

The first line of defense against run-time errors is anticipating where they could occur and coding around them. For example, the following line of code moves the record pointer to the next record in the table:

```
SKIP
```

This code works unless the record pointer is already past the last record in the table, at which point an error will occur.

The following lines of code anticipate this error and avoid it:

```
IF !EOF()
   SKIP
      IF EOF()
         GO BOTTOM
      ENDIF
ENDIF
```

As another example, the following line of code displays the Open dialog box to allow a user to open a table in a new work area:

```
USE GETFILE('DBF') IN 0
```

The problem is that the user could choose Cancel in the Open dialog box or type the name of a file that doesn't exist. The following code anticipates this by making sure that the file exists before the user tries to use it:

```
cNewTable = GETFILE('DBF')
IF FILE(cNewTable)
   USE (cNewTable) IN 0
ENDIF
```

Your end user may also type the name of a file that isn't a Visual FoxPro table. To circumvent this problem, you could open the file with low-level file I/O functions, parse the binary header, and make sure that the file is indeed a valid table. However, this would be a bit of work and it might noticeably slow down your application. You would be better off handling the situation at run time by displaying a message like "Please open another file. This one is not a table" when error 15, "Not a table," occurs.

You can't, and probably don't want to, anticipate all possible errors, so you'll need to trap some by writing code to be executed in the event of a run-time error.

Handling Procedural Errors

When an error occurs in procedural code, Visual FoxPro checks for error-handling code associated with an ON ERROR routine. If no ON ERROR routine exists, Visual FoxPro displays the default Visual FoxPro error message. For a complete list of Visual FoxPro error messages and error numbers, see Help.

Creating an ON ERROR routine

You can include any valid FoxPro command or expression after ON ERROR, but normally you call an error-handling procedure or program.

To see how ON ERROR works, you can type an unrecognizable command in the Command window, such as:

```
qxy
```

You'll get a standard Visual FoxPro error message dialog box saying "Unrecognized command verb." But if you execute the following lines of code, you'll see the error number, 16, printed on the active output window instead of the standard error message displayed in a dialog box:

```
ON ERROR ?ERROR()
qxy
```

Issuing ON ERROR with nothing after it resets the built-in Visual FoxPro error messaging:

```
ON ERROR
```

In skeletal form, the following code illustrates an ON ERROR error handler:

```
LOCAL lcOldOnError

* Save the original error handler
lcOldOnError = ON("ERROR")

* Issue ON ERROR with the name of a procedure
ON ERROR DO errhandler WITH ERROR(), MESSAGE(), LINENO()

code to which the error handling routine applies
```

```
* Reset the original error handler
ON ERROR &lcOldOnError

PROCEDURE errhandler
LOCAL aErrInfo[1]
AERROR(aErrInfo)
DO CASE
   CASE aErrInfo[1] = 1 && File Does Not Exist
      * display an appropriate message
      * and take some action to fix the problem.
   OTHERWISE
      * display a generic message, maybe
      * send high priority mail to an administrator
ENDPROC
```

Handling Errors in Classes and Objects

When an error occurs in method code, Visual FoxPro checks for error-handling code associated with the Error event of the object. If no code has been written at the object level for the Error event, the Error event code inherited from the parent class, or another class up the class hierarchy, is executed. If no code has been written for the Error event anywhere in the class hierarchy, Visual FoxPro checks for an ON ERROR routine. If no ON ERROR routine exists, Visual FoxPro displays the default Visual FoxPro error message.

The beauty of classes is that you can encapsulate everything a control needs, including error handling, so that you can use the control in a variety of environments. Later, if you discover another error the control might encounter, you can add handling for that error to the class, and all objects based on your class will automatically inherit the new error handling.

For example, the vcr class in the Buttons.vcx class library, located in the Visual Studio …\Samples\Vfp98\Classes directory, is based on the Visual FoxPro container class.

Four command buttons in the container manage table navigation, moving the record pointer in a table with the following commands:

```
GO TOP
SKIP - 1
SKIP 1
GO BOTTOM.
```

An error could occur when a user chooses one of the buttons and no table is open. Visual FoxPro attempts to write buffered values to a table when the record pointer moves. So an error could also occur if optimistic row buffering is enabled and another user has changed a value in the buffered record.

These errors could occur when the user chooses any one of the buttons; therefore, it doesn't make sense to have four separate error handling methods. The following code associated with the Error event of each of the command buttons passes the error information to the single error-handling routine of the class:

```
LPARAMETERS nError, cMethod, nLine
THIS.Parent.Error(nError, cMethod, nLine)
```

The following code is associated with the Error event of the vcr class. The actual code differs because of coding requirements for localization.

```
Parameters nError, cMethod, nLine
DO CASE
CASE nError = 13 && Alias not found
   cNewTable = GETFILE('DBF')
   IF FILE(cNewTable)
      SELECT 0
      USE (cNewTable)
      This.SkipTable = ALIAS()
   ELSE
      This.SkipTable = ""
   ENDIF
CASE nError = 1585 && Data Conflict
* Update conflict handled by a datachecker class
   nConflictStatus = ;
      THIS.DataChecker1.CheckConflicts()
   IF nConflictStatus = 2
      MESSAGEBOX "Can't resolve a data conflict."
   ENDIF
OTHERWISE
* Display information about other errors.

cMsg="Error:" + ALLTRIM(STR(nError)) + CHR(13) ;
   MESSAGE()+CHR(13)+"Program:"+PROGRAM()

nAnswer = MESSAGEBOX(cMsg, 2+48+512, "Error")
DO CASE
      CASE nAnswer = 3    &&Abort
         CANCEL
      CASE nAnswer = 4    &&Retry
         RETRY
      OTHERWISE           && Ignore
         RETURN
   ENDCASE
ENDCASE
```

You want to make sure that you supply information for an error that you haven't handled. Otherwise, the error event code will execute but won't take any actions, and the default Visual FoxPro error message will no longer be displayed. You, as well as the user, won't know what happened.

Depending on your target users, you might want to supply more information in the case of an unhandled error, such as the name and phone number of someone to call for help.

Returning from Error Handling Code

After the error handling code executes, the line of code following the one that caused the error is executed. If you want to re-execute the line of code that caused the error after you've changed the situation that caused the error, use the RETRY command.

> **Note**   The Error event can be called when the error encountered wasn't associated with a line of your code. For example, if you call a data environment's CloseTables method in code when AutoCloseTables is set to true (.T.) and then release the form, an internal error is generated when Visual FoxPro tries to close the tables again. You can trap for this error, but there is no line of code to RETRY.

CHAPTER 15

Optimizing Applications

When you use Visual FoxPro to design and run applications, you want to get the best performance from your operating system, from Visual FoxPro, and from your application.

For information about how to optimize your computer and operating system, see Chapter 4, "Optimizing Your System," in the *Installation Guide*.

This chapter describes:

- Optimizing Tables and Indexes
- Using Rushmore to Speed Data Access
- Optimizing Forms and Controls
- Optimizing Programs
- Optimizing ActiveX Controls
- Optimizing Applications in Multiuser Environments
- Optimizing Access to Remote Data
- Optimizing International Applications

Optimizing Tables and Indexes

You can speed access to data in tables by using indexes and by using buffering efficiently. In addition, you can use Rushmore technology to optimize your queries.

Using Indexes

To speed access to data in a table, use indexes. Adding an index to a table speeds searches, especially if you're able to use Rushmore technology to optimize your search. Indexing also allows you to work with data in a particular order, such as viewing a customer table in order by last name.

If the records in a table have unique keys, create a primary or candidate index on the field. These types of indexes allow Visual FoxPro to validate the key at a low level, resulting in best performance.

In addition to indexing fields used for searching and sorting, you should also index any fields involved in a join. If you join two tables on fields that are not indexed, the join operation can take as much as hundreds of times longer.

An important feature of Visual FoxPro is that you can create an index on any expression. (In some database products, you can index only on fields.) This capability allows you to use indexes to optimize searching, sorting, or joining on combinations of fields, or on expressions derived from fields. For example, you can index a name field based on an expression that uses the SOUNDEX( ) function. That way, your application can provide extremely quick access to names that sound alike.

When adding indexes to your tables, you must balance the benefit you get in retrieval times against a performance loss when updating the table. As you add more indexes to your table, updates and inserts to the table are slower because Visual FoxPro needs to update each index.

Finally, avoid using indexes on fields that contain only a few discrete values, such as a logical field. In these cases, the index contains only a small number of entries, and the overhead of maintaining the index probably outweighs the benefit it provides when searching.

For details about how to index effectively when using Rushmore technology, see "Using Rushmore to Speed Data Access" later in this chapter.

Optimizing Joins

When you create joins using SELECT – SQL, the following situations can degrade performance and produce unexpected results:

- Joining tables on data that is not a primary or unique key in one of the tables.

- Joining tables containing empty fields.

To avoid these situations, create joins based on the relationship between primary keys in one table and foreign keys in the other. If you create a join based on data that is not unique, the end result can be the product of two tables. For example, the following SELECT – SQL statement creates a join which can produce a very large result:

```
SELECT *;
   FROM  tastrade!customer INNER JOIN tastrade!orders ;
   ON  Customer.postal_code = Orders.postal_code
```

In the example, postal code uniquely identifies a location within a city, but has little value if your intent is to match customer rows and their order rows. The postal code doesn't necessarily uniquely identify a customer or an order. Instead, create a join using a statement such as the following:

```
SELECT *;
   FROM  tastrade!customer INNER JOIN tastrade!orders ;
   ON  Customer.customer_id = Orders.customer_id
```

In this example, the field `customer_id` uniquely identifies a specific customer and the orders belonging to that customer, and therefore creates a result set that combines the customer row with each order row.

In addition, use caution when joining tables with empty fields because Visual FoxPro will match empty fields. However, Visual FoxPro doesn't match fields containing null. When creating a join, qualify the field expressions in the join condition by testing for an empty string.

For example, if you think that the customer id field in the Orders table might be empty, use a statement such as the following to filter out order records with no customer number:

```
SELECT *;
   FROM  tastrade!customer INNER JOIN tastrade!orders ;
   ON  Customer.customer_id = Orders.customer_id;
   WHERE tastrade!orders <> ""
```

Tip You can also test for an empty string using the EMPTY( ) function, but including a function call within the filter expression is not as fast as comparing to a constant value.

Using the Project Manager

When you use the Project Manager, you can combine an unlimited number of programs and procedures into a single .app or .exe file. This can greatly increase program execution speed for a couple of reasons.

First, Visual FoxPro opens a program file and leaves it open. Later, When you issue a DO command on a program contained in the file, Visual FoxPro doesn't need to open an additional file.

Second, an application of only one or two files reduces the number of files necessary in the working directory. The speed of all file operations increases as the operating system has fewer directory entries to examine when opening, renaming, or deleting files.

For information on using the Project Manager to create applications, see Chapter 13, "Compiling an Application."

General Table and Index Optimization Hints

To create the fastest possible tables and indexes, follow the recommendations listed below.

- If record or table buffering is not enabled, use INSERT – SQL instead of APPEND BLANK followed by REPLACE, particularly with an indexed table in a multiuser environment, because indexes only need to be updated once.

- If you need to append a large number of records to an indexed table, it might be faster to remove the index, append the records, and then re-create the index.

- In SQL statements, avoid function calls if possible, especially in statements that will return more than one record, because the statement must be reevaluated (and the functions called again) for each record. If you are creating a SQL statement with variable data, use name expressions or macro substitution in favor of the EVALUATE( ) function. A better strategy yet is to construct the entire statement dynamically, not just individual clauses. For more information, see "Using Macros" and "Creating Name Expressions" in Help.

- If you usually use a certain index order, you can improve performance by periodically sorting the table in this order.

- Use .cdx instead of .idx files in multiuser environments because you can update one .cdx file faster than you can update multiple .idx files.

Using Rushmore to Speed Data Access

To help you optimize the performance of your applications, Visual FoxPro includes Rushmore data access technology. Using Rushmore, you can run certain complex table operations hundreds or even thousands of times faster than without it.

Understanding Rushmore Technology

Rushmore technology is a data access technique that uses standard Visual FoxPro indexes to optimize access to data. You can use Rushmore with any Visual FoxPro index, including FoxPro 1.*x* (.idx) indexes, compact (.idx) indexes, and compound (.cdx) indexes.

Both .cdx and compact .idx indexes use a compression technique that produces indexes as small as one-sixth the size of uncompressed old-format indexes. Visual FoxPro can process a compressed index faster because it requires less disk access, and because more of the index can be buffered in memory. Although Rushmore, like other file access techniques, benefits from the smaller size of compact indexes, it also functions very well with indexes in older formats.

When Visual FoxPro processes very large tables on computers with only the minimum amount of RAM, Rushmore might not find sufficient memory to operate. In that case, Visual FoxPro might display a warning message ("Not enough memory for optimization"). Although your program will function correctly and without losing any data, the query will not benefit from Rushmore optimization.

In its simplest form, Rushmore speeds the performance of single-table commands using FOR clauses that specify sets of records in terms of existing indexes. Also, Rushmore can speed the operation of certain commands such as LOCATE and INDEX. For a complete list of optimizable commands, see the next section, "Using Rushmore with Tables."

Visual FoxPro SQL commands use Rushmore as a basic tool in multi-table query optimization, using existing indexes and even creating new ad-hoc indexes to speed queries.

Using Rushmore with Tables

Use Rushmore to optimize data access according to the number of tables involved. When you access single tables, you can take advantage of Rushmore anywhere that a FOR clause appears. When you access multiple tables, SELECT – SQL queries supersede all Rushmore optimizations. In an SQL command, Visual FoxPro decides what is needed to optimize a query and does the work for you. You don't need to open tables or indexes. If SQL decides it needs indexes, it creates temporary indexes for its own use.

To use Rushmore

Choose one of the following options:

- To access data from a single table, use a FOR clause in a command such as AVERAGE, BROWSE, or LOCATE, or use SQL commands to update tables. For a complete list of commands that use the FOR clause, refer to the table below.

  – or –

  To access data from more than one table, use the SELECT – SQL, DELETE – SQL, and UPDATE – SQL commands.

The following table lists commands that use FOR clauses. Rushmore is designed so that its speed is proportional to the number of records retrieved.

Potentially Optimizable Commands with FOR Clauses

AVERAGE	BLANK
BROWSE	CALCULATE
CHANGE	COPY TO
COPY TO ARRAY	COUNT
DELETE	DISPLAY
EDIT	EXPORT TO
INDEX	JOIN WITH
LABEL	LIST
LOCATE	RECALL
REPLACE	REPLACE FROM ARRAY
REPORT	SCAN
SET DELETED	SET FILTER
SORT TO	SUM
TOTAL TO	

If you use a scope clause in addition to an optimizable FOR clause expression, the scope must be set to ALL or REST to take advantage of Rushmore. The NEXT or RECORD scope clauses disable Rushmore. Since the default scope is ALL for most commands, Rushmore works when you omit the scope clause.

Rushmore can use any open indexes except for filtered and UNIQUE indexes.

Note   For optimal performance, don't set the order of the table.

Creating an index or tags automatically sets the order. If you want to take maximum advantage of Rushmore with a large data set that must be in a specific order, issue SET ORDER TO to turn off index control, then use the SORT command.

Indexing Effectively for Rushmore

Rushmore cannot take advantage of all indexes. If you use a FOR clause in the INDEX command, Rushmore cannot use the index for optimization. For example, because it contains a FOR clause, the following statement cannot be optimized:

```
INDEX ON ORDNUM FOR DISCOUNT > 10 TAG ORDDISC
```

Similarly, Rushmore cannot use an index created with a NOT *condition*. For example, the following expression can be optimized:

```
INDEX ON DELETED() TAG DEL
```

But this one cannot:

```
INDEX ON NOT DELETED() TAG NOTDEL
```

In the special case that you want to exclude delete records from a query, using an index like the first example above will speed up operations when you've set SET DELETED to ON.

Operating Without Rushmore

Data retrieval operations proceed without Rushmore optimization in the following situations:

- When Rushmore cannot optimize the FOR clause expressions in a potentially optimizable command. For more information on creating an optimizable FOR expression, see the section "Combining Basic Optimizable Expressions" later in this chapter.

- When a command that might benefit from Rushmore contains a WHILE clause.

- When memory is low. Data retrieval continues, but is not optimized.

Disabling Rushmore

Though you rarely want to, you can disable Rushmore. When you issue a command that uses Rushmore, Visual FoxPro immediately determines which records match the FOR clause expression. These records are then manipulated by the command.

If a potentially optimizable command modifies the index key in the FOR clause, the record set on which Rushmore is operating can become outdated. In this case, you can disable Rushmore to ensure that you have the most current information from the table.

To disable Rushmore for an individual command

- Use the NOOPTIMIZE clause.

  For example, this LOCATE command is not optimized:

  ```
  LOCATE FOR DueDate < {^1998-01-01} NOOPTIMIZE
  ```

You can globally disable or enable Rushmore for all commands that benefit from Rushmore, with the SET OPTIMIZE command.

To disable Rushmore globally

- Use the following code:

  ```
  SET OPTIMIZE OFF
  ```

To enable Rushmore globally

- Use the following code:

  ```
  SET OPTIMIZE ON
  ```

The default setting of Rushmore optimization is ON.

For more information, search for SET OPTIMIZE in Help.

Optimizing Rushmore Expressions

Rushmore technology depends on the presence of a *basic optimizable expression* in a FOR clause or in an SQL WHERE clause. A basic optimizable expression can form an entire expression or can appear as part of an expression. You can also combine basic expressions to form a complex optimizable expression.

Creating Basic Optimizable Expressions

A basic optimizable expression takes one of the two following forms:

eIndex relOp eExp

– or –

eExpr relOp eIndex

A basic optimizable expression has the following characteristics:

- *eIndex* exactly matches the expression on which an index is constructed.

- *eExpr* is any expression and can include variables and fields from other unrelated tables.

- *relOp* is one of the following relational operators: <, >, =, <=, >=, <>, #, ==, or !=. You can also use the ISNULL( ), BETWEEN( ), or INLIST( ) functions (or their SQL equivalents such as IS NULL, and so on).

You can use BETWEEN( ) or INLIST( ) in the following two forms:

eIndex BETWEEN(*eIndex, eExpr, eExpr*)

– or –

eExpr INLIST(*eIndex, eExpr*)

> **Note**   ISBLANK( ) and EMPTY( ) are not optimizable by Rushmore.

If you create the indexes `firstname`, `custno`, `UPPER(lastname)`, and `hiredate`, each of the following expressions is optimizable:

```
firstname = "Fred"
custno >= 1000
UPPER(lastname) = "SMITH"
hiredate < {^1997-12-30}
```

An optimizable expression can contain variables and functions that evaluate to a specific value. For example, using the index `addr`, if you issue the command `STORE "WASHINGTON AVENUE" TO cVar`, then the following statements are also basic optimizable expressions:

```
ADDR = cVar
ADDR = SUBSTR(cVar,8,3)
```

Understanding When Queries Are Optimized

It is important to understand when queries will be optimized and when they will not. Visual FoxPro optimizes search conditions by looking for an exact match between the left side of a filter expression and an index key expression. Therefore, Rushmore can optimize an expression only if you search against the exact expression used in an index.

For example, imagine that you've just created a table and are adding the first index using a command such as the following:

```
USE CUSTOMERS
INDEX ON UPPER(cu_name) TAG name
```

The following command is not optimizable, because the search condition is based on the field `cu_name` only, not on an expression that is indexed:

```
SELECT * FROM customers WHERE cu_name ="ACME"
```

Instead, you should create an optimizable expression using a command such as the following, in which the expression for which you are searching exactly matches an indexed expression:

```
SELECT * FROM customers WHERE UPPER(cu_name) = "ACME"
```

Tip   To determine the level of Rushmore optimization being used, call SYS(3054).

Combining Basic Optimizable Expressions

You can combine simple or complex expressions based on the FOR clause or WHERE clause to increase data retrieval speed, if the FOR expressions have the characteristics of basic optimizable expressions.

Basic expressions might be optimizable. You can combine basic expressions using the AND, OR, and NOT logical operators to form a complex FOR clause expression that might also be optimizable. An expression created with a combination of optimizable basic expressions is fully optimizable. If one or more of the basic expressions are not optimizable, the complex expression might be partially optimizable or not optimizable at all.

A set of rules determines if an expression composed of basic optimizable or non-optimizable expressions is fully optimizable, partially optimizable, or not optimizable. The following table summarizes Rushmore query optimization rules.

Combining Basic Expressions

Basic Expression	Operator	Basic Expression	Query Result
Optimizable	AND	Optimizable	Fully Optimizable
Optimizable	OR	Optimizable	Fully Optimizable
Optimizable	AND	Not Optimizable	Partially Optimizable
Optimizable	OR	Not Optimizable	Not Optimizable
Not Optimizable	AND	Not Optimizable	Not Optimizable
Not Optimizable	OR	Not Optimizable	Not Optimizable
–	NOT	Optimizable	Fully Optimizable
–	NOT	Not Optimizable	Not Optimizable

You can use the AND operator to combine two optimizable expressions into one fully optimizable expression:

```
FIRSTNAME = "FRED" AND HIREDATE < {^1997-12-30}      && Optimizable
```

In this example, the OR operator combines a basic optimizable expression with an expression that is not optimizable to create an expression that is not optimizable:

```
FIRSTNAME = "FRED" OR "S" $ LASTNAME      && Not optimizable
```

Using the NOT operator on an optimizable expression creates a fully optimizable expression:

```
NOT FIRSTNAME = "FRED"      && Fully optimizable
```

You can also use parentheses to group combinations of basic expressions.

Combining Complex Expressions

Just as you can combine basic expressions, you can combine complex expressions to create a more complex expression that is fully optimizable, partially optimizable, or not optimizable. You can then combine these more complex expressions to create expressions that again might be fully or partially optimizable, or not optimizable at all. The following table describes the results of combining these complex expressions. These rules also apply to expressions grouped with parentheses.

Combining Complex Expressions

Expression	Operator	Expression	Result
Fully Optimizable	AND	Fully Optimizable	Fully Optimizable
Fully Optimizable	OR	Fully Optimizable	Fully Optimizable
Fully Optimizable	AND	Partially Optimizable	Partially Optimizable
Fully Optimizable	OR	Partially Optimizable	Partially Optimizable
Fully Optimizable	AND	Not Optimizable	Partially Optimizable
Fully Optimizable	OR	Not Optimizable	Not Optimizable
–	NOT	Fully Optimizable	Fully Optimizable
Partially Optimizable	AND	Partially Optimizable	Partially Optimizable
Partially Optimizable	OR	Partially Optimizable	Partially Optimizable
Partially Optimizable	AND	Not Optimizable	Partially Optimizable
Partially Optimizable	OR	Not Optimizable	Not Optimizable
–	NOT	Partially Optimizable	Not Optimizable
Not Optimizable	AND	Not Optimizable	Not Optimizable
Not Optimizable	OR	Not Optimizable	Not Optimizable
–	NOT	Not Optimizable	Not Optimizable

You can combine fully optimizable expressions with the OR operator to create one expression that is also fully optimizable:

```
* Fully-optimizable expression
(FIRSTNAME = "FRED" AND HIREDATE < {^1997-12-30}) ;
   OR (LASTNAME = "" AND HIREDATE > {^1996-12-30})
```

To create partially optimizable expressions, combine a fully optimizable expression with an expression that is not optimizable. In the following example, the AND operator is used to combine the expressions:

```
* Partially-optimizable expression
(FIRSTNAME = "FRED" AND HIREDATE < {^1997-12-30}) ;
   AND "S" $ LASTNAME
```

Partially optimizable expressions can be combined to create one expression that is also partially optimizable:

```
* Partially-optimizable expression
(FIRSTNAME = "FRED" AND "S" $ LASTNAME) ;
   OR (FIRSTNAME = "DAVE" AND "T" $ LASTNAME)
```

Combining expressions that are not optimizable creates an expression that is also not optimizable:

```
* Expression that is not optimizable
("FRED" $ FIRSTNAME OR "S" $ LASTNAME) ;
   OR ("MAIN" $ STREET OR "AVE" $ STREET)
```

Optimizing Forms and Controls

You can also make significant improvements in the forms and controls in your application.

Tip   For information about setting and getting properties efficiently, see "Referencing Object Properties Efficiently" later in this chapter.

Using the Data Environment

If you use the data environment of the Form Designer or Report Designer, table open performance is much faster than executing USE, SET ORDER, and SET RELATION commands in the form Load event. When you use the data environment, Visual FoxPro uses low-level engine calls to open the tables and set up the indexes and relations.

Limiting the Number of Forms in a Form Set

Use form sets only when it is necessary to have a group of forms share a private data session. When you use a form set, Visual FoxPro creates instances of all forms and all controls on all forms in the form set, even though the first form in the form set is the only one being displayed. This can be time consuming, and is unnecessary if the forms don't have to share a private data session. Instead, you should execute DO FORM for other forms when they're needed.

However, if you do use a form set, you will gain some performance back when you access the forms in the form set, because the forms will already be loaded but not visible.

Dynamically Loading Page Controls on a Page Frame

Page frames, like form sets, load all the controls for each page when the page frame is loaded, which can cause a noticeable delay when the page frame is loaded. Instead, you can dynamically load page controls, as needed, by creating a class out of the controls on each page, then loading them as the page is activated.

To dynamically load page controls

1. Design your form as you normally would, including all controls on all pages.

2. When your design is complete, go to the second page of your page frame, and save the controls you find there as a class.

3. Open the class you created, and ensure the controls are still properly laid out.

4. Repeat Steps 2 and 3 for the third and subsequent pages of the page frame.

5. In the Activate event of the second and subsequent pages of the page frame, add objects and make them visible.

   For example, if your controls class is named cnrpage1, you would add the following code:

```
IF THIS.ControlCount = 0
   THIS.AddObject("cnrpage1","cnrpage1")
   THIS.cnrpage1.Visible = .T.
ENDIF
```

Dynamically Binding Controls to Data

You can speed the load time for a form that contains many data-bound controls if you delay the binding of those controls until they're needed.

To dynamically bind controls to data

1. Put the tables and views for your form in the data environment so that they're opened when the form is loaded.

2. For each bound control, add code to its GotFocus event code that binds the control to the data value. For example, the following code binds a ComboBox control to the `customer.company` field:

```
* Check to see if the control has been bound yet.
IF THIS.RecordSource = ""
   * Set the record source to the right value
   * and set the record source type to "fields"
   THIS.RecordSource = "customer.company"
   THIS.RecordSourceType = 6
   THIS.Refresh
ENDIF
```

Delaying Screen Refresh

If you must make several changes to the screen — for example, change the values of several controls at once — you can reduce the overall time required to update the screen by delaying screen refresh until all changes are done. For example, if you make controls visible or invisible, change control colors, or move records in bound controls, it is much more efficient to delay the painting of those controls until after the changes have all been completed:

To delay screen refresh

1. Set the form's LockScreen property to true.

2. Update the controls as required.

3. Call the form's Refresh method.

4. Set the form's LockScreen property to false.

For example, the following example changes the display properties of several properties at once, moves to a new record, and only then refreshes the screen with new information. If LockScreen were not set to true, each of these operations would repaint the affected controls individually and the overall update performance would seem sluggish.

```
THISFORM.LockScreen = .T.
THISFORM.MyButton.Caption = "Save"
THISFORM.MyGrid.BackColor = RGB (255, 0, 0) && Red
SKIP IN customers
SKIP IN orders
THISFORM.Refresh
THISFORM.LockScreen = .F.
```

Tip   This technique doesn't provide any benefit if you're updating only a single control.

Reducing Code in Frequently-Used Methods

Because the Refresh method and Paint event are called frequently, you can improve performance in forms by reducing the amount of code in these methods. Similarly, to speed the load time for a form, you could move code from the Init event to a less frequently used event such as Activate, Click, and GotFocus. Then, you use a property on the control (such as Tag or a custom property) to keep track of whether the control has already run code that only needs to be run once.

Optimizing Programs

By writing your code carefully, you can write the fastest possible programs. There are several ways to improve program performance in Visual FoxPro:

- Following the general programming performance hints provided below.

- Using name expressions instead of macro substitution.

- Referencing object properties efficiently.

General Programming Performance Hints

To write the fastest programs possible, follow the recommendations listed below.

- Choose the correct data type for your data. In particular, use the Integer data type for numeric information whenever possible, as it is processed most efficiently. Wherever possible, use Integer data types for primary and foreign key values, which will result in smaller data files, smaller (and therefore faster) indexes, and faster joins.

    Note   For an example showing how to create a smaller (and therefore faster) index, run Solution.app, located in the Visual Studio ...\Samples\Vfp98\Solution directory. Choose **View Samples by Filtered List**, select **Indexes** from the drop-down list, and then choose **Create Small Indexes Using BINTOC( )** from the list that appears.

- Avoid reopening files, which slows performance. Instead, assign files to work areas as you open them, then use the SELECT command to choose a specific work area as needed.

- Use FOR ... ENDFOR loops rather than DO WHILE ... ENDDO loops when possible, because they're faster.

- When you copy data from multiple fields, SCATTER TO ARRAY is faster than SCATTER MEMVAR.

- To use memory most efficiently, avoid creating objects before you need them, and clear objects when you finish with them to free memory.

    Tip   You can test how much memory each object consumes by calling the SYS(1016) function.

- Send output to the topmost window whenever possible; updating windows behind the top window is substantially slower. Causing output to scroll behind a window is nearly a worst-case event.

- Disable status display with the SET TALK OFF command, which eliminates the overhead of screen update.

- Set the SET DOHISTORY command to OFF to avoid updating the command window each time a program runs.

Using Name Expressions Instead of Macro Substitution

If you use name expressions instead of macro substitution, program performance will greatly improve. For example, if you assign a value to the variable cFile, a name expression created with cFile is faster than macro substitution.

```
cFile = "CUST"
use &cFile        && Macro substitution, slow
use (cFile)       && Name expression: faster, preferred
```

Referencing Object Properties Efficiently

By understanding how Visual FoxPro works with properties and objects, you can make your applications run more efficiently.

Optimizing Repeated References to a Property

When you reference an object property with the *object.property* syntax, Visual FoxPro must search for the object before it can access the property. If you must access the property repeatedly, this search strategy can slow performance.

To avoid referencing the same procedure repeatedly (such as in a loop), read the property value into a variable, make changes, and then set the property once when you're through. For example, the following code fills a property array by first creating an array in memory, filling it, and then setting the property only once at the end:

```
* Copy string to a local variable
lcChar = THISFORM.cCharString
LOCAL laCharArray[256]   && Create local array
FOR nCounter = 1 to 256
   laCharArray[x] = SUBSTR(laChar,x,1)
ENDFOR
* Copy the local array to the property array
ACOPY(laCharArray,THISFORM.aCharArray)
```

Referencing Multiple Properties Efficiently

If you update more than one property for the object, Visual FoxPro must search for the object multiple times, which can affect performance. In the following example, the code causes Visual FoxPro to search through four objects (such as THISFORM, pgfCstInfo, pgCstName, and txtName) to find the property to be set. Because the code sets two properties, the fourfold search is done twice:

```
THISFORM.pgfCstInfo.pgCstName.txtName.Value = ;
 "Fred Smith"
THISFORM.pgfCstInfo.pgCstName.txtName.BackColor = ;
 RGB (0,0,0)   & Dark red
```

To avoid this overhead, use the WITH … ENDWITH command. This method causes Visual FoxPro to find the object once. For example, the following example accomplishes the same task as the previous one, but faster:

```
WITH THISFORM.pgfCstInfo.pgCstName.txtName
    .Value = "Fred Smith"
    .BackColor = RGB (0,0,0)   & Dark red
ENDWITH
```

You can also store an object reference in a variable, then include the variable in place of the object reference:

```
oControl = THISFORM.pgfCstInfo.pgCstName.txtName
oControl.Value = "Fred Smith"
oControl.BackColor = RGB (0,0,0)   & Dark red
```

Optimizing ActiveX Controls

If you use Automation or ActiveX controls in your application, you can fine-tune the application to get the best performance out of both ActiveX controls and Automation.

Using ActiveX Controls Efficiently

For best performance when using ActiveX controls in your forms, use the following suggestions:

- Start Automation servers in advance. Controls bound to general fields will generally perform better when the servers for those data types (like Microsoft Excel or Word) are already running on the client's machine.

- Insert objects "As Icon." When you insert an ActiveX control into a field, insert it as an icon or placeholder rather than as an entire object. This reduces the amount of storage space required because Visual FoxPro stores a presentation image with the object, which can consume a lot of storage space. Inserting an object as an icon also increases performance for drawing the object.

- Use image controls. If you want to display a bitmap (such as a company logo), image controls are much faster than OLE bound controls.

- Use manual links whenever possible. Manual links to objects are faster because they avoid the notification time required for automatic links, and because the server doesn't need to be started to draw the object. If you don't need to update an object frequently, use manual links.

Optimizing Automation Performance

If your application interacts with other applications, you can get the best performance using the following techniques.

Avoiding Multiple Instances of the Server

In some cases, Automation servers (such as Microsoft Excel) will always start a new instance, even if one is already running. To remedy this and improve performance, use the GetObject( ) function instead of CreateObject( ). For example, the following call will always use an existing instance, if it exists:

```
x = GetObject(,"excel.Application")
```

In contrast, the following call creates a new instance:

```
x = CreateObject("excel.Application")
```

If you call GetObject( ) but the server isn't already running, you will get error 1426. In that case, you can trap for the error and call CreateObject( ):

```
ON ERROR DO oleErr WITH ERROR()
x = GetObject(,"excel.application")
ON ERROR  && restore system error handler

PROCEDURE oleErr
PARAMETER mError
IF mError = 1426 then
x = CreateObject("excel.application")
ENDIF
```

Referencing Objects Efficiently

Executing expressions that use objects within the Automation server can be expensive, particularly when evaluated multiple times. It is much faster to store objects' references to variables for reference. For details, see "Optimizing Repeated References to a Property" earlier in this chapter.

Optimizing Applications in Multiuser Environments

If you're writing applications for a multiuser environment, performance is particularly important, because inefficiencies are multiplied. In addition, if multiple users are accessing data, your application must handle issues of concurrency and network access.

To handle these issues, you can:

- Adjust lock retry interval.
- Use transaction processing efficiently.

You might also benefit from the suggestions for working with data stored on remote servers. For details, see "Optimizing Access to Remote Data" later in this chapter.

Adjusting Lock Retry Interval

If your application attempts to lock a record or table and is unsuccessful, you can have Visual FoxPro automatically retry the lock after a small interval. However, each lock attempt results in more network traffic. If network traffic is already heavy, sending repeated lock requests adds a burden to the network, and results in overall slowdown for all users.

To address this situation, you can adjust the interval between lock attempts. By using a larger interval (which results in fewer retries per second), you reduce network traffic and gain performance.

To adjust the lock retry interval

- Call the SYS(3051) function, passing it the number of milliseconds to wait between each lock attempt.

Using Transaction Processing Efficiently

When using transaction processing, you must design transactions to minimize the impact that they have on other users. While a transaction is open, any locks set during the transaction remain locked until the transaction is committed or rolled back. Even if you issue an explicit UNLOCK command, locks are held until the END TRANSACTION or ROLLBACK command.

Furthermore, appending records to a table requires Visual FoxPro to lock the table header. The header remains locked for the duration of the transaction, preventing other users from also appending records.

To minimize the impact of transactions, design them so that they begin and end as close to the actual data update as possible; the ideal transaction contains only data update statements.

If you are adding transaction processing to data updates made in a form, don't open a transaction, run the form, and then commit the transaction when the form is closed. Instead, put the transaction processing statements in the event code for the Save button (for example):

```
* Save method from the cmdSave command button
BEGIN TRANSACTION
UPDATE PRODUCTS SET reorder_amt = 0 WHERE discontinued = .T.
END TRANSACTION
```

Optimizing Access to Remote Data

Data retrieval from any remote database is expensive. In order to get data from a server database, the following steps must occur:

1. The client issues the query to the remote database.

2. The server parses and compiles the query.

3. The server generates a result set.

4. The server notifies the client that the result is complete.

5. The client fetches the data over the network from the server. This step can happen all at once, or the client can request that results be sent in pieces as requested.

You can use a number of techniques to speed up the retrieval (or update) of data. The following section discusses these strategies:

- Retrieving only the data you need

- Updating remote tables efficiently

- Sending statements in a batch

- Setting packet size

- Delaying retrieval of memo and binary data

- Storing lookup data locally

- Creating local rules

Retrieving Only the Data You Need

In most applications that use remote data, forms and reports don't need to access all the data from a table at once. Therefore, you can speed performance by creating remote views that fetch or update only the fields and records you want, which minimizes the amount of data that needs to be transmitted across the network.

To create queries that minimize the overhead of data retrieval from remote sources, follow these suggestions:

- Specify only the fields you need. Don't use the statement `SELECT * FROM customers` unless you need all the fields from the table.

- Include a WHERE clause to limit the number of records downloaded. The more specific your WHERE clause, the fewer records are transmitted to your computer, and the faster the query will finish.

- If you cannot predict at design time what values to use in a WHERE clause, you can use parameters in the clause. When the query is executed, Visual FoxPro uses the value of a parameter variable or prompts the user for the search value. For example, this query allows the application or user to fill in the region at run time:

```
SELECT cust_id, company, contact, address ;
   FROM customers ;
   WHERE region = ?pcRegion
```

- Set the NoDataOnLoad property of the corresponding Data Environment Cursor object. This technique is commonly used with parameterized views in which the data for the parameter comes from the value of a control on a form.

Updating Remote Tables Efficiently

When you use a view to update a table on a remote data source, Visual FoxPro must check whether the record or records you are updating have been changed. To do so, Visual FoxPro must examine the data on the server and compare it to the data being held on your computer. In some instances, this can be a time-consuming operation.

To optimize the process of updating data on remote data sources, you can specify how Visual FoxPro should check for changed records. To do this, you indicate the WHERE clause that Visual FoxPro should generate in order to perform the update.

For example, imagine that you are using a view based on a customer table on a remote data source. You created the view using a SELECT – SQL statement such as this one:

```
SELECT cust_id, company, address, contact ;
   FROM customers ;
   WHERE region = ?vpRegion
```

You want to be able to update all four fields that you have specified in the view except the key field (`cust_id`). The following table illustrates the WHERE clause that Visual FoxPro will generate for each of the options available under the SQL WHERE clause.

Note   The OLDVAL( ) function returns the pre-update version of fields you modified, and the CURVAL( ) function returns the current value stored on the remote data source. By comparing them, Visual FoxPro can determine whether the record has changed on the remote data source since you downloaded it to your computer.

Setting	Resulting WHERE clause
Key fields only	`WHERE OLDVAL(cust_id) = CURVAL(cust_id)`

Key and updatable fields (default)	`WHERE OLDVAL(cust_id) = CURVAL(cust_id) AND`
	`   OLDVAL(<mod_fld1>) = CURVAL(<mod_fld2>) AND`
	`   OLDVAL(<mod_fld2>) = CURVAL(<mod_fld2>) AND`
	`   ...`

Key and modified fields	`WHERE OLDVAL(cust_id) = CURVAL(cust_id) AND`
	`   OLDVAL(company) = CURVAL(company) AND`
	`   OLDVAL(contact) = CURVAL(contact) AND`
	`   OLDVAL(address) = CURVAL(address)`

Key and timestamp	`WHERE OLDVAL(cust_id) = CURVAL(cust_id) AND` `   OLDVAL(timestamp) = CURVAL(timestamp)`

In general, you should choose an option for the SQL WHERE clause in this order of preference:

1. **Key and timestamp**, if the remote database supports timestamped fields, which is the fastest way to tell if a record has changed.

2. **Key and modified fields**, because the fields you update to the server are almost always a subset of the total number of fields that you could update.

3. **Key and updatable fields**.

4. **Key fields only**. Using this settings implies that the remote server will insert an entirely new record using the changed key, and will delete the old record.

Sending Statements in a Batch

Some servers (such as Microsoft SQL Server) allow you to send a batch of SQL statements in a single packet. This speeds performance because you reduce network traffic, and because the server can compile multiple statements at once.

For example, if you specify a batch size of four, then update 10 records in a database, Visual FoxPro sends four statements such as the following to the server database in one batch:

```
UPDATE customer SET contact = "John Jones" ;
   WHERE cust_id = 1;
UPDATE customer SET contact = "Sally Park" ;
   WHERE cust_id = 2;
UPDATE customer SET company = "John Jones" ;
   WHERE cust_id = 3;
UPDATE customer SET contact = "John Jones" ;
   WHERE cust_id = 4
```

To send statements in a batch

- In the **Options** dialog box, choose the **Remote Data** tab, and then under **Records to batch update**, specify the number of records to include in a batch.

  – or –

  Call the DBSETPROP( ) or CURSORSETPROP( ) functions to set these properties:

  - Set Transaction to 2.

  - Set BatchUpdateCount to the number of statements to send in a batch.

  – or –

1. In the **View Designer**, choose **Advanced Options** from the **Query** menu to display the **Advanced Options** dialog box.

2. In the **Performance** area, next to **Number of records to batch update**, specify the number of statements to send in a batch.

   Note   You should experiment with different values for this property and the PacketSize property to optimize your updates.

Setting Packet Size

You can optimize access to remote servers by fine-tuning the size of the network packet that is sent to and retrieved from the remote database. For example, if your network supports large packet sizes (greater than 4,096 bytes), you can increase the packet size in Visual FoxPro in order to send more data each time you read or write to the network.

To set packet size

- Call the DBSETPROP( ) or CURSORSETPROP( ) functions and set the PacketSize property to a positive integer value. The default value is 4,096.

  Note   Different network providers will handle this property differently, so you should consult your network service documentation. Novell NetWare, for example, has a maximum packet size of 512 bytes so setting the PacketSize property to a value greater than this will have no additional benefit.

Delaying Retrieval of Memo and Binary Data

If you're storing Memo or binary data on a remote server, you can improve performance by delaying the download of this data until your application actually requires it.

To delay retrieval of memo and binary data

- In the **Options** dialog box, choose the **Remote Data** tab, and then under **Remote view defaults**, set **Fetch memo**.

  – or –

  Call the DBSETPROP( ) or CURSORSETPROP( ) functions to set the FetchMemo property.

Storing Lookup Data Locally

Many applications include static lookup data such as state abbreviations, postal codes, and employee titles. If your application contains this type of data, and if the table is not too large, you might be able to speed up your application by keeping copies of this information on each user's computer, because lookups do not generate network traffic.

This technique is primarily useful for data that never changes or changes very rarely. If the data does change on occasion, you must devise a strategy for downloading a new copy of the lookup table to each user's computer.

Creating Local Rules

You can gain efficiency in your application by creating local field-level and record-level rules within Visual FoxPro, rather than relying on rules defined on the server. These rules can prevent data that doesn't conform to data or business rules from getting into the database.

By defining rules in Visual FoxPro, you trap the invalid data before it's sent across the network, which is faster, and which gives you better control for handling error conditions. However, using local rules also means that you must coordinate them with rules on the remote server. For example, if there are changes to the rules on the server, you might have to change your local rules to match.

For details about creating local rules, see the section "Updating Data in a View" in Chapter 8, "Creating Views."

Optimizing International Applications

If you're developing international applications, you might need to manage the collating sequence of your data for optimal performance. This section discusses:

- Using collating sequence efficiently.
- Using SELECT – SQL with multiple collating sequences.

Using Collating Sequence Efficiently

If your data doesn't include diacritical marks, such as accents (á) or umlauts (ü), you can improve performance by using the machine collating sequence because:

- Non-machine index keys are twice as large because they contain the diacritical information.
- Non-machine collation uses many special rules for indexing characters to return proper results.

Because the machine collate sequence is faster, it's usually preferred for joins and searching, while other collate sequences are perfect for ordering records.

When you create an index, Visual FoxPro uses the current setting of SET COLLATE. Therefore, if you want to create two indexes with two collating sequences, you can use a sequence of commands such as the following:

```
SET COLLATE TO "MACHINE"
INDEX ON lastname TAG _lastname       && join/seek index
SET COLLATE TO "GENERAL"
INDEX ON lastname TAG lastname   && sort index
```

When you want to seek, select, or join on the field lastname, issue the command SET COLLATE TO "MACHINE" before performing the operation. Rushmore will then use the index created in the machine collate sequence, and the search operation will be very fast.

Using SQL SELECT with Multiple Collating Sequences

When you issue a SELECT – SQL command, Visual FoxPro uses the current collating sequence for searching and for the ORDER BY and GROUP BY clauses. If you want to search and sort using different collating sequences, you can split your SQL commands into two steps as follows:

```
* Select records using one collating sequence
SET COLLATE TO "MACHINE"
SELECT * FROM table INTO CURSOR temp1 ;
WHERE lname = "Müller"
* Order records using a different collating sequence
SET COLLATE TO "GENERAL"
SELECT * FROM temp1 INTO TABLE output ORDER BY lastname
```

PART 5

Extending Applications

To extend a basic Visual FoxPro application, you can enable it to work for multiple users, take advantage of ActiveX controls and OLE-enabled applications, and add international capabilities.

Chapter 16 Adding OLE

Use ActiveX controls and object linking and embedding in your application to link to data and leverage the strengths of other applications.

Chapter 17 Programming for Shared Access

If your application runs on a network or contains forms that access the same data, the application needs to share that data efficiently to provide maximum productivity.

Chapter 18 Developing International Applications

Learn how to move your applications into the world market by designing them for effective international use.

CHAPTER 16

Adding OLE

You can extend the power of your Visual FoxPro applications by employing the strengths of other Automation-enabled applications or ActiveX controls. In your applications' forms or General fields, you can include specific functionality or data such as text, sound, pictures, and video from other applications. You can view or manipulate this data visibly by using the application that created it. Or, you can manipulate the data invisibly and automatically by controlling the application programmatically with Automation.

Other applications can also tap into the power of Visual FoxPro through Automation. You can even create Automation servers (COM components) in Visual FoxPro that your applications or other applications can access locally and remotely.

This chapter discusses:

- Designing an OLE Application
- Adding OLE Objects to Your Applications
- Using ActiveX Controls
- Manipulating Objects with Automation
- Subclassing Objects
- Controlling Visual FoxPro from Other Applications
- Creating Automation Servers
- Using Remote Automation

Designing an OLE Application

Automation-enabled applications and COM components can act as Automation servers, clients, or both. Components that act as servers can provide objects to another application; components that act as clients can create objects.

You can easily incorporate the power and flexibility of applications, such as Microsoft Excel and Word, in your Visual FoxPro applications. Because Visual FoxPro also acts as a server, you can also provide functionality that can be integrated into solution packages based around Microsoft Office or other COM components.

Insertable OLE objects come from OLE-capable applications such as Microsoft Excel and Word. Such objects include Word documents and Excel worksheets. On forms, you can link or embed these objects using the OLE Container control, and you can store such objects in General fields of a table, displaying them in your forms with the OLE Bound control.

In a Visual FoxPro application, you can use OLE and ActiveX technology in many ways. Before you create an application, consider the ways you can use it.

Linking or Embedding OLE Objects

You can embed or link files from other Windows applications in your tables and forms. For example, you can embed or link a Word document in a General field of a table, and you can embed or link an Excel worksheet on a form.

The difference between embedding and linking lies in where the data is stored. Embedding stores the data in the table or form, whereas linking does not. For example, when you embed an Excel worksheet on a form, the form contains a copy of the worksheet. When you link, however, the form contains only a reference to the worksheet — not the worksheet itself.

Embedding and linking data

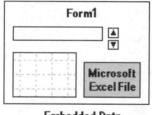

Embedded Data

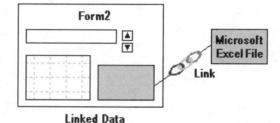

Linked Data

Both embedded and linked data start off with the original contents of the server file, as the illustration shows:

A spreadsheet embedded and linked in a form

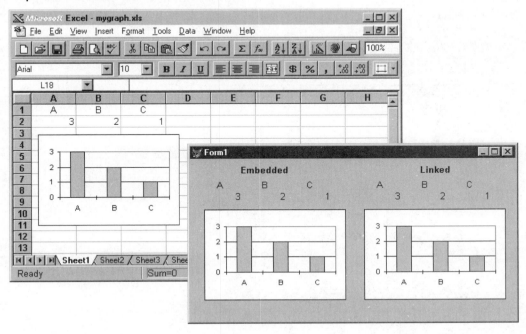

But when the original file is changed, linked data is automatically updated to reflect the change, whereas embedded data is not:

Linked data updated in a form

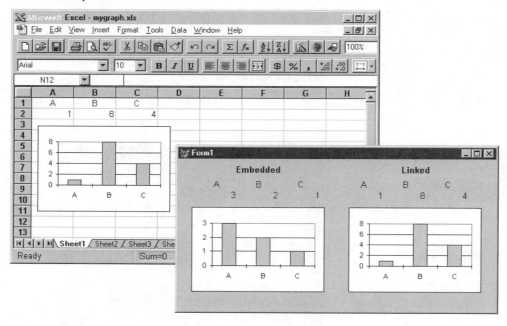

Embedded data is not necessarily static, though. Both embedded and linked data can be displayed, changed, and manipulated interactively and programmatically in Visual FoxPro.

Adding Bound or Unbound OLE Objects

On a form or in a report, you can create objects that are bound to General fields in tables. Such objects are called *bound OLE objects* and you use them to display the contents of OLE objects in General fields. You create bound OLE objects by using the OLE Bound control on the Form Controls toolbar. Alternatively, you create *unbound OLE objects* by using the OLE Container control. An unbound OLE object is not connected to a General field in a table.

Adding OLE Objects to Your Applications

You can add OLE objects to tables and forms interactively or programmatically.

Adding OLE Objects to Tables

While you're designing tables for your application, consider whether you need OLE objects in the tables. For instance, suppose you have a product table and want to include

Word documents containing nicely formatted descriptions of the products to be sent to potential customers. To include the Word documents, you must define a General field in the table. Then, you add the documents to the table by linking or embedding them in the General field.

To add an OLE object to a table

1. Use the Table Designer to create a table with General field.

2. Open the window for the General field by browsing the table and double-clicking the General field or by using the MODIFY GENERAL command.

3. From the **Edit** menu, choose **Insert Object**.

   – or –

   Use the APPEND GENERAL command.

For more information about adding OLE objects with the Table Designer, see Chapter 10, "Sharing Information with Other Applications," in the *User's Guide*.

Appending OLE Objects to Tables

You can add OLE objects to tables programmatically with the APPEND GENERAL command. With this command, you can import an OLE object from a file and place it in a General field. If the field already contains an object, the new object replaces it.

> **Note** Unlike APPEND and APPEND BLANK, APPEND GENERAL does not add a new record to the table.

You can use APPEND GENERAL to embed OLE objects or link to OLE objects created by applications such as Microsoft Excel and Word. These applications support both linking and embedding. However, some applications such as Microsoft Graph only support embedding.

Suppose you have Microsoft Word files that you want to store in a Visual FoxPro table. If the table has a General field named WordDoc, you can embed the documents by using the following code:

```
CREATE TABLE oletable (name c(24), worddoc g)
CD GETDIR()

nFiles = ADIR(aWordFiles, "*.doc")
IF nFiles > 0
   FOR i = 1 to nFiles
      APPEND BLANK
      REPLACE Oletable.Name WITH aWordFiles(i,1)
      APPEND GENERAL WordDoc FROM aWordFiles(i,1)
   ENDFOR
ELSE
   MESSAGEBOX("No Word files found.")
ENDIF
```

Note The preceding example looks only for files ending in .doc, the standard extension used by Word files. Because Microsoft Word and OLE are aware of this, the files are automatically associated with the Word server when you use APPEND GENERAL.

If you use a different extension from the one expected by the server, you must declare the class of the server, using the CLASS clause. For example, if you add the class for Word to the previous example, the code becomes:

```
APPEND GENERAL WordDoc FROM wordfiles(i,1) CLASS "Word.Document.6"
```

If you have files with common extensions (for example, .bmp) that other servers might use, you can use the CLASS clause to specify the particular server you want to use for those files. Alternatively, if you'd rather link than embed objects, use the LINK keyword.

```
APPEND GENERAL WordDoc FROM wordfiles(i,1) LINK CLASS "Word.Document.6"
```

In addition, you can replace data in an object by using the DATA keyword of APPEND GENERAL, as the following Microsoft Graph example illustrates.

Refreshing Microsoft Graph

Microsoft Graph is an embeddable application. The values in a Microsoft Graph chart are based on the values in the Microsoft Graph data sheet.

Microsoft Graph object in a general field

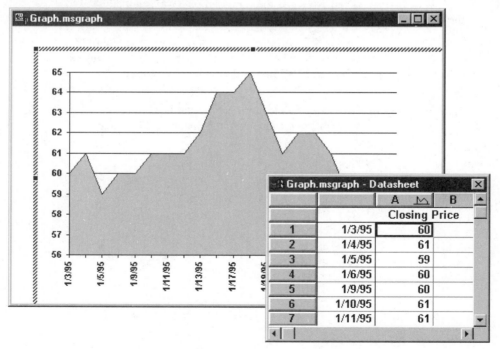

In order to programmatically change the data in a Microsoft Graph chart, you need to construct a string that contains the new data, including tabs, carriage returns, and line feeds, and pass this string to a Microsoft Graph object with the DATA clause of the APPEND GENERAL command.

The following example assumes you have a table, named stock, with, among other fields, date and close for the date and the closing price of the stock. The Microsoft Graph object is stored in the msgraph general field of a table named graph. The example refreshes a graph with stock closing prices from the previous 30 days.

Code	Comments
| ```
#DEFINE CRLF CHR(13)+CHR(10)
#DEFINE TAB CHR(9)
LOCAL lcData
``` | Define carriage return and tab characters. |
| ```
SELECT date, close;
   FROM Stock WHERE BETWEEN(date, ;
   DATE(),DATE() - 30) ;
   ORDER BY date INTO CURSOR wtemp
``` | Select the values that you want to update the graph with, in this case, the date and closing values for stocks for the last 30 days. |
| ```
SELECT wtemp
lcData = " " + ;
   TAB + "Closing Price" + CRLF
SCAN
   lcData = lcData + DTOC(date)
   lcData = lcData + TAB
   lcData = lcData + ;
   ALLTRIM(STR(close)) + CRLF
ENDSCAN
``` | Build a character string (lcData) of data from the cursor to refresh the graph.<br><br>"Closing Price," as the column header, is the text that will be displayed by default in the graph's legend. |
| ```
SELECT graph
APPEND GENERAL msgraph DATA lcData
``` | Send the new values to the graph in the DATA clause of the APPEND GENERAL command. |
| ```
USE IN wtemp
``` | Close the cursor. |

For more information on the APPEND GENERAL command, including a full description of its syntax, see Help.

Note   You can also display OLE objects from General fields in your reports. For details about displaying OLE objects in reports, see "Adding a General Field" in Chapter 7, "Designing Reports and Labels," in the *User's Guide*.
```

Adding OLE Objects to Forms

Using the Form Designer, you can add insertable OLE objects to forms with the OLE Container control. In addition, you can display OLE objects from General fields by using the OLE Bound control.

To add an OLE object to a form

1. In the Form Designer, add an OLE Container control to your form. The **Insert Object** dialog box opens.

2. In the **Insert Object** dialog box, select Create New or Create from File.

Insert Object dialog box

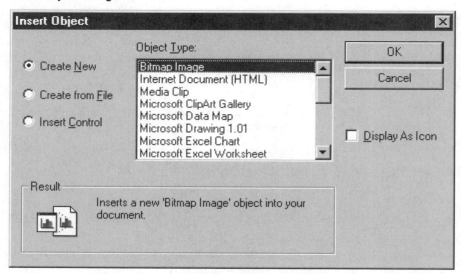

3. Choose the appropriate OLE object from the Object Type list.

You can also customize the Form Controls toolbar so that you can directly add specific OLE objects.

To add OLE objects to the Form Controls toolbar

1. From the **Tools** menu, choose **Options**.

2. In the **Controls** tab of the **Options** dialog box, choose **ActiveX controls**.

Controls tab of the Options dialog box

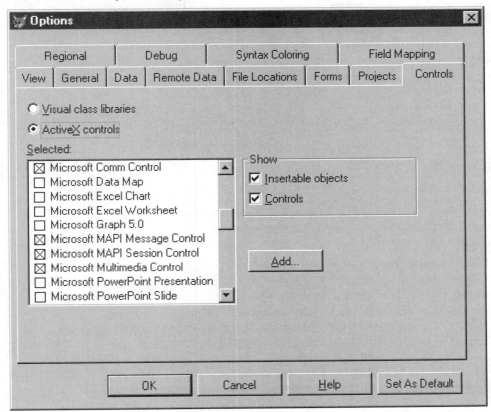

3. In the **Selected** list, select the OLE objects and ActiveX controls you want to be available from the **Form Controls** toolbar.

4. Choose **Set as Default**, and then choose **OK**.

5. In the **Form Controls** toolbar, choose **View Classes**, and then choose **ActiveX Controls**.

For more details about using the Options dialog box, see Help.

To display an OLE object from a General field

1. In the Form Designer, add an OLE Bound control to your form.

2. Specify the General field that contains the data by setting the object's ControlSource property.

    For example, if the table name is Inventory and the General field name is Current, then set the ControlSource property to Inventory.Current.

You can also display an OLE object from a General field programmatically:

Code	Comments
`frm1 = CREATEOBJECT("form")`	Create form.
`frm1.ADDOBJECT("olb1",` `"oleboundcontrol")`	Add control.
`frm1.olb1.ControlSource =` `"Inventory.Current"`	Bind the data to the control.
`frm1.olb1.Visible = .T.` `frm1.Visible = .T.`	Make the control and form visible.

Interacting with OLE Objects

If you add an OLE object to a form or General field, you can edit the data and display characteristics of the object at run time or design time.

Note   You cannot edit the data of an OLE object in an OLE Bound control at design time.

Some OLE objects support in-place editing so that you can edit the object in the window used by your application. For example, if you double-click a Microsoft Excel worksheet object in a General field, rather than starting a copy of Microsoft Excel in another window, the menu titles change to reflect the Microsoft Excel menu structure and the default Microsoft Excel toolbars are displayed. You or your application user can then edit the Microsoft Excel object without leaving your application.

Note   You can edit only embedded objects in place, not linked objects.

You can also open the Automation server in another window, edit the data or display characteristics there, and have the new values reflected in your application when you return to it.

To edit an OLE object in place in a General field window

- From the **Edit** menu, select the specific object type, and from the submenu, choose **Edit**.

  For example, if the object is a Word document, select the **Document Object** menu item; if the object is a Microsoft Graph chart, select the **Chart Object** menu item.

  – or –

  Double-click the object.

To open the application for an OLE object in a General field window

- From the **Edit** menu, select the specific object type, and from the submenu, choose **Open**.

When you add an OLE object to a form in either the OLE Container control or the OLE Bound control, you have more control over the opening and editing of the object.

You can determine whether the OLE object is opened or edited when the control gets the focus or when the user double-clicks the control by setting the AutoActivate property of an OLE bound or container control. The AutoVerbMenu property specifies whether the shortcut menu of the ActiveX control allows a user to open or edit the OLE object.

To control access so that the OLE object can only be opened or edited programmatically with the DoVerb method, set AutoActivate to 0 – Manual and AutoVerbMenu to false (.F.). For more information, see Help.

Controlling Menus

When a user is in-place editing an OLE object, the menu bar displays the menus for the OLE object, not the menus for your application. If you create a menu title and want it to be displayed even while the user edits an OLE object, select Negotiate in the Prompt Options dialog box of the Menu Designer. For more information, see Chapter 11, "Designing Menus and Toolbars," or the NEGOTIATE clause in the DEFINE PAD Help topic.

Using ActiveX Controls

ActiveX controls are objects with encapsulated functionality and exposed properties, events and methods. ActiveX controls provide a wide range of functionality that you can easily tap into. ActiveX controls that ship with Visual FoxPro include:

- Windows 95 controls, like the RichText and the TreeView controls.

- System controls, like the Communications and MAPI controls.

ActiveX controls are versatile because you can subclass them to create other controls and you can control them by using the events, methods, and properties associated with the controls. You cannot create ActiveX controls with Visual FoxPro; however, you can create them using the Microsoft OLE Custom Control Developer's Kit provided with Microsoft Visual C++ 4.0, and with the Microsoft Visual Basic Control Creation Edition version 5.0.

For more information about accessing ActiveX controls, see Chapter 27, "Extending Visual FoxPro with External Libraries." For more information on creating ActiveX controls specific to Visual FoxPro, see Chapter 28, "Accessing the Visual FoxPro API."

Adding ActiveX Controls to a Form

ActiveX controls in Visual FoxPro must be contained in an OLE Container control (the base class is OLEControl). When you add an OLE Container control to a form, you can choose the ActiveX control you want to add to the form.

To add an ActiveX control to a form

1. From the **Form Controls** toolbar, choose OLE Container Control and drag it to size in the form.

2. In the **Insert Object** dialog box, choose **Insert Control**.

Insert Object dialog box

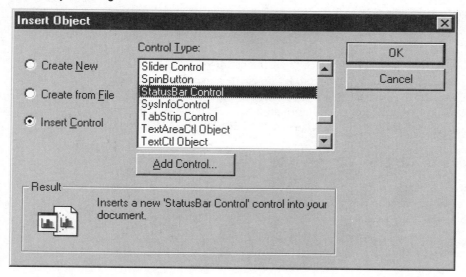

3. In the **Control Type** list, select the desired ActiveX control.

4. Choose **OK**.

Managing Bound ActiveX Controls

If an ActiveX control supports simple data binding, Visual FoxPro will expose a ControlSource property for the control. All you have to do is set the ControlSource property to a table field and the value displayed in the ActiveX control reflects that value in the underlying field. Changes to the value in the control are saved to the field.

For examples of using ActiveX controls, run Solution.app in the Visual Studio ...\Samples\Vfp98\Solution directory.

Note To ensure all ActiveX control events are processed, set the AutoYield property of the Visual FoxPro Application object to false (.F.).

For more information about OLE event processing, see the AutoYield Property and DOEVENTS Command topics in Help.

Manipulating Objects with Automation

OLE objects in your forms or programs, or ActiveX controls inside OLE Container controls, can be manipulated through code in the same way that you can program native Visual FoxPro objects.

Manipulating Extrinsic Object Properties

In code, you can manipulate an object using its properties. The way you reference a property depends on whether the object stands alone or is part of a container, such as the OLE Container control or OLE Bound control.

Note   ActiveX controls are always part of an OLE Container control.

An object in a container has two parts: the object itself and a container around the object. Both the object and the container have properties, and sometimes they have the same property names. To ensure you reference the object's properties, always append the container's Object property to the object's name. For example, the following code refers to the object's Left property.

```
frm1.olecontrol1.Object.Left = 25   && Object's Left
```

If you omit the Object property, you reference the container's Left property instead.

```
frm1.olecontrol1.Left= 25   && Container's Left property
```

For example, suppose you have an application that sends mail when the user clicks on a compose command button. If you've added a Microsoft MAPI message control to a form as olecontrol1, the code associated with the Click event of the command button might be:

```
THISFORM.olecontrol1.Object.Compose
THISFORM.olecontrol1.Object.Send(.T.)
```

In addition to using the Object property to reference properties of the contained object, you can use other properties of the container control. For example, you can reference the read-only OLEClass property to identify the type of object in the container and the Sizable property to prevent users from changing the size of an object. For details about container control properties, search for "OLE Container Control" in Help.

In the Form and Class Designers, the properties of ActiveX controls are displayed in the Visual FoxPro Properties window, but most ActiveX controls also have their own interface for setting common properties. You can see this properties interface by selecting the object-specific Properties option from the ActiveX control's shortcut menu. For example, to open the Properties dialog box for a rich text control, choose Microsoft RichText Control Properties from the shortcut menu.

Opening the RichText control properties dialog box

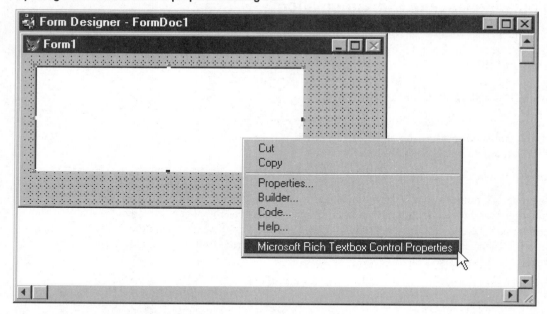

Using Extrinsic Object Methods

In addition to setting and retrieving properties of objects, you can manipulate an object using methods it supports. For example, you can use the Add method of a Microsoft Excel collection object to create a new Microsoft Excel workbook.

The following Automation example uses the Add method to create an Excel workbook, the Save method to save the workbook, and the Quit method to end Excel:

Code	Comments
`oleApp = CREATEOBJECT("Excel.Application")`	Start Excel.
`OleApp.Visible=.T.`	Display Excel.
`OleApp.Workbooks.Add`	Create a workbook.
`OleApp.Cells(1,1).Value=7`	Set a cell's value.
`OleApp.ActiveWorkbook.SaveAs("C:\TEMP.XLS")`	Save the workbook.
`OleApp.Quit`	Quit Excel.

If you create an object using the OLE Container control or OLE Bound control, you can use the DoVerb method of the control to execute a verb on the object. For example, use DoVerb(0) to execute the default verb, DoVerb(–1) to activate the object for visual editing, and DoVerb(–2) to open the object in a separate window. For details about the DoVerb method, see Help.

Note   See an application's documentation to determine what Automation commands it supports. For example, Microsoft Excel add-in components are not available for Automation.

Setting Time Outs

When you pass a request to an OLE object, the Automation server processes it. You don't have much control over the server processing, but you can specify how long you'll wait for a process to finish by setting the OLERequestPendingTimeout and OLEServerBusyTimeout properties. You can determine what happens when that time has expired by setting the OLEServerBusyRaiseError property. For more information about these properties, see Help.

Accessing Collections of Objects

An object type can represent a single object or a collection of related objects. For example, a Microsoft Excel Workbook object represents a single workbook, whereas the Workbooks object represents all the workbooks currently loaded. Because the Workbooks object represents a collection of objects, it's called a collection object.

In code, a collection is an unordered list in which the position of an object can change whenever objects are added to or removed from the collection. You access an object in a collection by iterating through the collection, using the Count property of the collection. The Count property returns the number of items in the collection. You can also use the Item method to return an item in a collection.

For example, to display the names of worksheets in a Microsoft Excel workbook, use the following code:

```
oleApp = CREATEOBJECT("Excel.Application")
oleApp.Workbooks.Add
FOR EACH x IN oleApp.Workbooks
 ? x.Name
ENDFOR
```

You can also access a collection within a collection. For example, you can access a cells collection within a range using the following code:

```
oleApp = CREATEOBJECT("Excel.sheet")
oleApp.Workbooks.Add
oleApp.Range(oleApp.Cells(1,1),oleApp.Cells(10,10)).Value=100
oleApp.Visible=.T.
```

Using Arrays of Objects

You can pass arrays to methods, and you can receive arrays back. However, you must pass arrays by reference by prefixing the array name with the @ sign.

For example, to send a Visual FoxPro array to Microsoft Excel, consider the following code. It creates an array in Visual FoxPro, assigns the array some values, starts Microsoft Excel, creates a workbook, sets a value to the first cell of a worksheet, and then copies that value to the other sheets in the array:

```
DIMENSION aV(3)
aV(1) = "Sheet1"
aV(2) = "Sheet2"
aV(3) = "Sheet3"
oleApp=CREATEOBJECT("Excel.Application")
oleApp.Workbooks.Add
oleI=oleApp.Workbooks.Item(1)
oleI.Sheets.Item(1).Cells(1,1).Value = 83
oleI.Sheets(@aV).;
FillAcrossSheets(oleI.Worksheets("Sheet1").Cells(1,1))

oleApp.Visible = .T.
```

Alternatively, the following example returns an array to Visual FoxPro and then displays the contents of the array:

```
oleApp = CREATEOBJECT("Excel.Application")
aOleArray = oleApp.GetCustomListContents(3)
FOR nIndex = 1 to ALEN(aOleArray)
    ? aOleArray(nIndex)
ENDFOR
```

> **Note** With Visual FoxPro, you cannot pass arrays larger than two dimensions to OLE objects. For more information about working with arrays in Visual FoxPro, see Chapter 3, "Object-Oriented Programming," or search for "Working with Arrays" in Help.

Releasing Extrinsic Objects

An Automation server is automatically released if it is not visible and no variables in scope reference the object. You can use the RELEASE command to release the variable associated with an object. If the server is visible, use the Quit method to release it.

Subclassing Objects

You can create custom objects by subclassing the base classes provided with
Visual FoxPro. For example, the following code subclasses the Outline control
provided with Visual FoxPro:

Subclassing the Outline Control

Code	Comments

``
PUBLIC frmMyForm, cFilename
SET SAFETY OFF
frmMyForm = CREATEOBJECT("form")
frmMyForm.Width = 100
frmMyForm.ADDOBJECT("oleOutl","myoutline")
DIMENSION aSection(3)
aSection(1) = "Table"
aSection(2) = "Field"
aSection(3) = "Index"
cFilename = GETFILE("dbc","Select a DBC")
USE (cFilename)
INDEX ON objecttype FOR (objecttype = "Table" ;
   OR objecttype = "Field" ;
   OR objecttype = "Index") ;
   TAG fname
FOR nIndex = 1 TO 3 STEP 1
   frmMyForm.oleOutl.AddItem(aSection(nIndex))
   frmMyForm.oleOutl.Indent;
   ((frmMyForm.oleOutl.ListCount-1)) = 1
   SCAN
      IF objecttype = aSection(nIndex)
         frmMyForm.oleOutl.Additem(objectname)
         frmMyForm.oleOutl.Indent;
         ((frmMyForm.oleOutl.ListCount-1)) = 2
      ENDIF
   ENDSCAN
   GO TOP
ENDFOR
frmMyForm.oleOutl.Visible = .T.
frmMyForm.Show
 	
DEFINE CLASS myoutline AS olecontrol
   OleClass = "msoutl.outline"
   Top = 5
   Left = 5
   Height = 10
   Width = 60
ENDDEFINE
``
	Declare variables and initialize.
	
	Create a form, add the custom outline control to the form, and then create an array for the items that the control lists.
	
	Prompt for a database that contains the information you want the control to list.
	
	Gather information from the database, and then add it to the control.
	
	Make the control visible, and then display the form.
	
	Define a subclass of the OLE Container control and add the outline control by setting the OleClass property of the container, and then defining other custom settings.

If you want to distribute your applications, there are some additional considerations.
For more information, see Chapter 25, "Building an Application for Distribution."

Controlling Visual FoxPro from Other Applications

Because Visual FoxPro acts as a server (with level 2 compliance) as well as a client, applications that support Automation can create instances of Visual FoxPro, run Visual FoxPro commands, and access Visual FoxPro objects.

You can even manipulate Visual FoxPro from applications that don't support Automation by using Fpole.dll. For more information, search for "Fpole.dll" in Help.

You control Visual FoxPro from other applications by using the Visual FoxPro Application object. An Application object is automatically created whenever Visual FoxPro is launched, either directly, through DDE or through Automation.

For example, the following lines of code in Visual Basic, or a Microsoft Excel module create a reference to a Visual FoxPro application object:

```
Dim oFox as Object
Set oFox = CreateObject("VisualFoxPro.Application")
```

Once you have a reference to the Visual FoxPro Application object, you can call methods associated with the application object and access other objects through the collection properties of the Application object.

Methods of the Application Object

DataToClip	Help
DoCmd	Quit
Eval	RequestData

The following example uses Visual Basic for Applications code in an Excel module to create a Visual FoxPro Application object, open a Visual FoxPro table, and add the results of a query to the active spreadsheet:

```
Sub FoxTest()
Dim oFox as Object
Set oFox = CreateObject("VisualFoxPro.Application")

oFox.DoCmd "USE customer"
oFox.DoCmd "SELECT contact, phone FROM customer
    WHERE country = " + Chr$(39) + USA+ Chr$(39) + " INTO CURSOR cust"
oFox.DataToClip "cust",,3
Range("A1:B1").Select
ActiveSheet.Paste
End Sub
```

The Visual FoxPro Application Object Model

An application object is automatically created whenever Visual FoxPro is launched, either directly, through Automation or DDE. This application object provides access to all other objects created in a Visual FoxPro session through Collection properties.

Visual FoxPro application object model

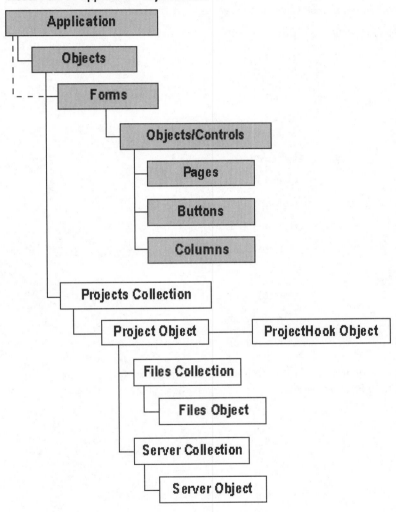

Accessing Objects Through Collection Properties

The Visual FoxPro application object and all container objects in Visual FoxPro have a count property and a collection property associated with them. The collection property is an array referencing each contained object. The count property is a numeric property indicating the number of contained objects.

The following table lists objects and the corresponding collection and count properties.

Object	Collection Property	Count Property
Application	Objects	Count
	Forms	FormCount
FormSet	Forms	FormCount
Form	Objects	Count
	Controls	ControlCount
PageFrame	Pages	PageCount
Page	Controls	ControlCount
Grid	Columns	ColumnCount
CommandGroup	Buttons	ButtonCount
OptionGroup	Buttons	ButtonCount
Column	Controls	ControlCount
ToolBar	Controls	ControlCount
Container	Controls	ControlCount
Control	Controls	ControlCount

These properties allow you to use a loop to programmatically manipulate all or specific contained objects. For example, the following lines of code set the Visible property of all forms to True (.T.):

```
FOR EACH Form IN Application.Forms
   Form.Visible = .T.
ENDFOR
```

Creating Automation Servers

With Visual FoxPro, you can create Automation servers (COM components) that package code to perform tasks common to many applications, or that implement complex business rules. These tasks and rules are then available to other programmers in your company, and to users of tools that support automation.

For example, you could create one or more classes to handle enterprise-wide business rules. A client application that uses the business rule objects would pass input parameters in a method call, and the Automation server might then do a great deal of work, retrieving data from various sources and performing complex calculations, before returning the answer.

Examples of Automation servers are installed in the Visual Studio
...\Samples\Vfp98\Servers directory.

Creating the Server

All you need to create an Automation server in Visual FoxPro is a project that contains classes defined as OLEPUBLIC. You can have as many OLEPUBLIC classes as you want in the project and they can be defined in program files (.prg) or class libraries (.vcx).

For example, the following class definition in a program file creates a custom OLE public class:

```
DEFINE class person AS CUSTOM OLEPUBLIC
    FirstName = SPACE(30)
    LastName = SPACE(45)

    PROCEDURE GetName
        RETURN THIS.FirstName + " " + THIS.LastName
    ENDPROC
ENDDEFINE
```

When you're designing a class in the Class Designer, select OLE Public in the Class Info dialog box to designate the class as OLEPUBLIC.

Class Info dialog box

Select OLE Public to build OLE servers. ————

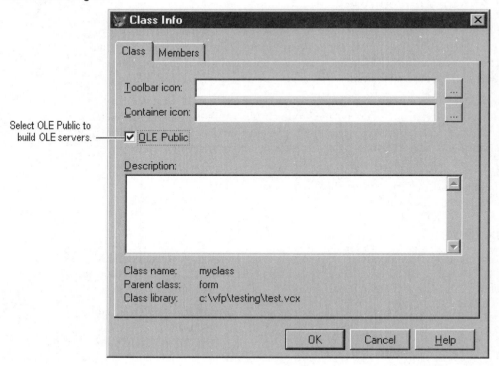

Compiling the Server

In Visual FoxPro, you can create either an out-of-process or an in-process Automation server. An *out-of-process* component is an executable (.exe file) that runs in its own process. Communication between a client application and an out-of-process server is therefore called *cross-process* communication. An *in-process* component is a dynamic-link library (DLL) that runs in the same process address space as the client that calls it.

There are benefits to each. An in-process server is faster because there is no inter-process communication overhead. On the other hand, an out-of-process server can be deployed remotely and an in-process server cannot. Additionally, because the in-process server and the client share a process address space, any serious error in the .dll will terminate the client whereas an error in an out-of-process .exe would only terminate the server.

When you create an executable with OLE Public classes, you don't lose any of your normal .exe capabilities. You can still run the executable, provide a user interface, and all the normal functionality you would include in an application. You increase the extensibility of your application, though, by allowing other applications to tap into the specific functionality you want to expose.

> **Note**   If more than one user is accessing the Automation server, there can be conflicts. If you've provided Automation access as well as a user interface for your functionality, provide an extra layer of consistency checking in the interface to make sure your environment hasn't been changed.

To compile an Automation server

1. From the **Project Manager**, choose **Build**.

2. In the **Build Options** dialog box, choose **Build Executable** or **Build OLE DLL**.

   Build Options dialog box

   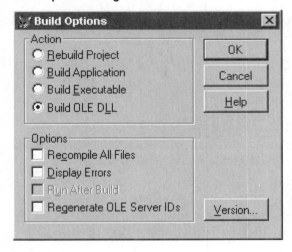

3. Choose **OK**.

   – or –

   Use the BUILD DLL or BUILD EXE commands.

Once you build the project, you can see the server classes displayed in the Project Information dialog box. Here you can also specify a help file and a Help context ID for each class. This help file can be opened from most generic object browsers.

Project Information dialog box

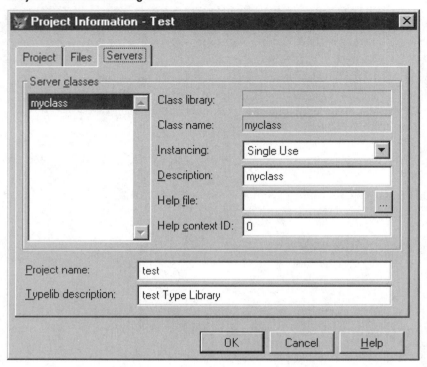

You can choose class-specific instancing values in the Project Information dialog box. The instancing options are:

- **Not Creatable**   Even though the class is marked OLE public, it will not be available to other applications. For example, you could have a standard library of OLE public classes used in multiple applications and disable automation of one or more classes for a single application.

- **Single Use**   Each client application that uses your server creates a separate instance of the server class. Each instance has a single thread of execution. Although separate instances require more memory, choosing Single Use allows the operating system to apply preemptive multitasking.

- **Multi Use**   Once the server has been created, other applications can use the same instance.

   Note   If you make changes in the Servers tab of the Project Information dialog box, you need to rebuild the .dll or .exe for the new settings to take effect.

When you build a project with OLE public classes, three files are created:

- The .dll or .exe
- A type library (.tlb) file
- A registry (.vbr) file

The type library file is a binary file that lists all the published classes in your Automation server, along with their properties, methods, and events. OLE object browsers read this information and present it in a readable interface.

The registry file lists the global unique IDs (GUID) for the classes in your server.

Note   A .vbr registry file is the same as a .reg registry file except that the .vbr file doesn't include hard-coded paths.

A .vbr file with GUIDs for each OLE public class in a project

```
test.vbr
REGEDIT

HKEY_CLASSES_ROOT\test.myclass = myclass
HKEY_CLASSES_ROOT\test.myclass\NotInsertable
HKEY_CLASSES_ROOT\test.myclass\CLSID = {3607DFE0-B166-11CF-8611-00AA0038BB65}
HKEY_CLASSES_ROOT\CLSID\{3607DFE0-B166-11CF-8611-00AA0038BB65} = myclass
HKEY_CLASSES_ROOT\CLSID\{3607DFE0-B166-11CF-8611-00AA0038BB65}\ProgId = test.myclass
HKEY_CLASSES_ROOT\CLSID\{3607DFE0-B166-11CF-8611-00AA0038BB65}\VersionIndependentProgId =
test.myclass
HKEY_CLASSES_ROOT\CLSID\{3607DFE0-B166-11CF-8611-00AA0038BB65}\InProcServer32 =
c:\vfp4\testing\test.dll
HKEY_CLASSES_ROOT\CLSID\{3607DFE0-B166-11CF-8611-00AA0038BB65}\TypeLib =
{3607DFE1-B166-11CF-8611-00AA0038BB65}


; TypeLibrary registration
HKEY_CLASSES_ROOT\TypeLib\{3607DFE1-B166-11CF-8611-00AA0038BB65}
HKEY_CLASSES_ROOT\TypeLib\{3607DFE1-B166-11CF-8611-00AA0038BB65}\1.0 = test Type Library
HKEY_CLASSES_ROOT\TypeLib\{3607DFE1-B166-11CF-8611-00AA0038BB65}\1.0\0\win32 =
c:\vfp4\testing\test.tlb
```

Registering an Automation server

Your Automation servers are available to other applications once the servers have been added to the Windows Registry. When you build an Automation server, it's automatically registered on the build machine. You can also register your servers on other machines.

When you use the Visual FoxPro Setup Wizard to create setup disks, the setup program registers your servers on your customers' machines. You can also manually register servers.

To register an .exe component

- Run the .exe file with the **/regserver** switch.

  For example, to register Myserver.exe, run the following command:

  ```
  myserver /regserver
  ```

To remove an .exe component registry entry

- Run the .exe file with the **/unregserver** switch.

  For example, to unregister Myserver.exe, run the following command:

  ```
  myserver /unregserver
  ```

To register a .dll component

- Run REGSVR32 with the name of the server.

  For example, to register Myserver.dll run the following command:

  ```
  REGSVR32 myserver.dll
  ```

To remove a .dll component registry entry

- Run REGSVR32 with the name of the server and the **/u** switch.

  For example, to register Myserver.dll run the following command:

  ```
  REGSVR32 /u myserver.dll
  ```

  Note The registry contains the full path name to the file, so if you move the file, you'll need to register it again.

Using the Automation server

Any application that can create Automation objects can create objects based on your Automation server, set properties that are not HIDDEN or PROTECTED, and call methods. For example, assuming that your server is named foxole and contains a class named person with a GetName method, the following code could be run in Visual FoxPro 3.0:

```
oTest = CREATEOBJECT("foxole.person")
cName = oTest.GetName()
```

Similar code could be run in Microsoft Excel or Visual Basic:

```
Set oTest = CreateObject("foxole.person")
cName$ = oTest.GetName()
```

Raising or Returning Errors from Automation servers

The only interaction with the objects provided by an Automation server (COM component) is through the methods and properties of the exposed classes. When a client application calls a method of an object, and an error occurs in the Automation server, the method either returns an error value or raises an error in the client application.

The client application decides whether to alert the user or proceed with another execution path. The Automation server itself never interacts with the user. This allows the location of the Automation server to be transparent to the client application. The Automation server can be local, running on the user's computer, or you can use the Remote Automation feature of Visual FoxPro to run it on a network server.

Using Remote Automation

In typical Automation scenarios, both the client and the server are on a single computer and share the same resources, such as memory and processor.

Automation on a single computer

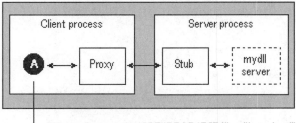

When you create local servers for Automation, you can deploy them remotely. Remote Automation allows you the same flexibility, extensibility, and power of local Automation, but over a network. Remote Automation allows:

- Servers to use separate resources.
- Many different users to access the same server.

You can configure a server and local computer for remote Automation with the Remote Automation Connection Manager, which saves the settings in the registry. The Automation Manager running on the server computer manages the Automation so that the same code that manipulates a local object can automatically manipulate a remote object.

Remote automation

Workstation   **Win32 remote computer**

Client process	Automation Manager	Server process
A ←→ Remote Automation proxy	Remote Automation stub ←→ Proxy	Stub ←→ mydll server

Object reference: A = CREATEOBJECT ("mydll.myclass")

Configuring the Server

The first step in enabling remote Automation is to configure the server computer for client access in the Remote Automation Connection Manager.

To configure the remote automation server

1. Copy the Automation server executable file (.exe) to the server and run it one time to register it in the Windows Registry.

2. On the server computer, run Racmgr32.exe, the Remote Automation Connection Manager.

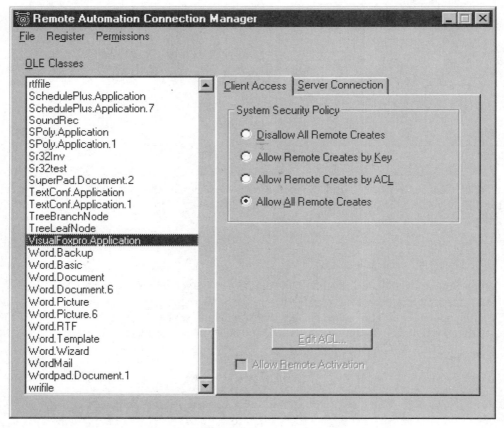

3. Select your class in the **COM Classes** list.

4. In the **Client Access** tab, choose **Allow Remote Creates by Key**.

5. In the **Client Access** tab, make sure **Allow Remote Activation** is selected.

After you've enabled client access in the Remote Automation Connection Manager, run the Automation Manager, Autmgr32.exe, on the server computer. Autmgr32.exe is installed in the System folder under Windows 95 or in the System32 folder under Windows NT. This will enable remote automation connections from other computers.

Configuring the Client

When the server computer is set up, you can configure the local client computer.

To configure the local computer for remote automation

1. Copy the .vbr file that was created when you created the Automation server to the client machine.

2. Run CLIREG32 with the name of the .vbr file. For example, if the file is Myserver.vbr, run the following command at the Command prompt:

   ```
   CLIREG32 MYSERVER.VBR
   ```

3. In the dialog box that opens, enter the network address of the server machine and choose the network protocol (usually TCP/IP).

System Security Policy Options

The following table describes the System Security Policy area options in the Client Access tab of the Remote Automation Connection Manager.

Name	Value*	Description
Disallow All Remote Creates	0	Do not allow any objects to be created.
Allow Remote Creates by Key	2	An object can be created only if the Allow Remote Activation check box is selected. This alters its CLSID in the Windows Registry to include the following subkey setting: AllowRemoteActivation = Y.
Allow Remote Creates by ACL	3	A user can create an object only if the Access Control List for the CLSID in the Windows Registry includes the user. Windows NT only.
Allow All Remote Creates	1	Allow any object to be created. Not recommended outside the development environment.

* The Value column lists the RemoteActivationPolicy preference setting of the Automation Manager in the Windows Registry.

Using Authentication in Remote Automation

For remote Automation servers running on any Windows operating system, remote call procedure (RPC) provides the following levels of authentication.

Name	Value	Description
Default	0	Use Network default.
None	1	No authentication.
Connect	2	Connection to the server is authenticated.
Call	3	Authenticates only at the beginning of each remote procedure call, when the server receives the request. Does not apply to connection-based protocol sequences (those that start with the prefix "ncacn").
Packet	4	Verifies that all data received is from the expected client.
Packet Integrity	5	Verifies that none of the data transferred between client and server has been modified.
Packet Privacy	6	Verifies all previous levels and encrypts the argument values of each remote procedure call.

The need for RPC authentication should be evaluated carefully, because as the level of RPC authentication increases, performance declines. You can specify an authentication level for each class in your Automation server, so that costly levels like encryption need not be applied to the entire component.

For example, a data service implemented as a remote Automation server might have a Logon class used to transmit user and password information, and this class might require Packet Privacy authentication. Other classes exposed by the server might use a much lower level of authentication.

Troubleshooting Remote Automation

Here are some suggestions in case you run into difficulties.

Problem	Action
OLE error code 0x800706d9: There are no more endpoints available from the endpoint manager.	Make sure the Automation manager is running on the server computer and that the name of the server computer is correctly entered in the Network Address box of the Remote Automation Connection Manager.
Visual FoxPro: Application doesn't appear in the Remote Automation Manager OLE Classes list.	1. Run Regedit.exe to open the registry. 2. Delete all references to Microsoft Visual FoxPro. 3. Run Visual FoxPro with the -r command line tag: `vfp6.exe -r`

Programming for Shared Access

If you create an application that will run on several machines in a network environment, or if several instances of a form will access the same data, then you need to program for shared access. Shared access means providing efficient ways of using and sharing data among users, as well as restricting access when necessary.

Visual FoxPro provides support for shared or exclusive access to data, locking options, data sessions, record and table buffering, and transactions. Although these features are particularly useful in shared environments, you can use them in single-user environments too.

This chapter discusses:

- Controlling Access to Data
- Updating Data
- Managing Conflicts

Controlling Access to Data

Since you access data in files, effective data management begins with control over the environment of these files. You must choose how to access the data and how and when to limit that access.

Accessing Data

In a shared environment, you can access data in two ways: from exclusive files or from shared files. If you open a table for shared access, other users also have access to the file. If you open a table for exclusive access, no other user can read or write to that file. Because exclusive use defeats many of the benefits of sharing data on a network, it should be used sparingly.

Using a Table with Exclusive Access

The most restrictive way to open a file is to open it exclusively. When you open a table through the interface, it opens for exclusive use by default. You can also explicitly open a table for exclusive use by using Visual FoxPro commands.

To open a table for exclusive use

- Type the following commands in the Command window:

```
SET EXCLUSIVE ON
USE cMyTable
```

– or –

Type the following command in the Command window:

```
USE cMyTable EXCLUSIVE
```

The following commands require you to open a table for exclusive use:

- ALTER TABLE
- INDEX when creating, adding, or deleting a compound index tag.
- INSERT [BLANK]
- MODIFY STRUCTURE

  To use this command to change a table structure, you must open the table exclusively. You can, however, use this command in read-only mode when you open the table for shared use.

- PACK
- REINDEX
- ZAP

Visual FoxPro returns the error, "Exclusive open of file is required," if you try to execute one of these commands on a shared table.

You can restrict access to a table by using the FLOCK( ) function. If you use FLOCK( ) to lock the table, other users cannot write to the table but they can read it.

For more information on these commands, see Help.

Using a Table with Shared Access

When you open a table for shared use, more than one workstation can use the same table at the same time. When you open a table through the interface, you can override the default ON setting for SET EXCLUSIVE. You can explicitly open a table for shared use by using Visual FoxPro commands.

To open a table for shared use

- Type the following commands in the Command window:

```
SET EXCLUSIVE OFF
USE cMyTable
```

– or –

Type the following command in the Command window:

```
USE cMyTable SHARED
```

When you add or change data in a shared table, you must first lock the affected record or the entire table. You can lock a record or a table opened for shared use in the following ways:

- Use a command that performs an automatic record or table lock. See the table of commands that perform automatic locking in the section, "Choosing Automatic or Manual Locks" later in this chapter.

- Manually lock one or more records or an entire table with the record and table locking functions.

- Initiate buffering with the CURSORSETPROP( ) function.

Associated memo and index files always open with the same share status as their table.

If your application uses a table for lookup purposes only and all users of the application access it, then you can improve performance by marking the table as read-only.

Locking Data

If you share access to files, you must also manage access to data by locking tables and records. Locks, unlike access permissions, can provide both long- and short-term control of data. Visual FoxPro provides both automatic and manual locking.

Choosing Record or Table Locks

Record locking, whether automatic or manual, prevents one user from writing to a record that's currently being written to by another user. Table locking prevents other users from writing to, but not reading from, an entire table. Because table locking prohibits other users from updating records in a table, it should only be used sparingly.

Choosing Automatic or Manual Locks

In addition to record or table locking, you can also choose automatic or manual locking. Many Visual FoxPro commands automatically attempt to lock a record or a table before the command is executed. If the record or table is successfully locked, the command is executed and the lock is released.

Commands that Automatically Lock Records and Tables

Command	Scope of lock
ALTER TABLE	Entire table
APPEND	Table header
APPEND BLANK	Table header
APPEND FROM	Table header
APPEND FROM ARRAY	Table header
APPEND MEMO	Current record
BLANK	Current record
BROWSE, CHANGE and EDIT	Current record and all records from aliased fields in related tables once editing of a field begins
CURSORSETPROP( )	Depends on parameters
DELETE	Current record
DELETE NEXT 1	Current record
DELETE RECORD n	Record *n*
DELETE of more than one record	Entire table
DELETE – SQL	Current record
GATHER	Current record
INSERT	Entire table
INSERT – SQL	Table header
MODIFY MEMO	Current record when editing begins
READ	Current record and all records from aliased fields

Commands that Automatically Lock Records and Tables   *(continued)*

Command	Scope of lock
RECALL	Current record
RECALL NEXT 1	Current record
RECALL RECORD *n*	Record *n*
RECALL of more than one record	Entire table
REPLACE	Current record and all records from aliased fields
REPLACE NEXT 1	Current record and all records from aliased fields
REPLACE RECORD *n*	Record *n* and all records from aliased fields
REPLACE of more than one record	Entire table and all files from aliased fields
SHOW GETS	Current record and all records referenced by aliased fields
TABLEUPDATE( )	Depends on buffering
UPDATE	Entire table
UPDATE – SQL	Entire table

For more information on these commands, see Help.

Record Lock Characteristics

Commands that attempt record locks are less restrictive than commands that lock tables. When you lock a record, other users can still add or delete other records. If a record or table is already locked by another user, an attempted record or table lock fails. Commands that attempt to lock the current record return the error, "Record is in use by another," if the record cannot be locked.

The BROWSE, CHANGE, EDIT, and MODIFY MEMO commands do not lock a record until you edit the record. If you're editing fields from records in related tables, the related records are locked if possible. The lock attempt fails if the current record or any of the related records are also locked by another user. If the lock attempt is successful, you can edit the record; the lock is released when you move to another record or activate another window.

Header and Table Lock Characteristics

Some Visual FoxPro commands lock an entire table while others only lock a table header. Commands that lock the entire table are more intrusive than commands that only lock the table header. When you lock the table header, other users cannot add records, but they can still change data in fields.

Users can share the table without causing a conflict when you issue the APPEND BLANK command, but an error can occur while another user is also appending a BLANK record to the table. You can trap for the error, "File is in use by another," which is returned when two or more users execute APPEND BLANK simultaneously. Commands that lock an entire table return the error, "File is in use by another," if the table cannot be locked. To cancel the attempted lock, press ESC.

Example: Automatic Locking

In the following example, the user automatically locks the table header by appending records from another table, even though `customer` was opened as a shared file:

```
SET EXCLUSIVE OFF
USE customer
APPEND FROM oldcust FOR status = "OPEN"
```

Locking Manually

You can manually lock a record or a table with locking functions.

To manually lock a record or a table

- Use one of the following commands:

```
RLOCK()
LOCK()
FLOCK()
```

RLOCK( ) and LOCK( ) are identical and lock one or more records. FLOCK( ) locks a file. The LOCK( ) and RLOCK( ) functions can apply to a table header. If you provide 0 as the record to LOCK( ) or RLOCK( ) and the test indicates the header is unlocked, the function locks the header and returns true (.T.).

Once you lock a record or table, be sure to release the lock by using the UNLOCK command as soon as possible to provide access to other users.

These manual locking functions perform the following actions:

- Test the lock status of the record or table.

- If the test indicates the record is unlocked, lock the record or table and return true (.T.).

- If the record or table cannot be locked, attempt to lock the record or table again, depending on the current setting of SET REPROCESS.

- Return true (.T.) or false (.F.), indicating whether the lock attempt was successful.

    Tip If you want to test the lock status of a record in your session without locking the record, use the ISRLOCKED( ) or ISFLOCKED( ) function.

If an attempt to lock a record or table fails, the SET REPROCESS command and your current error routine determine if the lock is attempted again. SET REPROCESS affects the result of an unsuccessful lock attempt. You can control the number of lock attempts or the length of time a lock is attempted with SET REPROCESS.

For more information, search for SET REPROCESS in Help.

Example: Manual Locking

The following example opens the `customer` table for shared access and uses FLOCK( ) to attempt to lock the table. If the table is successfully locked, REPLACE ALL updates every record in the table. UNLOCK releases the file lock. If the file cannot be locked because another user has locked the file or a record in the file, a message is displayed.

```
SET EXCLUSIVE OFF
SET REPROCESS TO 0
USE customer    && Open table shared
IF FLOCK()
   REPLACE ALL contact ;&& Replace and unlock
      WITH UPPER(contact)
   UNLOCK
ELSE  && Output message
   WAIT "File in use by another." WINDOW NOWAIT
ENDIF
```

Unlocking Data

After you establish a record or file lock and complete a data operation in a shared environment, you should release the lock as soon as possible. There are several ways to release locks. In some cases, simply moving to the next record is enough to unlock the data. Other situations require explicit commands.

To unlock a record that's been automatically locked, you need only move the record pointer, even if you set MULTILOCKS ON. You must explicitly remove a lock from a record that you've manually locked; simply moving the record pointer is not enough.

The following table describes the effects of commands on manual and automatic record and table locks.

Command	Effect
UNLOCK	Releases record and file locks in the current work area.
UNLOCK ALL	Releases all locks in all work areas in the current session.
SET MULTILOCKS OFF	Enables automatic release of the current lock as a new lock is secured.
FLOCK( )	Releases all record locks in the affected file before locking the file.
CLEAR ALL, CLOSE ALL, USE, QUIT	Releases all record and file locks.
END TRANSACTION	Releases automatic locks.
TABLEUPDATE( )	Releases all locks after updating the table.

Caution If a record was automatically locked in a user-defined function and you move the record pointer off and then back on the record, the lock will be released. Use table buffering to avoid this problem.

Using Data Sessions

To ensure that each user in a shared environment has a secure, exact duplicate of the working environment, and to ensure that multiple instances of a form can operate independently, Visual FoxPro provides data sessions.

A data session is a representation of the current dynamic work environment. You might think of a data session as a miniature data environment running inside one open Visual FoxPro session on one machine. Each data session contains:

- A copy of the items in the form's data environment.

- Cursors representing the open tables, their indexes, and relationships.

The concept of a data session is easily understood when you consider what happens when you open the same form simultaneously from separate workstations in a multi-user application. In this case, each workstation is running a separate Visual FoxPro session, and therefore has its own set of work areas: cursors representing open base tables, indexes, and relationships.

However, if you open multiple instances of the same form in a single project, on one machine, within the same Visual FoxPro session, the forms share the Default data session, representing a single dynamic work environment. Each instance of the open form open in the same Visual FoxPro session uses the same set of work areas, and actions in one instance of a form that move the record pointer in a work area automatically affect other instances of the same form.

Using Private Data Sessions

If you want to have more control over multiple instances of form, you can implement Private data sessions. When your form uses private data sessions, Visual FoxPro creates a new data session for each instance of the Form, FormSet, or Toolbar control your application creates. Each private data session contains:

- A separate copy of each table, index, and relationship in the form's data environment.
- An unlimited number of work areas.
- Record pointers for each copy of each table that are independent from the base tables for the form.

The number of available data sessions is limited only by available system memory and disk space.

You implement private data sessions by setting the DataSession property for the form. The DataSession property has two settings:

- 1 – Default data session (the default setting).
- 2 – Private data session.

By default, the DataSession property of a form is set to 1.

To enable private data sessions

Choose one of the following options:

- In the Form Designer, set the DataSession property of the form to **2 – Private data session**.

  – or –

  In code, set the DataSession property to 2.

  For example, type:

```
frmFormName.DataSession = 2
```

> **Note**   You can only set the DataSession property at design time. The DataSession property is read-only at run time.

When a form uses private data sessions, each instance of a form open on a single machine in a single Visual FoxPro session uses its own data environment. Using private data sessions is similar to running the same form simultaneously from separate workstations.

Equivalent multiple data sessions

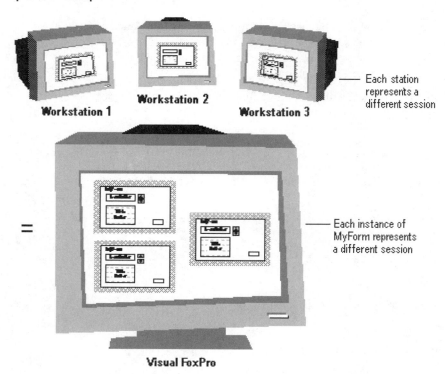

Identifying Data Sessions

Each private data session is identified separately. You can see the contents of each data session in the Data Session window. You can also change the data session description through commands in the Load event code.

You can view the identification number for each data session by using the DataSessionID run-time property. The following example displays the DataSessionID property of a form named frmMyForm:

```
DO FORM frmMyForm
? frmMyForm.DataSessionID
```

If you activate the form using the NAME clause, you can use the form's name to access the DataSessionID property, as in the following code:

```
DO FORM MyForm NAME one
? one.DataSessionID
```

The DataSessionID property is designed only to identify a particular data session. Avoid changing the DataSessionID of a form instance because data-bound controls lose their data sources when you change the DataSessionID.

Updating Data Using Multiple Form Instances

While private data sessions generate separate work areas containing separate copies of a form's open tables, indexes, and relationships, every copy of the form references the same underlying base tables and base index files. When a user updates a record from one instance of a form, the base table referenced by the form is updated. You see the changes made from another instance of the form when you navigate to the changed record.

Locks taken on records or tables in one private data session are respected by other private data sessions. For example, if the user of data session 1 takes a lock on a record, the user in data session 2 cannot lock the record. If the user in session 1 opens a table exclusively, the user in data session 2 cannot open the table. By respecting locks taken by other data sessions, Visual FoxPro protects the integrity of updates to the underlying base tables.

Customizing the Environment of a Data Session

Because data sessions control the scope of certain SET commands, you can use private data sessions to establish custom SET command settings within a single session of Visual FoxPro.

For example, the SET EXACT command, which controls the rules used when comparing character strings of different lengths, is scoped to the current data session. The default setting for SET EXACT is off which specifies that, to be equivalent, expressions must match, character for character, until the end of the expressions on the right side is reached. You might want to enable "fuzzy" or equivalent searches by leaving SET EXACT set to OFF for the default data session; however, your application might contain a specific form that requires exact matches. You could set the DataSession property for the form requiring exact matches to 2, to enable private data sessions, and then SET EXACT to ON for that form. By issuing a SET command only for the form using private data sessions, you preserve the global Visual FoxPro session settings while enabling customized session settings for a specific form.

Overriding Automatic Private Data Session Assignment

When private data sessions for a form are in use, changes you make to data in one form are not automatically represented in other instances of the same form. If you want all instances of a form to access the same data and to immediately reflect changes to common data, you can override automatic data session assignment.

To override automatic data session assignment

- Use one of these commands:

```
SET DATASESSION TO 1
```

– or –

```
SET DATASESSION TO
```

Both commands enable the default data session to be controlled by the Command window and the Project Manager.

Buffering Data

If you want to protect data during updates, use buffers. Visual FoxPro record and table buffering help you protect data update and data maintenance operations on single records and on multiple records of data in multi-user environments. Buffers can automatically test, lock, and release records or tables.

With buffering, you can easily detect and resolve conflicts in data update operations: the current record is copied to a memory or disk location managed by Visual FoxPro. Other users can then still access the original record simultaneously. When you move from the record or try to update the record programmatically, Visual FoxPro attempts to lock the record, verify that no other changes have been made by other users, and then writes the edits. After you attempt to update data, you must also resolve conflicts that prevent the edits from being written to the original table.

Choosing a Buffering Method

Before you enable buffering, evaluate the data environment to choose the buffering method and locking options that best suit the editing needs of your application, the record and table types and sizes, how the information is used and updated, and other factors. Once you enable buffering, it remains in effect until you disable buffering or close the table.

Visual FoxPro has two types of buffering: record and table.

Visual FoxPro record and table buffering

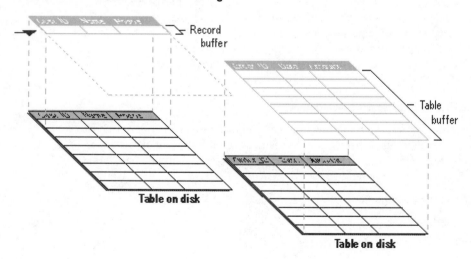

- To access, modify, and write a single record at a time, choose record buffering.

  Record buffering provides appropriate process validation with minimal impact on the data update operations of other users in a multi-user environment.

- To buffer the updates to several records, choose table buffering.

  Table buffering provides the most effective way to handle several records in one table or child records in a one-to-many relationship.

- To provide maximum protection for existing data, use Visual FoxPro transactions.

  You can use transactions alone, but you gain additional effectiveness by using transactions as wrappers for record or table buffering commands. For more details, see the section, "Managing Updates with Transactions," later in this chapter.

Choosing a Locking Mode

Visual FoxPro provides buffering in two locking modes: pessimistic and optimistic. These choices determine when one or more records are locked, and how and when they're released.

Pessimistic Buffering

Pessimistic buffering prevents other users in a multi-user environment from accessing a particular record or table while you're making changes to it. A pessimistic lock provides the most secure environment for changing individual records but it can slow user operations. This buffering mode is most similar to the standard locking mechanism in previous versions of FoxPro, with the added benefit of built-in data buffering.

Optimistic Buffering

Optimistic buffering is an efficient way to update records because locks are only taken at the time the record is written, thus minimizing the time any single user monopolizes the system in a multi-user environment. When you use record or table buffering on views, Visual FoxPro imposes optimistic locking.

The value of the Buffering property, set with the CURSORSETPROP( ) function, determines the buffering and locking methods.

The following table summarizes valid values for the Buffering property.

To enable	Use this value
No buffering. The default value.	1
Pessimistic record locks which lock record now, update when pointer moves or upon TABLEUPDATE( ).	2
Optimistic record locks which wait until pointer moves, and then lock and update.	3
Pessimistic table locks which lock record now, update later upon TABLEUPDATE( ).	4
Optimistic table lock which wait until TABLEUPDATE( ), and then lock and update edited records.	5

The default value for Buffering is 1 for tables and 3 for views. If you use buffering to access remote data, the Buffering property is either 3, optimistic row buffering, or 5, optimistic table buffering.

Note   Set MULTILOCKS to ON for all buffering modes above 1.

Enabling Record Buffering

Enable record buffering with the CURSORSETPROP( ) function.

To enable pessimistic record locking in the current work area

- Use this function and value:

```
CURSORSETPROP("Buffering", 2)
```

Visual FoxPro attempts to lock the record at the pointer location. If the lock is successful, Visual FoxPro places the record in a buffer and permits editing. When you move the record pointer or issue a TABLEUPDATE( ) command, Visual FoxPro writes the buffered record to the original table.

To enable optimistic record locking in the current work area

- Use this function and value:

```
CURSORSETPROP("Buffering", 3)
```

Visual FoxPro writes the record at the location of the pointer to a buffer and permits edits. When you move the record pointer or issue a TABLEUPDATE( ) command, Visual FoxPro attempts a lock on the record. If the lock is successful, Visual FoxPro compares the current value of the record on the disk with the original buffer value. If these values are the same, the edits are written to the original table; if these values are different, Visual FoxPro generates an error.

Enabling Table Buffering

Enable table buffering with the CURSORSETPROP( ) function.

To enable pessimistic locking of multiple records in the current work area

- Use this function and value:

```
CURSORSETPROP("Buffering", 4)
```

Visual FoxPro attempts to lock the record at the pointer location. If the lock is successful, Visual FoxPro places the record in a buffer and permits editing. Use the TABLEUPDATE( ) command to write the buffered records to the original table.

To enable optimistic locking of multiple records in the current work area

- Use this function and value:

```
CURSORSETPROP("Buffering", 5)
```

Visual FoxPro writes the records to a buffer and permits edits until you issue a TABLEUPDATE( ) command. Visual FoxPro then performs the following sequence on each record in the buffer:

- Attempts a lock on each edited record.

- Upon a successful lock, compares the current value of each record on the disk with the original buffer value.

- Writes the edits to the original table if the comparison shows the values to be the same.

- Generates an error if the values differ.

When table buffering is enabled, Visual FoxPro attempts updates only after a TABLEUPDATE( ) command.

Appending and Deleting Records in Table Buffers

You can append and delete records while table buffering is enabled: appended records are added to the end of the buffer. To access all records in the buffer, including appended records, use the RECNO( ) function. The RECNO( ) function returns sequential negative numbers on records you append to a table buffer. For instance, if you initiate table buffering, edit records 7, 8, and 9, and then append three records, the buffer will contain RECNO( ) values of 7, 8, 9, –1, –2, and –3.

Buffer after editing and appending records

TABLE BUFFER	
7	Edit Record
8	Edit Record
9	Edit Record
-1	Append Record
-2	Append Record
-3	Append Record

You can remove appended records from the buffer only by using the TABLEREVERT( ) command. For any appended record, both TABLEUPDATE( ) and TABLEREVERT( ) delete the negative RECNO( ) value for that record while maintaining the sequence.

For more information on CURSORSETPROP( ), TABLEUPDATE( ), and TABLEREVERT( ), see Help.

Buffer after editing, deleting an appended record, and appending another

TABLE BUFFER		
7		Edit Record
8		Edit Record
9		Edit Record
-1		Append Record
-2		Delete Record
-3		Append Record
-4		Append Record

While using a table buffer, you can use the GO command with the negative RECNO( ) value to access a specific appended record. For instance, using the previous example, you can type:

```
GO 7     && moves to the 1st buffered record
GO -3    && moves to the 6th buffered record (3rd appended)
```

To append records to a table buffer

- Use the APPEND or APPEND BLANK command after you enable table buffering.

Appended records have sequential ascending negative RECNO( ) numbers.

To remove an appended record from a table buffer

1. Use the GO command with a negative value to position the record pointer at the record to be deleted.

2. Use the DELETE command to mark the record for deletion.

3. Use the TABLEREVERT( ) function to remove the record from the buffer.

   Note The TABLEREVERT( ) function also affects the status of deleted and changed rows.

To remove all appended records from a table buffer

- Use the TABLEREVERT( ) function with a value of true (.T.).

TABLEREVERT( ) removes appended records from a table buffer without writing the records to the table. TABLEUPDATE( ) writes all current buffered records to a table, even if they've been marked for deletion.

Updating Data

To update data, you can use buffers, transactions, or views.

Performing Updates with Buffers

After choosing the buffering method and the type of locking, you can enable record or table buffering.

To enable buffering

Choose one of the following options:

- In the **Form Designer**, set the BufferModeOverride property of the cursor in the data environment of the form.

  – or –

  In code, set the Buffering property.

  For example, you can enable pessimistic row buffering by placing the following code in the Init procedure of a form:

  ```
  CURSORSETPROP('Buffering', 2)
  ```

You then place code for the update operations in the appropriate method code for your controls.

To write edits to the original table, use TABLEUPDATE( ). To cancel edits after a failed update operation in a table constrained by rules, use TABLEREVERT( ). TABLEREVERT( ) is valid even if explicit table buffering isn't enabled.

The following sample demonstrates how to update records when pessimistic record buffering is enabled.

Example of Updating Using Record and Table Buffers

Code	Comment

```OPEN DATABASE testdata```
```USE customers```
```CURSORSETPROP('Buffering', 2)```
```lModified = .F.```
	In the form Init code, open the table and enable pessimistic record buffering.

```FOR nFieldNum = 1 TO FCOUNT()```
```   IF GETFLDSTATE(nFieldNum) = 2```
```   lModified = .T.```
```   EXIT```
```   ENDIF```
```ENDFOR```
	Go through fields, checking for any field that's been modified.
	
	Note This code might be in the Click event of a "Save" or "Update" command button.

(continued)

Example of Updating Using Record and Table Buffers *(continued)*

Code	Comment
| ```
IF lModified
   nResult = MESSAGEBOX;
      ("Record has been modified. Save?", ;
      4+32+256, "Data Change")

   IF nResult = 7
      TABLEREVERT (.F.)
   ENDIF
ENDIF

SKIP
IF EOF()
   MESSAGEBOX( "already at bottom")
   SKIP -1
ENDIF
THISFORM.Refresh
``` | Locate the next modified record.<br><br><br><br>Present the current value and give the user the option to revert the change to the current field.<br><br><br><br><br>SKIP guarantees that the last change is written. |

Managing Updates with Transactions

Even with buffering, things can go wrong. If you want to protect update operations and recover from an entire section of code as a unit, use transactions.

Adding transactions to your application provides protection beyond Visual FoxPro record and table buffering by placing an entire section of code in a protected, recoverable unit. You can nest transactions and use them to protect buffered updates. Visual FoxPro transactions are available only with tables and views contained in a database.

Wrapping Code Segments

A transaction acts as a wrapper that caches data update operations to memory or to disk, rather than applying those updates directly to the database. The actual database update is performed at the end of the transaction. If for any reason the system cannot perform the update operations on the database, you can roll back the entire transaction and no update operations are performed.

> **Note** Buffered update operations made outside a transaction are ignored within a transaction in the same data session.
```

Commands that Control Transactions

Visual FoxPro provides three commands and one function to manage a transaction.

To	Use
Initiate a transaction	BEGIN TRANSACTION
Determine the current transaction level	TXNLEVEL( )
Reverse all changes made since the most recent BEGIN TRANSACTION statement	ROLLBACK
Lock records, commit to disk all changes made to the tables in the database since the most recent BEGIN TRANSACTION, and then unlock the records	END TRANSACTION

You can use transactions to wrap modifications to tables, structural .cdx files, and memo files associated with tables within a database. Operations involving variables and other objects don't respect transactions; therefore, you cannot roll back or commit such operations.

Note   When using data stored in remote tables, transaction commands control only updates to the data in the local copy of the view cursor; updates to remote base tables are not affected. To enable manual transactions on remote tables use SQLSETPROP( ), and then control the transaction with SQLCOMMIT( ) and SQLROLLBACK( ).

For more information on these commands, see Help.

In general, you should use transactions with record buffers rather than with table buffering, except to wrap TABLEUPDATE( ) calls. If you place a TABLEUPDATE( ) command in a transaction, you can roll back a failed update, address the reason for the failure, and then retry the TABLEUPDATE( ) without losing data. This ensures the update happens as an "all-or-nothing" operation.

Though simple transaction processing provides safe data update operations in normal situations, it doesn't provide total protection against system failures. If power fails or some other system interruption occurs during processing of the END TRANSACTION command, the data update can still fail.

Use the following code template for transactions:

```
BEGIN TRANSACTION
* Update records
IF lSuccess = .F. && an error occurs
   ROLLBACK
ELSE && commit the changes
   * Validate the data
   IF && error occurs
      ROLLBACK
   ELSE
      END TRANSACTION
   ENDIF
ENDIF
```

Using Transactions

The following rules apply to transactions:

- A transaction starts with the BEGIN TRANSACTION command and ends with the END TRANSACTION or ROLLBACK command. An END TRANSACTION statement without a preceding BEGIN TRANSACTION statement generates an error.

- A ROLLBACK statement without a preceding BEGIN TRANSACTION statement generates an error.

- A transaction, once begun, remains in effect until the corresponding END TRANSACTION begins (or until a ROLLBACK command is issued), even across programs and functions, unless the application terminates, which causes a rollback.

- Visual FoxPro uses data cached in the transaction buffer before using disk data for queries on the data involved in transactions. This ensures that the most current data is used.

- If the application terminates during a transaction, all operations roll back.

- A transaction works only in a database container.

- You cannot use the INDEX command if it overwrites an existing index file, or if any .cdx index file is open.

- Transactions are scoped to data sessions.

Transactions exhibit the following locking behaviors:

- Within a transaction, Visual FoxPro imposes a lock at the time a command directly or indirectly calls for it. Any system or user direct or indirect unlock commands are cached until the completion of the transaction by ROLLBACK or END TRANSACTION commands.

- If you use a locking command such as FLOCK( ) or RLOCK( ) within a transaction, the END TRANSACTION statement will not release the lock. In that case, you must explicitly unlock any locks explicitly taken within a transaction. You should also keep transactions containing the FLOCK( ) or RLOCK( ) commands as brief as possible; otherwise, users could be locked out of records for a long time.

Nesting Transactions

Nested transactions provide logical groups of table update operations that are insulated from concurrent processes. BEGIN TRANSACTION...END TRANSACTION pairs need not be in the same function or procedure. The following rules apply to nested transactions:

- You can nest up to five BEGIN TRANSACTION...END TRANSACTION pairs.

- Updates made in a nested transaction aren't committed until the outermost END TRANSACTION is called.

- In nested transactions, an END TRANSACTION only operates on the transaction initiated by the last issued BEGIN TRANSACTION.

- In nested transactions, a ROLLBACK statement only operates on the transaction initiated by the last issued BEGIN TRANSACTION.

- The innermost update in a set of nested transactions on the same data has precedence over all others in the same block of nested transactions.

Notice in the following example that because changes in a nested transaction aren't written to disk but to the transaction buffer, the inner transaction will overwrite the changes made to the same STATUS fields in the earlier transaction:

```
BEGIN TRANSACTION &&  transaction 1
   UPDATE EMPLOYEE ; && first change
      SET STATUS = "Contract" ;
      WHERE EMPID BETWEEN 9001 AND 10000
   BEGIN TRANSACTION &&  transaction 2
      UPDATE EMPLOYEE ;
         SET STATUS = "Exempt" ;
         WHERE HIREDATE > {^1998-01-01}  &&  overwrites
   END TRANSACTION &&  transaction 2
END TRANSACTION       &&  transaction 1
```

The following nested transaction example deletes a customer record and all its related invoices. The transaction will roll back if errors occur during a DELETE command. This example demonstrates grouping table update operations to protect updates from partial completion and to avoid concurrency conflicts.

Example of Modifying Records in Nested Transactions

Code	Comments

`DO WHILE TXNLEVEL( ) > 0`
`   ROLLBACK`
`ENDDO`
	Cleanup from other transactions.

`CLOSE ALL`
`SET MULTILOCKS ON`
`SET EXCLUSIVE OFF`
`OPEN DATABASE test`
`USE mrgtest1`
	Establish environment for buffering.

`CURSORSETPROP('buffering',5)`	Enable optimistic table buffering.
`GO TOP`	
`REPLACE fld1 WITH "changed"`	Change a record.
`SKIP`	
`REPLACE fld1 WITH "another change"`	Change another record.
`MESSAGEBOX("modify first field of both" + ;` `   "records on another machine")`	

(continued)

Example of Modifying Records in Nested Transactions *(continued)*

Code	Comments

```
BEGIN TRANSACTION
lSuccess = TABLEUPDATE(.T.,.F.)
```
Start transaction 1 and try to update all modified records without force.

```
IF lSuccess = .F.
   ROLLBACK
   AERROR(aErrors)
   DO CASE
   CASE aErrors[1,1] = 1539
   ...
   CASE aErrors[1,1] = 1581
   ...
   CASE aErrors[1,1] = 1582
   CASE aErrors[1,1] = 1585
      nNextModified = getnextmodified(0)
      DO WHILE nNextModified <> 0
         GO nNextModified
         RLOCK()
         FOR nField = 1 to FCOUNT()
            cField = FIELD(nField)


            if OLDVAL(cField) <> CURVAL(cField)


            nResult = MESSAGEBOX;
            ("Data was changed " + ;
            "by another user—keep"+ ;
            "changes?", 4+48, ;
            "Modified Record")
            IF nResult = 7
               TABLEREVERT(.F.)
               UNLOCK record nNextModified
            ENDIF
            EXIT
         ENDIF
      ENDFOR
   ENDDO

   BEGIN TRANSACTION
   TABLEUPDATE(.T.,.T.)
   END TRANSACTION
   UNLOCK
```

If the update failed, roll back the transaction.
Get the error from AERROR( ).
Determine the cause of the failure.
If a trigger failed, handle it.

If a field doesn't accept null values, handle it.
If a field rule was violated, handle it.

If a record was changed by another user, locate the first modified record.
Loop through all modified records, starting with the first record.
Lock each record to guarantee that you can update.
Check each field for any changes.

Check the buffered value against the value on disk, and then present a dialog box to the user.

If user responded "No," revert the one record and unlock it.

Break out of the "FOR nField..." loop.

Get the next modified record.

Start transaction 2 and update all non-reverted records with force.
End transaction 2.
Release the lock.

Example of Modifying Records in Nested Transactions   *(continued)*

Code	Comments
```CASE aErrors[1,1] = 109```	If the record is in use by another user, handle it.
```...```	
```CASE aErrors[1,1] = 1583```	
```...```	If a row rule was violated, handle it.
```CASE aErrors[1,1] = 1884```	
```...```	If there was a unique index violation, handle it.
```OTHERWISE```	
``` MESSAGEBOX("Unknown error "+;```	Otherwise, present a dialog box to the user.
``` "message: " + STR(aErrors[1,1]))```	
``` ENDCASE```	
```ELSE```	
``` END TRANSACTION```	End transaction 1.
```ENDIF```	

Protecting Remote Updates

Transactions can protect you from system-generated errors during data updates on remote tables. The following example uses a transaction to wrap data-writing operations to a remote table.

Example of a Transaction on a Remote Table

Code	Comment
```hConnect = CURSORGETPROP('connecthandle')```	Get the connect handle
```SQLSETPROP(hConnect, 'transmode',```	and enable manual transactions.
```DB_TRANSMANUAL)```	
```BEGIN TRANSACTION```	Begin the manual transaction.
```lSuccess = TABLEUPDATE(.T.,.F.)```	Try to update all records without force.
```IF lSuccess = .F.```	If the update failed,
``` SQLROLLBACK (hConnect)```	roll back the transaction on
``` ROLLBACK```	the connection for the cursor.
``` AERROR(aErrors)```	Get the error from AERROR( ).
``` DO CASE```	
``` CASE aErrors[1,1] = 1539```	If a trigger failed, handle it.
``` ...```	
``` CASE aErrors[1,1] = 1581```	If a field doesn't accept null values, handle it.
``` ...```	
``` CASE aErrors[1,1] = 1582```	If a field rule was violated, handle it.
``` ...```	

(continued)

Example of a Transaction on a Remote Table   *(continued)*

Code	Comment

```
CASE aErrors[1,1] = 1585
   nNextModified = GETNEXTMODIFIED(0)
   DO WHILE nNextModified <> 0
      GO nNextModified


      FOR nField = 1 to FCOUNT()
         cField = FIELD(nField)
         IF OLDVAL(cField) <> CURVAL(cField)
            nResult = MESSAGEBOX;
            ("Data has been changed ;
            by another user. ;
            Keep changes?",4+48,;
            "Modified Record")
            IF nResult = 7
               TABLEREVERT(.F.)
            ENDIF
            EXIT
         ENDIF
      ENDFOR
      nNextModified = ;
      GETNEXTMODIFIED(nNextModified)
   ENDDO
   TABLEUPDATE(.T.,.T.)
   SQLCOMMIT(hConnect)

CASE aErrors[1,1] = 109
      * Handle the error

CASE aErrors[1,1] = 1583
      * Handle the error

CASE aErrors[1,1] = 1884
      * Handle the error

OTHERWISE
      * Handle generic errors.
   MESSAGEBOX("Unknown error message:" ;
      + STR(aErrors[1,1]))
ENDCASE

ELSE
   SQLCOMMIT(hConnect)
   END TRANSACTION
ENDIF
```

If a record was changed by another user, handle it.

Loop through all modified records, starting with the first record.

Check each field for any changes.

Check the buffered value against the value on disk, and then present a dialog box to the user.

If user responded "No," revert the one record.

Break out of the "FOR nField..." loop.

Get the next modified record.

Update all non-reverted records with force and issue a commit.

Error 109 indicates that the record is in use by another user.

Error 1583 indicates that a row rule was violated.

Error 1884 indicates that the uniqueness of the index was violated.

Present a dialog box to the user.

End of error handling.

If all errors were handled and the entire transaction was successful, issue a commit and end the transaction.

Managing Performance

Once you have a working multi-user application, you can use the following suggestions to improve performance:

- Place temporary files on a local drive.

- Choose between sorting and indexing files.

- Schedule exclusive access to files.

- Time the locking of files.

Place Temporary Files on a Local Drive

Visual FoxPro creates its temporary files in the Windows default Temp directory. Text editing sessions can also temporarily create a backup copy of the file being edited (a .bak file).

If local workstations have hard drives with plenty of free space, you can improve performance by placing these temporary work files on the local drive or in a RAM drive. Redirecting these files to a local drive or a RAM drive increases performance by reducing access to the network drive.

You can specify an alternate location for these files by including the EDITWORK, SORTWORK, PROGWORK and TMPFILES statements in your Config.fpw configuration file.

Choose between Sorting and Indexing Files

When the data contained in a table is relatively static, processing sorted tables sequentially without an order set improves performance. This doesn't mean that sorted tables cannot or should not take advantage of index files — the SEEK command, which requires an index, is incomparable for locating records quickly. However, once you locate a record with SEEK, you can turn ordering off.

Schedule Exclusive Access to Files

Commands that run when no other users require access to the data, such as overnight updates, can benefit by opening the data files for exclusive use. When files are open for exclusive use, performance improves because Visual FoxPro doesn't need to test the status of record or file locks.

Time the Locking of Files

To reduce contention between users for write access to a table or record, shorten the amount of time a record or table is locked. You can do this by locking the record only after it's edited rather than during editing. Optimistic row buffering gives you the shortest lock time.

For more information on improving performance in your client/server applications, see Chapter 22, "Optimizing Client/Server Performance," in this book.

Managing Updates with Views

You can use the update conflict management technology built into Visual FoxPro views to handle multi-user access to data. Views control what is sent to the base tables underlying the view by using the WhereType property. You can set this property for both local and remote views. The WhereType property provides four settings:

- DB_KEY

- DB_KEYANDUPDATABLE

- DB_KEYANDMODIFIED (the default)

- DB_KEYANDTIMESTAMP

By choosing one of these four settings, you control how Visual FoxPro builds the WHERE clause for the SQL Update statement sent to the view's base tables. You can choose the setting you want using the Update Criteria tab of the View Designer, or you can use DBSETPROP( ) to set the WhereType for a view definition. To change the WhereType setting for an active view cursor, use CURSORSETPROP( ).

For example, suppose you have a simple remote view based on the Customer table that includes seven fields: cust_id, company, phone, fax, contact, title, and timestamp. The primary key for your view is cust_id.

The Update Criteria tab displays the updatable fields in your view.

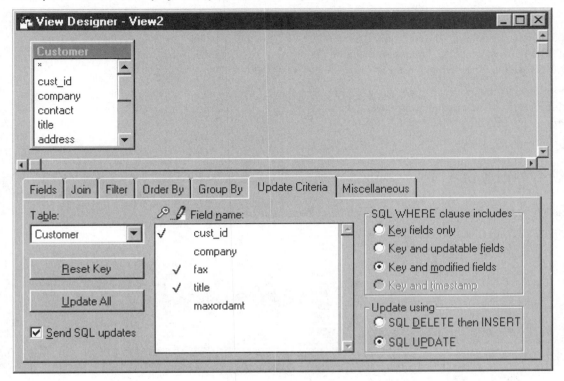

You've made only two fields updatable: `contact_name` and `contact_title`. You want the user to be able to change the company contact and their title from the view. However, if other facts about the company change, such as the company address, you want the changes to go through a coordinator who'll identify the impact of the changes on your company, such as whether the sales region for the customer will change. Now that your view has been set up to send updates, you can choose the WhereType according to your preferences.

Now suppose that you change the name in the `contact` field for a customer, but you don't change the value in the other updatable field, `title`. Given this example, the following section discusses how the WhereType setting would impact the WHERE clause that Visual FoxPro builds to send the new contact name to the base tables.

Comparing the Key Field Only

The least restrictive update uses the DB_KEY setting. The WHERE Clause used to update remote tables consists of only the primary key field specified with the KeyField or KeyFieldList property. Unless the value in the primary key field has been changed or deleted in the base table since you retrieved the record, the update goes through.

In the case of the previous example, Visual FoxPro would prepare an update statement with a WHERE clause that compares the value in the `cust_id` field against the `cust_id` field in the base table row:

```
WHERE OLDVAL(customer.cust_id) = CURVAL(customer_remote_view.cust_id)
```

When the update statement is sent to the base table, only the base table's key field is verified.

The key field in your view is compared against its base table counterpart.

```
WHERE OLDVAL(customer.cust_id) =
      CURVAL(customer_remote_view.cust_id) ;
```

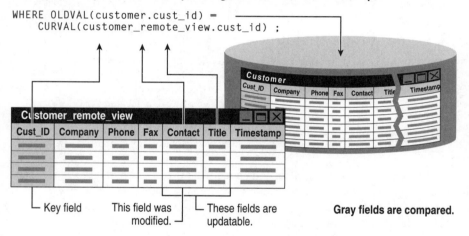

Key field   This field was   These fields are   **Gray fields are compared.**
               modified.   updatable.

Comparing the Key Field and Fields Modified in the View

The DB_KEYANDMODIFIED setting, the default, is slightly more restrictive than DB_KEY. DB_KEYANDMODIFIED compares only the key field and any updatable fields you've modified in the view against their base table counterparts. If you modify a field in the view, but the field isn't updatable, the fields are not compared to the base table data.

The WHERE clause used to update base tables consists of the primary fields specified with the KeyFieldList property and any other fields that are modified in the view. In the case of the previous example, Visual FoxPro would prepare an update statement that compares the values in the `cust_id` field because it is the key field, and the `contact` field because the contact name has been changed. Even though the `title` field is updatable, `title` is not included in the update statement because we haven't modified it.

The key and modified fields in your view are compared against their base table counterparts.

```
WHERE OLDVAL(customer.cust_id) =
    CURVAL(customer_remote_view.cust_id) ;
AND OLDVAL(customer.contact) =
    CURVAL(customer_remote_view.contact) ;
```

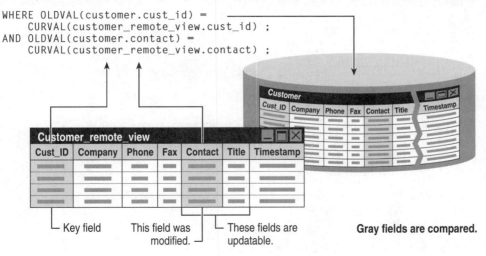

— Key field   This field was modified. —   — These fields are updatable.   **Gray fields are compared.**

Comparing the Key Field and All Updatable Fields

The DB_KEYANDUPDATABLE setting compares the key field and any updatable fields (whether modified or not) in your view against their base table counterparts. If the field is updatable, even if you haven't changed it in the view, if anyone else has changed that field in the base table, the update fails.

The WHERE clause used to update base tables consists of the primary fields specified with the Key Field or KeyFieldList property and any other fields that are updatable. In the case of the example, Visual FoxPro would prepare an update statement that compares the values in the cust_id, contact, and title fields against the same fields in the base table row.

All the updatable fields in your view are compared against their base table counterparts.

```
WHERE OLDVAL(customer.cust_id) =
    CURVAL(customer_remote_view.cust_id) ;
AND OLDVAL(customer.contact) =
    CURVAL(customer_remote_view.contact) ;
AND OLDVAL(customer.title) =
    CURVAL(customer_remote_view.title)
```

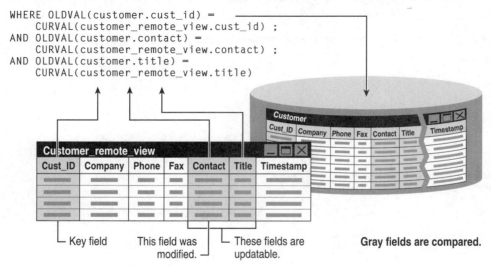

Key field   This field was   These fields are   **Gray fields are compared.**
                modified.   updatable.

Comparing the Timestamp for All Fields in the Base Table Record

The DB_KEYANDTIMESTAMP is the most restrictive type of update, and is only available if the base table has a timestamp column. Visual FoxPro compares the current timestamp on the base table record against the timestamp at the time the data was fetched into the view. If any field in the base table's record has changed, even if it's not a field you're trying to change, or even a field in your view, the update fails.

In the case of the example, Visual FoxPro prepares an update statement that compares the values in the cust_id field and the value in the timestamp field against those fields in the base table row.

The timestamp for your view's record is compared against the timestamp on the base table record.

```
WHERE OLDVAL(customer.cust_id) =
    CURVAL(customer_remote_view.cust_id) ;
AND OLDVAL(customer.timestamp) =
    CURVAL(customer_remote_view.timestamp)
```

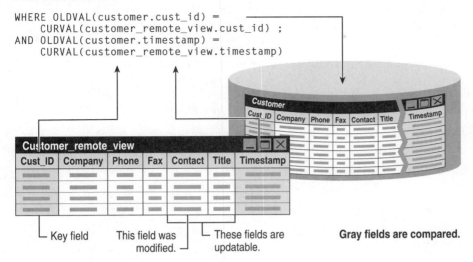

Key field — This field was modified. — These fields are updatable. — **Gray fields are compared.**

In order to successfully update data using the DB_KEYANDTIMESTAMP setting with a multi-table view, you must include the timestamp field in your view for each table that is updatable. For example, if you have three tables in a view and want to update only two of them, and you choose the DB_KEYANDTIMESTAMP setting, you must bring down the timestamp fields from the two updatable tables into your result set. You can also use logical values in the CompareMemo property to determine whether memo fields are included in conflict detection.

Managing Conflicts

Whether you choose buffering, transactions, or views, you must manage conflicts during the update process.

Managing Buffering Conflicts

You can make data update operations more efficient by carefully choosing how and when to open, buffer, and lock data in a multi-user environment. You should limit the time a record or table is subject to access conflicts. Still, you must anticipate and manage the inevitable conflicts that result. A *conflict* occurs when one user tries to lock a record or table that's currently locked by another user. Two users cannot lock the same record or table at the same time.

Your application should contain a routine to manage these conflicts. If your application doesn't have a conflict routine, the system can lock up. A *deadlock* occurs when one user has locked a record or a table and tries to lock another record that's locked by a second user who, in turn, is trying to lock the record that's locked by the first user. While such occurrences are rare, the longer that a record or table is locked, the greater the chance of deadlock.

Trapping Errors

Designing a multi-user application or adding network support to a single-user system requires that you deal with collisions and trap for errors. Using Visual FoxPro record and table buffers simplifies some of this work.

If you attempt to lock a record or table already locked by another user, Visual FoxPro returns an error message. You can use SET REPROCESS to automatically deal with unsuccessful lock attempts. This command, in combination with an ON ERROR routine and the RETRY command, enables you to continue or cancel the lock attempts.

The following example demonstrates automatic reprocessing of a failed operation, using SET REPROCESS.

Using SET REPROCESS and ON ERROR to Manage User Collisions

Code	Comment
```ON ERROR DO err_fix WITH ERROR(),MESSAGE()```	This routine runs if an error occurs.
```SET EXCLUSIVE OFF```	Open the files non-exclusively.
```SET REPROCESS TO AUTOMATIC```	Reprocessing of unsuccessful locks is automatic.
```USE customer```	Open the table.
```IF !FILE('cus_copy.dbf')```	
``` COPY TO cus_copy```	Create the APPEND FROM table if needed.
```ENDIF```	
```DO app_blank```	The main routine starts here. These commands are
```DO rep_next```	examples of codes that could be executed in the
```DO rep_all```	course of your program.
```DO rep_curr```	
```DO add_recs```	
```ON ERROR```	The main routine ends here.
```PROCEDURE app_blank```	Routine to append a blank record.
``` APPEND BLANK```	
```RETURN```	
```ENDPROC```	
```PROCEDURE rep_next```	Routine to replace data in the current record.
``` REPLACE NEXT 1 contact WITH ;```	
``` PROPER(contact)```	
```RETURN```	
```ENDPROC```	

Using SET REPROCESS and ON ERROR to Manage User Collisions   *(continued)*

Code	Comment

<pre>PROCEDURE rep_all
   REPLACE ALL contact WITH ;
      PROPER(contact)
   GO TOP
RETURN
ENDPROC</pre>
	Routine to replace data in all records.

<pre>PROCEDURE rep_curr
   REPLACE contact WITH PROPER(contact)
RETURN
ENDPROC</pre>
	Routine to replace data in the current record.

<pre>PROCEDURE add_recs
   APPEND FROM cus_copy
RETURN
ENDPROC</pre>
	Routine to append records from another file.

The following example demonstrates an error procedure that starts when the user presses ESC.

Error Handling Using the ESC Key

Code	Comment

<pre>PROCEDURE err_fix
   PARAMETERS errnum, msg</pre>
	This program is called when an error is encountered and the user escapes from the wait process.

<pre>DO CASE</pre>	Figure out what kind of error this is. Is it "File is in use by another?"
<pre> CASE errnum = 108 line1 = "File cannot be locked." line2 = "Try again later..."</pre>	
<pre> CASE errnum = 109 .OR. errnum = 130 line1 = "Record cannot be locked." line2 = "Try again later."</pre>	Or "Record is in use by another?"
<pre> OTHERWISE line1 = msg + " " line2 = ; "See your system administrator."</pre>	Or is it unknown?

<pre>ENDCASE
=MESSAGEBOX(line1 + line2, 48, "Error!")
RETURN</pre>
	Display the error message in a dialog box with an exclamation point and an OK button.

Detecting and Resolving Conflicts

During data update operations, especially in shared environments, you might want to determine which fields have changed or what the original or the current values are in changed fields. Visual FoxPro buffering and the GETFLDSTATE( ), GETNEXTMODIFIED( ), OLDVAL( ) and CURVAL( ) functions, enable you to determine which field has changed, find the changed data, and compare the current, original, and edited values so you can decide how to handle an error or conflict.

To detect a change in a field

- After an update operation, use the GETFLDSTATE( ) function.

GETFLDSTATE( ) works on unbuffered data; however, this function is even more effective when you've enabled record buffering. For instance, use GETFLDSTATE( ) in the code of a Skip button on a form. When you move the record pointer, Visual FoxPro checks the status of all fields in the record as in the following example:

```
lModified = .F.
FOR nFieldNum = 1 TO FCOUNT( ) && Check all fields
if GETFLDSTATE(nFieldNum) = 2   && Modified
lModified = .T.
EXIT && Insert update/Save routine here.
ENDIF && See the next example
ENDFOR
```

To detect and locate a changed record in buffered data

- Use the GETNEXTMODIFIED( ) function.

GETNEXTMODIFIED( ), with zero as a parameter, finds the first modified record. If another user makes changes to the buffered table, any changes encountered by a TABLEUPDATE( ) command in your buffer will cause conflicts. You can evaluate the conflicting values and resolve them using the CURVAL( ), OLDVAL( ), and MESSAGEBOX( ) functions. CURVAL( ) returns the current value of the record on disk, while OLDVAL( ) returns the value of the record at the time it was buffered.

To determine the original value of a buffered field

- Use the OLDVAL( ) function.

OLDVAL( ) returns the value of a buffered field.

To determine the current value of a buffered field on disk

- Use the CURVAL( ) function.

CURVAL( ) returns the current value on disk of a buffered field before any edits were performed.

You can create an error-handling procedure that compares the current and original values, enabling you to determine whether to commit the current change or to accept an earlier change to data in a shared environment.

For more information on these functions, see Help.

The following example uses GETNEXTMODIFIED( ), CURVAL( ), and OLDVAL( ) to provide the user with an informed choice in an update operation. This example continues from detection of the first modified record and might be contained in an Update or Save button on a form.

Click Event Code for an Update or Save Button

Code	Comment
```DO WHILE GETNEXTMODIFIED(nCurRec) <> 0```	Loop through buffer.
``` GO nCurRec```	
``` RLOCK( )```	Lock the modified record.
``` FOR nField = 1 TO FCOUNT(cAlias)```	Look for conflict.
``` cField = FIELD(nField)```	
``` IF OLDVAL(cField) <> CURVAL(cField)```	Compare the original value to the current value on the disk, and then ask the user what to do about the conflict.
``` nResult = MESSAGEBOX("Data was ;```	
``` changed by another user. ;```	
``` Keep changes?", 4+48+0, ;```	
``` "Modified Record")```	
``` IF nResult = 7```	If the user selects "No," revert this record, and then remove the lock.
``` TABLEREVERT(.F.)```	
``` UNLOCK RECORD nCurRec```	
``` ENDIF```	
``` ENDIF```	
``` ENDFOR```	
``` nCurRec = GETNEXTMODIFIED(nCurRec)```	Find the next modified record.
```ENDDO```	
```TABLEUPDATE(.T., .T.)```	Force update to all records.

Detecting Conflicts Using Memo Fields

You can use the CompareMemo property to control when memo fields are used to detect update conflicts. This view and cursor property determines whether memo fields (types M or G) are included in the update WHERE clause. The default setting, True (.T.), means that memo fields are included in the WHERE clause. If you set this property to False (.F), memo fields don't participate in the update WHERE clause, regardless of the settings of UpdateType.

Optimistic conflict detection on Memo fields is disabled when CompareMemo is set to False. For conflict detection on memo values, set CompareMemo to True (.T.).

Rules for Managing Conflicts

Managing conflicts encountered in multi-user environments can require extensive and repetitive code. A complete conflict management routine does the following:

- Detects a conflict.
- Identifies the nature and location of the conflict.
- Provides enough information so that the user can intelligently resolve the conflict.

For an example of a conflict management routine, see the data checker class in Samples.vcx, located in the Visual Studio ...\Samples\Vfp98\Classes directory. Just add the class to a form and call the CheckConflicts method before any operation that writes buffered data to the table, for example moving the record pointer if you're using row buffering, closing a table, or issuing TABLEUPDATE( ).

CHAPTER 18

Developing International Applications

To move into the world market, you must design your Visual FoxPro applications so that they're as effective internationally as domestically. This chapter describes how to use the international features of Visual FoxPro to produce applications for selected locales. A locale is a geographic area described by its culture, language, and conventions.

This chapter discusses:

- Planning an International Application
- Designing the Interface
- Entering International Data
- Working with Code Pages
- Sorting Data in International Applications
- Working with Double-Byte Character Sets
- Creating or Modifying Programs
- Managing Files in an International Application

Planning an International Application

Preparing an international application usually involves three steps: creating data, writing code, and designing a user interface. Before you take these steps, however, you need to consider the following questions:

- What data is acceptable?
- How do you write code for an international application?
- What should you consider when designing a user interface?

The following sections address these questions and pose others you need to consider before you prepare your application.

Tip You can reduce the cost of developing an international application and bring it to market more quickly by designing it as an international application initially rather than modifying it for international use later on.

Preparing the International Data

To create international data for an application, you can enter it manually, import it from other applications, or append it to existing files and memo fields. For details about importing and appending data, see Chapter 9, "Importing and Exporting Data," in the *User's Guide*.

What Data Is Acceptable?

To decide what data is acceptable, first consider the locales in which the application will be used. The locales will determine the cultural content of the data as well as the languages in which the data is prepared.

In addition, the languages will affect the code page with which the data is prepared. A code page is a character set that a computer uses to display data properly, often to handle *international characters*. International characters include characters that have diacritical marks. Diacritical marks are placed over, under, or through letters to indicate sound changes from the unmarked form. The most common diacritical marks are the grave accent (` as in à), acute accent (´ as in á), circumflex (^ as in â), tilde (~ as in ã), umlaut (¨ as in ä), ring (° as in å), and slash (/ as in ø), all used in conjunction with vowels.

Ordinarily, data is automatically marked with the appropriate code page when you work with it. However, if you manually assign a code page to a table, or if you otherwise cause the code page to change, users might not recognize some or all of the data displayed. For details about code pages, see "Working with Code Pages" later in this chapter.

Some languages, such as Chinese, Korean, and Japanese, use *DBCS* (double-byte character sets) to represent their data. If your application might run in these environments, you might need to use special string-handling functions and collation sequences for the application to work properly. For details about working in DBCS environments, see "Working with Double-Byte Character Sets" later in this chapter.

How Do You Write Code?

An application consists of a user interface component and an application component. The user interface component contains graphics, text strings, and settings related to various locales, such as dates, currencies, numeric values, and separators. The application component contains the code that is run for all locales, including code that processes the strings and graphics used in the user interface.

The components of an application

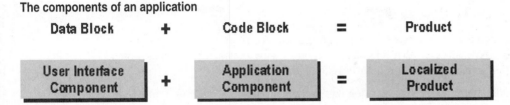

When designing your application, keep the application and user interface components separate, because independent components make the application easier to localize and maintain. For example, with separate components, you don't have to browse the source code to localize interface elements. For more information about writing code, see "Creating or Modifying Programs," later in this chapter.

How Do You Design a User Interface?

The menus, forms, controls, toolbars, and bitmaps used in the user interface must serve the locales for which you're designing the application. For example, if you design the application for users in Germany and France, dialog boxes must be large enough to display instructions properly when the instructions are localized in German and French. In addition, the images used in icons and bitmaps must be culturally correct so that they're understood in the target locales. For more information about designing user interfaces, see "Designing the Interface" later in this chapter.

Testing the Application

To test an international application, you need to check the country and language dependencies of the locale for which the application is designed. Testing involves checking the application's data and user interface to ensure that they conform to the locale's standards for date and time, numeric values, currency, list separators, and measurements.

Designing the Interface

Because text tends to increase when you localize an application, be careful when designing the following user interface components:

- Application messages
- Menus and forms
- Icons and bitmaps

Creating Application Messages

When you create messages in your application, English text strings are usually shorter than equivalent text strings in other languages. The following table shows the additional average growth for strings, based on their initial length.

English length (in characters)	Additional growth for localized strings
1 to 4	100%
5 to 10	80%
11 to 20	60%
21 to 30	40%
31 to 50	20%
over 50	10%

Designing Menus and Forms

As with messages, menus and forms can grow when the application is localized. For instance, consider the following forms, which are part of an Automated Teller Machine sample application. The first figure shows the English form, and the second figure shows the Spanish equivalent. You can see that extra space was allocated for text to increase in the form.

Tip   If you allow room for text to increase in an interface, localizers need less time to resize controls and to redesign the interface.

Text needs more room when localized.

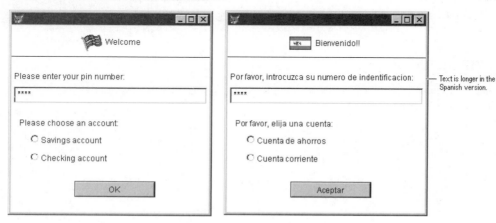

In menus and forms, avoid crowding status bars. Also, avoid abbreviations, because they might not exist in other languages.

Using Icons and Bitmaps

Used properly, icons and bitmaps can be an important part of a user interface. However, the meaning of icons and bitmaps can be more ambiguous than the meaning of words. Therefore, consider the following guidelines when using icons and bitmaps:

- Use images that are universally recognized. For example, use an envelope to represent mail, but don't use a mailbox because it's not a universal symbol.

- Use culturally sensitive images. For example, avoid using images of religious symbols and animals.

- Avoid using text in bitmaps, because text growth can become a problem, just as it can in other parts of the interface.

- Avoid jargon, slang, humor, extravagant language, and ethnic stereotypes.

- Use ToolTips to help explain icons, which have the added advantage of expanding automatically to the size of the text they display.

- If you portray men and women, ensure that their gender roles are suitable, and that gestures and images of the human body are appropriate in the target culture.

- Use color appropriately. For example, avoid using color combinations associated with national flags or political movements.

If you're not sure whether an icon or bitmap is appropriate, consult someone in the locale for which you're designing the application.

Entering International Data

An important aspect of developing international applications is knowing how to enter data into your application. Data can come into your application in two ways:

- Users enter the data.

- You or your users import the data from existing files.

The following sections discuss these two methods.

Entering International Characters

You can enter international characters into Visual FoxPro using your keyboard. The exact method you use depends on the language you're working with. In single-byte character environments, you can enter the characters directly, or by pressing a combination of keys on the keyboard. On the other hand, DBCS environments often provide an Input Method Editor (IME), which is an application you can use to enter characters.

Entering Characters Using the Keyboard

With an international keyboard, you can display international characters by simply pressing the keys dedicated to those characters. If your keyboard doesn't have keys for international characters, you can enter such characters by using the character map provided with Windows or by pressing the ALT key in conjunction with keys on the numeric keypad.

The easiest way to enter an international character is to copy it from the character map. In Windows 95, the character map is available from the Accessories menu.

Alternatively, you can enter an international character by pressing ALT combined with a four-digit number beginning with zero that you enter from the numeric keypad.

Note You cannot enter international characters in FoxFont. For example, if you open the Command window, switch to FoxFont, and then press a dedicated key, the result isn't the character on the key. For best results, avoid FoxFont in international applications.

To create an international character

- Copy the character from the character map, and then paste it into your document.

  – or –

  Hold down ALT and then type a zero followed by the appropriate three-digit ASCII code.

    Tip The status bar on the character map shows the key combination that corresponds to each character selected on the map.

For instance, to type ö (ANSI code 246), press NUM LOCK on the numeric keypad, and then press ALT+0246. Be sure to use a standard Windows font — not FoxFont or FoxPrint.

  Troubleshooting If characters don't transport correctly, see if you're using FoxFont. For example, FoxFont is the default for user-defined windows created with DEFINE WINDOW (if the FONT clause is omitted). Be sure to use the FONT clause to specify a font other than the standard Windows font when creating user-defined windows so that international characters display correctly.

Entering Characters Using an IME

If you're working in an IME environment, you can use an Input Method Editor to enter characters into Visual FoxPro. The IME is an application provided with your environment that allows you to type characters on the keyboard to display a selection of international characters and then choose the specific character you want. For example, an IME for Chinese might allow you to enter a Pinyin representation of a Chinese word and then display a list of characters that match the representation. When you select the character you want, the IME pastes it into Visual FoxPro.

You can control when Visual FoxPro displays an IME by setting the IMEMode property or calling the IMESTATUS( ) function. If you turn the IME window on, Visual FoxPro automatically displays the IME when you're editing in a system window such as the Browse or Edit windows. If you turn the IME window off, you can invoke the IME by pressing the appropriate keys on your keyboard.

Appending and Copying International Data

If you're importing or copying data from delimited files using the APPEND FROM or COPY TO commands, you can specify what character is being used in the file to separate fields. For example, it's common in many European countries to use a semicolon (;) as a field delimiter, whereas the common delimiters in the United States are comma (,), TAB, or SPACE.

To import or copy files and specify a delimiter, add the DELIMITED WITH CHARACTER clause to the APPEND FROM or COPY TO commands:

```
COPY TO mytxt.txt DELIMITED WITH _ WITH CHARACTER ";"
```

For more details, see APPEND FROM and COPY TO in Help.

Working with Code Pages

Data stored in Visual FoxPro is often tagged with a *code page*, which is a table of characters and corresponding numbers in memory that Windows uses to display data properly. For example, if you enter the letter C in a .dbf file, the letter is stored on your hard disk as the number 67. When you open the file, Visual FoxPro determines its code page, inspects the code page to find the character corresponding to the number 67, and then displays the character (C) on your monitor.

Code pages correspond roughly to different alphabets. For example, Windows supplies code pages for English, German, Scandinavian languages, and so on. By using a different code pages, applications can properly display characters from these different alphabets.

Understanding Code Pages in Visual FoxPro

Visual FoxPro displays data using one code page. By default, this is the current code page used by Windows. However, you can override the Windows code page by specifying an alternative code page in your configuration file (you must specify a valid code page).

Tables in Visual FoxPro are tagged with the code page that was in use when the table was created. When you use the table, Visual FoxPro checks the code page for the table against the current code page. If they match, Visual FoxPro displays the data as is. If there is no code page for the table (for example, the table was created in an earlier version of FoxPro), Visual FoxPro prompts you for a code page and then marks the file with it.

If the table code page does not match the system code page, Visual FoxPro attempts to translate characters from the table code page into the current one. For example, if you're using Visual FoxPro and the current system code page is the English code page, the character ü is represented by ANSI value 252. If the code page for the table represents the ü character as ANSI value 219, Visual FoxPro translates all instances of ANSI value 219 into ANSI 252 so that they display properly.

Code page translation doesn't work perfectly in all instances, because code pages usually contain characters that are not represented one-for-one in other code pages. For example, you cannot map data that contains the MS-DOS line-drawing characters into Windows, because the Windows code pages don't contain line-drawing characters. Similarly, you cannot translate data created in the Russian code page into an English code page, because there isn't a one-to-one correspondence between the alphabets for these languages. Finally, Visual FoxPro might not contain a character translation map for a particular code page. In that case, the data is displayed with no code page translation. (Visual FoxPro does not display an error to indicate that no code page translation is occurring.) Any of these situations can cause some characters to display improperly.

If you want to create an application for a specific locale, you can avoid code page translation problems by creating the application's components using the code page designed for that locale and environment. For example, to create an application for use in Russia, you should use code page 1251, 866, or 10007 for users in the Windows, MS-DOS, or Macintosh environments, respectively. For a complete list, search for "Code Pages Supported By Visual FoxPro" in Help.

If you need to enter some characters not represented by keys on your keyboard, you can enter these characters using ALT in conjunction with keys on the numeric keypad. However, remember that the same key combination in different environments often displays different results. For example, if you enter ALT+0182 with code page 1252 in Visual FoxPro, you see a paragraph symbol. In contrast, if you enter ALT+0182 with code page 437 in FoxPro for MS-DOS, you see a graphic character with a double vertical line meeting a single horizontal line.

Although Visual FoxPro supports many code pages, only a few are used often. With Visual FoxPro for Windows, for example, English-speaking users typically use code page 1252, while in Visual FoxPro for Macintosh, English-speaking users typically use code page 10000. However, in FoxPro for MS-DOS, English-speaking users typically use code page 437.

When working with code pages, be sure to test that the user interface and data display correctly by using the code page designed for a particular locale. If you see unexpected characters on the screen, check the underlying code page.

Specifying the Code Page of a .dbf Files

When you create .dbf files, Visual FoxPro automatically gives them code page marks so that you can tell which code pages they use. However, if you use .dbf files from previous versions of FoxPro, they might not have code page marks.

You can determine whether a .dbf file has a code page mark by using the CPDBF( ) function after opening the file or by having Visual FoxPro check when you open the file.

To check for code page marks automatically

1. From the **Tools** menu, choose **Options**.

2. Select the **Data** tab.

3. Set the **Prompt for code page** check box, if it's not already set.

    To save this setting for future sessions of Visual FoxPro, choose **Set as Default**.

    > **Tip**   Instead of setting the **Prompt for code page** check box, you can use the SET CPDIALOG command to check for code pages. For details, search for SET CPDIALOG in Help.

If a file doesn't have a code page mark, you must add a mark, as described in the following section.

Adding Code Page Marks

If you use a .dbf file from a previous version of FoxPro, the file might not have a code page mark; without such a mark, the file might not display properly. If automatic code page checking is enabled, when you open the file you can tell if it has a code page mark. If it doesn't have one, you can add one.

To manually add a code page mark to a .dbf file

1. Ensure automatic code page checking is in effect (see the previous procedure).

2. Open the file.

    If the file doesn't have a code page mark, the Code Page dialog box appears.

The Code Page dialog box

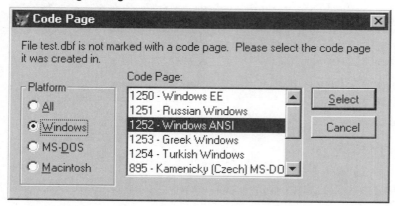

3. Choose the appropriate code page.

4. View the file to see if you assigned the proper code page.

    If you can't see some of the data, or if you can't recognize some of it, the code page is not correct.

5. If the code page is incorrect, remove the code page mark by using the CPZERO program in the Visual FoxPro Tools\Cpzero directory. For details, see "Removing Code Page Marks" later in this chapter.

6. Repeat this procedure until the code page is correct.

    Note   Text files such as program (.prg) and query (.qpr) files don't have code page marks. This means that you can't tell which code pages the files use. However, if you include such files in a project, the project can keep a record of the code pages used. For details, see "Specifying the Code Page of a Text File" later in this chapter.

Removing Code Page Marks

If a .dbf file doesn't display properly, it might have the wrong code page mark. You can remove the code page mark with the CPZERO program located in Tools\Cpzero. Running CPZERO sets the code page to 0, meaning none. For more details, search for CPZERO in Help.

To remove a code page mark

*   Run CPZERO using the following syntax:

    DO CPZERO WITH "*filename*", 0

    Note   When you remove the code page mark of a .dbf file, the data in the file doesn't change. To change the code page of the data, you must mark the file with the proper code page. For details, see "Adding Code Page Marks" earlier in this chapter.

Changing Code Page Marks

You can change the code page of a .dbf file by removing its code page mark and then adding a new one, by copying the file to another file, or by using the CPZERO program.

To change the code page of a .dbf file by copying the file

- Use the COPY TO command, specifying the target code page with the AS clause. (To set the code page to the current system code page, omit the AS clause.)

  For example, to copy Test.dbf to Test866.dbf, while changing the code page to 866, use the following commands:

  ```
  USE TEST.DBF
  COPY TO TEST866.DBF AS 866
  ```

When the COPY TO completes, the data in the resulting file will have the new code page. For details, search for COPY TO in Help.

To change a code page mark using CPZERO

- Run CPZERO using the following syntax:

  DO CPZERO WITH "*filename*", *newCodePage*

  Note   Some characters cannot be translated between code pages successfully. In addition, some code page translations aren't supported by Visual FoxPro. Always check the results of a code page change to be sure that your data has been translated successfully.

Specifying the Code Page of a Text File

If you forget the code page of a text file that's not part of a project, you cannot determine the code page, because a text file doesn't have a code page mark as .dbf files have. The best way to remember the code page of a text file is to add the file to a project.

To specify the code page of a text file

1. Open the Project Manager.

2. Select the text file whose code page you want to specify.

3. From the **Project** menu, choose **Project Info**.

4. In the **Project Information** dialog box, click the **Files** tab.

5. Right-click the selected file.

6. From the submenu, choose **Code Page**.

Visual FoxPro displays the **Code Page** dialog box.

7. Choose the appropriate code page.

Visual FoxPro displays the available code pages.

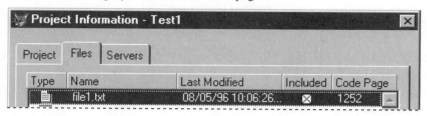

If you know the code page of a text file, you can specify it by using the AS clause of the appropriate Visual FoxPro command. For files you want to import or append, you can specify the code page in the IMPORT or APPEND commands. For query, program, and other text files already on your computer, you can change the code page using the MODIFY QUERY, MODIFY COMMAND, and MODIFY FILE commands. For details about these commands, see the corresponding Help topics.

If you're not sure which code page to apply, substitute the GETCP( ) function for the code page number in the command. GETCP( ) displays the Code Page dialog box, allowing you to select the appropriate code page. For details, see the GETCP( ) and SET CPDIALOG topics in Help.

Note   Some characters cannot be translated between code pages successfully. In addition, some code page translations aren't supported by Visual FoxPro. Always check the results of a code page change to be sure that your data has been translated successfully.

Determining the Code Page of a Project File

After adding a file to a project, you can determine its code page. The method you use depends on whether the file is a table (.dbf file) or a text file.

To determine the code page of a text file

1. Open the Project Manager.

2. Under **Other**, select the text file whose code page you want to know.

3. From the **Project** menu, choose **Project Info**.

To determine the code page of a table

- Use the CPDBF( ) function.

When you build an application from a project, the Project Manager automatically integrates the files in the project, no matter how many different code pages they have. The resulting application has the current code page.

> **Note**   When you add a .dbf file to a project, you don't have to specify a code page for the file, because Visual FoxPro automatically determines the code page from the file's code page mark. However, when you add a text file to a project, you must specify a code page for the file, because Visual FoxPro cannot determine the code page automatically.

To prepare a program for use with another code page, specify the original code page when you save or compile the program on the new platform. For example, to prepare a program created with Visual FoxPro for Macintosh for use with Visual FoxPro, specify the appropriate MS-DOS code page when you save or compile the program with Visual FoxPro. If you use the COMPILE command, specify the code page using the AS clause. Alternatively, specify the code page with SET CPCOMPILE before compiling the program. For details, search for COMPILE and SET CPCOMPILE in Help.

Specifying Code Pages for Variables

You might want to manipulate international data in certain ways. For example, you might want to translate the data in a variable to another code page, or you might want to prevent translation of data in a character or memo field.

Translating Data in Variables

If the code in your application includes a variable containing data from another code page, you can translate the data to the proper code page using the CPCONVERT( ) function. For example, suppose the variable x contains data created with the Macintosh code page (10000). To translate the data to the Windows code page (1252), issue the following command:

```
cConvert=CPCONVERT(10000,1252,x)
```

In Windows, the converted data looks just as you see it on the Macintosh. For example, a character that looks like "ä" on the Macintosh looks identical in Windows.

Preventing Translation of Data in Character or Memo Fields

In some cases, you don't want automatic code page translation. For instance, if a character field contains an encrypted password, you don't want Visual FoxPro to automatically translate the password, because doing so would alter it.

To prevent translation of data in a character or memo field

1. Open the project containing the table.

2. Select the table.

3. Choose the **Modify** button.

   The Table Designer appears.

4. Select the field whose data you want to protect.

5. From the **Type** list, select **Character (Binary)** for a Character field, or **Memo (Binary)** for a memo field.

6. Choose **OK**, and then choose **Yes** to make the changes permanent.

7. Verify the changes by displaying the structure of the table with the DISPLAY STRUCTURE command.

   Alternatively, use the MODIFY STRUCTURE command to protect the appropriate fields. For details, see the MODIFY STRUCTURE command topic in Help.

You can also prevent translation of selected characters in text files by using the CHR( ) function. For details, search for CHR( ) in Help.

Code Pages Supported by Visual FoxPro

A code page is a set of characters specific to a language or hardware platform. Accented characters are not represented by the same values across platforms and code pages. In addition, some characters available in one code page are not available in another.

Code page	Platform	Code page identifier
437	U.S. MS-DOS	x01
620 *	Mazovia (Polish) MS-DOS	x69
737 *	Greek MS-DOS (437G)	x6A
850	International MS-DOS	x02
852	Eastern European MS-DOS	x64

(continued)

Code page	Platform	Code page identifier
861	Icelandic MS-DOS	x67
865	Nordic MS-DOS	x66
866	Russian MS-DOS	x65
895 *	Kamenicky (Czech) MS-DOS	x68
857	Turkish MS-DOS	x6B
1250	Eastern European Windows	xC8
1251	Russian Windows	xC9
1252	Windows ANSI	x03
1253	Greek Windows	xCB
1254	Turkish Windows	xCA
10000	Standard Macintosh	x04
10006	Greek Macintosh	x98
10007 *	Russian Macintosh	x96
10029	Macintosh EE	x97

* Not detected when you include CODEPAGE=AUTO in your configuration file.

Sorting Data in International Applications

After creating a table of international data, check to see if your application sorts the data correctly. How the data sorts depends on the code page associated with the table, because the code page specifies the available sort orders or collation sequences. For more information about the sort orders that code pages support, search for "Sort Orders" in Help.

Understanding Sort Orders

Sort orders incorporate the sorting rules of different locales, allowing you to sort data in those languages correctly. In Visual FoxPro, the current sort order determines the results of character expression comparisons and the order in which records appear in indexed or sorted tables.

> **Note**   Sorting works differently in double-byte character (DBCS) environments. For details, see "Sorting DBCS Data" later in this chapter.

Use the appropriate sort order, because different sort orders produce different results, as shown in the following table.

Unsorted	Machine	General	Spanish
!@#$	Space	space	space
1234	!@#$	!@#$	!@#$
space	1234	1234	1234
Caesar	Caesar	äa	äa
cæsar	Car	ab	ab
Strasse	Char	äb	äb
straße	Czech	Caesar	Caesar
Car	Strasse	cæsar	cæsar
Char	Ab	Car	Car
Czech	Cæsar	Çar	Çar
ab	Straße	Char	Czech
Çar	Çar	Czech	Char
äa	Äa	Strasse	Strasse
äb	Äb	straße	straße

Sort Order Guidelines

Consider the following guidelines when choosing a sort order:

- Avoid the Machine sort order if you want to sort international characters properly, because Machine sorts international characters in ASCII order. For example, notice that Çar follows straße.

- Characters with diacritical marks sort differently than characters without diacritical marks. For example, in the General and Spanish sort orders, notice that äa sorts before ab but ab sorts before äb.

- Ligatures such as ß sort the same as their equivalent character expansions. For example, straße sorts the same as Strasse, and cæsar sorts the same as Caesar.

- In some languages, two characters sort as a single character. For example, in Spanish the Ch in Char sorts as a character between C and D.

The following sections describe how to specify sort orders, check the current sort order, and recognize the effects of sort orders.

Specifying Sort Orders

You can specify a sort order for character fields used in subsequent indexing and sorting operations.

To specify a sort order

1. From the **Tools** menu, choose **Options**.

2. Select the **Data** tab.

3. In the **Collating sequence** box, select the appropriate sort order.

   To save this setting for future sessions of Visual FoxPro, choose **Set as Default**.

   > **Tip**   You can also specify a sort order with the SET COLLATE TO command or the COLLATE statement in your Config.fpw file. For details about Config.fpw, see Chapter 3, "Configuring Visual FoxPro," in the *Installation Guide*.

The current sort order doesn't affect previously created indexes; however, it does affect the results of comparisons and commands such as SEEK and SELECT – SQL. For details, see "Recognizing the Effects of Sort Orders" later in this chapter.

You can change the sort order at any time. For instance, after opening a customer table, you can create index tags representing different sort orders, as shown in the following code. Then, you can change the sort order by simply using a different tag:

```
USE customer
SET COLLATE TO "GENERAL"
INDEX ON fname TAG mygeneral ADDITIVE
SET COLLATE TO "MACHINE"
INDEX ON custid TAG mymachine ADDITIVE
SET COLLATE TO "DUTCH"
INDEX ON lname TAG mydutch ADDITIVE
```

> **Note**   The sort order for an index overrides the current sort order.

The current code page determines which sort orders are available. If you use SET COLLATE to specify a sort order not supported by the current code page, Visual FoxPro generates an error. Also, if you specify a sort order in Config.fpw that isn't supported by the current code page, the sort order defaults to Machine.

Checking Sort Orders

You can determine the current sort order by using the SET ('COLLATE') function. For example, you can save the current sort order, set the current sort order to Machine, perform whatever work is necessary, and then restore the original sort order by using the following code:

```
cCurrentOrder=SET('COLLATE')
SET COLLATE TO 'MACHINE'
```

```
*
* code that requires the Machine sort order
*
SET COLLATE TO cCurrentOrder   && return to the previous sort order
```

You can also determine the sort order of an index or index tag by using the IDXCOLLATE( ) function. For details, search for IDXCOLLATE( ) in Help.

Recognizing the Effects of Sort Orders

The sort order affects the results of string comparisons, SEEK, and SELECT – SQL, as described in the following sections.

Comparing Strings

All sort orders except for Machine and Unique Weight ignore case. This means that you don't have to use UPPER( ) in your index expressions.

The current sort order affects string comparisons. For example, when you set the sort order to General, the following statements return true (.T.):

```
?"A" = "a"
?"Straße"="Strasse"
?"æ" = "ae"
```

However, when you use the Machine sort order, all of these statements return false (.F.). because the strings are matched for an exact comparison, byte by byte.

The character string comparison operator (==) gives you the same result as when you compare by value or when you compare using the Machine sort order; that is, it compares strings byte by byte. For example, the following statement returns false (.F.):

```
? "Straße" == "Strasse"
```

> **Note**   Visual FoxPro ignores SET EXACT when you use the character string comparison operator (==).

Using SEEK

Visual FoxPro ignores diacritical marks when you perform a *partial seek*. A partial seek occurs when you make the length of the expression less than the length of the key. If diacritics are important, consider using SCAN FOR...ENDSCAN or LOCATE FOR...CONTINUE instead of SEEK.

The advantages of using SCAN and LOCATE instead of SEEK include the following:

- SCAN and LOCATE are sensitive to diacritics.

- Visual FoxPro fully optimizes the results of SCAN or LOCATE if the current sort order is Machine or Unique Weight, whereas Visual FoxPro only partly optimizes the results of SEEK.

- SCAN and LOCATE remember the condition that invoked them, allowing you to use them for looping on a condition. In contrast, SEEK positions you somewhere in the index, and SKIP continues down the index from that point. Accordingly, SEEK might not produce the results you want with international data.

Using SELECT – SQL

The SELECT – SQL command uses the current sort order. For example, if you have an index tag based on the General sort order, and the current sort order (returned by SET ('COLLATE')) is Machine, the result of SELECT SQL is based on Machine.

To employ the current sort order, use the ORDER BY clause of SELECT – SQL. For details, search for SELECT – SQL in Help.

Using Indexes

Sort orders determine the order of records in indexed tables. Consider the following guidelines for using indexes with sort orders:

- Rebuild indexes created in earlier versions of FoxPro if you want the indexes to use a sort order other than Machine.

- Rebuild dBASE indexes to take advantage of Visual FoxPro sort orders.

- Use the REINDEX command to rebuild an index, because REINDEX leaves the sort order unchanged.

Working with Double-Byte Character Sets

Visual FoxPro supports DBCS (double-byte character sets) — character sets that require more than one byte to represent a character. Some examples of languages that require a double-byte character set are Simplified Chinese, Traditional Chinese, Japanese, and Korean.

Visual FoxPro DBCS support allows you to create international applications. For example, you can create a Japanese application with a U.S. version of Visual FoxPro if you're running the Japanese version of Windows. The Visual FoxPro DBCS functions operate properly on the Japanese character set, and the Japanese collation sequence is supported.

> **Note**   Visual FoxPro provides special programming functions for use with string in DBCS environments. For details, see "Working with Strings in DBCS Environments" later in this chapter.

Using DBCS Characters When Naming Objects

Visual FoxPro allows you to use DBCS characters when naming elements of your applications. As with Visual FoxPro generally, elements can:

- Be up to 254 characters in length with the combination of double-byte characters and single characters. For example, if you use all double-byte characters, the name you're creating can be only 127 characters long.

- Begin with a letter, number, underscore or leading-trailing byte combination.

- Contain only letters, numbers, underscores, or DBCS characters.

These rules apply to variables, objects (windows, menus, and so on), function and procedure names, class and subclass names, aliases, and constants. You can also use double-byte characters for file names. To avoid the possibility that characters in the file name are inadvertently treated as delimiters, it's safest to always enclose the file name in quotation marks.

Note   Visual FoxPro length limits are expressed using single-byte characters. Using double-byte characters in field names, index expressions, variable names, window names, and so on, effectively shortens the length of the name. For example, a field name can be up to 10 bytes long in a free table, so a field name can consist of 10 single-byte characters, but only 5 double-byte characters. For more information about Visual FoxPro system capacities, search for "system capacities" in Help.

Sorting DBCS Data

To help you order information in DBCS environments, Visual FoxPro supports collation sequences for Simplified Chinese, Traditional Chinese, Japanese, and Korean. Collation sequences allow you to properly order character fields in tables for each language.

The following table lists the Visual FoxPro collation sequence options and the corresponding language.

Options	Language
JAPANESE	Japanese
KOREAN	Korean
PINYIN	Simplified Chinese
STROKE	Simplified and Traditional Chinese

For more information about specifying collation sequences, see "Specifying Sort Orders" earlier in this chapter.

Creating or Modifying Programs

You can prevent localization problems with code by observing the guidelines described in the following sections.

Testing for International Versions

If it's important for your application to be able to determine what language Visual FoxPro is running in, you can call VERSION( ). Knowing the language environment can help you determine what text to display, how to format data, and so on. For example, the following code determines what language environment Visual FoxPro is running in and then runs a language-specific form:

```
IF VERSION(3) = 34 THEN
    * Running in Spanish--display Spanish form
    DO FORM CST_SPN.SCX
ELSE
    * Display English form
    DO FORM CST_ENU.SCX
ENDIF
```

> **Note**   Support for double-byte characters strings has been available in Visual FoxPro only since version 3.0b. If your application is relying on the availability of DBCS functions, you should also call the VERSION(1) function to test the Visual FoxPro version number.

Using Strings

Avoid including strings directly in code because they make localization difficult. For instance, don't include dates and currencies as strings in code. If possible, write your code so that it retrieves strings from files or tables separate from the program.

> **Note**   The performance of your program might suffer if you remove all strings from it. For example, performance might suffer if the program searches for strings while inside a loop.

One way to work with strings in an application that will be translated is to use string constants throughout the application. You can then define the text for these constants in a separate text file that is referenced from your programs using the #INCLUDE preprocessor directive. For example, instead of embedding the error message "file not found," you can use the constant ERR_FILE_NOT_FOUND. The text for this constant could be in a file called ERR_TEXT.H. A program that uses this technique might look like this:

```
#INCLUDE ERR_TEXT.H

* processing here
```

```
IF ERR THEN
    MESSAGEBOX( ERR_FILE_NOT_FOUND )
ENDIF
```

When your application is localized, the translator can create a locale-specific version of the error text file and then recompile the application.

Working with Strings in DBCS Environments

Visual FoxPro includes functions for manipulating character expressions containing any combination of single-byte or double-byte characters. By using DBCS string functions, you can develop applications without having to write extra code that tests for double-byte characters when counting, locating, inserting, or removing characters in a string.

Most DBCS functions are equivalent to their single-byte counterparts except that they're named with a C suffix to distinguish them. You can use these functions with both single-byte and double-byte data; the DBCS functions return exactly the same value as their single-byte counterparts when single-byte data is passed to them. A few other functions help you work with strings specifically in double-byte environments.

DBCS string functions	Description
AT_C( )	Returns the position of one string within another (case-sensitive), starting at the left.
ATCC( )	Returns the position of one string within another (case-insensitive).
CHRTRANC( )	Replaces characters in a string.
IMESTATUS( )	Toggles double-byte editing in the Browse window.
ISLEADBYTE( )	Tests whether a character is a DBCS character.
LEFTC( )	Returns leftmost characters from a string.
LENC( )	Returns the number of characters in a string.
LIKEC( )	Determines whether two strings match.
RATC( )	Returns the position of one string within another (case-sensitive), starting at the right.
RIGHTC( )	Returns rightmost characters from a string.
STRCONV( )	Converts characters between single-byte and double-byte representations.
STUFFC( )	Replaces characters in a string with another string.
SUBSTRC( )	Returns a substring.

When working with double-byte string functions, remember that the maximum-length limit for variables, names, and so on is effectively cut in half. For more information about Visual FoxPro system capacities, search for "system capacities" in Help.

Note   The Visual FoxPro DBCS functions are not supported in earlier versions of Visual FoxPro, and calling them might cause unpredictable results. If you use any DBCS functions in your application, use VERSION(1) to verify that the Visual FoxPro version is later than version 3.0.

Working with Date, Time, and Currency Formats

To help you format dates, times, and currency to match what your users are accustomed to, you can use a variety of formatting techniques. You can:

- Allow Visual FoxPro to use the settings established in the Control Panel.

- Specify a language or a specific format in the Visual FoxPro Options dialog box that you want to use.

- Format dates, times, and currency information in code.

To set a format for date, times, and currency

1. From the **Tools** menu, choose **Options**, and then click the **Regional** tab.

2. To use the settings made with the Windows Control Panel, choose **Use system settings**.

   – or –

   Choose a language or format for dates and times and then choose options for formatting currency and numbers. If you choose the format **Short** or **Long** for the date format, you cannot specify any further options for the date format, and the settings are read from the Windows Control Panel.

3. Choose **OK** to use the options for this session, or **Set As Default** to make the changes the default settings for this copy of Visual FoxPro.

You can also make these settings using the SET SYSFORMATS and SET DATE commands. As a rule, you would issue this command during the initialization of your application (for example, in the configuration file). The default for SET SYSFORMATS is OFF, so you must explicitly set it to ON when starting your application.

For more information on these commands, see Help.

You can establish data validation in individual text boxes by setting the Format property of the text box. However, because text box formatting takes precedence over system-wide formatting, this can make it more difficult to localize your application to an environment that uses a different format for dates, currency, and so on.

Using Preprocessor Directives

You can create application variants for different locales by using preprocessor directives. These control compilation of code in the application and include the #INCLUDE, #DEFINE, #UNDEF, and #IF...#ENDIF constructs.

Using preprocessor directives can produce variants quickly; however, such directives have the following drawbacks:

- To use preprocessor directives, you bracket code, and extensive bracketing can increase the code's complexity.

- Compile-time constants are available only in the program that creates them.

Managing Files in an International Application

The Project Manager can help you organize an international application. In a project, you can integrate the parts of an application, such as forms, menus, programs, and reports. The project ensures that the parts are current when you build the application for its target market.

Unlike .dbf files, text files such as query and program files don't have code page marks. This means that you must keep track of the code pages used by text files so that you can use the files properly. With the Project Manager, you can track the code pages used by text files. For details, see "Specifying the Code Page of a Text File" earlier in this chapter.

Distributing Locale-Specific Run-Time Files

If you're distributing your application along with the run-time version of Visual FoxPro, you might need to include a locale-specific *resource file*. This file contains the dialog boxes and other user-interface elements that Visual FoxPro uses to interact with the user. There is a different run-time resource file for each language in which Visual FoxPro is available.

You would normally need to concern yourself about a locale-specific run-time resource only if all of the following are true:

- You are including the run-time version of Visual FoxPro with your application.

- You are distributing your application to users who use a language different from the one in which you developed it. For example, if you develop in English for an English-speaking user base, you don't need to worry about including a locale-specific resource file. However, if you use the English version of Visual FoxPro to develop but are distributing your run-time application in a French-speaking country, you should consider including the run-time resource file.

- Your application displays Visual FoxPro dialog boxes, menus, or error messages. Typically, if you've designed and localized your own versions of these interface elements, you don't need to include the locate-specific resource file.

For information about distributing run-time files with your application, see Chapter 25, "Building an Application for Distribution," and Chapter 26, "Creating Distribution Disks."

Run-time resource files are named using the format Vfpaaa.dll, where "aaa" is a three-letter code representing the language. For example, the code ENU stands for United States English, the code DEU stands for German, and the code FRA for French. The run-time resource files for these languages are therefore Vfpenu.dll, Vfpdeu.dll, and Vfpfra.dll, respectively.

You must always include at least one run-time resource file, even if you don't intend to use any of the user interface elements in Visual FoxPro as part of your application. By default, Visual FoxPro includes the resource file that's provided with your copy of the program. For example, if you're developing an application using the United States version of Visual FoxPro, Visual FoxPro automatically includes Vfpenu.dll if you include run-time files with your application. If you have no reason to use a locale-specific resource file, you can simply distribute the default resource file as part of your application.

When the application is installed, users can specify the run-time resource file to use by making an entry in the Windows system registry or by using a command-line switch.

To specify a run-time resource file

- In the command line that starts your application, include the L switch and the name of the resource file that you want to use (including a path if necessary). Do not put a space between the switch and the file name.

  For example, the following command specifies the file Vfpdeu.dll as the resource file:

  ```
  C:\Program Files\Microsoft Visual ;
  Studio\Vfp98\MYAPP.EXE -LC:\Myapp\Vfpdeu.dll
  ```

  – or –

  Set the Windows registry on the user's machine (using code or an application such as Regedit.exe) to point to the resource file to use. The registry entry containing the name of the run-time resource file is:

  HKEY_CLASSES_ROOT\VisualFoxProRuntime.5\RuntimeResource.5

When the run-time application starts, Visual FoxPro searches for a resource file, first according to the L switch and then according to the Registry setting. If neither of these settings specifies a locale-specific resource file, Visual FoxPro uses the current system (Windows) locale to dynamically construct a DLL file name. Therefore, if the locale-specific resource file for your application matches the system locale on the user's version of Windows, you don't need to explicitly specify the resource file name. However, it's always safest not to rely on the system default if you want to be sure that the proper file is loaded.

PART 6

Creating Client/Server Solutions

Client/server applications combine the functionality of Visual FoxPro on your local computer with the storage and security benefits provided by a remote server. You can prototype your application locally, then use the Upsizing Wizard to transform the application for a client/server environment.

Chapter 19   Designing Client/Server Applications

Building on multiuser development technologies, learn how to design a powerful client/server application.

Chapter 20   Upsizing Visual FoxPro Databases

Creating local prototypes of your design can reduce development time and costs. Once you have a tested local prototype, it's easy and beneficial to upsize your application so it can take advantage of all the features provided by the remote server.

Chapter 21   Implementing a Client/Server Application

You can use SQL pass-through technology to enhance your upsized application. While remote views provide access to server data, SQL pass-through lets you send commands directly to the server using native server syntax, increasing your control and flexibility.

Chapter 22   Optimizing Client/Server Performance

After upsizing and implementing, you can take additional steps to optimize the performance of your application. Find out what you can do in Visual FoxPro and on the remote server to optimize your client/server application.

CHAPTER 19

Designing Client/Server Applications

Visual FoxPro provides you with the tools to create powerful client/server applications. A Visual FoxPro client/server application combines the power, speed, graphical user interface and sophisticated querying, reporting, and processing of Visual FoxPro with the seamless multi-user access, massive data storage, built-in security, robust transaction processing, logging, and native server syntax of an ODBC data source or server. The synergy of Visual FoxPro and server strengths provides a powerful client/server solution for your users.

The most important step in building a successful client/server application is creating a good design. This chapter builds on the multi-user application development information provided in previous chapters. From that foundation, we define a methodology for developing client/server applications.

If you want information on building and upsizing a local prototype, see Chapter 20, "Upsizing Visual FoxPro Databases." For information on using SQL pass-through technology, see Chapter 21, "Implementing a Client/Server Application." To speed up data retrieval and processing, see Chapter 22, "Optimizing Client/Server Performance."

This chapter discusses:

- Goals for Client/Server Design
- Designing for High Performance
- Developing Applications Quickly
- Building in Accuracy and Data Integrity

Goals for Client/Server Design

When you design a client/server application, you're balancing several sets of requirements. You want to build the fastest, most productive application for your users. You also want to ensure the integrity of application data, make the most of existing hardware investments, and build in scalability for the future. In addition, as a Visual FoxPro developer, you want to make the development process as streamlined and cost-efficient as possible.

The best way to meet these requirements is to design your application with these goals in mind. Let's set the stage by outlining the techniques that provide maximum client/server performance.

Designing for High Performance

Building a fast, high-performance client/server application with Visual FoxPro involves taking advantage of the tremendous speed of the Visual FoxPro engine. You accomplish this with new techniques such as using set-based data access rather than traditional local navigation, building parameterized queries to download just the data you need, locating tables on the optimal platform, and leveraging both Visual FoxPro and remote stored procedures.

Before you can take advantage of new techniques, you must analyze the systems you'll be using. When you design a local or file-server application, you determine the queries, forms, menus, and reports your application will use or create. When you design a client/server application, you perform all the normal system analysis plus additional analysis that relates specifically to client/server applications. You need to think about where the data used by queries, forms, menus and reports will be located, and how you'll access that information. For example, you might ask yourself questions such as:

- Which tables will be stored on the remote server once the application is implemented?
- Which tables would be more efficiently stored as local lookup tables?
- What views will you need to access remote data?
- What business rules are enforced by the server, and how will your application interact with these rules?

Once you've determined the basic components of your client/server application, you can begin to design how your application will access and update data.

Downloading Just the Data You Need

One of the most important factors in building a fast, efficient client/server application is minimizing the amount of data you pull down from the server. Because client/server applications can access potentially huge amounts of data on a remote server, using traditional local navigation techniques could result in a slow client/server application. To speed performance, you use set-based data access techniques to filter the amount of data you download.

Accessing Set-Based Data Efficiently

Remote data is set-based; you access remote data by selecting a *set* of data from a large data store using SELECT – SQL statements. The most important difference between building a traditional local application and building a client/server application is the contrast between traditional Visual FoxPro navigational techniques and set-based server data access techniques.

Using Traditional Navigational Techniques

In traditional local database programming, you can access discrete and often large amounts of data by using the GOTO BOTTOM command, which you then query against. You can navigate through data by issuing a SET RELATION command to create a temporary relationship between two tables and then issuing a SKIP command to move through the related records.

While this method of navigating records could be used against remote data, it can be inefficient against large remote data stores. For example, if you create a remote view that accesses a large table on a remote data source and then issue the GOTO BOTTOM command, you must wait while all the data in the view is retrieved from the data source, sent across the network, and loaded into your local system's view cursor.

Using Parameterized Queries

A more efficient approach for accessing remote data is to download just the data you need and then requery to obtain specific additional or new records. Use a SELECT statement based on parameters to download a specific small set of data and then access new records by using the REQUERY( ) function to request a new set of data.

You don't issue the GOTO BOTTOM command against remote server data because this would:

- Unnecessarily burden network resources by downloading huge amounts of data.

- Slow performance of your application by handling unneeded data.

- Potentially reduce accuracy of the data in the local cursor because changes to remote data aren't reflected in the local cursor until you requery.

For example, if you want to create a client/server application that accesses the orders for a particular customer, create a remote view that accesses the Customer table. Create another remote view that accesses the Orders table, but parameterize the view based on the cust_id field. Then use the current customer record as the parameter for the view of the Orders table.

You can use the parameter to scope the downloaded data set to just the right amount of data. If you request too little data, you can lose performance because you'll have to requery the remote server more frequently. If you request too much data, you can waste time downloading data you won't use.

Choosing the Best Client/Server Design

The following examples describe how to gain the benefits of client/server technology and avoid the pitfalls of poor programming techniques. The first method uses traditional programming practices to retrieve all the data from a remote data source into local cursors which are then related with the SET RELATION command. The second, third, and fourth methods adopt progressively smarter data-fetching techniques, effectively limiting the amount of data downloaded with a "just-in-time" methodology that provides the freshest data and fastest response time over a network.

Using an Unoptimized Client/Server Strategy

A straightforward, unoptimized client/server application uses local data navigation techniques with remote data. For example, if you have 10-million customer records and 100-million order records on a remote data source, you can create an inefficient application that downloads all the Customer and Order records into local cursors. You could then index on 100-million order records, create a temporary relationship between the Customer and Orders tables in your local cursors, and use the SKIP command to navigate through the records.

This method is not optimized for performance, but might, however, be useful if the one side is local and the many side is remote.

Filtering the Many Side

A slightly improved client/server application limits the many side of the relationship, but retrieves all of the one side so you can skip through the records. In this scenario, you create a remote view of the many side of the relationship, the Orders table, parameterized on the customer ID. You then download the entire Customer table.

While creating a parameterized view on the Orders table is an improvement over downloading all of the orders, you still retrieve unnecessary information by continuing to download the entire Customer table. The Customer table is also increasingly out-of-date as changes are made by other users on your system. This method might be beneficial if the one side of the relationship contains a small data set.

Filtering the One Side

A better client/server programming technique creates remote views for all remote data. You limit the number of Customer records downloaded into the remote view of the Customer table by using the SELECT statement in the view to select just the customers for one region. You then create a remote view of the many side of the relationship, the Orders table, parameterized on the customer ID.

This scenario retrieves a smaller set of records. You use the SKIP command to skip on the one side of the relation (the Customer view). You use the REQUERY( ) function to access new data on the many (Orders) side.

In this example, you limit, or filter, both the one side and the many side of the relationship, and can still use the SKIP command to navigate through the filtered data. This method is be recommended if the one side of the relationship, even after being filtered, is still sufficient to provide information for a successive set of queries before you requery the remote server.

Using the Primary Key to Access the One-to-Many Relationship

The most efficient client/server programming paradigm gives up the luxury of using the SKIP command, and creates a form that requests input or selection of the customer ID, which is then used as a parameter for a remote view of the Customer table. This parameter is also used as a parameter for a remote view of the Orders table.

For example, you could create a one-to-many form in which the customer information forms the one side, and a Grid control displays the many side of the relationship. The Grid control can be bound to the customer ID chosen in the one side of the form. You can then set the MaxRecords property of CURSORSETPROP( ) to 1, and use the following code to populate the one side of the form:

```
SELECT * FROM customer WHERE customer.cust_id = ?cCust_id
```

When the user wants to view a different customer's record, they input or select a new customer ID. The form requeries the data source for the orders for the new customer ID and refreshes the Grid control with the new order data.

Using these techniques, your application downloads just the data you need, at the time it's needed. You speed response over the network by limiting the amount of data downloaded, and you provide fresher information to the user by requerying the data source just before you display requested information.

This method is recommended when you want to access the one-to-many relationship randomly using any primary key value. You might want to download the primary keys into a control, such as a drop-down list, when you open the form and then provide a control that the user can choose to refresh the list of primary key values on demand.

Using the Data Environment in Client/Server Applications

When you use remote data in a form, include the views in the form's data environment. You can set the AutoOpenTables property for the data environment to false (.F.) so that you can specify when the application refreshes the views with the remote data. Set the ControlSource property for text boxes or other data-bound controls after you call the data environment's OpenTables method, typically in the code associated with the Init event of the form. For more information on setting form properties, see Chapter 9, "Creating Forms," in Part 3, "Creating the Interface."

Locating Data on the Optimal Platform

You get maximum performance when you store data and other attributes of your database on the optimal platform. The best platform for a particular element depends on how the element is accessed and updated. For example, you might want to store a local copy of a server table, such as a postal code directory that is used as a lookup table, and refresh the local copy only when the back-end table changes.

The following table lists some common application elements and examples of where to locate them for optimal performance.

Locating Elements by Platform

Element	Location	Type	Notes
Tables	Local	Local copies of server lookup tables; small, infrequently changed tables	Use a time stamp, if supported by your remote server, to compare and optionally refresh the local table to match any changes to the back-end source table.
	Remote	Large or frequently changing tables	
Rules	Local	Rules on remote views	You can use DBSETPROP( ) to store field- and record-level rules on a remote view. Your application can use these local rules to check the validity of data before sending the data to the back-end as an update to remote tables.
	Remote	Row-level and column-level rules on remote base tables	
Stored procedures	Local	Visual FoxPro stored procedures	
	Remote	Back-end server stored procedures	Use the SQL pass-through SQLEXEC( ) function to call server stored procedures.
Transactions	Local	Visual FoxPro transactions	
	Remote	Server transactions	
Triggers	Local views	No triggers on views	
	Remote	Server triggers	

To reduce network traffic during lookups, you can choose to store not only infrequently changing but also frequently changing lookup tables locally. For example, you can download your company's customer list and refresh it only when customer information changes.

To accomplish this, you can program your application to compare the time stamp on the local copy of the table with the time stamp on back-end data (if your remote server supports time stamps) and update the local copy only if the server table has changed. You can also add a command button to your form that forces an immediate download of the table, allowing users to refresh their copy of the local table on demand.

Choosing the Right Methods

You can use remote views, SQL pass-through, or both to create your client/server application. You can combine both methods for powerful results: use views for the majority of your data management requirements and use SQL pass-through to enhance the power of your application.

Using Views

You can use views as the core method for developing a robust client/server application. Remote views are a powerful technology; they're designed to allow you to select just the data you need from a remote server into a local Visual FoxPro cursor, which you can then use to view and update remote data. A view is basically a result set from a SQL SELECT statement.

Views are persistent: the view definition is stored in a database. View definitions have properties that you can set and then customize further for the active view cursor. Views are the best tool for data definition of an updatable result set.

You can use local views to build a local prototype, then use an Upsizing Wizard to transform local views into remote views. For information on using the Upsizing Wizards, see Chapter 20, "Upsizing Visual FoxPro Databases."

If your application's users want to use data for mobile work, you can employ offline views. Offline views make data portable, allowing laptop or other portable computer users to work with a stored copy of source data that they can update while they're on the road. When the user reconnects to the server, your application can easily merge offline changes into the source tables.

You might also want to use offline view technology to allow local users to work with data "offline," merging their updates at a later time. For information on working with offline data, see Chapter 8, "Creating Views," in Part 2, "Working with Data."

Using SQL Pass-Through

SQL pass-through technology provides you with direct access to a remote server with the Visual FoxPro SQL pass-through functions. These functions permit additional server access and control beyond the capability of views. For example, you can perform data definition on the remote server, set server properties, and access server stored procedures.

SQL pass-through is the best tool for creating read-only result sets and for using any other native SQL syntax. In contrast to a view, which is a result set from a SQL SELECT statement, SQL pass-through enables you to send anything you want to the server using the SQLEXEC( ) function. The following table lists the Visual FoxPro SQL pass-through functions.

SQL Pass-Through Functions

SQLCANCEL( )	SQLCOLUMNS( )	SQLCOMMIT( )
SQLCONNECT( )	SQLDISCONNECT( )	SQLEXEC( )
SQLGETPROP( )	SQLMORERESULTS( )	SQLPREPARE( )
SQLROLLBACK( )	SQLSETPROP( )	SQLSTRINGCONNECT( )
SQLTABLES( )		

You can create cursors yourself using SQL pass-through technology. Though SQL pass-through provides more direct server access, it provides less persistent access than views. In contrast to views, whose definitions are stored persistently in a database, cursors created using SQL pass-through exist only for the current session. For more information on using SQL pass-through technology, see Chapter 21, "Implementing a Client/Server Application." For more information on any of the individual functions, see Help.

Combining Views and SQL Pass-Through

The most powerful paradigm for building a Visual FoxPro client/server application combines view and SQL pass-through technologies. Because views are easy to build and provide automatic buffering and update capabilities, use views for the majority of your data management tasks. Then use SQL pass-through to accomplish specific tasks on the remote server, such as data definition and the creation and execution of server stored procedures.

Developing Applications Quickly

Regardless of the programming method you choose, you need a good strategy to make developing client/server applications quick and efficient. Because Visual FoxPro makes it easy to quickly prototype and build applications, you can choose to design and build a local prototype of your application and then upsize and implement it in stages against a remote data source. If you have access to a remote data source during the development process, you might choose to prototype your application against the remote data source, using remote views.

Building a Prototype with Views

The first step in developing a Visual FoxPro client/server application can be to build a prototype. By prototyping your application, perhaps module by module, you discover changes and enhancements to your application's design early in the development process. You can then fine-tune your design efficiently against small sample data stores before adding the additional layer of complexity inherent in working with large sets of remote, heterogeneous data. Building a prototype is described in Chapter 20, "Upsizing Visual FoxPro Databases."

Creating a Local Prototype with Local Views

A local prototype for a client/server application is a functioning Visual FoxPro application that uses local views to access local tables. You use views in your client/server prototype because the final client/server application will use remote views to access remote data. By prototyping your application with local views, you're one step closer to the final application.

Building a local prototype is especially practical if you don't have constant access to a remote data source during development, or if you don't want to use remote data to prototype your application. Local views access local Visual FoxPro tables, rather than remote data source tables. You create the local data, however, to mimic the structure of the data on the server. Using local data to represent remote data is one method of quickly developing and testing your application's basic design. You can also speed development by limiting the amount of data selected into the views. For more information on building local and remote views, see Chapter 8, "Creating Views," in Part 2, "Working with Data."

Planning for Upsizing

Upsizing is the process that creates a database on the remote server with the same table structure, data, and potentially many other attributes of the original Visual FoxPro database. With upsizing, you take an existing Visual FoxPro application and migrate it to a client/server application. For more information on upsizing, see Chapter 20, "Upsizing Visual FoxPro Databases."

When you build an application that you'll eventually upsize, you make choices about the design of your application's architecture and the programming model based on eliciting maximum performance against a remote data source. These choices are described earlier in this chapter in "Designing for High Performance."

Prototyping with Remote Views

If you have access to a remote data source and you want to use remote data directly as you develop your client/server application, you can build your prototype using remote views. When you prototype using remote views, you skip the upsizing step because your data is already located on a remote server and you already have remote views to access that data.

Implementing your Client/Server Application

You can simplify testing and debugging your application by implementing your prototyped application in stages. When you implement a prototyped application in stages, you add multi-user enhancements, move the data to the remote data source, and test and debug the application, module by module, in a systematic manner.

As you implement your application, you can use native server syntax and access server specific functionality, such as server stored procedures, with SQL pass-through technology. For information about SQL pass-through, see Chapter 21, "Implementing a Client/Server Application."

Optimizing Your Application

Once your application is fully implemented against remote data and you've completed the testing and debugging phase, you can fine-tune the speed and performance of the entire application. For more information about enhancements you can make to your implemented application, see Chapter 22, "Optimizing Client/Server Performance."

Building in Accuracy and Data Integrity

You can combine the power of Visual FoxPro data validation rules and stored procedures with the data source's data validation rules and stored procedures to build client/server applications that protect data integrity.

Maintaining Data Integrity

You can create local versions of remote server validation rules to provide friendly messages to the user; for example, about updates that would not be allowed when sent to the remote server because the data entered had violated some server relational integrity or data validation rule.

Using Visual FoxPro Rules on a Remote or Offline View

You can create field- and record-level rules on remote and offline views to validate data entered locally before the data is sent to the remote data source. Because the purpose of these view rules is to prevent sending data to the data source that will be rejected by the server's data integrity rules, you want to replicate the data source's rules in the rules you create for your remote view. You use the DBSETPROP( ) function to create rules for views.

> **Tip**   You can create a local validation rule on a remote view that calls a remote server stored procedure and sends the value you want to validate to the server as a parameter. However, using a remote stored procedure adds to processing time during data entry.

Using Server Rules

You can choose to rely on the rules established on the server for data validation. If an error occurs, your error handling routine can call the AERROR( ) function to obtain information, including the error message number, the text of the remote error message, and the connection handle associated with the error. For more information on AERROR( ), see Help.

Using Server Triggers

Though you can create Visual FoxPro triggers on local tables, you can't create them on views. You can, however, use triggers on the remote data source. Server triggers can be used to process secondary data updates, such as cascading updates or deletes. Using server triggers to process secondary updates is more efficient than sending multiple commands to the remote server from your Visual FoxPro application.

Protecting Against Data Loss

Both Visual FoxPro and most remote data sources provide transaction logging capabilities to protect against data loss. For more information on using Visual FoxPro transactions, see Chapter 17, "Programming for Shared Access," in Part 5, "Extending Applications."

You can use Visual FoxPro transactions for local prototypes and for processing local data. Use server transactions for remote data updates, inserts, and deletes. For more information on using remote transactions, see Chapter 22, "Optimizing Client/Server Performance."

CHAPTER 20

Upsizing Visual FoxPro Databases

Once you've designed your client/server application, you're ready to build and upsize a local prototype. A local prototype is a working model of your application using Visual FoxPro tables, views, and databases to represent data that will eventually be accessed on a remote server. Use the upsizing wizards to move databases, tables, and views from your system to a remote SQL Server or Oracle server.

This chapter discusses:

- Goals for Prototyping
- Building a Local Prototype of an Application
- Using the Upsizing Wizards
- Upsizing to SQL Server
- Upsizing to Oracle

Goals for Prototyping

When you use Visual FoxPro to build a prototype of your application, you're leveraging the power of visual forms, wizards, builders, designers, and the Project Manager to quickly develop a working application. While your ultimate goal is to implement your application across client/server platforms, you gain a great deal by choosing to build a solid prototype.

Reducing Development Time

By building a quick prototype, you can refine your application's design and local architecture quickly and easily, without having to access the remote server to rebuild server tables and databases. You can also test and debug your application's forms against smaller data stores, allowing you to more quickly correct and enhance your application's user interface. Because you're keeping architectural overhead low, you prevent wasting development time in rebuilding, reindexing, and reconnecting remote data just to test your prototype.

Decreasing Development Costs While Increasing Customer Satisfaction

Because the local prototype is self-contained on your computer, you can easily demonstrate a working model of your application to the end user early in the development cycle. Being able to see your application as it progresses gives clients confidence in your ability to deliver a solution that meets their needs. It also provides you with the opportunity to get customer feedback about the user interface and reports before you've invested resources in implementing it against a remote server.

As users see and interact with your prototype, they can begin to identify areas they'd like to change, as well as see the potential for adding additional functionality into their application. You can implement changes and redemonstrate the application in an iterative process until both you and the customer are satisfied with the design and function of the prototyped application. Your prototype then serves as a working specification for the final, implemented client/server application.

Contributing to Successful Implementation

You can also potentially provide the prototyped application as a demonstration for your users, allowing them to experiment with the working model as you move forward in the implementation process of the actual application. As they gain experience with the prototype, their learning curve decreases and they become better partners with you in refining and fine-tuning the application. They're also positioned to be more productive and satisfied in the final implementation stage because they already understand the basic framework of the application.

Having a working model increases the lead time the end user has to become familiar and comfortable with the application. It also provides a framework to allow staff at your company or the customer site to design and develop a training plan for the application. The prototype can even be used to train end users before the final application is delivered, thus contributing to a successful implementation of the final, implemented client/server application.

Building a Local Prototype of an Application

When you build a local prototype of your application, you might be starting from scratch, or you might be converting an existing Visual FoxPro application to a client/server application. The primary difference between building a local prototype of a client/server application and developing any other Visual FoxPro application is in using local views and tables to represent data that will eventually be upsized.

To build and upsize a local prototype

1. Create your application using local views and local tables to represent data you want to move to a remote server.

2. Use local views in your application's data environment for forms and reports.

3. Upsize local views and tables using the SQL Server Upsizing Wizard or Oracle Upsizing Wizard:

   - In the **Set Upsizing Options** step, in the **Changes to make locally** area, select **Redirect views to remote data**.

     When you select this option, the upsizing wizard copies the local tables you select to the remote server, and redirects local views to use remote data where applicable.

For more information on creating views, see Chapter 8, "Creating Views." For information on creating forms and using a data environment, see Chapter 9, "Creating Forms." For information on developing an application, see Chapter 2, "Developing an Application."

Using the Upsizing Wizards

Visual FoxPro provides two upsizing wizards: the SQL Server Upsizing Wizard, and the Oracle Upsizing Wizard. These wizards create SQL Server or Oracle databases that duplicate, as much as possible, the functionality of a set of tables in a Visual FoxPro database. You can also choose to redirect Visual FoxPro views so that they use the newly created remote data instead of local data. You can use the upsizing wizards to:

- Move local data to a remote server.

- Transform local base tables and local views into remote base tables and remote views.

- Migrate a local application to a client/server application.

  Note   Though the upsizing wizards access SQL Server or Oracle servers, you can create a client/server application for any remote ODBC data source. For servers other than SQL Server or Oracle, you can use SQL pass-through functions to create remote tables, then use Visual FoxPro to create remote views that access server tables. For more information on using SQL pass-through functions, see Chapter 21, "Implementing a Client/Server Application." For information on creating remote views, see Chapter 8, "Creating Views."

Upsizing to SQL Server

Before you run the SQL Server Upsizing Wizard, you must prepare both the client and server sides.

Preparing the SQL Server Side

Before upsizing, you must ensure that you have necessary permissions on the server, estimate the size of your database, and check that the server has sufficient disk space. There are also special preparations for upsizing to multiple disks or devices.

Checking Free Disk Space

Make sure you have enough disk space on the server.

> **Caution**   If the SQL Server Upsizing Wizard runs out of disk space on the server, it halts, leaving a partial database and any devices it created on the server. You can remove devices, databases, and tables with the SQL Server Administration tool.

Setting Permissions on SQL Server Databases

In order to run the SQL Server Upsizing Wizard, you must have certain permissions on the SQL server to which you will be upsizing. The permissions you need depend on the tasks you want to accomplish.

- To upsize to an existing database, you need CREATE TABLE and CREATE DEFAULT permissions.

- To build a new database, you need CREATE DATABASE and SELECT permissions on the system tables in the master database.

- To create new devices, you must be a system administrator.

For more information on granting server permissions, see your SQL Server documentation.

Estimating SQL Server Database and Device Size

When you create a new database, the SQL Server Upsizing Wizard asks you to select devices for your database and log. It also asks you to set the size of the database and your devices.

Estimating SQL Server Database Size

When SQL Server creates a database, it sets aside a fixed amount of space for that database on one or more devices. Not all this space is necessarily used by the database — the database size simply limits how large a database can grow before it runs out of space.

> **Note**   You can increase the size of a SQL Server database after it's created. For more information, see the ALTER DATABASE command in your SQL Server documentation.

To estimate the space needed for your database, calculate the total size of your Visual FoxPro .dbf files for the tables you want to upsize plus the rate at which your new SQL Server database will grow. In general, every megabyte of Visual FoxPro data requires at least 1.3 to 1.5 MB in the SQL Server.

If you have ample disk space on your server, multiply the size of your Visual FoxPro tables by two. This ensures that the SQL Server Upsizing Wizard has enough space to upsize your database and also leaves some room to grow. If you expect to add a lot of data to the database, increase the multiple.

Estimating SQL Server Device Sizes

All SQL Server databases and logs are placed on devices. A device is both a logical location at which to put databases and logs, and a physical file. When a device is created, SQL Server creates a file, thus reserving a set amount of disk space for its own use.

The SQL Server Upsizing Wizard displays the amount of free space available on the existing SQL Server devices. Select a device that has at least enough free space for your estimated database size.

If no existing devices have enough free space, you can use the SQL Server Upsizing Wizard to create a new device. New devices should be at least as big as your estimated database size. If possible, make the device larger than your database size, so you can expand your database later, or place other databases or logs on the same device.

Important   Device size cannot be changed. Make sure you create sufficiently large devices.

Using Multiple SQL Server Disks or Devices

In most cases, the SQL Server Upsizing Wizard provides more than enough control over SQL Server devices. However, if your server has multiple disks or if you want to place a database or log on multiple devices, you might want to create devices before running the SQL Server Upsizing Wizard.

Servers with Multiple Physical Disks

If your server has more than one physical hard disk, you might want to place your database on one disk and the database log on a different disk. In the event of a disk failure, you'll be more likely to recover your database if the log and the database are stored on different physical disks.

The SQL Server Upsizing Wizard allows you to create new devices but only on one physical disk — the same disk as the Master database device.

To place a database and log on separate disks, make sure you have devices that are big enough on both disks, creating new devices if necessary. Then run the SQL Server Upsizing Wizard.

Placing Databases or Logs on Multiple Devices

SQL Server allows databases and logs to span several devices. However, the SQL Server Upsizing Wizard allows you to specify only one device for your database and one device for the log.

If you want to specify multiple devices for a database or log, make those devices (and no other devices) the default devices. Then run the SQL Server Upsizing Wizard and choose Default for the database or log device.

> **Note**   If the new SQL Server database or log sizes don't require using all the default devices, SQL Server uses only the devices necessary to accommodate the database or log.

Preparing the Client

Before upsizing, you must have access to a SQL Server through an ODBC data source or named connection. You must also have a Visual FoxPro database, which you should back up before running the SQL Server Upsizing Wizard.

Creating an ODBC Data Source or Named Connection

When you create a new remote database, you select an ODBC data source or named connection in your Visual FoxPro database that accesses the SQL Server to which you want to upsize. Because you can't proceed through the Upsizing Wizard until you select a named connection or data source, you should create the appropriate named connection or data source before you start the upsizing process.

For information on creating a named connection, see Chapter 8, "Creating Views." If you want to create an ODBC data source, run the ODBC Administrator. For information on setting up ODBC data sources, see Chapter 1, "Installing Visual FoxPro," in the *Installation Guide*.

Backing Up Your Database

It's a good idea to create a backup copy of your database (.dbc, .dct, and .dcx files) before upsizing. While the SQL Server Upsizing Wizard doesn't modify .dbf files, it does operate on the .dbc directly by opening the .dbc as a table at times and indirectly by renaming tables and views when creating new remote views. If you back up your database, you can revert your database to its original pre-upsizing state by overwriting the upsized .dbc, .dct, and .dcx files with the original backup copies, which reverses the renaming and creation of new views.

Closing Tables

The SQL Server Upsizing Wizard attempts to exclusively open all the tables in the database to be upsized; if any tables are already open and shared, the wizard closes them and reopens them exclusively. Opening tables exclusively before upsizing protects against other users attempting to modify records in the tables you're exporting during data export. If any tables can't be opened exclusively, the SQL Server Upsizing Wizard displays a message; those tables are not available for upsizing.

Starting the SQL Server Upsizing Wizard

After you create an ODBC data source and complete the necessary preparations on the client and server, you're ready to begin upsizing.

To start the SQL Server Upsizing Wizard

1. From the **Tools** menu, choose **Wizards**, and then choose **Upsizing**.

2. From the **Wizard Selection** dialog box, choose **SQL Server Upsizing Wizard**.

3. Follow the directions in the wizard screens, as described in the following sections.

   You can choose **Cancel** at any time to exit the wizard; the wizard performs no actions on the server until you choose **Finish**.

4. When you're ready to upsize, choose **Finish**.

After you choose Finish, the SQL Server Upsizing Wizard begins exporting the database to the server.

The Finish button is available after you provide the basic information needed for upsizing. If you choose Finish before you complete all the wizard screens, the SQL Server Upsizing Wizard uses default values for the remaining screens.

How the SQL Server Upsizing Wizard Works

The SQL Server Upsizing Wizard makes upsizing a Visual FoxPro database to SQL Server practically transparent. This section explains exactly what happens after you choose Finish — how the SQL Server Upsizing Wizard exports data and maps Visual FoxPro objects to SQL Server objects.

Data Export Methods

The SQL Server Upsizing Wizard exports data using one of two methods. The first method creates a stored procedure that performs multiple row inserts. This method can be very fast, because stored procedures are precompiled and execute quickly.

However, stored procedures can't accept variable length binary variables as parameters. If you're exporting data that's to be stored in SQL Server tables using text or image data types, or tables with more than 250 fields, the SQL Server Upsizing Wizard uses a different exporting method. This second method creates a SQL INSERT statement for each row in the table and then executes the statement.

If the SQL Server Upsizing Wizard encounters errors while exporting data using the SQL INSERT method, and the number of errors exceeds 10 percent of the number of records in the table or 100 records (whichever is larger), the wizard cancels the export for that table and saves the number of export errors for the error report. The exported server table is not dropped, however, and any records that were successfully exported are left in the server table.

Overview of Object Mapping

To upsize a Visual FoxPro database to a server, the SQL Server Upsizing Wizard creates server objects that, as far as possible, do everything the Visual FoxPro database did. Mapping some Visual FoxPro objects to server objects is very straightforward: Visual FoxPro databases, tables, fields, defaults, and indexes map to SQL Server databases, tables, fields, defaults, and indexes in a direct, one-to-one mapping.

However, not all local objects map directly to server objects. Validation rules and referential integrity in Visual FoxPro are part of the data dictionary and are enforced at the engine level. SQL Server validation rules and referential integrity aren't part of the data dictionary, and are enforced through code bound to a table. These differences, as well as design decisions made by the SQL Server Upsizing Wizard, mean that much of the Visual FoxPro data dictionary cannot be mapped directly to SQL Server constructs.

The following table summarizes how objects are mapped from Visual FoxPro to SQL Server:

Visual FoxPro objects	SQL Server objects
Database	Database
Table	Table
Indexes	Indexes
Field	Field
Default	Default
Table validation rule	SQL Server stored procedures, called from UPDATE and INSERT triggers
Field validation rule	SQL Server stored procedures, called from UPDATE and INSERT triggers
Persistent relationships (where used for referential integrity constraints)	Update, Insert, and Delete triggers or table constraints

The following sections discuss each Visual FoxPro object and the SQL Server object (or objects) to which it maps.

Naming Conventions for Upsized Objects

As it migrates objects to a data source, the SQL Server Upsizing Wizard creates named objects on the server. The wizard uses prefixes for objects that need new names because no such stand-alone object existed in Visual FoxPro (defaults and rules, for example). Following the prefix is a table name and then a field name, if appropriate. This naming convention enables all objects of the same kind to have the same prefix and sort together when viewed with data source administration tools. Objects created on the same table also group together when viewed.

Database and Table Objects

A Visual FoxPro database maps directly to a SQL Server database. A Visual FoxPro table, excluding part of its data dictionary, maps to a SQL Server table.

Database, table, index, and field names might change during upsizing, if they violate SQL Server naming conventions. SQL Server names must be 30 characters or less, and the first character must be a letter or the symbol "@". The remaining characters may be numbers, letters, or the "$," "#," and "_" symbols; no spaces are allowed. The SQL Server Upsizing Wizard replaces any illegal characters with the "_" symbol.

Any names that are identical to SQL Server reserved words are given a suffix of "_". For example, FROM and GROUP become FROM_ and GROUP_. The SQL Server Upsizing Wizard also places the "_" symbol in front of object names that begin with a number.

Tables

The SQL Server Upsizing Wizard gives each upsized table the same name as the local table unless the table name contains a space or is a keyword for the data source.

Views of New Server Tables

If you select Create Remote Views On Tables, the SQL Server Upsizing Wizard creates remote views and gives them many of the properties of the fields in the original local table.

Mapping Visual FoxPro Field Names and Data Types to SQL Server Equivalents

Field names and data types are automatically translated into SQL Server fields when a Visual FoxPro table is exported by the SQL Server Upsizing Wizard.

Visual FoxPro data types map to SQL Server data types as follows:

Abbreviation	Visual FoxPro Data Type	SQL Server Data Type
C	Character	char
Y	Currency	money
D	Date	datetime
T	DateTime	datetime
B	Double	float
F	Float	float
G	General	image
I	Integer	int
L	Logical	bit
M	Memo	text
M (binary)	Memo binary	image
C (binary)	Character binary	binary
N	Numeric	float

Timestamp and Identity Columns

Timestamp columns are created using the Transact-SQL timestamp datatype. When you select the Timestamp column checkbox for a specific table in Step 4 – Map Field Data Types, the SQL Server Upsizing Wizard creates a timestamp field for that table.

If a table contains one or more memo (M) or picture (P) fields, the SQL Server Upsizing Wizard selects the Timestamp column check box for that table by default and creates a timestamp field on the upsized version of the table.

Identity columns are created using the Transact-SQL IDENTITY property fields.

Indexes

SQL Server and Visual FoxPro indexes are very similar. The following table shows how Visual FoxPro index types are converted to SQL Server index types:

Index Type Conversion

Visual FoxPro Index Type	SQL Server Index Type
Primary	Clustered Unique
Candidate	Unique
Unique, Regular	Non-unique

The SQL Server Upsizing Wizard uses Visual FoxPro tag names as names for indexes on SQL Server. If the tag name is a reserved word on the server, the wizard alters the tag name by appending the "_" character.

> **Note**   SQL Server doesn't support ascending or descending indexes, or permit expressions within server indexes. The SQL Server Upsizing Wizard removes Visual FoxPro expressions from index expressions as the index is upsized; only field names are sent to the server.

SQL Server Defaults

A Visual FoxPro default expression maps directly to a single SQL Server default. The SQL Server Upsizing Wizard tries to create a SQL Server default based on the default expression for a Visual FoxPro field. If the default is successfully created, the SQL Server Upsizing Wizard binds it to the appropriate SQL Server field. The upsizing report on fields indicates if the SQL Server Upsizing Wizard was successful in translating the Visual FoxPro expression to SQL Server Transact-SQL. For details on translation, see "Expression Mapping" later in this chapter.

While SQL Server and Visual FoxPro defaults are largely similar, there are some differences in the way defaults are created and behave in the two products. SQL Server defaults are stand-alone objects, independent of any particular field or table. Once a default has been created, it can be used by, or bound, to any number of different fields.

Naming Conventions for Defaults

The SQL Server Upsizing Wizard names defaults using the prefix Dflt_ plus the table name and field name. For example, a default value for the ordamt field in the Customer table might be named Dflt_Customer_Ordamt on the server. If combining the prefix with the table and field names causes the default name to exceed 30 characters, Visual FoxPro truncates the excess characters.

Fields with a default expression of zero are bound to a default named UW_ZeroDefault. If two or more fields have the same non-zero default expression, the SQL Server Upsizing Wizard creates two defaults, with two different names, that are functionally identical.

Default Values for Visual FoxPro Logical Fields

Logical fields in SQL Server prohibit null values; Visual FoxPro logical fields allow them. To manage this difference, the SQL Server Upsizing Wizard automatically creates and binds a default value called UW_ZeroDefault to each exported logical field, whether or not you chose to export defaults. This default sets the value of the server field to 0 (or false (.F.), if you look at the field in Visual FoxPro) when you don't supply a value.

If the local Visual FoxPro table contains a default value for a logical field that sets the field equal to true (.T.), the SQL Server Upsizing Wizard doesn't bind the UW_ZeroDefault default to the server table. Instead, the wizard creates a default that sets the field equal to 1, and names the default according to the naming conventions outlined earlier in this chapter.

SQL Server defaults behave differently than Visual FoxPro defaults. For more information, see "Default Values" later in this chapter.

SQL Server Triggers

A SQL Server trigger is a series of Transact-SQL statements associated with a particular SQL Server table. When you choose to upsize Validation rules and Relationships in Step 8, the SQL Server Upsizing Wizard converts Visual FoxPro field- and record-level validation rules and persistent table relationships into stored procedures that are called from SQL Server triggers. Each server trigger can contain code to emulate the functionality of several validation and referential integrity rules.

Note   The SQL Server Upsizing Wizard does not upsize Visual FoxPro triggers.

A server table can have three triggers, one for each of the commands that can modify data in the table: UPDATE, INSERT, and DELETE. The trigger is automatically executed when the associated command is carried out.

The following table describes the triggers created by the SQL Server Upsizing Wizard. Any specific trigger might contain code to emulate some or all of the Visual FoxPro functionality listed.

Trigger	Visual FoxPro Functionality Emulated
UPDATE	Validation rules (Field- and record-level validation)
	Referential integrity
INSERT	Validation rules (Field- and record-level validation)
	Referential integrity (Child table triggers only)
DELETE (Parent table only)	Referential integrity

Naming Conventions for Triggers

The SQL Server Upsizing Wizard names server triggers by combining a prefix that indicates the type of trigger being created with the table name of the SQL Server table to which the trigger belongs. The prefix ("TrigU_" for UPDATE triggers, "TrigD_" for DELETE triggers, and "TrigI_" for INSERT triggers) is placed in front of the table name. For example, the UPDATE trigger on the Customer table might be called TrigU_Customer.

Validation Rules

The SQL Server Upsizing Wizard can export Visual FoxPro field- and record-level validation rules, which it converts to stored procedures on SQL Server. The wizard names field-level rules by combining a prefix "vrf" (for "validation rule, field") with the names of the table and the field; an example might be vrf_customer_lname. Table validation rules are named with the prefix "vrt" (for "validation rule, table") plus the name of the table, to create a name such as vrt_customer.

The SQL Server Upsizing Wizard uses triggers that call stored procedures rather than SQL Server rules to enforce field level validation because SQL Server rules don't allow you to display custom error messages. For more information about SQL Server rules, see the CREATE RULE command in your SQL Server documentation.

Referential Integrity

Your Visual FoxPro application supports referential integrity through triggers on UPDATE, DELETE, and INSERT events on persistent table relationships that are enforced at the engine level. You can choose to implement referential integrity constraints on SQL Server using either of two methods:

- Trigger-based referential integrity

   – or –

   Declarative referential integrity

When you choose trigger-based referential integrity, the SQL Server Upsizing Wizard creates triggers that include the Transact-SQL code required to duplicate Visual FoxPro referential integrity constraints. If you choose to implement declarative referential integrity, the SQL Server Upsizing Wizard creates SQL Server constraints using the ALTER TABLE command with the CONSTRAINT keyword.

Trigger-based Referential Integrity

In the trigger-based method, referential integrity is enforced on SQL Server by Transact-SQL code in triggers. You can use triggers to provide restrictions on UPDATE, DELETE, and INSERT statements, and to cascade changes resulting from DELETE and INSERT statements.

The SQL Server Upsizing Wizard creates SQL Server triggers by evaluating the Visual FoxPro triggers used to enforce referential integrity on persistent relationships in your Visual FoxPro database. The following table lists the mapping between Visual FoxPro Referential Integrity constraints and the SQL Server triggers generated by the SQL Server Upsizing Wizard.

Visual FoxPro Referential Integrity Constraint		SQL Server Trigger
UPDATE	Cascade	Cascade UPDATE trigger
	Restrict	Restrict UPDATE trigger
	Ignore	No trigger generated
DELETE	Cascade	Cascade DELETE trigger
	Restrict	Restrict DELETE trigger
	Ignore	No trigger generated
INSERT	Restrict	Restrict INSERT trigger
	Ignore	No trigger generated

A Visual FoxPro persistent relationship that's used in a referential integrity constraint can become up to four triggers on a SQL Server data source: two for the parent table and two for the child table.

Note   If only one of the tables in a relationship is upsized, or if referential integrity isn't enforced in Visual FoxPro, the relationship isn't exported.

Parent Table

The SQL Server Upsizing Wizard creates an UPDATE trigger that either prevents the user from changing the parent table's primary key or cascades that change through the child table, depending on the type of relationship that was created in Visual FoxPro.

The SQL Server Upsizing Wizard also creates a DELETE trigger that prevents the user from deleting a record with related child records, or that deletes the child records, again depending on the type of relationship between the tables in Visual FoxPro.

Child Table

The SQL Server Upsizing Wizard creates an UPDATE trigger that prevents the user from making changes to the foreign key that would orphan the record. Similarly, an INSERT trigger is created to prevent the user from adding a new record that has no parent.

Custom Error Values

If, at run time, the referential integrity established by the SQL Server Upsizing Wizard-created triggers is violated, SQL Server places a custom error value into the @@ERROR variable. Potential error values are defined by the SQL Server Upsizing Wizard as a part of the trigger code. The specific error value returned at run time depends on the action the user was attempting: updating, inserting, or deleting.

The following table lists the error numbers generated for each action:

Action	SQL Server Error
Violated validation rule	44444
Attempted delete	44445
Attempted update	44446
Attempted insert	44447
Update or Delete statement affected more than one row; statement is automatically rolled back	44448

Declarative Referential Integrity

If you choose to implement declarative referential integrity, the SQL Server Upsizing Wizard creates SQL Server constraints using the ALTER TABLE command with the CONSTRAINT keyword. The parent table constraint uses the PRIMARY KEY keyword. The child table constraint uses the FOREIGN KEY and REFERENCES keywords. Declarative referential integrity is supported at the RESTRICT, RESTRICT updates, and RESTRICT deletes levels.

You can use SQL Server constraints to provide restrictions on UPDATE, DELETE, and INSERT statements.

Expression Mapping

Although Visual FoxPro and Transact-SQL have some functions in common, many Visual FoxPro functions aren't supported by SQL Server. The SQL Server Upsizing Wizard attempts to convert Visual FoxPro expressions in field- and record-level validation rules and default values to Transact-SQL, using the following expression mapping.

Visual FoxPro expression	SQL Server expression
True (.T.)	1
False (.F.)	0
#	<>
.AND.	AND
.NOT.	NOT
.NULL.	NULL
.OR.	OR
=<	<=
=>	>=
ASC( )	ASCII( )
AT( )	CHARINDEX( )
CDOW( )	DATENAME(dw, ...)
CHR( )	CHAR( )
CMONTH( )	DATENAME(mm, ...)
CTOD( )	CONVERT(datetime, ...)
CTOT( )	CONVERT(datetime, ...)
DATE( )	GETDATE( )
DATETIME( )	GETDATE( )
DAY( )	DATEPART(dd, ...)
DOW( )	DATEPART(dw, ...)
DTOC( )	CONVERT(varchar, ...)
DTOR( )	RADIANS( )
DTOT( )	CONVERT(datetime, ...)
HOUR( )	DATEPART(hh, ...)
LIKE( )	PATINDEX( )
MINUTE( )	DATEPART(mi, ...)
MONTH( )	DATEPART(mm, ...)
MTON( )	CONVERT(money, ...)
NTOM( )	CONVERT(float, ...)

(continued)

(continued)

Visual FoxPro expression	SQL Server expression
RTOD( )	DEGREES( )
SUBSTR( )	SUBSTRING( )
TTOC( )	CONVERT(char, ...)
TTOD( )	CONVERT(datetime, ...)
YEAR( )	DATEPART(yy, ...)

The following expressions are the same on Visual FoxPro and on SQL Server.

Expressions That Map Directly from Visual FoxPro to SQL Server

CEILING( )	LOG( )	LOWER( )
LTRIM( )	RIGHT( )	RTRIM( )
SOUNDEX( )	SPACE( )	STR( )
STUFF( )	UPPER( )	

Files Created by the SQL Server Upsizing Wizard

The SQL Server Upsizing Wizard creates tables for its own use during the upsizing process. These files are removed from the hard disk unless:

- You choose to produce an upsizing report.

- You want to save the generated SQL.

- Errors occur during upsizing and you choose to save the error information.

If any of the conditions above are true, the SQL Server Upsizing Wizard creates a project (named Report, Report1, Report2, and so on) and a database (named Upsize, Upsize1, and so on) in a subdirectory (named UPSIZE) of the defined by the SET DEFAULT command for your Visual FoxPro session. The wizard adds to the database the tables used to produce the Upsizing Report, a table to store the generated SQL, and any error tables. The following table lists the files potentially created by the upsizing process.

Local Tables Created During Upsizing

File Purpose	Table Name	Contents
Report Tables	Errors_uw	Information on any error that occurred during upsizing.
	Fields_uw	Information about all the tables upsized.
	Indexes_uw	Information about all the indexes upsized.
	Misc_uw	Miscellaneous upsizing information.
	Relations_uw	Information about all the referential integrity constraints stored in the Visual FoxPro database.
	Tables_uw	Information on all the tables in the database you choose to upsize.
	Views_uw	Information about the local views redirected to access remote data.
Script Table	SQL_uw	One memo field containing all the SQL code generated by the SQL Server Upsizing Wizard.
Data Export Error Tables	ExportErrors_*table_name*	For each table that experiences a data export error during upsizing, the SQL Server Upsizing Wizard generates a table containing the records that aren't successfully exported.

If the wizard is canceled during processing or if the wizard halts because of an error, no tables are left on your hard disk.

Using Generated SQL

The Script table stored on your hard disk contains all the SQL code generated by the SQL Server Upsizing Wizard, whether it executes without error on the server or not. If you want to use this code, the best approach is to look at the generated SQL, copy the parts of it you want to use, run the extracted pieces of code, and repeat the process to obtain the results you want. You can't run the entire SQL script as a substitute for running the SQL Server Upsizing Wizard, because the wizard performs additional steps that aren't reflected in the generated SQL code.

Completing the SQL Server Upsizing Process

You can now take additional steps, both on your server and in your Visual FoxPro application, to ensure your application and data are secure and functioning properly.

You can also use the information in this section when you build an application from remote views rather than by upsizing. Regardless of how you created remote tables, you take certain steps to ensure the server and client are prepared to work together in your client/server application.

SQL Server Steps

You can complete the upsizing process on your server by:

- Making sure the tables you want to edit from Visual FoxPro are updatable.

- Setting permissions on the database so that users can access the objects they need.

- Protecting your work by making your new database recoverable, in case it's damaged or lost.

Adding Unique Indexes for Updatability

A remote table should have a unique index to be updatable in Visual FoxPro. The SQL Server Upsizing Wizard can export an existing unique index, but it doesn't create one where none exists. Make sure that tables you want to edit from Visual FoxPro are updatable.

Setting Permissions

The new SQL Server database and its objects receive a set of default permissions from the SQL Server. Set permissions on the remote database so that your users have access to the objects they need.

Database Logon Permissions

The default permissions of a new database make it accessible only to system administrators and the database owner.

You can add new users and groups by using the SQL Server Security Manager or the system procedures sp_adduser and sp_addgroup.

For more information on adding users and groups, see "SQL Server Security Manager Help" and the documentation of the system procedures sp_adduser and sp_addgroup in the *Microsoft SQL Server Transact-SQL Reference*.

Object Permissions

All objects created by the Visual FoxPro-to-SQL Server Upsizing Wizard, including tables, triggers, and defaults, are accessible initially only to the database owner and system administrators. This is true whether you upsized to a new or existing database. If you overwrite existing objects, you also overwrite all object permissions.

To grant permissions on tables, use SQL Enterprise Manager or the GRANT and REVOKE commands. For more information on setting object permissions, see the "Managing Object Permissions" section in the *Microsoft SQL Server Administrator's Companion*, and the GRANT and REVOKE commands in the *Microsoft SQL Server Transact-SQL Reference*.

Ensuring Recoverability

Protect your work by making your new database recoverable in case it's damaged or lost.

Dumping the Master Database

When a database is created on a SQL Server, new records are added to the system tables in the Master database. Dumping the Master database also provides you with a backup copy, including all the latest changes. For more information on dumping the Master database, see "Backing Up the Master Database" in the *Microsoft SQL Server Administrator's Companion*, and the DUMP Statement and "Dumping the Master Database" in the *Microsoft SQL Server Transact-SQL Reference*.

Scheduling Backups

Schedule regular backups of your database so that you can restore your database from this backup copy in the event of a serious problem. For details on backing up SQL Server databases, see "Database Maintenance Plan Wizard" and "Backup and Recovery" in *What's New in SQL Server 6.5* and "Database Design and Backup Strategy" in the *Microsoft SQL Server Transact-SQL Reference*.

Device Mirroring

Mirroring a device continuously duplicates the information from one SQL Server device to another. In the event that one device fails, the other contains an up-to-date copy of all transactions.

If you anticipate that many changes will be made to a database between backups and you can't afford to lose those changes, consider device mirroring. Device mirroring is most effective when the devices are located on separate disks, as both devices might be lost if they're on the same disk and the disk fails.

For more information on mirroring devices, see "Mirroring a Database Device," "About SQL Server Device Mirroring," and "Using SQL Server Mirroring" in the *Microsoft SQL Server Administrator's Companion*.

Visual FoxPro Client Steps

Once you've transferred objects from Visual FoxPro to a SQL Server, you probably need to modify code in the original Visual FoxPro database so that it functions properly with the new SQL Server database.

Optimizing Views

Views created by the SQL Server Upsizing Wizard aren't parameterized and therefore are not optimized. For most efficient processing, add parameters to views created by the SQL Server Upsizing Wizard to download just the data you need. For information on adding a parameter to a view, see Chapter 8, "Creating Views."

Some Visual FoxPro functions aren't supported by SQL Server. If the remote view created by the SQL Server Upsizing Wizard uses functions that couldn't be mapped to Transact-SQL functions, the view will not work. For more information on mapping Visual FoxPro expressions to Transact-SQL expressions, see "Expression Mapping" earlier in this chapter.

Creating Stored Procedures and Triggers

The SQL Server Upsizing Wizard doesn't upsize Visual FoxPro stored procedures and triggers. If you want to create SQL Server stored procedures or triggers, you can use Transact-SQL on the server or use SQL pass-through in Visual FoxPro. For more information on using Transact-SQL, see your SQL Server documentation. For information on using SQL pass-through, see Chapter 21, "Implementing A Client/Server Application."

Comparing Event Order

In Visual FoxPro, some events occur in a different order, depending on whether your application is using SQL Server data or Visual FoxPro data. These differences might require changes to your code.

Default Values

Visual FoxPro default field values appear when you begin editing a new record. Default values generated by SQL Server defaults appear only after a record has been inserted. You need to change any code that depends on having values before the record is committed, such as the code for lookups.

Validation Rules

In Visual FoxPro, field validation occurs when the focus leaves a field. When you edit SQL Server data in attached tables, triggers and rules aren't fired until you leave the record. You might need to modify any record validation rules that rely on field validation occurring when a field is exited.

Handling Unconverted Expressions

The upsizing report indicates whether each Visual FoxPro table validation rule, field validation rule, and default expression was successfully converted. If a default expression or validation rule was not translated, you should rewrite it in Transact-SQL.

You can also perform validation at the form level in Visual FoxPro. However, if server data is then modified without using a particular form, the validation will not be applied and invalid data might be entered.

For more information about expression conversion, see "Expression Mapping" earlier in this chapter. For more information about Transact-SQL functions, see your SQL Server documentation.

Record Locking

Visual FoxPro uses optimistic locking internally when accessing tables on a SQL server. Optimistic locking means that the row is locked only when the edited value is committed and the update process occurs — usually a very brief interval.

Optimistic locking is used rather than pessimistic locking on SQL Server because pessimistic locking on SQL Server is provided by page locking, potentially locking many records at a time. While page locking prevents other users from making changes to the same record you're editing, it can also prevent users from accessing many other records in the same (locked) page. Optimistic locking provides the best multi-user access for a Visual FoxPro client/server application.

You can optimize updates and control how update conflicts are handled with the SQL WhereType property. For more information on controlling update conflicts, see Chapter 8, "Creating Views."

Upsizing to Oracle

The Oracle Upsizing Wizard is similar in behavior to the SQL Server Upsizing Wizard. For step-by-step instructions, search for "Oracle Upsizing Wizard" in Help. For specific information on Oracle servers, see your Oracle documentation.

Starting the Oracle Upsizing Wizard

After you create a named connection or ODBC data source connecting to an Oracle server, and complete the necessary preparations on the client and server, you're ready to begin upsizing.

To start the Oracle Upsizing Wizard

1. From the **Tools** menu, choose **Wizards**, and then choose **Upsizing**.

2. From the **Wizard Selection** dialog box, choose **Oracle Upsizing Wizard**.

3. Follow the directions in the wizard screens.

   You can choose **Cancel** at any time to exit the wizard; the wizard performs no actions on the server until you choose **Finish**.

4. When you're ready to upsize, choose **Finish**.

   Finish is available after you provide the basic information needed for upsizing. If you choose **Finish** before you complete all the wizard screens, the Oracle Upsizing Wizard uses default values for the remaining screens.

After you choose Finish, the Oracle Upsizing Wizard begins exporting the database to the server.

CHAPTER 21

Implementing a Client/Server Application

Whether you've created and upsized a working local prototype or developed your application against remote data using remote views, you've gained access to the large data stores typically available in a server database. You can also take advantage of the security and transaction processing capabilities of the remote server. While remote views handle the main data management tasks, you can enhance your application by using SQL pass-through (SPT) technology to create objects on the server, run server stored procedures, and execute commands using native server syntax.

This chapter discusses techniques for implementing client/server technology in a working application that uses remote views. If you want to know more about designing and creating a client/server application, see Chapter 19, "Designing Client/Server Applications," and Chapter 20, "Upsizing Visual FoxPro Databases." For more information on creating remote views, see Chapter 8, "Creating Views."

This chapter discusses:

- Using SQL Pass-Through Technology
- Working with Remote Data Using SQL Pass-Through
- Handling SQL Pass-Through Errors

Using SQL Pass-Through Technology

Your client/server application can access server data by using:

- Remote views
- SQL pass-through

Remote views provide the most common and easiest method for accessing and updating remote data. The upsizing wizards can automatically create remote views in your database as part of upsizing, or you can use Visual FoxPro to create remote views after upsizing. For more information on remote views, see Chapter 8, "Creating Views."

SQL pass-through technology enables you to send SQL statements directly to a server. SQL pass-through statements, because they execute on the back-end server, are powerful ways to enhance the performance of your client/server applications. The following table compares remote views with SQL pass-through:

Comparison of Remote View and SQL Pass-Through Technologies

Remote View	SQL Pass-Through
Based on a SQL SELECT statement.	Based on any native server SQL statement, enabling data definition statements or execution of server stored procedures.
Can be used as data source for controls at design time.	Can't be used as a data source for controls.
Provides no ability to execute DDL commands on data source.	Provides method for using DDL commands on data source.
Fetches one result set.	Fetches one or multiple result sets.
Provides built-in connection management.	Requires explicit connection management.
Provides built-in default update information for updates, inserts, and deletes.	Provides no default update information.
Provides implicit SQL execution and data fetching.	Provides explicit SQL execution and result fetching control.
Provides no transaction handling.	Provides explicit transaction handling.
Stores properties persistently in database.	Provides temporary properties for SQL pass-through cursor, based on session properties.
Employs asynchronous progressive fetching while executing SQL.	Fully supports programmatic asynchronous fetching.

SQL pass-through technology offers the following advantages over remote views:

- You can use server-specific functionality, such as stored procedures and server-based intrinsic functions.

- You can use extensions to SQL supported by the server, as well as data-definition, server administration, and security commands.

- You have more control over SQL pass-through Update, Delete, and Insert statements.

- You have more control over remote transactions.

> **Tip** Visual FoxPro can handle SQL pass-through queries that return more than a single result set. For more information, see "Processing Multiple Result Sets" later in this chapter.

SQL pass-through queries also have disadvantages:

- By default, a SQL pass-through query always returns a non-updatable snapshot of remote data, which is stored in an active view cursor. You can make the cursor updatable by setting properties with the CURSORSETPROP( ) function. An updatable remote view, in contrast, usually doesn't require that you set properties before you can update remote data, because property settings are stored in the database with the view definition.

- You must enter SQL commands directly into the Command window or into a program, rather than using the graphical View Designer.

- You create and manage the connection to the data source.

Whether you use remote views or SQL pass-through, you can query and update remote data. In many applications, you'll use both remote views and SQL pass-through.

Using SQL Pass-Through Functions

To use SQL pass-through to connect to a remote ODBC data source, you first call the Visual FoxPro function SQLCONNECT( ) to create a connection. You then use the Visual FoxPro SQL pass-through functions to send commands to the remote data source for execution.

To use Visual FoxPro SQL pass-through functions

1. Confirm your system's ability to connect your computer to your data source. Use a utility such as ODBC Test for ODBC.

2. Establish a connection to your data source with the SQLCONNECT( ) or the SQLSTRINGCONNECT( ) function.

   For example, if you're connecting Visual FoxPro to the SQL Server data source sqlremote, you might log on as system administrator (user id sa) using the password secret with the following command:

   ```
   nConnectionHandle = SQLCONNECT('sqlremote','sa','secret')
   ```

   Note   You can also use the SQLCONNECT( ) function to connect to a named connection.

3. Use Visual FoxPro SQL pass-through functions to retrieve data into Visual FoxPro cursors and process the retrieved data with standard Visual FoxPro commands and functions.

   For example, you might query the authors table and browse the resulting cursor using this command:

   ```
   ? SQLEXEC(nConnectionHandle,"select * from authors","mycursorname")
   BROWSE
   ```

4. Disconnect from the data source with the SQLDISCONNECT( ) function.

Visual FoxPro SQL Pass-Through Functions

The following table lists the Visual FoxPro SQL functions that support working with remote data sources, grouped according to task.

Task	Function	Purpose
Connection management	SQLCONNECT( )	Connects to a data source for SQL pass-through operations.
	SQLSTRINGCONNECT( )	Connects to a data source using ODBC connection string syntax.
	SQLDISCONNECT( )	Breaks a connection to an ODBC data source, making the specified connection handle obsolete.
SQL statement execution and control	SQLCANCEL( )	Cancels an asynchronously executing SQL query on an active connection.
	SQLEXEC( )	Executes a SQL pass-through query on an active connection; returns the number of result sets generated, or 0 if SQLEXEC( ) is still executing (asynchronous processing).
	SQLMORERESULTS( )	Puts another result set into a cursor. Returns 0 if the statement creating the result set is still executing.
	SQLPREPARE( )	Pre-compiles the SQL statement on the data source and binds the Visual FoxPro parameters, i.e. saves the actual parameter expressions for all the parameters in the SQL statement.
	SQLCOMMIT( )	Requests a transaction commitment.
	SQLROLLBACK( )	Requests a transaction rollback.
Data source information	SQLCOLUMNS( )	Stores a list of column names and information about each to a cursor. Returns 1 if the function succeeds, or 0 if the function is still executing.

(continued)

Task	Function	Purpose
	SQLTABLES( )	Stores the names of tables in the source into a cursor. Returns 1 if the function succeeds, or 0 if the function is still executing.
Miscellaneous control	SQLGETPROP( )	Gets a connection property from an active connection.
	SQLSETPROP( )	Sets a property of an active connection.

The SQLEXEC( ), SQLMORERESULTS( ), SQLTABLES( ), and SQLCOLUMNS( ) statements can be canceled in synchronous mode by pressing ESC if SET ESCAPE is set to ON. You can cancel these statements at any time in asynchronous mode by issuing SQLCANCEL( ). All other SQL pass-through statements function synchronously and are not interruptible.

For more information on the SQL pass-through functions, see Help.

Creating Result Sets

When you use the SQL pass-through functions SQLEXEC( ) or SQLMORERESULTS( ) to query data, Visual FoxPro returns the data to you in one or many result sets. Result sets originate from cursors in the server data source and become cursors in Visual FoxPro. The default name for a result set is SQLRESULT.

Accessing Server Stored Procedures with SQL Pass-Through Functions

You can use Visual FoxPro SQL pass-through technology to create and execute stored procedures on a remote server. Stored procedures can greatly enhance the power, efficiency, and flexibility of SQL, and dramatically improve the performance of SQL statements and batches. Many servers provide stored procedures for defining and manipulating server database objects and for performing server system and user administration.

> **Note**   The examples in this chapter use Microsoft SQL Server syntax unless otherwise noted.

To call a server stored procedure

- Use the SQLEXEC( ) function with the stored procedure name.

For example, the following code displays the results of calling a stored procedure named sp_who on SQL Server using an active connection to the data source sqlremote:

```
nConnectionHandle = SQLCONNECT('sqlremote')
? SQLEXEC(nConnectionHandle, 'use pubs')
? SQLEXEC(nConnectionHandle, 'sp_who')
BROWSE
```

For more information on creating and executing server stored procedures, see your server documentation.

Returning Multiple Result Sets

If you execute a stored procedure that contains native server syntax SELECT statements, each result set is returned to a separate Visual FoxPro cursor. You can use these cursors to return values or parameters from a server stored procedure to the Visual FoxPro client.

To return multiple result sets

- Use the SQLEXEC( ) function to select multiple results sets using your native server syntax.

For example, the following code creates and executes a SQL server stored procedure, my_procedure, that returns three Visual FoxPro cursors: sqlresult, sqlresult1, and sqlresult2:

```
=SQLEXEC(nConnectionHandle,'create procedure my_procedure as ;
     select * from sales; select * from authors;
     select * from titles')
=SQLEXEC(nConnectionHandle,'execute my_procedure')
```

How the Server Processes Result Sets and Errors

Because the server compiles each stored procedure when you create it, you receive any server syntax errors at create time. When you execute the stored procedure, the server executes the compiled SQL statements sequentially (as in a Visual FoxPro program) and Visual FoxPro fetches each result set from each SQL statement within the stored procedure separately, in the order executed.

Result sets and errors are returned in the order received, and processing stops if an error is encountered. For example, if a run-time error occurs when the server executes the third statement in a four-statement stored procedure, you receive the first two result sets and then receive the error that occurred upon processing the third result set. Processing stops after the error is returned; the fourth result set is not retrieved. You can use the AERROR( ) function to obtain information about the most recent error.

> **Note** You can execute server stored procedures from Visual FoxPro only by using Visual FoxPro SQL pass-through functions. Views don't support server stored procedures, because each view contains an explicit SQL SELECT statement in its SQL definition.

Passing a SQL Statement to the Data Source

The SQLEXEC( ) function enables you to send a SQL statement to the data source without interpretation. In the simplest case, any string you enclose in the second parameter of the SQLEXEC( ) function is passed to your data source without interpretation. This allows you to execute any statement using your data source's native SQL.

You can also use the SQLEXEC( ) function to create a parameterized query, or to pass ODBC extensions to SQL to the data source.

Creating a Parameterized Query

Just as you can create parameterized views using the View Designer or the language, you can create a parameterized SQL pass-through query.

To create a parameterized query with SQL pass-through

- Precede a Visual FoxPro parameter with a question mark (?) symbol, and then include the parameter in a SQL string you send with SQLEXEC( ).

  The parameter you supply is evaluated as a Visual FoxPro expression and the value is sent as part of the view's SQL statement. If the evaluation fails, Visual FoxPro prompts for the parameter value.

  Tip If your parameter is an expression, enclose the parameter expression in parentheses. This ensures the entire expression is evaluated as part of the parameter.

  For example, if you have the `customer` table from the Testdata database on a remote server, the following code creates a parameterized query that limits the view to those customers whose country matches the value supplied for the `?cCountry` parameter:

```
? SQLEXEC(1,'SELECT * FROM customer WHERE customer.country = ?cCountry')
```

If you want to prompt the user for a parameter value, enclose the parameter expression in quotation marks. For more information on prompting for a parameter value, see Chapter 8, "Creating Views."

Your ODBC data source doesn't accept parameters in the following locations:

- In a SELECT fields or tables list.

- As both expressions in a comparison predicate.

- As both operands of a binary operator.

An ODBC data source will not accept parameters in the following locations in the WHERE or HAVING clause of a SELECT statement:

- As both the first and second operands of a BETWEEN predicate.

- As both the first and third operands of a BETWEEN predicate.

- As both the expression and the first value of an IN predicate.

- As the operand of a unary + or – operator.

- As the argument of a SET function.

For more information about the SQLEXEC( ) function, see Help.

Using SQL Server Input/Output Parameters

You can use input/output parameters to pass values between Visual FoxPro and SQL Server. Input/output parameters are available only using SQL pass-through; they can't be used in views.

The following table provides an example using input/output parameters to pass values from Visual FoxPro to a SQL Server stored procedure, returning the result to a Visual FoxPro variable.

Using Input/Output Parameters with a SQL Server Stored Procedure

Code	Comments
```resultCode = SQLExec(connHand,` ` "CREATE PROCEDURE sp_test;` ` @mult1 int, @mult2 int, @result int;` `OUTPUT AS SELECT` ` @result = @mult1 * @mult2")` `outParam = 0```	Create a stored procedure, sp_test, that multiplies two variables (mult1 and mult2), then stores the resulting amount in the variable result. Create a Visual FoxPro variable to receive the output parameter value when it's passed from SQL Server to Visual FoxPro.
```resultCode = SQLExec(connHand, ;` `"{CALL sp_test (2, 4, ?@outParam)}")```	Execute the SQL Server stored procedure, passing the values "2" and "4" to be multiplied together in the stored procedure.
```? "outParam =", outParam && the value is 8```	Display the value of the output parameter.

Defining Parameters

The syntax for output parameters is:

?@parameter_name

When you implement input/output parameters, define the Visual FoxPro variables you want to include in your SQL pass-through command before you use the variables in the SQL statement. To successfully send and receive information with input/output parameters, you must define:

- A stored procedure parameter, with an output type, that returns a value.

  For example, if your stored procedure parameter is @result, you must assign an output type, such as int, to @result, and you must assign a value to @result.

- An output parameter (@*parameter_name*) expression that evaluates to an existing Visual FoxPro variable.

  For example, if your output parameter expression is ?@outParam, your application must have defined the Visual FoxPro variable outParam.

  > **Note**   If you don't use an output parameter, either in Visual FoxPro or in the stored procedure, or you don't define a Visual FoxPro variable to receive the return value, the Visual FoxPro parameter value will not change.

Converting Data Types

Visual FoxPro converts returned variable values using the following rules:

- Floating point data type (N, F, B) variables are converted to N.

- The display size is set to 20.

- The decimal setting is set to the current session setting. The decimal setting affects only the default display format, and doesn't affect the decimal precision.

- Date and time variables (D, T) are converted to time (T) variables.

You can't use Memo, General, Picture, or NULL data types in input/output parameters.

If your application uses cursor fields as parameters, Visual FoxPro will attempt to convert the result back to the original field data type.

Returning Parameter Values

Input/output parameters are available only after the last result set of a statement has been fetched. This means that input/output values are returned to Visual FoxPro only after:

- SQLEXEC( ) returns (1) in batch mode

  – or –

  SQLMORERESULTS( ) returns (2) in non-batch mode.

If your SQLEXEC( ) statement requests multiple result sets, the output parameters are only guaranteed to be available after the last result set has been fetched from the data source.

Creating Outer Joins with Remote Data

You can use SQL pass-through to perform outer joins on remote data using native server syntax, if your server supports outer joins. An outer join combines information from one or more tables regardless of whether matching rows are found.

To perform an outer join on a server

- Use the SQLEXEC( ) function with the server's outer join syntax.

For example, the following code uses the Visual FoxPro SQL pass-through function SQLEXEC( ) to display the results of an outer join on SQL Server using the active named connection sqlremote:

```
? SQLEXEC(sqlremote, 'select au_fname, au_lname, pub_name ;
               from authors, publishers ;
               where authors.city *= publishers.city')
BROWSE
```

For more information on outer join syntax and types of outer joins, see your server documentation. For information on creating a named connection, see "Defining a Connection" in Chapter 8, "Creating Views."

Using ODBC Extensions to SQL

You can use SQLEXEC( ) to execute ODBC extensions to SQL by enclosing the SQL statement with SQL Access Group standard or extended escape syntax. For more information about ODBC extensions to SQL, refer to the SQL Grammar appendix in your ODBC documentation.

Creating Outer Joins Using the ODBC Escape Clause

You can use SQL pass-through to perform outer joins on remote data using the ODBC escape syntax, if your server supports outer joins. An outer join combines information from one or more tables regardless of whether matching rows are found.

The syntax for outer joins using the ODBC escape clause is:

{oj *outer-join expression*}

The following example creates a result set of the names and departments of employees working on project 544:

```
SELECT employee.name, dept.deptname;
   FROM {oj employee LEFT OUTER JOIN dept;
           ON employee.deptid = dept.deptid};
   WHERE employee.projid = 544
```

For more information on outer join syntax and types of outer joins, see your server documentation. For information on creating a named connection, see "Defining a Connection" in Chapter 8, "Creating Views."

Managing Connections with SQL Pass-Through

When you create a remote view, you choose an ODBC data source name or a connection name that is then used as a pipeline to the remote server upon activation of the view. To access remote data directly with SQL pass-through, you must have the handle for an active connection. A handle is a value that refers to an object; in this case, the handle refers to a data source connection. To obtain a handle, you request a connection to the data source using the SQLCONNECT( ) or SQLSTRINGCONNECT( ) function. If the connection is successful, your application receives a connection handle for use in subsequent Visual FoxPro calls.

Your application can request multiple connections for one data source. You can also work with multiple ODBC data sources by requesting a connection to each data source you want to access. If you want to reduce the number of connections used, you can configure remote views to share the same connection. You disconnect from a data source with the SQLDISCONNECT( ) function.

> **Tip**   Visual FoxPro relies on the definition of the ODBC data source that's stored in your Windows Odbc.ini file or Windows NT registry to connect to a data source. If you change the name or the login information for a data source, keep in mind that these changes might affect whether an application using that data source can connect to the desired remote server.

Controlling Environment and Connection Properties

The client/server environment is established each time you open Visual FoxPro. The environment exists for that session of Visual FoxPro and disappears when you close Visual FoxPro. The client/server environment contains:

- Global properties that act as the prototypes for new connections.

- Error values for errors that occur outside a specific connection.

You can use a handle of 0, the environment handle, to refer to global property settings. You use the SQLSETPROP( ) function to control default property settings in the connection environment and properties within individual connections. The methods you use for entering SQLSETPROP( ) values are consistent for both the environment and individual connections:

- Properties specified with one of two values can use a logical value (.F. or .T.) for *eExpression*.

- A property name can be abbreviated to its shortest unambiguous truncation. For example, you can use "Asynchronous," "Asynch," or "A" to specify the Asynchronous property. Property names aren't case-sensitive.

When you initiate a connection, the connection inherits default connection property values. You can use SQLSETPROP( ) to change these values.

Setting Connection Properties

To view the current property settings for a connection, use SQLGETPROP( ) with the respective connection handle. The following table lists the connection properties you can access with SQLGETPROP( ).

Visual FoxPro Connection Properties

To	Use this property	Purpose
Display the information used to create the active connection	ConnectString	The login connection string.
	DataSource	The name of the data source as defined by ODBC.
	Password	The connection password.
	UserID	The user identification.
Work with shared connections	ConnectBusy	True (.T.) if a shared connection is busy; false (.F.) otherwise.
Control interface display	DispLogin	Controls when the ODBC Login dialog box is displayed.
	DispWarnings	Controls whether non-fatal warning messages are displayed or not.
Control time intervals	ConnectTimeout	Specifies the time (in seconds) to wait before returning a connection time-out error.
	IdleTimeout	Specifies the idle time-out interval (in seconds). Qualifying active connections are deactivated after the specified time interval.[1]
	WaitTime	Controls the amount of time in milliseconds that elapses before Visual FoxPro checks whether the SQL statement has completed executing.
	QueryTimeout	Controls the time (in seconds) to wait before returning a general time-out error.

(continued)

To	Use this property	Purpose
Manage transactions	Transactions	Determines how the connection manages transactions on the remote table.
Control fetching of result sets into view cursors	Asynchronous	Specifies if result sets are returned synchronously (the default) or asynchronously.
	BatchMode	Specifies if SQLEXEC( ) returns result sets all at once (the default), or individually with SQLMORERESULTS( ).
	PacketSize	Specifies the size of the network packet used by the connection.
Display internal ODBC handles	ODBChdbc[2]	The internal ODBC connection handle that can be used by external library files (.fll files) to call the ODBC API functions.
	ODBChstmt[2]	The internal ODBC statement handle that can be used by external library files (.fll files) to call the ODBC API functions.

1. If in manual transaction mode, the connection is not deactivated.

2. If a connection is deactivated, the ODBChdbc and ODBChstmt values are no longer valid. Do not free or drop these values in a user library.

For more information on connection properties and their default settings, see SQLSETPROP( ) in Help.

Controlling Environment Property Settings

The values you set in the Visual FoxPro environment using handle 0 are used as prototypes or default values for each subsequent connection or attachment.

To view the current environment property settings

- Use SQLGETPROP( ) with 0 as the value for the handle.

The following example displays the current environment's WaitTime property setting:

```
? SQLGETPROP(0, "WaitTime")
```

If you set the DispWarnings property to true (.T.), Visual FoxPro displays any environment errors from that point on, and also sets DispWarnings to true (.T.) for newly-created connections.

Although the values you set for handle 0 are used as prototype values for each connection, you can also set custom properties for an individual connection by issuing SQLSETPROP( ) for that connection handle. The exceptions are the ConnectTimeout, PacketSize, and DispLogin properties, whose settings the connection inherits at connect time. If you change the setting of the ConnectTimeout, PacketSize, or DispLogin property, the new setting isn't used until you reconnect.

Controlling Connection and View Objects

You can control connections and views by setting properties on the connection or view object. Properties that control databases, tables, table fields, view definitions, view fields, named connections, active connections, or active view cursors are called *engine properties*. You can display or set engine properties with one of the following Visual FoxPro functions:

To display engine properties use	To set engine properties use
CURSORGETPROP( )	CURSORSETPROP( )
DBGETPROP( )	DBSETPROP( )
SQLGETPROP( )	SQLSETPROP( )

The function you use depends on whether you want to set properties on object 0 (connection 0 and cursor 0), the object definition in a database (named connection or view definition), or the active object (active connection or active view cursor). The following table lists objects and the functions you use to set properties on each object:

To set properties for	Connection	View
Object 0	SQLSETPROP( )	CURSORSETPROP( )
Object definition in a database	DBSETPROP( )	DBSETPROP( )
Active object	SQLSETPROP( )	CURSORSETPROP( )

Engine Properties

The following table lists engine properties alphabetically along with the objects that use each property.

LEGEND

O Read-only
◑ Read-only local ; read-write remote
● Read-write

Properties	Database	Table	Table Field	View Definition	View Field	Connection Definition	Active Connection	Active Cursor
Asynchronous						●	●	
BatchMode						●	●	
BatchUpdateCount				●				●
Buffering								●
Caption			●		●			
Comment	●	●	●	●	●	●		
CompareMemo				●				●
ConnectBusy							O	
ConnectHandle								O
ConnectName				●			O	O
ConnectString						●	O	
ConnectTimeout						●	●	
Database								O
DataSource						●	O	
DataType					◑			
DefaultValue			O		●			
DeleteTrigger		O						
DispLogin						●	●	
DispWarnings						●	●	
FetchAsNeeded				●				●
FetchMemo				●				O
FetchSize				●				●
IdleTimeout						●	●	
InsertTrigger		O						
KeyField					●			
KeyFieldList								●
MaxRecords				●				●
ODBChdbc							O	
ODBChstmt							O	
Offline				O				O
PacketSize						●	●	
ParameterList				●				●
Password						●	O	
Path		O						
Prepared				●				●
PrimaryKey		O						
QueryTimeout						●	●	
RuleExpression		O	O	●	●			
RuleText		O	O	●	●			
SendUpdates				●				
ShareConnection				●				O
SourceName								O
SourceType				O				O
SQL				O				O
Tables				●				●
Transactions						●	●	
Updatable					●			
UpdatableFieldList								●
UpdateName					●			
UpdateNameList								●
UpdateTrigger		O						
UpdateType				●				●
UseMemoSize				●				O
UserID						●	O	
Version	O							
WaitTime						●	●	
WhereType				●				●

For complete information on a property, including the property type, description, and read-only or read-write status, see the associated function topic in Help.

Engine property	Applies to
Asynchronous	Connection definitions: see DBSETPROP( ). Active connections: see SQLSETPROP( ).
Batchmode	Connection definitions: see DBSETPROP( ). Active connections: see SQLSETPROP( ).
BatchUpdateCount[1]	View definitions: see DBSETPROP( ). Active view cursors: see CURSORSETPROP( ).
Buffering	Active view cursors: see CURSORSETPROP( ).
Caption	Fields in tables, fields in view definitions: see DBSETPROP( ).
Comment	Databases, tables, fields in tables, view definitions, fields in view definitions, connection definitions: see DBSETPROP( ).
CompareMemo	View definitions: see DBSETPROP( ). Active view cursors: see CURSORSETPROP( ).
ConnectBusy	Active connections: see SQLGETPROP( ).
ConnectHandle	Active view cursors: see CURSORGETPROP( ).
ConnectName[1]	View definitions: see DBSETPROP( ). Active connections: see SQLGETPROP( ). Active view cursors: see CURSORGETPROP( ).
ConnectString	Connection definitions: see DBSETPROP( ). Active connections: see SQLGETPROP( ).
ConnectTimeout	Connection definitions: see DBSETPROP( ). Active connections: see SQLSETPROP( ).
Database	Active view cursors: see CURSORGETPROP( ).
DataSource	Connection definitions: see DBSETPROP( ). Active connections: see SQLGETPROP( ).
DataType	Fields in view definitions: see DBSETPROP( ).
DefaultValue	Fields in tables, fields in view definitions: see DBSETPROP( ).
DeleteTrigger	Tables: see DBGETPROP( ).
DispLogin	Connection definitions: see DBSETPROP( ). Active connections: see SQLSETPROP( ).

(continued)

Engine property	Applies to
DispWarnings	Connection definitions: see DBSETPROP( ). Active connections: see SQLSETPROP( ).
FetchAsNeeded	View definitions: see DBSETPROP( ). Active view cursors: see CURSORGETPROP( ).
FetchMemo[1]	View definitions: see DBSETPROP( ). Active view cursors: see CURSORGETPROP( ).
FetchSize[1]	View definitions: see DBSETPROP( ). Active view cursors: see CURSORSETPROP( ).
IdleTimeout	Connection definitions: see DBSETPROP( ). Active connections: see SQLSETPROP( ).
InsertTrigger	Tables: see DBGETPROP( ).
KeyField	Fields in view definitions: see DBSETPROP( ).
KeyFieldList[2]	Active view cursors: see CURSORSETPROP( ).
MaxRecords[1]	View definitions: see DBSETPROP( ). Active view cursors: see CURSORSETPROP( ).
ODBCHdbc	Active connections: see SQLGETPROP( ).
ODBCHstmt	Active connections: see SQLGETPROP( ).
Offline	View definitions: see DBGETPROP( ).
PacketSize	Connection definitions: see DBSETPROP( ). Active connections: see SQLSETPROP( ).
ParameterList	View definitions: see DBSETPROP( ). Active view cursors: see CURSORSETPROP( ).
Password	Connection definitions: see DBSETPROP( ). Active connections: see SQLGETPROP( ).
Path	Tables: see DBGETPROP( ).
Prepared	View definitions: see DBSETPROP( ).
PrimaryKey	Tables: see DBGETPROP( ).
QueryTimeOut	Connection definitions: see DBSETPROP( ). Active connections: see SQLSETPROP( ).

(continued)

(continued)

Engine property	Applies to
RuleExpression	Tables, fields in tables, view definitions, fields in view definitions: see DBSETPROP( ).
RuleText	Tables, fields in tables, view definitions, fields in view definitions: see DBSETPROP( ).
SendUpdates[2]	View definitions: see DBSETPROP( ). Active view cursors: see CURSORSETPROP( ).
ShareConnection	View definitions: see DBSETPROP( ). Active view cursors: see CURSORGETPROP( ).
SourceName	Active view cursors: see CURSORGETPROP( ).
SourceType	View definitions: see DBGETPROP( ). Active view cursors: see CURSORGETPROP( ).
SQL	View definitions: see DBGETPROP( ). Active view cursors: see CURSORGETPROP( ).
Tables[2]	View definitions: see DBSETPROP( ). Active view cursors: see CURSORSETPROP( ).
Transactions	Connection definitions: see DBSETPROP( ). Active connections: see SQLSETPROP( ).
Updatable	Fields in view definitions: see DBSETPROP( ).
UpdatableFieldList[2]	Active view cursors: see CURSORSETPROP( ).
UpdateName	Fields in view definitions: see DBSETPROP( ).
UpdateNameList[2]	Active view cursors: see CURSORSETPROP( ).
UpdateTrigger	Tables: see DBGETPROP( ).
UpdateType	View definitions: see DBSETPROP( ). Active view cursors: see CURSORSETPROP( ).
UseMemoSize[1]	View definitions: see DBSETPROP( ). Active view cursors: see CURSORGETPROP( ).
UserID	Connection definitions: see DBSETPROP( ). Active connections: see SQLGETPROP( ).
Version	Databases: see DBGETPROP( ).
WaitTime	Connection definitions: see DBSETPROP( ). Active connections: see SQLSETPROP( ).
WhereType	View definitions: see DBSETPROP( ). Active view cursors: see CURSORSETPROP( ).

1. Property primarily useful for remote views; setting has no effect on performance of local views. You can set this property on local views if you want to pre-set the property on the local view and then upsize later to create a remote view.

2. Property must be set for updates to be sent to remote data source.

Using Transactions with Remote Data

You can wrap transactions around updates, deletes, and inserts to remote data using one of two methods:

- Automatic transaction mode
- Manual transaction mode

The transaction mode you select determines how Visual FoxPro handles transactions on your local machine.

Using Automatic Transaction Mode

By default, Visual FoxPro automatically wraps every transactable command sent to the remote server in a transaction. This default automatic transaction handling is provided when the Transactions property is set to 1, or DB_TRANSAUTO.

To use automatic transaction mode

- Use the DBSETPROP( ) function to set the Transactions property on the connection to 1 or DB_TRANSAUTO.

  – or –

  Use the SQLSETPROP( ) function to set the Transactions property on the active connection to 1 or DB_TRANSAUTO.

Transaction processing for the remote table is automatically handled.

  Note   The Visual FoxPro commands BEGIN TRANSACTION and END TRANSACTION create a transaction for the local Visual FoxPro cursor only. They don't extend the transaction to the remote server.

Controlling Transactions Manually

If you want to control transactions manually, you can set the Transactions property to 2, or DB_TRANSMANUAL. With manual transaction handling, Visual FoxPro automatically begins a transaction for you when you issue the first transactable SQL statement, but you must submit the Visual FoxPro SQLCOMMIT( ) or SQLROLLBACK( ) functions to end the transaction.

To use manual transaction mode

- Use the DBSETPROP( ) command to set the Transactions property on the connection to 2 or DB_TRANSMANUAL.

  – or –

  Use the SQLSETPROP( ) command to set the Transactions property on the active connection to 2 or DB_TRANSMANUAL.

Transaction processing is handled manually through SQLCOMMIT( ) and SQLROLLBACK( ).

After committing or rolling back the prior transaction, Visual FoxPro automatically begins a new transaction when you issue the next transactable SQL statement. For more information about transactions, see Chapter 17, "Programming for Shared Access." For details on DBSETPROP( ) and other transaction commands, see Help.

Nested Transactions

Visual FoxPro supports transactions nested up to five levels for local data. A single level of transaction support is built into SQL pass-through.

If your server supports multiple levels of transactions, you can use SQL pass-through to manage transaction levels explicitly. Explicit transaction management is complex, however, because it can be difficult to control the interaction between the built-in transaction and the timing of remote server transactions. For more information on explicit transaction management, see your ODBC documentation.

Working with Remote Data Using SQL Pass-Through

After you retrieve a result set using SQL pass-through, you can view and control the properties of your result set cursor using the Visual FoxPro functions CURSORGETPROP( ) and CURSORSETPROP( ). These are the same functions you use to set properties on an active view cursor.

> **Note**   Cursors aren't objects and aren't tied to the object model. However, you can view their properties, or attributes, with CURSORGETPROP( ) and set their properties with CURSORSETPROP( ).

For more detailed information about these functions, see CURSORGETPROP( ) or CURSORSETPROP( ) in Help.

Setting Cursor Properties for Remote Data

The following table lists the Visual FoxPro cursor properties that support working with views and connected result sets, grouped according to task categories.

Visual FoxPro Cursor Properties

Task	Property	Purpose
View cursor definition	SQL	Contains the SQL statement from which the cursor was created.
Control interactions between Visual FoxPro and ODBC	ConnectHandle	Handle to remote connection that's used by cursor.

(continued)

Task	Property	Purpose
	ConnectName	Name of connection used by the cursor.
	Prepare	Specifies whether the query for the view is prepared before it's executed.
	FetchAsNeeded	Specifies whether rows are fetched automatically during the idle loop or only on an as-needed basis.
	CompareMemo	Specifies whether Memo and General fields participate in the WHERE clause of an UPDATE statement, regardless of the setting of the UpdateType property
	FetchMemo	Specifies whether Memo and General fields are fetched automatically with result sets, or fetched later, on demand, as the Memo or General field is opened.
	UseMemoSize	Specifies the minimum column size (1 to 255) in result sets for which columns are returned in Memo fields.
	FetchSize	Specifies the number of rows that are fetched at one time from the remote result set.
	MaxRecords	Specifies the maximum number of rows fetched when result sets are returned.
Update data	SendUpdates[*]	Specifies whether updates to the cursor are sent to the tables on which the cursor is based.
	BatchUpdateCount	Specifies the number of update statements sent to the back end for buffered tables.
	Tables[*]	Comma-delimited list of table names on the data source; used to define scope for UpdateNameList and UpdatableFieldsList properties.

(continued)

(continued)

Task	Property	Purpose
	KeyFieldList*	Comma-delimited list of Visual FoxPro fields that represent the primary key of the result set used for updates.
	UpdateNameList*	Comma-delimited list pairing Visual FoxPro fields in the cursor with the table and column names of fields to which you want to send updates.
	UpdatableFieldList*	Comma-delimited list of the Visual FoxPro fields for which updates are sent.
	Buffering	Specifies the type of buffering being performed on the cursor.
	UpdateType	Specifies whether updates should occur using UPDATE, or DELETE and then INSERT commands.
	WhereType	Specifies what should be included in the WHERE clause for updates to table data.

* Properties that must be set before you can update data.

You use these properties to control the way your application interacts with remote data, such as establishing the number of rows retrieved during progressive fetching, and controlling buffering and updates to remote data.

Using the Remote Data Tab in the Options Dialog Box

Some cursor properties inherit their initial values from the environment; other properties only become available at the cursor level. Some properties are available to cursors representing remote views and ODBC or SQL pass-through connected tables.

You can control some cursor and connection property settings through the Remote Data tab of the Options dialog box. When you display the Remote Data tab, the values in the dialog box represent the cursor settings for the current session and the Visual FoxPro global default settings for the connection. When you change values in the Remote Data tab and choose OK, the new values are saved to the cursor's current session and the connection's global default settings. If you choose Set As Default, the values are written to the configurable system settings on your machine. The following diagram illustrates these interactions.

View and set global and session settings with the Options dialog box

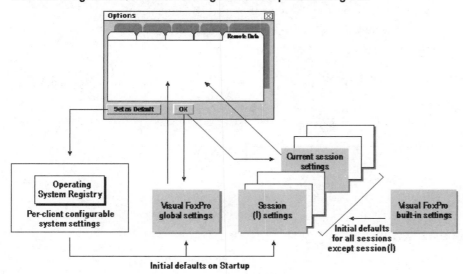

Setting Properties with SQL Pass-Through

When you create a cursor, the cursor inherits property settings, such as UpdateType and UseMemoSize, from the environment cursor, or cursor 0 of the current session. You can change these default property settings by using the CURSORSETPROP( ) function with 0 as the cursor number.

After you create a view cursor with SQL pass-through, you can change the active cursor's property settings by using the CURSORSETPROP( ) function for the view cursor. Changes you make with CURSORSETPROP( ) are temporary: the temporary settings for the active view disappear when you close the view, and the temporary settings for cursor 0 go away when you close the Visual FoxPro session.

Connections inherit properties in a similar fashion. Default properties for connection 0 are inherited when you create and store a named connection in a database. You can change these default property settings for connection 0 with the SQLSETPROP( ) function. After the connection has been created and is stored in a database, you can change connection properties with the DBSETPROP( ) function. When you use a connection, the property settings stored for the connection in the database are inherited by the active connection. You can change these properties on the active connection using the SQLSETPROP( ) function for the connection handle.

Both SQL pass-through view cursors and named connections can use a named ODBC data source. If you use an ODBC data source in a SQL pass-through view cursor, the connection inherits properties from the session defaults. For more information on CURSORSETPROP( ), DBSETPROP( ), and SQLSETPROP( ), see Help.

The following diagram illustrates property inheritance for cursors and connections created with SQL pass-through. The gray lines represent the flow of property inheritance; the black lines represent Visual FoxPro commands.

SQL pass-through (SPT) connection and cursor property inheritance

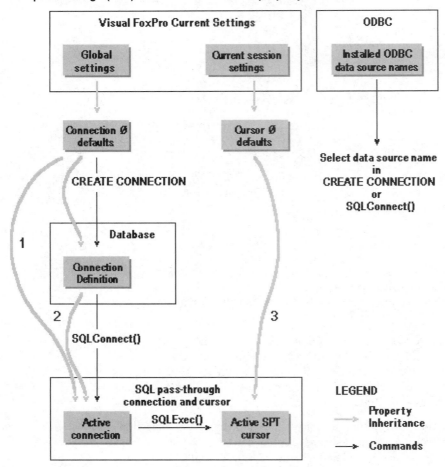

[1] If the active connection is based on an ODBC data source, its properties are inherited from connection Ø.
[2] If the active connection is based on a database connection, its properties are inherited from the connection definition in the database.
[3] Active SQL pass-through cursor properties are inherited from cursor Ø defaults.

Updating Remote Data with SQL Pass-Through

When you use SQL pass-through functions to update data on a remote server, you control whether data is updated, as well as specific details about the updates, by setting properties on the result set cursor. Visual FoxPro checks these properties when an update is requested before committing the update.

To update remote data you must set five properties: Tables, KeyFieldList, UpdateNameList, UpdatableFieldList, and SendUpdates. You can specify additional properties such as Buffering, UpdateType, and WhereType to best fit the requirements of your application.

To enable updates on an active view cursor

- Use the CURSORSETPROP( ) function to specify the view cursor's update properties: Tables, KeyFieldList, UpdateNameList, UpdatableFieldList, and SendUpdates.

   Tip   SQL pass-through view cursors aren't updatable until you specify update properties for the view cursor. If you want to store update property settings persistently, create a view definition. Visual FoxPro supplies default values that prepare the view to be updatable when you create a view using the View Designer or the language. You can use the CURSORSETPROP( ) function to add additional information to supplement or customize the default values.

The update properties you set on the active view cursor have slightly different names than their DBSETPROP( ) counterparts. The following table lists the names used for both view definitions and active cursors.

View and Cursor Update Properties

Purpose	View definition properties[1]	Active cursor properties[2]
Make remote table updatable.	Tables	Tables
Specify the remote names for view fields.	UpdateName (field-level property)	UpdateNameList
Specify view fields you want to use as keys.	KeyField (field-level property)	KeyFieldList
Specify the view fields that are updatable.	Updatable (field-level property)	UpdatableFieldList
Turn updates on.	SendUpdates	SendUpdates

1. Set with DBSETPROP( ).

2. Set with CURSORSETPROP( ).

For more information on setting update properties, see Chapter 8, "Creating Views," or see DBSETPROP( ) or CURSORSETPROP( ) in Help.

Controlling the Timing of Remote Updates

You control how updates to remote data are buffered by setting the cursor's Buffering property. Of the five possible buffering property settings, two are valid for remote views:

- 3, or DB_BUFOPTROW, the default, which optimistically locks the row.
- 5, or DB_BUFOPTTABLE, which optimistically locks the table.

Visual FoxPro supports only optimistic locking on remote cursors.

> **Note**   The pessimistic row and table buffering settings, 2 and 4, don't apply to remote views, because Visual FoxPro doesn't take locks on the server data. Buffering property setting 1 doesn't apply to remote views because views are always buffered.

Using Optimistic Row Buffering

The default Buffering setting, DB_BUFOPTROW, optimistically locks remote data on a row-by-row basis. For example, if you want changes to the titles table to be committed on a row-by-row basis, such as when using the SKIP command, you could set the Buffering property to 3:

```
CURSORSETPROP('buffering', 3, 'titles')
```

When Buffering is set to row buffering, you have two methods of sending updates to the remote server. You can:

- Call the TABLEUPDATE( ) function.
- Use a command that moves the record pointer off the row, such as SKIP or GO BOTTOM.

The TABLEUPDATE( ) function updates the server without moving the record pointer. Commands that move the record pointer send updates to the remote server as a by-product of moving off the updated record.

If you use row buffering and want to be able to revert changes to rows, you must wrap the changes in manual transactions using SQL pass-through transaction functions.

Using Optimistic Table Buffering

If you want changes to a table to be committed a batch at a time, such as when the user clicks a Save or OK button in a form, you can set the Buffering property to 5, or DB_BUFOPTTABLE. You must call the TABLEUPDATE( ) function to send the update to the server.

In the following example, you set the Buffering property in your form's initialization code and then commit the changes in the save code.

Code	Comments
`CURSORSETPROP('buffering', 5, 'sqltitles')`	Set in Init code

`* Update batched changes;`
`* ignore changes made by others`
`TABLEUPDATE(.T., .T., 'titles')`
	Set in Save code

To restore the original values to a table and prevent updates from being sent to the remote server, you call TABLEREVERT( ). You can control whether a single row or all rows are reverted by combining the setting of the cursor's Buffering property with the TABLEREVERT( ) command. The following example reverts only the current row. You might want to invoke this code when the user clicks on a Cancel button in a form:

```
= TABLEREVERT(.F., 'titles')     && Revert current row
```

If you wanted to revert all rows, such as when the user presses ESC to leave a form, you could use the same example, this time changing the settings of the Buffering property and TABLEREVERT( ) command to revert all rows, with the entire table buffered:

```
= TABLEREVERT(.T., 'titles')     && Revert all rows
```

For more information about buffering, see Chapter 17, "Programming for Shared Access." For more information on the TABLEUPDATE( ) and TABLEREVERT( ) commands, see Help.

Detecting Changes by Other Users

In multi-user applications, conflicts with other users' updates are detected by the SQL Update query, which is generated when a write is attempted locally. The level of detection depends on the setting of the WhereType property. For more information on setting the WhereType property, see Chapter 8, "Creating Views."

Forcing Updates

You can use the TABLEUPDATE( ) function to control whether changes made to a table or cursor by another user on a network are overwritten when you send your updates. If you set the Force parameter of TABLEUPDATE( ) to true (.T.), and the CURSORSETPROP( ) UpdateType property is set to the default value, 1, old data is updated with the new data you send, as long as the value in the record's key field on the remote table hasn't been changed. If the value in the remote table's key field has changed, or if the UpdateType property is set to 2, Visual FoxPro sends a DELETE and then an INSERT statement to the remote table.

Troubleshooting Update Error Messages

The following table lists the Visual FoxPro and ODBC error messages that apply specifically to remote updates. The Action column contains the action you take to resolve the error condition.

Error Message	Meaning	Action
No update table(s) specified. Use the Tables cursor property.	The cursor property Tables contains no remote table names. At least one table is required to enable updates to the remote server.	Use the Tables property to specify at least one table for the cursor.
No key column(s) specified for the update table *table_name*. Use the KeyFieldList cursor property.	The primary key for the remote table specified in the error message isn't included in the KeyFieldList property for the cursor; a primary key is required for each table being updated.	Use the KeyFieldList property to specify the primary key for the remote table.
No valid update table specified for column *column_name*. Use the UpdateNameList and Tables cursor properties.	The UpdateName property for column *column_name* has an invalid table qualifier.	Set the table qualifier with the UpdateNameList property, or add the table qualifier to the Tables property setting, or both.
The KeyField List cursor property doesn't define a unique key.	More than one remote record has the same key.	Use the KeyField List property to define a unique key for the remote table.
From ODBC: ODBC invalid object.	ODBC cannot find the remote table or column because it doesn't exist as named. Visual FoxPro field names are validated by Visual FoxPro; remote table and column names are validated only by the remote server.	Check the object name.

For more information on error handling, see "Handling SQL Pass-Through Errors" later in this chapter.

Choosing an Efficient SQL Pass-Through Processing Mode

Visual FoxPro provides two processing modes for retrieving and updating remote data using SQL pass-through: synchronous and asynchronous. When you use SQL pass-through functions you can choose the method you prefer. You don't need to choose a method for remote views; Visual FoxPro automatically employs progressive fetching and manages the processing mode for you for remote views.

Benefits of Synchronous Mode

By default, Visual FoxPro SQL functions are processed synchronously: Visual FoxPro doesn't return control to an application until a function call is completed. Synchronous processing is useful when you're working with Visual FoxPro interactively.

Benefits of Asynchronous Mode

Asynchronous processing provides greater flexibility than synchronous processing. For example, when your application is processing a function asynchronously, your application can build a progress indicator to display the progress of the executing statement, display movement of the mouse pointer, create loops, and set timers to allow interruption of processing that is taking too long.

Using SQL Pass-Through Asynchronously

Your application can request asynchronous processing for the four functions that submit requests to a data source and retrieve data: SQLEXEC( ), SQLMORERESULTS( ), SQLTABLES( ), and SQLCOLUMNS( ). You enable asynchronous processing by setting the Asynchronous property of the connection with the SQLSETPROP( ) function. When asynchronous communication is established for the connection, all four of these functions operate asynchronously.

To check the setting of the Asynchronous property

- Use the SQLGETPROP( ) function to view the Asynchronous property setting. In the following example, `nConnectionHandle` represents the handle number for your active connection:

   ```
   ? SQLGETPROP(nConnectionHandle,'Asynchronous')
   ```

To enable asynchronous processing

- Use the SQLSETPROP( ) function to specify the Asynchronous property:

   ```
   ? SQLSETPROP(nConnectionHandle,'Asynchronous', .T.)
   ```

In Asynchronous mode, you must call each function repeatedly until it returns a value other than 0 (still executing). While the function is still executing, you can cancel processing of the function by pressing the ESC key if the SET ESCAPE property is set to true (.T.).

Until the function has finished processing, the application can use a connection handle only with SQLCANCEL( ) or with the asynchronous function — SQLEXEC( ), SQLMORERESULTS( ), SQLTABLES( ), or SQLCOLUMNS( ) — originally associated with the handle. You can't call any of the other three asynchronous functions or SQLDISCONNECT( ) with the same connection handle until the function has finished.

Processing Multiple Result Sets

Your application retrieves multiple result sets when you use the SQLEXEC( ) function to issue more than one SQL SELECT statement, or to execute a stored procedure that issues multiple SELECT statements. The results of each SQL SELECT statement are returned in a separate Visual FoxPro cursor.

The default name SQLRESULT is used for the first cursor; subsequent cursors are assigned unique names by indexing the default name. For example, the default names for the cursors returned by a SQLEXEC( ) statement requesting three result sets are Sqlresult, Sqlresult1, and Sqlresult2.

In batch mode, if a function returns multiple result sets, the respective cursor names in Visual FoxPro have unique suffixes and can have up to 255 characters. For example, the following example sets the BatchMode property to batch mode, and then issues a SQLEXEC( ) statement containing four SQL SELECT statements that build four result sets:

```
? SQLSETPROP(nConnectionHandle,'BatchMode', .T.)
? SQLEXEC(nConnectionHandle,'select * from authors ;
                 select * from titles ;
                 select * from roysched ;
                 select * from titleauthor','ITEM')
```

When the function above has completed processing, Visual FoxPro returns the four result sets as the Visual FoxPro cursors Item, Item1, Item2, and Item3.

You can change the default name by using the *cCursorname* parameter with the SQLEXEC( ) or SQLMORERESULTS( ) functions. If the name you specify for a result set has already been used, the new result set overwrites the existing cursor.

When your application retrieves multiple result sets, you can choose between asynchronous or synchronous processing and batch or non-batch modes.

Using Batch Mode Processing

The BatchMode property, set with SQLSETPROP( ), controls how SQLEXEC( ) returns multiple result sets. The default value is .T., for batch mode. Batch mode processing means that Visual FoxPro doesn't return any results from a still-executing SQLEXEC( ) call until all of the individual result sets have been retrieved.

Using Non-Batch Mode Processing

If you use SQLSETPROP( ) to set the BatchMode property to .F., for non-batch mode, each result set is returned individually. The first result set is returned by the SQLEXEC( ) function call. Your application must then call SQLMORERESULTS( ) repeatedly until a value of 2 is returned, indicating that no more results are available.

In non-batch mode, the cursor name can be changed in each subsequent SQLMORERESULTS( ) call. In the previous example, if the first cursor name in a SQLEXEC( ) sequence is Item, and the second SQLMORERESULTS( ) call changes the *cCursorName* parameter to Otheritem, the resulting cursors will be named Item, Item1, Otheritem, and Otheritem1.

The next section describes batch mode and non-batch mode processing with synchronous and asynchronous detail added. The following diagram provides a representation of the four possible processing combinations. The numbers 0, 1, and 2 represent the values returned when you call each function.

Visual FoxPro synchronous and asynchronous processing modes

A	B	C	D	
Visual FoxPro Synchronous, Batch	Visual FoxPro Synchronous, No Batch	Visual FoxPro Asynchronous, Batch	Visual FoxPro Asynchronous, No Batch	Data Source
SQLExec( )	SQLExec( )	SQLExec( ) 0	SQLExec( ) 0	Prepare, send, and fetch result set #1.
		SQLExec( ) 0	SQLExec( ) 0	
		SQLExec( ) 0	SQLExec( ) 1	
		SQLExec( ) 0		
	SQLMoreResults( )	SQLExec( ) 0	SQLMoreResults( ) 0	Prepare, send, and fetch result set #2.
		SQLExec() 0	SQLMoreResults( ) 0	
		SQLExec( ) 0	SQLMoreResults( ) 1	
	1	SQLExec() 0		
	SQLMoreResults( )	SQLExec( ) 0	SQLMoreResults() 0	Prepare, send, and fetch result set #3.
		SQLExec( ) 0	SQLMoreResults() 0	
		SQLExec() 3	SQLMoreResults() 1	
3	1		SQLMoreResults() 2	
	SQLMoreResults( ) 2			

time   time   time   time   time

The behavior of each type of processing is explained below: the labels A, B, C, and D reference the preceding diagram. Each explanation assumes the execution of a statement that will return three result sets, represented in the diagram by three horizontal bands.

Using Synchronous Processing

In synchronous mode, control doesn't return to your application until the execution of a function is complete.

A: Synchronous Batch Mode

When you execute a SQL pass-through statement synchronously in batch mode, control isn't returned until all result sets have been retrieved. You specify the name of the first cursor by using the *cCursorname* parameter in the original function. If the cursor you specify already exists, the result set overwrites the existing cursor. When you request multiple result sets in synchronous batch mode, Visual FoxPro creates the names of additional cursors by uniquely indexing the name of the first cursor.

B: Synchronous Non-Batch Mode

When you execute a SQL pass-through statement synchronously in non-batch mode, the first statement retrieves the first result set and returns a 1. You must then call the SQLMORERESULTS( ) function repeatedly, and optionally specify a new name for the cursor. If you don't specify a new name for the cursor, multiple names for multiple result sets are created by uniquely indexing the base name. When SQLMORERESULTS( ) returns a value of 2, there are no more results available.

Using Asynchronous Processing

In asynchronous mode, your application must continue calling the same SQL pass-through function until it returns a value other than 0 (still executing). The default result set name, Sqlresult, can be explicitly changed with the *cCursorname* parameter the first time you call the function. If the name you specify for a result set has already been used, the new result set overwrites the information in the existing cursor.

C: Asynchronous Batch Mode

When you execute asynchronously in batch mode, each repeat call of the original function returns a 0 (still executing) until all of the multiple result sets have been returned to the specified cursors. When all results have been retrieved, the return value is either the number of cursors, or a negative number indicating an error.

D: Asynchronous Non-Batch Mode

When processing asynchronously in non-batch mode, SQLEXEC( ) returns a value of 1 when it completes the retrieval of each result set. Your application must then call SQLMORERESULTS( ) repeatedly until a value of 2 is returned, indicating that no more results are available.

> **Tip**   Remote result sets are retrieved in two stages: first, the result set is prepared on the server; then the result set is fetched into a local Visual FoxPro cursor. In asynchronous mode, you can call the USED( ) function to see whether Visual FoxPro has started fetching the cursor you requested.

Controlling Data Type Conversion

When you move data between a remote server and Visual FoxPro, you may encounter differences in the richness of data types available either on your server or in Visual FoxPro, because there is rarely a one-to-one correlation between data types available on a remote data source and those available in Visual FoxPro. To handle these differences, Visual FoxPro uses ODBC data types to map remote data types to local Visual FoxPro data types. By understanding how data types are mapped between ODBC and Visual FoxPro, you can predict how your server's remote data will be handled in your Visual FoxPro application.

If you need to, you can also adjust the data types used on your server or in your application. The default Visual FoxPro field data type can be overridden by creating a view for the remote data set and then setting the DataType view field property in the database. The DataType property is a character property indicating the desired data type for each field of a remote view. For more information on the DataType property, see DBSETPROP( ) in Help.

Downloading and Uploading Remote View Data

When you retrieve data from a remote ODBC data source, Visual FoxPro converts the data type of each ODBC field into an equivalent Visual FoxPro data type in the result set cursor. The following table lists the data types available on ODBC data sources and their Visual FoxPro equivalents.

ODBC data type of remote field	Field data type in Visual FoxPro cursor
SQL_CHAR SQL_VARCHAR SQL_LONGVARCHAR	Character or Memo[1]
SQL_BINARY SQL_VARBINARY SQL_LONGVARBINARY	Memo

(continued)

ODBC data type of remote field	Field data type in Visual FoxPro cursor
SQL_DECIMAL SQL_NUMERIC	Numeric or Currency[2]
SQL_BIT	Logical
SQL_TINYINT SQL_SMALLINT SQL_INTEGER	Integer
SQL_BIGINT	Character
SQL_REAL SQL_FLOAT SQL_DOUBLE	Double; the number of decimal places is the value of SET DECIMAL in Visual FoxPro
SQL_DATE	Date
SQL_TIME	DateTime[3]
SQL_TIMESTAMP	DateTime[4]

1. If the ODBC field width is less than the value of the cursor property UseMemoSize, it becomes a Character field in the Visual FoxPro cursor; otherwise, it becomes a Memo field. For more information on UseMemoSize, see Help.

2. If the server field is a money data type, it becomes a Currency data type in Visual FoxPro.

3. The day defaults to 1/1/1900.

4. If the value in the SQL_TIMESTAMP field contains fractions of seconds, the fractions are truncated when the value is converted to a Visual FoxPro DateTime data type.

Note   Null values in ODBC data source fields become null values in the Visual FoxPro cursor, regardless of the SET NULL setting in Visual FoxPro at the time your application retrieves remote data.

Converting Visual FoxPro Parameters to Remote View Data Types

If Visual FoxPro data exists in a cursor that originated from remote data, the data goes back to its original ODBC type when sent to the remote server. If you send data that originated in Visual FoxPro to the remote server via SQL pass-through, the following conversions apply.

Visual FoxPro data type	ODBC data type
Character	SQL_CHAR or SQL_LONGVARCHAR[1]
Currency	SQL_DECIMAL
Date	SQL_DATE or SQL_TIMESTAMP[2]
DateTime	SQL_TIMESTAMP
Double	SQL_DOUBLE
Integer	SQL_INTEGER
General	SQL_LONGVARBINARY
Logical	SQL_BIT
Memo	SQL_LONGVARCHAR
Numeric	SQL_DOUBLE

1. If the Visual FoxPro variable that maps to a parameter creates an expression whose width is less than 255, it becomes a SQL_CHAR type in the ODBC data source; otherwise, it becomes a SQL_LONGVARCHAR type.

2. Visual FoxPro Date data is converted to SQL_DATE for all ODBC data sources except SQL Server, where it becomes SQL_TIMESTAMP.

Mapping a Visual FoxPro Parameter into a Remote Data Type

You can map a Visual FoxPro parameter value to a particular remote data type by formatting the parameter as a character expression that uses the syntax for the desired remote data type. For example, if your server provides a DateTime data type, you can create your Visual FoxPro parameter as a character expression in the format used by your server to represent DateTime data. When your server receives the parameter value, it attempts to map the formatted data to the DateTime data type.

Note   When you send a parameter to the remote server, be sure the data type in the WHERE clause matches the data type that's used for the parameter expression.

Handling SQL Pass-Through Errors

If a SQL pass-through function returns an error, Visual FoxPro stores the error message in an array. The AERROR( ) function provides information about errors that are detected in any of the component levels: Visual FoxPro, the ODBC data source, or the remote server. By examining the values returned by AERROR( ), you can determine the server error that occurred and its error message text. For more information on AERROR( ), see Help.

Important   You must call AERROR( ) immediately to obtain error information. If you generate any other error before you call AERROR( ), the error information is lost.

CHAPTER 22

Optimizing Client/Server Performance

Once you've implemented your client/server application, you might find areas where you'd like to improve performance. For example, you can fine-tune your application to gain maximum performance by speeding up forms and queries and increasing data throughput.

This chapter discusses optimization strategies for application performance on the client, network, and server. For information about implementing client/server applications, see earlier chapters in this book.

This chapter discusses:

- Optimizing Connection Use
- Speeding Up Data Retrieval
- Speeding Up Queries and Views
- Speeding Up Forms
- Improving Performance on Updates and Deletes

Optimizing Connection Use

Establishing a connection uses time and memory on both the client and the server. When you optimize connections, you balance your need for high performance against the resource requirements of your application.

The number of connections used by Visual FoxPro depends on whether you force the closing of unused connections, and how you set the length of the connection idle time-out.

Using Shared Connections

You can use connections exclusively or share a connection. Each method has its benefits. When you use a connection exclusively, your application experiences no contentions for connection resources once a connection is established. If each result set uses an exclusive connection, you can also intermingle asynchronous processing on multiple result sets.

When you use a shared connection, you have one connection for multiple result sets. You must serialize data manipulation operations on the result sets sharing the same connection, and design the application to test the connection for busyness any time conflicts might occur. For information on sharing a connection, see Chapter 8, "Creating Views," in Part 2, "Working with Data."

Controlling Connection Timeouts

If your application doesn't take any action for a long time, you can reduce connection use by setting the IdleTimeout property on the connection. The IdleTimeout property controls the interval of time connections are allowed to idle before they're closed by Visual FoxPro. By default, connections wait indefinitely and are not deactivated until specifically closed by the user.

You set the idle time for a connection definition with the IdleTimeout property of the DBSETPROP( ) function; you can set the IdleTimeout property for an active connection with the SQLSETPROP( ) function. For more information, search for DBSETPROP( ) and SQLSETPROP( ) in Help.

Visual FoxPro closes connections even if Browse windows and forms displaying remote data are still open, and then automatically reconnects when the connection is needed again. However, Visual FoxPro cannot close a connection if:

- Results of a query from the server are pending.

- The connection is in manual transaction mode. You must commit or roll back the transaction and switch to automatic transaction mode before the connection can be closed.

You set the transaction mode for a connection definition with the Transactions property of the DBSETPROP( ) function; you can set the transaction mode for an active connection with the SQLSETPROP( ) function.

Releasing Connections

You can improve performance by closing connections that your application is no longer using. Connections are closed automatically for you when you close a view. If the connection is shared by multiple views, Visual FoxPro closes the connection when the last view using the connection is closed.

You can control the connection for a query manually if you don't want to update the data in a cursor. Use a SQL pass-through query to select the data you need into a local cursor and then close the connection.

Speeding Up Data Retrieval

You can speed up data retrieval by managing the number of rows fetched during progressive fetching, controlling fetch size, and by using delayed Memo fetching.

You can also use the UseMemoSize view property to return character fields as memo fields and then turn FetchMemo off to enable your application to selectively fetch those character fields converted to memo fields.

Using Progressive Fetching

When you query a remote data source, Visual FoxPro retrieves complete rows of data and builds a Visual FoxPro cursor. To speed retrieval of remote data, Visual FoxPro employs progressive fetching of view cursors and cursors created asynchronously with SQL pass-through. Rather than requiring you or your application to wait while an entire data set is retrieved, Visual FoxPro executes a query and fetches only a small subset of the result set rows into the local cursor. The size of this subset is 100 rows by default.

Note   Synchronous SQL pass-through statements don't employ progressive fetching. The entire result set requested by a SQLEXEC( ) statement is retrieved before control is returned to your application.

As Visual FoxPro retrieves additional rows of data, the local cursor contains increasingly more of the queried data. Since rows are retrieved at different times from the data source, the information in the rows isn't automatically current. If your connection is operating in asynchronous mode, Visual FoxPro returns control to you or your program as soon as it fetches the first subset of data. During idle time, Visual FoxPro performs a background fetch of the remaining rows in the queried data, one subset at a time, into the local cursor. This scenario allows you to use the already fetched data in the cursor without having to wait for the rest of the data.

Note   Increasing the number of rows fetched improves performance, but decreases the responsiveness of the user interface. Decreasing the number of rows fetched has the inverse effect.

Fetching Data on Demand

You can disable progressive fetching and fetch rows only on an as-needed basis by using the FetchAsNeeded database and view cursor property. This can result in more efficient data retrieval for remote views or views retrieving extremely large results sets.

The FetchAsNeeded property is set by default to false (.F.), which means that progressive fetching is employed by default. When you set the FetchAsNeeded property to true (.T.), rows are fetched only when needed. When the FetchAsNeeded property is set to true, you cannot perform an update until you either complete the fetch, call the SQLCANCEL( ) function on the current connection handle, or close the view.

If you want to see the impact of using the FetchAsNeeded property, set the FetchAsNeeded property on a view retrieving a large result set to .T. and then open a browse window on the view and scroll down. The status bar is updated to show the number of rows retrieved as you move through the browse window.

Controlling Cursor Fetching

If you want to fetch the entire cursor, you can issue the GOTO BOTTOM command, or any command requiring access to the entire data set.

> **Tip**   While you can use the GOTO BOTTOM command to fetch the entire cursor, it's often more efficient to build a parameterized view that fetches only a single row at a time and requeries as the user changes records. For more information on building high-performance views, see Chapter 8, "Creating Views," in Part 2, "Working with Data."

Programs don't provide idle loop processing. To fetch view cursors programmatically, use the GO *nRecordNumber* or GOTO BOTTOM commands. To fetch cursors created with SQL pass-through in asynchronous mode, call the SQL pass-through asynchronous function once for each row subset.

Canceling a SQLEXEC( ) Statement

You can use the SQLCANCEL( ) function to cancel a SQLEXEC( ) statement or a view at any time. However, if the server has completed building the remote result set and Visual FoxPro has begun fetching the remote result set into a local cursor, the SQLCANCEL( ) function cancels the SQLEXEC( ) statement and leaves the local cursor. If you want to delete the local cursor you can issue the USE command, which closes the cursor and cancels the fetch.

The USE command will not cancel a SQLEXEC( )statement if the statement hasn't yet created a local cursor. To determine whether Visual FoxPro has created a local cursor, you can call the USED( ) function.

Controlling Fetch Size

You control the number of rows fetched at one time by your application from a remote server by setting the FetchSize property on your view. The FetchSize property specifies how many records are fetched into the local cursor from the remote server at one time, through progressive fetching or asynchronous SQL pass-through calls. The default value is 100 rows.

To control the number of records fetched at one time into a view

- In the View Designer, choose **Advanced Options** from the **Query** menu. In the **Data Fetching** area of the **Advanced Options** dialog box, use the spinner to set a value for **Number of Records to Fetch at a time**.

  – or –

Set the FetchSize property with the DBSETPROP( ) function to set the view definition's fetch size.

– or –

Set the FetchSize property with the CURSORSETPROP( ) function to set the active view cursor's fetch size.

For example, the following code sets the view definition to progressively fetch 50 rows at a time into `Customer_remote_view`:

```
? DBSETPROP('Customer_remote_view', 'View', 'FetchSize', 50)
```

Using Delayed Memo Fetching

A well-designed application frequently uses delayed Memo fetching to speed downloading of result sets that contain Memo or General fields. Delayed Memo fetching means that Memo and General field contents are not automatically downloaded when you download a result set. Instead, the rest of the fields in the row are quickly downloaded, and Memo and General field contents aren't fetched until you request them by opening the Memo or General field. Delayed Memo fetching provides the fastest downloading of rows, and allows Memo or General field contents, which can be quite large, to be fetched only if needed by the user.

For example, your form might include a General field that displays a picture. To speed performance, you can use delayed Memo fetching to prevent downloading of the picture until the user chooses a "Preview" button on your form. The code behind the "Preview" button then fetches the General field and displays it on the form.

To control delayed Memo fetching, you use the FetchMemo property on your view or cursor. The FetchMemo property specifies whether to fetch the contents of the Memo or General fields when the row is downloaded. The default value is true (.T.), which means that Memo and General fields are downloaded automatically. If your data contains large amounts of Memo or General field data, you might notice increased performance when you set the FetchMemo property to false (.F.).

> **Note**   The view must be updatable to allow delayed Memo fetching to work, because Visual FoxPro uses the key field values established by the update properties to locate the source row on the server when it retrieves the Memo or General field. For information on making a view updatable, see Chapter 8, "Creating Views," in Part 2, "Working with Data."

Use DBSETPROP( ) to set the FetchMemo property on a view, and CURSORSETPROP( ) to set the FetchMemo property on a cursor.

Optimizing Data Fetching Performance

You can use the following recommendations for setting connection and view properties to optimize data fetching. The PacketSize property on your connection has the greatest influence on performance. Also, you can optimize fetch performance using synchronous connections.

Object	Property	Setting
Connection	PacketSize	4K to 12K[1]
Connection	Asynchronous[2]	.F.
View	FetchSize[3]	Maximum

1. Set a higher value for rows containing more data; you should experiment to find the best value.
2. Use synchronous connections to increase performance up to 50%, unless you want to be able to cancel SQL statements while executing on the server.
3. The effect of FetchSize is highly dependent on the record size of the fetched result set. In synchronous mode, it does not significantly affect performance, so set it as needed for SQL pass-through asynchronous processing view progressive fetching. FetchSize, if reduced, provides significantly better responsiveness while progressively fetching a view, but slows down the fetch speed. If increased, it increases view fetch performance.

Actual performance depends greatly on your system configuration and application requirements. These recommendations are based on a client machine running Windows NT version 3.5, with ODBC version 2.10 and a SQL Server ODBC driver version 2.05; and a server machine running Windows NT version 3.5 with SQL Server version 4.21 and version 6.0.

Speeding Up Queries and Views

You can improve query and view performance by adding indexes, optimizing local and remote processing, and optimizing parameter expressions.

Adding Indexes to Remote Tables

Remote indexes can make queries significantly faster. Multiple-table queries are faster if the tables are indexed on the joining fields. Having indexes on fields that are included in a query's WHERE clause can also improve performance.

Clustered indexes provide the best performance. On SQL Server, each table can have one clustered index. The SQL Server Upsizing Wizard automatically creates clustered indexes on tables that had a primary key in Visual FoxPro.

Tip   While indexes on table fields used in queries can speed processing, indexes on result sets can slow performance. Use indexes on result sets with care.

Optimizing Local and Remote Processing

If you need to process a combination of local and remote data, create a remote view that combines all remote data in a single view. You can then join the remote view with the local data in a local view. Because Visual FoxPro fetches both views completely before joining and filtering the combined view, it's important to limit the size of the view result set.

You gain speed in remote processing by limiting the remote view result set to the minimum amount of data needed by your application. When you retrieve less data into a remote result set, you minimize the time required to download remote data into your local query or view cursor.

Optimizing Parameterized Views

You can speed data retrieval during REQUERY( ) operations on an open, parameterized view by compiling the view before it's executed. To precompile or "prepare" a view, set the Prepared property on the view to true (.T.). For more information on the Prepared property, see Help.

Optimizing Parameter Expressions

View and SQL pass-through parameters are Visual FoxPro expressions and are evaluated in Visual FoxPro before being sent to the remote server. Evaluation time for the expression is important, because it lengthens the query execution time.

Speeding Up Forms

When you design a form based primarily on server data, take a minimalist approach for the best performance. Determine the data and functionality needed, and delay asking the server for this data and functionality until requested by the user. Requesting data from the server uses processing time and creates network traffic. To request less data in your forms:

- Request as few records as possible. For example, use a filter or query to limit the size of the record set. Make sure that the server can process any restrictions you use.

- Use as few remote fields as possible in views underlying your forms.

- Use as few forms that access remote views as possible in your form set. When you open a form set, all the forms in the form set are opened and populated with data as applicable. By limiting the number of forms in your form set, especially those that must connect to a server and retrieve remote data, you shorten the time the form set takes to load.

- Use fewer bound controls that access remote data. Each combo box, list box, and grid that's bound to a remote table or query requires a separate query to the server when the form is opened. Avoid controls containing totals, or list boxes and combo boxes that have large row sources.

- If users need to compare multiple sets of data, consider storing the data returned by the server in temporary local tables. Provide a form in which the user can use the previously stored data, or execute a new query.

Storing Lookup Tables Locally

Often, an application contains several forms that use the same remote table. If the data in the table doesn't change frequently, you can speed up form loading and reduce server load using one of the following techniques:

- Store tables that never change and aren't too large (such as the names and abbreviations of the regions or states in your country) in the local Visual FoxPro application database. If the table is joined in queries or views with remote tables, you should also keep a copy of it on the server to avoid joining local and remote data.

- Store tables that rarely change (such as a list of company buildings) both on the server and in the local application database. Provide a way for the user to download the table when the data does change.

- Store tables that change occasionally but not daily (such as a list of employees in a small company or department) both on the server and in the local application database. Your application should automatically refresh the local version each time it starts. This method uses extra time when the application starts, but speeds up queries when the application is running.

Displaying Fields Only on Request

Display fields that take a long time to retrieve data from the server, such as Memo or General fields, only when requested. You can use the following techniques:

- If your form is based on a view, place Memo or General fields off screen on another form page. Add a label to the form, such as "Page down to see notes and pictures," that informs the user how to display the information. Set the FetchMemo property on the view or cursor to false (.F.), so that Visual FoxPro doesn't retrieve Memo or General fields until they're displayed on screen.

- Set the Visible property to false (.F.) for controls bound to Memo or General fields. Add a toggle button or command button that sets the property to true (.T.), so that the user can choose to view the contents of these controls.

- Display the most important fields on a main form, and provide a button labeled "More Information" that opens another form containing other fields. Base the second form on a view that's parameterized by the primary key field on the main form. For example, suppose you have a main form based on a view whose SQL SELECT statement includes the following code:

```
SELECT customer_id, company_name, address, city, region, country
FROM customers
```

In the preceding form, `cust_id` is bound to `thisform.txtCust_id`. You could base the second form on the following view, which is used only when the user chooses the "More Information" button:

```
SELECT orders.order_id, orders.order_date, orders.shipper_id, ;
    employee.emp_id, employee.last_name, employee.first_name ;
FROM orders, employee ;
WHERE orders.cust_id = ?THISFORM.txtCust_id ;
AND orders.employee_id = employees.emp_id
```

Improving Performance on Updates and Deletes

You can speed up Update and Delete statements by:

- Adding timestamps to your remote tables.
- Using the CompareMemo property.
- Using manual transaction mode.
- Using server-stored procedures.
- Batching updates.

Adding Timestamps

You can improve performance when you update, insert, or delete data in a remote table that contains many fields by adding a timestamp field to the remote table, if your server provides the Timestamp field type.

The presence of a timestamp field in a remote table allows you to use the Visual FoxPro SQL WhereType update option DB_KEYANDTIMESTAMP. This option saves processing time because Visual FoxPro compares only two fields in your view, the key field and the timestamp field, against a remote table to detect update conflicts. By comparing only two fields, rather than all the updatable fields (with the DB_KEYANDUPDATABLE option) or all the modified fields (with the DB_KEYANDMODIFIED option), the DB_KEYANDTIMESTAMP option reduces the time it takes to update remote data. For more information on WhereType options, see Chapter 8, "Creating Views," in Part 2, "Working with Data."

Note   The DB_KEYANDTIMESTAMP option compares the key and timestamp fields only when your remote table contains a timestamp field. If you use the DB_KEYANDTIMESTAMP option against a remote table that doesn't contain a timestamp field, Visual FoxPro compares the key fields only.

The Upsizing Wizard can automatically add timestamp fields as appropriate to tables you export. For more information, see "Timestamp and Identity Columns" in Chapter 20, "Upsizing Visual FoxPro Databases."

Tip   If you do something that alters the structure of a view's base table, such as adding a timestamp field, you might need to re-create the view. The fields in a view definition are stored in the database, and any changes to the base tables for a view after the view is used aren't reflected in the view definition until you re-create the view.

Excluding Memo Fields from the Update WHERE Clause

Whenever appropriate, you can speed updates by preventing view memo fields (fields of type Memo, General, or Picture) from being compared against their base table counterparts. By default, the CompareMemo property is set to true (.T.), which automatically includes memo fields in the SQL WHERE clause generated when you create an updatable view. You can set the CompareMemo property to false (.F.) to exclude memos from the SQL WHERE clause.

Using Transactions

For optimum performance, use manual transaction mode and manage transactions yourself. Manual transaction mode allows you to control when you commit a group of transactions, which enables the server to process more statements quickly.

Automatic transaction mode is more time-consuming, because by default every single update statement is wrapped in a separate transaction. This method provides maximum control over each individual update statement, but also increases overhead.

You can improve performance in automatic transaction mode by increasing the setting of the BatchUpdateCount property on the view or cursor. When you use a large BatchUpdateCount setting, many update statements are batched in a single update statement, which is then wrapped in a single transaction. However, if any statement in the batch fails, the entire batch is rolled back.

Tip   The BatchUpdateCount property isn't supported by some servers; you should test this property against each remote server before deploying it in your application.

Using Server-Stored Procedures

You can create stored procedures on the server, which are precompiled and therefore run very quickly. You can execute stored procedures, send parameters with SQL pass-through, and move additional processing to the server as appropriate for your application.

For example, you might want to collect user input locally and then execute a SQL pass-through query to send the data to the server, calling the appropriate stored procedure. To do this, you might want to create a form on a local cursor or array to collect data and then write code that constructs a SQLEXEC( ) statement by using the name of the server-stored procedure and the parameters to be supplied. You could then add this code to the Click event of a command button titled "OK" or "Commit." When the user chooses the button, the SQLEXEC( ) statement runs. Using server stored procedures to update remote data can be more efficient, because the stored procedures are compiled on the server.

Batching Updates

If your application updates a number of records, you might want to batch updates so they're handled more efficiently by the network and server. Update or Insert statements are batched before being sent to the server, according to the setting of the BatchUpdateCount property of the view. The default value is 1, which means that each record is sent to the server with an update statement. You can reduce network traffic by increasing the value to package multiple updates in a statement.

> **Tip**   The BatchUpdateCount property isn't supported by some servers; you should test this property against each remote server before deploying it in your application.

To use this feature efficiently, the view connection should be set to Buffering mode 5, for optimistic table buffering, and changes ideally should be confined to the same fields in each row of the cursor. You can use DBSETPROP( ) to set the BatchUpdateCount property for the view definition; to change the value for an active view cursor, use CURSORSETPROP( ).

Optimizing Performance of Updates and Deletes

You can use the following guidelines for setting view and connection properties to optimize performance of updates and deletes. The BatchSize property on your view has the greatest influence on performance.

Object	Property	Setting	Notes
View	BatchUpdateCount	10–30 rows	Set a higher value for smaller-sized updates.[1] Set to increase performance by up to 50%. The default is 1.
Connection	Asynchronous	(.F.)	Use synchronous connections to increase performance up to 50%, unless you want to be able to cancel SQL statements while executing on the server. The default is synchronous.
Connection	WaitTime	N/A	To increase performance in asynchronous mode, use a shorter wait time; to reduce network traffic, increase the wait time.
Connection	PacketSize	4K to 12K	Has little effect on performance.

* Your best value also depends on the speed of your server.

Actual performance depends greatly on your system configuration and application requirements. Experiment with the listed values to determine the best settings for your configuration. The previous recommendations were optimal based on a client machine running Windows NT version 3.5 with ODBC 2.10 and SQL Server Driver 2.05; and a server machine running Windows NT, Version 3.5 with Microsoft SQL Server 4.21 and 6.0.

PART 7

Creating Help Files

Help files are a valuable source of information for users of your application. With Visual FoxPro, you can choose to create Winhelp, HTML Help, or .DBF-style Help.

Chapter 23   Creating Graphical Help

Graphical Help can be Winhelp, for a Windows look and feel, or HTML Help, for a Web look and feel.

Chapter 24   Creating .DBF-Style Help

.DBF-style Help is character-based and gives you the flexibility to move your Help file to other platforms. This style of Help is easy to create because it's based on a Visual FoxPro table.

Creating Graphical Help

You can add professional polish to your application by adding a graphical Help file in the form of HTML or WinHelp Help. Graphical Help can include graphics and formatted text; .dbf-style Help is limited to a single font without graphics. For information about creating .DBF–style Help, see Chapter 24, "Creating .DBF–Style Help."

Note Microsoft Visual Studio 6.0 includes Microsoft HTML Help Workshop (Hhw.exe) for creating HTML Help files. It does not include Microsoft Help Workshop 4.0 (Hcw.exe) for creating Winhelp files. Previous versions of Microsoft Visual FoxPro include Microsoft Help Workshop 4.0.

This chapter discusses:

- HTML Help
- WinHelp 4.0

HTML Help

HTML Help provides many of the features of Winhelp, and adds the following features:

- Support for HTML.
- Support for ActiveX, Java, and scripting (Javascript and Microsoft Visual Basic Script).
- Support for HTML image formats (.jpg, .gif, .png).
- Capability to jump from a Help topic to a site on the Internet.
- Capability to view the HTML code for a Help topic.

HTML Help is created with Microsoft HTML Help Workshop, which is included with Visual Studio and stand-alone Visual FoxPro. HTML Help Workshop provides a complete authoring system for HTML Help, and includes backwards compatibility that allows you to easily create HTML Help files from existing Winhelp projects. To create HTML Help files for your application, consult the online Help for the HTML Help Workshop.

A sample HTML Help project, part of the Solutions sample, is included in …\Samples\Vfp98\Solution\Help. It includes the following files:

File	Description
Solution.chm	Compiled Help file.
Solution.hhp	Project file — a text file that brings together all the elements of a help project and contains information about how a compiled help file will appear.
Solution.hhk	Index file — contains the index entries (keywords) for your index.
Solution.hhc	Table of Contents file.
Solution.ali	Alias file for context-sensitive Help support. Maps product Ids to Help topics.
Solution.hh	Header file for context-sensitive Help support. Includes product Ids.
Solution.chi	Index file used when you ship .chm files that are likely to remain on a CD–ROM, as in the case of the MSDN Library. The .chi file allows certain navigation information to be installed locally on a hard disk for quick access, while the main content lives on the CD–ROM. A .chi file should not be used in a non-CD–ROM scenario. When a .chi file is not used all the information that would be in it remains in the .chm itself.
MSDN_ie3.css	Cascading style sheet.
MSDN_ie4.css	Cascading style sheet.
FileName.htm	Source content files.
FileName.gif	Source graphics files.

Planning Access to Online HTML Help

In addition to creating an HTML Help file that contains useful information, you need to provide a means for users of your application to access Help. There are three ways to deliver Help:

- A Help menu — a menu that appears on the main menu bar of your application.

- Context-sensitive Help — Help that appears when a user presses F1 (or another key that you specify) while a particular object, control, or menu option is selected.

- "What's This?" Help — Help that appears when a user calls for help on a particular object or control.

Implementing HTML Help is similar to implementing WinHelp. The following sections describe how you can implement HTML Help for your application.

Planning a Help Menu

A Help menu typically contains commands that provide access to the topics in your Help system. It is strongly recommended to have a single command on your Help menu that opens your HTML Help system. Beyond that, you can place additional commands on the Help menu that provide system information, or copyright and version information about your application.

Adding Context Sensitivity

Context-sensitive Help allows users to easily access Help topics relating to what they are doing or seeing in your application at any given time. For example, if a user is viewing a data entry form, context-sensitive Help could provide a topic relating specifically to that data entry form.

You decide the level of detail at which context-sensitive Help is implemented in your application. For example, you can associate a context-sensitive Help topic with a form, or you can associate more detailed Help topics with each control and field on your form.

Context-sensitive Help is typically accessed by pressing F1, but you can specify any key to activate context-sensitive Help with ON KEY LABEL.

Using Context-Sensitive Help on a Form

To implement context-sensitive Help, you must specify a Help file for your application, and then associate specific Help topics with different objects in your application.

To add context-sensitive Help

1. Specify a Help file for your application.

2. Assign a Help topic to each object for which you plan to provide context-sensitive Help.

Specifying a Help File

You determine the Help file that can be accessed in your application by including the command SET HELP TO file in your code, where *file* is the name of your Help file. For example, if your Help file is called Myhelp.chm, you can use the following command:

```
SET HELP TO MYHELP.CHM
```

This command is typically included in the setup code for the main program of your application.

Assigning Help Topics

You can assign a Help topic to specific objects in your Visual FoxPro application.

To assign a Help topic to an object

1. In Design mode, open the object — a form, control, or toolbar, for example — that you want to assign context-sensitive Help to.

2. View the object's properties.

3. Set the HelpContextID property to the number representing a specific topic in your HTML Help file.

For more information about mapping HTML Help topics to context ID numbers, consult the online Help for the HTML Help Workshop.

Note   To assign Help topics to menu titles or menu commands, you must include the SET TOPIC TO command in the procedure associated with the menu title or menu command. For more information, search for SET TOPIC in Help.

Implementing "What's This?" Help

"What's This?" Help is similar to context-sensitive Help because it provides Help related to the specific object or control that currently has focus.

For WinHelp, instead of invoking the Help file and displaying the Help topic in the full default-sized Help window, "What's This?" Help displays the topic in a small pop-up window that disappears as soon as the user clicks anywhere on the screen. "What's This?" Help is useful for providing brief tip-style descriptions or definitions for specific controls.

Unlike WinHelp, HTML "What's This?" Help is displayed in the full default-sized Help window.

You associate "What's This?" Help with a particular form, form control, or toolbar by setting its WhatsThisHelpID property to a number representing a specific topic in your Help file.

Use the following properties and methods to implement "What's This?" Help:

Property	Description
WhatsThisHelp	Set this property to true (.T.) on a form to enable "What's This?" Help for the form and any controls on the form.
WhatsThisButton	Set this property to true (.T.) if you want a "What's This?" Help button to appear in the title bar of the form.
WhatsThisHelpID	For a form, control, or toolbar, set this property to an ID number corresponding to a topic in your HTML Help file.
WhatsThisMode	Use this method to display the "What's This?" Help question mark mouse pointer and enable "What's This?" Help mode. Clicking an object displays the "What's This?" Help topic specified by the WhatsThisHelpID property for the object.

To implement "What's This?" Help

1. In design mode, open the form you want to enable "What's This?" Help for.

2. Set the form's WhatsThisHelp property to true (.T.).

3. To display a "What's This?" Help button in the form's title bar, set the form's WhatsThisButton property to true (.T.).

4. To associate a "What's This?" Help topic with the form, set the form's WhatsThisHelpID property to an ID number corresponding to a topic in your HTML Help file.

5. To associate a "What's This?" Help topic with a specific control on the form, select the control and set its WhatsThisHelpID property to an ID number corresponding to a topic in your HTML Help file.

Programming Help Features

You can program your application so that users can access your HTML Help system. Although an HTML Help system can consist of one or more separate files, Help appears to users as part of your application.

You can program your Visual FoxPro application to use graphical and .dbf-style Help with the SET HELP TO and SET TOPIC TO commands. SET HELP TO specifies the name of a custom Help file for your application. SET TOPIC TO sets the identifying keyword for a topic in the custom Help file.

Reserving F1

When a user presses F1 in your application, Visual FoxPro can display a context-sensitive Help topic. To do this, assign a Help context ID to a topic in your Help table and assign the same value to the HelpContextID property of your form or control. When the form or control has the focus and the user presses F1, Visual FoxPro displays the matching topic.

Note   F1 is enabled for context-sensitive Help by default. Because this is a recognized standard for Help, redefining this key is not recommended.

Including Help Buttons on Forms

If you add Help buttons to your forms, users can access Help more easily. You should especially consider adding a Help button if your user is a novice.

To set context sensitivity and add a Help button

1. In the Init event for your form, set the HelpContextID property for all the form's objects to the same value you assigned to the Help topic. For example, if the value is 7, you can use the following command:

    ```
    THIS.SetAll("HelpContextID", 7)
    ```

2. Add a command button to your form.
3. Set the Caption property of the command button to Help.
4. In the Click event of the command button, add the following command:

    ```
    HELP ID THIS.HelpContextID
    ```

    Tip   Save the Help button as a class so that you can easily add it to any form. For more information about saving objects as classes, see Chapter 9, "Creating Forms," in Part 3, "Creating the Interface."

Distributing a Compiled HTML Help System

In addition to the .chm file you create for your HTML Help system, you can use a free-distributable setup program, Hhupd.exe, that will install and register the HTML Help run-time components listed below. Internet Explorer or the Internet Explorer run-time engine must be installed on your users' machines.

Component Name	Description
Hhctrl.ocx	HTML Help ActiveX control
Itss.dll	Dynamic link library that handles compiled HTML
Itircl.dll	Full-text search Dynamic link library
Hh.exe	HTML Help viewer

You will find this setup program in the Redist folder in the folder where HTML Help Workshop has been installed. This setup program can be called from other setup programs, and can be made to run in 'quiet' mode so that it does not interfere with the setup program you may have already created. For a complete list of command line options, run Hhupd.exe/?.

WinHelp 4.0

Use the Microsoft Help Workshop, provided with previous versions of Visual FoxPro, to create Winhelp files. The Microsoft Help Workshop includes a Help Authoring Guide. The Help Authoring Guide (Hcw.hlp) is a graphical Help file that contains much of the information you will need to author a robust Help system.

Choosing Help Features

WinHelp systems can have some or all of the following features:

- A contents page that provides a hierarchical view of the topics in your Help system.

- An index, based on keywords you provide, that guides a user to specific information.

- Full-text search capabilities that allow users to search for information in Help based on specific words and phrases.

- Text with multiple fonts, font sizes, and colors.

- Graphics, including bitmaps with multiple resolutions.

- Macros that automate or extend the operation of the Help system.

- Hot spots — mouse-sensitive areas you create to give users jumps that link topics; pop-up windows that display additional text; and macro commands that you add to the Help system.

- Segmented hypergraphics: graphics with one or more hot spots.

- Secondary windows.

- Customizable menus.

- Graphics in Windows metafile format.

- .DLLs.

Planning Access to Online Help

In addition to creating a WinHelp file that contains useful information, you need to provide a means for users of your application to access Help. There are three ways to deliver Help:

- A Help menu — a menu that appears on the main menu bar of your application.

- Context-sensitive Help — Help that appears when a user presses F1 (or another key that you specify) while a particular object, control, or menu option is selected.

- "What's This" Help — Help that appears as a brief pop-up tip when a user calls for help on a particular object or control.

Planning a Help Menu

A Help menu typically contains commands that provide access to the topics in your Help system. WinHelp 4.0 features the Help Finder window, which is a single dialog box providing access to contents, index, and full-text searching.

The Help Finder Window

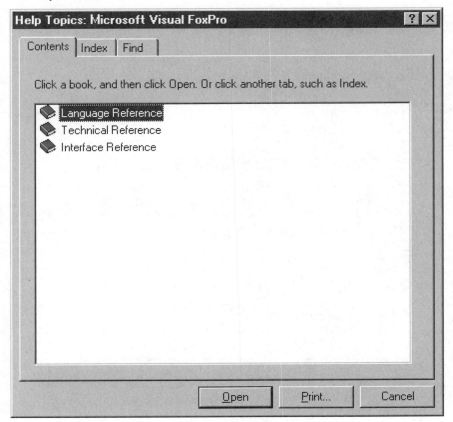

It is strongly recommended to have a single command on your Help menu that opens the Help Finder window. Beyond that, you can place additional commands on the Help menu that provide system information, or copyright and version information about your application.

You can call the Help Finder window programmatically using the WinHelp function with the HELP FINDER parameter. For more information, see "Using the WinHelp Function" later in this chapter, and the WinHelp topic in the *Help Authoring Guide*.

Adding Context Sensitivity to Help

Context-sensitive Help allows users to easily access Help topics relating to what they are doing or seeing in your application at any given time. For example, if a user is viewing a data entry form, context-sensitive Help could provide a topic relating specifically to that data entry form.

You decide the level of detail at which context-sensitive Help is implemented in you application. For example, you can associate a context-sensitive Help topic with a form, or you can associate more detailed Help topics with each control and field on your form.

Context-sensitive Help is typically accessed by pressing F1, but you can specify any key to activate context-sensitive Help with ON KEY LABEL.

Using Context-Sensitive WinHelp on a Form

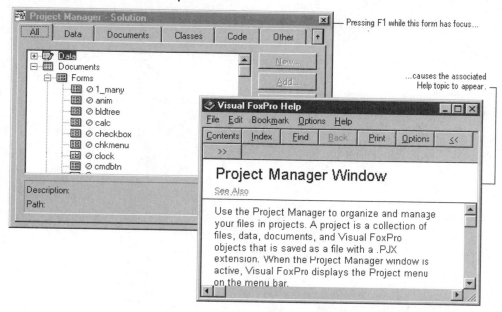

To implement context-sensitive Help, you must specify a Help file for your application, and then associate specific Help topics with different objects in your application.

To add context-sensitive Help

1. Specify a Help file for your application.

2. Assign a Help topic to each object for which you plan to provide context-sensitive Help.

Specifying a Help File

You determine the Help file that can be accessed in your application by including the command SET HELP TO file in your code, where *file* is the name of your Help file. For example, if your Help file is called Myhelp.hlp, you can use the following command:

```
SET HELP TO MYHELP.HLP
```

This command is typically included in the setup code for the main program of your application.

Assigning Help Topics

You can assign a Help topic to specific objects in your Visual FoxPro application.

To assign a Help topic to an object

1. In Design mode, open the object — a form, control, or toolbar, for example — that you want to assign context-sensitive Help to.

2. View the object's properties.

3. Set the HelpContextID property to the number representing a specific topic in your Help file.

For more information about mapping Help topics to context ID numbers, see the *Help Authoring Guide*.

> **Note**   To assign Help topics to menu titles or menu commands, you must include the SET TOPIC TO command in the procedure associated with the menu title or menu command. For more information, search for SET TOPIC in Help.

Implementing "What's This?" Help

"What's This?" Help is similar to context-sensitive Help because it provides Help related to the specific object or control that currently has focus. However, instead of invoking the Help file and displaying the Help topic in the full default-sized Help window, "What's This?" Help displays the topic in a small pop-up window that disappears as soon as the user clicks anywhere on the screen. "What's This?" Help is useful for providing brief tip-style descriptions or definitions for specific controls.

> **Tip**   Keep your "What's This?" Help topics brief and concise so that the window doesn't grow too large to obscure the feature you're describing.

"What's This?" Help

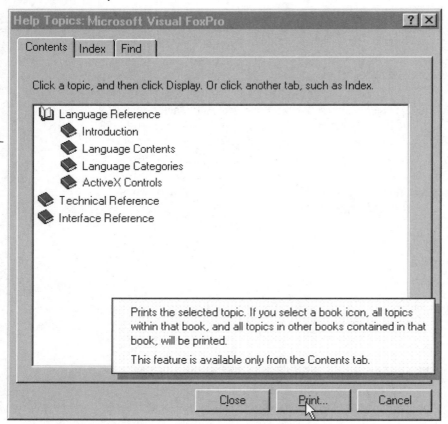

You associate "What's This?" Help with a particular form, form control, or toolbar by setting its WhatsThisHelpID property to a number representing a specific topic in your Help file.

Use the following properties and methods to implement "What's This?" Help:

Property	Description
WhatsThisHelp	Set this property to true (.T.) on a form to enable "What's This?" Help for the form and any controls on the form.
WhatsThisButton	Set this property to true (.T.) if you want a "What's This?" Help button to appear in the title bar of the form.
WhatsThisHelpID	For a form, control, or toolbar, set this property to an ID number corresponding to a topic in your Help file.
WhatsThisMode	Use this method to display the "What's This?" Help question mark mouse pointer and enable "What's This?" Help mode. Clicking an object displays the "What's This?" Help topic specified by the WhatsThisHelpID property for the object.

Using a "What's This?" button

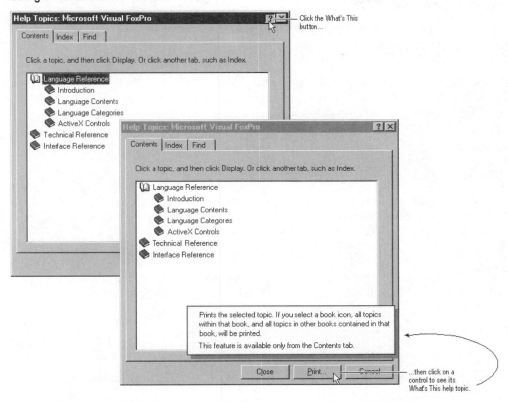

Click the What's This button...

Prints the selected topic. If you select a book icon, all topics within that book, and all topics in other books contained in that book, will be printed.

This feature is available only from the Contents tab.

...then click on a control to see its What's This help topic.

To implement "What's This?" Help

1. In design mode, open the form you want to enable "What's This?" Help for.

2. Set the form's WhatsThisHelp property to true (.T.).

3. To display a "What's This?" Help button in the form's title bar, set the form's WhatsThisButton property to true (.T.).

4. To associate a "What's This?" Help topic with the form, set the form's WhatsThisHelpID property to an ID number corresponding to a topic in your Help file.

5. To associate a "What's This?" Help topic with a specific control on the form, select the control and set its WhatsThisHelpID property to an ID number corresponding to a topic in your Help file.

Programming Help Features

You can program your application so that users can access your Help system in Microsoft Help. Although a Help system can consist of one or more separate files, Help appears to users as part of your application.

You can program your Visual FoxPro application to use graphical and .dbf-style Help with the SET HELP TO and SET TOPIC TO commands or with the WinHelp function described later in this chapter. SET HELP TO specifies the name of a custom Help file for your application. SET TOPIC TO sets the identifying keyword for a topic in the custom Help file.

Using the WinHelp Function

Another way to program your application to use Help is to call the WinHelp function. The WinHelp function is part of the Windows application programming interface (API). The WinHelp function is only available on the Windows platform.

You can use the WinHelp function in addition to the HelpContextID property, especially to call a second Help file.

Tip   If you use SET HELP TO, HELP ID, and SET TOPIC TO, you don't need to use the WinHelp function.

To use the WinHelp function

1. Define the command parameters that you'll pass in your application.

   For a description of these parameters, see "The wCmd Parameter" later in this chapter.

2. Set the library with SET LIBRARY TO and define the variables to be used, typically in the initialization code for your application's main file.

```
SET LIBRARY TO SYS(2004) + "FOXTOOLS.FLL" ADDITIVE
Help = RegFn("Help", "LCIC", "I")
```

   The library must be set to Foxtools.fll. SYS(2004) returns the Visual FoxPro root directory, where Foxtools.fll is installed.

   If you want to open a Help topic by sending its K keyword, define a variable with RegFn( ), like the Help variable in the previous example. If you want to open a Help topic mapped with a number, define a variable with RegFn like the HelpI variable in the previous example and use a number instead of a string for *dwData*. If you pass numbers, you must map them in the [MAP] section of the .hpj file to unique context strings defined with the number sign (#) footnote.

3. Use CallFn( ) to call the function.

   For example, if your Help file is called Myhelpfile.hlp, use CallFn( ) to open a topic in Myhelpfile.hlp by including the topic's K keyword:

```
#define HELP_KEY 0x0101
wCmd = HELP_KEY
cFilename = Myhelpfile.hlp"
dwData = "Add Menu Items at Run Time"
CallFn(Help, MainHWND(), cFileName, wCmd, dwData)
```

For more information on SET LIBRARY TO and SYS(2004), see the *Language Reference*. For more information on FoxTools functions, see Foxtools.chm in the Vfp98\Tools directory.

Specifying WinHelp Parameters

The following parameters specify options for the WinHelp function.

The hWnd Parameter

The *hWnd* parameter identifies the window requesting Help. Help uses this identifier to track which applications have requested Help. In Visual FoxPro, use the MainHWND( ) function included in the Foxtools.fll library for the *hWnd* parameter.

The lpzFileName Argument

The *lpzFileName* argument represents a text string designating a valid path and file name for the Help file containing the desired topic. It is passed by value.

The wCmd Parameter

The *wCmd* parameter specifies either the type of search that Help uses to locate the specified topic or that the application no longer requires Help. It can be set to any of the following values.

Constant	Value	Meaning
HELP_FINDER	0x000B	Displays the Help Finder window.
HELP_CONTEXT	0x0001	Displays Help for a particular topic identified by a context number.
HELP_HELPONHELP	0x0004	Loads Help.hlp and displays the Using Help index topic.
HELP_INDEX	0x0003	Displays the main Help index topic as defined in the [OPTIONS] section of the Help Project file (.hpj).
HELP_KEY	0x0101	Displays the first topic found in the keyword list that corresponds to the keyword in the *dwData* parameter.
HELP_QUIT	0x0002	Informs the Help application that Help is no longer needed. If no other applications have requested Help, Windows closes the Help application.
HELP_SETINDEX	0x0005	Sets a specific topic as the index topic.

The dwData Parameter

The *dwData* parameter represents the topic for which the application is requesting Help. Its content and format depend on the value of *wCmd* passed when your application calls the WinHelp function.

In most calls to Help you pass the *dwData* argument by value. This is the default in Visual FoxPro.

Depending on the circumstances, *dwData* in the preceding line can either represent a text string, indicating a keyword to look up, or a numeric value, indicating the context number that identifies a specific topic.

The following list describes the format of *dwData* for each value of *wCmd*.

wCmd Value	dwData Format
HELP_CONTEXT	A numeric value containing the context number for the topic. Instead of using HELP_INDEX, HELP_CONTEXT can use the value –1.
HELP_HELPONHELP	Ignored.
HELP_INDEX	Ignored.
HELP_KEY	A long pointer to a string that contains a keyword for the desired topic.
HELP_QUIT	Ignored.
HELP_SETINDEX	A numeric value containing the context number for the topic you want as the index.

Because the WinHelp function can specify either a context number or a keyword, it supports both context-sensitive Help and topical searches of the Help file.

Note   If a Help file contains two or more indexes, the application must assign one as the default. To ensure that the correct index remains set, the application should call Help with *wCmd* set to HELP_SETINDEX (with *dwData* specifying the corresponding context identifier). Each call to Help should be followed with a command set to HELP_CONTEXT. You should never use HELP_INDEX with HELP_SETINDEX.

Reserving F1 for Help

When a user presses F1 in your application, Visual FoxPro can display a context-sensitive Help topic. To do this, assign a Help context ID to a topic in your Help table and assign the same value to the HelpContextID property of your form or control. When the form or control has the focus and the user presses F1, Visual FoxPro displays the matching topic.

Note   F1 is enabled for context-sensitive Help by default. Because this is a recognized standard for Help, redefining this key is not recommended.

Including Help Buttons on Forms

If you add Help buttons to your forms, users can access Help more easily. You should especially consider adding a Help button if your user is a novice.

To set context sensitivity and add a Help button

1. In the Init event for your form, set the HelpContextID property for all the form's objects to the same value you assigned to the Help topic. For example, if the value is 7, you can use the following command:

```
THIS.SetAll("HelpContextID", 7 )
```

2. Add a command button to your form.

3. Set the Caption property of the command button to Help.

4. In the Click event of the command button, add the following command:

```
HELP ID THIS.HelpContextID
```

Tip   Save the Help button as a class so that you can easily add it to any form. For more information about saving objects as classes, see Chapter 9, "Creating Forms," in Part 9, "Creating the Interface."

Quitting Help

The Help application is a shared resource available to all Windows applications. Because it is also a stand-alone application, the user can execute it like any other application. As a result, your application has limited control over the Help application.

While your application cannot directly close the Help application window, it can inform the Help application that Help is no longer needed. Before closing its main window, your application should call Help with the *wCmd* parameter set to HELP_QUIT, which informs Help that your application will not need it again.

An application that has called Help at some point during its execution must call Help with the *wCmd* parameter set to HELP_QUIT before the application terminates.

If an application opens more than one Help file, it must call the WinHelp function to quit the Help application for each file.

If an application or dynamic-link library (DLL) has opened a Help file but no longer wants the associated instance of the Help application to remain active, then the application or DLL should call Help with the *wCmd* parameter set to HELP_QUIT to quit that instance of the Help application.

Note   Before terminating, an application or DLL should always call Help for any of the opened Help files. A Help file is opened if any other Help call has been made using the Help file name.

The Help application does not exit until all windows that have called Help have subsequently called it with *wCmd* set to HELP_QUIT. If an application fails to do so, then the Help application will continue running, even after all applications that requested Help have terminated.

CHAPTER 24

Creating .DBF-Style Help

.DBF-style Help is simple to create and uses standard Visual FoxPro tables that port easily to other Visual FoxPro platforms. If you want a simple solution to providing help, if you're developing cross-platform applications, or if you prefer to maintain a backward-compatible help file, you can provide .DBF-style help for your users.

This chapter discusses:

- Designing .DBF-Style Help
- Viewing the Sample .DBF-Style Help File
- Using .DBF-Style Help
- Customizing .DBF-Style Help

Designing .DBF-Style Help

.DBF-style Help files, or Help tables, are free tables that are displayed in the .DBF Help window. With this style of Help, your users can:

- Get context-sensitive Help for the current dialog box, menu command, or object by pressing F1.
- Jump to related topics within the Help file by selecting a topic from the See Also drop-down list.
- Select a keyword or phrase in the middle of a topic and jump to it by clicking the Look Up button.
- Copy any selected text in the Help window to the clipboard.

A sample .DBF-style Help file, Ttrade.DBF, is included in Visual FoxPro and is located in the Visual Studio …\Samples\Vfp98\Tastrade\Help directory. The following sections use the Ttrade.DBF sample to describe designing and navigating .DBF-style Help.

Viewing the Sample .DBF-Style Help File

To view the Ttrade.DBF sample Help file

- In the Command window, with the default directory set to the directory containing Ttrade.DBF, type:

```
SET HELP TO TTRADE.DBF
HELP
```

Visual FoxPro displays the Ttrade .DBF-style Help in its own window.

The .DBF Help window has two modes, Topics and Details. The Topics mode displays a list of all the topics in the Help file. Note that the font for the .DBF Help window is MS Sans Serif and cannot be changed.

.DBF Help window in Topics mode

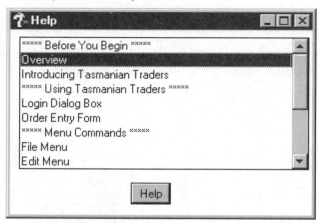

When you double-click a topic, the contents of that topic appear in Details mode.

.DBF Help window in Details mode

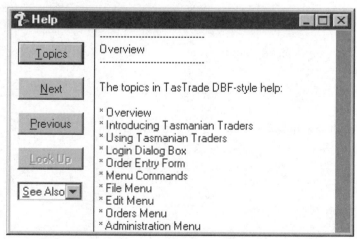

Help Table Requirements

Help tables hold a maximum of 32,767 records and must contain at least two fields. The table may have an optional first field for context sensitivity. The following example shows you the setup of a typical Help table:

TTRADE table in Browse mode

There are no requirements for the field names. The field types are, in order:

Numerical   This field is optional and contains the Help context ID used with context-sensitive Help.

Character   This is the topic name that appears in the Topics mode of the Help window.

Memo   This field holds the information displayed in the Details mode of the Help window.

Beyond these requirements, you can add as many additional fields as you wish.

Understanding Ttrade.DBF

Ttrade.DBF is a small example of a .DBF-style Help file. You can pattern your Help file after Ttrade.DBF, or you can create your own design. Because a Help file is a table, you can create your own Help file by creating a new table or by copying and changing an existing one.

To view or edit the Ttrade.DBF table, open it and browse through it as you would any other table. If you've previously run the command SET HELP TO TTRADE.DBF, you must first use the SET HELP OFF command before opening Ttrade.DBF.

TTRADE Topics

Several kinds of topics are included in Ttrade.DBF, including:

- Step-by-step instructions.

- Interface topics for context-sensitive Help, including menu commands and dialog boxes.

- General information.

You might consider these and other categories for your own Help file.

TTRADE Details

When a user selects a topic from the Topics mode, the Help window displays the contents of the memo field named Details.

TTRADE Cross-References

See Also cross-references appear at the end of the Details information for most Help topics. These references are displayed automatically in the See Also box and act as direct links to related topics.

To create a See Also cross-reference

1. At the end of the memo field, type **See Also** followed by a colon and optional spaces.

2. On the same line, type a comma-delimited list of the desired topics.

3. Enter a carriage return to signal the end of the list.

Case doesn't matter in the See Also list, and Visual FoxPro trims leading and trailing spaces from each referenced topic. For example, cross-references for the Overview topic appear in the following illustration.

Contents of the Overview topic's memo field

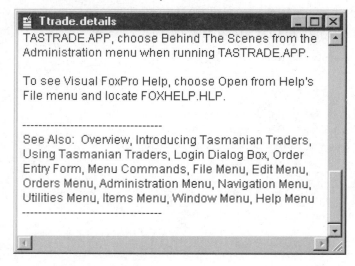

> **Tip**   Add lines above and below your See Also section at the end of your topic to separate it visually from the contents of the topic.

When locating a topic in the See Also box, Visual FoxPro tries to match the user's selection with the first Help topic that consists of or begins with the same text string. If Visual FoxPro cannot find a match, it displays "No help found for *topicname*" in the status bar.

Using .DBF-Style Help

Your user will be able to easily access Help if you include a Contents command on your Help menu that uses the HELP command. When a user chooses the Contents command, the Help window appears in Topics mode. The user can either scroll through the list to find the desired topic or type a letter to select the first topic starting with that letter. Once a topic is selected, there are three ways to display information about the topic:

- Double-click the topic in the list.
- Click the Help button.
- Press ENTER.

Customizing .DBF-Style Help

In your application code, you specify which Help file is used, which and when topics are displayed, and other optional settings. If you include context-sensitive Help, your users can easily get Help on demand from your application's dialog boxes and menu commands.

Specifying a Help Table

Specify your Help table by issuing the command SET HELP TO *filename*. This closes the current Help table if one is already open and opens *filename* as the new Help table.

In a typical programming scenario, save the name of the current Help file in a variable and specify the name of your Help file in your initialization code, as in the following example:

```
cUserHlp = SET("HELP", 1)
SET HELP TO MYHELP.DBF
```

When the application exits, you can restore the original Help file:

```
SET HELP TO (cUserHlp)
```

Displaying Topics in the Help Window

After specifying the Help table, you can specify which topics you want to display in these ways:

- For topic selection by topic name, use either the HELP Topic or the SET TOPIC TO cHelpTopicName commands.
- For context-sensitive topics, use the HelpContextID property.
- To display a subset of topics, use the SET HELPFILTER command.

For more information on these commands, see Help.

Selecting Topics by Topic Name

To select topics by name, use the HELP Topic command. When you use this command, Visual FoxPro searches the Help table to find the record whose topic field matches *Topic*. The search is case-insensitive.

When Visual FoxPro finds a match, it displays the contents of the Details memo field in the Details mode of the Help window. If Visual FoxPro cannot find a match, it displays all the topics in a list in the Help Topics dialog box with the closest match highlighted.

Enabling Context-Sensitive Help

You can design your application so that your user is able to get context-sensitive Help in two ways:

- By pressing F1 at any time.
- By clicking a Help button that you include in your forms and dialog boxes.

Reserving F1

When a user presses F1 in your application, Visual FoxPro can display a context-sensitive Help topic. To do this, assign a Help context ID to a topic in your Help table and assign the same value to the HelpContextID property of your form or control. When the form or control has the focus and the user presses F1, Visual FoxPro displays the matching topic.

> **Note**   F1 is enabled for context-sensitive Help by default. Because this is a recognized standard for Help, redefining this key is not recommended.

Including Help Buttons in Forms

If you add Help buttons to your forms, users can access Help more easily. You should especially consider adding a Help button if your user is a novice.

To create a context-sensitive Help topic

1. In the first field of a record in your Help table, enter a numerical value.

2. Fill in the record's Topic and Details fields.

Now you're ready to map the Help topic to your form. It's a good idea to map a Help button, the form, and its objects to the same Help topic.

To set context-sensitivity and add a Help button

1. In the Init event for your form, set the HelpContextID property for all the form's objects to the same value you assigned to the Help topic. For example, if the value is 7, you can use the following command:

```
THIS.SetAll("HelpContextID", 7)
```

2. Add a command button to your form.

3. Set the Caption property of the command button to Help.

4. In the Click event of the command button, add the following command:

```
HELP ID THIS.HelpContextID
```

> **Tip**   Save the Help button as a class so that you can easily add it to any form. In the Form Designer, choose Save As Class from the File menu. For more information about saving objects as classes, see Chapter 9, "Creating Forms."

Controlling the Location of the Help Window

To specify a location for your Help, you must create your own window using the DEFINE WINDOW command. Use this command in your initialization code to specify the size and location of the window and then display the window by activating or showing it.

For example, the following commands define a window named test and display the current Help table within that window:

```
DEFINE WINDOW test FROM 1,1 TO 35,60 SYSTEM
ACTIVATE WINDOW test
HELP IN WINDOW test
```

Tailoring Help to Your Application

Because you can add any number of fields to a Help table and can use any logical expression to select Help topics, only your imagination limits the kind of Help system you can create.

For example, you can:

- Define one or many program variables that control the behavior of your Help system and then assign values to these variables based on the operating mode of your program.

- Provide more detail in Help files for novice users than you provide in files for experienced users.

- Permit users to access Help only if they enter an appropriate password.

Distributing Applications

After you've developed an application, you can prepare to distribute it by including all
needed files and creating distribution disks.

Chapter 25   Building an Application for Distribution

Learn how to customize your application and how to ensure that it has all the correct
files and resources before you create an executable file to distribute.

Chapter 26   Creating Distribution Disks

Creating disks and a setup routine for your users is straightforward with the Visual
FoxPro Setup Wizard.

Building an Application
for Distribution

Building an application for distribution is similar to developing a standard Visual FoxPro application. You work in the Visual FoxPro development environment as usual, but then you create an executable file or Automation server (a COM component) and test it in the run-time environment. You then distribute your application and any related files to your distribution sites.

This chapter describes changes you need to make to prepare an application for distribution, as well as some suggested changes that help make a distributed application look unique.

This chapter addresses:

- The Distribution Process
- Preparing an Application for Distribution
- Customizing an Application for Distribution
- Preparing to Make Distribution Disks

The Distribution Process

The following list identifies the steps you need to follow to distribute a Visual FoxPro application:

- Create and debug the application using the Visual FoxPro development environment.
- Prepare and customize your application for the run-time environment. For more information, see the sections "Customizing an Application for Distribution" and "Preparing an Application for Distribution" later in this chapter.

    Important   Certain development environment features aren't available in the run-time environment and must be removed from your application. These features are listed in "Removing Restricted Visual FoxPro Features and Files" later in this chapter.

- Create documentation and online Help. For more information about creating Help for your application, see Part 7, "Creating Help Files."
- Build an application or executable file. For more information about building an application, see Chapter 13, "Compiling an Application."

- Create a distribution directory containing all the files a user needs to run your application.

- Create distribution disks and an installation routine using the Setup Wizard. For more information, see Chapter 26, "Creating Distribution Disks."

- Package and distribute your application disks and any printed documentation.

Preparing an Application for Distribution

The following sections describe the steps you might need to take to prepare your application for the run-time environment. These steps include:

- Choosing the type of build.

- Considering environment issues.

- Ensuring correct run-time behavior.

- Including resources in your application.

- Removing restricted features and files.

- Customizing your application.

Choosing the Type of Build

Before you can distribute your application, you must build either an application file, with an .app extension, or an executable file, with an .exe extension. The following table lists the differences between the builds.

Build Type	Characteristics
Application (.app) file	10K to 15K smaller than an .exe file. User must own a copy of Visual FoxPro.
Executable (.exe) file	Application includes the Visual FoxPro loader so users don't need to own Visual FoxPro. You must provide the two support files Vfp6r.dll and Vfp6renu.dll (EN denotes the English version). These files must be placed in the same directory as the executable file or along the MS-DOS path. See BUILD EXE for more information about creating and distributing executables.
OLE DLL	Used to create a file that can be called by other applications. For details about using this build option, see Chapter 16, "Adding OLE."

When you choose the type of build, consider the size of your final application file and whether your users own Visual FoxPro.

Considering Hardware, Memory, and Network Issues

You should consider and test the minimum environment your application can operate in, including the amount of disk space and memory. The results of your testing and the resolution of other issues covered in this chapter can help determine the type of build you choose, the files you include with your application, and the way you structure your distribution directory.

The applications you create have the same hardware, memory, and network requirements as Visual FoxPro. For more information on those requirements, see "System Requirements" in Chapter 1, "Installing Visual FoxPro," in the *Installation Guide*. For additional information on creating applications for multi-user environments, see Chapter 17, "Programming for Shared Access."

An executable application file always checks for the presence of the Visual FoxPro run-time library, Vfp6r.dll. To run an application .exe file using the development version of Visual FoxPro, you must force the application to use the Visual FoxPro .exe file instead.

To run an executable application in Visual FoxPro

- Start Visual FoxPro, and then from the **Project** menu, choose **Do**. In the Do dialog box, select your application's .exe file name.

  – or –

  In the Command window, enter DO followed by the name of your application's .exe file name.

  – or –

  In the command line that starts Visual FoxPro, specify the E switch. For example, if your application is called MYAPP, you can run it with the following command line:

  ```
  MYAPP.EXE -E
  ```

  This command line switch forces the application to use the executable file Vfp6.exe. For this switch to work, Vfp6.exe must be in the search path.

Ensuring Correct Run-Time Behavior

An application consisting only of modeless forms will not function properly in a run-time environment unless you provide a READ EVENTS command. You can ensure that the application runs properly by adding a calling program or setting the WindowType property.

To run a form in a run-time environment

- Run the form from a program containing a READ EVENTS command.

  – or –

  Set the form's WindowType property to **Modal**.

Some Visual FoxPro applications rely heavily on Visual FoxPro system menus. At run time, some menus and commands are unavailable, and without a provision for a READ EVENTS command, a menu-driven application ends as quickly as it starts. Use the following section to review any menus you include in your application.

For more information on structuring an application with the READ EVENTS command, see "Controlling the Event Loop," in Chapter 13, "Compiling an Application."

Menu Options

If you use the Visual FoxPro system menu, your application file includes only the following default menus and menu commands.

Menu	Menu items
File	Close, Save, Save As, Exit
Edit	Undo, Redo, Cut, Copy, Paste, Paste Special, Select All, Find, Replace
Window	Arrange All, Hide, Hide All, Show All, Clear, Cycle, all open windows
Help	Contents, Search for Help on, Technical Support, About Visual FoxPro

You can disable or remove any of the default menus and menu commands, or add your own menus and menu commands to run-time applications.

> **Troubleshooting**   If your menu system works in the development environment but closes prematurely in your application, make sure you have a READ EVENTS command active while your menu system is running. Also be sure to include a CLEAR EVENTS command when you exit the menu system.

For more information about customizing menus, see Chapter 11, "Designing Menus and Toolbars."

Including Resources in Your Applications

Visual FoxPro provides several resource files that extend the basic functionality of your applications, including FOXUSER resource files, API libraries, and ActiveX controls. If you use these files, you must include them in your project or distribution tree.

Including FOXUSER Resource Files

Visual FoxPro resource files store useful information for your application, including window positions, Browse window configurations, and label definitions. If your application relies on specific settings for any of these resource items, you must also distribute the FOXUSER database and memo files or the resource files you create specifically for your application. These resource files consist of a Visual FoxPro table with an associated memo file, usually named Foxuser.dbf and Foxuser.fpt.

> **Note**   The FOXUSER resource file isn't the same as the locale-specific resource file that contains dialog boxes and error messages. The FOXUSER resource file stores application information such as macros you've defined; the locale-specific resource file stores system text strings. For more information, see "Including a Locale-Specific Resource File" later in this chapter.

Including External Library Files

If your application includes external library files such as ActiveX controls (.ocx files) or Visual FoxPro API libraries (.fll files), use the Setup Wizard to ensure they're placed in the appropriate directory. You can distribute the Visual FoxPro file Foxtools.fll with your applications. For more information on creating external libraries to access the Visual FoxPro API, see Part 9, "Accessing APIs."

Including COM Components

If you include ActiveX controls or have created an Automation server (a COM component) as part of your application, include any .ocx files in your project and ensure the necessary support files are installed on the user's machine in the Windows system directory. Note that you can only distribute ActiveX controls for which you are licensed. For Automation servers, you must also include registration files, such as type libraries (.tlb files) and registry files (.vbr files), with your application.

If you use the Setup Wizard to create the distribution disks, you can include these files automatically. In Step 6, make sure the ActiveX column contains check marks for the ActiveX controls you're shipping. When you do this, the Setup program created by the Setup Wizard will ensure that COM components are registered properly on the user's computer when the application is installed. For more information on the Setup Wizard, see Chapter 26, "Creating Distribution Disks" and Help.

All users can run forms containing ActiveX controls; however, your application cannot accomplish certain tasks if it is running under the run-time version of Visual FoxPro. Remember the following guidelines:

- Your application must be running under a full version of Visual FoxPro to change forms, classes, or subclasses that include ActiveX controls.

- Your application must be running under a full version of Visual FoxPro to add ActiveX controls to forms at run time. For example, the full version of Visual FoxPro is required to add the Outline control to a form by running the following code:

```
PUBLIC frmOleNewForm
frmOleNewForm = CREATEOBJECT("form")
frmOleNewForm.Show
frmOleNewForm.ScaleMode = 3
frmOleNewForm.Addobject("NewOutline","OLEControl",;
"MSOutl.Outline")
```

   Note   When a form is closed, controls added at run time aren't saved.

- Your application can be running under either the run-time or full version of Visual FoxPro to add subclassed ActiveX controls to a form at run time. For example, you can define the RedOutline subclass from the Outline class, and distribute the subclass in Olelib.vcx; all users can then add the RedOutline control to a form by running the following code:

```
PUBLIC frmOleNewForm
frmOleNewForm = CREATEOBJECT("form")
frmOleNewForm.Show
frmOleNewForm.ScaleMode = 3
SET CLASSLIB TO CURR() + OLELIB.VCX
frmOleNewForm.Addobject("NewOutline","RedOutline")
```

Including a Configuration File

The configuration file, Config.fpw, can establish many default Visual FoxPro settings. For instance, you can change the Visual FoxPro title, the background color, and the way a user navigates with the keyboard.

If you want the configuration file to be read-only, place it in your project and mark it as included. If you want the configuration to be modifiable, place the file in your project and mark it as excluded. Then distribute the configuration file with your application or executable file, as a separate file. By default, Visual FoxPro looks for a configuration file named Config.fpw. However, you can specify a different configuration file name using the -C command-line switch when starting Visual FoxPro.

For more information about options that you can set in the configuration file, see "Using a Configuration File" in Chapter 3, "Configuring Visual FoxPro," in the *Installation Guide*.

Including a Locale-Specific Resource File

If you're distributing your application along with the run-time version of Visual FoxPro, you might need to include a locale-specific *resource file*. This file contains the dialog boxes and other user-interface elements that Visual FoxPro uses to interact with the user. There's a different run-time resource file for each language in which Visual FoxPro is available.

For more information about using locale-specific run-time files, see "Distributing Locale-Specific Run-Time Files" in Chapter 18, "Developing International Applications."

> **Note** The locale-specific resource file isn't the same as the FOXUSER resource file, which stores application information such as macros you've defined. The locale-specific resource file stores system text strings. For more information, see "Including FOXUSER Resource Files" earlier in this chapter.

Including All Your Files

You can freely reproduce and distribute some Visual FoxPro files, graphics, and programs with the applications you create. For detailed information, see "Removing Restricted Visual FoxPro Features and Files" later in this chapter.

Before you build your application, make sure that your project includes the necessary files for your application as well as any additional resource files, such as graphics files or templates.

The following table list files you can add to your project.

If you are	Add these files to your projects
Applying a custom configuration to your application	Config.fpw
Applying custom settings to your application	Foxuser.dbf and Foxuser.fpt
Distributing a .dbf-style Help file	Your .dbf-style Help file

To add files to your application

- Include the files in your project.

  If you don't want to change them in the distributed application, place the files in your project and mark them as included. The files are then read-only and cannot be modified.

  – or –

  Add the files to your application directory. For details, see Chapter 26, "Creating Distribution Disks."

  If you want to modify them, place the files in your project and mark them as excluded. Then distribute them with your application as separate files.

For more information about creating a project, and including or excluding files in a project, see Chapter 13, "Compiling an Application."

Removing Restricted Visual FoxPro Features and Files

The development environment of Visual FoxPro contains many features and files that are licensed for your use only. If your application contains any of these features or files, remove them.

Restricted Visual FoxPro Features

You cannot include the following Visual FoxPro menus and their menu commands in a distributed executable file.

Restricted menus

Database	Project
Form	Query
Menu	Table
Program	

If your application includes the following commands, it will return the error "Feature not available." Although you cannot include commands that create or modify menus, forms, or queries, you can run compiled menu, form, or query programs in your application.

Unavailable commands

BUILD APP	MODIFY FORM
BUILD EXE	MODIFY MENU
BUILD PROJECT	MODIFY PROCEDURE
COMPILE	MODIFY PROJECT
CREATE FORM	MODIFY QUERY
CREATE MENU	MODIFY SCREEN
CREATE QUERY	MODIFY STRUCTURE
CREATE SCREEN	MODIFY VIEW
CREATE VIEW	SUSPEND
MODIFY CONNECTION	SET STEP
MODIFY DATABASE	

If used in a distributed application, the following commands are ignored.

Ignored commands

SET DEBUG	SET DOHISTORY
SET DEVELOPMENT	SET ECHO

Restricted Visual FoxPro Files

Visual FoxPro installs files on your computer that are restricted and may not be reproduced or distributed, including:

- Wizard files
- TrueType fonts
- SpellCheck utility files
- Help files

Although you cannot distribute Visual FoxPro sample applications with your applications, you can refer to portions of sample application code as examples for building your own application. You can also include the wizard class library, Wizstyle.vcx, and the sample class libraries in your application.

License.txt

Visual FoxPro contains many files that are licensed for your use for design, development, and testing purposes only. See License.txt, located in your Visual FoxPro directory, for a list of restricted files.

If your application contains any of these files, remove them. Under the terms of the Microsoft License Agreement you received with this product, you aren't permitted to ship these files in your application or on your disks.

Distributable Files

You may distribute any Visual FoxPro file that isn't restricted. Pursuant to the Microsoft License Agreement you received with this product, files must be distributed in conjunction with a corresponding application. The following guidelines apply to distributable files.

Setup Wizard

The Setup Wizard checks for restricted files and will exclude them from distributable disk sets. Do not assign these file names to any files you will distribute. The Setup Wizard will exclude any file that has a name identical to one on this list.

Any files in the Visual FoxPro Distrib.src and SETUP directories that are required to support a corresponding application may be distributed. When you use the Setup Wizard to create distribution disks, it automatically places the required files from these directories on the distributable disks in a compressed format. Upon installation, these file are decompressed and are installed by name in the appropriate directories on the user's machine. It isn't necessary to copy these files to your distribution tree.

Samples

Files in the Visual Studio …\Samples\Vfp98 folders and in the Vfp98\Api\Samples folders are provided for you to learn from and build on. Although you may not distribute unmodified Visual FoxPro sample applications, you may refer to portions of sample application code as examples for building your own application.

If you use any files in these directories (including all .bmp, .ico, and .cur files), they must be included in your project and in the application build. They must not appear by name on the distributable disks and may not be distributed independently of your applications.

Class Libraries

You can use any .vcx file, including those in the Vfp98\Ffc and Vfp98\Gallery directories, without modification in your applications. The libraries must be included in your project and in your application build.

ODBC Files

Please refer to the Microsoft License Agreement you received with this product for specific restrictions with respect to your redistribution of ODBC files.

ActiveX Controls

Visual FoxPro includes a set of ActiveX controls (.ocx files) you can add to and distribute with your applications.

Customizing an Application for Distribution

The Visual FoxPro default run-time environment looks like the development environment: it displays Visual FoxPro icons and menus. To give your application a unique appearance, you might want to customize some of its features by:

- Protecting and documenting your source code.

- Calling error-handling and shutdown routines.

- Changing the default Visual FoxPro menu and menu commands.

- Including a configuration file to specify custom title, icon, keyboard, and Help settings.

- Modifying the main Visual FoxPro window.

- Adding Help to your application.

Protecting and Documenting Your Source Code

To prevent users from viewing or changing the source code of your application, encrypt your source code and remove debugging information.

> **Tip**   Always back up your source code before encrypting it.

To protect your source code

1. Open your application project.

2. From the **Project** menu, choose **Project Info**.

3. In the **Project Information** dialog box, select **Encrypted** and clear **Debug info**.

4. In the Project Manager, choose **Build**.

5. In the **Build Options** dialog box, select **Recompile all files** and choose **OK**.

6. In the setup section of your application, include the SET DEBUG OFF command.

Before you begin the distribution process, if you haven't already done so, you can comment and format your code so it has a consistent appearance and is easier to maintain. You can use the Beautify option from the Tools menu or the Documenting Wizard to customize your application documentation in several ways, including:

- Capitalizing keywords and variables.

- Indenting source code.

- Adding headers to files, procedures, and methods.

To use the Documenting Wizard

1. From the **Tools** menu, choose **Wizards**.

2. From the submenu, choose **Documenting**.

You can also use the Documenting Wizard to create cross-references of symbols you've used in your application and to produce an analytical summary of your project. For more information, search for "Documenting Wizard" in Help.

Calling Error-Handling and Shutdown Routines

At times, errors occur when users run your application. You can call your own error-handling routine by including ON ERROR. Typically, ON ERROR uses a DO command to run a routine which handles the error, as in:

```
ON ERROR DO My_Error
```

If your application contains no error-handling routines when an error occurs, the application pauses and Visual FoxPro displays an error message with the following options:

- **Cancel**   If a user chooses Cancel, Visual FoxPro immediately stops running the application and returns control to the system.

- **Ignore**   If a user chooses Ignore, Visual FoxPro ignores the line that caused the error and continues to the next line in the program.

For more information about error handling, see "Handling Run-Time Errors" in Chapter 14, "Testing and Debugging Applications." Also see ON ERROR in Help.

For a complete list and explanation of Visual FoxPro error messages, search for "Error Messages" in Help.

> **Tip**   Be sure to provide documentation to your users that describes the errors that they might see, and suggests ways in which they can correct errors.

Create your own shutdown routine by including the command ON SHUTDOWN in your code. Typically, ON SHUTDOWN uses a DO command to call a routine if you try to exit the application, as in the following example:

```
ON SHUTDOWN DO My_Shutdown
```

This routine typically includes a dialog box that asks if the user is sure they want to quit the current application. If the user wants to quit the application, the routine can close open files and clean up the environment, and then issue the QUIT command. If the user doesn't want to exit the current application, the routine can return control to the application.

For more information about creating a shutdown routine, see ON SHUTDOWN in Help.

Adding Help to Your Application

You can integrate context-sensitive Help into your applications, so that users can press F1 or choose Help from a menu to get assistance with your application. The Help that you provide with your application has the same features as the Help in Visual FoxPro. For more information, see Part 7, "Creating Help Files."

If you create graphical Help for your application, include the .chm or .hlp file in your application distribution directory so that the Setup Wizard includes it on your distribution disks.

> **Note**   You cannot distribute Winhelp.exe or the Help files shipped with Visual FoxPro. For more information, see "Removing Restricted Visual FoxPro Features and Files" earlier in this chapter.

Modifying the Appearance of Your Application

You can modify the appearance of your application without changing your application code by:

- Changing the default menu system.
- Changing the default title.
- Changing the default application icon.
- Specifying platform-specific keyboard navigation.

Changing the Default Visual FoxPro Menus

You can add your own menus and menu options to distributed applications by using the Menu Designer. If you don't create your own menu, the run-time environment displays a default Visual FoxPro menu.

For details on the default menus, see "Ensuring Correct Run-Time Behavior" earlier in this chapter. For more information about the Menu Designer, see Chapter 11, "Designing Menus and Toolbars."

Changing the Default Title

Your application runs in the main Visual FoxPro window. By default, the text "Microsoft Visual FoxPro" appears in the title bar.

To customize the title of the main Visual FoxPro window

- Add the following statement to your configuration file.

```
TITLE = cMyTitle
```

Replace cMyTitle with the title of the main window of your application.

To include a Visual FoxPro function as part of the title, use the Caption property of the main window as in the following example.

```
COMMAND=_SCREEN.Caption=;
"Visual FoxPro " + SUBSTR(VERSION(),25,3)
```

Changing the Default Application Icon

After your application is compiled, the default Visual FoxPro icon appears in the Windows Explorer or Start Menu as the application icon. You can use the generic icon that is supplied by Visual FoxPro or design your own.

If you want to display your own icon, create an icon (.ico) file with two images: one small (16 by 16) and one standard (32 by 32). Create both images as 16-color icons.

You can change the default Visual FoxPro icon in the Project Info dialog box of the Project menu. If you use the Setup Wizard to create distribution disks for your application, you can also specify an application icon there.

To change the default application icon using the Project Manager

1. In the Project Manager, select the main file for your project.

2. From the **Project** menu, choose **Project Info** and then select the **Project** tab.

3. Choose **Attach icon**.

4. Choose **Icon** and then select an icon (.ico) file to assign to your project.

Backing Up Your Source Code

In all application development, it's a good practice to make complete backup copies of your original program files before you build an application. Store the backup copies separately from your compiled applications.

> **Important**   Be sure to maintain separate copies of your original source programs for future use. You cannot re-create your source programs from their compiled code.

Building Your Application

When your application project contains all the necessary files, you're ready to build a distributable file. You can build your project as a standard application that only runs when Visual FoxPro is present, or as an executable application that runs without Visual FoxPro.

> **Note**   You can also build your application as an Automation server. For details, see "Creating Automation Servers" in Chapter 16, "Adding OLE."

Building a Standard Visual FoxPro Application

You can build a standard Visual FoxPro application with the Project Manager or with the BUILD APP command. However, more build options are available when you create an application through the Project Manager.

To build a standard application

- In the Project Manager, choose **Build**, then in the **Build Options** dialog box, choose **Build Application**.

    – or –

    Use the BUILD APP command.

Building an Executable File

You can build a Visual FoxPro executable file with the Project Manager or with the BUILD EXE command.

To build an executable file

- In the Project Manager, choose **Build**, then in the **Build Options** dialog box, choose **Build Executable**.

    – or –

    Use the BUILD EXE command.

    If you include the STANDALONE or EXTENDED clauses of the BUILD EXE command, Visual FoxPro generates a "Feature not available" error message.

You can also build an Automation server, which creates a DLL that can be called from other Windows programs.

To compile an Automation server

- In the Project Manager, choose **Build**, then in the **Build Options** dialog box, choose **Build OLE DLL**.

    – or –

    Use the BUILD DLL command.

Preparing to Make Distribution Disks

Now that you've considered all the requirements and options that Visual FoxPro provides, and built an application from your files, follow these steps:

- Create a distribution directory.

- Copy your application files from the project to the appropriate locations in your distribution directory.

- Create distribution disks.

Creating a Distribution Directory

The distribution directory contains copies of all the project files that comprise your application. The structure of this *distribution tree* represents the way the Setup routine created by the Setup Wizard will install files on a user's machine.

Mapping the project files to the distribution tree

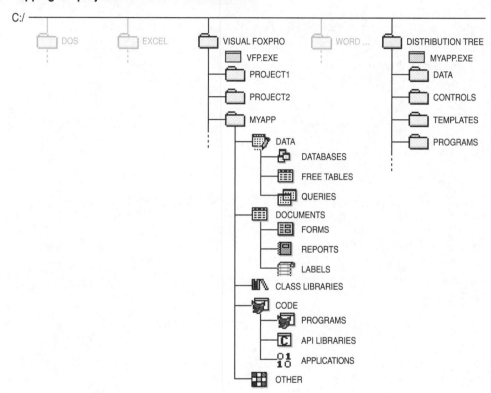

To create the distribution directory

1. Create a directory named as you want it to appear on a user's machine.

2. Divide the distribution directory into any subdirectories folders that are appropriate for your application.

3. Copy files from the application project into the directory folder.

You can use this directory to test your application in the run-time environment. If necessary, temporarily reset defaults on your development machine to reflect the minimum settings on a target user machine. When everything works correctly, use the Setup Wizard to create disk images that will reproduce the correct environment when you distribute copies of your application.

Creating the Distribution Disks

To create distribution disks, use the Setup Wizard. The Setup Wizard compresses the files in the distribution tree and copies these compressed files to the disk image directory, placing them in a separate subdirectory for each disk. After you use the Setup Wizard to create images of your application disks, copy the contents of each disk image directory to a separate disk.

When you distribute the package, the user can install all the files for your application by running Setup.exe from Disk 1.

For details on using the Setup Wizard, see Chapter 26, "Creating Distribution Disks."

Creating Distribution Disks

After you've designed and tested an application, you can use the Setup Wizard to create a setup routine and distribution disks for your application. If you plan to distribute your application in more than one disk format, the Setup Wizard creates routines and disks for all the formats you specify.

For detailed information on preparing an application for distribution, see Chapter 25, "Building an Application for Distribution." For more information on creating an application, see Chapter 13, "Compiling an Application."

This chapter outlines how to create distribution disks, including:

- Understanding the Distribution Process
- Using the Setup Wizard

Understanding the Distribution Process

When you distribute an application, you copy all your application and support files to a distribution medium, commonly disks, and provide a method for users to install the application on their computers. Because copying and installing the right files can be complicated, use the Project Manager and the Setup Wizard to streamline this process.

In the Project Manager, you create and manage your application files and identify the files that you want to distribute.

With the Setup Wizard, you create one or more sets of distributable disks that contain a setup routine for your application. To simplify the task of creating a setup routine, the Setup Wizard asks you a series of questions about your application and how you would like the setup routine to appear. When you answer the questions, the Setup Wizard creates a customized setup routine for you.

Each time you run the Setup Wizard, the options you select for that distribution tree are recorded. That way, the next time you run the Setup Wizard, the process is even simpler.

Note If you just copy your application's files to a user's machine, the application might not function properly. Windows setup routines, such as the one created by the Setup Wizard, require version checking and registration of various DLL and ActiveX files. To ensure proper installation, use the Setup Wizard. For more information, see "The Setup Wizard" later in this chapter.

The Distribution Tree

Before you create disks with the Setup Wizard, you must create a directory structure, or distribution tree, that contains all the distribution files as you'd like them to appear on your user's hard drive. Place all the files that you want to be on your distribution disks into this distribution tree.

Mapping the distribution tree to the disk images

This distribution tree can assume almost any form. However, your application or executable file must reside in the root directory of the tree.

Many Visual FoxPro applications require additional resource files. For example, you might want to include a configuration or Help file. If you need to add a resource file and haven't included it in your project, place the file in the application directory structure.

The following table lists some typical files that are placed in the application directory.

If you are	Add these files to your application directory
Applying a custom configuration to your application	Config.fpw or other configuration file
Supplying custom settings for your application	Foxuser.dbf and Foxuser.fpt
Distributing Visual FoxPro fonts	Foxfont Foxprint
Distributing a support library	*LibraryName*.ocx or *LibraryName*.fll
Including a locale-specific resource file	Vfp6raaa.dll, where "aaa" is the three-letter language code.

When you run the Setup Wizard, it creates a separate distribution directory for each disk format you specify. These directories contain all the necessary files for your disk images.

For example, if you specify both 1.44-MB and Netsetup disk images, the Setup Wizard creates two subdirectories called DISK144 and NETSETUP. If your application requires four distribution disks, the Setup Wizard creates four subdirectories named DISK1, DISK2, DISK3, and DISK4 in the DISK144 directory.

> **Important**   Because the Setup Wizard creates two new subdirectories on your hard disk, be sure you have enough disk space for three uncompressed copies of your application.

The Setup Wizard

The Setup Wizard creates a setup routine for your application, which includes a Setup.exe file, some information files, and the compressed or uncompressed application files (stored in .cab files). The end result is a set of files that can be put onto diskettes, a network, or a web site. Users can then install your application the way they install any Windows application. While they're installing your application, users will see options that you specify when using the Setup Wizard.

After you create the distribution tree, use the Setup Wizard to create a set of disk image subdirectories containing all the files needed to install your application. You copy the files from these subdirectories to create the distribution disks for your application.

The Setup Wizard performs the following steps:

1. Creates a file called Wzsetup.ini that contains your Setup Wizard choices for this distribution tree.

2. Ensures all the files needed to run your distributed application are included with the application.

3. Copies the compressed files into subdirectories it creates in the distribution disk directory.

4. Creates setup files in the specified image directories, including Setup.inf and Setup.stf that specify installation parameters for the setup routine.

5. Creates files named Dkcontrl.dbf and Dkcontrl.cdx in your distribution tree. These files contain statistical information about how files were compressed, and assigned to disk subdirectories.

Using the Setup Wizard

Use the Setup Wizard to create distribution disks from the files in your distribution tree. The Setup Wizard enables you to create new setup routines or use information in the distribution tree as defaults.

The Setup Wizard requires a working directory called Distrib.src. If this is the first time you are using the Setup Wizard, or if for some reason the Distrib.src directory is in a location different from where the Setup Wizard is looking for it, you will see a message indicating that the directory cannot be found.

To create a setup routine and distribution directory

1. From the **Tools** menu, choose **Wizards**.

2. From the **Wizards** submenu, choose **Setup**.

3. If the Setup Wizard prompts you to create or locate the Distrib.src directory, confirm that you want to create it, or choose **Locate** and specify the location of the directory.

For details about the options available in each screen of the Setup Wizard click the Help button in that screen or press F1.

Specifying the Distribution Tree

To specify the distribution tree, use Step 1 of the Setup Wizard. You should identify the distribution tree directory that you created to model the user installation of your application files.

The Setup Wizard expects the specified directory to contain all files and subdirectories you want to create in a user's environment. The Setup Wizard uses this directory as the source for files that it will compress into the disk image directory.

The Setup Wizard records the options you set for each distribution tree and uses them as default values the next time you create a setup routine from the same distribution tree.

Selecting Optional Components

To specify the optional components your application uses or supports, use Step 2 of the Setup Wizard. For example, if you want to make your application available using the run-time version of Visual FoxPro, choose Visual FoxPro Run-Time so that the Setup Wizard includes the necessary runtime support file (Vfp6r.dll). If you're making your application available as an automation server, choose that option.

> **Note**   If your application includes an automation server, the Setup program will register it automatically on the user's computer when the user installs the application.

Specifying Disk Images

To specify the different disk types that your application can be loaded from, use Step 3 of the Setup Wizard.

The Setup Wizard asks you to specify the different types of disks that your application can be loaded from. You can choose any or all of the following options:

- 1.44 MB (3.5 inch) disks

- Compress Netsetup

- Uncompressed Netsetup

The Setup Wizard also prompts you for the name of a distribution subdirectory containing disk images for each type of disk you specify. You can create the disk image directory before you run the Setup Wizard, or you can let the Setup Wizard create the directory for you.

If you select one of the Netsetup options, the Setup Wizard creates a single directory that will contain all the files.

Customizing Distributed Installation Dialog Boxes

To customize the distributed installation dialog boxes, use Step 4 of the Setup Wizard.

The Setup Wizard asks you to specify the setup routine dialog box titles and the contents of the copyright statement.

The Setup Wizard creates installation dialog boxes with the title you specify.

Specifying a Post-Setup Action

To specify a program or action that Setup should run when the installation is finished, use Step 4 of the Setup Wizard. Typical post-setup actions might be to display a readme file or launch the setup process for a related product.

The Setup Wizard asks you to specify the name of the executable. Enter the complete command line required to run the executable, including the full path of the executable, the name of any files to pass to the program, and any command-line switches.

> **Note**   The program that you specify must exist on the user's system, or an error will result.

Identifying Default File Destinations

To identify the default destinations for your application files, use Step 5 of the Setup Wizard.

The Setup Wizard asks you to specify:

- The default name of the directory in which the installation program will place your application on a user's machine.

- The default program group in which to place the startup icon for your application on a user's machine.

The setup routine will place your application in the directory folder you specify and the default application icon (or any icon you specify) in the named program group.

You can specify whether the completed setup routine will enable the user to modify either the default program group or both the default destination directory and program group.

Reviewing the File Summary

To display the results of all your choices, use Step 6 of the Setup Wizard.

The Setup Wizard displays a summary of your files and the results of all your choices and allows you to make changes in file names, file destinations, and other specifications.

Finishing the Setup Wizard Process

To start creating the setup routine for your application, choose Finish in Step 7 of the Setup Wizard. In this step you can also can also create a dependency (.dep) file that allows you to use other setup utilities to install your application.

When you choose Finish, the Setup Wizard performs the following steps:

- It records the configuration for use the next time you create distribution disks from the same distribution tree.

- It launches the process of creating the application disk images.

After the Setup Wizard creates the disk images you specified, you can copy the images to master disks, then copy and combine the disks with the rest of your distribution package. After you create a set of master disks, you can delete the disk image directories.

PART 9

Accessing APIs

If your application has requirements that cannot be met by the features already built into Visual FoxPro, you can extend the program by taking advantage of external libraries — ActiveX controls or dynamic-link libraries (DLLs). Using external libraries, you can add objects to your application, everything from enhanced text boxes to calendars and other full-featured applications, and you can take advantage of the functionality offered by other programs (including Windows itself) through their application programming interfaces (APIs).

Chapter 27   Extending Visual FoxPro with External Libraries

You can easily add ActiveX controls (.OCX files) to your application, which provides you with new objects to use in forms, to subclass, and to manage the way you work with native Visual FoxPro controls. In addition, you can link to an external library such as a .DLL and call the library's functions to use in your own programs. If you already have Visual FoxPro external libraries (.FLL files), you can link those as well and call their functions.

Chapter 28   Accessing the Visual FoxPro API

If an external library is not available to suit your needs, you can write your own ActiveX control or Visual FoxPro-specific dynamic-link library (.FLL file). By calling the functions available in the API available in Visual FoxPro, you can create controls or libraries that are tightly integrated with and optimized for use in Visual FoxPro.

CHAPTER 27

Extending Visual FoxPro with External Libraries

You can extend the native capabilities of Visual FoxPro by taking advantage of the facilities of ActiveX controls (.ocx files), ActiveX objects, and dynamic-link libraries (DLLs). External libraries allow you to access not only the capabilities of other programs, but of Windows itself. For example, you can use an ActiveX control to read and update the Windows registry directly, or it can call system-level functions by linking to one of the DLLs in Windows.

If the functionality you need isn't already available in an external library, you can create your own ActiveX control in C++ using a 32-bit compiler such as Microsoft Visual C++ version 4.0 or later, or with the Microsoft Visual Basic Control Creation Edition version 5.0. For details, see Chapter 28, "Accessing the Visual FoxPro API."

This chapter discusses:

- Using External Libraries
- Accessing ActiveX Controls and Objects
- Accessing Dynamic-Link Libraries
- Accessing a Visual FoxPro Library

Using External Libraries

In most cases, Visual FoxPro provides all the tools you need to complete your application. However, occasionally you might find that an application requires additional functionality not already available in Visual FoxPro. In those cases, you can reach outside Visual FoxPro and take advantage of the capabilities of external libraries.

Visual FoxPro allows you to access these kinds of external libraries:

- **ActiveX controls (.ocx files) and Objects**. ActiveX controls and objects are programs that include objects designed to accomplish specific tasks. Most ActiveX controls and objects add new objects to Visual FoxPro — everything from a new type of text box to a calendar, calculator, or other complex object. Some ActiveX controls and objects also incorporate additional facilities, such as access to your e-mail system or to the communications ports on your computer. As a rule, after incorporating an ActiveX control or object into Visual FoxPro, you can use the objects in them as you would any Visual FoxPro base class.

- **Dynamic-link libraries (.dll files).** A .dll file is a library of functions that you can call from Visual FoxPro programs as you would any user-defined function in Visual FoxPro. Many Windows programs — and Windows itself — make their functionality available using .dll files. For example, you can access the system color settings for Windows by linking to a system .dll file and calling functions in it.

- **Visual FoxPro external libraries (.fll files).** An .fll file is like a .dll file, but uses special protocol for sharing data with Visual FoxPro, and often contains calls to internal Visual FoxPro functions. As a consequence, .fll files are specific to Visual FoxPro, unlike .dll files, which can be called from any Windows program. You can call the functions in an .fll as you would any user-defined function in Visual FoxPro.

Before you use any library, you must be familiar with the conventions used to access its controls or functions. For example, if you want to include an ActiveX control on a form, you must know what properties, events, and methods you can use to manage the control. For an ActiveX control, you can use a Visual FoxPro Class Browser to determine the properties, events, and methods you can use. Similarly, if you want to call a function in a .dll file, you must know the function name, the number and data types of the parameter it requires, and the data type of its return value. In general, you can obtain this type of information from the documentation that accompanies a library, whether in a book or a Help system. For information about system .dll files for Windows, you can refer to the Software Development Kit (SDK) appropriate to your version of Windows.

Accessing ActiveX Controls and Objects

You can use any ActiveX control that is available on your computer. To use an ActiveX control, you add it to a form, then set its properties, write handlers for its events, or call its methods. You can add an ActiveX control to a form using the Form Controls toolbar or the OLE Container control, or by using code. For details about adding an ActiveX control in the Form Designer, see Chapter 16, "Adding OLE," in Part 5, "Extending Applications."

You can create an ActiveX control in code in much the same way you would create any Visual FoxPro control. However, before creating the control you must determine the name of the control's class library, which is stored in the Windows registry. If you have no other way to determine the class library name, use the Form Designer to create the control (as described in the previous section), and then get the control's OLEClass property.

ActiveX objects can be created directly with CREATEOBJECT( ), and don't require an instance of a form.

To create an ActiveX control in code

1. Call CREATEOBJECT( ) to create a form.

2. Call the new form's AddObject method to add the control, specifying `olecontrol` as the class. You must pass the control's class library name as the third parameter of the AddObject method.

For example, the following program creates a new form and adds an outline control to it:

```
oMyForm = CREATEOBJECT("form")
oMyForm.AddObject("oleOutline","olecontrol", ;
"MSOutl.Outline")
```

After you've created the form and control, you can display the form by calling its Show method, and display the control by setting its Visible property to true:

```
oMyForm.oleOutline.Visible = .T.
oMyForm.Show
```

Some ActiveX controls aren't designed primarily to be used interactively by a user. For example, a timer control doesn't support methods for user interaction. Even then, you can still create the control on a form because the control will usually make available a default visible component, such as an icon. Frequently you will not be able to change or resize the icon.

If you don't want your application to display the icon for non-interactive controls, you can hide the control by setting the Visible property of its OLE container control to false, or set its Left property to a negative value (such as −100) that moves it off the visible portion of the screen. Alternatively, you can place the control on a form that's never made visible (that is, for which the Show method is never called). In all cases, you can still call the control's methods as if the control were visible.

Accessing Dynamic-Link Libraries

If the functionality you require is available in a DLL, you can link to the library and call its functions. Before calling a DLL function, you must determine its calling protocol, including the name of the function, the number and data types of its parameters, and the data type of its return value.

In Visual FoxPro, you can only use DLLs that have been written for a 32-bit environment. However, if you require access to a 16-bit DLL, you can call it using functions available in Foxtools.fll. For details, see Help for Foxtools (Foxtools.chm).

To call a DLL function

1. Register the DLL function using the DECLARE - DLL command. Function names are case-sensitive.

    Note   If you specify WIN32API for the library name, Visual FoxPro searches for the 32-bit Windows DLL function in Kernel32.dll, Gdi32.dll, User32.dll, Mpr.dll, and Advapi32.dll.

2. Call the function as you would any Visual FoxPro function.

For example, the following program registers the GetActiveWindow( ) function from the Windows USER system DLL, which displays the handle of the Visual FoxPro main window. The GetActiveWindow( ) takes no parameters, but returns a single integer:

```
DECLARE INTEGER GetActiveWindow IN win32api
MESSAGEBOX(STR( GetActiveWindow() ) )
```

The DLL containing the function you're registering must be available in the default directory, in the Windows or System directories, or along the DOS path.

If the function you want to call has the same name as another function already available in Visual FoxPro (either a native function or a DLL function previously declared), you can assign an alias to the function with the duplicate name, then call it using the alias.

```
DECLARE INTEGER GetActiveWindow IN win32api AS GetWinHndl
MESSAGEBOX(STR( GetWinHndl() ) )
```

Linked DLL functions remain available until you quit Visual FoxPro, so you only need to declare them once per session. If you don't intend to call the functions in a DLL again, you can issue the CLEAR DLLS command to remove it from memory and free resources.

Note   Issuing CLEAR DLLS clears all declared DLL functions from memory.

Passing Parameters to a DLL

When you register a DLL function, you must specify the number and data types of its parameters. By default, data is passed by value. You can force a parameter to be passed by reference by including an at sign (@) in front of the parameter.

In general, DLL functions follow the data type conventions used for C, which differ from those used in Visual FoxPro. For example, DLL functions do not support a data type for a date or for currency. If the data you're passing to a DLL function is in a data type not supported by the function, you must convert it to an appropriate type before passing it. For example, you can convert a date to a numeric Julian format using commands such as the following:

```
cDate = sys(11, date())
nDate = val( cDate )
```

Some DLL functions require more complex parameters, such as structures or arrays. If the function requires a pointer to a structure, you must determine the layout of the structure, then emulate it as a string in Visual FoxPro before passing it or receiving it from the DLL function. For example, the Windows system function GetSystemTime( ) expects a pointer to a structure consisting of eight words or unsigned 16-bit integers indicating the year, month, day, and so on. The structure is defined this way:

```
typedef struct _SYSTEMTIME {
    WORD wYear ;
    WORD wMonth ;
    WORD wDayOfWeek ;
    WORD wDay ;
    WORD wHour ;
    WORD wMinute ;
    WORD wSecond ;
    WORD wMilliseconds ;
} SYSTEMTIME
```

To pass data between Visual FoxPro and the GetSystemTime( ) function, you must create a 40-byte string buffer (consisting initially of spaces) and then pass the address of this string to the function for it to fill in. When the string is returned, you must parse it in 2-byte increments to extract the individual fields of the structure. The following fragment illustrates how you could extract three of the fields from the structure:

```
DECLARE INTEGER GetSystemTime IN win32api STRING @
cBuff=SPACE(40)
=GetSystemTime(@cBuff)

tYear = ALLTRIM(STR(ASC(SUBSTR(cBuff,2)) * ;
    256 + ASC(SUBSTR(cBuff,1))))
tMonth = ALLTRIM(STR(ASC(SUBSTR(cBuff,4)) * ;
    256 + ASC(SUBSTR(cBuff,3))))
tDOW = ALLTRIM(STR(ASC(SUBSTR(cBuff,6)) * ;
    256 + ASC(SUBSTR(cBuff,5))))
```

For more information, you can examine the sample form Systime.scx in the Visual Studio ...\Samples\Vfp98\Solution\Winapi directory. For other examples of how to pass parameters to DLL functions, see the program Registry.prg in the Visual Studio ...\Samples\Vfp98\Classes directory.

If the data you're working with in Visual FoxPro is in an array, you must loop through the array and concatenate it into a single string representing a C-style array before passing it to the DLL function. If the Windows function expects 16-bit or 32-bit values, you must convert the values to their hex equivalents before concatenating them into string. When you pass the string containing the array data, Visual FoxPro passes the address of the string variable to the DLL, which can then manipulate it as an array. For an example of this, see the sample form Syscolor.scx in the Visual Studio ...\Samples\Vfp98\Solution\Winapi directory.

Accessing a Visual FoxPro Library

Like a DLL, a Visual FoxPro library (.fll file) contains functions you can call as you would any other function. Because .fll files are created specifically to be called from Visual FoxPro, it's generally easier to pass parameters to and from .fll functions.

To use a Visual FoxPro library, you specify the name of the .fll file, then call the function normally. Unlike registering DLL functions, you don't need to register individual functions within the .fll file, nor do you need to specify information about the parameters or data types used by the function.

Note If you want to use an .fll library from an earlier version of Visual FoxPro, the library must be recompiled to work with Visual FoxPro version 5.0.

To call an .fll function

1. Register the .fll function by issuing a SET LIBRARY command.

2. Call any of the functions in the library as you would any function.

For example, the following program calls a function from the Foxtools.fll library to determine what type of drive the C: drive is:

```
SET LIBRARY "C:\Program Files\Microsoft ;
Visual Studio\Vfp98\Foxtools.fll"
? DriveType("C:")
```

If you need to register more than one .fll file, include the ADDITIVE keyword in the SET LIBRARY command. If you don't, the previously-registered .fll file is cleared and replaced by the one most recently registered.

If a function name conflicts with that of another function already available in Visual FoxPro, the last function defined takes precedence. If the function name in a linked library has the same name as that of an intrinsic Visual FoxPro function, the Visual FoxPro function takes precedence.

The functions in an .fll file remain available until you quit Visual FoxPro, so you only need to register them once per session. If you don't intend to call the functions in a .fll file again, issue RELEASE LIBRARY, RELEASE ALL, or SET LIBRARY TO to remove it from memory and free resources.

For more information on these commands, see Help.

CHAPTER 28

Accessing the Visual FoxPro API

If Visual FoxPro doesn't already include the features you require for your application, you can extend its capabilities by creating an ActiveX control (.ocx file) or library (.fll file) specific to Visual FoxPro, using a 32-bit compiler such as Microsoft Visual C++ version 4.0 and greater. The information in this chapter addresses both types of programs.

> **Note** If you're using Visual C++ version 2.x to develop an ActiveX control, you need the Control Development Kit. The procedures in this chapter assume Visual C++ version 4.0.

For information about using ActiveX controls or FLLs, see Chapter 27, "Extending Visual FoxPro with External Libraries."

This chapter discusses:

- Creating a Library or ActiveX Object
- Adding Visual FoxPro API Calls
- Passing and Receiving Parameters
- Returning a Value to Visual FoxPro
- Passing Parameters to Visual FoxPro API Functions
- Accessing Visual FoxPro Variables and Fields
- Managing Memory
- Building and Debugging Libraries and ActiveX Controls

Creating a Library or ActiveX Object

You can extend the capabilities of Visual FoxPro by creating programs in C or C++ that accomplish tasks required by your application. For example, if your application requires direct access to Windows facilities, you can write a C or C++ program that makes calls to the Windows API, then returns information to Visual FoxPro.

You can create three types of programs to access the Visual FoxPro API:

- An ActiveX control (.ocx file).

- A COM object.

- A DLL specific to Visual FoxPro. Because the DLL can be called only from Visual FoxPro, it is customary to name it with the extension .fll.

Each type of program has advantages. An ActiveX control:

- Can be accessed using standard object-oriented techniques, such as setting its properties and invoking its methods.

- Can be subclassed, and its methods overridden.

- Is encapsulated, and can be called (instantiated) multiple times without complex environment management to preserve user states.

- Features simpler parameter passing.

- Can also be called from other Windows programs, if you program it with this in mind.

A COM object:

- Can be accessed using standard object-oriented techniques, such as setting its properties and invoking its methods.

- Its methods can be overridden.

- Is encapsulated, and can be called (instantiated) multiple times without complex environment management to preserve user states.

- Features simpler parameter passing.

- Can also be called from other Windows programs, if you program it with this in mind.

On the other hand, an .fll library:

- Might be familiar to you if you've used previous versions of Visual FoxPro.

   Note If you want to use an .fll library from a version of Visual FoxPro earlier than 5.0, the library must be recompiled to work with Visual FoxPro 6.0.

Creating a Basic ActiveX Object

You can create COM objects with the ActiveX Template Library provided with Microsoft Visual C++ 5.0. For more information about creating COM objects with Visual C++ 5.0, search for "ATL" in the MSDN Library.

You create ActiveX controls specific to Visual FoxPro as you would any similar control. Most C++ compilers allow you to create skeletons of the control, and they can also be created with the Microsoft Visual Basic Control Creation Edition version 5.0.

The follow sections describe the steps for creating an ActiveX control with Microsoft Visual C++ for use in Visual FoxPro.

To create a project for the ActiveX control

1. Start Microsoft Visual C++.

2. From the **File** menu, choose **New**.

3. In the **New** dialog box, choose **Project Workspace**.

4. In the **New Project Workspace** dialog box, specify a project name.

5. In the **Type** list, choose **OLE ControlWizard**.

6. Choose **Create**, and then follow the steps in the wizard.

When the wizard is finished, you can build the ActiveX control immediately. However, you'll also need to define properties and methods for the control.

To add properties and methods to the ActiveX control

1. From the **View** menu, choose **ClassWizard**.

2. Choose the **OLEAutomation** tab.

3. Choose **Add Method** or **Add Property**.

4. Fill in the name, parameter, and other information required by the element you are creating, and then choose **OK**.

5. Choose **Edit Code** to display the editor, and then enter the code that defines the property or method you're creating.

For example, to create a Version property that returns the .ocx file version as an integer (such as 101), you create the property with a return type of long, and add code similar to the following:

```
#define VERSION 101

long CPyCtrl::GetVersion()
{
    // set the version number here
    return VERSION;
}
```

Because the version number is ordinarily read-only, you wouldn't create a SetVersion( ) function.

Creating a Basic FLL Library

Because an FLL library is essentially a DLL with calls to the Visual FoxPro API, you create an FLL library by following the steps in your development environment for creating a DLL.

To create a project for the FLL library

1. Start Microsoft Visual C/C++.

2. From the **File** menu, choose **New**.

3. In the **New** dialog box, choose **Project Workspace**.

4. In the **New Project Workspace** dialog box, specify a project name.

5. In the **Type** list, choose **Dynamic-Link Library.**

After creating the basic DLL structure, you add the functions you want to be able to call from Visual FoxPro. The following sections provide skeletons for creating functions in both C and C++.

Setting Up a Library Template

Each function library that you create has the same basic structure. By using a template for the structure, all you have to do is fill in the blanks that apply to your specific library routine.

There are five elements in a Visual FoxPro library template:

1. #include statement

2. Function definition

3. Function code

4. FoxInfo structure

5. FoxTable structure

A Sample C Template

You can use the following template to create libraries written in C:

```
#include <Pro_ext.h>

void Internal_Name(ParamBlk *parm)
{
// function code goes here.
}
```

```
FoxInfo myFoxInfo[] = {
   {"FUNC_NAME", (FPFI) Internal_Name, 0, ""},
};

FoxTable _FoxTable = {
   (FoxTable *)0, sizeof(myFoxInfo)/sizeof(FoxInfo), myFoxInfo
};
```

A Sample C++ Template

For C++ routines, you can use the following template. This template differs from the C template because it declares the FoxTable structure as external:

```
#include <Pro_ext.h>

void Internal_Name(ParamBlk  *parm)
{
// function code goes here.
}

   FoxInfo myFoxInfo[] = {
      {"FUNC_NAME", (FPFI) Internal_Name, 0, ""},
   };

extern "C" {
   FoxTable _FoxTable = {
      (FoxTable *)0, sizeof(myFoxInfo)/sizeof(FoxInfo), myFoxInfo
   };
}
```

Using the Template

To use the header file and create a compiled library, you need:

- The header file Pro_ext.h. You can print this file to see the function declarations, typedefs, and structs used in the Visual FoxPro API.

- The file Winapims.lib.

Both of these files are installed in the API subdirectory when you install Visual FoxPro.

The function definition returns void and expects the following parameter: ParamBlk *parm. The ParamBlk structure is discussed under "Passing and Receiving Parameters" later in this chapter.

Other than the files listed above, the only other required elements of a Visual FoxPro library are the FoxInfo and FoxTable structures.

Using FoxInfo and FoxTable Structures

Your library functions communicate with Visual FoxPro through the FoxInfo structure. From this structure, Visual FoxPro determines the function name and the number and type of parameters. The FoxTable structure is a linked list that keeps track of the FoxInfo structures. See Pro_ext.h in the Visual FoxPro API directory for the FoxInfo and FoxTable struct definitions.

FoxInfo Structure

The FoxInfo structure is the vehicle used to communicate function names and parameter descriptions between Visual FoxPro and your library. A generic FoxInfo structure looks like this:

FoxInfo *arrayname*[ ] = {
    {*funcName1*, FPFI *function1*, *parmCount1*, *parmTypes1*}
    {*funcName2*, FPFI *function2*, *parmCount2*, *parmTypes2*}
     . . .
    {*funcNameN*, FPFI *functionN*, *parmCountN*, *parmTypesN*}
};

The placeholders are defined as follows:

arrayname
    A variable of type FoxInfo. Note that you can include several FoxInfo structure lines in this array.

funcName
    Contains the name (in uppercase and no more than 10 characters) that the Visual FoxPro user calls to invoke your function.

function
    The address of your C language routine. This is the exact (case-sensitive) name you use to define your function.

parmCount
    Specifies the number of parameters described in the *parmTypes* string or one of the following flag values.

Value	Description
INTERNAL	Specifies that the function cannot be called directly from Visual FoxPro.
CALLONLOAD	Specifies that the routine is to be called when the library is loaded. CALLONLOAD can't call any routine that returns results to Visual FoxPro.
CALLONUNLOAD	Specifies that the routine is to be called when the library is unloaded or when the Visual FoxPro QUIT command is issued. CALLONUNLOAD cannot call any routine that returns results to Visual FoxPro.

parmTypes

Describes the data type of each parameter. The following table lists the valid values for *parmTypes*.

Value	Description
""	No parameter
"?"	Any type can be passed. In the body of the function, you'll need to check the type of the passed parameter.
"C"	Character type parameter
"D"	Date type parameter
"I"	Integer type parameter
"L"	Logical type parameter
"N"	Numeric type parameter
"R"	Reference
"T"	DateTime type parameter
"Y"	Currency type parameter
"O"	Object type parameter

Include a type value for each parameter passed to the library. For example, if you create a function that accepts a character and a numeric parameter, substitute "CN" for *parmType*.

Note   To indicate that a parameter is optional, precede it with a period. Only trailing parameters can be omitted.

The following FoxInfo structure defines a library with one function — internally called dates and externally accessed as DATES — that accepts one Character type parameter:

```
FoxInfo myFoxInfo[] = {
    { "DATES", (FPFI) dates, 1, "C" }
};
```

When you've compiled the library with this FoxInfo structure and loaded it in Visual FoxPro with the SET LIBRARY TO command, you can call this function in Visual FoxPro with the following line of code:

```
=DATES("01/01/95")
```

FoxTable Structure

The FoxTable structure is a linked list that keeps track of all the FoxInfo structures you have for a given library:

FoxTable _FoxTable = {*nextLibrary*, *infoCount*,*infoPtr*};

where the placeholders are defined as follows:

nextLibrary
> A pointer used internally by Visual FoxPro; should be initialized to 0.

infoCount
> The number of Visual FoxPro external routines defined in this library.

infoPtr
> The address of the first element of an array of FoxInfo structures. This name must match the array name listed in the FoxInfo statement.

The following is an example of a FoxTable statement. If your FoxInfo array name is myFoxInfo, you'll never need to change this statement:

```
FoxTable _FoxTable = {
   (FoxTable   *) 0,
   sizeof( myFoxInfo) / sizeof( FoxInfo ),
   myFoxInfo
};
```

Adding Visual FoxPro API Calls

To integrate your program with Visual FoxPro, you can call Visual FoxPro API routines. These API routines are functions you can call from any C or C++ program, including an .ocx or .fll file, that give you access to variables, manage database operations, and accomplish many other Visual FoxPro-specific tasks.

The following table lists the general categories of API calls available in Visual FoxPro. For details about individual API functions, see "API Library Routines A–Z" or "API Library Routines by Category," and search for "API Library Routines" in Help. These routines are listed in Help both alphabetically and by category.

To use the Visual FoxPro API routines, you must include the file Pro_ext.h, available in the Visual FoxPro API directory. This file includes the prototypes for the functions and structures that allow you to share information with Visual FoxPro.

If you're writing an ActiveX control, you must also add calls to initialize and clear the API.

To add Visual FoxPro API routines to your ActiveX object

1. Use #INCLUDE to include the Pro_ext.h file along with any other required header files.

2. In the Constructor (Init method) of the control, call _OCXAPI( ) to initialize the interface to Visual FoxPro using this code:

    ```
    _OCXAPI(AfxGetInstanceHandle(),DLL_PROCESS_ATTACH);
    ```

3. Include calls to the Visual FoxPro API as required in your object.

4. In the Destructor (Destroy method) for the object, call _OCXAPI( ) again to release the process created in the Constructor, using this code:

    ```
    _OCXAPI(AfxGetInstanceHandle(),DLL_PROCESS_DETACH);
    ```

For an example .ocx file that includes calls to the Visual FoxPro API, see Foxtlib.ocx in the Vfp98\Api\Samples directory. For an example of an .fll library that includes calls to the Visual FoxPro API, see the sample programs in Vfp98\Api\Samples directory that have the extension C: EVENT.C, HELLO.C, and so on.

If you use Visual FoxPro API calls in your ActiveX control, COM object, or .fll library, the code containing the calls is incompatible with other applications. You might therefore want to build one or more tests into the program to determine whether the object is being called from Visual FoxPro.

For example, if you're creating an ActiveX control using the Microsoft Foundation Classes, you can change the control's constructor code to include a test and then alert the user if the control has been called from a program other than Visual FoxPro:

```
if (!_OCXAPI(AfxGetInstanceHandle(),DLL_PROCESS_ATTACH))
{
    ::MessageBox(0,"This OCX can only be hosted by Visual FoxPro","",0);
        //Here you can do whatever you want when the host isn't VFP:
        // you might want to reject loading or you
        // might want to set a property
        // saying that the host isn't VFP and the control will use other
        // means to achieve it's purpose.
}
```

If you're creating an ActiveX control using the Microsoft ActiveX Template Library, use the following code:

```
if (!_OCXAPI(_Module.GetModuleInstance(),DLL_PROCESS_ATTACH))
{
    ::MessageBox(0,"This OCX can only be hosted by Visual FoxPro","",0);
        //Here you can do whatever you want when the host isn't VFP:
        // you might want to reject loading or you
        // might want to set a property
        // saying that the host isn't VFP and the control will use other
        // means to achieve it's purpose.
}
```

In this example, the control doesn't exit, and will continue running after the user has acknowledged the message. The strategy you choose depends on how you anticipate the control will be used. For example, if you detect that the control is being used outside of Visual FoxPro, you can set a flag that you test at each point in the control where you call the Visual FoxPro API. If the flag indicates that the control is outside Visual FoxPro, you can branch around the API call to an alternative means of accomplishing the same task.

Passing and Receiving Parameters

When your program is called from Visual FoxPro, it can receive parameters. For example, an ActiveX control might receive parameters when one of its methods is invoked. Similarly, a Visual FoxPro program might call a function in your FLL library and pass parameters to it.

Visual FoxPro can pass parameters to your program by value or by reference. By default, parameters respect the setting made with SET UDFPARMS. Other variables (such as arrays or fields) and expressions are passed by value.

To force a parameter to be passed by reference, precede the variable reference with the @ operator. To force a parameter to be passed by value, enclose it in parentheses.

> **Note** In Visual FoxPro, individual array elements are always passed by value. When SET UDFPARMS is set to VALUE and no array element is specified, the array name by itself refers to the first element of the array (unless it is prefixed with @).

Because ActiveX controls and COM objects are Windows-standard programs, no special mechanism is required to pass parameters from Visual FoxPro and your program. You can write the program as if it were receiving parameters from any C or C++ program.

In contrast, functions in an FLL library use the FoxInfo structure to receive data from Visual FoxPro. The FoxInfo structure lists your library functions and the number and type of parameters they expect. For example, the following `FoxInfo` structure belongs to a library with one function, internally called `dates`, that accepts one Character parameter:

```
FoxInfo myFoxInfo[] = {
    { "DATES", (FPFI) dates, 1, "C" }
};
```

Functions you define in your libraries actually receive only one parameter, a pointer to the parameter block. This parameter block, defined in the `ParamBlk` structure, holds all the information about the parameters that were passed from the Visual FoxPro function call. Your function declaration follows this format:

void *function_name*(ParamBlk **parm*)

For example, the function definition for dates is:

```
void dates(ParamBlk *parm)
```

The `ParamBlk` structure consists of an integer that represents the number of parameters, immediately followed by an array of parameter unions. The structure definition is included in Pro_ext.h:

```
/* A parameter list to a library function.      */
typedef struct {
    short int pCount;        /* number of parameters passed */
    Parameter p[1];          /* pCount parameters */
} ParamBlk;
```

The `Parameter` typedef included in the `ParamBlk` structure is a union of a Value structure and a Locator structure. Call by value is handled by a Value structure; call by reference is handled by a Locator structure. You use these structures to access the parameters passed to your function when the function is called in Visual FoxPro.

The following information is extracted from the file `Pro_ext.h` and shows the definition of the `Parameter` type:

```
/* A parameter to a library function.           */
typedef union {
    Value val;
    Locator loc;
} Parameter;
```

Value Structure Definition

If a parameter is passed to your function by value, use the Value structure to access it. The following `Value` structure definition is extracted from the Pro_ext.h file:

```
// An expression's value.
Typedef struct {
    char        ev_type;
    char        ev_padding;
    short       ev_width;
    unsigned    ev_length;
    long        ev_long;
    double      ev_real;
    CCY         ev_currency;
    MHANDLE     ev_handle;
    ULONG       ev_object;
} Value;
```

Value Structure Fields

The following table is a guide to the values you can pass and receive in the Value structure for different types of data. Only the structure fields listed for a data type are used for that data type.

Contents of Value structure for different data types

Data type	Structure field	Value
Character	ev_type	'C'
	ev_length	string length
	ev_handle	MHANDLE to string
Numeric	ev_type	'N'
	ev_width	Display width
	ev_length	Decimal places
	ev_real	Double precision
Integer	ev_type	'I'
	ev_width	Display width
	ev_long	Long integer
Date	ev_type	'D'
	ev_real	Date[1]
Date Time	ev_type	'T'
	ev_real	Date + (seconds/86400.0)
Currency	ev_type	'Y'
	ev_width	Display width
	ev_currency	Currency value[2]
Logical	ev_type	'L'
	ev_length	0 or 1
Memo	ev_type	'M'
	ev_wdith	FCHAN
	ev_long	Length of memo field
	ev_real	Offset of memo field
General	ev_type	'G'

(continued)

Data type	Structure field	Value
	ev_wdith	FCHAN
	ev_long	Length of general field
	ev_real	Offset of general field
Object	ev_type	'O'
	ev_object	Object identifier
Null	ev_type	'0' (zero)
	ev_long	Data type

1. The date is represented as a double-precision floating-point Julian day number calculated using Algorithm 199 from Collected Algorithms of the ACM.

2. The currency value is a long integer, with an implied decimal point in front of the last four digits.

Note ev_length is the only true indicator of a string's length. The string can't have a null terminator because the string can contain embedded null characters.

Locator Structure Definition

Use the Locator structure to manipulate parameters passed by reference. The following Locator structure definition is extracted from the Pro_ext.h file:

```
typedef struct {
   char  l_type;
   short l_where,     /* Database number or -1 for memory */
   l_NTI,             /* Variable name table offset*/
   l_offset,          /* Index into database*/
   l_subs,            /* # subscripts specified 0 <= x <= 2 */
   l_sub1, l_sub2;    /* subscript integral values */
} Locator;
```

Locator Structure Fields

The following table is a guide to the fields in the Locator structure.

Locator field	Field use
l_type	'R'
l_where	The number of the table containing this field, or –1 for a variable.
l_NTI	Name Table Index. Visual FoxPro internal use.
l_offset	Field number within table. Visual FoxPro internal use.

(continued)

(continued)

Locator field	Field use
l_subs	For variables only, the number of subscripts (0–2).
l_sub1	For variables only, the first subscript if l_subs is not 0.
l_sub2	For variables only, the second subscript if l_subs is 2.

Note It's good programming practice to check for the parameter type in ev_type to help determine which fields to access from the Value structure.

An Example of Accessing Parameters in an FLL Library

The following example uses _StrCpy( ) to return a Character type to Visual FoxPro that's the concatenation of its two Character parameters. Notice that although the handle of each parameter's Value structure is used as working memory to perform the concatenation, changes to this memory allocation don't affect the Visual FoxPro argument that was passed by value.

For an example that uses the Locator structure to manage a parameter passed by reference, see "Returning a Value from an FLL Library" later in this chapter.

```
#include <Pro_ext.h>

Example(ParamBlk *parm)
{
// make the paramBlk structure easier
// to manage by using #define shortcuts
#define p0 (parm->p[0].val)
#define p1 (parm->p[1].val)

// make sure there is enough memory
if (!_SetHandSize(p0.ev_handle, p0.ev_length + p1.ev_length))
   _Error(182); // "Insufficient memory"

// lock the handles
_HLock(p0.ev_handle);
_HLock(p1.ev_handle);

// convert handles to pointers and make sure the
// strings are null-terminated
((char *)_HandToPtr(p0.ev_handle))[p0.ev_length] = '\0';
((char *)_HandToPtr(p1.ev_handle))[p1.ev_length] = '\0';

// concatenate strings using the API function _StrCpy
_StrCpy((char *)_HandToPtr(p0.ev_handle) + p0.ev_length,
_HandToPtr(p1.ev_handle));
```

```
// return the concatenated string to Visual FoxPro
_RetChar(_HandToPtr(p0.ev_handle));

// unlock the handles
_HUnLock(p0.ev_handle);
_HUnLock(p1.ev_handle);
}

FoxInfo myFoxInfo[] = {
   {"STRCAT", Example, 2, "CC"},
};

FoxTable _FoxTable = {
   (FoxTable *) 0, sizeof(myFoxInfo)/sizeof(FoxInfo), myFoxInfo
};
```

Returning a Value to Visual FoxPro

The method you use to return a value from your program to Visual FoxPro depends on whether you're creating an ActiveX control or an FLL library.

Returning a Value from an ActiveX Control

To return a value from the ActiveX control to Visual FoxPro, use the RETURN statement in the control, passing a single value, as in the following example:

```
#define VERSION 101

// other code here

long CPyCtrl::GetVersion()
{
   // set the version number here in variable fVersion
   return VERSION;
}
```

Returning a Value from an FLL Library

To return values from an FLL library, use API functions, not native C or C++ commands. The following functions allow you to return values to Visual FoxPro.

Note   Don't use the following API function to return a value from an .ocx file; use the RETURN statement. The API return functions should only be used in FLL libraries.

Function	Description
_RetChar(char *string)	Sets the function return value to a null-terminated string.
_RetCurrency(CCY cval, int width)	Sets the function return value to a currency value.
_RetDateStr(char *string)	Sets the function return value to a date. The date is specified in mm/dd/yy[yy] format.
_RetDateTimeStr(char *string)	Sets the function return value to a date and time specified in mm/dd/yy[yy] hh:mm:ss format.
_RetFloat(double flt, int width, int dec)	Sets the function return value to a float value.
_RetInt(long ival, int width)	Sets the function return value to a numeric value.
_RetLogical(int flag)	Sets the function return value to a logical value. Zero is considered FALSE. Any non-zero value is considered TRUE.
_RetVal(Value *val)	Passes a complete Visual FoxPro Value structure; any Visual FoxPro data type except for memo can be returned. You must call _RetVal( ) to return a string that contains embedded null characters or to return a .NULL. value.

Note   To return the value of an object data type, use the _RetVal() function, filling in the ev_object field in the Value structure.

The following example, Sum, accepts a reference to a numeric field in a table and uses _RetFloat to return the sum of the values in the field:

```
#include <Pro_ext.h>

Sum(ParamBlk *parm)
{
// declare variables
double tot = 0, rec_cnt;
int i = 0, workarea = -1; // -1 is current workarea
Value val;

// GO TOP
_DBRewind(workarea);

// Get RECCOUNT( )
rec_cnt = _DBRecCount(workarea);

// Loop through table
for(i = 0; i < rec_cnt; i++)
{
    //Place value of the field into the Value structure
    _Load(&parm->p[0].loc, &val);
```

```
    // add the value to the cumulative total
    tot += val.ev_real;

    // SKIP 1 in the workarea
    _DBSkip(workarea, 1);
}

// Return the sum value to Visual FoxPro
_RetFloat(tot, 10, 4);
}
// The Sum function receives one Reference parameter
FoxInfo myFoxInfo[] = {
    {"SUM", Sum, 1,"R"}
};
FoxTable _FoxTable = {
    (FoxTable *) 0, sizeof(myFoxInfo)/sizeof(FoxInfo), myFoxInfo
};
```

Assuming there's a numeric field named amount in the currently open table, the following line of code in a Visual FoxPro program calls the function:

```
? SUM(@amount)
```

Passing Parameters to Visual FoxPro API Functions

Often the Visual FoxPro API routines will require parameters of a particular Visual FoxPro data structure. The following sections provide a list of Visual FoxPro data types and additional data structures. For the actual type definitions and structure definitions, refer to the Pro_ext.h file.

Visual FoxPro API Data Types

The following data types are used in Visual FoxPro API routines.

Data type	Description
EDLINE	The number of a line in an open file in an editing window. The first line is 1.
EDPOS	The offset position of a character in an open file in an editing window. The offset position of the first character in the file or memo field is 0.
FCHAN	File channel. Every file opened by Visual FoxPro, or through the API by using _FCreate( ) and _FOpen( ), is assigned an FCHAN.
FPFI	A 32-bit pointer to a function returning an integer.
ITEMID	A unique identifier assigned to a single command on a menu.
MENUID	A unique identifier assigned to a menu. *(continued)*

(continued)

Data type	Description
MHANDLE	A unique identifier given to every block of memory allocated by Visual FoxPro, or allocated through the API using _AllocHand( ). It can be de-referenced to its pointer using _HandToPtr( ).
NTI	Name table index. Every variable and table field's name has an entry in this table.
WHANDLE	Window handle. A unique identifier assigned to every window opened by Visual FoxPro, or opened through the API using _WOpen( ).

Note   Because FAR pointers are not appropriate for 32-bit compilers, #define statements in Pro_ext.h redefine FAR, _far, and __far as null values.

Visual FoxPro API Data Structures

The primary data structures used in the Visual FoxPro API library are listed in the following table.

Structure	Description
EventRec	A structure used to describe what the system is doing at a given time.
FoxInfo	Used in FLL libraries for communicating between Visual FoxPro and your program; not used in .ocx files. Discussed under "Using FoxInfo and FoxTable Structures" earlier in this chapter.
FoxTable	Used in FLL libraries for communicating between Visual FoxPro and your program; not used in .ocx files. Discussed under "Using FoxInfo and FoxTable Structures" earlier in this chapter.
Locator	A structure used to access parameter values (FLL) or Visual FoxPro variables or fields (FLL and ocx).
ParamBlk	Used in FLL libraries for communicating between Visual FoxPro and your program; not used in .ocx files. Discussed under "Using FoxInfo and FoxTable Structures" earlier in this chapter.
Parameter	Used in FLL libraries for communicating between Visual FoxPro and your program; not used in .ocx files. Discussed under "Using FoxInfo and FoxTable Structures" earlier in this chapter.
Point	A structure that defines the horizontal and vertical coordinates of a single point on the screen. Coordinates are specified in rows and columns.
Rect	A structure that defines the coordinates of a rectangle on the screen. The upper-left corner of the rectangle is defined by (*top*,*left*) and the lower-right corner is defined by (*bottom*-1,*right*-1). Coordinates are specified in rows and columns.
Value	A structure used to access parameter values (FLL) or Visual FoxPro variables or fields (FLL and OCX).

Accessing Visual FoxPro Variables and Fields

You can access Visual FoxPro variables or field values in your ActiveX control or FLL function, either to read them or to set them. In addition, you can create new variables that can be accessed from within Visual FoxPro.

Variables and fields are made available in Visual FoxPro in a name table, which is an array containing the names of all currently-defined variables and fields. You can access an individual element in the array using a name table index (NTI). A special API function, _NameTableIndex( ), returns the index of an existing variable or field based on a name that you provide. After you've determined the NTI for a given variable, you can read it using the _Load( ) API function or set it using the _Store( ) API function. To create a new variable, you can call the API function _NewVar( ).

To access Visual FoxPro variables or fields, you use the Value and Locator structures defined in Pro_ext.h. If you're creating an FLL library, you can use the same technique you used to access parameters passed to your functions. For details about the Value and Locator structures, see "Passing and Receiving Parameters" earlier in this chapter.

The following example, drawn from the Foxtlibctl.cpp program in the Vfp98\Api\Samples\Foxtlib directory, illustrates how you can use the Value and Locator structures in an ActiveX control to access Visual FoxPro variables:

```
long CFoxtlibCtrl::TLGetTypeAttr(long pTypeInfo, LPCTSTR szArrName)
{
   int nResult = 1;
   TYPEATTR *lpTypeAttr;
   Locator loc;
   Value val;
   OLECHAR szGuid[128];
   char *szBuff;
__try {
   if (_FindVar(_NameTableIndex(( char *)szArrName),-1,&loc)) {
      ((ITypeInfo *)pTypeInfo)->GetTypeAttr(&lpTypeAttr);
      if (_ALen(loc.l_NTI, AL_ELEMENTS) < 16) {
         _Error(631); //Array argument not of proper size.
      }

      //1 = Guid
      StringFromGUID2(lpTypeAttr->guid, (LPOLESTR )&szGuid,sizeof(szGuid));
      OLEOleToAnsiString(szGuid,&szBuff);
      val.ev_type = 'C';
      val.ev_length = strlen(szBuff);
      val.ev_handle = _AllocHand(val.ev_length);
      _HLock(val.ev_handle);
      _MemMove((char *) _HandToPtr( val.ev_handle ), szBuff, val.ev_length);
      OLEFreeString((void **)&szBuff);
      _HUnLock(val.ev_handle);
      loc.l_sub1 = 1;
      _Store(&loc,&val);
      _FreeHand(val.ev_handle);
```

```
            //2 = LCID
            loc.l_sub1 = 2;
            val.ev_type = 'I';
            val.ev_long = lpTypeAttr->lcid;
            _Store(&loc,&val);

            // code for values 3 - 16 here
            ((ITypeInfo *)pTypeInfo) -> ReleaseTypeAttr(lpTypeAttr);
        }
    } __except  (EXCEPTION_EXECUTE_HANDLER) {
        nResult = 0;
    }
    return nResult;
```

Managing Memory

The Visual FoxPro API provides direct access to the Visual FoxPro dynamic memory
manager. For API routines that request memory allocations, a memory identifier — or
handle — is returned. The Visual FoxPro segment-loading architecture uses handles
instead of pointers so it can manage memory more efficiently.

Note   The techniques described in this section for managing memory using the
Visual FoxPro API apply to both ActiveX controls and FLL libraries.

Using Handles

A *handle* refers to a memory handle, which is essentially an index into an array of pointers.
The pointers point to blocks of memory that Visual FoxPro knows about. Nearly all
references to memory in the API are made through handles instead of the more traditional
C pointers.

To allocate and use memory in your library

1. Allocate a handle with _AllocHand( ).

2. Lock the handle with _HLock( ).

3. Convert the handle into a pointer with _HandToPtr( ).

4. Reference the memory by using the pointer.

5. Unlock the handle with _HUnLock( ).

    Note   To avoid memo file corruption, don't write to a memo file before calling
    _AllocMemo( ).

In order to address the allocated memory, your API routines must convert the handle to a
pointer by calling the _HandToPtr( ) routine. Even if the Visual FoxPro memory manager
needs to reorganize memory to obtain more contiguous memory for subsequent memory
requests, the handle remains the same. Routines that grow, shrink, free, and lock memory
allocations are also provided.

When you're creating external routines, try to minimize memory use. If you create an external routine that dynamically allocates memory, try to use the least amount of memory possible. Be especially careful about locking large memory allocations for long periods of time. Remember to unlock memory handles with _HUnLock( ) when they no longer need to be locked, because the performance of Visual FoxPro can be adversely affected by locked memory handles.

> **Caution**   Excessive use of dynamic memory deprives Visual FoxPro of memory for buffers, windows, menus, and so on, and degrades performance, because the memory given to fill API requests is managed by the Visual FoxPro memory manager. Allocating large handles and retaining them could cause Visual FoxPro to run out of memory and terminate abnormally.

> The Visual FoxPro environment has no memory protection. The external API routine cannot provide all the validation that's inherent in a standard Visual FoxPro program. If you corrupt memory, you receive messages such as "Transgressed handle," "Internal consistency error," and "Transgressed node during compaction."

The following function from an FLL library illustrates memory allocation. The example uses _RetDateStr( ) to return a Visual FoxPro Date type (assuming that the Character parameter is a proper date):

```
#include <Pro_ext.h>

void dates(ParamBlk  *parm)
{
    MHANDLE mh;
    char *instring;

    if ((mh = _AllocHand(parm->p[0].val.ev_length + 1)) == 0) {
        _Error(182); // "Insufficient memory"
    }
    _HLock(parm->p[0].val.ev_handle);
    instring = _HandToPtr(parm->p[0].val.ev_handle);
    instring[parm->p[0].val.ev_length] = '\0';
    _RetDateStr(instring);
    _HUnLock(parm->p[0].val.ev_handle);
}
FoxInfo myFoxInfo[] = {
    {"DATES", (FPFI) dates, 1, "C"}
};
FoxTable _FoxTable = {
    (FoxTable *) 0, sizeof(myFoxInfo)/sizeof(FoxInfo), myFoxInfo
};
```

Understanding Stacks

The control or library you create doesn't have a stack of its own. Instead, it uses the stack of its calling program, in this case the Visual FoxPro stack. You cannot control the size of the Visual FoxPro stack or affect the amount of stack space available to an ActiveX control or .fll file.

Under normal circumstances, this distinction isn't important. The Visual FoxPro stack is generally large enough to hold the automatic variables you might need to allocate in a control or library. If you run out of stack space, you can always allocate additional memory on the heap dynamically.

Following Handle Rules

The following rules apply to ownership of handles and the responsibility for freeing them:

- Users must free all handles they allocate, including handles allocated by functions such as _Load().

- _Load() only creates a handle when the variable you're loading is a character string (that is, ev_type = 'C'). All the other data types store their values in the Value structure itself, while loading a character string puts an MHANDLE in the ev_handle of the Value structure.

- In an FLL library, Visual FoxPro assumes responsibility for freeing all handles returned with _RetVal( ). Users must not free these handles, even if they allocate them.

- Users must not free handles passed to them in their ParamBlk.

   Caution   When you write an external routine that calls functions, be careful to follow all rules and check the return results. A stray pointer or handle reference could damage the Visual FoxPro internal data structures, causing an immediate abnormal termination or delayed problems, which could result in data loss.

Building and Debugging Libraries and ActiveX Controls

After creating a project, you're ready to build and debug it.

Building the Project

Before building, you need to establish the project settings. Some of the settings you make depend on whether you want to create a debug or release version of the control or library. As a rule, you create debug versions of the program until you're satisfied that it's working correctly, and then you create a release version.

To specify a debug or release version

1. From the **Build** menu, choose **Set Default Configuration.**

2. Choose whether you're creating a debug or release version of the control.

3. Choose **OK**.

To establish project settings

1. From the **Build** menu, choose **Settings**.

2. Under **Settings For**, choose whether you're creating a debug or release version of the program.

3. Click the **C/C++** tab and then make these settings:

   - In the **Category** list, choose **Code Generation**.

   - In the **Calling Convention** list, choose **_fastcall**.

   - In the **Use run-time library** list, choose **Multithreaded DLL**.

4. Choose the **Link** tab and then in the **Object/Library Modules** text box, add one of the following libraries:

   - If you're building an .ocx, add `OCXAPI.LIB` from the Visual FoxPro API directory.

   - If you're building an .fll, add `WINAPIMS.LIB` from the Visual FoxPro API directory.

5. Unmark **Ignore all default libraries**.

6. Choose **OK**.

To make sure the compiler can find the necessary files

1. From the **Tools** menu, choose **Options**.

2. Click the **Directories** tab.

3. In the **Show directories for** list, choose **Include files**.

4. In the **Directories** toolbar, click the **Add** button.

5. Add the directory with Pro_ext.h.

6. In the **Show directories for** list, choose **Library files**.

7. In the **Directories** toolbar, click the **Add** button.

8. Add the directory with Ocxapi.lib from the Visual FoxPro API directory (when creating a control) or add the Winapims.lib from the Visual FoxPro API directory (when creating an FLL)

9. In the **Options** dialog box, choose **OK**.

After you've specified the settings, you can compile and link your program.

To compile and link an .ocx file

- From the **Build** menu, choose **Build** *projname***.ocx**.

When you compile and link the .ocx file, Visual C++ automatically registers the control on the computer on which it was built. If for any reason you must register the control manually, you can do so using the following procedure.

To register the ActiveX control

- From the **Tools** menu in the Visual C++ Developer Studio, choose **Register Control**.

  – or –

  Declare and call DLLRegisterServer( ) from your program.

Debugging an ActiveX Control or FLL Library

Debugging the control or library in the context of a full Visual FoxPro application is more difficult than debugging it separately from the application. It's a good idea to create a simple test program to test the operation of your control or library.

Debugging with Microsoft Visual C++

Microsoft Visual C++ version 4.0 and higher offers an integrated debugging environment that makes it easy to set break points and to step through your code. You can even run Visual FoxPro from Visual C++.

To start debugging with Microsoft Visual C++

1. From the **Build** menu, choose **Settings**.

2. In the **Project Settings** dialog box, click the **Debug** tab.

3. In the **Executable for debug session** text box, type the path followed by Vfp6.exe.

   For example, type
   C:\Program Files\Microsoft Visual Studio\Vfp98\Vfp6.exe

4. Choose **OK**.

5. Set a break point in your library.

6. From the **Build** menu, choose **Debug**. Then, from the submenu choose **Go**.

7. When Developer Studio displays a message that says "Vfp6.exe doesn't contain debugging information," choose **Yes** to continue.

For more information about debugging in Visual C++, see the Visual C++ documentation set.

Debugging with Other Debuggers

You should be able to debug a control or library with any debugger that correctly handles an INT 3 (_BreakPoint( )) embedded in your program. You can use any debugger for symbolic debugging as long as it can do all of the following:

- Make a symbol table from a map file.
- Load the symbol table independent of the program.
- Relocate the symbols to a new address.

To debug a library

1. Add a _BreakPoint( ) call to the routine at the point where debugging will begin.

2. Build the control or library.

3. Invoke your debugger.

4. If your debugger supports symbols, load the symbol table for your library.

5. Start Visual FoxPro.

6. Call your library routine from Visual FoxPro.

7. When the breakpoint is reached, make adjustments to the symbol base to align your symbols with the actual location where the library was loaded.

8. Increment the instruction pointer (IP) register by 1 to skip over the INT 3 instruction.

9. Continue debugging as with a normal program.

    Note   Always remove any breakpoints specified in your debugger before you release your product.

Creating Enterprise Solutions

By taking advantage of features in Visual FoxPro, you can extend your development efforts to create complex, multifaceted applications. You can create your applications using a team of developers, which allows you to work more quickly and to develop applications that might be difficult for an individual developer to create. You can also combine the power of Visual FoxPro with that of other programs to create rich, enterprise-wide solutions to your application requirements.

Chapter 29   Developing in Teams

To work successfully as a team, developers must coordinate their efforts and avoid duplicating effort or overwriting one another's work. To help you manage team development, Visual FoxPro allows you to integrate source control software into the Project Manager, so that you can check Visual FoxPro files out and in, merge changes, view differences, and more. You can also work concurrently in the same database.

Chapter 30   Visual FoxPro Enterprise Solutions

In addition to creating your applications entirely in Visual FoxPro, you can extend Visual FoxPro by using it as a front end for other data sources, and you can use it as a data source for other Windows programs. You can also use Visual FoxPro in other innovative ways, such as a search engine for the World Wide Web or as a data warehousing tool.

Developing in Teams

You can create complex applications quickly by combining the skills of a team of developers. However, team development requires some extra coordination to keep the development effort working smoothly. One strategy is to use source control software, such as Microsoft Visual SourceSafe, to manage the files in a project.

This chapter provides strategies that you can follow to make team development successful. It assumes that you're already familiar with creating a Visual FoxPro application, as discussed in previous chapters of this book.

This chapter includes information on:

- Understanding Team Development
- Working with Source Control Software in Visual FoxPro
- Managing Visual FoxPro Projects Under Source Control
- Managing Files in a Source-Controlled Project
- Developing and Modifying Databases in Teams
- Developing Class Libraries in Teams

Understanding Team Development

By working with a team of developers, you can create applications faster, and can develop more complex applications. You can blend the skills of different developers to create applications that would be difficult or impossible for a single developer to create.

However, team development requires extra effort in the development process. Successful team development depends on:

- Allowing several developers to work with the same projects and databases at the same time.
- Coordinating the changes that are made to the same programs, forms, or other application elements, so that one developer's changes don't overwrite those of another developer.
- Allowing developers to enhance existing application elements (for example, programs or class libraries) without affecting the work of other developers who are currently using these elements.

For example, imagine that your team is developing a complex application. Because the application is large, Visual FoxPro must allow several developers to be working at once on different components of the application. However, you want to be sure that only one developer at a time works on an individual element, such as a form, so that one developer doesn't overwrite the changes made by another developer.

Furthermore, you want that developer to be able to code, test, and debug a form without affecting the other developers (and users) who continue working with an earlier version of the form. When the first developer is finished with the new form, the enhancements can then be integrated into the application.

You can follow the methods recommended in this chapter for coordinating the work of multiple developers. For example, this chapter provides information on how you can work with projects and class libraries in a multi-developer environment. For details, see "Integrating Source Control with Visual FoxPro Projects" and "Developing Class Libraries in Teams" later in this chapter.

Understanding Source Control

Visual FoxPro provides a number of features that support team development. A significant feature of team development is the use of a source code control system to coordinate who can access and modify files in a project.

Source control is the generic term for tools that manage files in a multi-developer environment. Most source control tools work something like a traditional public library, maintaining a central repository of files — documents, programs, or any other files — in a location accessible to all developers. In addition, source control tools include the ability to track the changes that developers make to files and revert to earlier versions if necessary.

Generally speaking, source control tools provide some or all of these features:

- **Check out, check in**   Developers check out a file by downloading a copy from the central repository to their local computer before modifying it. As a rule, while a file is checked out, other developers cannot check it out or modify it, but they can usually view it by synchronizing, or getting a read-only copy of it. (If the file is a text file, such as program source code, it's possible for several developers to check out the same file, and then merge others' changes with their local copy.) When developers are done with a file, they can check in their changes by checking in, or uploading, their local copy to the central repository. As part of the file check-in process, most source control tools prompt the developer to enter any comments about changes made to the file.

- **Merging**   To allow several developers to work concurrently on the same file, source control software allows multiple developers to check out the file at the same time. (This can usually be done only with text files such as program source code.) If another developer has changed the file, the source control system can integrate those changes into your version of the file.

- **Project control**   Developers can organize files into projects or other work-specific categories. Files can often be shared between projects if necessary.

- **Change tracking**   Most source control systems keep track of the changes made in a file when it's checked in. This allows developers to reconstruct earlier versions of the file, which is useful for recovering earlier work.

- **Difference checking**   Source control software allows developers to compare versions of a file and review the differences between them.

- **History**   Developers can examine the check-in history for each file, including the comments made by each developer when checking in the file.

    Tip   If your source control software supports comments, take advantage of it. Comments can greatly aid in the process of tracking changes and provide a useful history of application development.

To use source code control, users must join a source-controlled project (sometimes referred to as "enlisting" in a project). When users have joined a project, they can check out and check in the files that belong to that project.

    Note   You must enable your source control system's option to check out the same file multiple times in order for several developers to work in a project concurrently. For details, refer to the documentation for your source code control software.

Working with Source Control Software in Visual FoxPro

One of the most critical aspects of developing in teams is the ability to control who is allowed to change files. For example, if there are no controls on files, and if more than one developer is changing a program at the same time, there is a strong likelihood that one set of changes will end up being overwritten or discarded, wasting time and effort.

Visual FoxPro helps your team manage files in your projects by allowing you to integrate a source code control system into the Visual FoxPro Project Manager. By doing so, you can manage project files in a team development environment and ensure that development efforts proceed smoothly.

Integrating Source Control with Visual FoxPro Projects

Visual FoxPro supports source code control tools by allowing you to integrate commercially-available source control software directly into your projects. You can use many of the version control systems currently available. (Contact the software vendor to find out if the software can be integrated with Microsoft development tools.) For example, if your development team already uses Microsoft Visual SourceSafe, you can specify that as the source control software to use with Visual FoxPro.

All source control in Visual FoxPro is managed through the Project Manager. When you set up a project in Visual FoxPro, you have the option to create a corresponding source code control project, which is referred to as "putting the project under source control." After you've put a project under source control, Visual FoxPro helps you manage the files in the source-controlled project. When you want to modify a file — for example, if you edit a program or modify a form — Visual FoxPro prompts you to check out that file.

In Visual FoxPro, source control is used to manage files of all types, not just .prg files, but .scx, .frx, .lbx, .mnx, and .vcx files, and others as well. Although individual files can be shared between different Visual FoxPro projects, all source control operations are conducted on files within the context of a particular project.

Note Visual FoxPro doesn't prompt you to put data tables such as .dbf and .dbc files under source control when you create them, but you can add them manually to your source-controlled project.

When you work in the Project Manager with a project that's under source control, Visual FoxPro displays icons next to files that are under source control to indicate their status.

Project Manager showing source control icons

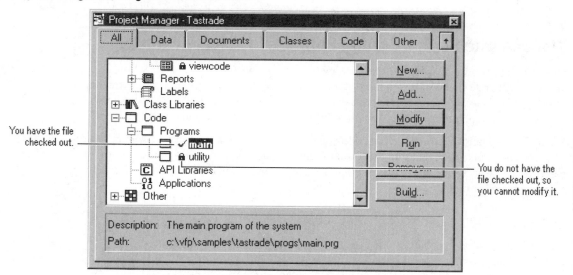

The following table summarizes the icons used in the Project Manager to indicate source
control status.

Icon	Meaning
✓	The file is checked out to you.
✓	The file is checked out to you and to one or more other developers.
🧍	The file is checked out to another developer.
🔒	The file is not checked out; you cannot change the file until you check it out.
↟	The file has been merged. After examining the changes, you can check the file in.
↟	The file has been merged and there are conflicts that need to be resolved.
?	Visual FoxPro cannot determine the source control status of the file.

If a file isn't under source control, no icon appears next to it.

> **Note**   For details about merging files and merge conflicts, see "Checking In Text Files"
> later in this chapter.

Enabling Source Control

To enable source control, first install your source control program according to the
documentation provided with it. Typically, you install an administrator version on a server
where the source code will be maintained, and then install the client version of the product
on local machines.

> **Note**   All developers on a project must use the same source code control software.

After installing the source control software, you can set options so that Visual FoxPro will
recognize it, and to specify defaults for your projects.

To enable source control in Visual FoxPro

1. From the **Tools** menu, choose **Options**.

2. In the **Options** dialog box, choose the **Projects** tab.

3. In the **Source control options** area, select the name of your source control program
    in the **Active source control provider** list.

4. To have Visual FoxPro prompt you to add new projects to source control, select
    Automatically add new projects to source control.

Each time you start Visual FoxPro, it checks for a source control provider. If one is found,
you can put or manage projects under source control.

Managing Visual FoxPro Projects Under Source Control

To use source control software in Visual FoxPro, you put projects under source control, add files to your source-controlled projects, and update the project list for each project.

Working with the Project File and Project List File

In Visual FoxPro, project information is maintained in a set of table and memo files with the extensions .pjx and .pjt. For example, if you've created a project called "MyProj," the information about the project, including the list of files, their location, and whether they're compiled into the application file (.app or .exe file), is stored in the files called Myproj.pjx and Myproj.pjt.

When working in a team development environment, developers don't share the same project files (.pjx and .pjt files). Instead, developers maintain their own local copies of the .pjx and .pjt files.

To coordinate changes that individual developers make to a project under source control, Visual FoxPro maintains a project file list (or .pjm file, short for "project metafile"). The file containing the project file list is a text file that stores the same information as the .pjx and .pjt files, such as which files are currently included in the project.

The source code control software maintains a central project file list file stored with the other files in the central repository. In addition, each developer has a local copy of the project file list checked out that reflects his or her current version of the project.

Imagine you're working with a project, and that you're adding a new program (.prg file). When you add the new file (and assuming that you put this file under source control), Visual FoxPro updates your local copy of the project and shows the file when you use the Project Manager on your computer. Other developers aren't initially aware of your change, and their local copies of the project don't show the file you have added. Even though you haven't updated the project file list, you can still check in the new file for safekeeping and check it back out again as needed.

When you're finished with the new file — for example, when you've finished testing your new program — you can update the project file list. When you do, Visual FoxPro merges the information in your local project file list with that in the central project file list.

Visual FoxPro in turn updates your local project file list with changes it finds in the central project file list. If other developers have added files to the project, your local project file list is updated, local copies of the new files are placed on your computer, Visual FoxPro rebuilds your project (.pjx and .pjt files), and the Project Manager displays the added files for you to work with.

Managing project files using the project list

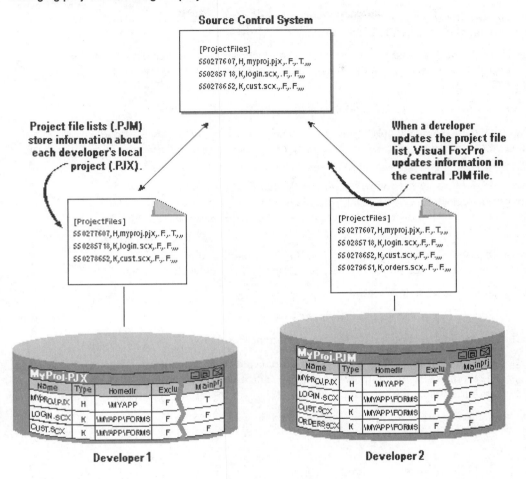

Note   The project file list tracks only the project files that are explicitly under source control. If your project includes files that aren't under source control, they will not appear in the project file list, and Visual FoxPro will not add these files to other developers' projects when they update their own project lists.

Putting Projects Under Source Control

You must specify that a Visual FoxPro project will be source-controlled before you can take advantage of your source control software. You do this by adding a project to your source control system.

If source control software is enabled, you can specify that any new projects you create are automatically put under source control.

To create a new source-controlled project

1. In the **Options** dialog box, choose the **Projects** tab, and then select a source code control provider if you haven't already done so.

2. Make sure **Automatically add new projects to source control** is selected, and then choose **OK**. To make this setting the default, choose **Set as Default**, and then choose **OK**.

3. From the **File** menu, choose **New**, and then start a new Visual FoxPro project.

   After you've named the new project, Visual FoxPro will prompt you to create the new source-controlled project. The default name for the new project will be the same as the name of the Visual FoxPro project.

After you create the new source-controlled project, Visual FoxPro finishes creating the Visual FoxPro project. Before other developers can use the file, they must enlist in the project. For details, see "Joining an Existing Source-Controlled Project" later in this chapter.

If you're working with an existing project that isn't already under source control, you can create a new source-controlled project for it, and then put its files under source control.

To put an existing project under source control

1. Open your Visual FoxPro project in the Project Manager.

2. From the **Project** menu, choose **Add Project to Source Control**.

   Visual FoxPro displays the dialog box for your source control system that allows you to create a new project. By default, the name of the source-controlled project is the same as that of the Visual FoxPro project.

3. Create the source-controlled project as you normally do with your source control software.

When you add an existing project to source control, Visual FoxPro prompts you to add the project's files to the source-controlled project. For details, see the next section, "Adding Files to a Source-Controlled Project."

Adding Files to a Source-Controlled Project

After you put a Visual FoxPro project under source control, you can add individual files to the source-controlled project. If the Visual FoxPro project already contains files when you put it under source control, you can add them to the source-controlled project.

Note If the source control software supports it, Visual FoxPro allows you to keep the file checked out when you add it to the source-controlled project. If not, the file is checked in and you must check it out again in order to work with it. For details about checking files out and in after they're added to a project, see "Managing Files in a Source-Controlled Project" later in this chapter.

To add existing files to a controlled project

1. From the **Project** menu, choose **Source Control** and then choose **Add Files to Source Control**.

2. In the **Add Files to Source Control** dialog box, select the files you want to add.

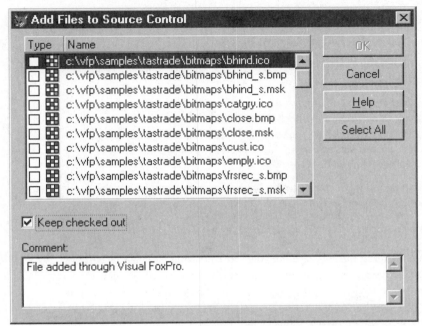

> **Note**   **Keep checked out** and **Comment** appear only if your source code control software supports these options.

3. Choose **OK**.

   Visual FoxPro generates the control files necessary for the source control software, and then adds the files to the project. If you've selected many files, this process can take some time.

You can set it up so that when you add a file to a project, Visual FoxPro will prompt you to put it under source control.

To specify that Visual FoxPro prompts you to put new file under source control

- In the **Projects** tab of the **Options** dialog box, make sure **Automatically add new projects to source control** is selected, and then choose **OK**.

  To make this setting the default, choose **Set as Default**, and then choose **OK**.

After you've added files to a project, you must update the project list before other developers can work with the new files. For details, see "Updating the Project List" later in this chapter.

Joining an Existing Source-Controlled Project

If you are a new developer on a project that's already under source control, you must join the project before you can check files out and in. When you join a project, Visual FoxPro creates a local project list file and generates a current project file (.pjx file) for you.

To join an existing project

1. From the **File** menu, choose **Join Source Control Project**.

2. In the **Open Project** dialog box, select the server and directory that contains the Visual FoxPro project file you want to join.

3. Set the working directory on your local machine; this specifies where the source control system will place files when you check them out and where it will look when you check them back in. For example, if you're using Visual SourceSafe as your source control provider, choose **Browse** from the **Directory** area and select an existing directory, or type the name of a new directory.

   Tip   All developers on a project must use the same directory structure for the files in a project, although the names of individual subdirectories can differ.

Updating the Project List

Even after files have been added to the source-controlled project, other developers will not be able to work with them. Developers will be able to manually use their source control system to check files out and in if they need to, but the added files will not be displayed in the Project Manager for any developer except the developer who added the files. To make the files available to other developers, update the project list.

When you update the project list, Visual FoxPro:

- Generates a new local project file list (.pjm file).

- Checks in the new project file list (with the option set to keep the file checked out).

- Merges the local and central project file lists if there are differences. If a merge conflict occurs, Visual FoxPro displays a dialog box to help you resolve the merge conflicts.

- Rebuilds the local project (.pjx) file based on the merged project file list.

- Gets local copies of files added to the project by other developers.

- Prompts you to get the latest versions of the project files.

- Refreshes the display in the Project Manager to reflect changes.

To update the project list

- From the **Project** menu, choose **Source Control**, and then choose **Update Project List**.

As part of the update procedures, Visual FoxPro prompts you to get the latest versions of files. If you have a file already checked out, as a general rule you shouldn't get the latest version, because your version is almost certainly more current than the one on the network.

If you're getting the latest version of a text file (such as a program), the source control software can attempt to merge the latest changes with your version. For more information about merging text files, see "Checking In Files" later in this chapter.

When you're finished, other developers should also then update their project list (using the same procedure) in order to be able to work with the files you've added.

Detaching a Project from Source Control

If you no longer want to control the files in a project, you can detach the project from source control. When you do so, files remain in the source control project so that other developers can continue to use them and so you can examine their history or use them with other projects.

If you have project files on your computer that are tagged as read-only — that is, you have copies of files, but they're not checked out — you can remove their read-only attribute when the project is detached from source control.

> **Note**   When you detach a project from source control, you break the link between your local project files and the source-controlled project, and your local files become read/write. Be sure to institute manual version control procedures after detaching the project, or you run the risks inherent in working with files that are not under source control.

To detach a project from source control

1. Check in all the files under source control.

2. From the **Project** menu, choose **Detach Project from Source Control**.

Removing Files from a Source-Controlled Project

You can remove individual files from source control if you no longer want them to be part of your source-controlled project. You might do this, for example, if a program or form becomes obsolete and is no longer part of your project

To remove a file from source control

1. In the Project Manager, select the file to remove.

2. From the **Project** menu, choose **Source Control**, and then choose **Remove Files from Source Control**.

3. In the **Remove Files from Source Control** dialog box, select the files to remove, and then click **OK**.

If you remove a file from a Visual FoxPro project that's under source control, Visual FoxPro prompts you as usual whether you want only to remove the file from the project or to delete it from disk. A setting in the Options dialog box determines whether Visual FoxPro also prompts you to remove the file from the source-controlled project.

- If **Remove files from source control upon removal from project** is checked, Visual FoxPro also prompts you to remove the file from the source-controlled project.

- If **Remove files from source control upon removal from project** isn't checked, you're not prompted, and the file is left under source control.

After a file has been removed from source code control, copies of it might still exist on other developers' computers. If so, the file is treated as a local file only for those developers.

Sharing Files Between Source-Controlled Projects

You can set up a file so that it's a member of two or more source-controlled projects at the same time. This is useful if you use common files, such as standard programs, libraries, or dialog boxes, in more than one project. When you share files between projects, changes you check in to a file are reflected in all the projects that share the file.

The specific method for sharing files between source-controlled projects depends on your source control software. If file sharing options aren't supported by your source control provider, file sharing commands will not be available on the menu.

The first step of the following procedure applies to all source control systems that support file sharing. The subsequent steps may differ, depending on your source control software.

To share files between controlled projects

1. From the **Project** menu, choose **Source Control** and then choose **Share Files**.

2. In the dialog box that appears, indicate what files you want to share with your current project, and what project they currently belong to.

   The specific options available from this menu command depend on your source control system. For details, choose **Help** in the **Share** dialog box or refer to the documentation for your source control system.

   Tip   In Microsoft Visual SourceSafe, you can see what projects a file is a member of by using the **Project Properties** command and choosing the **Links** tab.

Managing Files in a Source-Controlled Project

After you have put a Visual FoxPro project under source control, you can work with individual files or manage the project as a whole.

Working with Multi-File Components

Some project components in Visual FoxPro actually consist of multiple files: a primary file and one or more implicit files. For example, when you create a form, Visual FoxPro creates an .scx file (the primary file) and an .sct file (the implicit file). The following components have multiple files:

Component	Primary file type	Implicit file type(s)
Form	.scx	.sct
Report	.frx	.frt
Label	.lbx	.lbt
Class Library	.vcx	.vct
Menu	.mnx	.mnt
Table	.dbf	.fpt, .cdx, .idx
Database	.dbc	.dct, .dcx

When a developer checks out a component file, such as a form, Visual FoxPro also manages the corresponding implicit file or files. Likewise, when a file is checked back in, or a new file added, Visual FoxPro manages the implicit file or files automatically.

> **Note** If you generate and compile a menu, you create local .mpr and .mpx files as well. These aren't initially under source control, but you can add them as files to your project, and then put them under source control as you would other files.

Checking Out Files

When you're working in a source-controlled project, Visual FoxPro can prompt you to check files out when you modify them by opening the appropriate editor. For example, if you select a form and choose Modify to open the Form Designer, Visual FoxPro can first prompt you to check out the files for the form. (If you don't check out the files, the form is displayed in the Form Designer, but is read-only.)

However, you can also check out files manually, which is useful if you want exclusive access to the file, but don't want to open the editor for the file just at the moment. You might do this, for example, if you intended to work with a file offsite.

To specify that Visual FoxPro prompts you to check out files being modified

- In the **Projects** tab of the **Options** dialog box, make sure the option **Check out files upon modify** is checked, then choose **OK**.

  To make this setting the default, choose **Set as Default**, and then choose **OK**.

To check out a file manually

1. In the **Project Manager**, select the file to work with.

2. From the **Project** menu, choose **Source Control**, and then choose **Check Out**.

3. In the **Check Out Files** dialog box, select the file or files you want to work with, and then click **OK**.

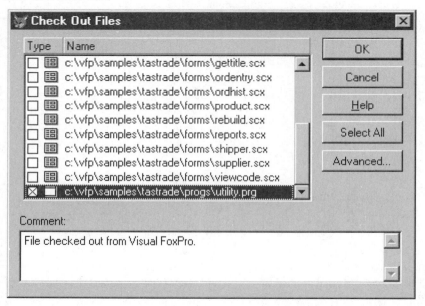

Checking In Files

You must always check in files manually. Visual FoxPro doesn't automatically check in a file; for example, it doesn't check in a form when you close the Form Designer. Instead, it leaves the file checked out so you can continue to edit it, take it offsite, or work with it in some other fashion.

The exact result of the check-in process depends on the file you're checking in and on your source control software. For forms, menus, labels, class libraries, and other types of files, the file is treated as a binary file, and the source control software makes your new version of the file into the current one for other developers to check out.

Tip   Always remember to check in files when you're done editing them. If you keep them checked out for long periods, you might prevent other developers from working with them, and you'll prevent the latest version of the file from being backed up during the course of your network backup.

To check in a file

1.   In the Project Manager, select the file to work with.

2.   From the **Project** menu, choose **Source Control**, and then choose **Check In**.

3.   Enter a comment describing the changes you've made.

4.   In the **Check In Files** dialog box, select the file, and then click **OK**.

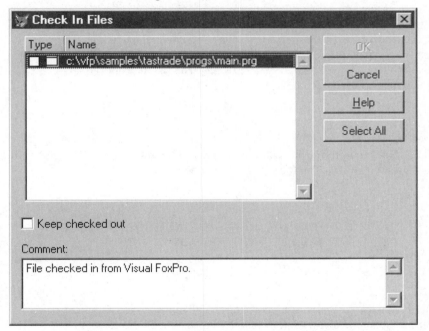

Checking In Text Files

When you check in a text file such as a .prg file, and if multiple versions of the file are checked out, the source control software doesn't simply overwrite the central version. Instead, it checks whether there have been changes to the file since you last checked it out. If so, it attempts to merge those changes with your file. To do so, it adds, deletes, and changes lines in your copy of the file.

When it's finished merging, the source control software might also give you the opportunity to check in your file. Don't check in your file right away. Instead, test your application using the new version of the file that incorporates both your changes and those of other developers. Only when you're satisfied that the application works correctly, check in your file. If other developers have made further changes to the same file, you might have to merge, test, and check in again.

In some instances, the source control software might report a merge conflict, which indicates that it cannot resolve changes between your changes and those of other developers. This can occur, for example, if you and another developer have been updating the same lines of the same program. If the source control software cannot merge successfully, it creates a version of the file that contains the original text plus your changes, marks the conflicts, and writes that file to your computer. (The exact means by which the conflicts are marked depends on the source control software you're using.) The file then appears in the Project Manager with a merge conflict icon:

To resolve the merge conflict, you must edit the file again, make your changes, and remove the merge conflict markers. When you're finished editing, Visual FoxPro prompts you to confirm that you've resolved all conflicts. The file is then marked with the merge icon:

Test your application to be sure that the changes are working properly. You can then attempt to check the file in again. If no more merge conflicts occur, your file becomes the current version.

Discarding Changes

If you've checked out a file, but decide to discard any changes you've made, you can undo the checkout. This has the effect of checking the file back in (that is, other users can then check the file out), but doesn't update it with changes. For example, if you mistakenly checked out a file instead of simply getting the latest version, undo the checkout instead of checking the file back in. This prevents the source code control system from having to create another version of the file, thus saving time and space.

> **Tip**   If you want to view a file but don't need to check it out, you can get the latest version of it. For details, see the next section, "Getting the Latest Version of Files."

To undo a checkout

1. In the Project Manager, select the file to work with.

2. From the **Project** menu, choose **Source Control**, and then choose **Undo Check Out**.

3. In the **Undo Check Out of Files** dialog box, make sure the file you want is selected, and then click **OK**.

Getting the Latest Versions of Files

If you want to view the latest version of a file, you can check it out. However, if the file is already checked out, or if you only want to view the file (not modify it), you can get the latest version of a file. When you do, Visual FoxPro copies the most current checked-in version of a file to your computer, but leaves it as a read-only file. You can get the latest version of a file even if it's currently checked out.

If the file you're getting is a text file, the source control software will merge the most current one with your version instead of simply overwriting it.

Note   To merge files when getting the latest version, you might need to enable this as an option in your source control software. For details, see the documentation for your source control software.

To get the latest version of a file

1. In the Project Manager, select the file for which you want the latest version.

2. From the **Project** menu, choose **Source Control,** and then choose **Get Latest Version**. If the file is currently checked out, you're prompted to replace or merge your checked-out version with the current version from the source control project.

    Important   If you already have the file checked out, Visual FoxPro prompts you to overwrite it. If you've made changes to the file since last checking it out, choose No when prompted to replace the file.

Comparing Files or Projects

When working with files and with a project, you might need to compare the current local copy in your working directory with the current master copy in the source-controlled project. This can help you determine whether another user has changed a file, or it can help you pinpoint where you've made changes since you checked out the file.

Most source control systems can only compare and display differences between files if they're in text format. When Visual FoxPro compares forms, reports, menus, labels, and class libraries, it uses the text representations of those files. For details, see the next section, "Checking for Differences in Forms, Reports, and Other Table Files."

Note   If file comparison options aren't supported by your source control provider, they aren't available on the menu.

To see differences between projects

- From the **Project** menu, choose **Source Control,** and then choose **Show Project Differences**.

  The resulting report is produced by your source control software, so the specific information provided can vary. In general, however, the source control system will display a window with two panes, and will highlight or otherwise mark the differences between the local and master copies of the file.

To see differences between files or the project list

1. If you're viewing differences for a single file, in the **Project Manager**, select the file for which you want to see differences.

2. For a single file, from the **Project** menu, choose **Source Control,** and then choose **Show Differences**. For the project list, from the **Project** menu, choose **Source Control,** and then choose **Show Project List Differences**.

   The resulting report is produced by your source control software, so the specific information provided can vary. In general, however, the source control system will display the two versions side-by-side, and will highlight or otherwise mark new, deleted, and changed lines.

Checking for Differences in Forms, Reports, and Other Table Files

In Visual FoxPro, only a few types of files are treated as text files by the source control software. These include program source code (.prg) files and the project file list (.pjm file). Forms, reports, and other types of files are actually stored as tables of information about their components. For example, a form's .scx file is a table of the controls in that form, plus information about the form itself. Table-type files are used to store information about forms (.scx files), reports (.frx files), menus (.mnx files), labels (.lbx files), and class libraries (.vcx files).

Because these files are stored as Visual FoxPro tables, source control systems cannot treat them as text files (the source control system treats them as "binary" files). As a result, tools for viewing differences between versions of these files cannot pinpoint the differences, nor can you see a history of changes.

In order to allow you to use source control to view differences in forms, reports, and similar files, Visual FoxPro creates text representations of them. Then, when you put one of these files under source control, Visual FoxPro creates a text version of the file, which it maintains automatically as you make changes.

Text representation of Visual FoxPro file

MyForm.SCX

MyForm.SCA

[PLATFORM] WINDOWS

[UNIQUEID] _RA40Z2APO

[CLASS] commandbutton

[BASECLASS] commandbutton

[OBJNAME] commandbutton

[PARENT] frmLogin

Form as table file

Text representation of
form file

To support the capability to generate text representations of table-type files, Visual FoxPro includes the utility program Scctext.prg, or you can use a different program that you obtain from another source or write yourself.

To specify a text conversion utility

1. In the **Options** dialog box, choose the **Projects** file.

2. In the **Text generation** box, enter the name of the conversion program.

3. Choose **Set as Default**, and then choose **OK**

Visual FoxPro automatically calls the text conversion program whenever you add a form, report, menu, label, or visual class file to a source-controlled project. The utility generates a text file that has the same name as the primary file, but uses "A" as the last letter of the extension. For example, for a form called Myform.scx, the utility generates a text file called Myform.sca. When you check in the form (or other file) after changing it, the source control software automatically creates and checks in the text file.

If you specify a text conversion utility when you already have forms, reports, and similar files in your source-controlled project, you must temporarily remove them from the project, and then re-add them with text generation enabled.

To generate text representations for existing files in a project

1. Back up all the files that will be affected: forms, reports, menus, labels, and class libraries.

2. Verify that the files aren't already checked out.

3. From the **Project** menu, choose **Source Control**, and then choose **Remove Files from Source Control**.

4. Select the files to remove from the project, and then choose **OK**.

5. Enable text generation, following the steps described earlier.

6. From the **Project** menu, choose **Source Control,** and then choose **Add Files to Source Control**.

7. Select the files to add, and then choose **OK**.

As it puts the each file under source control, Visual FoxPro also creates the corresponding text representation for the file.

Displaying File and Project Information

You can display information about individual files and about the project as a whole. For example, you can display the checkout history for an individual file or for the project list file. Information typically available includes:

*   The version number, which indicates how many times a new version of the file or project list has been checked in.

*   Who checked in the file or project file each time.

*   The date and time it was checked in.

*   What comments the developer added when checking in the file or project list.

To view checkout history for a file or the project list

1. If you're viewing the history of a single file, in the **Project Manager**, select the file for which you want to see the history.

2. For an individual file, from the **Project** menu, choose **Source Control**, then choose **Show History**. For the project list, from the **Project** menu, choose **Source Control**, and then choose **Show Project List History**.

    The specific options available from this menu command depend on your source control system. For details, choose **Help** in the dialog box that's displayed or refer to the documentation for your source control system.

You can also view the information about an individual or about the project that's being maintained by the source control system. This usually includes information such as the checkout status of the file or project list, whether the file is a text or binary file (which determines if you can merge your changes with the centrally-stored file), and so on.

To view source control information for a file or the project list

1. If you're viewing the history of a single file, in the **Project Manager**, select the file for which you want to see the history.

2. For an individual file, from the **Project** menu, choose **Source Control**, and then choose **Source Control Properties**. For the project list, from the **Project** menu, choose **Source Control**, and then choose **Project Properties**.

The specific options available from this menu command depend on your source control system. For details, choose **Help** in the dialog box that's displayed or refer to the documentation for your source control system.

Developing and Modifying Databases in Teams

In addition to working together with projects and project files, your team must be able to share information in databases. Working with databases as a team involves not only the issues of ordinary concurrency control for data in tables, but the need to be able to share database control information as well.

For several developers to work with a database at the same time, they must be able to share the database (.dbc) file. In Visual FoxPro, the .dbc file can be shared between developers as an ordinary data table. The .dbc file must therefore be stored centrally with the tables making up the database. Developers shouldn't keep local copies of a .dbc file because changes that they make to the database will not be reflected in other developers' versions of the file.

If you do need to change the .dbc file, note the following restrictions:

- Developers cannot modify the same database element (such as a table structure, view, or connection) at the same time. When a developer modifies a database element, Visual FoxPro locks its entry in the .dbc file; other users can read the entry (that is, they can issue a USE command), but they cannot modify it (MODIFY STRUCTURE).

- If a database element is in use, you cannot modify its structure. For example, if one developer has a table open, no other developer can modify its structure.

- If you call the DBSETPROP( ) function to change the properties of a database, the function puts a write lock on the object being updated. If there's a lock conflict, DBSETPROP( ) follows the rules established with SET REPROCESS.

Working with Views and Connections

Views and connections work somewhat differently than tables. When you're first defining the view, Visual FoxPro uses the tables in a database, but doesn't lock them. However, because the tables are in use, other developers cannot modify their structures.

From the time you first save a new view or connection definition, Visual FoxPro locks it exclusively until you close the View or Connection Designer. In other words, as long as you have the view or connection open in a designer, it's locked exclusively. While the view is locked, no one else can modify it.

When you use a view, its structure is cached locally. This ensures that if the view is modified while you're using it — for example, if you call REFRESH( ) or REQUERY( ) — your form or report continues to run correctly.

Developing Class Libraries in Teams

Because class libraries (.vcx files) are a crucial part of most Visual FoxPro applications, teams must be able to coordinate development efforts when creating them. Working with class libraries in a team involves many of the same coordination issues that any set of application components does, but adds some issues unique to classes:

- Changes to classes are propagated not just to applications that use those classes, but to all subclasses derived from them.

- Multiple classes are often stored in a single library file, the minimum unit that can be managed by a source control system.

As with complex forms and programs, it's good practice to isolate development in a class library, so that one developer can make changes to the library without affecting the work of other developers. Ideally, the team of developers can work with a class library while it's being enhanced by another developer, without having to worry about whether changes to the libraries will cause problems in the application.

When a class is used, Visual FoxPro caches it on the user's computer, even after a form that uses the class has been released. You must explicitly release the class before Visual FoxPro will recognize it as no longer in use. If you've used a class during the current session (and it's therefore cached), but want to load a new version of the class, be sure to release the class to force Visual FoxPro to reload it from the changed library.

Putting Class Libraries Under Source Control

When you put a class library under source control, only one developer can check the library out at a time. The library becomes read-only for other developers. As a rule, this doesn't interfere with application development, because developers can use and subclass a library even if it's read-only. While the application developers work with the read-only version of the library, the class library developer can modify all the classes in the library.

If you use this approach, the developer who is updating the library shouldn't check in the file until it has been finished and tested. Otherwise, other developers will get the incomplete version of the file when they update their project file lists or get the latest versions of files.

If the library is very complex, you can also consider breaking it into smaller libraries for development. Another advantage of this approach is that smaller library files load faster. However, this means that different classes might be finished and available at different times.

Because each approach has its advantages, you should examine the requirements of your development team and choose the strategy that best fits how you work.

Visual FoxPro Enterprise Solutions

In addition to using to create stand-alone applications, you can make it part of a larger, enterprise-wide business solution. By doing so, you can integrate the features of Visual FoxPro with other Windows applications to create a comprehensive, powerful solution to your application needs.

This chapter provides an overview of where and how you can use Visual FoxPro as part of your business-wide development efforts. It doesn't include procedural information on how to accomplish particular tasks; instead, this chapter is a guided tour that outlines the features of Visual FoxPro that make it uniquely suitable for enterprise solutions.

The chapter includes information on:

- Developing for the Enterprise
- Using Visual FoxPro as an Application Front End
- Using Visual FoxPro as a Data Source

Developing for the Enterprise

Many applications that you create with Visual FoxPro are self-contained solutions to a specific business requirement. For example, you might create a Visual FoxPro application to track your customers, which can include not only database information about the customers, but tools for taking orders, invoicing, and so on. You can create all the features your application needs using the facilities already available in Visual FoxPro, including its database engine, visual design tools, and reporting capabilities.

But you can also use Visual FoxPro as part of a larger-scale application that involves two or more development tools. Using Visual FoxPro this way — referred to as "enterprise development" — allows you to take advantage of the unique capabilities of each product. Enterprise development can be as simple as maintaining a customer database in Visual FoxPro and creating a mail merge letter in Microsoft Word, or it can involve creating a complex application using client/server databases, Automation servers, electronic mail, and more.

Visual FoxPro is an ideal tool for creating enterprise-wide business solutions because it features:

- Powerful, easy-to-use application development tools, including a Form Designer and wizards.

- A fast database engine.

- Excellent connectivity with other products, including both other Windows programs such as Microsoft Excel and Word, and client/server systems such as Microsoft SQL Server.

- Integrated source control and other team development tools.

These features allow you to develop with Visual FoxPro in several roles in an enterprise-wide application. You can use Visual FoxPro:

- As a front end for other applications. In this scenario, you work primarily with Visual FoxPro; for example, you create the user interface for the application in Visual FoxPro. You then access other applications that contain data needed for the application or that can provide services that enhance those already available in Visual FoxPro. You can also upsize your Visual FoxPro data or move it to another platform.

- As a data source for other applications. To do so, you would create the user interface for the application using another program, and then access Visual FoxPro data as needed.

The strategy you choose depends on what your application goals are and what programs you want to use.

The following sections provide ideas and scenarios that illustrate how you can use Visual FoxPro in each of the ways described above. However, don't think that the applications presented here are the only types that you can create — use the ideas here as a springboard for inventing and designing your own enterprise solutions.

Using Visual FoxPro as an Application Front End

As a Visual FoxPro developer, you probably find it natural to design your applications around the program's visual design tools. For example, you probably think of your application's user interface in terms of Visual FoxPro forms, menus, and reports. In addition, when you develop applications in Visual FoxPro, you most likely think of storing the application's data in Visual FoxPro tables.

One way to integrate Visual FoxPro into an enterprise-wide application is to use the visual design tools in Visual FoxPro, but enhance them with the capabilities of other products. Another way is to create your application's look and feel using Visual FoxPro, but to extend the data storage capabilities of your application by taking advantage of the capabilities of other programs or of non-Visual FoxPro data storage options. You can also upsize your Visual FoxPro data by moving it to a database server.

Extending the Visual Design Tools in Visual FoxPro

The base classes of Visual FoxPro controls were designed to accommodate the vast majority of application interface needs. Visual FoxPro provides all the basic controls and interface elements that are required to create a standard Windows application. However, you will often find that your application requires objects or controls beyond those provided in the base Visual FoxPro classes. If so, you can extend the visual design tools by creating subclasses and by using ActiveX controls.

Creating Subclasses

An extremely powerful feature of Visual FoxPro is the ability to create subclasses of the base controls. By creating one or more subclasses, you can customize the basic Visual FoxPro controls in almost any way that's required for your application. This ability extends to being able to create new objects or controls that combine the features of other controls. For example, the grid control in Visual FoxPro contains not only its own container, properties, and methods, but those of the objects that appear in the grid such as buttons, text boxes, and so on.

Similarly, by subclassing base controls, you can extend the capabilities of Visual FoxPro by creating objects that add new features to existing base classes, or that combine the capabilities of several objects. For example, you can add visual features such as frames or three-dimensional effects to a text box. Or you could combine an image control, buttons, and a text box to create a bitmap-viewing control in which users can move through a series of .bmp files. Creating custom classes in this way can help you manage company-wide development by allowing you to create standardized controls that appear in all your applications. For more information about creating subclasses, see Chapter 3, "Object-Oriented Programming," in Part 1, "Programming in Visual FoxPro."

Using ActiveX Controls

An alternative to creating a new control using subclasses in Visual FoxPro is to use an ActiveX control (.ocx file). These controls are created independently from Visual FoxPro, and can be integrated not only into Visual FoxPro, but into many other Windows applications as well.

In effect, ActiveX controls are off-the-shelf components that you can integrate seamlessly into your application. Using ActiveX controls provides several benefits:

- It saves you the time and effort required to create, test, and maintain a Visual FoxPro-specific control to accomplish the same tasks. The more capable the ActiveX control, the more time you save.

- Many ActiveX controls are already available from third-party suppliers to answer common application requirements. For example, if your application calls for you to display a calendar and allow users to choose dates on it, you can probably find an ActiveX control (perhaps several) that already manages this task.

- The same control can be used in multiple programs. For example, if it makes sense to do so, you can use the same ActiveX control in Visual FoxPro and Visual Basic. The same properties and methods are used in each case to manage the control, and the control will have the same appearance in all programs, making it easier for users to work with.

- ActiveX controls often provide access to Windows functionality that can otherwise be awkward or time-consuming to include using only Visual FoxPro tools. For example, you can find ActiveX controls that provide access to electronic mail (using Windows MAPI functions), to low-level Windows graphics functions, and so on. By including an ActiveX control, you can add these types of features to your application in a way that's easy to control using the ActiveX control's properties, methods, and events.

In short, using ActiveX controls enables you to extend your applications not only by integrating Windows-wide functionality, but by adding a common look-and-feel between your application and others in the same enterprise. For more information about using ActiveX controls, see Chapter 16, "Adding OLE," in Part 5, "Extending Applications." For information about creating your own ActiveX controls, see Chapter 28, "Accessing the Visual FoxPro API," in Part 9, "Accessing APIs."

Integrating Functionality from Other Programs

You might find when developing an application that other programs are uniquely suited to accomplishing certain tasks. For example, Microsoft Word has unsurpassed merge letter capabilities, while Microsoft Excel is optimized to calculate complex formulas and easily create charts and graphs from them.

Rather than emulating these capabilities in Visual FoxPro, you can make your application an enterprise-wide solution by integrating them into your application. This way you can match the requirement of your application to the best possible tool to address it.

You can integrate the functionality of other applications into Visual FoxPro in these ways:

- Run a Visual FoxPro wizard that makes Visual FoxPro data available for use by another application.

- Write Visual FoxPro programs that use Automation to communicate with, control, and share data with other Windows programs.

The following sections provide details about these methods of extending the capabilities of Visual FoxPro.

Using Wizards

A number of Visual FoxPro wizards allow you to integrate Visual FoxPro data with the functionality of other Windows programs. For example, you can send form letters to your customers by using the Mail Merge Wizard. When you run the wizard, you can specify a table or view that contains the Visual FoxPro data to use, and then either export the data to a suitable file format (such as comma-delimited) or specify that your word processing program use the Visual FoxPro ODBC driver to access the data. If you use Microsoft Word, the wizard will even start the word processing program, create the blank merge document, and display the Mail Merge toolbar for you to link fields to your Visual FoxPro data.

Similarly, using Microsoft Excel and Microsoft Query, you can analyze your data using a pivot table, which summarizes data in columns and allows you to rearrange it to view it in different ways. By using the PivotTable Wizard in Visual FoxPro, you can use your application data as the source data for Microsoft Excel, and generate the pivot table in Microsoft Excel.

For details about running the Mail Merge Wizard and PivotTable Wizard, see Help.

Using Automation

A more powerful way to interact with other applications is to use Automation. Using Visual FoxPro programs, you can access the objects exposed by other applications, and then control them by setting their properties and calling their methods. For example, Microsoft Excel exposes an application object as well as worksheets, columns, rows, and cells within the application object. You can directly manipulate any of these objects, including getting or setting data in them. In addition, you can usually control the application object using the full range of commands available in the program itself. For example, by managing the application object in Microsoft Excel, you can open, save, or print worksheets, invoke the Microsoft Excel Chart Wizard, and so on.

Automation is a particularly attractive and powerful way to tie Windows programs for several reasons:

- You have direct access to the other program, including all its objects and commands.

- You can share data directly with the other program without having to export it or convert it to another format.

- You can control the other program using the familiar properties and methods model.

- The other program doesn't necessarily need to be visible to the user when you invoke it. For example, you can invoke Microsoft Excel, place some data into cells, run a complex calculation on the data, read the result, and then display it in Visual FoxPro, all without ever displaying Microsoft Excel. Your user would continue to see only Visual FoxPro, unless you explicitly wanted to display Microsoft Excel.

- The commands (methods and properties) to control the other program are embedded within familiar Visual FoxPro programs. You don't need to learn a different programming language in order to be able to control the other program.

Automation is particularly powerful because it's an open-ended method for working with other programs. In essence, Automation simply makes available to you the data and commands from other applications, for you to use in the way best suited to your application.

A sample scenario illustrates how you can integrate several Windows programs. Imagine that you store your customer and sales data in Visual FoxPro. You'd like to create a sales report that summarizes quarterly sales.

One solution would be to use Automation to copy the Visual FoxPro sales data to cells in a Microsoft Excel worksheet. You can then invoke the Microsoft Excel Chart Wizard to create a chart of the data and copy it to the Windows Clipboard. Still using Automation, you can invoke Microsoft Word and create or open a sales report document (if you create it as a new document, you can insert standard text that you store in Visual FoxPro), and then paste in the chart you created in Microsoft Excel.

This is just one way you can use Automation to make Visual FoxPro part of an enterprise-wide solution. By becoming familiar with the objects and methods available in programs that you typically use, you can imagine many more ways to make each program enhance the capabilities of the other. For details about Automation, see "Manipulating Objects with Automation" in Chapter 16, "Adding OLE," Part 5, "Extending Applications."

Extending Data Storage Capabilities in Visual FoxPro

The data table and indexing capabilities of Visual FoxPro are usually more than adequate to the requirements of an application, whether you're concerned about speed or database size. However, there are times when you might want to extend Visual FoxPro by using data that's stored in some other format. This might be true if:

- Your application needs access to legacy data that's created and maintained by an existing application. For example, suppose that, as part of your sales application, you need access to data being maintained by an accounting application that was written using a different program, perhaps even on a different platform.

- You want to optimize data access by using a database server, which can greatly speed data access, particularly in very large databases.

- You want to share data with other programs, and therefore want to store the data in a format that's accessible to all the programs.

- The data is best suited to the format of a particular program (such as a spreadsheet). This might be true, for example, if your application required only occasional access to data that was otherwise being maintained by the other program.

    If the data you need is in the format of a spreadsheet, word processing document, or other Windows program, you can access it using Automation. For example, you might do this if your application required a collection of form letters. In that case, the letters might be stored as Microsoft Word documents, and your application would use Automation to invoke Word, open the appropriate letter, and insert or substitute text as necessary.

A more common approach to using non-Visual FoxPro data is to use ODBC to access it. ODBC drivers allow you to connect to data in the format of other programs — typically other database programs — and query or edit it using standard SQL commands.

For example, you might decide that security and transaction processing capabilities are a vital part of your application, so you want to store the data using the Microsoft SQL Server. To access the data, you define a connection to the SQL Server, using the ODBC driver for it. You can then run ordinary queries (and other SQL commands) as if the data were in Visual FoxPro format.

Other applications can access the same data and take advantage of the same features. For example, a Microsoft Excel worksheet can get its data from the same SQL Server database. Not only will the worksheet enjoy the same performance advantages that your application does, it can also take advantage of the security and transaction processing features of the server, which aren't otherwise available in a Microsoft Excel worksheet.

In some instances, you might want to go further and use SQL commands that are specific to the data source you're accessing with ODBC. For example, Microsoft SQL Server allows you to create and run stored procedures, which can manipulate data at the server (rather than in your application). To take advantage of stored procedures, you can send "native" SQL statements to the database server. Pass-through SQL commands also allow you to perform system administration tasks on the server, and in some instances they will execute faster than similar SQL statements executed in Visual FoxPro.

For more details about extending data storage capabilities in Visual FoxPro, refer to the documentation in the following table.

For details about	See
Automation	"Manipulating Objects with Automation" in Chapter 16, "Adding OLE"
Using ODBC to access data	"Accessing Remote Data" in Chapter 8, "Creating Views"
Using Visual FoxPro in a client/server environment	Chapter 19, "Designing Client/Server Applications"

Upsizing Visual FoxPro Data

You can choose to keep your data in Visual FoxPro tables or on another platform such as a database server. Or you can do both: keep your data in Visual FoxPro tables while you're developing, or until your database grows large, and then move (or *upsize*) the data to another platform.

For example, you can prototype your application by keeping all the data in local Visual FoxPro tables. This gives you the flexibility to modify your tables, views, and indexes as you develop the application without the complexities of managing tables on a database server. You can keep sample data in the local tables so you test your forms, reports, and other programs. When the database structure is complete, you can upsize your data to a database server and put the application into production.

Another way to work is to keep your data in Visual FoxPro tables only as long as is practical. When the database grows large, you can upsize it and take advantage of the optimized performance provided by a database server. The exact point at which it makes sense to upsize your database depends on many factors, including the complexity of the database, the performance of your local computer or network, and the demands of your application.

Finally, you can prototype your database in Visual FoxPro, and then upsize it in order to share the data with other applications that can also access a database server. Similarly, you can upsize the database in order to take advantage of the security and server-side transaction processing capabilities of the database server.

For details on upsizing databases, see Chapter 20, "Upsizing Visual FoxPro Databases," in Part 6, "Creating Client/Server Solutions."

Using Visual FoxPro as a Data Source

A different way to integrate Visual FoxPro into an enterprise solution is to use it as one component, but not necessarily as the primary application. In effect, you'd be treating it as a back end for an application written using another product. In this case, the user wouldn't directly see Visual FoxPro. Instead, the application's user interface would be written using tools in the other application, and would communicate with Visual FoxPro in the background to get or manipulate data.

Visual FoxPro works well in this role because it can make available its database engine, which provides rapid data access to other applications. In addition, Visual FoxPro can make its objects and command sets available to other programs, including custom objects that you create.

Making Visual FoxPro Data Available to Other Programs

One way for an enterprise-wide application to take advantage of Visual FoxPro is to use the Visual FoxPro database engine for storing and managing data. This provides high-performance storage and query capability to other programs.

Programs can connect to Visual FoxPro data using the Visual FoxPro ODBC driver. This driver exposes the Visual FoxPro database engine to standard SQL commands.

For example, an application might use Microsoft Excel as a calculation tool for complex data analysis. If the data to be manipulated is highly fluid, it might make sense not to store it in a worksheet, but in a database. The worksheet could then be written to use the Visual FoxPro ODBC driver to connect to the database, extract the relevant information, and display it in a worksheet for further processing.

Another example might be a kiosk application, such as an information stand at an airport or convention center. You could create the information display using a multimedia authoring program. But if some of the data in the application changed often, it would be cumbersome to change pages in the presentation. Instead, the presentation program could connect to a Visual FoxPro database using the ODBC driver, and then extract data at run time.

For more information, see Visual FoxPro ODBC Driver Help (Drvvfp.hlp) installed in the …\Vfp98\Distrib\Src\System directory. It's also available from the ODBC program group if you installed ODBC during Visual FoxPro Setup.

Making Visual FoxPro Objects and Commands Available to Other Programs

In addition to making Visual FoxPro data available to other programs as part of an enterprise solution, you can expose Visual FoxPro objects and commands. Other applications can call the methods and set properties of objects in Visual FoxPro; including not only the base objects, but objects defined in custom classes.

For example, you can create an application in Microsoft Excel that stores data in a Visual FoxPro database. In addition to simply reading and writing the data, Microsoft Excel can call Visual FoxPro commands to display a form as a dialog box. One use might be to gather data for a parameterized view.

Another way to expose Visual FoxPro objects is to create an Automation server. This allows you to create application-specific objects that can perform almost any function that you can program Visual FoxPro to accomplish, with the further advantage that you can distribute the server.

One use for a custom server is to create an object that includes a set of business rules that ensure the integrity of data that another application passes to it. For example, you can create an object in Visual FoxPro for storing employee information that not only validates that the application has passed valid employee information, but checks the user's access level to ensure that the user has security access to make the employee changes.

A custom server can also expose an object that incorporates complex logic for updating or reading information. For example, an order entry object might not only be able to store the order, but could also maintain a transaction log of orders, update inventory, calculate a sales commission, and so on.

This type of Automation server is ideal for creating the "middle layer" of a three-tiered enterprise application. In this model, the data forms the lowest level and the application forms the highest. The functionality is in the middle, and provides a specific, application-independent view of the data that incorporates business rules (or other data processing capabilities) that don't properly belong with the data or with the application alone.

For information about creating custom Automation servers, see "Creating Automation Servers" in Chapter 16, "Adding OLE," in Part 5, "Extending Applications."

Creating a Data Warehouse Using Visual FoxPro

In addition to creating your application in Visual FoxPro, you can use the program to create and maintain a data warehouse, or version of your data that is optimized for reporting. To create a data warehouse, you make a copy of the data required for reporting, and then make it available to users who need it. By maintaining this data separately from your live data, you can:

- Structure it to make reporting easier or faster than if users created reports from the live data.

- Place data for reports in a location separate from the live data, which reduces contention for data, improves performance, and can make data available to users who shouldn't see live data for security purposes.

A data warehouse is a "snapshot" of the data at the time you create it. You refresh the data in the warehouse periodically, scheduling the update according to the reporting needs for your application.

For example, imagine that you're creating an application to manage a library, including an inventory of materials. During the day, the system is in constant use as patrons check materials in and out, and query the system to locate or reserve books. In addition to managing these individual transactions, librarians want to be able to analyze their library, to determine facts such as what materials are the most popular, what books are overdue, and so on.

To help with the analysis, the application can create a data warehouse out of the transaction information. The application can warehouse the data periodically, perhaps every night, and the librarians can create queries without affecting the performance of the system during the day. In addition, the data warehouse can exclude details about the patrons using the library, because this information isn't required for the analysis and might be considered confidential information.

To get the most benefit from a data warehouse, you create it on a server separate from the live data. If the live data and data warehouse are on the same server, you can still get the benefit of having optimized data in the warehouse. However, as users make queries against the warehouse, they can generate a large amount of network traffic which might affect performance of the live system.

When you create the data warehouse, you can simply copy the live files over to parallel files in the data warehouse. Alternatively, you can restructure the data in the warehouse to optimize it for reporting. For example, you might create indexes for the warehouse data that reduce reporting overheard.

As another example, data in the live application should be normalized in order to avoid data duplication. However, in the data warehouse it might be useful to combine tables that would otherwise be separate; this can eliminate the need to join tables, making it easier for less experienced users to create reports.

You can also match the level of detail in the data warehouse to the reporting requirements of your application. For the most flexibility, you should store the same level of detail in the data warehouse as you have in the live data. However, if users wanted to create only summary reports (such as spreadsheets or charts), you could roll up detail data from the application and store only summary data in the data warehouse.

Using Visual FoxPro as a World Wide Web Search Engine

If your enterprise solution involves creating a World Wide Web server for the Internet, you can incorporate Visual FoxPro into the application as a search engine. This allows you to make the power of your Visual FoxPro database available to anyone who can access your Web server, whether on the Internet or via a company intranet.

For example, imagine that as part of your company-wide intranet you want to make available an employee directory. Employees could point their browsers to a "Search for Employee" page, which would display a page that looks like a Visual FoxPro form, containing text boxes to enter criteria. To perform a search, users would enter the employee's name, phone extension, department, position, or any other information they had available, and then choose a Search Now button. In a moment or two they would see a listing of the employees who met the search criteria. They could then save this listing as a text file that could then be imported into another program, such as a word processor.

Understanding Visual FoxPro as a Web Search Engine

In general, in order to use Visual FoxPro as an information server for the Web, you need these components:

- An existing Web server with HTTP service, running on Microsoft Windows NT operating system.

- A Visual FoxPro application that can be called as an Automation server. This application can run on any server accessible to the Web server.

- A means displaying search results, which usually consists of a Web page template into which you can insert data.

The usual sequence of events that involve a Visual FoxPro search on the Web are these:

1. The user displays your application's search page by pointing a Web browser to it. The search page includes any text and graphics that you want, plus text boxes in which users can enter search text.

2. The user chooses a "Search Now" button. The data from the completed form is sent to the Web server for processing, along with the name of your Web page search application.

3. The Web server calls your application using ISAPI (Internet Server API) protocol, passing to it a parameter containing the search information.

4. Your application searches the database. When it gets results, it inserts them into a Web page template, and then sends the Web page back to the server as a stream of characters.

5. The Web server sends the results page to the browser that initiated the search.

6. The browser displays the results page for the user.

If you've created Web pages, most of the steps in this process are probably familiar. For example, you might already know how to create Web pages. Even if you aren't already familiar with Web page design, you'd probably find the process of creating these pages relatively easy.

For an example of how to use Visual FoxPro as a Web search engine, see the sample Foxisapi.dll in the in the Visual Studio ...\Samples\Vfp98\Servers\Foxisapi directory. Refer to the Readme.txt file in that directory for details about how to run the example.

PART 11

What's New in Visual FoxPro

The following chapters describe the new features in Visual FoxPro 6.0. These features make creating Visual FoxPro applications faster and easier than ever, and allow you to create applications for the Internet and intranets.

Chapter 31   Interoperability and the Internet

Use OLE drag-and-drop to develop applications that let you move data between Windows-based applications and within a Visual FoxPro application. Create applications and Visual FoxPro servers for use with the Internet.

Chapter 32   Application Development and Developer Productivity

Component Gallery and Foundation Classes, Coverage Profiler Application, Project Manager Hooks, and Wizards.

Chapter 33   Programming Improvements

New programming features designed to improve developer productivity, including Access and Assign methods, support for more graphic file formats, and new language to simplify programming tasks. Also, many of the file name manipulation functions available in Foxtools.fll, a Visual FoxPro API library, have been added to Visual FoxPro.

CHAPTER 31

Interoperability and the Internet

Microsoft Visual FoxPro 6.0 now supports OLE drag-and-drop, which allows you to move data between Visual FoxPro and other applications, and within Visual FoxPro applications.

Visual FoxPro 6.0 also makes it easy to create applications for use with the Internet and other Windows-based applications such as Microsoft Excel and Microsoft Visual Basic. Visual FoxPro 6.0 lets you create Active Documents that can be hosted by Active Document hosts such as Internet browsers.

Visual FoxPro 6.0 features improved Automation servers to work better with the Internet, Microsoft Transaction Server, and the Active Desktop.

This chapter covers:

- OLE Drag-and-Drop
- Active Documents
- Automation Server Improvements

OLE Drag-and-Drop

Visual FoxPro now supports OLE drag-and-drop, a powerful and useful tool that allows you to move data between other applications that support OLE drag-and-drop (such as Visual FoxPro, Visual Basic, the Windows Explorer, Microsoft Word and Excel, and so on). In a distributed Visual FoxPro application, you can move data between controls in the application, or between controls and other Window applications that support OLE drag-and-drop.

Note that previous versions of Visual FoxPro supported a programmatic drag-and-drop feature for controls, allowing you to move controls on a form. This form of drag-and-drop is still supported in Visual FoxPro 6.0. However, if you choose to implement drag-and-drop support in your applications, you should exclusively use either programmatic drag-and-drop for controls or OLE drag-and-drop — don't mix the two types of drag-and-drop support.

Understanding some of the basics of OLE drag-and-drop applications makes it easier to take full advantage of their features.

Dragging and Dropping Data

The mouse is used to drag-and-drop data between applications and controls. For example, you can select a set of files in the Windows Explorer. You can then press and hold the mouse button down while dragging the files, then release the mouse button to drop them onto the Visual FoxPro Project Manager, or you can select text in a Word document and drop the text into a text box on a Visual FoxPro form. During the OLE drag-and-drop operation, the mouse cursor changes to indicate that an OLE drag-and-drop operation is in effect.

Drag Source

The application or control from which data is moved is called the drag source.

Drag Source Properties, Events, and Methods

The following table lists the properties, events, and methods available for an OLE drag source.

Property, Event, or Method	Description
OLECompleteDrag Event	Occurs when data is dropped on the drop target or the OLE drag-and-drop operation is canceled.
OLEDrag Method	Starts an OLE drag-and-drop operation.
OLEDragPicture Property	Specifies the picture displayed under the mouse pointer during an OLE drag-and-drop operation. You can specify a picture file of type .bmp, .dib, .jpg, .gif, .ani, .cur, and .ico.
OLEDragMode Property	Specifies how a drag source manages OLE drag operations.
OLEGiveFeedBack Event	Occurs after every OLEDragOver event. Allows the drag source to specify the type of OLE drag-and-drop operation and the visual feedback.
OLESetData Event	Occurs when a drop target calls the GetData method and there is no data in a specified format on the OLE drag-and-drop DataObject.
OLEStartDrag Event	Occurs when the OLEDrag method is called.

Drop Target

The application or control to which the data is moved is called the *drop target*.

Drop Target Properties and Events

The following table lists the properties, events, and methods available for an OLE drop target.

Property or Event	Description
OLEDragDrop Event	Occurs when data is dropped on a drop target and the drop target's OLEDropMode property is set to 1 – Enabled.
OLEDragOver Event	Occurs when data is dragged over a drop target and the drop target's OLEDropMode property is set to 1 – Enabled.
OLEDropEffects Property	Specifies the type of drop operations an OLE drop target supports.
OLEDropHasData Property	Specifies how a drop operation is managed.
OLEDropMode Property	Specifies how a drop target manages OLE drop operations.

Moving Data

To perform a drag-and-drop operation to move data using the default (left) mouse button, select the data you want to move in the drag source. After selecting the data, press and hold down the mouse button as you move the mouse pointer over the drop target. Release the mouse button to drop the data onto the drop target. During the OLE drag-and-drop operation, the mouse cursor changes to indicate that an OLE drag-and-drop operation is in effect.

You can also click the non-default (right) mouse button on the data in a drag source and drag it to a drop target. Depending on the drop target, a context menu may be displayed when you drop the data on the drop target. The context menu contains a set of options that let you choose how the data is processed by the drop target.

Copying Data

You can also copy data from a drag source and paste it in a drop target. Press the CTRL key as you click the mouse on the data selected in the drag source. The mouse cursor displays a plus sign (+) while the mouse is dragged to indicate a Copy operation is in effect.

Targets and Sources Not Supporting OLE Drag-and-Drop

You can only move or copy data from a drag source that supports OLE drag-and-drop, and the drop target must also support OLE drag-and-drop. Note that while a drop target may support OLE drag-and-drop, the drop target doesn't have to accept the data you attempt to drop on it. For example, the data you're moving or copying may be in a format the drop target doesn't support. During a drag-and-drop operation, the mouse cursor changes to a No Drop symbol (a slashed circle) to indicate the mouse is positioned over an area of an application or control where the data cannot be dropped.

Canceling an Operation

To cancel the OLE drag-and-drop operation, press ESC during the operation.

Design Time OLE Drag-and-Drop Support

Design time support for OLE drag-and-drop in Visual FoxPro makes developing applications even faster than previous versions. OLE drag-and-drop makes it easy to drop files into the Project Manager and the Visual FoxPro designers from the Windows Explorer. Text can be easily moved or copied from other applications to the Command Window, the Visual FoxPro text editors, and the Properties Window.

The following table lists the Visual FoxPro design time features that support OLE drag-and-drop with a description of the support.

Interface item	Description
Command Window	Drop target for files, drag source and drop target for text.
	If a file created in Visual FoxPro is dropped on the Command window, the file is opened with the appropriate Visual FoxPro command. For example, if a database is dropped on the Command window, Visual FoxPro issues the OPEN DATABASE and MODIFY DATABASE commands to open the file for modification. If a table is dropped on the Command window, the table is opened with the USE … AGAIN and BROWSE commands. If SET EXCLUSIVE is ON, the table is opened for exclusive use. If SET EXCLUSIVE is OFF, the table is opened for shared use.
	Other Visual FoxPro files are opened with the appropriate MODIFY command — forms are opened with MODIFY FORM, queries are opened with MODIFY QUERY, text and header (.H) files are opened with MODIFY FILE, and so on.
	If a file that has been created in another application is dropped on the Command window, the file is opened in the application with which it is associated. For example, dropping a Microsoft Excel spreadsheet on the Command window starts Excel and opens the spreadsheet.
Project Manager	Drop target for files.
	Files are added to the appropriate Project Manager categories, based on their file extensions. If a file with an extension Visual FoxPro does not recognize is dropped on the Project Manager, the file is added to the Other category.
	If a table contained in a database is dropped on the Project Manager, the database is added to the Databases category of the Data item and is marked as Excluded. If a free table is dropped on the Project Manager, the table is added to the Free Tables category of the Data item and is marked as Excluded. If a database is dropped on the Project Manager, the database is added to the Databases category of the Data item and is marked as Excluded.
	While OLE drag-and-drop makes it easy to add files to the Project Manager, remember that the Project Manager automatically adds any referenced files to the project when you build the project. For example, if a program you add to the project executes a second program, the second program is automatically added to the project when the project is built. It isn't necessary to manually add the second program to the project.

(continued)

Interface item	Description
Text Editors	Drag source and drop target for text.
	Text editors include editing windows opened with MODIFY COMMAND, MODIFY FILE, and MODIFY MEMO, the Command window, snippet editing windows in the Form, Class, Menu, and Data Environment Designers, and the Stored Procedure editor in the Database Designer.
Debugger	Drag source and drop target for text.
	The Watch window text box and Name list are drag sources and drop targets for text. The Trace window and the Debug Output window are drag sources for text.
Database Designer	Drop target for files.
	Dropping a table onto the Database Designer adds the table to the current database.
Class Designer	Drop target for text and files.
	By default, dropping text on a container object in the Class Designer creates a label with the text as the value of its Caption property. You can change the default control created when text is dropped on the Form Designer in the Field Mapping Tab of the Options Dialog Box.
	If you drop text onto a non-container control (a CheckBox, CommandButton, Header, Label, or OptionButton control), the control's Caption property is set to the text.
	Dropping a graphics file (.ani, .bmp, .cur, .gif, .ico, or .jpg) onto the Class Designer creates an Image control with the Picture property set to the name of the graphics file.
Data Environment Designer	Drop target for files.
	Dropping a table onto the Data Environment Designer adds the table to the data environment. Dropping a database onto the Data Environment Designer displays the Add Table or View dialog, allowing you to add a table or view to the data environment.
Query Designer	Drop target for files.
	Dropping a table onto the Query Designer adds the table to the query. Dropping a database onto the Query Designer displays the Add Table or View dialog, allowing you to add a table or view to the query.
View Designer	Drop target for files.
	Dropping a table onto the View Designer adds the table to the view. Dropping a database onto the View Designer displays the Add Table or View dialog, allowing you to add a table or view to the view.

(continued)

(continued)

Interface item	Description
Properties window	Drag source and drop target for text.
	You can drag text from and drop text onto the text box or combo box that appears at the top of the Properties window when a design time property is selected.
Component Gallery	Drag source and drop target for files.
	You can drag objects out of the Component Gallery and drop them onto the Form Designer. You can also drag files out of the Component Gallery and drop them onto the Project Manager.
	Files can be dropped on the Component Gallery.

Run-Time OLE Drag-and-Drop Support

OLE drag-and-drop support is available at run time for Visual FoxPro controls and the text editor. The controls and the text editor support OLE drag-and-drop interactively at run time, and the controls provide programmatic support at run time. The DataObject object provides programmatic OLE drag-and-drop support for the controls.

Two modes of OLE drag-and-drop are available for Visual FoxPro controls: intrinsic mode and manual mode. In intrinsic mode, Visual FoxPro intrinsically handles an OLE drag-and-drop operation. In manual mode, OLE drag-and-drop operations are handled programmatically. The events that occur are determined by the OLE drag-and-drop mode. For more information, see "Intrinsic and Manual OLE Drag-and-Drop Modes," later in this section.

Drag-and-Drop in Previous Versions of Visual FoxPro

Previous versions of Visual FoxPro supported programmatic drag-and-drop for controls, allowing you to move controls on a form. This form of drag-and-drop is still supported. If you use the default settings for the OLEDragMode and OLEDropMode properties, your existing applications will run as before without any changes.

The DataObject Object

The DataObject object is a container for data being transferred from an OLE drag source to an OLE drop target, and exists only for the duration of an OLE drag-and-drop operation. The DataObject object cannot be created programmatically and references to it become invalid once the OLE drag-and-drop operation is completed. The DataObject is passed as the oDataObject parameter in the OLEStartDrag, OLEDragOver, OLEDragDrop, and OLESetData events.

The DataObject can store multiple sets of data, each in a different format. The existence of a specific format in the DataObject can be determined with the GetFormat method. See the GetFormat Method for a listing of the formats supported by the DataObject.

DataObject Object Methods

The DataObject object has methods that allow you to programmatically manipulate the data being dragged and dropped. The following table lists the methods available at run time for the DataObject.

Method	Description
ClearData	Clears all data and data formats from the OLE drag-and-drop DataObject object.
GetData	Retrieves data from the OLE drag-and-drop DataObject object.
GetFormat	Determines if data in a specified format is available on the OLE drag-and-drop DataObject.
SetData	Places data and its format on the OLE drag-and-drop DataObject.
SetFormat	Places a data format without data on the OLE drag-and-drop DataObject.

Intrinsic and Manual OLE Drag-and-Drop Modes

Visual FoxPro supports two OLE drag-and-drop modes for controls: intrinsic and manual. In intrinsic mode, OLE drag-and-drop operations are handled by Visual FoxPro. In manual mode, OLE drag-and-drop operations are under programmatic control.

Intrinsic OLE Drag-and-Drop Mode

Intrinsic OLE drag-and-drop mode can be implemented in an application to provide standard OLE drag-and-drop support without any additional programming.

To implement intrinsic OLE Drag-and-Drop support for a control

1. Set its OLEDragMode property to **1 – Automatic**, allowing the control to act as an OLE drag source.

2. Set the control's OLEDropMode property to **1 – Enabled**, to allow the control to act as an OLE drop target.

For intrinsic OLE drag-and-drop operations, Visual FoxPro determines if the drop target supports the format of the data being dropped on it; if the drop target supports the format, the drop occurs, otherwise the drop is not allowed.

The following table lists the Visual FoxPro controls and the data formats they support as drag sources in intrinsic mode. Note that CF_TEXT is text, such as text you would enter in a text box, and CFSTR_VFPSOURCEOBJECT is an object type reference to a Visual FoxPro control or object. For the controls below that support the CF_TEXT data format, you can drag text from the text portion of the control.

Drag Source Data Formats

Control	Data Format (defined in Foxpro.h)
Container, Image, Line, PageFrame, and Shape	CFSTR_VFPSOURCEOBJECT
CommandButton and Label	CFSTR_VFPSOURCEOBJECT and CF_TEXT
CheckBox, ComboBox, EditBox, ListBox, Spinner, and TextBox	CFSTR_VFPSOURCEOBJECT, CF_TEXT, and CFSTR_OLEVARIANT

The Visual FoxPro controls and data formats they support as drop targets in intrinsic mode are listed in the following table. For the controls listed in this table, you can drop text onto the text portion of the control. The text is inserted at the insertion point.

Drop Target Data Formats

Control	Data Format
EditBox and ComboBox (When the ComboBox Style property is set to 0 – Dropdown Combo)	CF_TEXT
Spinner and TextBox	CFSTR_OLEVARIANT

Manual OLE Drag-and-Drop Mode

There may be cases where you'd like to control the type of data that can be dropped on a drop target, or provide additional functionality for a drag-and-drop operation. For example, you can convert data to a format supported by the drop target, or you can display a dialog that asks the user if they're sure they want to drop the data on the drop target. In cases such as these, override the intrinsic OLE drag-and-drop support to provide greater control over drag-and-drop operations.

To implement manual OLE drag-and-drop support for a control, override the drag or drop events or methods you want to control to by writing your own event or method code. Include the NODEFAULT keyword in the event or method code to override the intrinsic Visual FoxPro drag-and-drop behavior.

Backward compatibility (no OLE drag support) is provided for existing applications when OLEDragMode is set to 0 (the default) and you do not include additional OLE drag-and-drop coding.

Active Documents

Visual FoxPro 6.0 allows you to create Active Documents. Active Documents enable you to view non-HTML documents in a Web browser host such as Microsoft Internet Explorer. Active Document technology allows you to view multiple types of documents from multiple sources within a single Active Document host.

An Active Document is a specific type of OLE embeddable document. It displays in the entire client area of an Active Document host and does menu merging with the host. The Active Document is full-frame and always in-place active.

The following are some of the features that Active Documents provide:

- Active documents are always in-place active.

- Active Document menu and toolbar commands can be routed to the Active Document host.

- Active Documents provide seamless integration with other web pages when viewed in Internet Explorer.

- Active Documents provide an evolutionary step along the migration path from pure Visual FoxPro client applications to Active Platform applications that use a client interface based on HTML.

Creating an Active Document

Visual FoxPro Active Documents are easy to create. A Visual FoxPro Active Document, like any other Visual FoxPro application, can manipulate data, run forms, reports, and labels, instantiate classes, and run code.

A Visual FoxPro Active Document is an application (.app) created from a Visual FoxPro project. Earlier versions of Visual FoxPro allowed you to create applications, so you may already be familiar with creating applications. For more information about creating applications, see Chapter 13, "Compiling an Application."

Any application can be run in Internet Explorer. However, only applications based on the ActiveDoc base class, described below, support the properties, events, and methods that provide communication with the Active Document host.

The ActiveDoc Base Class

Visual FoxPro Active Documents differ slightly from other applications (.app). The most notable difference is that the "main file" for an Active Document must be set to a class based on the ActiveDoc base class. Other types of applications require that the main file be a program or a form.

A class based on the ActiveDoc base class is created with the Class Designer and serves as the basis for all Visual FoxPro Active Documents. The ActiveDoc base class provides properties, events, and methods for an Active Document, and provides communication with the Active Document host. For example, the ContainerRelease event occurs when an Active Document is released by its host. You can place code in the ContainerRelease event to close files, complete transactions, and perform other clean up duties before the Active Document is released.

To set the main file to a class based on the ActiveDoc base class

1. Add the visual class library (.vcx) containing the class based on the ActiveDoc base class to the project.

2. Expand the visual class library (.vcx) hierarchy by clicking the plus (+) box to the left of the library name, or right-click the library and choose **Expand All** from the shortcut menu.

3. Select the class based on the ActiveDoc base class. Right-click the class and choose **Set Main** from the shortcut menu.

The ActiveDoc Object

When a Visual FoxPro Active Document is run in Internet Explorer, an ActiveDoc object is created from the ActiveDoc base class. The ActiveDoc object responds to events and method calls for the ActiveDoc base class.

ActiveDoc Object Properties, Events, and Methods

The following tables list the properties, events, and methods supported by the ActiveDoc object.

Properties

BaseClass	Caption	Class
ClassLibrary	Comment	ContainerReleaseType
Name	Parent	ParentClass
Tag		

Events

CommandTargetExec	CommandTargetQuery	ContainerRelease
Destroy	Error	HideDoc
Init	Run	ShowDoc

Methods

AddProperty	ReadExpression	ReadMethod
ResetToDefault	SaveAsClass	WriteExpression

Active Document Event Sequences

When an Active Document application is opened in Internet Explorer, the Active Document runs and the Active Document's Init event occurs. Then the Active Document's ShowDoc event occurs. When Internet Explorer successfully hosts the Active Document,

the Active Document's Run event occurs. In general, the Active Document program code should be placed in this event. Typically, the Run event contains code that executes your menu code, executes the main form in the application, and contains READ EVENTS to start event processing, just like a standard Visual FoxPro application.

You can put setup code in your Active Document's Init event, but if the code takes too long to execute, the Active Document container might generate a time out error. If you do put setup code in the Init event, it should not require user interaction or create a user interface.

The HideDoc event occurs if you navigate from an Active Document, and the ShowDoc event occurs when you navigate back to the Active Document.

If Internet Explorer is closed when the Active Document is hosted, the HideDoc event occurs, and then the ContainerRelease Event occurs. The ContainerRelease event also occurs if the Active Document falls out of the Internet Explorer 3.0 cache.

When the ContainerRelease event occurs, the program code in the event can do the following:

- Close files, clean up after itself, and issue QUIT to close the Active Document.

- Set the ContainerReleaseType property to 0 (the default), which opens the Active Document in the Visual FoxPro run-time. The Active Document continues to run in the main Visual FoxPro window of the run-time.

  Note   The CommandTargetExec event occurs if Internet Explorer 4.0 is about to close the Active Document or navigate from the Active Document. In this case, the CommandTargetExec event *nCommandID* parameter is set to 37, and you can set the *eArgOut* parameter to false (.F.) to prevent the Active Document from being closed by Internet Explorer. Internet Explorer 3.0 doesn't support the CommandTargetExec event.

New Active Document Functions

Two new functions, GETHOST( ) and ISHOSTED( ), have been added to Visual FoxPro to provide information about an Active Document's host. GETHOST( ) returns an object reference to an Active Document's host. ISHOSTED( ) returns a logical value indicating if an Active Document is hosted.

Changes to the Form Object

The user interface in a Visual FoxPro Active Document is defined by its program code. In general, a Visual FoxPro form should be displayed as the initial user interface. The following form properties, events, and methods have been added to Visual FoxPro to allow forms to work well in Active Documents.

Properties

ContinuousScroll	HscrollSmallChange	Scrollbars
TitleBar	ViewPortHeight	ViewPortLeft
ViewPortTop	ViewPortWidth	VScrollSmallChange

Event

Scrolled

Method

SetViewPort

Forms in Active Documents

Forms in an Active Document are displayed in the client area provided by Internet Explorer. To make a form display entirely within the Internet Explorer client area, set the following form properties to these values:

BorderStyle = 0 (No Border)
TitleBar = 0 (Off)
WindowState = 2 (Maximized)

Also, if scrollbars should be displayed when the Internet Explorer's client area is smaller than the Active Document viewport (the area determined by a rectangle that encloses all the controls on the form), the Scrollbars property should be set to the following value:

ScrollBars = 3 (Both horizontal and vertical scrollbars)

Menus in Active Documents

If menu code is run in a Visual FoxPro Active Document, the menus are merged with the Internet Explorer menus, following specific menu merging rules. Once the Active Document menus are merged with those of Internet Explorer, the Active Document menus appear as if they would in a traditional Visual FoxPro application.

Menu Negotiation

In Visual FoxPro 6.0 and earlier versions, you can specify menu negotiation behavior for menus when OLE visual editing occurs for an ActiveX control contained in a Visual FoxPro form. In Visual FoxPro 6.0, menu negotiation has been enhanced to provide control over where menus in an Active Document appear in Internet Explorer.

When an Active Document is open in Internet Explorer, it shares menu space with Internet Explorer and menus are merged together. Menus from Internet Explorer are merged with menus from the Active Document. The merged menus fall into six groups, and each group is owned by Internet Explorer, the Active Document, or both.

Group	Owner
File Group	Internet Explorer
EditGroup	Active Document
Container Group	Internet Explorer
Object Group	Active Document
Window Group	Internet Explorer
Help Group	Active Document or Internet Explorer

Help Menu Merging

The Active Document shares its Help menu with Internet Explorer. If Internet Explorer has a help menu, the Active Document can add its help menu to the end of Internet Explorer's help menu.

Language Enhancements for Menu Negotiation

The DEFINE PAD NEGOTIATE clause has been enhanced to allow you specify how menu negotiation occurs for menus in an Active Document. A new second option, *cObjectPosition*, specifies the location of a menu title in the Internet Explorer menu bar.

See DEFINE PAD in the *Microsoft Visual FoxPro 6.0 Language Reference* for more information.

Menu Negotiation and the Menu Designer

The Prompt Options dialog box in the Menu designer has been enhanced, allowing you to specify menu negotiation for menus created in the Menu Designer and included in Active Documents. An **Object** drop-down has been added; this drop-down specifies how the menu title is negotiated when a Visual FoxPro Active Document is hosted in Internet Explorer.

Menu Negotiation Information

The menu negotiation information is stored in the Location field of a menu's .mnx file. The following table lists the values in this field and the type of menu negotiation for each value. See DEFINE PAD for more information about *cContainerPosition* and *cObjectPosition*.

Value	cContainerPosition	cObjectPosition
0	None	None
1	Left	None
2	Middle	None
3	Right	None
4	None	Left
5	Left	Left
6	Middle	Left
7	Right	Left
8	None	Middle
9	Left	Middle
10	Middle	Middle
11	Right	Middle
12	None	Right
13	Left	Right
14	Middle	Right
15	Right	Right

Note that in Visual FoxPro 6.0 the Location field size was increased from 1 digit to 2 digits. This is the only change made in Visual FoxPro 6.0 to the structures of tables, including database (.dbc), form (.scx), label (.lbx), project (.pjx), report (.frx), and visual class library (.vcx) tables.

CommandTargetExec and CommandTargetQuery Events

Two Active Document events, CommandTargetExec and CommandTargetQuery, allow you to manage Internet Explorer menu selections (and other Internet Explorer events) from an Active Document. The CommandTargetExec event occurs when Internet Explorer notifies an Active Document of a command (including a menu command) to be executed. The CommandTargetQuery event occurs when Internet Explorer updates its user interface. See CommandTargetExec Event and CommandTargetQuery Event in the *Microsoft Visual FoxPro 6.0 Language Reference* for more information about each event.

Running Active Documents

Visual FoxPro Active Documents require Vfp6.exe and Vfp6run.exe, or Vfp6run.exe, Vfp6r.dll, and Vfp6renu.dll (enu denotes the English version) to run. These files must be installed and registered on the computer on which Internet Explorer is installed. When Visual FoxPro is installed, Vfp6.exe is installed in the Visual FoxPro directory, and the remaining files are installed in the Windows 95 Windows\System directory or the Windows NT WinNT\System32 directories.

Running Active Documents from the Tools Menu

The Visual FoxPro Tools menu contains a **Run Active Document** command that you can choose to display the **Run Active Document** dialog box. In this dialog you can specify how an Active Document is run. The following options are available:

Option	Description
In Browser (Default)	The Active Document is run in Internet Explorer using the Visual FoxPro Run-Time.
Stand-Alone	The Active Document is run as a stand-alone application with the Visual FoxPro Run-Time.
In Browser (Debugging)	The Active Document is run in Internet Explorer using the Visual FoxPro executable (Vfp6.exe). Debugging capabilities, the Command window, and all features of the Visual FoxPro development environment are available.
Stand-Alone (Debugging)	The Active Document is run as a stand-alone application with the Visual FoxPro executable (Vfp6.exe), providing debugging capabilities, the Command window, and all features of the Visual FoxPro development environment.
	Choosing this option is identical to issuing DO <Active Doc Name> in the Command window.

You can also run an Active Document by opening the Active Document from the Open File dialog box in Internet Explorer, or by navigating to the Active Document from another Web page with a hyperlink to the Active Document.

The Visual FoxPro Run-Time and Active Documents

From Visual FoxPro you can run an Active Document by double-clicking the Active Document icon in the Windows Explorer. You can also run an Active Document from a Visual FoxPro run-time application. The Visual FoxPro Run-Time consists of two files, Vfp6run.exe and Vfp6r.dll. Both must be installed and registered to run Active Documents. The run time can also be used to run other Visual FoxPro distributable files such as compiled Visual FoxPro programs (.fxp files).

Vfp6run.exe, once registered, can be used to run Active Documents (and other Visual FoxPro distributable files) directly.

Syntax for Vfp6run.exe

VFP6RUN [/embedding] [/regserver] [/unregserver] [/security] [/s] [/version] [*FileName*]

Arguments

/embedding
> Loads Vfp6run.exe as an active document server. In this mode, Vfp6run.exe is registered as a COM server capable of creating a Visual FoxPro Active Document object ("Visual.FoxPro.Application.6"). Without this argument, Vfp6run.exe doesn't act as a COM server.

/regserver
> Registers Vfp6run.exe.

/unregserver
> Unregisters Vfp6run.exe.

/security
> Displays the Application Security Settings dialog box, allowing you to specify the security settings for Active Documents and other application (.app) files. For more information, see the next section, "Active Document Security."

/s
> Silent. Specifies that an error is generated if Vfp6run.exe is unable to load the Vfp6r.dll run-time component.

/version
> Displays Vfp6run.exe and the Vfp6r.dll version information.

FileName
> Specifies the Visual FoxPro file to run.

Vfp6run.exe requires that the run-time support dynamic link library Vfp6r.dll be installed and registered. To register Vfp6r.dll, run Regsvr32 with the name of the run time:

```
Regsvr32 Vfp6r.dll
```

Active Document Security

The /security option for the Vfp6run.exe Visual FoxPro Run-Time allows you to set security levels for Active Documents and other application (.app) files. Executing `Vfp6run.exe /security` displays the **Application Security Settings** dialog box where you can set security levels for Active Documents and other .app files.

The following options are available in the Application Security Settings dialog box:

Hosted

Choose this application mode setting to specify a security level for an Active Document or application (.app) that is run from an Active Document container such as Internet Explorer.

Non-hosted

Choose this application mode setting to specify a security level for an Active Document or application (.app) that is run from the Window Explorer by double-clicking its icon, or is run with the Visual FoxPro Vfp6run.exe run time.

High (most secure)

Choose this setting to prevent an Active Document or application (.app) from being run.

Medium (more secure)

Choose this setting to display a warning before an Active Document or application (.app) is run. Medium is the default setting for non-hosted Active Documents and applications.

Low (no security)

Choose this setting to run an Active Document or application (.app) without displaying a warning. Low is the default setting for hosted Active Documents and applications.

Reset

Restores the default security level for the currently selected application mode (hosted or non-hosted).

OK

Saves the settings you choose in the dialog box.

Internet Explorer Notes

To increase performance, Internet Explorer 3.0 caches the last four pages visited in memory. This means that an Active Document can fall out of the Internet Explorer 3.0 cache, causing the ContainerRelease event to occur. Internet Explorer 4.0 does not have a page cache, so the ContainerRelease event occurs as soon as you navigate from an Active Document.

Active Document Sample

The Visual FoxPro Solutions Sample application includes a sample named "Create Active Documents for the Web" that demonstrates many of the Active Document features.

To run the Solutions Sample application

- Enter the following in the Command window:

```
DO (HOME(2) + 'solution\solution')
```

– or –

1. From the **Program** menu, choose **Do**.
2. Choose the …**\Samples\Vfp98\Solution** folder.
3. Double-click **Solution.app**.

To run the "Create Active Documents for the Web" sample

1. After starting Solution.app, double-click **New Features for Visual FoxPro 6.0**.
2. Click **Create Active Documents for the Web** and then click the **Run Sample** button.

The "Create Active Documents for the Web" sample allows you to open a project that contains all of the files necessary to create an Active Document from the project. When the project is open, you can examine the code in the Actdoc class to see how Active Document events are managed and how forms are run. Note that Actdoc, a class based on the ActiveDoc base class, is set as the main file in the project. An Active Document must have a class based on the ActiveDoc base class as its main file.

You can also create build an Active Document from the project by choosing **Build** in the Project Manager. After the Active Document is built, choose **Run Active Document** from the **Tools** menu to run the Active Document.

Automation Server Improvements

This topic describes improvements made to Visual FoxPro 6.0 Automation servers, and includes discussions of how Visual FoxPro Automation servers can work with products and technologies such as Microsoft Transaction Server and Microsoft Visual Basic.

Visual FoxPro allows you to create Automation servers. An Automation server is a component application that exposes functionality that can be used and reused by other applications through Automation. For example, using Visual FoxPro you can create an Automation server that displays reusable forms (in an out-of-process .exe), or packages a complex routine into a simple component that other programmers can use. In addition, you could create one or more classes to handle enterprise-wide business rules. A client application that uses the business rule objects would pass input parameters in a method call, and the Automation server might then do a great deal of work, retrieving or storing data from various sources and performing complex calculations, before returning the answer.

In Visual FoxPro, you can create either an out-of-process or an in-process Automation server. An *out-of-process* component is an executable (.exe) file that runs in its own process. Communication between a client application and an out-of-process server is therefore called *cross-process* communication. An *in-process* component is a dynamic-link library (.dll) file that runs in the same process address space as the client that calls it or in a Microsoft Transaction Server process.

For more information about creating Visual FoxPro Automation servers, see "Creating Automation Servers," in Chapter 16, "Adding OLE."

Visual FoxPro 6.0 Automation Server Improvements

The following topics describe the new and improved Visual FoxPro 6.0 Automation server features.

Apartment Model Threading

Visual FoxPro Automation servers now support Apartment Model Threading. The Microsoft Transaction Server takes advantage of servers marked as apartment threaded and offers better thread protection and scalability.

Each apartment model object (such as a Visual FoxPro Automation server) may only be entered by one thread, the thread that created the object (for example, called CoCreateInstance in Microsoft Visual C++. However, an object server (such as Microsoft Transaction Server) can support multiple objects, each being entered simultaneously by different threads. Common data held by the object server must be protected against thread collisions. The object server creates an apartment model object in the same thread that called CoCreateInstance. Calls to the object from the apartment thread are not marshaled.

For more information about apartment model threading, search for "Apartment-Model Threading in Visual Basic" in the MSDN library.

User Interfaces and In-Process Servers

The new apartment model threading support requires that in-process .dll Automation servers not have user-interfaces. In Visual FoxPro 5.0, one could create (although it was not recommended) an in-process .dll Automation server that had a user-interface such as a form. The form could be used only for display because the form events are not supported. In Visual FoxPro 6.0, any attempts to create a user-interface in an in-process .dll Automation generates an error.

An out-of-process .exe Automation server can have a user-interface. A new Visual FoxPro 6.0 function, SYS(2335), has been added so you can disable modal events for an out-of-process .exe Automation server, which may be deployed remotely without intervention from a user. Modal events are created by user-defined modal forms, system dialogs, the MESSAGEBOX( ) function and the WAIT command, and so on.

Early (vtable) Binding

Visual FoxPro 6.0 now supports both early (vtable) binding as well as the existing IDispatch interface (together known as dual-interface support). Early (vtable) binding provides performance benefits for Automation controllers such as Visual Basic and the Microsoft Transaction Server that support early (vtable) binding.

The Visual FoxPro Run-Time Vfp6r.dll

A single Visual FoxPro 6.0 Run-Time, Vfp6r.dll, no longer services multiple in-process .dll Automation servers. Each in-process .dll now uses a separate instance of the Vfp6r.dll run time. The following rules determine how in-process .dlls use the Vfp6r.dll run time:

- The in-process .dll first called has exclusive use of the Vfp6r.dll run time library (typically installed in the Windows 95 System folder or the Windows NT System32 folder).

- If an in-process .dll already has exclusive use of the Vfp6r.dll run time, a renamed copy of the Vfp6r.dll run time is created on disk and loaded into memory for each in-process .dll called. The Vfp6r.dll run time is assigned a name based on that of the in-process .dll. For example, if an in-process .dll with the name Myserver.dll is called, a copy of the Vfp6r.dll run time is renamed to Myserverr.dll (note the "r" appended to the name) and is loaded into memory to service the in-process .dll.

- Visual FoxPro Run-Times are renamed only for in-process .dlls that run within the same process. This means that two separate clients, each running in their own process, can load two different Visual FoxPro in-process .dlls without the run time being renamed. In this case, both Visual FoxPro in-process .dlls use Vfp6r.dll because the clients load in separate processes.

- Multiple Automation servers (created with OLEPUBLIC in DEFINE CLASS) in a single in-process .dll share the same Vfp6r.dll run time. In this case, it's possible that the Automation servers can affect each other by sharing public memory variables, setting the same SET commands, and so on. Be careful that multiple Automation servers in a single in-process .dll don't interfere with each other.

Type Libraries

Visual FoxPro 6.0 now supports intrinsic (Visual FoxPro) properties, events, and methods in an Automation server's type library. Only properties declared as Public are included in the type library; protected and hidden properties do not appear in the type library. Note that the Visual FoxPro Release method isn't included in the type library because it already exists as a COM method.

Both PUBLIC custom user-defined properties and methods appear in Visual FoxPro type libraries as long as they are marked Public. For methods, Visual FoxPro also includes a return value type (variant) and list of parameters (variants) parsed from the original method definition.

Note that in Visual FoxPro 6.0 a single Help file can be designated the type library.

Exception Handling

Visual FoxPro Automation servers are now more robust, so they can more gracefully terminate when an exception occurs. When exceptions occur in a Visual FoxPro 6.0 Automation server, the Automation server now sets the COM ErrorInfo object (via IErrorInfo) and cancels out of the current method. The Automation client has the option of releasing the Visual FoxPro Automation server or handling the exception, based on the information in the COM ErrorInfo object (and the client has access to the COM ErrorInfo object).

A new function, COMRETURNERROR( ), has been added to Visual FoxPro 6.0 to handle errors that occur on an Automation server. COMRETURNERROR( ) can be used in the Error method, and populates the COM exception structure with information that Automation clients can use to determine the source of Automation server errors. For more information, see COMRETURNERROR( ) in the *Microsoft Visual FoxPro 6.0 Language Reference*.

Passing Arrays

Visual FoxPro 5.0 passes arrays to COM objects (such as Automation servers created in Visual FoxPro, Visual Basic, or Visual C) by value; the array elements are the same after a method call, and the COM object changes aren't propagated to the elements on the client. This restriction prevents passing large amounts of data back and forth between Visual FoxPro 5.0 and COM objects.

Also, the array passed to the COM object is assumed be a one-based array, meaning that the first element, row, and column in the array is referenced with 1 (for example, Myarray[1]). However, some COM objects require that the array passed is zero-based (the first element, row, and column in the array is referenced with 0; for example, Myarray[0]).

A new Visual FoxPro 6.0 function, COMARRAY( ), lets you specify how an array is passed to a COM object, and lets you specify if the array is zero or one-based. For more information, see COMARRAY( ) in the *Microsoft Visual FoxPro 6.0 Language Reference*.

Note that COMARRAY( ) is only used when arrays are passed to COM objects using the following syntax:

```
oComObject.Method(@MyArray)
```

If the @ token is omitted, only the first element of the array is passed to the COM object and COMARRAY( ) has no effect. This is the same behavior for earlier versions of Visual FoxPro.

Building .dlls and .exes from Projects

Because in-process .dll and out-of-process .exe Automation servers are invoked through class instantiation, it isn't necessary to specify a main file for them. In Visual FoxPro 6.0 you can now build an in-process .dll or an out-of-process .exe Automation server without first specifying a main file in the Project Manager.

Language

The following table lists the properties and functions added to Visual FoxPro 6.0 to make it easier to manage Automation clients and servers. See each topic for further information.

New Server Improvements language	Description
COMARRAY( ) Function	Specifies how arrays are passed to COM objects.
COMCLASSINFO( ) Function	Returns registry information about a COM object such as a Visual FoxPro Automation server.
CREATEOBJECTEX( ) Function	Creates an instance of a registered COM object (such as a Visual FoxPro Automation server) on a remote computer. For a Visual FoxPro in-process .dll, you can use Microsoft Transaction Server to create an instance of the .dll on a remote computer.
COMRETURNERROR( ) Function	Populates the COM exception structure with information that Automation clients can use to determine the source of Automation server errors.
ServerName Property	Contains the full path and file name for an Automation server. The ServerName property is a property of the Application object.
StartMode Property	Contains a numeric value that indicates how the instance of Visual FoxPro was started.
SYS(2334) – Automation Server Invocation Mode	Returns a value indicating how a Visual FoxPro automation server method was invoked.
SYS(2335) – Unattended Server Mode	Enables or disables support for modal states in distributable Visual FoxPro .exe Automation servers.

Automation Server Programming Notes

The following section provides additional programming information for Automation servers.

The Application Object

The Application object isn't exposed in an Automation server's type library. This prevents access to the Application object's DoCmd and Eval methods, which can potentially provide access to the entire Visual FoxPro language. You can expose the Application object by creating a custom property and setting its value to the Application object, or provide a method that accesses the Application object.

Automation Server Samples

Visual FoxPro 6.0 includes two sample ISAPI Automation servers, FoxWeb and FoxIS. These samples manage sending selected records of Visual FoxPro data as HTML back to an Internet browser. For more information about these samples, see "FoxISAPI: An OLE Server Sample" in Help.

CHAPTER 32

Application Development and Developer Productivity

Microsoft FoxPro has always provided developer tools for application development within the FoxPro application and the XBase language. Visual FoxPro has added object-oriented language and behaviors. This version of Visual FoxPro includes an enhanced application framework and object creation and maintenance tools designed to aid rapid application development and to streamline your maintenance tasks.

This chapter discusses:

- Component Gallery
- Coverage Profiler Application
- Project Manager Hooks
- New and Enhanced Wizards and Builders
- Enhanced Application Framework

Component Gallery

The Component Gallery is a container for catalogs of software objects such as class libraries, forms, buttons, and so on. The Component Gallery also contains new Visual FoxPro classes. You can use the Component Gallery to organize components into object, project, application, or other groupings. These visual groupings are dynamically customizable so that you can use, duplicate, or rearrange components among several classifications within the Component Gallery. You can access a specific item from any of the places in the Component Gallery that you place a reference to that component. You can have several references in different catalogs or folders to a single object. For instance, a button might appear in one or more Component Gallery project categories (represented as folders), but might also be visible in a "Tools" category that holds references to all the buttons you use.

You can use the Component Gallery for all the functions provided by the separate Project Manager, Class Browser, and Form Controls toolbar. Each of the other Visual FoxPro components provides very specific focus to the projects or classes from within the special environment of either Project file or Class library. The Component Gallery allows you to manage the relationships between components and many of the behaviors of those components from either an abstract design level as well as from a more intimate development perspective.

You can drag and drop components within the Component Gallery and from the Component Gallery to projects or forms. You can also change properties of objects or classes from within the Component Gallery.

The Component Gallery can contain any Visual FoxPro element, including local and remote documents, files, or folders, Automation servers like Microsoft Excel and Word, and HTML locations and files. You can also include .prg files containing code snippets, classes, wizards, builders, or art.

To open the Component Gallery

- From the **Tools** menu, click **Component Gallery**.

  – or –

  Type **DO (_GALLERY)** in the **Command** window.

Managing Projects with the Component Gallery

You can use the Component Gallery to create Projects and Applications and to manage their development. Use the Component Gallery to arrange components within the Component Gallery or use the templates, builders, and wizards in the Component Gallery to create the project or application you want.

To create a project or an application from the Component Gallery

- Use the **Application Wizard** or **New Application template** in the **Applications** folder of the **Visual FoxPro** catalog.

For catalogs and folders, select tabs and options for the change you want to make. For details, see Component Gallery Options dialog box in Help.

Moving and Viewing Items in the Component Gallery

You can move items in the right, Object, pane of the Component Gallery window to the desktop or to an open project or form. The Project Manager recognizes the item referenced by the Component Gallery item and places it in the proper location in the Project Manager. Component Gallery items placed on the desktop are nonfunctional. There is no desktop representation for the Database, Folder, and gallery items representing nonvisual files.

To move items from the Component Gallery

1. In the right pane, click the item you want to move.

   The Move icon, located in the upper-left corner of the Component Gallery window, changes according to what item you select.

2. Drag and drop the Move icon to the desktop or to an open project or form.

When the Component Gallery cannot find the original item represented by the gallery item, a Find dialog box opens so that you can locate the item.

The following table identifies the gallery items included in Visual FoxPro and their default behaviors.

Component Gallery item type	Drag-and-Drop targets			
	Project	Form	Screen	Controls
Class (_ClassItem)			6	
File (_FileItem)				
URL (_UrlItem)		1		
Form (_FormItem)		9	11	
Report (_ReportItem)		9	11	
Program (_ProgramItem)			11	
Menu (_MenuItem)		10	11	
Image (_ImageItem)		2	7	2
Sound (_SoundItem)		3		
Video (_VideoItem)		3		
ActiveX (_ActiveXItem)				
Data (_DataItem)		4		
Template (_TemplateItem)	5			
Catalog (_CatalogItem)			8	
Sample (_SampleItem)				
Project (_ProjectItem)			11	

1 – Add hyperlink class
2 – Add an image class or set a Picture property
3 – Add a multimedia class
4 – Add a grid class
5 – Depending on the type (e.g., form) creates a new file and adds it to the project
6 – Creates an instance in Screen
7 – Sets the Visual FoxPro wallpaper
8 – Launches a new Gallery window with that catalog
9 – Add a Button class to launch a form/report
10 – Add a shortcut menu to a form
11 – Opens in a designer (modifies)

Using Shortcut Menus in the Component Gallery

You can right-click on a selected item in the right, Object, pane to display an Item Shortcut menu containing all the action options for that item, including **Add to Project** or **Add to Form** options. Use the shortcut menu to modify or, in some cases, run the gallery item.

The shortcut menus are characteristic for each type of gallery item. You can change some properties of the selected item by clicking **Properties** on the shortcut menu to open the Item Properties dialog box.

Organizing Visual FoxPro or Windows Components into User-Defined Groups

The Component Gallery folders represent an arbitrary grouping of gallery items. You can reassemble the gallery items using drag-and-drop or you can duplicate items into other folders. You can copy and rename a catalog or folder and reassemble the items it contains. There are few, if any, limits on how you can use, modify, or create catalogs or folders.

Reviewing and Modifying Classes

Since Component Gallery items represent real items that can be objects or classes, you can review or modify these classes by accessing the original object through the Component Gallery.

To review a class

1. In the Component Gallery, right-click a class.

2. On the shortcut menu, click **View in Browser**.

   This opens the Class Browser so you can view the properties and methods of the selected class.

To modify a class

1. In the Component Gallery, right-click a class.

2. On the shortcut menu, click **Modify**.

   This opens the class in the **Class Designer**.

Creating and Modifying Forms

You can use the Component Gallery to duplicate or modify forms and to add forms and other gallery items to a project.

To create a form from the Component Gallery

- Double-click any template or select New Form from the shortcut menu of any template in the Forms folder of the Component Gallery.

  – or –

  Double-click the Form Wizard in the Forms folder of the Component Gallery.

  – or –

  Select Create Form from the shortcut menu of Component Gallery items in the Forms folder of the Component Gallery.

Advanced Editing Features in the Component Gallery

The default settings for catalogs and folders enable you to perform basic review and management with gallery items. If you want to modify characteristics of catalogs or folders, or if you want greater access to gallery properties, select **Advanced editing enabled** in the Component Gallery Options dialog box.

Component Gallery Catalogs

When you open the Component Gallery, the left, Catalog, pane displays the default catalog shipped with the Component Gallery. A catalog is a visual representation of items that belong to a Visual FoxPro or user-defined group of items. Within a catalog you can create folders to further organize subgroups of items. Items can be forms, queries, programs, templates, art files, sound files, or other objects. The Visual FoxPro Component Gallery default catalog includes items grouped into several categories, including forms, controls, and others. The default catalog also includes an empty folder named Favorites that you can use to create or copy gallery items into. You can also copy and rename the default catalog, or create your own catalogs.

Component Gallery catalog options are set for catalog content and opening behavior. *Global* catalogs can contain any Component Gallery item type. *Default* catalogs open automatically when you start the Component Gallery. For details, see the Catalogs tab of the Component Gallery Options dialog box in Help.

The Component Gallery includes the following catalogs.

Catalog	Description
VFPGLRY	Contains components used by other catalogs in the gallery. Contains all the catalogs shipped with Visual FoxPro. Default and Global catalog.
Visual FoxPro	Contains the Visual FoxPro Foundation classes. Default catalog.
Favorites	An empty folder. Global catalog.
My Base Classes	Contains subclassed Visual FoxPro base classes. Default catalog.
ActiveX	A dynamic catalog containing either a list of all registered ActiveX Controls or a list of all Visual FoxPro ActiveX Controls. Default catalog.
World Wide Web	A collection of Web site URLs.
Multimedia	A variety of images, sounds, and video items you can use in your applications.
Samples	References to the Solutions, Tastrade, ActiveX Servers and Client/Server samples.

When you click a catalog in the list view, the right, Object, pane, displays the contents of that catalog. You can open other catalogs by double-clicking the catalog in either panel. Several Catalogs are included in the Gallery folder.

Customizing the Component Gallery

You can customize the Component Gallery by changing the default behavior of catalog, folder, and gallery items through the appropriate Properties dialogs.

To create a Component Gallery catalog

1. Select the **Options** button on the Component Gallery toolbar.

2. Click the **Catalogs** tab in the **Component Gallery Options** dialog box.

3. Click **New** and name the new catalog in the **Open** dialog.

4. Click **OK**.

   The **Component Gallery** adds the catalog to the treeview so you can begin using it as you would any existing catalog.

To change a catalog or folder configuration

1. Right-click the catalog or folder.

2. From the shortcut menu, click **Properties**.

3. In the **Catalog Properties** dialog box or **Folder Properties** dialog box, select the tab containing the options you want to configure.

   Gallery catalogs and folders, as displayed in the Component Gallery window **Catalog pane**, can represent URLs, folders, or files on your hard disk. You can view a Gallery folder as Web view or as an Explorer-level view, depending on the way you specify the name in the **General** tab of the **Folder** properties dialog.

Web Views

You can specify URLs or files as Gallery catalogs or as Gallery items. When you configure an item as a Gallery folder, the item automatically opens as a Web view in the **Object** (right) **pane** when you select it in the **Catalog pane**.

To configure a Gallery catalog or folder as a web view

1. In the Folder Properties Dialog_Box, select the **Node** tab.

2. In the **Dynamic folder** field, specify the Web page or file name as in the following examples:

   http:\\www.microsoft.com\

   file:\\c:\my documents\testpage.htm

   file:\\c:\my documents\Wordfile.doc

When you highlight the Eeb view icon in the **Catalog pane**, the toolbar changes to include Web navigation buttons. The Web view will reflect the settings of your Windows Explorer.

Explorer-level Views

You can specify a directory as a Gallery folder or catalog that has characteristics of Windows Explorer.

To configure a Gallery catalog or folder as an Explorer-level view

1. In the Folder Properties Dialog_Box, select the **Node** tab.

2. In the **Dynamic folder** field, specify a folder or file name and backslash (\) as the value as in the following examples:

   C:\My Documents\

   Note   This specification creates a view of actual files, unlike other Component Gallery views. In this view you *can* delete files from your disk.

   To create an Explorer-level view that maintains protection of displayed files, specify the target using a wildcard designation as in the following example:

   C:\My Documents*.*

Avoid using wildcards to create dynamic folders when you can expect to find more than 512 items, unless you have a fast machine with a large amount of RAM.

Component Gallery Object Members

The Component Gallery is comprised of an interface, whose classes are contained in Vfpglry.vcx, and items that reference the following Visual FoxPro Foundation Classes.

Object	Description	Class library
About Dialog	Provides a simple About dialog box for custom applications.	_dialogs.vcx
ActiveX Calendar	A calendar control that can be tied to a date field.	_datetime.vcx
Array Handler	Provides methods for handling array operations not performed by native product array functions.	_utility.vcx
Cancel Button	Releases a form and discards any outstanding buffered data.	_miscbtns.vcx
Clock	A simple clock control for a form or container.	_datetime.vcx
Conflict Catcher	A dialog box for resolution of row conflicts encountered while editing under optimistic buffering.	_dataquery.vcx
Cookies Class	A simple Web class for handling cookies between Web pages.	_internet.vcx

(continued)

(continued)

Object	Description	Class library
Cross Tab	Generates a cross tab.	_utility.vcx
Data Edit Buttons	A complete set of edit buttons (as used by Form Wizards).	Wizbtns.vcx
Data Navigation Buttons	A Top, Next, Prev, Bottom navigation button group and the DataChecker class to check for conflicts when moving records.	_datanav.vcx
Data Navigation Object	A nonvisual navigation object that other classes can use.	_table.vcx
Data Session Manager	Manages data sessions and handles data updates.	_app.vcx
Data Validation	Traps for data conflicts on buffered data.	_datanav.vcx
DBF -> HTML	Converts a Visual FoxPro cursor (.dbf) to HTML.	_internet.vcx
Distinct Values Combo	Performs a lookup of unique values from the controlsource field to populate a combo box.	_dataquery.vcx
Error Object	A generic error handler that works for both object and procedural code.	_app.vcx
Field Mover	A supermover list box that automatically loads fields from current data source.	_movers.vcx
File Registry	Provides a set of registry functions that return application-specific information.	Registry.vcx
File Version	Retrieves information from the version resource of a file.	_utility.vcx
Filter Button	Displays dialog to specify a data filter on a particular field.	_table2.vcx
Filter Dialog	A dialog that enables you to specify filter conditions on data.	_table.vcx
Filter Expression Dialog	Creates an advanced filter expression dialog.	_table.vcx
Find (Findnext) Buttons	A generic find/findnext buttonset.	_table.vcx
Find Button	Locates a record based on specific criteria.	_table.vcx
Find Dialog	A find dialog with simple options such as Field choice.	_table.vcx
Find Files/Text	Uses the Filer.DLL COM object to search for files.	_utility.vcx

(continued)

Object	Description	Class library
Find Object	Creates a generic object that locates a record based on specified criteria.	_table.vcx
Font Combobox	A combo box that lists available fonts. It is also used by tbrEditing and rtfControls classes.	_format.vcx
Fontsize Combobox	A combo box that lists available font sizes. It is also used by tbrEditing and rtfControls classes.	_format.vcx
Format Toolbar	Provides a toolbar for applying font formatting to text of the active control.	_format.vcx
FRX -> HTML	Converts a Visual FoxPro reporting output (.frx) to HTML.	_internet.vcx
GetFile and Directory	Retrieves both a file and a folder name.	_controls.vcx
Goto Dialog Button	Creates a button that displays the Goto dialog box.	_table2.vcx
Goto Dialog	Creates a Goto record dialog box.	_table.vcx
Graph By Record Object	A navigation button group that allows you to refresh a new graph per record on the fly.	_utility.vcx
Graph Object	Generates a Graph using the core Graph Wizard engine.	Autgraph.vcx
Help Button	Displays the Help file as it starts searching for the specified HelpContextID.	_miscbtns.vcx
Hyperlink Button	Launches a Web browser from a button.	_hyperlink.vcx
Hyperlink Image	Launches a Web browser from an image.	_hyperlink.vcx
Hyperlink Label	Launches a Web browser from a label.	_hyperlink.vcx
INI Access	A set of registry functions that access old INI-style file settings.	Registry.vcx
Item Locator	This button brings up a dialog to locate a record.	_dialogs.vcx
Keywords Dialog	Creates a dialog like the Component Gallery keywords dialog.	_dialogs.vcx
Launch Button	Launches an application with an optional document.	_miscbtns.vcx
Locate Button	Displays a dialog to locate a record.	_table2.vcx
Lookup Combobox	Performs a lookup of values in a field to populate a combo box.	_dataquery.vcx

(continued)

(continued)

Object	Description	Class library
Mail Merge Object	Generates a Word Mail Merge using the core Mail Merge Wizard engine.	Mailmerge.vcx
Messagebox Handler	A simple wrapper around the MessageBox function.	_dialogs.vcx
MouseOver Effects	Highlights a control as the mouse passes over it.	_ui.vcx
Mover	Provides a simple mover list box class with move/remove buttons.	_movers.vcx
Navigation Shortcut Menu	A shortcut menu that can be dropped onto a form.	_table2.vcx
Navigation Toolbar	A set of navigation buttons in a toolbar.	_table2.vcx
Object State	Determines the state of an object and saves/restores object property settings.	_app.vcx
ODBC Registry	A set of registry functions that return ODBC-specific information	Registry.vcx
Offline Switch	Provides a view of online data for use offline.	_dataquery.vcx
OK Button	Performs a simple form release.	_miscbtns.vcx
Output Control	Displays a complex dialog box that prompts the user for a reporting output option.	_reports.vcx
Output Dialog	Displays a dialog box that prompts the user for a reporting output option.	_reports.vcx
Output Object	Various reporting output options.	_reports.vcx
Password Dialog	A simple Password dialog for custom applications.	_dialogs.vcx
Pivot Table	Generates a Microsoft Excel Pivot Table using the core PivotTable Wizard engine.	Pivtable.vcx
Preview Report	A generic button to run a report.	_miscbtns.vcx
QBF	Provides a buttonset for Query-By-Form querying.	_dataquery.vcx
Registry Access	Provides access to information in the Windows Registry.	registry.vcx
Resize Object	Causes form objects to resize/move with the Form's resize event.	_controls.vcx
RTF Controls	Provides a set of buttons for applying font formatting to text of the active control.	_format.vcx
Run Form Button	A button that runs a form.	_miscbtns.vcx

(continued)

Object	Description	Class library
SCX -> HTML	Converts an .scx form to an HTML.	_internet.vcx
SendMail Buttons	Uses the MAPI ActiveX Control to send a mail message from a form.	_miscbtns.vcx
Shell Execute	Provides Windows Explorer double-click behavior.	_environ.vcx
Shortcut Menu Class	This wrapper class dynamically creates shortcut pop-up menus.	_menu.vcx
Simple Edit Buttons	Provides simple Add, Edit, Delete, Duplicate, Save, and Cancel buttons (as used by Form Wizards).	Wizbtns.vcx
Simple Navigation Buttons	Provides a set of Next and Previous navigation buttons.	_table.vcx
Simple Picture Navigation Buttons	This is a set of simple picture navigation buttons.	_table2.vcx
Sort Button	Displays a dialog that enables you to perform an ascending or descending data sort on a particular field.	_table2.vcx
Sort Dialog	Enables you to perform an ascending or descending data sort on a particular field.	_table2.vcx
Sort Mover	This subclass of the supermover list box class automatically handles sorting of data.	_movers.vcx
Sort Object	Performs a sort on a data source.	_table.vcx
Sort Selector	Performs an ascending or descending sort based on the current control.	_table2.vcx
Sound Player	This class loads and plays a sound file.	_multimedia.vcx
Splash Screen	Provides a simple Splash Screen for custom applications.	_dialogs.vcx
SQL Pass Through	Provides SQL Pass Thru and can allow you to execute stored procedures on your host database.	_dataquery.vcx
Stop Watch	Provides a stop watch control for a form or container.	_datetime.vcx
String Library	Performs various string conversions.	_utility.vcx
Super Mover	Provides Move, Remove, Moveall, and Removeall buttons.	_movers.vcx

(continued)

(continued)

Object	Description	Class library
System Toolbars	A manager class that handles and tracks Systoolbars.	_app.vcx
Table Mover	This subclass of the supermover list box class automatically loads tables and fields from the current data source.	_movers.vcx
Text Preview	Provides a viewer of output text.	_reports.vcx
Thermometer	Provides a standard thermometer class.	_controls.vcx
Trace Aware Timer	This is an application utility that determines whether the trace window is open.	_app.vcx
Type Library	The main routine ExportTypeLib creates a text file with Typelib output.	_utility.vcx
URL Combo	Creates a combo box for typing in a Web URL. It launches Microsoft Internet Explorer and navigates to the site.	_internet.vcx
URL Open Dialog	Provides a dialog that creates a drop-down list that stores URL history.	_internet.vcx
VCR Buttons	A Top, Next, Prev, and Bottom navigation button group.	_table.vcx
VCR Picture Navigation Buttons	A set of VCR picture navigation buttons.	_table2.vcx
Video Player	Loads and plays a video file using MCI commands.	_multimedia.vcx
Web Browser control	A subclass of the Internet Explorer 4.0 Browser control, which provides hooks for Visual FoxPro code.	_webview.vcx
Window Handler	Performs several common window operations typical of applications.	_ui.vcx

For full details on these class libraries, see the "Visual FoxPro Foundation Classes" topic in Help. You can get information on how to use the foundation classes in "Guidelines for Using Visual FoxPro Foundation Classes" in Help.

Component Gallery Class Library (Vpfgallery.vcx)

The Component Gallery class library, Vpfgallery.vcx, provides the item types as classes.

Item type	Description
Class (_ClassItem)	The generic item type for any Visual FoxPro class. This can be either from .vcx or .prg files.
File (_FileItem)	This is any file. Visual FoxPro reads the Registry for shell functions and adds them to the menu. The gallery includes a look up routine that checks for specific extensions and redirects the item type.
	The gallery supports UNC naming conventions for team development (sharing of Catalogs across networks).
ActiveX (_ActiveXItem)	This is an ActiveX Control or Server such as an .ocx created by Visual Basic CCE or .exe/.dll created by Visual FoxPro.
Data (_DataItem)	This is a Visual FoxPro datasource (.dbc, .dbf, View, etc.).
Image (_ImageItem)	This is a File Item Type whose file has an image file extension such as .bmp, .jpg, .gif, .ico, .cur, .ani, and so on.
Sound (_SoundItem)	This is a File Item Type whose file has either a .wav or .rmi extension.
Video(_VideoItem)	This is a File Item Type whose file has a .avi extension.
URL (_UrlItem)	This is a Web Item Type and includes Web and local documents such as HTML files or Visual FoxPro Active Documents.
Sample (_SampleItem)	This is a File Item Type for files that run in Visual FoxPro and can be an executable Visual FoxPro file such as .app, .exe, .prg, .scx, or .frx files.
Template (_TemplateItem)	This is a Script Item Type that opens a builder for the Visual FoxPro element represented by the type of the highlighted item, including forms and reports.
Catalog (_CatalogItem)	This is a Component Gallery type that allows you to Add and Open Visual FoxPro catalogs.
Form(_FormItem)	This is a type for Visual FoxPro forms (.scx).
Report (_ReportItem)	This is a type for Visual FoxPro reports (.frx).
Menu (_MenuItem)	This is a type for Visual FoxPro menus (.mnx).
Program (_ProgramItem)	This is a type for Visual FoxPro programs (.prg).
Project (_ProjectItem)	This is a type for Visual FoxPro projects (.pjx).

You can use the Class Browser to examine the details of any of these classes.

For details on other classes used in the Component Gallery, see the "Visual FoxPro Foundation Classes" topic in Help or use the Class Browser to examine the libraries in the Ffc folder.

Component Gallery Table Structure

The Visual FoxPro Component Gallery is described in the following table structure.

Field	Field Name	Type	Width	Index
1	TYPE	Character	12	No
2	ID	Character	12	No
3	PARENT	Memo	4	No
4	LINK	Memo	4	No
5	TEXT	Memo	4	No
6	TYPEDESC	Memo	4	No
7	DESC	Memo	4	No
8	PROPERTIES	Memo	4	No
9	FILENAME	Memo	4	No
10	CLASS	Memo	4	No
11	PICTURE	Memo	4	No
12	FOLDERPICT	Memo	4	No
13	SCRIPT	Memo	4	No
14	CLASSLIB	Memo	4	No
15	CLASSNAME	Memo	4	No
16	ITEMCLASS	Memo	4	No
17	ITEMTPDESC	Memo	4	No
18	VIEWS	Memo	4	No
19	KEYWORDS	Memo	4	No
20	SRCALIAS	Memo	4	No
21	SRCRECNO	Numeric	6	No
22	UPDATED	DateTime	8	No
23	COMMENT	Memo	4	No
24	USER	Memo	4	No

Coverage Profiler Application

A coverage application writes information about which lines of code in a file were run. A profiler application provides information about which lines actually run, how many times a line is run, duration, and more. Coverage and profiling enable a developer to identify problem areas in an application, especially skipped code and performance bottlenecks.

Visual FoxPro Coverage Profiler is provided in two parts — a Coverage engine you can use or customize, and a multiwindow application you can use to analyze programs and projects.

The Coverage Profiler application provides several ways to view the data provided by the Coverage Engine. Coverage.app is a subclass of the Coverage engine. You can automate coverage, or modify the User Interface to suit your needs, run Coverage Profiler in unattended mode and not display the application window, or use engine features without using the interface.

Upon startup the coverage application suspends coverage logging enabled with a SET COVERAGE TO command. When you release the coverage object, the application provides a choice to restore the SET COVERAGE setting.

Coverage Profiler Log File

Coverage Profiler uses a log file generated by Visual FoxPro when you use the Coverage option in the Debugger Tools menu or use SET COVERAGE TO as in the following command:

```
SET COVERAGE TO cCoverage.log
```

When you use the command, the ADDITIVE clause allows you to avoid overwriting an existing log. This command starts data streaming and opens the file *cCoverage*.log, a text file that will gather the stream of details on the file or application you examine.

A coverage log file consists of records in comma-delimited lines. The following list describes the structure of each record.

Item	Description
1	execution time
2	class executing the code
3	object, method, or procedure in which the code is found or called
4	line number within the method or procedure
5	fully defined file
6	call stack level (Visual FoxPro 6.0 only)

After specifying the log file name, run the program or application you want to examine. When you end the program you can use the SET COVERAGE TO command to stop the data stream to the coverage log.

You can view the coverage log by starting Coverage Profiler from the Tools menu or by using DO as in the following command:

```
DO (_COVERAGE) [WITH cCoverage]
```

Visual FoxPro prompts you for the name if you do not specify a log file. The _COVERAGE System variable in Visual FoxPro 6.0 defaults to the Coverage Profiler application, Coverage.app.

Examining Application Coverage and Profile

To use the Coverage Profiler effectively, prepare your application and your environment carefully. If you use the following guidelines, the Coverage Profiler can provide accurate and useful information about your project or application.

To use the Coverage Profiler to examine application coverage

1. Use the **Coverage Logging** option of the Debugger **Tools** menu or the SET COVERAGE command to start the coverage data stream and to open the file to log that data.

2. Run the program or application you want to examine for coverage.

3. Run the coverage application from the **Tools** menu or use DO (_COVERAGE) in the command window.

   The Coverage Profiler application starts in **Coverage Mode** by default.

To use Coverage Profiler to examine application profile

1. Use the SET COVERAGE command to start the coverage data stream and to open the file to log that data.

2. Run the program or application you want to profile.

3. Run the coverage application from the **Tools** menu or use DO (_COVERAGE) in the command window.

4. Click the **Profile Mode** button in the **Coverage Profiler** dialog box.

   If you find that you are most often interested in profiling, you can change the default to Profile Mode in the Coverage Profiler Options dialog box.

To use the Coverage Profiler with a specific log file

- Run the coverage application using the WITH option and the log file name as in the following example:

```
DO (_COVERAGE) WITH "Mylog.LOG"
```

This example uses the log file Mylog.log and opens the Coverage Profiler application window to display the results. If you specify no file name, the Coverage Profiler uses the log specified in a current SET COVERAGE TO command or displays the Open file dialog box when coverage logging is OFF.

To use the Coverage Profiler without the User Interface

- Run the coverage application using the WITH option and specify true (.T.) for unattended mode running as in the following example:

```
DO (_COVERAGE) WITH "Mylog.LOG",.T.
```

In this example, the Coverage Profiler application uses the log file Mylog.log and runs without displaying the Coverage Profiler application window.

To use the Coverage Profiler with a specific Add-In file

- Run the coverage application using the WITH option and the add-in file name as in the following example:

```
DO (_COVERAGE) WITH "Mylog.LOG",, "add_ui.prg"
```

This example uses the log file Mylog.log and opens the Coverage Profiler application window to display the results, and then the Add-In program ADD_UI.PRG runs. The second, unspecified, parameter is a logical value that specifies whether the coverage engine operates in unattended mode. In the default setting, false (.F.), the Coverage Profiler window displays.

Besides viewing the profiler information, you can insert comments or markers and you can save the information as a file to use later.

Modifying the Coverage Profiler

By default the Coverage Profiler application runs in a separate window. You can reconfigure it to run inside the main Visual FoxPro window by changing the Environment Option. In the Coverage Profiler Options dialog box, change the **Environment** selection from **Coverage frame** to **FoxPro frame**, and then restart the Coverage Profiler.

You can also use the **Coverage Profiler Options** dialog box to modify the following Coverage Profiler characteristics.

Characteristic	Description
Add-Ins	Specifies whether Add-Ins are registered in the Coverage Profiler as they are used. For more information, see "Coverage Profiler Add-Ins," later in this section.
Coverage Marks	Specifies whether the Coverage Profiler marks code that is run or code that is not run. Specifies the character(s) used to mark code. Specifies when code is marked.
Fonts	Specifies the fonts used in the Coverage Profiler as code and in displays.
Smart Pathing	Specifies whether Coverage Profiler automatically seeks files in previously specified locations.
Start Mode	Specifies whether Coverage Profiler opens in Coverage or Profile Mode.

Ensuring Relevance in the Coverage Profiler

To help ensure that the files processed by the Coverage Profiler are the correct files:

- Set your project directory as the default before you start coverage logging so that the referenced files are relative.

- Avoid renaming objects dynamically. The Coverage Profiler will not find objects if you rename them at run time.

- Avoid using source files with exactly the same root name, even with different extensions. Internally, the Coverage Profiler cannot distinguish between them.

- Make sure that your project contains only the correct versions of much-modified files.

- Make sure your project does not contain multiple copies of a file in subdirectories.

- Perform a compile for the coverage run:

  - Make sure Debug information is in your application.

  - Turn Encrypt OFF.

  - Use RECOMPILE or Build All to force a fresh compile of all source code.

  - Perform the compile immediately before the coverage run so that you know that the source code exactly matches the object code.

Some lines in code, such as comments, DEFINE CLASS and ELSE statements, and lines within TEXT … ENDTEXT do not appear in coverage logs because they are not even potentially executable. Also, lines broken by continuation symbols (semicolons) are considered as a single line of code and marked only on the last line.

Coverage Profiler Add-Ins

Add-Ins are code files (usually .prg or .scx) that provide an easy way for you to adjust the Coverage Profiler. The cov_standard subclass of the coverage engine which comprises the User Interface of Coverage.app shows only a small part of what you can do with the engine. The engine analyzes the coverage log; cov_standard just displays the results in one of many ways you could want to see them.

You could create a different subclass of cov_engine with a very different display. For example, your subclass might display a dialog that runs queries against the coverage statistics gathered by the engine. The display options might provide a view of the marked code for a filtered set of log entries, or only a graph of the profiling results.

You may not want to subclass cov_engine to create a new interface from scratch because the cov_engine class provides an easier process. You can add functionality to cov_standard, or any cov_engine subclass, using Add-Ins. Cov_standard exposes this feature through a button in the main dialog of Coverage Profiler. When you run an Add-In on an instance of cov_standard such as Coverage Profiler, the Add-In can manipulate the capabilities of cov_engine, the coverage tables, as well as cov_standard. Add-Ins might also add new dialogs and features to the cov_standard visual interface.

Writing Add-Ins

You can write Add-Ins to enhance the standard interface or you can subclass cov_standard to create your own wholly new interface.

Enhancing the Standard Application

The following list includes features you might want to provide through Add-Ins:

- Add a visible feature to the main dialog.

- Add a dialog into the coverage engine formset (reference limitation below on how to make sure your dialog shows up in the right place).

- Display a separate dialog that accesses a Coverage engine feature (reference limitation below on how to make sure your dialog shows up in the right place).

- Provide a querying interface that uses the Source table and presents a list of all lines that meet your criteria, and filters or orders the results.

   Note   You can use the Adjust... methods (AdjustCoverageFilenameCursor( ), AdjustSourceCursor( ), and AdjustTargetCursor( )) of the Engine to add fields to the Source and Target tables when the engine creates them, and use these fields in your Add-Ins.

- Add file names to the IgnoredFiles cursor, to eliminate those files from analysis. This can save analysis time.

- Use the special Init hook for Add-Ins.

- Register Add-Ins for retrieval and easy access to a list of Add-Ins.

  The modal dialog class cov_AddInDialog in the standard coverage engine subclass, presents previously registered dialogs in a drop-down list. When you set the coverage engine lRegisterAdd-In option ON, the full path name of successfully run Add-Ins are added to the Windows Registry so you can easily run these Add-Ins again. The Standard UI class also allows you to set this property in the Coverage Profiler Options dialog box.

  The Coverage Engine object maintains a list of all registered Add-Ins in the aAddIns property.

- Use the final coverage.log field information, callstack, to design your own interface or your own view of the coverage log.

When you write Add-Ins, consider the following information:

- You can use any of the supported file types as Add-Ins. The supported file types are .qpr, .qpx, .mpr, .mpx, .app, .exe, .scx, and procedures (if the procedures are already available in an open procedure library).

- The Coverage Engine formset has an "invisible" toolbar. If your Add-In is nonvisual you can use this toolbar to contain it. If your Add-In is a visual control, the standard subclass main dialog .Cov_tools member container is probably the most convenient place to put it. This allows the position and size to be automatically synchronized with the rest of the dialog when it is resized.

- All the engine methods that use the Source and Target tables take optional arguments that will allow you to point these methods at the appropriate aliases while you're working with them. You can also change the current cSourceAlias and cTargetAlias property contents to match the pair of cursors in which you are interested. This allows you to compare multiple Coverage log runs to each other within the same interface.

- Limitations:

  - Add-Ins must accept one parameter (the Coverage engine passes a reference to itself).

  - An Add-In must be one of the permitted file types, listed above.

  - Procedures you use as Add-Ins should be available in a currently loaded procedure library (see SET PROCEDURE) in Help. The Engine does not use the IN *FileName* syntax, and it does not call procedures or .prg files as functions and RETURN their values. It does not use the NAME or LINK keywords on the DO FORM command; you can either manage the reference yourself, or allow the Engine to scope a form for you by making your form a member of the Engine formset.

  - If you run an Add-In at startup, you must use a reference because the public _oCoverage variable is not yet available. At other times, you can use the public variable reference within your own code, if you prefer.

- When you write an Add-In as a form, if you create the form as ShowWindow = 1 and run Coverage in its own frame, your Add-In forms should display in the Coverage frame.

- If you use .RunAddIn from the Command window, make sure the coverage frame is the active MDI frame before you instantiate your forms.

Subclass Cov_Standard Class

You can subclass either the coverage engine or its standard subclass. The following list describes the structure of the COVERAGE project source file set.

File	Description
Coverage.prg	A "wrapper" for the coverage object, which instantiates the object.
Coverage.vcx Coverage.vct	All classes for the engine and its standard subclass.
Cov_short.mnx Cov_short.mnt	Shortcut menu.
Cov_pjx.frx Cov_pjx.frt	Default mechanism to deliver project-level results.

Coverage.h	Header file for all Coverage code, incorporating the following elements:
	
	*— Coverage character constants for log and parsing:
	   #INCLUDE COV_CHAR.H
	
	*— Coverage localized strings (can use some log and parsing constants):
	   #INCLUDE COV_LOCS.H
	
	*— Coverage common dialog component constants:
	   #INCLUDE COV_DLGS.H
	
	*— Coverage specs & requirements:
	   #INCLUDE COV_SPEC.H
	
	*— Coverage registry object constants:
	   #INCLUDE COV_REGS.H
	
	*— Coverage tune-able options:
	   #INCLUDE COV_TUNE.H

The COVERAGE project source file set also includes various .ico .bmp, and .msk files.

Use the file COV_TUNE.H (containing appropriate comments and explanations) to become familiar with options available to you without rewriting code.

Since Add-In use is governed by the coverage engine superclass, any other coverage subclass you create can use Add-Ins in the same manner as the standard subclass.

The coverage engine subclass instantiated by the default Coverage.app does not augment the coverage engine RunAddIn( ) method in any way. It does, however, invoke a modal dialog box to allow the user to pick an Add-In before it invokes the coverage engine RunAddIn( ) method. The modal dialog box receives a reference to the Coverage object and sets the coverage engine cAddIn property.

If you write your own coverage engine subclass, ensure that your subclass can use the same modal dialog class (cov_AddInDialog) to handle Add-Ins as the standard Coverage application; the dialog box does not rely on any features of the standard subclass.

You can call a different modal dialog box, set the cAddIn file name directly in the cAddIn property, or override the contents of the cAddIn property by passing the name of the Add-In file you wish to run to the RunAddIn( ) method.

However you access an Add-In to run in your subclass, you can investigate the list of Add-Ins registered to Coverage.app by checking the file names in the coverage engine aAddIns property.

For details on the Properties, Events, and Methods of the coverage engine, see "Coverage Engine Object" in Help.

Project Manager Hooks

In previous versions of Visual FoxPro, the only access to a project was through direct table manipulation of the project's .pjx file. In Visual FoxPro 6.0, you can access a project programmatically, allowing you to manipulate a project as an object. A project can be manipulated at design time while the project is open in the Project Manager, or at design time and run time without the Project Manager visible.

The following are some of the actions you can perform programmatically on a project:

- Add or delete files from a project.

- Add files in the project to source code control applications (such as Microsoft Visual SourceSafe) and check files in and out of source code control.

- Determine the number of files in a project and their types.

- Open and modify files in the project.

- Change properties of the project.

- Change properties of files in the project.

- Change properties of Automation servers (.dll dynamic-link libraries or .exe executable files) built from the project.

- Execute code when events occur in the project.

- Rebuild the project, or build .app, .exe, or .dll files from the project.

With the new project manager hooks, advanced developers can create their own project managers with unique customized user interfaces.

The Project Object Hierarchy

The object hierarchy for a project consists of the project, a project object, and its associated ProjectHook object. A project object contains a files collection, consisting of files in the project, and a servers collection, consisting of Automation servers created from the project. The following diagrams illustrates the project object hierarchy within the Visual FoxPro object model:

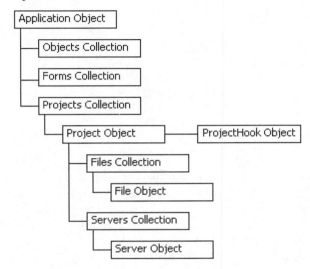

Projects Collection

The projects collection gives direct access to a project object, allowing you to manipulate the project and the files and servers the project contains. A project object is added to the projects collection whenever a project is created, opened or an .app, .dll, or .exe is built from the project.

Like other OLE collections, you can obtain information about a project from the projects collection. For example, the following code uses the projects collection Count and Item properties to display the names of all the projects in the projects collection, and then uses the FOR EACH command to display the same information:

```
nProjectCount = Application.Projects.Count

FOR nCount = 1 TO nProjectCount
    ? Application.Projects.Item(nCount).Name
NEXT

FOR EACH oProj IN Application.Projects
    ? oProj.Name
ENDFOR
```

This line of code uses the ActiveProject property to add a program, Main.prg, to the currently active project:

```
Application.ActiveProject.Files.Add('Main.prg')
```

This line of code adds Main.prg to the first project added to the projects collection:

```
Application.Projects[1].Files.Add('Main.prg')
```

A projects collection has the following property and method:

Property

Count

Method

Item

The Project Object

The project object is instantiated whenever a project is opened from the File menu or with the CREATE PROJECT, MODIFY PROJECT, BUILD APP, BUILD DLL, BUILD EXE, or BUILD PROJECT commands. The project object allows you to programmatically manipulate the project, and can be accessed through the Visual FoxPro Application object. Note that the Application object supports a new ActiveProject property that provides a project object reference to the project open in the currently active Project Manager.

A project object has the following properties and methods:

Properties

Application	AutoIncrement
BaseClass	BuildDateTime
Debug	Encrypted
HomeDir	Icon
MainClass	MainFile
Name	Parent
ProjectHook	ProjectHookClass
ProjectHookLibrary	SCCProvider
ServerHelpFile	ServerProject
TypeLibCLSID	TypeLibDesc

TypeLibName	VersionComments
VersionCompany	VersionCopyright
VersionDescription	VersionLanguage
VersionNumber	VersionProduct
VersionTrademarks	Visible

Methods

Build	CleanUp
Refresh	SetMain

The ProjectHook Object

A ProjectHook object is a Visual FoxPro base class that is instantiated by default whenever a project assigned to the ProjectHook object is opened. (You can include the NOPROJECTHOOK clause in CREATE PROJECT and MODIFY PROJECT to prevent a ProjectHook object from being instantiated for the project.)

The ProjectHook object allows programmatic access to events that occur in a project. For example, you can execute code whenever a file is added to a project.

You can specify a default ProjectHook class for new projects in the Projects tab of the Options dialog box. If a default ProjectHook class isn't specified in the Projects tab, new projects aren't assigned a ProjectHook class. You can specify a project hook class for an individual project (overriding the default ProjectHook class) in the Project Information dialog box. At runtime, you can use the ProjectHook property to specify a project hook class for a project. If you change the ProjectHook class for a project, the new ProjectHook class doesn't take effect until the project is closed and opened again.

A ProjectHook object has the following properties, events, and methods:

Properties

BaseClass	Class
ClassLibrary	Comment
Name	OLEDropEffects
OLEDropHasData	OLEDropMode
Parent	ParentClass
Tag	

Events

AfterBuild	BeforeBuild
Destroy	Error
Init	OLEDragDrop
OLEDragOver	OLEGiveFeedBack
QueryAddFile	QueryModifyFile
QueryRemoveFile	QueryRunFile

Methods

AddProperty	ReadExpression
ReadMethod	ResetToDefault
SaveAsClass	WriteExpression

Project Object and the ProjectHook Object Interaction

When you open the Project Manager from the File menu, or with the CREATE PROJECT or MODIFY PROJECT commands, the Project Manager window appears and a project object is instantiated with its associated ProjectHook object. Project build commands (BUILD PROJECT, BUILD APP, BUILD DLL, and BUILD EXE) also instantiate the project and ProjectHook objects.

When an event occurs in a project, the project object passes the event to the ProjectHook object. User code in the event in the ProjectHook object is executed and control is passed back to the Project object. The value returned to the project object from the ProjectHook object determines if the project object finishes the operation. Placing NODEFAULT in the event code prevents the default action from being performed. For example, placing NODEFAULT in the QueryAddFile event prevents a file from successfully being added to a project.

Files Collection

The files collection gives direct access to a file object, allowing you to manipulate file objects in a project while the project is open. Like other OLE collections, you can obtain information about a file in a project from the files collection. For example, the following code uses the files collection Count and Item properties to display the names of all the files in the files collection, and then uses the FOR EACH command to display the same information:

```
nFileCount = Application.ActiveProject.Files.Count

FOR nCount = 1 TO nFileCount
    ? Application.ActiveProject.Files.Item(nCount).Name
NEXT
```

```
FOR EACH oProj IN Application.ActiveProject.Files
    ? oProj.Name
ENDFOR
```

This line of code uses the ActiveProject property to add a file, Main.prg, to the currently active project:

```
Application.ActiveProject.Files.Add('Main.prg')
```

This line of code adds Main.prg to the first project added to the projects collection:

```
Application.Projects[1].Files.Add('Main.prg')
```

The files collection has the following property and methods:

Property

Count

Methods

Add	Item

File Object

The file object allows you to manipulate individual files in a project.

A file object has the following properties and methods:

Properties

CodePage	Description
Exclude	FileClass
FileClassLibrary	LastModified
Name	ReadOnly
SCCStatus	Type

Methods

AddToSCC	CheckIn
CheckOut	GetLatestVersion
Modify	Remove
RemoveFromSCC	Run
UndoCheckOut	

Servers Collection

The servers collection gives direct access to a server object, allowing you to manipulate the servers that a project contains. A server object is added to the servers collection whenever a .dll dynamic-link library or .exe executable file containing an Automation server is built from the project. For more information about creating Automation servers, see "Creating Automation Servers" in Chapter 16, "Adding OLE."

A servers collection has the following property and method:

Property

Count

Method

Item

Server Object

The server object lets you determine information (including type library information) about Automation servers contained in a project. This information is also available in the Servers tab of the Project Information dialog box. Note that a server object isn't created until the project containing the OLEPUBLIC class (specified in the DEFINE CLASS command) is built.

A server object has the following properties:

Properties

CLSID	Description
HelpContextID	Instancing
ProgID	ServerClass
ServerClassLibrary	

Project Object Architecture

A Visual FoxPro project object exposes an IDispatch interface so that Automation clients, ActiveX controls, and other COM objects can access the project object through standard OLE interfaces. Because a project object now exposes an IDispatch interface, the errors that can be generated when manipulating projects are OLE errors.

Language Enhancements

Two new clauses have been added to the CREATE PROJECT and MODIFY PROJECT commands. The first clause, NOPROJECTHOOK, prevents the ProjectHook object from being instantiated for a project. The second clause, NOSHOW, opens a project without displaying it in the Project Manager, allowing you to programmatically manipulate the project without displaying it. You can use the Visible property to later display the Project Manager. For more information about these new clauses, see CREATE PROJECT and MODIFY PROJECT.

Project Events

The following sections describe events and the order in which they occur when projects are created, modified, closed, built, and so on.

Creating a New Project

The following events occur when you execute CREATE PROJECT, create a new project from the **File** menu, or click the **New** toolbar button and specify to create a new project:

1. The project object is created.

2. The ProjectHook object is instantiated.

3. The Init event for the ProjectHook object occurs. If the Init event returns true (.T.), the default, the project is created and the project is displayed in the Project Manager.

    If the Init event returns false (.F.), the project isn't created, the project and ProjectHook objects are released, and the Project Manager isn't displayed.

Modifying an Existing Project

The following events occur when you execute MODIFY PROJECT, modify an existing project from the **File** menu, or click the **Open** toolbar button and specify an existing or new project:

1. The project object is created. The project object obtains its values from the project's .pjx file.

2. The ProjectHook object is instantiated.

3. The Init event for the ProjectHook object occurs. If the Init event returns true (.T.) (the default), the project is opened for modification in the Project Manager.

    If the Init event returns false (.F.), the project isn't opened for modification, the project and ProjectHook objects are released, and the Project Manager isn't displayed.

Closing a Project

The following events occur when an open project is closed:

1. The ProjectHook Destroy event occurs and the ProjectHook object is released.

2. The Project object is released.

Issuing BUILD APP, BUILD DLL, or BUILD EXE

The following events occur when BUILD APP, BUILD DLL, or BUILD EXE is issued:

1. The project object is created. The project object obtains its values from the project's .pjx file.

2. The ProjectHook object is instantiated.

3. The Init event for the ProjectHook object occurs. If the Init event returns true (.T.), the default, the ProjectHook BeforeBuild event occurs. If NODEFAULT is included in the BeforeBuild event, the .app, .dll, or .exe isn't built. Otherwise, the build process continues.

   If any files are added to the project during the build process, the ProjectHook QueryAddFile event occurs before each file is added. If NODEFAULT is included in the QueryAddFile event, a file isn't added to the project. Otherwise, the file is added to the project. When the .app, .dll, or .exe is successfully built, the ProjectHook AfterBuild event occurs, and then the ProjectHook Destroy event occurs.

   If the Init event returns false (.F.), the app, .dll, or .exe isn't built, and the project and ProjectHook objects are released.

Issuing BUILD PROJECT

The following events occur when BUILD PROJECT with the FROM clause is issued. If the FROM clause is omitted, the events occur in the order described above when BUILD APP, BUILD DLL, or BUILD EXE is issued.

1. The project object is created. The project object obtains its values from the project's .pjx file.

2. The ProjectHook object is instantiated.

3. The Init event for the ProjectHook object occurs. If the Init event returns true (.T.), the default, the files specified in the FROM clause are added individually to the project. The ProjectHook QueryAddFile event occurs before each file is added to the project. If NODEFAULT is included in the QueryAddFile event, the file isn't added to the project. Otherwise, the file is added to the project.

   The ProjectHook BeforeBuild event then occurs. If NODEFAULT is included in the BeforeBuild event, the project isn't built. Otherwise, the project is built. When the project build is complete, the ProjectHook AfterBuild event occurs, and then the ProjectHook Destroy event occurs.

   If the ProjectHook Init event returns false (.F.), the project isn't built. The project and ProjectHook objects are released and a new .pjx file isn't created.

Using a Drag-and-Drop Operation

The following events occur when you drag a file or a set of files over the outline section (treeview) of the Project Manager:

1. When the mouse pointer is positioned over the outline section of the Project Manager, the ProjectHook OLEDragOver event occurs with the *nState* parameter set to 0 (DRAG_ENTER in Foxpro.h). The OLEDragOver event then occurs repeatedly with the *nState* parameter set to 2 (DRAG_OVER in Foxpro.h). If the mouse pointer moves outside of the outline section of the Project Manager, the OLEDragOver event occurs with the *nState* parameter set to 1 (DRAG_LEAVE in Foxpro.h).

2. The ProjectHook OLEDragDrop event occurs if you release the mouse button while the mouse pointer is positioned over the outline section of the Project Manager. By default, Visual FoxPro adds each file dropped on the Project Manager to the project. The ProjectHook QueryAddFile event occurs before each file is added to the project.

Adding a File with the Add Button

The following events occur when you add a file to a project by clicking the **Add** button in the Project Manager:

1. The **Open** dialog box appears.

2. If you select a file and choose **OK**, a file object is created for the file you select.

3. The ProjectHook QueryAddFile event occurs and the name of the file object is passed to the event. If NODEFAULT is included in the QueryAddFile event, the file isn't added to the project. Otherwise, the file is added to the project.

Adding a File with the New Button

The following events occur when you add a new file to a project by clicking the **New** button in the Project Manager:

1. The appropriate designer or editor for the file is displayed.

2. When the new file is saved, the **Save As** dialog box is displayed. Clicking **Save** creates a file object for the new file.

3. The ProjectHook QueryAddFile event occurs and the name of the file object is passed to the event. If NODEFAULT is included in the QueryAddFile event, the file isn't added to the project. Otherwise, the file is added to the project.

Modifying a File with the Modify Button

The following events occur when you modify a file in a project by clicking the **Modify** button in the Project Manager:

1. The ProjectHook QueryModifyFile event occurs before the appropriate designer or editor for the file is displayed.

2. The file object for the file to modify is passed as a parameter to the QueryModifyFile event. If NODEFAULT is included in the QueryModifyFile event, the appropriate designer or editor for the file isn't displayed and the file isn't modified. Otherwise, the file is opened in the appropriate designer or editor for modification.

Removing a File with the Remove Button

The following events occur when you remove a file in a project by clicking the **Remove** button in the Project Manager:

1. The ProjectHook QueryRemoveFile event occurs.

2. The file object for the file to be removed is passed as a parameter to the QueryRemoveFile event. If NODEFAULT is included in the QueryRemoveFile event, the file isn't removed from the project. Otherwise, the file is removed from the project.

Executing a File with the Run Button

The following events occur when you execute a file in a project by clicking the **Run** button in the Project Manager:

1. The ProjectHook QueryRunFile event occurs.

2. The file object for the file to be executed is passed as a parameter to the QueryRunFile event. If NODEFAULT is included in the QueryRunFile event, the file isn't executed. Otherwise, the file is executed.

Rebuilding a Project or Building a File with the Build Button

The following events occur when you rebuild the project or build an .app, .dll, or .exe from a project by clicking the **Build** button in the Project Manager:

1. The **Build Options** dialog box is displayed.

2. You can choose **Rebuild Project**, **Build Application**, **Build Executable**, or **Build COM DLL**, and specify additional build options. If you click **Cancel**, the build doesn't occur.

3. The ProjectHook BeforeBuild event occurs if you click **OK**, and the build process begins.

4. When the build is completed, the ProjectHook AfterBuild event occurs.

Project Manager Hooks Sample

The Visual FoxPro Solutions Sample application includes a sample named "Track activities in a project" that demonstrates many of the new Project Manager hooks.

To run the Solutions Sample application

- Enter the following in the Command window:

```
DO (HOME(2) + 'solution\solution')
```

– or–

1. From the **Program** menu, choose **Do**.

2. Choose the …**Samples\Vfp98\Solution** folder.

3. Double-click **Solution.app**.

To run the "Track activities in a project" sample

1. After starting Solution.app, double-click **New Features for Visual FoxPro 6.0**.

2. Click **Track activities in a project** and then click the **Run Sample** button.

The "Track activities in a project" sample allows you to open a project and then manipulate the project in any manner. Any changes you make to the project are stored in a table. When you close the project, you can view the changes you made to the project in a Browse window.

For more information about how the "Track activities in a project" sample works and to take a closer look at the code behind the sample, you can open the form used to create the sample.

To open the "Track activities in a project" form

1. After starting Solution.app, double-click **New Features for Visual FoxPro 6.0**.

2. Click **Track activities in a project** and then click the **See Code** button.

Acttrack.scx, the form used to create the "Track activities in a project" sample, is opened in the Form designer.

You may also want to take a closer look at the ProjectHook class library, Project_hook.vcx, that is assigned to the project you open in the "Track activities in a project" sample. Most of the code that is executed when project events occur is in the event procedures in this class library. Project_hook.vcx is located in the …\Samples\Vfp98\Solution\Tahoe directory.

New and Enhanced Wizards and Builders

The following wizards and builders are either new or enhanced.

Application Wizard   *New*

The Application Wizard for Visual FoxPro 6.0 provides support for the enhanced Application Framework and the new Application Builder. You can run the Application Wizard from the Component Gallery or from the Visual FoxPro **Tools** menu by clicking **Wizards** and then **Application**.

> **Note**   The Application Wizard (5.0) from Visual FoxPro 5.0 is available from the Wizard Selection dialog box for backward compatibility.

Connection Wizards   *New*

The Connection Wizards include the **Code Generation Wizard** and the **Reverse Engineering Wizard**. These wizards let you easily manage transfers between Visual FoxPro class libraries and Microsoft Visual Modeler models.

Database Wizard   *New*

The Visual FoxPro Database Wizard uses templates to create a database and tables. You can also use the wizard to create indexes and relationships between the tables in a new database.

Documenting Wizard   *Enhanced*

The Visual FoxPro Documenting Wizard now provides an option to use the Code Analyzer as documentation is created.

Form Wizard   *Enhanced*

The updated Visual FoxPro Form Wizard provides input mask, format, and a field mapping class for specific fields as stored in a database. This wizard also includes more form style options, including scrolling forms.

Graph Wizard   *Enhanced*

The Visual FoxPro Graph Wizard creates a graph from a Visual FoxPro table using Microsoft Graph. This updated wizard supports the Graph 8.0 component of Microsoft Office 97, including automation of the datasheet and the Series by Row/Col option.

Import Wizard   *Enhanced*

The updated Visual FoxPro Import Wizard supports Office 97 and Microsoft Excel multisheet handling and provides the option to import a table to a database.

Label Wizard   *Enhanced*

The Visual FoxPro Label Wizard now includes greater control of label fonts and direct access to the Add Label wizard.

Mail Merge Wizard   *Enhanced*

The Visual FoxPro Mail Merge Wizard creates either a data source for a Microsoft Word merged document or a text file that can be used by any word processor. This updated wizard supports the Microsoft Word 8.0 component of Office 97 and true VBA Automation with Application object and collection support.

Pivot Table Wizard   *Enhanced*

The Visual FoxPro PivotTable Wizard helps you create interactive worksheet tables that summarize and analyze data between two or more fields in a table. This updated wizard supports the Microsoft Excel 8.0 component of Office 97. You can choose either to save a pivot table directly in Excel or to add one as an object on a form.

Report Wizard   *Enhanced*

The Visual FoxPro Report Wizard now includes advanced grouping and summary functionality so you can more easily customize your reports inside this single wizard. There are also more report styles to choose from.

Remote View Wizard   *Enhanced*

The Visual FoxPro View Wizard now provides access to System tables so you can use the functionality of ODBC drivers that support these.

Sample Wizard   *New*

The Visual FoxPro Sample Wizard provides simple steps to creating your own wizard. The output is an HTML file created from records in the data source you specify.

Setup Wizard   *Enhanced*

The Visual FoxPro Setup Wizard now provides enhanced support for ActiveX controls and override of the Windows file number limit for use in NT setups. It also enables you to add external .DLLs to your application through the setup and to create Web-based installs.

Table Wizard   *Enhanced*

The Visual FoxPro Table Wizard now provides new table templates, optional style settings, support for both Character and Memo binary data types, and access to databases. You can add your table to a database and you can use database settings to determine the formats of fields you add to your table. You can also establish relationships between tables in the database.

Web Publishing Wizard   *New*

The Visual FoxPro Web Publishing Wizard generates an HTML file created from records in the data source you specify.

Enhanced Application Framework

The Visual FoxPro 6.0 Application Framework is designed to make it easier to develop Visual FoxPro applications. You can access the enhanced Application Framework through the Application Wizard or through the **New Application** item of the Component Gallery. This enhanced framework supports the framework available in Visual FoxPro 5.0 including the following:

- A project (.pjx) file.

- A main program file (Main.prg) for global and environmental settings, launching any Splash Screen or other specific calls, and launching any Quick Start form.

- A main menu.

- The Application object for running the main menu, forms toolbars and report management, error handling, and data session management.

The Visual FoxPro 6 framework uses an enhanced Application Object and provides the following additional elements:

- A master Include file that contains the APP_GLOBAL value to ease localization and for use by components with settings and strings.

- An optional configuration file (Config.fpw) for certain types of applications.

- Uses the ProjectHook class for control of events related to the project.

- An Application Meta table to hold information used by the project hook class and application builders for creating forms within the new project.

- Use the Application Builder to make it easy to add components to the project.

Starting the Application Builder

You can start the Application Builder from the Visual FoxPro **Tools** menu or from the **Component Gallery**.

To start the Application Builder from the Tools menu

1. Click **Wizards**, and then click **All**.

2. Click **Application Builder** from the **Wizard Selection** dialog box.

To start the Application Builder from the Component Gallery

- Double click the **New Application** item.

    When you choose **OK**, the builder closes, applying the property settings from all tabs.

You can also start the Application Builder with a right-click in the Project Manager window, but when opened this way, Application Builder creates only meta tables for your Application — you will see only three tabs in the Application Builder. The only way to provide the full Enhanced Application Framework to your application is through the Application Wizard or through the New Application item of the Component Gallery.

For details on the contents and use of the enhanced Application Framework and the Application Builder, see Developing Applications Using the Application Framework in Help.

Files

Master Include File

This common #INCLUDE file is used by components with settings and strings. The file also includes the APP_GLOBAL value, the name used by components for referencing.

Configuration File

An optional Config.fpw used for applications such as top-level forms in order to implement settings such as SCREEN=OFF.

Project Hook Class

Controls events related to the project such as adding new files. It also can access Application Builder for setting actions and properties of file interaction within the application.

Application Meta Table

Contains information such as project settings made or used by the Application Builder and Project Hooks.

Application Builder

Facilitates adding components to the project and setting properties such as navigation options.

An application framework includes the project file and a starter class library subclassed from the Visual FoxPro base classes, ready for you to populate with new or existing tables and documents.

The framework allows you to specify whether to create a complete application or just an application framework. If you choose to create a complete application, you can either include in the application a database and forms or reports you have already created, or you can create a new application from scratch using a database template. If you choose to create a framework, you can go back later and add components to the framework.

Creating a Framework

You can create an Application Framework by using the Application Wizard or by using the New Application item in the Component Gallery. When you use the Component Gallery, a new project folder item is added to your Favorites folder.

Whichever method you use, Visual FoxPro displays an Application Builder so you can add information to be stored in a meta table.

To create an application

- From the **Tools** menu, click **Wizards**, and then click **Application**.

  – or –

1. In the Catalogs folder of the **Component Gallery**, double-click the **New Application** item.

2. In the **Enter Project Name** dialog box:

   - Specify the project name.

   - Accept or locate the project file.

   - Choose your options to **Create project directory structure** (default) and **Add to Favorites catalog** (default).

For details on the contents and use of the enhanced Application Framework and the Application Builder, see Developing Applications Using the Application Framework in Help.

You can also use the Component Gallery to add forms, reports, data, and service objects to your new application framework and controls to forms.

When you use the Component Gallery to add a form to an application, you can create a new form or subclass from an existing class.

CHAPTER 33

Programming Improvements

Microsoft Visual FoxPro now includes new programming features designed to improve developer productivity. These features include Access and Assign methods that let you execute code when the value of a property is queried or when you attempt to change the property's value, support for more graphic file formats, and new language to simplify programming tasks. Also, many of the file name manipulation functions available in Foxtools.fll, a Visual FoxPro API library, have been added to Visual FoxPro.

This chapter covers:

- Access and Assign Methods
- GIF and JPEG Graphics Support
- New and Enhanced Language Elements
- Year 2000 Date Support

Access and Assign Methods

Visual FoxPro has been enhanced to support Access and Assign methods. These user-defined methods let you execute code when the value of a property is queried, or when you attempt to change the property's value.

The code in an Access method is executed when the value of a property is queried, typically by using the property in an object reference, storing the value of the property to a variable, or displaying the value of property with a question mark (?).

The code in an Assign method is executed when you attempt to change the value of a property, typically by using the STORE or = command to assign a new value to the property.

Access and Assign methods are executed when property values are queried or changed at run time only. Querying or changing property values at design time doesn't execute Access and Assign methods.

> **Note** Because the value you attempt to assign to the property is passed to the Assign method, you must include a PARAMETERS or LPARAMETERS statement in the Assign method to accept the value.

Access and Assign methods can be created independently — you can create an Access method without an Assign method, or an Assign method without an Access method.

Access and Assign methods can be created for properties created programmatically within a DEFINE CLASS statement, or interactively for a form or class with the Form and Class designers. Access and Assign methods

> **Note**   Access and Assign methods can also be created for all native Visual FoxPro properties. For example, you can create an Access method for the Left property of a form, allowing you to execute code whenever the form's Left property is queried. You can create an Assign method for a native Visual FoxPro property that is read-only (for example, the ParentClass property), but the method will never be executed.

Benefits of Access and Assign Methods

Access and Assign methods provide the following benefits:

- You can create a public interface for a class or object that separates the interface from the implementation.

- You can easily implement property validation.

- You can easily protect properties in subclassed ActiveX controls.

Creating Access and Assign Methods

Enhancements to the DEFINE CLASS command and the Form and Class designers allow you to create Access and Assign methods both programmatically and interactively.

New DEFINE CLASS Suffixes

Two suffixes, _ACCESS and _ASSIGN, have been added to the DEFINE CLASS command to create Access and Assign methods. Appending one of these keywords to a function or procedure name creates an Access or Assign method for a property with the same name as the function or procedure.

For example, the following code example uses DEFINE CLASS to create a custom class named MyClass. A user-defined property, MyProperty, is created for the class. An Access method for MyProperty is then created with the PROCEDURE statement.

When the property value is queried, the code in the procedure (WAIT WINDOW 'This is the Access method') is executed. An Assign method for MyProperty is also created, again with a PROCEDURE statement. When an attempt is made to change the property value, the code in the procedure (WAIT WINDOW 'This is the Assign method') is executed.

Note the use of an LPARAMETERS statement to accept the value passed to the Assign method. This example also demonstrates how you can create read-only properties.

```
DEFINE CLASS MyClass AS Custom
   MyProperty = 100 && A user-defined property

   PROCEDURE MyProperty_ACCESS && Access method
      WAIT WINDOW 'This is the Access method';
         + ' ' + PROGRAM( )
      RETURN THIS.MyProperty
   ENDPROC

   PROCEDURE MyProperty_ASSIGN && Assign method
      LPARAMETERS tAssign  && Required to accept value
      WAIT WINDOW 'This is the Assign method';
         + ' ' + PROGRAM( )
   ENDPROC
ENDDEFINE
```

This next example demonstrates how you can add an Assign method for a native Visual FoxPro property and perform simple validation on the property value you attempt to set. Note that in this example an Assign method is created without a corresponding Access method.

DEFINE CLASS is used to create a Form class named frmMyForm. An Assign method named Left_ASSIGN is created with a PROCEDURE statement. The code in the Assign method is executed whenever an attempt is made to assign a value to the form's Left property.

If you attempt to change the Left property value to a negative value, a message is displayed and the Left property value is left unchanged. If you attempt to change the Left property value to a non-negative value, the form's Left property is set to that value.

```
DEFINE CLASS frmMyForm AS Form

   PROCEDURE Left_ASSIGN && Assign method
      LPARAMETERS tAssign  && Required to accept value

      DO CASE
         CASE tAssign < 0 && Left value negative
            WAIT WINDOW 'Value must be greater than 0'
         OTHERWISE  && Left value not negative
            THIS.Left = tAssign
      ENDCASE
   ENDPROC
ENDDEFINE
```

See DEFINE CLASS for further information about the syntax used to create Access and Assign methods.

The Form and Class Designers

To create an Access or Assign method in the Form Designer

1. Choose **New Property** from the **Form** menu.

   The **New Property** dialog box is displayed.

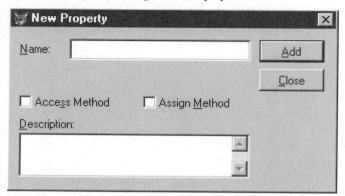

2. Enter the name of the property to create in the **Name** text box, and then select the **Access Method** check box or **Assign Method** check box (or both).

3. Choose **Add** to create a property for the form, and to create Access or Assign methods for the property.

To create an Access or Assign method for an intrinsic Visual FoxPro property in the Form Designer

1. Choose **New Method** from the **Form** menu.

   The **New Method** dialog box is displayed.

2. Enter the name of the intrinsic property followed with _Access or _Assign in the **Name** text box. For example, to create an Access method for the Left property, enter Left_Access in the **Name** text box.

3. Choose **Add** to create an Access or Assign methods for the intrinsic property.

   Note   In the Form Designer, you can create properties with Access and Assign methods only for a form or formset. To create properties with Access and Assign methods for a control or object, use the Class Designer to create the control or object class. In the Class Designer, add properties with Access and Assign methods to the control or object, and then add the control or object class to the Form in the Form Designer.

To create an Access or Assign method for a class in the Class designer

1. Choose **New Property** from the **Class** menu.

   The **New Property** dialog box is displayed.

2. Enter the name of the property to create in the **Name** textbox, then select the **Access Method** check box or **Assign Method** check box (or both).

3. Choose **Add** to create a property for the class, and to create Access or Assign methods for the property.

For more information about creating Access or Assign methods, see "New Property Dialog Box."

THIS_ACCESS Method

A new global class method, THIS_ACCESS, has been added to Visual FoxPro 6.0. The code in a THIS_ACCESS method is executed whenever you attempt to change the value of a member of an object or a member of an object is queried.

A THIS_ACCESS method is created in code within a DEFINE CLASS command, or in the New Method or Edit Properties dialog boxes for .vcx visual class libraries. A THIS_ACCESS method must always return an object reference, otherwise an error is generated. The THIS object reference is typically returned. A THIS_ACCESS method must also include a parameter to accept the name of the member of the object that is changed or queried.

The following simple example demonstrates how to create a THIS_ACCESS method in code within a DEFINE CLASS command. When this example is run as a program, 'Caption' is displayed twice, first when the Caption property is assigned a value, and again when the Caption property value is queried. The value of the Caption property ('abc') is then displayed.

```
CLEAR
oTempObj = CREATEOBJECT('MyForm')  && Instantiate the Form
oTempObj.Caption = 'abc'  && Assign a value, triggers THIS_ACCESS
? oTempObj.Caption  && Query a value, triggers THIS_ACCESS

DEFINE CLASS MyForm AS Form
    PROCEDURE THIS_ACCESS
        LPARAMETER cMemberName  && Object member name

        IF cMemberName = 'caption'
            ? cMemberName  && Display the object member name
        ENDIF
        RETURN THIS
    ENDPROC
ENDDEFINE
```

Note that THIS_ACCESS is not intended to be a global replacement for Access and Assign methods — it only provides information about which object member is accessed or queried. Unlike an Access or Assign method, THIS_ACCESS does not provide control over values returned to specific object members.

Access and Assign Programming Notes

The following sections describe programming information for Access and Assign methods.

Scoping

Access and Assign methods are protected by default — you cannot access or make changes to an Access or Assign method from outside of the class in which the Access or Assign method is created.

Include the HIDDEN keyword when you create an Access or Assign method to prevent access and changes to the properties from outside of the class definition. Only methods and events within the class definition can access the hidden properties. While protected properties can be accessed by subclasses of the class definition, hidden properties can only be accessed from within the class definition.

> **Note**   If you don't include the HIDDEN keyword, you can subclass Access and Assign methods.

Debugging

You can view the code for Access and Assign methods in the Trace window of the Debugger window. However, Access and Assign methods cannot be executed from within the Watch and Local windows of the Debugger window.

Passing Arrays to Assign Methods

Arrays are passed to Access and Assign methods in the same manner as standard Visual FoxPro procedures.

The entire array is passed to an Access or Assign method if you issue SET UDFPARMS TO REFERENCE or preface the array name with @. The first element of the array is passed by value if you issue SET UDFPARMS TO VALUE or enclose the array name by parentheses. Array elements are always passed by value. See SET UDFPARMS for more information about passing values and arrays.

ActiveX Controls

Access and Assign methods are not supported for an ActiveX control's native properties, events, or methods. However, Access and Assign methods are supported for properties, events, and methods for the Visual FoxPro OLE Container in which the ActiveX control is contained.

ResetToDefault Method

Executing the ResetToDefault method for an Access or Assign method changes the code in the Access or Assign method to the default snippet. The result is that the inherited method code, if any, does not get executed. The technique used to ensure that code inherited from the parent class does get executed varies according to the method type.

Place the following code in the subclass of an Access method to execute the code in the parent class:

```
RETURN DODEFAULT( )
```

Place the following code in the subclass of an Assign method to execute the code in the parent class:

```
LPARAMETERS vnewval
DODEFAULT(vnewval)
THIS.<property name> = vnewval
```

Place the following code in the subclass of a THIS_ACCESS method to execute the code in the parent class:

```
LPARAMETERS cmember
RETURN DODEFAULT(cmember)
```

GIF and JPEG Graphics Support

Visual FoxPro has been enhanced to support the GIF (Graphics Interchange Format) and JPEG (Joint Photographic Electronic Group) graphic file formats, widely used throughout the Internet.

In general, any areas that supported .bmp (bitmap) format in previous versions of Visual FoxPro now also support the following graphic file formats.

Graphic format	File extension
Bitmap	.bmp
Device Independent Bitmap	.dib
Graphics Interchange Format	.gif
Joint Photographic Electronic Group	.jpg
Cursor	.cur
Animated Cursor	.ani
Icon	.ico

Note In Visual FoxPro, cursor, animated cursor, and icon files can be used as graphics files. For example, you can specify an animated cursor file for the Picture property for the Image control (however, the Image control displays the static representation of the cursor).

Graphics support is provided in Visual FoxPro in three areas: language, controls and objects, and the interface.

The Visual FoxPro Language

The following commands and functions have been enhanced to support the new graphic file formats.

GETPICT( )

The **Open** dialog displayed by issuing the GETPICT( ) function in the Command window has been enhanced, allowing you to quickly locate all the graphic files supported in Visual FoxPro. The **Files of Type** drop-down list box now includes the following items.

Item	File specifications
All Files	*.*
All Graphics Files	*.bmp, *.dib, *.jpg, *.gif, *.ani, *.cur, *.ico
Bitmap	*.bmp, *.dib
Cursor	*.cur
Animated Cursor	*.ani
Icon	*.ico
JPEG	*.jpg
GIF	*.gif

Check the **Preview** check box to display the currently selected graphics file. In previous versions of Visual FoxPro, it was necessary to choose the **Preview** button each time a new graphics file was selected. The size of the **Picture** area has also been increased.

CLEAR RESOURCES

The CLEAR RESOURCES command in Visual FoxPro now clears all cached graphic files, including .gif and .jpg files.

Visual FoxPro Controls and Objects

The following table lists Visual FoxPro controls and objects with properties for which you can specify graphics files. You can now specify .gif, .jpg, cursor, animated cursor, and icon graphic files for these properties, in addition to the .bmp and .dib graphic files supported in previous versions of Visual FoxPro.

Control or Object	Properties
CheckBox Control	DisabledPicture DownPicture Picture
Command Button Container	DisabledPicture DownPicture Picture
Container Object	Picture
Control Object	Picture
Custom Object	Picture
Form Object	Picture
Image Control	Picture
OptionButton Control	DisabledPicture DownPicture Picture
Page Object	Picture
_Screen Object	Picture

The Visual FoxPro Interface

Several of the Visual FoxPro designers allow you to specify graphics files with the **Open** dialog. The **Open** dialog for the following designers have been enhanced to include the new graphic file formats.

Form Designer and Class Designer

In the Properties window, by double-clicking the property or choosing the property's dialog button you can display the **Open** dialog for a property that supports graphic files.

Project Manager

You can add graphics files to a project from the Project Manager **All** and **Other** tabs. When the **All** or **Other** tab is selected, select the **Other Files** item and then choose **Add**. The **Open** dialog is displayed, allowing you to add a graphics file to the project.

Report Designer

The **Report Controls** toolbar contains the **Picture/OLE Bound Control** button. Click this button and drag the cursor over a band in the Report Designer to display the **Report Picture** dialog box. To display the **Open** dialog, choose the **File** dialog button.

New and Enhanced Language Elements

Many new and enhanced language elements have been added to Visual FoxPro. The new language elements listed in this section include Active Documents, Project Manager Hooks, OLE drag-and-drop, Server Improvements, and miscellaneous language.

The enhanced elements are also listed.

In addition, many of the file name manipulation functions available in Foxtools.fll, a Visual FoxPro API library, have been added to Visual FoxPro. It's no longer necessary to use SET LIBRARY TO FOXTOOLS.FLL to call these Foxtools functions; you can call them directly in your Visual FoxPro programs.

This section also describes improvements to Visual FoxPro performance, robustness, and usability.

New Active Documents language	Description
ActiveDoc Object	Creates an Active Document that can be hosted in an Active Document container such as Microsoft Internet Explorer.
CommandTargetExec Event	Occurs when the user clicks on a menu item or toolbar item belonging to the Active Document container.
CommandTargetQuery Event	Occurs when the Active Document host needs to find out if the Active Document supports various host menu and/or toolbar commands so that it can enable or disable the corresponding menu items and/or toolbar buttons.
ContainerRelease Event	Occurs when an Active Document is released by its host.
ContainerReleaseType Property	Specifies if an Active Document is opened in the Visual FoxPro run time when the Active Document is released by its host.
ContinuousScroll Property	Specifies if scrolling within a form is continuous, or if scrolling only occurs when a scroll box is released.
DEFINE PAD Command	Supports new NEGOTIATE options for specifying menu title location for Active Documents.
GETHOST( ) Function	Returns an object reference to the container of an Active Document.
GoBack Method	Navigates backwards in the history list of an Active Document host.
GoFoward Method	Navigates forwards in the history list of an Active Document host.
HideDoc Event	Occurs when you navigate from an Active Document.
HScrollSmallChange Property	Specifies the increment a form scrolls in the horizontal direction when you click on a horizontal scroll arrow.
Hyperlink Object	Creates a Hyperlink object.
ISHOSTED( ) Function	Returns a logical value indicating if an Active Document is hosted in an Active Document container.

(continued)

New Active Documents language	Description
NavigateTo Method	Navigates in an Active Document container to a specified location.
Run Event	Occurs when an Active Document has finished coordinating with its host and with COM and is ready to run user code.
_RUNACTIVEDOC System Variable	Specifies an application that launches an Active Document.
ScrollBars Property	Now available for forms. If a form is in an Active Document, the scroll bars are displayed automatically when the size of the Active Document container is less than the size of the form.
Scrolled Event	Now available for forms, allowing you to determine if the horizontal or vertical scroll bars are clicked or a scroll box is moved.
SetViewPort Method	Sets the values of the ViewPortLeft and ViewPortTop properties for a form.
ShowDoc Event	Occurs when you navigate to an Active Document.
SYS(4204) – Active Document Debugging	Enables or disables debugging support for Active Documents in the Visual FoxPro debugger.
ViewPortHeight Property	Contains the viewport height for a form.
ViewPortLeft Property	Contains the left coordinate of the form that is visible in the viewport.
ViewPortTop Property	Contains the top coordinate of the form that is visible in the viewport.
ViewPortWidth Property	Contains the viewport width for a form.
VScrollSmallChange Property	Specifies the increment a form scrolls vertically when you click on a scroll arrow.

New Project Manager Hooks language	Description
ActiveProject Property	Contains an object reference to the project object for the currently active Project Manager window.
Add Method	Adds a file to a project.
AddToSCC Method	Adds a file in a project to source code control.
AfterBuild Event	Occurs after a project is rebuilt or an application file (.app), dynamic link library (.dll), or executable file (.exe) is created from a project.
AutoIncrement Property	Specifies if the build version of a project is automatically incremented each time a distributable .exe or in-process .dll is built.

(continued)

(continued)

New Project Manager Hooks language	Description
BeforeBuild Event	Occurs before a project is rebuilt or an application file (.app), dynamic link library (.dll), or executable file (.exe) is created from a project.
Build Method	Rebuilds a project, or creates an application file (.app), dynamic link library (.dll), or executable file (.exe) from a project.
BuildDateTime Property	Contains the last build date and time for a project.
CheckIn Method	Checks in changes made to a file in a project under source code control.
CheckOut Method	Checks out a file in a project under source code control, allowing you to make changes to the file.
CleanUp Method	Cleans up a project table by removing records marked for deletion and packing memo fields.
Close Method	Closes a project and releases the project's ProjectHook and project objects.
CLSID Property	Contains the registered CLSID (Class Identifier) for a server in a project.
CodePage Property	Contains the code page of a file in a project.
Count Property	A count of the number of project, file or server objects in a project, file or server collection.
CREATE PROJECT Command	Enhanced in Visual FoxPro 6.0. Supports two new options, NOSHOW and NOPROJECTHOOK, for use with the new Project Manager hooks.
Debug Property	Specifies if debugging information is included with compiled source code in a project.
Description Property	For a file object, the description for the file. For a server object, the description of the server class.
Encrypted Property	Specifies if compiled source code in a project is encrypted.
Exclude Property	Specifies if a file is excluded from an application (.app), dynamic link library (.dll), or executable file (.exe) when it is built from a project.
FileClass Property	Contains the name of the form class on which a form in a project is based.
FileClassLibrary Property	Contains the name of the class library containing the class on which a form in a project is based.
File Object	Provides references to specific files in a project.

(continued)

New Project Manager Hooks language	Description
Files Collection	A collection of file objects.
GetLatestVersion Method	Gets the latest version of a file in a project from source code control and copies a read-only version to your local drive.
HomeDir Property	Specifies the home directory for a project.
Instancing Property	Specifies how a server in a project can be instantiated.
Item Method	Returns an object reference to the specified item in a project collection.
LastModified Property	Contains the date and time of the last modification made to a file in a project.
MainClass Property	Contains the name of an ActiveDoc class set as the main program in a project.
MainFile Property	Contains the name and path of the file set as the main program in a project.
Modify Method	Opens a file in a project for modification in the appropriate designer or editor.
MODIFY PROJECT Command	Enhanced in Visual FoxPro 6.0. Supports two new options, NOSHOW and NOPROJECTHOOK, for use with the new Project Manager hooks.
ProgID Property	Contains the registered PROGID (Programmatic Identifier) for a server in a project.
Project Object	Instantiated when a project is created or opened.
ProjectHook Object	Instantiated whenever a project is opened, providing programmatic access to project events.
ProjectHook Property	An object reference to the ProjectHook object instantiated for a project.
ProjectHookClass Property	The default ProjectHook class for a project.
ProjectHookLibrary Property	The .vcx visual class library containing the default ProjectHook class for a project.
Projects Collection	A collection of project objects.
QueryAddFile Event	Occurs just before a file is added to a project.
QueryModifyFile Event	Occurs just before a file is modified in a project.
QueryRemoveFile Event	Occurs just before a file is removed from a project.
QueryRunFile Event	Occurs just before a file is executed or a report or label is previewed in a project. *(continued)*

(continued)

New Project Manager Hooks language	Description
Remove Method	Removes a file from its files collection and project.
RemoveFromSCC Method	Removes a file in a project from source code control.
Run Method	Runs or previews a file in a project.
SCCProvider Property	The name of the source code control provider for a project.
SCCStatus Property	Contains a numeric value indicating the source control status of a file in a project.
Server Object	An object reference to a server in a project.
Servers Collection	A collection of server objects.
ServerClass Property	Contains the name of a server class in a project.
ServerClassLibrary Property	Contains the name of the class library or program containing a server class.
ServerHelpFile Property	The help file for the type library created for server classes in a project.
ServerProject Property	The name of the project containing server classes.
SetMain Method	Sets the main file in a project.
Type Property	The file type for a file in a project.
TypeLibCLSID Property	The registry CLSID (Class Identifier) for a type library created for server classes in a project.
TypeLibDesc Property	The description for a type library created for server classes in a project.
TypeLibName Property	The name of the type library created for server classes in a project.
UndoCheckOut Method	Discards any changes made to a file and checks the file back into source code control.
VersionComments Property	The comments for a project.
VersionCompany Property	The company name information for a project.
VersionCopyright Property	The copyright information for a project.
VersionDescription Property	The description for a project.
VersionLanguage Property	The language information for a project.
VersionNumber Property	The build number for a project.
VersionProduct Property	The product name information for a project.
VersionTrademarks Property	The trademarks information for a project.

New OLE drag-and-drop language	Description
ClearData Method	Clears all data and data formats from the OLE drag-and-drop DataObject.
DataObject Object	Container for data being transferred from an OLE drag source to an OLE drop target.
GetData Method	Retrieves data from the OLE drag-and-drop DataObject.
GetFormat Method	Determines if data in a specified format is available on the OLE drag-and-drop DataObject.
OLECompleteDrag Event	Occurs when data is dropped on the drop target or the OLE drag-and-drop operation is canceled.
OLEDrag Method	Starts an OLE drag-and-drop operation.
OLEDragDrop Event	Occurs when data is dropped on a drop target and the drop target's OLEDropMode property is set to 1 – Enabled.
OLEDragMode Property	Specifies how a drag operation is initiated.
OLEDragOver Event	Occurs when data is dragged over a drop target and the drop target's OLEDropMode property is set to 1 – Enabled.
OLEDragPicture Property	Specifies the picture displayed under the mouse pointer during an OLE drag-and-drop operation. You can specify a picture file of type .bmp, .dib, .jpg, .gif, .ani, .cur, and .ico.
OLEDropEffects Property	Specifies the type of drop operations an OLE drop target supports.
OLEDropHasData Property	Specifies how a drop operation is managed.
OLEDropMode Property	Specifies how a drop target manages OLE drop operations.
OLEDropTextInsertion Property	Specifies if you can drop text in the middle of a word in the text box portion of a control.
OLEGiveFeedBack Event	Occurs after every OLEDragOver event. Allows the drag source to specify the type of OLE drag-and-drop operation and the visual feedback.
OLESetData Event	Occurs on a drag source when a drop target calls the GetData method and there is no data in a specified format in the OLE drag-and-drop DataObject.
OLEStartDrag Event	Occurs when the OLEDrag method is called.
SetData Method	Places data on the OLE drag-and-drop DataObject.
SetFormat Method	Places a data format on the OLE drag-and-drop DataObject.

New Server Improvements language	Description
COMARRAY( ) Function	Specifies how arrays are passed to COM objects.
COMCLASSINFO( ) Function	Returns registry information about a COM object such as a Visual FoxPro automation server.
COMRETURNERROR( ) Function	Populates the COM exception structure with information that COM clients can use to determine the source of Automation errors.
CREATEOBJECTEX( ) Function	Creates an instance of a registered COM object (such as a Visual FoxPro automation server) on a remote computer.
ServerName Property	Contains the full path and file name for an automation server.
StartMode Property	Contains a numeric value that indicates how the instance of Visual FoxPro was started.
SYS(2335) – Unattended Server Mode	Enables or disables modal states for distributable Visual FoxPro .exe automation servers.
SYS(2334) – Automation Server Startup	Returns a value indicating how a Visual FoxPro automation server was invoked or if a stand-alone executable (.exe) application is running.

New Miscellaneous language	Description
AddProperty Method	Adds a new property to an object.
AGETFILEVERSION( )	Creates an array containing information about files with Microsoft Windows version resources such as .exe, .dll, and .fll files, or automation servers created in Visual FoxPro. Corresponds to the GetFileVersion( ) function in Foxtools.
AGETCLASS( ) Function	Displays class libraries in the Open dialog box and creates an array containing the name of the class library and class chosen.
ALINES( ) Function	Copies each line in a character expression or memo field to a corresponding row in an array.
AMOUSEOBJ( ) Function	Returns mouse pointer position information and object references for the object and the object's container over which the mouse pointer is positioned.
ANETRESOURCES( ) Function	Places the names of network shares or printers into an array and then returns the number of resources.
AVCXCLASSES( ) Function	Places the information about classes in a class library into an array.
DisplayCount Property	Specifies the number of items displayed in the list portion of a ComboBox control.

(continued)

New Miscellaneous language	Description
FILETOSTR( ) Function	Returns the contents of a file as a character string.
_GALLERY System Variable	Specifies the program that is executed when you choose Component Gallery from the Tools menu.
_GENHTML System Variable	Specifies an HTML (Hypertext Markup Language) generation program that creates a text file that contains a hypertext markup language version of a form, menu, report, or table.
_GETEXPR System Variable	Specifies the program that is executed when you issue the GETEXPR command or the Expression Builder dialog box is displayed.
GridHitTest Method	Returns, as output parameters, the components of a grid control corresponding to specified horizontal (X) and vertical (Y) coordinates.
_INCLUDE System Variable	Specifies a default header file included with user-defined classes, forms, or form sets.
INDEXSEEK( ) Function	Without moving the record pointer, searches an indexed table for the first occurrence of a record whose index key matches a specified expression.
NEWOBJECT( ) Function	Creates a new class or object directly from a .vcx visual class library or program.
NewObject Method	Adds a new class or object to an object directly from a .vcx visual class library or program.
_SAMPLES System Variable	Contains the path of the directory in which the Visual FoxPro samples are installed.
SET BROWSEIME Command	Specifies if the Input Method Editor is opened when you navigate to a text box in a Browse window.
SET STRICTDATE Command	Specifies if ambiguous Date and DateTime constants generate errors.
STRTOFILE( ) Function	Writes the contents of a character string to a file.
SYS(3055) – FOR and WHERE Clause Complexity	Sets the complexity level of the FOR and WHERE clauses in commands and functions that support them.
SYS(3056) – Read Registry Settings	Forces Visual FoxPro to read its registry settings again and update itself with the current registry settings.
TitleBar Property	Specifies if a title bar appears at the top of a form.
VARTYPE( ) Function	Returns the data type of an expression.

Enhanced language elements	Description
= Operator	Can be used in Visual FoxPro 6.0 to determine if two object references refer to the same object.
ALTER TABLE – SQL Command	Supports a new FOR clause for the ADD PRIMARY KEY and ADD FOREIGN KEY clauses. FOR allows you to create filtered primary and foreign indexes.
APPEND FROM Command	Supports a new XL8 option for importing data from a Microsoft Excel 97 worksheet, and a new CSV option for importing data from a comma separated value file.
Century Property	The default for is now 1 – On. The century portion of the date is displayed in a text box to provide Year 2000 compliance.
CheckBox Control	Now supports the ReadOnly property.
Column Object	Now supports the Comment and Tag properties and the SaveAsClass method.
COMPILE DATABASE Command	COMPILE DATABASE now packs memo fields in the .dct memo file for the database to remove unused space from the memo file.
Container Object	Now supports the Tag property.
Control Object	Now supports the Tag property.
COPY TO Command	Supports a new CSV option for exporting data as a comma separated value file.
CREATE FORM Command	Supports a new AS clause that allows you to create a new form or formset from a form or formset in a .vcx visual class library.
Cursor Object	Now supports the Comment and Tag properties, and the ReadExpression, ReadMethod, SaveAsClass, and WriteExpression methods.
Custom Object	Now supports the Tag property.
DataEnvironment Object	Now supports the Comment and Tag properties, and the ReadExpression, ReadMethod, SaveAsClass, and WriteExpression methods.
DATE( ) Function	Now supports optional numeric arguments that let you create year 2000 compliant Date values.
DATETIME( ) Function	Now supports optional numeric arguments that let you create year 2000 compliant DateTime values.
DEFINE CLASS Command	Supports new Access and Assign methods, allowing you to execute code whenever a property is queried or you attempt to change the value of a property.

(continued)

Enhanced language elements	Description
FDATE( ) Function	Now supports an optional argument that lets you determine the time when a file was last modified without using character manipulation functions.
Form Object	Now supports the Scrollbars property and the Scrolled event.
FormSet Object	Now supports the Parent and Tag properties.
GETDIR( ) Function	The Select Directory dialog box has been enlarged to display more directory information.
GETFILE( ) Function	Supports a new *cTitleBarCaption* option that lets you specify the title bar caption in the Open dialog box.
GETFONT( ) Function	Allows you to specify a font, font size, and font style that are initially selected when the Font dialog box is displayed.
Header Object	Now supports the Comment and Tag properties, and the SaveAsClass method.
HOME( ) Function	Now lets you determine the Visual FoxPro and Visual Studio samples, tools, graphics, and common directories.
Image Control	Now supports the ToolTipText property.
IMPORT Command	Supports a new XL8 option for importing data from a Microsoft Excel 97 worksheet.
Label Control	Now supports the ToolTipText property.
MODIFY MEMO Command	Syntax coloring is now disabled in memo field editing windows in distributed run-time applications.
OS( ) Function	Now supports an option that lets you determine if the operating system supports DBCS (double-byte character sets).
Page Object	Now supports the Tag property and the SaveAsClass method.
PageFrame Control	Now supports the Tag property.
PEMSTATUS( ) Function	PEMSTATUS( ) supports a new 6 option for *nAttribute* that lets you determine if a property, event, or method was inherited from an object or class.
PROGRAM( ) Function	Now supports −1 as an argument, allowing you to determine the current program level.

(continued)

(continued)

Enhanced language elements	Description
Refresh Method	Now allows you to refresh the visual display of the Project Manager, and supports a new parameter to update the source control status for files in a project.
Relation Object	Now supports the Comment and Tag properties, the Destroy, Error, and Init events, and the ReadExpression, ReadMethod, and WriteExpression methods.
REPORT Command	Now supports a PREVIEW IN SCREEN clause, allowing you to place the preview window in the main Visual FoxPro window.
Separator Object	Now supports the Comment and Tag properties, and the ReadExpression, ReadMethod, SaveAsClass, and WriteExpression methods.
SET BELL	A waveform sound duration is no longer required.
SET('PRINTER')	Supports a new 3 option that allows you to determine the current Visual FoxPro default printer set in the Visual FoxPro Print or Print Setup dialog boxes.
SET('BELL')	Can now be used to determine the waveform sound played when the bell sounds.
STRCONV( ) Function	Supports a new *nLocaleID* argument that allows you to specify the Locale ID to use for the conversion.
SYS(2333) — ActiveX Dual Interface Support	Now allows you to determine its current setting, and the default startup setting for ActiveX dual interface support has been changed from enabled in Visual FoxPro 5.0 to disabled in Visual FoxPro 6.0.
TABLEUPDATE( ) Function	If an error other than a simple commit error occurs while updating records, the first element of the error array will now contain −1 and you can then use AERROR( ) to determine why the changes could not be committed.
ToolBar Object	Now supports the Tag property and the Release method.
TRANSFORM( ) Function	The *cFormatCodes* format code is now optional. A default transformation is used if the *cFormatCodes* format code is omitted.
VERSION( ) Function	Supports two new *nExpression* options, 4 and 5, to return just the Visual FoxPro version number in formats that can be easily parsed.

Foxtools functions	Description
The following functions have been added to Visual FoxPro 6.0 from Foxtools; they can now be used without executing SET LIBRARY TO FOXTOOLS.	Note that you must recompile any programs, class libraries, labels, or reports created in earlier versions of Visual FoxPro if they contain any of the following functions.
ADDBS( ) Function	Adds a backslash (if needed) to a path expression.
AGETFILEVERSION( ) Function	Creates an array containing information about files with Windows version resources such as .exe, .dll, and .fll files, or automation servers created in Visual FoxPro. Corresponds to the GetFileVersion( ) function in Foxtools.
DEFAULTEXT( ) Function	Returns a file name with a new extension if one doesn't already exist.
DRIVETYPE( ) Function	Returns the type of the specified drive.
FORCEEXT( ) Function	Returns a string with the old file name extension replaced by a new extension.
FORCEPATH( ) Function	Returns a file name with a new path name substituted for the old one.
JUSTDRIVE( ) Function	Returns the drive letter from a complete path.
JUSTEXT( ) Function	Returns the three-letter extension from a complete path.
JUSTFNAME( ) Function	Returns the file name portion of a complete path and file name.
JUSTPATH( ) Function	Returns the path portion of a complete path and file name.
JUSTSTEM( ) Function	Returns the stem name (the file name before the extension) from a complete path and file name.

Improvements to Visual FoxPro Performance

The performance of string concatenation in Visual FoxPro 6.0 has been increased dramatically. String concatenation is typically used to create Web pages with code like the following:

```
cMyString = cMyString + <html tags>
cMyString = cMyString + <more html tags>
cMyString = cMyString + <even more html tags>
```

Object creation and instantiation performance has also been improved and is typically 10 or more times faster than in previous versions.

Improvements to Visual FoxPro Robustness

Visual FoxPro 6.0 now captures General Protection Faults (GPFs) in ActiveX controls placed on a form, or COM objects instantiated from within Visual FoxPro. A GPF in an ActiveX control or COM object is now treated as a trappable Visual FoxPro error (Error 1440 – OLE object may be corrupt).

Improvements to Visual FoxPro Usability

You can specify the Visual FoxPro editor comment string in the Windows registry. Using the Windows Registry Editor (RegEdit), open the Visual FoxPro 6.0 Options folder, and right-click the folder. Choose **New**, and then **String Value**. Enter the name "EditorCommandString" for the name of the new string value. Right-click the string value, and choose **Modify**. Enter the editor comment string (*!* is the default value used when this registry entry doesn't exist in the Registry).

The Form menu is now accessible from within the form code window. Also, you can run a form with the CTRL+E keyboard shortcut, even from within a form code window.

Year 2000 Date Support

Visual FoxPro 6.0 has been enhanced to provide better year 2000 date support. This section describes the enhancements made to Visual FoxPro to make it easier to create year 2000 compliant applications.

SET CENTURY TO

The Visual FoxPro 5.0 documentation states that issuing SET CENTURY TO without additional arguments sets the century to the current century. This is only true in the 20th century, because the century is set to 19 regardless of the current century. In Visual FoxPro 6.0, SET CENTURY TO sets the century to the current century. Additionally, the value of SET CENTURY TO in new data sessions is initialized to the current century.

Also, in Visual FoxPro 6.0, the default ROLLOVER value for SET CENTURY has changed to the last two digits of the current year plus 50 years — if the current year is 1998, *nYear* is 48, the last two digits of 2048 (1998 + 50). In Visual FoxPro 5.0 the default value is 0.

See SET CENTURY for more information.

Strict Date Formats

Normally, Date and DateTime constants or expressions are interpreted based on the current settings of SET DATE and SET CENTURY at the time the constants or expressions are compiled or evaluated. This means that many date constants are ambiguous since they might evaluate to different values depending upon when they were compiled and what date settings were in effect at compilation time.

For example, is the date constant {10/11/12} October 11, 1912, October 11, 2012, November 10, 1912, November 12, 1910, or November 12, 2010?

It all depends on the current settings of SET DATE and SET CENTURY TO. This can introduce errors into existing Visual FoxPro code wherever Date or DateTime constants or expressions are either compiled or are evaluated at run time, such as in report and object expressions. This can introduce year 2000 noncompliance into existing code when the setting of SET CENTURY rolls over into the year 2000 and a four-digit year isn't specified.

To avoid noncompliance, a strict date format is now available in Visual FoxPro 6.0 (and Visual FoxPro 5.0). A strict date always evaluates to the same Date or DateTime value regardless of any date settings. The strict date format is:

^yyyy-mm-dd[,][hh[:mm[:ss]][alp]]

The caret character (^) always denotes the strict date format and causes Dates and DateTimes to be interpreted in a YMD format. Valid Date and DateTime separators are hyphens, forward slashes, periods, and spaces.

Empty Dates and DateTimes are considered nonambiguous and are always valid. Valid empty Date and DateTime formats include {}, {--}, and {--,:}.

With strict date formats, a greater range of Date and DateTime values are available. In Visual FoxPro 5.0, the smallest date value that can be expressed is {^0100/1/1}, January 1st, 100 A.D. This is because year values less than 100 were always rounded up to the nearest century based on the setting of SET CENTURY.

The smallest valid date in Visual FoxPro 6.0 is {^0001-01-01}, January 1st, 1 A.D. The largest valid date in Visual FoxPro 6.0 is {^9999-12-31}, December 31st, 9999 A.D.

Note that the strict date format ignores the TAIWAN setting for SET DATE, so the year of a strict format Date or DateTime is always in the Western calendar. (Note that this is not true in Visual FoxPro 5.0.)

SET STRICTDATE

A new command, SET STRICTDATE, can be used to enforce year 2000 compliant date constants and date strings.

SET STRICTDATE TO 0

Setting STRICTDATE to 0 means that strict date format checking is off. This is Visual FoxPro 5.0 compatible. 0 is the default setting for the Visual FoxPro run-time and ODBC driver. When STRICTDATE is set to 0, invalid Date and DateTimes evaluate to the empty date.

SET STRICTDATE TO 1

Setting STRICTDATE to 1 requires that all Date and DateTime constants be in the strict date format. Any Date or DateTime constant that is not in the strict format or evaluates to an invalid value generates an error, either during compilation, at run time, or during an interactive Visual FoxPro session. 1 is the default setting for an interactive Visual FoxPro session.

SET STRICTDATE TO 2

Identical to setting STRICTDATE to 1, but also generates a compilation error (2033 – CTOD and CTOT can produce incorrect results) whenever CTOD( ) and CTOT( ) functions appear in code.

Because the values returned by CTOD( ) and CTOT( ) rely on SET DATE and SET CENTURY to interpret the date string they contain, they are prone to year 2000 noncompliance errors. Use DATE( ) and DATETIME( ) with the optional numeric arguments to create Date and DateTime constants and expressions.

This setting is most useful during debugging sessions to trap for code that may contain year 2000 compliance errors.

Strict Date Format Errors

The following new errors have been added to Visual FoxPro 6.0, and can be generated when SET STRICTDATE is set to 1 or 2.

Error 2032: Ambiguous Date/DateTime constant.

This error occurs when a Date or DateTime did not adhere to the strict format. The following conditions will produce this error:

- The caret (^) is missing.

- The date separators are not the required hyphen, forward slash, period, or space separators.

- The year field contains less than four characters ({^98-02-16}).

- The month or day field is empty ({^1998-02}).

Error 2033: CTOD and CTOT can produce incorrect results.

This error occurs for the same reasons as error 2032, but CTOD( ) and CTOT( ) may be non-compliant or ambiguous. Use the DATE( ) or DATETIME( ) functions instead.

Error 2034: Date/DateTime evaluated to an invalid value.

A Date or DateTime is not in the valid Date or DateTime format, or is outside the valid Date or DateTime range.

When SET STRICTDATE is set to 0, invalid Date and DateTime constants evaluate to the empty Date or DateTime. When SET STRICTDATE is set to 1 or 2, invalid date constants, such as {^2000-02-31}, February 31st, or {^2000-01-01,25:00}, 25 o'clock, generate this error.

Examples of invalid Dates and DateTimes include:

- {^2000-02-31}, February 31st, 2000.

- {^2000-01-01,25:00} 25 o'clock.

- {^2000-01-01, 14a}, 14 A.M.

Error 2035: Date/DateTime contains illegal characters.

The Date or DateTime constant contains characters that are not supported in Date and DateTime constants.

When SET STRICTDATE is set to 0, the Date or DateTime constant containing the illegal characters evaluates to the empty Date or DateTime. When SET STRICTDATE is set to 1 or 2, the Date or DateTime constant containing the illegal characters generates this error.

Note that the StrictDateEntry property isn't affected by the setting of SET STRICTDATE. The StrictDateEntry property remains unchanged in Visual FoxPro 6.0.

Options Dialog

The General tab of the **Options** dialog box now includes a **Year 2000 Compliance** drop-down list box, which specifies the setting of SET STRICTDATE. Like all other Options dialog items, the value is set for the current Visual FoxPro session, and choosing **Set As Default** saves the setting to the Windows registry for the next Visual FoxPro session.

DATE( ) and DATETIME( ) Functions

The DATE( ) and DATETIME( ) functions now support optional numeric arguments that let you create year 2000 compliant Date or DateTime values. The enhancements to these functions now provide a preferable method for creating Date and DateTime values; it's no longer necessary to use character manipulation functions to create Date and DateTime values.

FDATE( ) Function

The FDATE( ) function now supports an optional argument that lets you determine the time when a file was last modified without using character manipulation functions. For example, in previous versions of Visual FoxPro, it was necessary to write code like the following to determine when the Visual FoxPro resource file was last modified:

```
tLastModified = CTOT(DTOC(FDATE('Foxuser.dbf')) + ' ' ;
   + FTIME('Foxuser.dbf')
```

This code can now be replaced with the following:

```
tLastModified = FDATE('Foxuser.dbf', 1)
```

Century Property

The default for the Century property in Visual FoxPro 6.0 is 1 – On. The century portion of the date is displayed in a text box. In previous versions of Visual FoxPro, the default is 2 — the SET CENTURY setting determines if the century portion of the date is displayed.

Index

C

G

M

O

Register Today!

Return this
Microsoft® Visual FoxPro® 6.0
Programmer's Guide
registration card for
a Microsoft Press® catalog

U.S. and Canada addresses only. Fill in information below and mail postage-free. Please mail only the bottom half of this page.

1-57231-868-6   *MICROSOFT® VISUAL FOXPRO® 6.0*   *Owner Registration Card*
PROGRAMMER'S GUIDE

_____
NAME

_____
INSTITUTION OR COMPANY NAME

_____
ADDRESS

_____

_____
CITY   STATE   ZIP

Microsoft®*Press*
Quality Computer Books

**For a free catalog of
Microsoft Press® products, call
1-800-MSPRESS**

BUSINESS REPLY MAIL
FIRST-CLASS MAIL   PERMIT NO. 53   BOTHELL, WA

POSTAGE WILL BE PAID BY ADDRESSEE

MICROSOFT PRESS REGISTRATION
MICROSOFT® VISUAL FOXPRO® 6.0
PROGRAMMER'S GUIDE
PO BOX 3019
BOTHELL WA   98041-9946